Wielding Words like Weapons

Selected Essays in Indigenism, 1995–2005

Ward Churchill

Wielding Words like Weapons: Selected Essays in Indigenism, 1995–2005
Ward Churchill
© 2017 Ward Churchill
This edition © 2017 PM Press

ISBN: 978–1–62963–101–1
Library of Congress Control Number: 2015930882

Cover by John Yates / www.stealworks.com
Interior design by briandesign

10 9 8 7 6 5 4 3 2 1

PM Press
PO Box 23912
Oakland, CA 94623
www.pmpress.org

Printed in the USA by the Employee Owners of Thomson-Shore in Dexter, Michigan.
www.thomsonshore.com

This one's for Russ

I want my words to be as eloquent
As the sound of a rattle snake.

I want my actions to be as direct
As the strike of a rattle snake.

I want results as conclusive
As the bite of the beautiful red and black coral snake.

—Jimmie Durham
from *Columbus Day*
(1983)

Contents

FOREWORD **"And Then They Build Monuments to You"** xiii

INTRODUCTION **A Few Thoughts on a Book Long Overdue** 1

ONE **Remembering Bob Thomas** 9
His Influence on the American
Indian Liberation Struggle

TWO **Subverting the Law of Nations** 29
American Indian Rights and U.S.
Distortions of International Legality

THREE **The United States and the Genocide
Convention** 56
A Half-Century of Obfuscation and Obstruction

FOUR **Charades, Anyone?** 81
The Indian Claims Commission in Context

FIVE **In the Spirit of Gunga Din** 111
A Response to John LaVelle

SIX **History in Service to Liberation** 139
Ron Welburn's *Roanoke and Wampum*

SEVEN **Broadening Our View of the Penal Colony** 142
Luana Ross' *Inventing the Savage*

EIGHT   **Contours of Enlightenment**   144
Reflections on Science, Theology, Law, and
the Alternative Vision of Vine Deloria Jr.

NINE   **Science as Psychosis**   174
An American Corollary to Germany's
Blood Libel of the Jews

TEN   **American Indians in Film**   217
Thematic Contours of Cinematic Colonization

ELEVEN   **Distorted Images and Literary
Appropriations**   279
Gretchen Bataille's *Native American Representations*

TWELVE   **Finding a "Middle Place"?**   282
Not in Joni Adamson's *American Indian Literature,
Environmental Justice, and Ecocriticism*

THIRTEEN   **Kizhiibaabinesik**   289
A Bright Star, Burning Briefly

FOURTEEN   **The Ghosts of 9-1-1**   363
Reflections on History, Justice
and Roosting Chickens

FIFTEEN   **"To Judge Them by the Standards of
Their Time"**   409
America's Indian Fighters, the Laws of War,
and the Question of International Order

APPENDIX   **"*Some* People Push Back"**   520
On the Justice of Roosting Chickens

ABOUT THE AUTHORS   544

INDEX   545

Other Books by Ward Churchill

A Decolonizing Encounter: Ward Churchill and Antonia Darder in Dialogue (2012)

"Kill the Indian, Save the Man": The Genocidal Impact of American Indian Residential Schools (2004)

On the Justice of Roosting Chickens: Reflections on the Consequences of U.S. Imperial Arrogance and Criminality (2003)

Acts of Rebellion: A Ward Churchill Reader (2003)

Pacifism as Pathology: Reflections on the Role of Armed Struggle in North America, with Michael Ryan (1998, 2007, 2017)

Perversions of Justice: Indigenous Peoples and Angloamerican Law (2003)

A Little Matter of Genocide: Holocaust and Denial in the Americas, 1492 through the Present (1997)

From a Native Son: Selected Essays in Indigenism, 1985–1995 (1996, 2017)

Since Predator Came: Notes from the Struggle for American Indian Liberation (1995, 2005)

Indians "R" Us? Colonization and Genocide in Native North America (1994)

Struggle for the Land: Indigenous Resistance to Genocide, Ecocide and Colonization in Contemporary North America (1993, 2002)

Fantasies of the Master Race: Literature, Cinema and the Colonization of American Indians (1992, 1998)

The COINTELPRO Papers: Documents from the FBI's Secret Wars Against Domestic Dissent, with Jim Vander Wall (1990, 2002)

Agents of Repression: The FBI's Secret Wars Against the Black Panther Party and the American Indian Movement, with Jim Vander Wall (1988, 2002)

Culture versus Economism: Essays on Marxism in the Multicultural Arena, with Elisabeth R. Lloyd (1984, 1989)

Edited volumes

Islands in Captivity: The Record of the International Tribunal on the Rights of Indigenous Hawaiians, with Sharon H. Venne (2004)

Leah Renae Kelly, In My Own Voice: Explorations in the Sociopolitical Context of Art and Cinema (2001)

Cages of Steel: The Politics of Imprisonment in the United States, with J.J. Vander Wall (1992)

Critical Issues in Native North America, Vol. 2 (1991)

Critical Issues in Native North America (1989)

Marxism and Native Americans (1983)

"And Then They Build Monuments to You"

Barbara Alice Mann

Being Indigenous in the United States has never been easy, not a little because the settler script called for all the "Indians" of Turtle Island (North America) to have died politely in the first act of invasion. Our continued existence into the present is thus perceived as a Deliberate Affront to the Established Order, to be slapped down as hard and as often as necessary. The slapping continues into the present and, in the service of ethnically cleansing the ranks of intellectuals, it may even escalate into the gang-slapping of a particularly pesky offender, as it did for Ward Churchill in 2005.

Just why Churchill was singled out for sustained abuse is a long and tempestuous story, which attaches to forces substantially beyond individual personalities or the caprice of a news cycle. Instead, the dedicated character assassination of Churchill was orchestrated politically as a sort of demonstration project in intimidation, aimed as much at American dissenters, generally, as at Churchill, personally. The point was to head off at the pass any but the official settler version of the U.S. metanarrative, in a preemptive measure to delegitimize not just Indigenous but also any "minority" commentary, against the prospect of a future that will be less and less European as the twenty-first century wears on.

Westerners will doubtless face a harder task in this now than they did in earlier centuries, because simply wiping out those annoying "lower races" is no longer socially acceptable. The burden has necessarily shifted from physical to verbal attack, which has morphed from a sort of warm-up exercise for physical violence into the primary modus operandi. This is the good news, for in such a contest, Indigenous peoples are fully armed. As exemplified in this book, Ward Churchill can devastatingly wield his words as weapons. To aid in locating opposition bunkers, I have identified the four basic, Western tactics, as successively deployed, in verbal warfare. In order, the ploys are: 1) Amnesia, 2) Denial, 3) Minimization, 4) Hostility.

Amnesia

Amnesia is always the first strategy, should any unpleasantness bubble up beneath the surface of an official story. This tactic requires little organization, since Euro-Americans are impressively adept at simply forgetting that any unpleasantness ever transpired. Choctaw scholar Devon Mihesuah attributes the amnesia to the raw truth's violation of the settler myth of self, which prefers "comfy" to factual history.[1] Personally, I have wondered whether the general settler amnesia is genuinely hysterical in origin, a psychological defense mechanism against a reappraisal of self.

Comfy history helpfully glosses over the criminality of Native American genocide as well as that of African slavery—and, indeed, of the mistreatment of American Others of *any* "wrong" ethnicity. It prevents students from hearing of the Chinese race riots in the 1880s and realizing with a jolt that the rioters were Euro-Americans who murdered helpless Chinese immigrants in the heat of the shamefully racist Chinese Exclusion Act of 1882.[2] It keeps students from learning that *latinos* residing on lands seized from Mexico in the unprovoked Mexican-American War (1846–1848) had been promised U.S. citizenship in Articles 8 and 9 of the 1848 Treaty of Guadalupe Hidalgo, only to have had the deal yanked out from under them for over a century, should they have attempted to invoke the articles' guarantees.[3]

Shushing such challenging facts as these worked for quite some time to preserve amnesia. For instance, in 1851 when the historian Francis Parkman published his *Conspiracy of Pontiac*, he detailed the disturbing fact that British commanders had deliberately distributed smallpox to the Indigenous peoples of Ohio in 1763 during peace conferences at Fort Pitt.[4] The documents that Parkman had used unaccountably disappeared thereafter, so that settler historians were able to pretend for the next 158 years that no one could *prove* a deliberate distribution. This dodge held until in 2009, when I pointed to direct admissions in two official fort journals and a negotiator's report, along with two oral traditions of the deed, first published in 1912, all documenting the smallpox distribution and all missed in the post-Parkman sanitizing.[5]

Of course, the settlers would rather discuss just about anything other than such facts, even to the point of forcing, instead, mind-numbing repetitions of catechisms about their "Founding Fathers." Privileging dogma over data forefends any awkward discoveries, say, of the fact that most of the Founding Fathers were Indian-hating slave-holders, whose unsung reasons for mounting the Revolution included the 1768 British Treaty of Fort Stanwix, which forbade any further encroachment on Iroquoian lands, and England's Mansfield Decision, which cut off the Slave trade in 1772. The dogma of amnesia now wears thin, however. I will never forget, during a class discussion of the Founding Fathers at the Constitutional Convention, one of my African American students mumbling, "Yeah. They found they were fathers, all right!"

There is calculation in the amnesia, as well. I am convinced that such fraught facts as those just canvassed, and there are many more, are why history is no longer taught in K–12 schools in the U.S., and only selectively taught in the universities, for they confer no glory on their perpetrators. Direct lies are no longer possible, yet truly told, American history would rip the veil of sanctity from the official story of *The Winning of the West*, as Teddy Roosevelt phrased his 1889 celebration of genocide in the service of land seizure.[6] Movies, such as the star-studded 1962 hit, *How the West Was Won*, showcasing Roosevelt's take on the issue, will no longer fly, even though the old movies can still make settler lists of *The Hundred Greatest Western Movies of All Time* (2011).[7]

Sponsored amnesia has been pretty well broken through the careful documentation by non-Western scholars of the behavior of European settlers on Turtle Island. With official history assailed, its ramparts of amnesia cannot hold. The last hurrah of racist triumphalism is passing, even as I write, with the death throes of the Tea Party. What necessarily follows is a collapse of European pomp, as other stories, hard stories, unforgiving stories, unsettle the settlers. From his earliest work, Churchill was in the forefront of those successfully chipping away at settler amnesia, a deed his enemies have found hard to forgive.

Denial

Once there is no longer any hiding from the unsavory facts of settler history, a strategy other than amnesia must be adopted. Denial works just fine, for a while, and in Churchill's case, denial prompted a full-court press to insist that what had happened to Native America was *not* genocide. This effort cynically used the pain and the power of the Jewish Shoah to shore up its shoddy arguments by wrapping itself in moral authority of the Jewish experience.

Puzzling as it may seem today, with both historical and modern genocides being freely named and studied *as genocide*, heading into the

1990s, the mere suggestion that anyone other than the Jews of mid-twentieth-century Europe had ever suffered genocide was ferociously repudiated as "anti-Semitic." Every era has a name, the mere calling of which suffices to shut down any commentator, besmirching him or her to the point that rehabilitation is nearly impossible. In 1920, that name was "nigger." In 1950, that name was "commie." In 1980, that name was "anti-Semite." Name-calling is a really efficient method of silencing an otherwise perplexing opponent, for once the era-appropriate slur is applied, the target must answer to the unanswerable name; nothing else is heard. *Ad hominem* attacks remain as handy as they are unethical for deniers.

Thus, the move was on to label Churchill an "anti-Semite," not for any untoward assertions he had ever made, let alone actions he had ever taken, against a people whom he had always pointedly defended.[8] He was smeared, instead, solely for his gall in having used the word "genocide" to describe what had happened to Native America. Painful as it may be to claimants of the uniqueness of the Shoah, however, neither the experience of genocide nor the term "holocaust" belongs exclusively to the twentieth-century Jews. In fact, the historical designation of holocaust arguably belonged first to the eighteenth-century Iroquois and was demonstrably used by the Iroquois in 1926 to describe their experience in the American Revolution.

The Iroquois had been naming their experience "the holocaust" since 1779, calling George Washington *Ganondaganious*, literally, "He Burns It," for ordering the cruelly complete destruction of Iroquoia.[9] Washington certainly did order and rejoice in the destruction of the towns of Iroquoia—sixty of them in upstate New York and sixteen more in Pennsylvania, along with four Lenape-held towns in southeastern Ohio[10]—but translated as "Town Destroyer," *Ganondaganious* omits the horrendous death, wrought mostly by subsequent starvation and exposure, that the conflagrations occasioned. It also avoids mention of the fact that, like Hitler, Washington was ordering the creation of *lebensraum*, for Revolutionary War soldiers were being paid in warrants for Indian land, which had to be seized before the warrants could be honored.[11] This is the post-traumatic context of the letter from the Seneca chiefs, *Gaiantwake* ("Cornplanter"), *Achiout* ("Half-Town"), and *Nihorontagoioa* ("Great-Tree") to Washington in 1791, remarking that "we call you the town destroyer; and to this day, when that name is heard, our women look behind them and turn pale, and our children cling close to the necks of their mothers."[12]

In 1926, the Seneca scholar Arthur C. Parker used the actual word "holocaust" (spelled "Hollocaust") in print to describe this Revolutionary War experience, finding it the most cogent English rendering of the Seneca term. This use of "Hollocaust," as Parker's section header for his discussion of Washington's ordered assaults on Iroquoia, appeared a good six years before the first Nazi concentration camps opened in 1933 and well before the term "holocaust" was generally applied to the Shoah.[13]

Moreover, a good decade before Churchill published *A Little Matter of Genocide* in 1997, other scholars, not all of them Native American, had openly used the terms "genocide" and "holocaust" to describe what had happened to Indigenous America. In 1987, Cherokee scholar Russell Thornton published *American Indian Holocaust and Survival*, followed in 1988 by Lyman Legters in an article on the subject entitled "The American Genocide."[14] David Stannard's *American Holocaust*, published in 1992, and now a staple of history courses, did not mince words on the issue, but opened with searing chapters on the topic of the Native American genocide.[15] In 1993, the Eagle Clan, Osage scholar George Tinker in his *Missionary Conquest* (1993), talked openly of cultural genocide.[16] The list could continue, but the point is clear: by the early 1990s, scholarly studies were intensively linking genocide and holocaust with the Native American experience.

By the time that Churchill's *A Little Matter of Genocide* appeared in 1997, attempts to deny that the settler invasion was genocidal had slipped significantly, yet as late as 2008 in *Anti-semitism*, author Avner Falk held Churchill up as a veritable poster boy for antisemitism. In Avner's mind, because Churchill had used the term "Holocaust" to describe the 500-year genocide against Native America, Churchill was a "racist Holocaust denier."[17] Had Avner but checked his facts, he would have found *au contraire*, that Churchill had been forthright in *denouncing* Shoah-denial, when that shameful "debate" was raging. Apparently, however, close enough is good enough in the practice of denial.

Minimization

Once denials started looking laughably weak, Euroamerican scholars migrated to minimization. This was not a new tactic, as I noted in 2009 in *The Tainted Gift*. Instead, it was a tactic practiced by Euro-scholars, fidgety with guilty knowledge, from the turn of the twentieth century on.[18] Once the sidewinding of land seizure had been rawly exposed in 1881 by social critic Helen Hunt Jackson in *A Century of Dishonor*, scholars began presenting the U.S. government as stuck in the bleachers, desperately wringing its impotent hands while watching the scene unfold. As historian Hiram Chittenden put it in 1902, the U.S. was simply "powerless to save the Indian's lands" from its rapacious citizens.[19] Yeah, sure, you betcha.

That old dog no longer hunts, but the new and improved version of minimization from the latter twentieth century is still dogging birds. This handy method insists that things were just not all that bad by rechristening invasion "contact" and chattering breezily about "middle grounds." Yes, what happened in the Americas was smiley-faced *contact*, as two great societies, previously unaware of one another, discovered each other's cultures. This patter was not confined to fifth-grade social studies texts, either. "Contact" became a favorite linguistic sidestep used, for instance, throughout the twenty volumes of the touchstone Smithsonian work, *Handbook of North American Indians*, particularly in volume 4, entitled *History of Indian-White Relations*.[20]

The *Handbook* used the noncommittal "contact" terminology to frame its uncomfortable discussions in innocent-sounding ways. Europeans did not invade, but somehow just "came into contact" with the Indians.[21] Trade was not a way to run the Indians into land-stripping debt, but was used to provide the Indians with "prestige items," including fancy clothing and glass beads.[22] Epidemic disease and abduction into slavery were euphemized as merely "unfortunate consequences of contact."[23]

This is the Argument of European Innocence, under which Europeans are first presumed innocent and next declared powerless to change anything, because their ethereal innocence in the first place prevents their puissance in the second. Uh-huh. James Baldwin called out this sophistry as far back as 1963 in *The Fire Next Time*, but perhaps conservatives missed that book.[24]

Notwithstanding Baldwin's analysis of the mechanics of the Innocence Project, disease as accidental became a favorite ambiguity. Jared Diamond was particularly active in muddying these waters, initially setting up his microbial argument of unintentionally spread disease in chapter 14 of *The Third Chimpanzee* (1992).[25] Returning to this theme in 1997, he argued hard in *Guns, Germs, and Steel* that epidemic disease had been inadvertently disseminated in the Americas.[26] (As it happened, the same, blameless process that obtained in the Americas was also operative when Australia and Africa were Euro-invaded.) The theme of European innocence thus continued unabated, but now re/presented as unassailable science.

Diamond left unaddressed why all those harmless Europeans did not simply reverse the death toll by abandoning their schemes of invasion, probably because preventing Indigenous death was never the point. The point of clever minimization was, instead, to show that settler design had never been in the mix, at all. No siree, Bob: everything was all the fault of those doggoned microbes doing their tiny dirty work, while the blameless settlers looked on, helpless to turn the tide of the Indians' biological fate. Notably, that fate had not budged one inch from square one. It was still the Manifestly Destined duty of Indians to vanish, making way for the biologically superior European.

Beguiling as Diamond's elegant lift off the hook was for Euroamerican readers, the fact remained that disease had most emphatically been distributed to the Indians with full intent to do harm, as Churchill maintained in *A Little Matter of Genocide*. Although he was heavily clobbered for having directed attention to the man behind the curtain, the documentation of disease as deliberately spread had existed in the archives all along, as I showed in 2009 in *The Tainted Gift*.

Another prime minimalist tack was to focus histories on those brief eras during which Indigenous lands were apparently still in contention. Zeroing in on the seventeenth and eighteenth centuries, Western scholars were able to present European and Indigenous casualties in any fracas as roughly equal numerically, thus to write off the strife as mutual. This was, of course, deplorably false accounting, for the *percentages* of those killed show that Indigenous populations were literally gutted in those affairs, whereas an ever-increasing number of apparently disposable European immigrants continually arrived to take the place of any fallen settlers.[27]

This form of minimizing was pulled off brilliantly in 1991 by Richard White, in his book actually entitled *The Middle Ground*.[28] Under this approach, which conveniently ignores the rigged time frames and carefully managed areas of examination, Western scholars could pretend that the struggle for America had been fought between equal forces, each giving as good as it got. Settlers even gave each other awards for discovering as much. White won four prestigious *awards* for *The Middle Ground*: The 1992 Francis Parkman Prize, for best book on American History, the 1992 Albert J. Beveridge Award, for best English-language book on American History, the 1992 Albert B. Corey Prize, for best book on U.S.-Canadian history, and the 1992 James A. Rawley Prize, for a book on the history of race relations in the U.S. Although White did not also take a Pulitzer for *The Middle Ground*, his book was a nominated finalist for that prize in 1992.

Alas for awards committees, it is only Euroamericans to whom it comes as a shock that "contact" in the "middle grounds" of Native America constituted genocide. Why, in the twenty-first century, minimization continues to be required to soften that shock deserves some examination. In "White Studies," reprinted in *From a Native Son*, Churchill fingers the ardently colonial bent of "higher" education in the U.S., which to this day marginalizes all non-Western subject matter.[29] Some folks call these margins "ghettos," but ghettos are walled up spaces in the midst of the mainstream, so that one can holler over the walls to people on the other side. By contrast, Indigenous scholars are confined at quite a remove, in outright townships, from which to exit they must still obtain white-signed passes.

The urge to minimize may also extend beyond the delicacy of settler sensibilities and into cold calculation. During a workshop that I conducted at Denver University in 2014, one student preferred hushing to exploring the topics of land theft and genocide. "Someone might mention restitution," he said softly. When I responded at normal volume, "What do you have against restitution?" dead silence prevailed in the room. It was palpable.

Notwithstanding some very clever minimizations, by the late twentieth century, it was obvious that the slappees were running off the reservation, slapping back, and that the slappers did not like it, not one little bit. This has led to the final stage of cultural repression: Hostility, teeth-bared, fist-curled, blood-in-its-eye, burn-at-the-stake hostility.

Hostility

Cherokee elders of my acquaintance tell me that a leader is one who walks out front and gets whacked first. If whacking be the sign of leadership, then Ward Churchill is a leader. After a long history of Native American advocacy, in 2005, he was savaged by a gang beating that just would not quit. Oddly enough, even though his 2005–2009 whacking was ferociously *ad hominem*, it was not necessarily personal, for the settler establishment is as skittish as a fawning doe, easily frightened by its own fears into exaggerating threats and even taking action against phantom perils.

Under these conditions, *any* Indigenous leader who had challenged Eurosupremacy as effectively as Churchill stood to have been targeted—and was. Activist Russell Means (1939–2012) of the Oglala Lakota, for example, survived *thirteen* assassination attempts.[30] Churchill argued in 2005 that this settler irritability is more than just a bilious attack of nerves, being a longstanding suppression technique by which a dominant force legitimizes its control. First, power invents a nonexistent threat, and next, it moves forcefully to forestall that ballyhooed threat in a public spectacle. This "two-fer" cements the establishment's dazzling reputation for efficacy against evil at the same time that it demonizes potential insurgents.[31]

Apparently, free-range Indians are just too explosive to leave lying about unguarded, so the U.S. government had been guarding against Churchill since 1969. The spectacular whacking that began in 2005 needs to be understood as a culmination of a thirty-six-year effort to neutralize him, for the Federal Bureau of Investigation opened its file on Ward Churchill on August 20, 1969, and has demonstrably watched him since, as files Churchill has obtained under the Freedom of Information Act (FOIA) attest. One was even sent by the "DIRECTOR, FBI," J. Edgar Hoover, himself, and captioned "WARD L. CHURCHILL, Bufile 100–457301." (See Figure 1.) "Bufile" indicated a headquarters file, and the unredacted portion of the caption included "SM," which (while it might also have been sadomasochistic) technically meant "security matter." "SAC" stood for "special agent in charge." The numerical prefix 100 indicated that an Internal Security investigation was afoot. Churchill's main file number was 100–11632, while 100–12044 indicated "INTENSIFICATION NEW LEFT," and 105–2711 stood for the FBI's notorious Counterintelligence Program ("COINTELPRO"). The rest of the mumbo-jumbo is still any non-initiate's guess.

The cover sheet on the FBI's release of Churchill's files under his FOIA request was stamped "May 25, 1989" and indicated that there were 462 pages reviewed pursuant to that request, of which but 285 pages were released. Thus, 183 pages remain withheld altogether. Moreover, every word of text on at least fifty pages of the material that was released was blacked out, along with roughly one-third of the overall text in the remaining 235 pages. No federal documents have been secured since 1989, but undoubtedly, Churchill's file has grown significantly since the FOIA release.

Notably, all of this was collected against a man who has never in his life been charged with, much less convicted of, an act of violence. To be sure, he strongly advocates for Indigenous rights, as well as the rights of "racial minorities" generally, and apparently that is enough to mark him as a peril in certain fearful minds, but there is no justification for the employment of COINTELPRO techniques against Churchill—or *anyone* (which was why COINTELPRO was a secret program). Worse, the FBI's

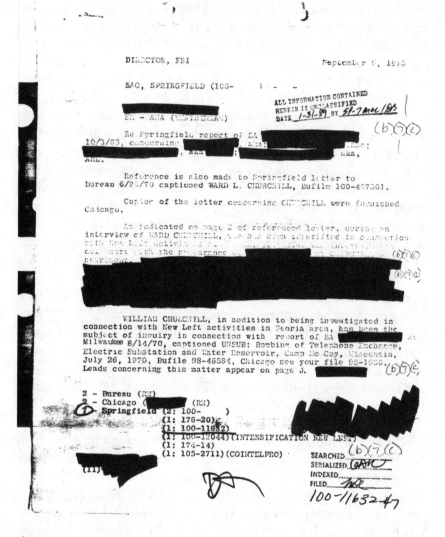

Figure 1

activities arguably generate more violence than they ever avert, often creating the appearance of guilt where there is none. Perhaps, that is the point.

Churchill worried the government enough that agents in Peoria and/or Springfield, Illinois, covertly attempted to neutralize him in 1969 by claiming that he had evaded his legal obligation to assume active reserve status with the army upon his discharge in 1968. Instructively, they did not inquire about his duties through regular military channels but instead went directly to the 113th Military Intelligence Group in Chicago, because the 113th was running its own illegal surveillance and counterintelligence operations against antiwar activists throughout the Midwest at the time, often in collaboration with the FBI and local officials.[32] This attempt to foil Churchill was itself foiled when the 113th revealed that, as a Vietnam veteran, Churchill was legally exempt from active reserve service.

At this point, the FBI decided to turn Churchill over to COINTELPRO. Run by Hoover's FBI, COINTELPRO was in operation, illegally, between 1956 and 1971, when it was purportedly shut down.[33] (Activists have their doubts.) COINTELPRO set *agents provocateurs* on "hostiles," including Native American advocates, to disrupt and discredit their efforts. The terminology of "hostiles" is resonant for Native Americans, since the descriptor "hostile," as attached to "Indians," has been used as a pretext to justify settler attack on Indians ever since the first Englishmen arrived on Turtle Island.[34]

Amid much redaction, the document subject misstated Churchill's first name as "William," although later in the document, it was correctly given as "Ward." The first page of the 1970 document states: "WILLIAM CHURCHILL, in addition to being investigated in connection with New Left activities in the Peoria area, has been the subject of an inquiry in connection with report of SA [redacted] Milwaukee 8/14/70, captioned UNSUB ["Unknown Subject"]: Bombing of Telephone Exchange, Electric Substation, and Water Reservoir, Camp McCoy, Wisconsin, July 26, 1970, Bufile 98–46584." It is unclear whether falsely connecting Churchill to this bombing derived from the same sloppy field work as misstating his first name or was intended to help "neutralize" him legally by smearing him. No further action was taken against him in regard to the Camp McCoy bombing, in any case, because Churchill was not at all involved. The investigation of Churchill in this connection was apparently closed when, later in August 1970, agents concluded that the bombing had been carried out by three active-duty GIs, who were subsequently convicted of it.[35]

The second page of this memo begins with two completely redacted paragraphs. The third and final paragraph, however, includes this key sentence: "Springfield should be advised so that appropriate recommendations may be maintained for Cointelpro action, which might neutralize the activities of this individual," meaning Churchill. Importantly, the document shows that COINTELPRO action against Churchill was authorized by Hoover, with several of the preceding and subsequent documents withheld in their entirety. Thus, it is impossible to determine what or how many federal actions were actually taken against him.

Exhibiting standard Indigenous cheek, instead of feeling intimi-
dated, Churchill gathered up what official documents on COINTELPRO
he could, and in 1988 with Jim Vander Wall, critiqued the FBI's shock-
ingly illicit behavior in a sharp exposé, *Agents of Repression: The FBI's Secret
War against the Black Panther Party and the American Indian Movement.*[36] This
book was followed in 1990 by *The COINTELPRO Papers: Documents from the
FBI's Secret Wars against Domestic Dissent.*[37] Both books were republished in
2001 in a series of "South End Press Classics." Anyone this hard to shut
up seriously spooks the settler establishment.

Churchill remained under continual surveillance from 1970 on,
his file classified. A two-page missive dated February 19, 1985, came
from the "Assistant Director in Charge" (ADIC) at the New York field
office. Sent to the Director of the FBI, then William Hedgcock Webster,
the report stated that, "This communication is classified 'Secret' in its
entirety." Virtually all the remaining text was redacted, including the
caption, so that its agenda was unclear, but it might have pertained to
the FBI's having believed that Churchill was in Mexico City at that point,
a date on which he was actually in Geneva, Switzerland.

Going into the 1990s, assassination became an option for dealing
with Churchill. Through a court-ordered release of documents following an ACLU lawsuit, Churchill's American Indian Movement (AIM)
colleague in Colorado AIM, Glenn Morris, obtained a copy of the two-
document "Person File Report" on himself compiled by Detective Dave
Pontarelli of the Denver Police, Intelligence Section. The second document in this file used information from a confidential informant (CI)
and was labeled an "Incident File Report." Although the names of Ward
Churchill and Russell Means were redacted from Morris' FOIA copy,
both Churchill and Means subsequently filed independent requests for
all file material in which their names were revealed, thereby receiving
copies separately from the one released to Morris. (See Figure 2.) The
pattern of redacting the other two parties' names was followed in each
case, but in combination with Morris's copy, Means and Churchill were
able to reconstruct the unredacted names in the original, except for the
name of the CI. As reconstructed, the file contained the following entry
toward the bottom of page 2:

> 11–22–94, Det. Pontarelli reported that information was received
> from the FBI that a CI had information that Glenn Morris, Ward
> Churchill, and Russell Means would be the target of a "hit" arranged
> by the National members of AIM. This is an attempt to get Colorado

---

Incident File Report

(Incident Number:)

Task Force:	**Incident Type:**
Occurrence Date/Time Begin: '	**Occurrence Date/Time End:** '
Discovered Date:	**Reported By:**
Reported Date: 01/02/1986	**Classification:** Law Enforcement
Author Name: Detective Dave Pontarelli	**Author Facility:** DPD Intelligence Section
Information Type: Intelligence	**Source of Information:** Investigation
Evaluation of Source: Reliable	**Evaluation of Information:** Confirmed

Narrative Summary:

Narrative: The following information contained in this report relating to Glenn Morris is from the DPD Intelligence Bureau reports on the subject from 1-2-86 to 3-3-98. 1-2-86, Information was reported that Glenn Morris and ▮▮▮▮▮▮▮▮ had sent a letter to the editor indicating ▮▮▮▮▮▮▮ ▮▮▮▮▮▮▮ of Colorado AIM. 1-25-86, Det. Potter reported that the subject is a Political Science professor at UCD. 2-20-86, Det. Potter reported that on 2-17-86 a program was held on the Auraria campus, which included ▮▮▮▮▮▮▮▮s, ▮▮▮▮▮ra, Glenn Morris, and ▮▮▮ ▮▮s, who are supporters of ▮▮▮▮▮▮▮▮in Nicaragua; other members of AIM who were present and led by Larry Mosqueda are Pro-Sandinista, a split in the leadership of AIM was foreseen. 3-1-86, Det. Potter prepared an AIM report indicating that a meeting had taken place at Auraria to celebrate the anniversary of Wounded Knee. Only Pro-Sandinistas faction showed. Present wer ▮▮▮▮▮▮▮▮▮▮▮▮▮▮▮rt, ▮▮▮▮▮▮▮▮▮ns and Glenn Morris were not present and were believed to be in So. Dakota. Det. Potter further reported that ▮▮▮▮▮▮▮▮Glenn Morris, active AIM members, professors of political science at Auraria. The report included a list of campus group affiliations for ▮▮▮▮▮▮, which included ▮▮▮▮▮▮▮▮▮▮▮▮ City, International ▮▮▮▮▮▮▮▮▮▮▮▮ 3-26-86, Information was received, a packet of articles from local papers on AIM and ▮▮▮▮▮▮▮▮▮▮trip to Nicaragua. 7-16-86, A report was prepared on a Prayer Vigil, demonstration at the Federal Building, which took place on 7-6-86 and 7-7-86, over ▮▮▮▮▮▮▮▮▮▮ protesting US take-over of tribal lands, Glenn Morris was a participant. 12-10-86, Det. Buysse prepared a report on ▮▮▮▮▮▮▮ ▮▮▮▮▮▮▮▮▮▮▮ giving a speech on 12-9-86 at Auraria. The report included a list of sponsors, ▮▮▮▮▮▮▮▮▮▮, et al, and a list of individuals seen. 2-10-87, Det. Potter reported that Glenn Morris was a participant in a 2-10-87 demonstration protestingCIA recruitment at Auraria, which was sponsored by 'Students Against CIA Terrorism'. 4-13-88, Information was reported on an article from Westword 'Colorado's Peace of Action' on Glenn Morris as a UCD Professor involved in Central America, protesting CIA actions. 10-9-89, Det Potter prepared a report in regards to an AIM demonstration at the Capitol on Columbus Day, protesting the National Holiday honoring the 'Indian killing Spaniards'; Glenn Morris, ▮▮▮▮▮▮▮▮▮▮spoke, as di▮▮▮▮▮▮▮▮, who was ordered-in to court after defacing the Columbus statue in Civic Center Park. The report also has information in regards to the October 12 protest to be held at the Federal Building, over Big Mountain issue, which is sponsored by amalgam of AIM ▮▮▮▮▮▮▮▮, ▮▮▮▮▮▮▮, and ▮▮▮▮▮▮▮▮. 11-7-89, Det. Potter prepared a follow-up report in regards to the AIM report of 10-18-89, which indicated that local Indian activists were involved in supplying illegal weapons to Indians in Latin America; further reported was that ▮▮▮▮ ▮▮▮▮s now strung out on druugs and stolefrom the persons who tried to help him. He was apparently confused about guns being in a church, but it appears tha ▮▮▮▮▮▮▮▮ Morris, et al may be invloved in gun running. 12-7-89, A report was prepared in regards to a news article on Pledge of resistance demonstration planned at Currigan Hall on 12-8-89, at President Bush visit. Glenn Morris was listed as the spokesperson/contact. 10-5-90, Information was reported that 'Means renews Columbus protest' ▮▮▮▮▮▮▮s of AIM vows to disrupt Columbus Day parade. Glenn Morris was quoted as supporting the protest. 10-8-90, It was reported that the Columbus Day protest was avoided, and the Columbus Day parade was peaceful. AIM protesters were allowed to join the parade. The report has quotes from ▮▮▮▮▮ and Morris. The report contained a list of support groups, which included, Nations of Islam and Big Mountain Support Group. The report quotes ▮▮▮▮▮▮▮▮▮▮▮▮▮▮▮▮▮▮▮. 10-15-90, Report indicated 'Newsmaker', a profile on Glenn Morris in the RMN. 11-23-90, A report indicated that Indians congregated at the Capitol for fasting. ▮▮▮▮▮▮▮▮▮▮nd Glenn Morris spoke out for AIM. Others spoke about US holiday celebrating the Indians welcoming Pilgrims; then the Indians were killed off by white

Figure 2

AIM "back in the fold" with the national Indian agenda. The report indicated that Morris and Churchill would be killed and that Means would be injured. It was feared that the incident would happen at an Indian Convention in Denver the previous week, bkut [*sic*] none of the persons involved was seen at the convention.

Although Detective Pontarelli had clear knowledge of a murder plot, neither he nor anyone in the Denver police contacted or made any known attempt to protect Churchill, Morris, or Means. The FBI was no less obligated than the Denver police to warn the trio of what was viewed as a credible threat of lethal violence against them. Instead, one or both agencies assigned *observers* to witness whatever happened at the conference.[38] Nothing happened, but only because neither Means, Morris, nor Churchill showed up at the expected location.

Instead of warning the targets of their danger, the Denver Police, Intelligence Section's files classified Colorado AIM as a "Criminal Extremist G—Organization." "G" stands for "gang" in this parlance, although as the files reflect, Colorado AIM has *never* been accused or, apparently, even suspected of engaging in a criminal enterprise. Notwithstanding, the Intelligence Section intensified its surveillance of the group. The FBI seems to have gone much further than the Denver Police, putting Colorado AIM under investigation as a "terrorist" organization. The basis for this classification is unknown, as the relevant files have not been released.[39]

The "Criminal Extremist G" classification assigned to Colorado AIM seems to have been unique, yet Colorado AIM was hardly the only political organization in the Denver area scrutinized by the Police Intelligence Section. When the spy files were disclosed in 2002, it was revealed that, although the files on Colorado AIM were by far the most extensive, the Intelligence Section had also been keeping tabs on a range of other groups during the 1990s. In fact, files had been opened on 208 Denver area organizations and nearly 3,200 individuals. Groups included such unoffending outfits as Amnesty International and the American Friends Service Committee (i.e., the Quakers!), none of which were shown to have been involved in any criminal activity whatsoever. Among the dangerous perps surveilled were Sister Antonia Anthony, a seventy-four-year-old Maryknoll nun, and Helen Henry, an eighty-two-year-old Quaker activist. The only thing many of the groups might have been accused of, or even had in common, was that each had voiced opposition to state or federal policies, at some point. In other words, they were "guilty" only of exercising their First Amendment rights, a matter which did not afford the police any lawful basis for having placed them under surveillance.[40]

Although the revelations concerning these spy files supposedly signaled the end of political snooping by the Denver Police Intelligence Section, it should be emphasized that not only was no one ever charged for having run the illegal police operation, but many of those previously spied upon—Colorado AIM members in particular—*continued* to have been targeted for harassment. In retrospect, it is easy to see that the unremitting surveillance applied to Churchill, most of all.

Prior to 2005, the primary strategy for unhinging Churchill seems to have been to convict him of charges stemming from his role in the ever-mounting protests of the annual Columbus Day parade in Denver. The assumption apparently was that, if he could be locked up for a while, the University of Colorado at Boulder could use his conviction as a basis for revocation of his faculty tenure. The subsequent loss of status would then undermine the credibility of his future activities. The first effort to get at Churchill around the Columbus Day parade occurred after protests had halted one in October 1991. At the subsequent trial in July of 1992, Churchill was one of the four "ringleaders" acquitted of all charges.[41]

The much-anticipated October 1992 celebration of the Columbian Quincentennial in Denver had to be called off at the last moment in the face of a massive AIM-organized protest, thereby greatly embarrassing local authorities, and parades were not resumed until 2000. Colorado AIM correspondingly resumed its protests, and the City of Denver, while still targeting those it saw as "key agitators," shifted to a policy of making mass arrests in an effort to quell their resistance.

The City was forced to dismiss all charges twice, beginning in 2002, before Churchill and seven other "ringleaders" of the protest were finally brought to trial in mid-January 2005. To the dismay of their enemies, all eight were acquitted on all counts, with Churchill defending himself *pro se*, although the other seven had retained lawyers. One of the prosecutors was later quoted in the *Rocky Mountain News* as crediting Churchill's testimony and courtroom tactics with having been the deciding factor in the acquittal of the eight.[42]

In 2001 and again in 2003, while the Columbus Day strategy was still in process, the golden alternative of "little Eichmanns" presented itself, although it would not emerge into public consciousness until 2005, after the Columbus Day strategy was conclusively dead. If Churchill was acquitted in mid-January 2005, on the protest charges, then in early February 2005, the University of Colorado at Boulder undertook to hector him openly for the comments of 2001 and 2003. Using this pretext, the university removed him from its teaching faculty in 2006 with the intention of finding a pretext on which to fire him outright, a feat it ultimately accomplished in 2007.

In this effort, there was a seeming confluence of interests involved, both national and local. It was in that respect a "perfect storm" propelling the astonishingly intense and sustained feeding frenzy on the part of the mainstream media in Denver. Churchill surmised that, among the

principal motives was the goal of utterly destroying his credibility as a
potential defendant or witness in any future court actions.

The odyssey began unnoticed in the immediate wake of the New
York's World Trade Center attack of September 11, 2001. In the emotional
whirl immediately following the Twin Towers' collapse, the media was
inviting commentary on the event by soliciting writers, literally right
and left. Like many others, on September 12, 2001, Churchill offered his
take on the fall of the towers in "*Some* People Push Back: On the Justice
of Roosting Chickens," the subtitle an allusion to Malcolm X's famous
response to the Kennedy assassination, that "chickens come home to
roost." Citing the half-million Iraqi children who had died "needless
deaths" as the result of U.S. actions since the close of the first Gulf War
(1990–1991), Churchill noted that those chickens had just come home to
roost "in a very big way."[43] This was hardly a new critique by Churchill,
who had been decrying the U.S. war drive against Islam since 1990.[44]

Between 1991 and 1996, well over 500,000 Iraqi children under
twelve years of age are estimated to have died of malnutrition and readily
curable diseases as a direct result of the U.S.-orchestrated and -enforced
sanctions.[45] Among other things, after the first Gulf War, U.S. sanctions
had prevented Iraq from obtaining certain medicines and foodstuffs, as
well as the materials necessary to repair or rebuild its infrastructure—
water purification and sanitation facilities, for example—causing great
suffering to the Iraqi people.[46] Madeleine Albright, then-U.S. ambassador to the United Nations and subsequently secretary of state, sought
to justify the attendant mass death and misery during a Leslie Stahl
interview on *60 Minutes* in May 1996, saying that if it accomplished U.S.
policy objectives, then "the price is worth it."[47]

In 1997 in *A Little Matter of Genocide*, Churchill indicted such unilateral
U.S. actions against Iraq as the massacre of retreating Iraqi troops and
the postwar bombings, as cynically motivated by economic and political considerations, not by any high-minded concern for democracy.[48]
Thus, in his 2001 response and his 2003 book, Churchill was *revisiting* the
topic of designer genocide that had been carried out continuously since
1991, albeit largely unremarked by ordinary Americans, under the Bush
I, Clinton, and Bush II administrations.

In "*Some* People Push Back," Churchill expanded on his theme by
stressing that those planning the longstanding bombing raids on Iraqi
targets had had their office in the Trade Towers. Both the CIA and the
Department of Defense (DoD) maintained offices that, together, encompassed some two-thirds of the space on the twenty-fifth floor of the

building known as "World Trade Center 7."[49] In describing the function-
aries of the CIA and Department of Defense as they targeted who was
to be bombed and when, Churchill used the phrase "little Eichmanns."
(Adolf Eichmann had been the hands-off, logistical architect of the
death-camp roundups and deportations for Nazi Germany.) In 2001,
Churchill's usage of "little Eichmanns" not only passed without hysteria, but was also republished in his 2003 book, *On the Justice of Roosting
Chickens.*[50] Far from a public roasting, this book received an honorable
mention for the Gustavus Meyers Award for Best Writing on Human
Rights for 2003.

Churchill's major argument had pertained to the rules of engagement regarding aerial bombardment, as articulated by the U.S. government during the first Gulf War. General Colin Powell, General "Stormin'"
Norman Schwarzkopf, and other high U.S. officials, military and civilian,
routinely justified their pinpoint bombings of Iraqi hospitals, schools,
and other civilian facilities on grounds that the Iraqi government had
deliberately situated its command and control infrastructure in those
buildings.[51] On the one hand, if those choosing the targets of the U.S.
air attacks sat in the Towers, then the U.S.'s own rules of bombardment
made the entire complex a "legitimate target." On the other hand, if
military siting did not make civilians a legitimate target in the U.S., then
how could it have ever made civilians a legitimate target in Iraq?

If these "legitimate targeting" premises were so very reasonable,
Churchill mused, were Americans then entitled to bitter complaints
when precisely the same rules were applied to them? Churchill contended that, if Americans did not like the prospect of being treated in
a manner identical to that in which they were accustomed to seeing
their military treat others, then they needed to reconsider a few things.
In particular, they needed to ensure that the U.S. military valued the
lives of "enemy" noncombatants no less highly than those of Americans.
Churchill recommended an insistence upon U.S. compliance with the
international laws of war, which prohibit the targeting of civilian facilities as objectives. The International Committee of the Red Cross agrees,
saying in 1987 that the laws of war "do *not* provide any justification for
attacks which cause extensive civilian losses and damages. Incidental
losses and damages should *never* be extensive" (emphasis mine).[52] If
Americans refuse to agree to these rules, then they, too, should be considered fair game, Churchill argued.

Ignoring such ethical and logical conundrums, U.S. officials instead
hurried on to term the Iraqi civilian casualties "collateral damage," rather

than real human beings with families, hopes, and dreams, all blown to bits because they happened to be in the targeted schools, hospitals, and domestic facilities. The psychological screening of obscurantist diction is magical, and luckily, the DoD did not have to invent new diction on the fly in 2003, for "collateral damage" had been in play since the First Gulf War. "Despite" the military's best efforts "to minimize collateral civilian casualties," the DoD moaned in July of 1991, "some collateral damage and injury did occur." This was because the "Government of Iraq located military assets (personnel, weapons, and equipment) in populated areas and adjacent to protected objects (mosques, medical facilities, histori-cal/cultural sites) in an effort to obtain protection for its military forces." The U.S. just had to bomb these facilities, for "military supplies were stored in mosques, schools, and hospitals in Iraq and Kuwait."[53] Thus was the responsibility for killing civilians off-loaded onto the Iraqis, at the same time the civilian casualties were dehumanized as mere "col-lateral damage."

Native Americans have had a long and painful acquaintance with this sort of wiggling off the hook to bathe in the light fantastic of inno-cence. The standard Indigenous response has been to expose the tactic in all its naked malice. The eighteenth-century Lenapes, for instance, called it out, warning those with less experience of the settlers than themselves that "the long knives will, in their usual way, speak fine words to you, and at the same time murder you."[54] "Long knives" did not just indicate the Virginia militias, but all the land speculators, financiers, timber companies, and other exploiters among the settlers, who lusted after Indian assets.

Churchill was coming out of this Indigenous space when he referred to "technocratic corps at the very heart of America's global financial empire" who were "inhabiting the sterile sanctuary of the twin towers."[55] His intention was to name just how many of those who profited from clearly immoral acts worked in the Towers, including all those interna-tional trade and finance technicians, brokers, and corporate attorneys busily maximizing profits, and their own commissions, while knowing full well that it was achieved by imposing mass immiseration and trun-cated lifespans on whole populations of Others, worldwide.

Churchill concluded that, individually, these technocrats were desk murderers every bit as much as those targeting the bombs and cruise missiles.[56] In the aggregate, they were symbolic of a systemic reality com-monly referred to as "globalization," although Churchill preferred simply to call it "imperialism." Whatever the term, it quietly generated precisely the sort of carnage that Indigenous America had experienced (and still experiences), but with an efficiency never before seen. For Churchill, the system was not especially different in substance from that envisioned by the Nazis during the postconquest era of their "Thousand Year Reich."[57]

Preserving that system, Churchill held, is the fundamental task harnessing both the U.S. military and veiled entities such as the CIA and NSA. It follows that, given the complexity of its reach, the soft technocracy is far more significant than the military technocracy. He argued that the desk murderers hiding behind the mask of supposedly harmless "free trade" should be called out, or at least called by their right name. To date, very few of them have been called to account, because the propaganda engines shifted into overdrive to proclaim their inherent innocence as mere agents of "commerce." Thus, we once more circle back to James Baldwin's critique of putative "innocence" as "powerlessness." Notably equivalent claims of "innocence" did not spare Nazi collaborators from prosecution in the 1945–1946 Nuremburg Trials.[58]

Importantly, unlike DoD spokesmen, Churchill took care to humanize the "collateral damage" of September 11 by exempting the true innocents in the attack from excoriation: children, custodial and janitorial staff, food service workers, secretarial and clerical personnel, emergency responders, sightseers, and random passers-by, as well as, perhaps, a few homeless folks who had sought refuge in the Towers' basement. By no reasonable method could Churchill's "technocrats" have stretched to them. Lost in the heat of media hysteria, however, was the distinction Churchill had drawn between the technocrats and the innocents, as the media screamed that Churchill had styled *everyone* in the Towers "little Eichmanns."

The long knives never have much appreciated being called out, but luckily, they have long since learned how to deflect such prickly critics as Churchill. Killing the messenger usually works, hence the ensuing media frenzy, not over Churchill's actual argument, but over his diction in using the term, "little Eichmanns." Churchill did not, however, coin the term. Along with related analogies to the "Good Germans," who denied responsibility for the consequences of Nazism on grounds that they were merely obeying orders, terms such as "little Eichmanns" have been clichés in casual usage since World War II to ping banal bureaucrats acting in prosaic ways that result, indirectly but quite predictably, in the systemic infliction of serious injury to Others.

During the late 1950s, following the work of Hannah Arendt and others, Edgar Zodiag Friedenberg was reputed to have uttered the term "creeping Eichmannism" to explain the spread and ever-growing institutionalization of such attitudes and attendant behavior as the banality of Eichmann's death-dealing bureaucracy.[59] Subsequently, the term was adopted by other scholars concerned with the same issues, not least by Noam Chomsky in his widely-read 1967 book *American Power and the New Mandarins* and, a couple of years later, Neil Postman and Charles Weinberger in their *Teaching as a Subversive Activity*.[60]

The formulation "little Eichmanns" is perhaps best-known for having been twice used by the anarchist philosopher John Zerzan in defending Ted Kaczynski—the so-called Unabomber—several years before Churchill applied it in the context of September 11.[61] The term has, however, a far longer and more expansive pedigree. It was certainly in common usage by the early 1960s, a matter readily attested by its use in a noticeably Churchillian manner by historian John Dornberg in a 1961 book on the psychosocial implications of Nazism.[62] In 1964, Oliver Walker used it in *Kaffirs Are Livelier*, a book on apartheid South Africa.[63] By 1981, in a book review by Richard Schickel, "a regular little Eichmann" had even made its appearance in the pages of the *New York Times*.[64] It is worth noting that Schickel's review was of Earl Shorris, *The Oppressed Middle: Politics of Middle Management*. Schickel was thus applying the term in very much the same sense—and to much the same cast of characters—as Churchill had been in "*Some* People Push Back."

A sampling of just a few others who employed the term "little Eichmanns" before—and often *long* before—Churchill includes social philosopher Lewis Mumford, poet Anne Sexton, psychoanalyst Ralph Greenson, and genocide scholar Eric Geldbach.[65] Moreover, independently of any reference to Churchill, scholars Michael Schwartz and Debra C. Comer have recently quoted M.W. Jackson's 1988 description of the "numerous little Eichmanns" surrounding Oskar Schindler during the Nazi Judeocide.[66] Most striking of all is the fact that the term "Eichmannism" is used to explain the perils integral to bureaucracy in the current edition of a standard college textbook, *Political Science: An Introduction*.[67]

With national emotions running amok, however, none of this context mattered. Churchill's historical arguments, grounded in the first Gulf War; his social commentary in noting that Islam had been styled an official enemy of "Christendom" since the Crusades; his appeal for the Twin Tower attacks to be viewed in the sweep of that history; his adoption of an oft-used sobriquet—all went for naught. What was pulled forward, and all that was heard, was the quip about "little Eichmanns," and the media, ever in search of a lip-smackin' controversy, was none too scrupulous about reporting it in context. The right-wing press, especially, devolved into in a perfect feeding frenzy that rivaled the thrashing of pirañas in a virgin kill zone.[68]

To this day, authors continue running with scissors, cutting Churchill's comment about "little Eichmanns" from its intended context in 2001 oblivious of its clichéd status and ignoring its long history of print usages, to present it as a unique coinage meaning something other than what it did.[69] Instead, proffering no citation other than popular gossip, authors continue to castigate Churchill for the phrase, as if the term "little Eichmanns" had been coined in 2001 and Churchill had intended it to encompass the child victims of September 11. Even those who acknowledge what Churchill actually meant by "little Eichmanns," including those in agreement with his premise, tend to misattribute the term's coinage to him, as did Phil Rockstroh, for instance, in describing it as "Ward Churchill's much scorned, career purge-inducing—but never-the-less accurate phrase."[70] Even true believers on a mission have a duty to honesty in citing Churchill's thesis accurately and responding to the arguments he actually made as opposed to some media-induced illusion of what he said.

Perhaps, as an Indian, Churchill should already have realized that Iraqi life was not nearly as valuable as Euroamerican life, and thus 500,000 dead Iraqi children would not fly as a critique of U.S. actions.[71] If surveillance and assassination plots had not already alerted him to the fact, then the supervening mess at the University of Colorado at Boulder certainly brought it to his attention. In pursuit of Churchill, in February 2005, the university's interim chancellor Philip DiStefano put together an *ad hoc* committee, which proceeded to investigate every last word that Churchill had ever written, even going to the ridiculous lengths of reviewing documents he had written *as a student*.[72] One spurious accusation after another was lobbed, impelling Churchill to resign from his chairmanship of the Department of Ethnic Studies in 2006 to devote all his time to self-defense.

In 2011, the Colorado Council of the American Association of University Professors (AAUP) published an exhaustive, two-year investigation of Churchill's case, ultimately publishing a 135-odd page report detailing the deviousness and even outright fraudulence of the charges against him. The AAUP not only found that Churchill was not guilty of *any* of the scholarly offenses of which he had been "convicted" by the CU committees, but also that the university administration had systematically rigged the process while its committees deliberately suppressed, distorted, and in some instances literally falsified evidence in order to create the necessary appearance of wrongdoing on Churchill's part.[73]

Notwithstanding the facts, matters heated to the point that the United Keetoowah Band of Cherokee Indians distanced itself from Churchill—after having invited him to enroll in 1994.[74] Although the Keetoowahs never disenrolled him, its rabbiting gave Churchill foes yet another cudgel with which to whack him, largely because "federal recognition" is poorly understood in the U.S. by non-Indians—and even by some Indians. Indian enrollment was one of those prophylactic measures presciently taken to insulate the West from the rest.

Under the infamous Allotment Act of 1887 and its associated regulations, "federal recognition" of Indians was cooked up as a *benefits determination* for receiving "allotted" land—from, of course, what had all been Indian lands. Upon receipt of their allotted land, people were expunged from the rolls in what the Commissioner of the Bureau of Indian Affairs characterized in 1905 as the "final solution" to the inconvenience of Indian existence.[75] This scam assigned federal recognition to just one-third of the 300,000 Indians who defied their elders to sign up.[76] The 300,000 was nowhere near the head count of all living Indians at the time, either. Nevertheless, the "Dawes Rolls" were gotten up, guessing at the "quantum" of "Indian" blood of each enrollee, based on the same racist pseudoscience under which Hitler's Nuremburg Laws parceled out racial identity to Jews in Nazi Germany.[77] This is why the Non-Treaty People of the east characterize governmental enrollment as "federal wreck-cognition."

The resultant "Dawes Rolls" are a gift that just keeps on giving. Today, a century-and-a-quarter later, the federal government is still able to use those knowingly fraudulent rolls to divide and conquer living Indians. The "federal recognition" originally cooked up as eugenics today allows the government to refuse to listen to the descendants of those Indians capriciously rejected from the Dawes rolls. The minority still enrolled is now pitted against the troublesome majority left out in the cold, punished by the government, which still withholds from them its imprimatur as "real" Indians, against the moment it might need to neutralize Indigenous critics as "not federally recognized."[78] After the bandwagon dumping on Churchill by the Keetoowahs, the Churchill-haters had the final pleasure of disparaging him *both* as an Indian *and* as a "fake." Life does not get much better than this for bigots.

Unbowed, Churchill promptly sued the University of Colorado at Boulder. At trial in 2009, even in Colorado, where public sentiment was leaning toward lynching Churchill at dawn, the jury rejected the university's case. The upshot of its slipshod "investigation" was that Churchill won his lawsuit on April 9, 2009, when—finding exactly as did the AAUP upon real examination of the facts—that that he had been wrongly dismissed, with his free speech rights massively violated. Because Churchill had argued throughout the trial that he was looking for justice, not a monetary reward, the jury awarded him just one dollar in damages.[79]

The permission granted by the fraught attacks on Churchill after the "little Eichmanns" comment went viral in 2005 brought America's white supremacists out of the woodwork, showing what the attacks on Churchill had *really* been about, all along. Not only Churchill but his wife—a non-Indian who had not been involved in the brouhaha in any way—received death threats. The harassment intensified to the point that a professional bodyguard volunteered his services to Churchill. Having long despised "ethnic studies," racists also seized the opportunity to flog the university's entire Department of Ethnic Studies (DES). Not only faculty, but also students of the program became the targets of racist threats. The menacing grew so intense, that on April 25, 2005, the DES faculty wrote an "Open Letter" to the Colorado Board of Regents, protesting the attacks and defending its right to exist.

The open letter included an eight-page sampling of the e-mails it had been receiving by way of illustrating the disgraceful attacks being mounted on all sides. The messages were breathtakingly hateful, homophobic, and racist, as these representative excerpts show:[80]

To Churchill's wife:
Subject: How squaw bitch . . .

> tell um Chief Ward Wigwam: Look like pale face who want um to be um red face is um disgraced. Why don't you BOTH come on a tour of the east coast when u do your little stop in NY. We'll go out and have some fire water. On an unrelated note, Is it possible for "indian givers" to give "indian burns."?

To the Department of Ethnic Studies:
Subject: Ward Churchill is a dickhead

> I must laugh at your so called college department. Tell Ward, my ancestors killed a lot of Indians and I'm proud of it.

To Churchill, personally:

> Dear Ward . . .
> Why don't you take a silly-ass muslim name like Mohammed
> Mohammed Mohammed and wear a diaper on your head.

To: Ward.Churchill [sic]

> Your people are a lazy bunch of scum! . . . I am a 52 year old son of
> the people that have made this miserable patch of ground called
> America the greatest force of good in the world! . . . [A]s a native
> of Colorado I will force you to become a piece of trash in the dust
> bin of history with the rest of your "ancestors."

To: Ward Churchill

> Hey Chief – the "7th Cavalry" is coming after your worthless ass.

To: Ward.Churchill@Colorado.EDU

> What I would like to know is why you liberal commi [sic] scumbags
> in this country hate it here so much . . . WHY THE FUCK ARE
> YOU HERE . . . WE ARE SICK OF YOU LIBERALS RUNNING THIS
> COUNTRY . . . YOU ARE A SICK MF AND HOPE YOU FRIGIN GET
> ANAL CANCER FROM YOUR HOMO STUDENTS.

To: Ward Churchill
Subject: PLEASE READ

> Dear Squanto/Crazy Horse
> . . . IF AMERICA IS SO EVIL WHY DON'T YOU GET THE FUCK
> OUT OF HERE? . . . I SUGGEST YOU LEAVE THIS CAMPUS,
> LEAVE THIS COUNTRY AND GO PREACH YOUR BULLSHIT IN
> SAUDI ARABIA OR WHERE ELSE THERE ARE "SAND NIGGERS"
> BECAUSE YOU WILL BE PUT TO DEATH . . . AND MANY PEOPLE
> WOULD BE HAPPY.

To: Ward Churchill

> I don't giva FUCK, ME AND YOU, MY MAN, LETS GET IT ON . . .
> ME AND U M/F. JUNGLE KNOTS COMMING [sic] YOUR WAY,
> SWEETIE PIE . . . 40 CAL, 9MIL, AK47, 50 CAL, H TO H, HOW U

WANT IT, IT WILL BE SHOVED UP YOUR RED ASS THE WORLD
TO SEE.

To: Ward Churchill

> Subject: Commie-pinko bed-wetting left-wing long-haired
> faggot . . . Given my way, you'd be throw into a dark cell for ten
> years, then execute you after that, you homo . . .
> PS: You may be interested in knowing that my god son has killed
> over 30 ragheads, destroyed 15 tanks and 10 Toyota pickup trucks
> from his F–18.

The sweet nothings continued, *ad nauseam*, but the reader has the gist of
them by now.

Monuments

In his remarks of May 15, 1918, to the Amalgamated Clothing Workers of
America, unionist Nicholas Klein summed up the process of civil struggle, invoking one, final stage that goes beyond my own list:

> And, my friends, in this story you have a history of this entire
> movement. First they ignore you. Then they ridicule you. And then
> they attack you and want to burn you. And then they build monu-
> ments to you.[81]

Whether Klein was right that today's turmoil will end in monuments to Native America remains to be seen, for, being vastly outnumbered in their own land, Indians have only the clout of moral authority.
So far, moral authority and Churchill's dollar will not buy anyone cup
of coffee.

Starbucks may not be the issue, however. I have made it a point
for the last several years of asking every Indigenous elder I encounter
whether they have any knowledge of just who invited the Europeans over
in the first place. It is the dangdest thing, but not one has had any tradition of having issued the invitation. Worse, the Europeans have been very
bad houseguests, and the hosts are getting restless.

Today, with the doctrine of discovery not only revealed as the
wretched rationale for invasion that it always was but also condemned
by the United Nations in 2009, the Indigenous push of the twenty-first
century is toward an emphatic decolonization, one that boldly challenges the "right" of Euroamerican settlers to:[82]

1. rest easy in their "sovereignty" over the land,
2. retain the "right" to "recognize" who the indigenous peoples are,
3. continue fouling Turtle Island with the rip-and-run economics of environmental desolation.

Maybe there will be a monument to this agenda.

Notes

1   Devon Abbott Mihesuah, "Academic Gatekeepers," in Devon Abbott Mihesuah and Angela Cavender Wilson, eds., *Indigenizing the Academy: Transforming Scholarship and Empowering Communities* (Lincoln: University of Nebraska Press, 2004) p. 42.

2   See, for instance, Isaac H. Bromley, *The Chinese Massacre at Rock Springs, Wyoming Territory, September 2, 1885* (Boston: Franklin Press; Rand, Avery & Company, 1886).

3   David Kazanjian, *The Colonizing Trick: National Culture and Imperial Citizenship in Early America* (Minneapolis: University of Minnesota Press, 2003) pp. 12, 175–76, 206–209.

4   Francis Parkman, *The Conspiracy of Pontiac and the Indian War after the Conquest of Canada* (1851; 1898; Boston: Little Brown and Company, 1910) pp. 44–45.

5   Barbara Alice Mann, *The Tainted Gift: The Disease Method of Frontier Expansion* (Santa Barbara, CA: Praeger, 2009) pp. 1–18.

6   Theodore Roosevelt, *The Winning of the West: An Account of the Exploration and Settlement of Our Country from the Alleghenies to the Pacific*, 6 vols. (1889; New York: G.P. Putnam's Sons, 1903).

7   The editors of *American Cowboy* magazine, *The 100 Greatest Western Movies of All Time* (Guilford, CT: TwoDot, 2011) p. 132.

8   Ward Churchill, *A Little Matter of Genocide: Holocaust and Denial in the Americas, 1492 to the Present* (San Francisco: City Lights, 1997) pp. 19–25.

9   Washington had boastingly used *Conotocaurious* ("Town Destroyer"), a different rendering of *Ganondaganious*, since 1755, in Charles E. Congdon, *Allegany Oxbow: A History of Allegany State Park and the Allegany Reserve of the Seneca Nation* (Salamanca, NY: self-published, 1967) p. 142.

10   *George Washington's War on Native America* (Westport, CT: Praeger, 2005), New York, p. 67; Pennsylvania, p. 37; Ohio, pp. 138–39 and 155–60.

11   For land warrants, see Mann, *George Washington's War*, pp. 39, 113, 13, 147–49, 177.

12   *American State Papers*, Class II, 2 vols. (1832, reprint; Buffalo, NY: William S. Hein, 1998) Vol. 1, p. 140.

13   Arthur C[aswell] Parker, *An Analytical History of the Seneca Indians: Researches and Transactions of the New York State Archaeological Association, Lewis H. Morgan Chapter* (1926, reprint; New York: Kraus Reprint Co., 1970 reprint of 1926 original) p. 126.

14   Russell Thornton, *American Indian Holocaust and Survival: A Population History since 1992* (Norman: University of Oklahoma Press, 1987); Lyman Legters, "The American Genocide," *Policies Studies Journal* 16 (1988) pp. 768–70.

15   David E. Stannard, *American Holocaust: Columbus and the Conquest of the New World* (New York: Oxford University Press, 1992).

16   George E. Tinker, *Missionary Conquest: The Gospel and Native American Cultural Genocide* (Minneapolis: Augsburg Fortress, 1993).

17 Avner Falk, *Anti-semitism: A History and Psychoanalysis of Contemporary* (Westport, CT: Praeger, 2008) p. 152.

18 Mann, *Tainted Gift*, p. xv.

19 Helen Hunt Jackson, *A Century of Dishonor: A Sketch of the United States Government's Dealings with Some of the Indian Tribes* (1881, reprint; Norman: University of Oklahoma Press, 1995); quotation, Hiram Martin Chittenden, *The American Fur Trade of the Far West*, 3 vols. (New York: Francis P. Harper, 1902) Vol. 1, p. 11.

20 William C. Sturtevant, ed., *Handbook of North American Indians*, vol. 4, *History of Indian-White Relations* (Washington, DC: Smithsonian Institution, U.S. Government Printing Office, 1988); for examples of "contact" terminology, see pp. 47, 89, 243, 301, 304, 351, 353, 397, 401, and 545.

21 Ibid., p. 3.

22 Ibid., p. 397.

23 Ibid., p. 110.

24 James Baldwin, "My Dungeon Shook: A Letter to My Nephew on the One-Hundredth Anniversary of Emancipation," in *The Fire Next Time* (1963; New York: Vintage International, 1993) pp. 3–10.

25 Jared M. Diamond, *The Third Chimpanzee: The Evolution and Future of the Human Animal* (New York: HarperCollins, 1992), "Accidental Conquerors," pp. 235–48.

26 Jared M. Diamond, *Guns, Germs, and Steel: The Fates of Human Societies* (New York: W.W. Norton & Co., 1997) p. 27.

27 See my close examination of false numerical equivalencies in Barbara Alice Mann, "Fractal Massacres in the Old Northwest: The Example of the Miamis," *Journal of Genocide Research*, Vol. 15, No. 2 (2013) pp. 167–82.

28 Richard White, *The Middle Ground: Indians, Empires, and Republics in the Great Lakes Region, 1650–1815* (Cambridge: Cambridge University Press, 1991).

29 Ward Churchill, "White Studies: The Intellectual Imperialism of U.S. Higher Education," in *From a Native Son* (Cambridge, MA: South End Press, 1996) pp. 271–94.

30 Gerald Robert Vizenor, *Fugitive Poses: Native American Scenes of Absence and Presence* (Lincoln: University of Nebraska Press, 1998) p. 101.

31 Ward Churchill, presentation, recorded September 2005, posted April 17, 2008 by Freemixradio, at minutes 8:48 to 10:48, http://www.youtube.com/watch?v=14W5hYRHjD0.

32 Athan Theoharis, *Spying on Americans: Political Surveillance from Hoover to the Huston Plan* (Philadelphia: Temple University Press, 1978) 178–79; Frank Donner, *Protectors of Privilege: Red Squads and Police Repression in Urban America* (Berkeley: University of California Press, 1990) pp. 146–47.

33 For the most comprehensive official overview, see "COINTELPRO: The FBI's Covert Action Programs Against American Citizens," in U.S. Senate, Select Committee to Study Government Operations, *Final Report, Book III: Supplementary Detailed Staff Reports on Intelligence Activities and the Rights of Americans* (Washington, DC: Report No. 94–755, 94th Cong., 2nd Sess., U.S. Government Printing Office, 1976) pp. 1–78.

34 See, for instance, Increase Mather on King Philip's War that "[t]hus did the War begin, this being the first English blood which was spilt by the Indians in a Hostile way," italics in the original, Increase Mather, *The History of King Philip's War* (1676; Albany: J. Munsell, 1862) p. 55.

35 Tyler C. Kennedy and David Null, "Archives & Oral History: Protests & Social Action at UW–Madison during the 20th Century; 1970s," 4, accessed March 23, 2014, http://archives.library.wisc.edu/uw-archives/exgibits/protests/1970s/html.

36 Ward Churchill and Jim Vander Wall, *Agents of Repression: The FBI's Secret War against the Black Panther Party and the American Indian Movement* (Boston: South End Press, 1988).

37 Ward Churchill and Jim Vander Wall, *The COINTELPRO Papers: Documents from the FBI's Secret Wars against Domestic Dissent* (Boston: South End Press, 1990).

38 Amy Herdy and Carol Kreck, "'Spy File' Target Seeks Scrutiny of Cops: Police Didn't Tell Activist of Rival's Plot to Kill Him," *Denver Post*, December 19, 2002.

39 "Spy Files Reveal Political Spying by FBI's Joint Terrorism Task Force," Colorado ACLU Press Release, September 12, 2002, accessed 23 March 2014, available at http://aclu-co.org/spyfiles/fbifiles.

40 Tom Gorman, "Denver in Uproar over Police 'Spy' Files: Dossiers on Individuals and 'Criminal Extremist Groups Are Called an Invasion of Privacy," *Los Angeles Times*, September 10, 2002, accessed 23 March 23, 2014, http://articles.latimes.com/2002/sep/10/nation/na-spies10.

41 M.A. Jaimes, "The Trial of the 'Columbus Day Four': Missing the Point in Denver," *Lies of Our Times* (September 1992) pp. 8–9. For the best overview of the Columbus Day protests in Denver and elsewhere during the late 1980s and early '90s, see Timothy Kubal, *Cultural Movements and Collective Memory: Christopher Columbus and the Rewriting of the National Origin Myth* (New York: Palgrave-Macmillan, 2008).

42 Charlie Brennan, "Ward Churchill: A Contentious Life," *Rocky Mountain News*, March 26, 2005, accessed March 20, 2014, http://www.freerepublic.com/focus/f-news/1371635/posts.

43 Ward Churchill, "*Some People Push Back: On the Justice of Roosting Chickens*," in this volume, p. 520.

44 See, e.g., Ward Churchill, "On Gaining 'Moral High Ground': An Ode to George Bush and the 'New World Order,'" in Cynthia Peters, ed., *Collateral Damage: The 'New World Order' at Home and Abroad* (Boston: South End Press, 1992) pp. 359–71.

45 Ramsey Clark, ed., *Reports by the UN Food and Agriculture Organization: The Impact of Sanctions on Iraq: The Children Are Dying* (New York: International Action Center, 1998) p. 166.

46 Ramsey Clark, "The Devastation of Iraq by War and Sanctions," in Ramsey Clark et al., eds., *Challenge to Genocide: Let Iraq Live* (New York: International Action Center, 1998) pp. 10–14, 24–26.

47 Leslie Stahl, "Punishing Saddam," produced by Catherine Olian, CBS, *60 Minutes*, May 12, 1996. Albright later repudiated her statement, although she was still held culpable for it, see "Democracy Now! Confronts Madeleine Albright on the Iraq Sanctions: Was It Worth the Price?" July 30, 2004, http://www.democracynow.org/2004/7/30/democracy_now_confronts_madeline_albright_on.

48 Churchill, *A Little Matter of Genocide*, p. 389.

49 See table 5.1, titled "WTC 7 Tenants" in Ramon Gilsanz, Edward M. DePaola, Christopher Marrion, and Harold "Bud" Nelson, "WTC 7," in FEMA, *World Trade Center Building Performance Study* (Washington, DC: FEMA, 2002) p. 5–2. Available online at http://www.fema.gov/pdf/library/fema403_ch5.pdf.

50 "The Ghosts of 9-1-1: Reflections on History, Justice, and Roosting Chickens," *On the Justice of Roosting Chickens: Reflections on the Consequences of U.S. Imperial Arrogance and Criminality* (Oakland, CA: AK Press, 2003) pp. 19, 33n126, 34n130.

51 For a representative selection of official statements in this connection, see Middle East Watch, *Needless Deaths in the Gulf War: Civilian Casualties During the Air Campaign and Violations of the Laws of War* (New York: Human Rights Watch, 1991) pp. 76–87, 171–93;

on so-called dual-use targets specifically, see pp. 76, 81; on the deliberate targeting of more explicitly civilian targets, see pp. 158–71.

52 International Committee of the Red Cross, *Commentary on the Additional Protocols of 8 June 1977 to the Geneva Conventions of 12 August 1949* (Geneva: Martinus Nijhoff, 1987) 626.

53 United States Department of Defense, *Conduct of the Persian Gulf Conflict: An Interim Report to Congress* (Washington, DC: U.S. Department of Defense, July 1991) p. 12–3.

54 John Heckewelder, *A Narrative of the Mission of the United Brethren among the Delaware and Mohegan Indians* (1820, reprint; New York: Arno Press, Inc., 1971) p. 219.

55 Churchill, "Some People Push Back."

56 Variations of the term "desk murderers," long and commonly used in the field of holocaust/genocide scholarship, originated on exactly the same basis as "little Eichmanns," and may in fact be considered a synonym. See, e.g., Hannah Arendt, *Responsibility and Judgment* (New York: Schocken, 2005) pp. 228, 237, 241, 242, 247, 250, 251; David Cesarani, *Becoming Eichmann: Rethinking the Life, Crimes, and Trial of a "Desk Murderer"* (Cambridge, MA: Da Capo Press, 2007), esp. p. 260.

57 Although this theme has been at least implicit to any number of studies and commentaries on Nazi expansionism over the past sixty-five years, it has of late been developed much more explicitly. See, e.g., Mark Mazower's well-received *Hitler's Empire: How the Nazis Ruled Europe* (New York: Penguin Press, 2008), esp. pp. 576–604.

58 See, e.g., Joseph Borkin, *The Crime and Punishment of I.G. Farben* (New York: Free Press, 1978) pp. 135–56.

59 Neil Postman and Charles Weingartner, *Teaching as a Subversive Activity* (New York: Delta Press, 1969) p. 9; "Children . . . and Ourselves: Diatribe Plus," MANAS *Reprints*, Vol. 22, No. 46 (November 12, 1969) pp. 12–13, accessed March 24, 2014, http://www.manasjournal.org/pdf_library/VolumeXXII_1969/XXII-46.pdf.

60 Noam Chomsky, *American Power and the New Mandarins* (1967; New York: New Press, 2002) p. 342; Postman and Weingartner, *Teaching as a Subversive Activity*, p. 9.

61 Anonymous Antiauthoritarian [John Zerzan], "Whose Unabomber?" *Green Anarchist*, 41–42 (Spring 1996) pp. 21–22; reprinted under the same title and Zerzan's own name in *Anarchy: A Journal of Desire Armed* 44 (Vol. 15, No. 2; Winter 1997–98) pp. 50–51; and collected in John Zerzan, *Running on Emptiness: The Pathology of Civilization* (Los Angeles: Feral House, 2002) p. 154.

62 John Dornberg, *Schizophrenic Germany* (New York: Macmillan, 1961) p. 52.

63 Oliver Walker, *Kaffirs Are Livelier* (London: Frederick Muller, 1964) p. 199.

64 Richard Schickel, "The Choking White Collar," *New York Times*, March 15, 1981, accessed March 24, 2014 http://www.nytimes.com/1981/03/15/books/the-choking-white-collar.html.

65 Respectively, Lewis Mumford, *The Pentagon of Power: The Myth of the Machine, Vol. II* (New York: Harcourt Brace Jovanovich, 1970) p. 279; Anne Sexton, "The Wonderful Musicians," in *Anne Sexton: Complete Poems* (New York: Houghton-Mifflin, 1981) p. 267; Robert A. Nemiroff, Alvin Robbins, and Alan Sugarman, eds., *On Loving, Hating, and Living Well: The Psychoanalytical Lectures of Ralph R. Greenson* (Madison, CT: International Universities Press, 1992) p. 191; and Eric Geldbach, "Goldhagen— Another Kind of Revisionism," in Franklin Hamlin Littell, ed., *Hyping the Holocaust: Scholars Answer Goldhagen* (East Rockaway, NY: Cummings and Hathaway, 1997) p. 96.

66 Michael Schwarz and Debra C. Comer, "The Difficulty of Being a Moral Exemplar When an Exemplar Is Needed Most: The Case of Oskar Schindler," in Howard Schwarz and Howard Harris, eds., *Moral Saints and Moral Exemplars* (Bingley, UK:

Emerald Group, 2013) pp. 163, 164. The quoted article was M. W. Jackson, "Oskar Schindler and Moral Theory," *Journal of Applied Philosophy*, Vol. 5, No. 2 (1988) p. 178.

67   Michael G. Roskin, Robert L. Cord, James A. Medeiros, and Walter S. Jones, *Political Science: An Introduction*, 12th ed. (Boston: Pearson, 2012) p. 271.

68   See, e.g., Brian Montopoli, "Of Agendas, Fetishes, and Crusades," *Columbia Journalism Review*, May 23, 2005, accessed March 24, 2014, http://www.cjr.org/politics/of_agendas_fetishes_and_crusad.php?page=all.

69   Ward Churchill, "Some People Push Back."

70   Phil Rockstroh, "Tales of Angst, Alienation and Martial Law: Roasting Marshmallows on the Reichstag Fire to Come," *Dissident Voice*, July 26, 2007, accessed March 23, 2014, http://dissidentvoice.org/2007/07/tales-of-angst-alienation-and-marshal-law-roasting-marshmallows-on-the-reichstag-fire-to-come/.

71   See Edward S. Herman and Noam Chomsky, "Worthy and Unworthy Victims," in *Manufacturing Consent: The Political Economy of the Mass Media* (1988; New York: Pantheon Books, 2002) pp. 37–86.

72   See generally Elizabeth Mattern Clark, "CU to Study Professor's Work, Consider Firing," *Boulder Daily Camera*, February 4, 2005, p. 1. Among other things, Churchill was asked to provide a copy of his MA thesis.

73   Don Eron, Suzanne Hudson, and Myron Hulen, *Report on the Termination of Ward Churchill* (Colorado Council of the American Association of University Professors, Committee to Protect Faculty Rights, November 1, 2011), published in *Journal of Academic Freedom*, Vol. 3 (2012), accessed March 24, 2014, http://www.aaup.org/reports-publications/journal-academic-freedom/volume-3.

74   Johnny Flynn, "Ward Churchill Finds a Home with the Friendly United Keetoowah Band," *Indian Country Today*, December 15, 1994, accessed March 24, 2014, http://www.highbeam.com/doc/1P1-2302597.html.

75   Department of the Interior, *Annual Report of the Commissioner of Indian Affairs for the Fiscal Year Ended June 30, 1905*, Part I (Washington, DC: U.S. Government Printing Office, 1906) p. 5.

76   Kent Carter, "Federal Indian Policy: Cherokee Enrollment, 1898–1907," *Prologue*, Vol. 23, No. 1 (1991) p. 36.

77   For an extended discussion of the entire, fraudulent process, see Barbara Alice Mann, *Native Americans, Archaeologists, and the Mounds* (New York: Lang Publishing, 2003) pp. 282–96.

78   For my further discussion of the recognition/nonrecognition issue, see Barbara Alice Mann, "Slow Runners," in *Daughters of Mother Earth: The Wisdom of Native American Women* (Westport, CT: Praeger, 2006) pp. 69–109.

79   Felisa Cardona, "Churchill Wins CU Suit but Awarded Just $1," *The Denver Post*, April 2, 2009, accessed March 3, 2014, http://www.denverpost.com/breakingnews/ci_12055632, Michael Roberts, "Juror Bethany Newill Talks about the Ward Churchill Trial," *Westword*, April 3, 2009, accessed March 24, 2014, http://blogs.westword.com/latestword/2009/04/juror_bethany_newill_talks_abo.php.

80   All extracts quoted in Faculty, Department of Ethnic Studies, University of Colorado at Boulder, "An Open Letter from the Department of Ethnic Studies, University of Colorado at Boulder to the Board of Regents, President Betsy Hoffman and Interim Chancellor Phil DiStefano," April 25, 2005, pp. 5–10.

81   Amalgamated Clothing Workers of America, "General Executive Board Report and Proceedings of the Third Biennial Convention of the Amalgamated Clothing Workers of America, Held in Baltimore, Maryland, May 13 to 18, 1918," in *Documentary History*

of the Amalgamated Clothing Workers of America, 1916–1918 (Baltimore: Amalgamated Clothing Workers of America, 1918) p. 53. This statement is often massaged and falsely attributed to Mohandas Gandhi.

82 Tonya Gonnella Frichner, "Impact on Indigenous Peoples of the International Legal construct known as the Doctrine of Discovery: A Preliminary Study," United Nations, E/C.19/2010/13 (February 3, 2010) pp. 1–2.

A Few Thoughts on a Book Long Overdue

> I write what I like.
> —Steve Biko
> (1969)

This one's been a long time comin'. More precisely, it's nearly ten years overdue. *Wielding Words like Weapons*, the second volume of my selected essays, composed of material published during the decade 1995 to 2005, should by rights have come out no later than 2006, and was even announced as forthcoming in that timeframe. That being so, its tardiness rather obviously had nothing to do with problems finding a publisher willing to handle my work. Nor was I suffering the least shortage of material with which to assemble the volume. If anything, precisely the opposite situation prevailed. The period at issue having been perhaps my most productive in terms of writerly output, my quandary at the time—and still, for that matter—arose from the bittersweet necessity of selecting from an overabundance of otherwise deserving candidates only those essays that might be accommodated within a book of roughly five hundred pages.

The delay—derailment might be a better way of putting it—was of course precipitated by the concerted attack launched against me/ my scholarship toward the end of January 2005 by the full spectrum of U.S. doctrinal enforcement, from the FoxNoise machine and its cohorts throughout mass media to a raft of republicratic officials on the order of Colorado's Cro-Magnon then-governor, Bill Owens, to the mainstream intelligentsia in its veritable entirety, to a centrally coordinated torrent of "spontaneous" vitriol spewing from the depths of euroamerica's bottomless pool of mentally jackbooted louts in waves of boilerplated e-mails, and on and on. The onslaught, summarized and contextualized quite well by Barbara Alice Mann in her foreword, will not be further belabored here apart from the observations that being targeted in such fashion was a fascinating—in many respects validating—experience, and that the matter will be taken up in my forthcoming but as yet untitled third volume of selected essays, spanning the decade 2005–2015.

It must nevertheless be acknowledged that certain effects of the "Ward Churchill Controversy" upon the book at hand have proven well-nigh unavoidable, and not only by way of its protracted postponement as I waded through a couple of years' worth of hearings before academic tribunals, the composition and comportment of which were worthy of Roland Freisler,[1] prepared for the month-long 2009 trial of my lawsuit against the University of Colorado's board of regents for firing me as an act of political retaliation, and thereafter commenced a lengthy series of appeals after the judge vacated the jury's unanimous verdict in my favor. By the time the case reached the U.S. Supreme Court—which declined to review it in early 2013—I'd already moved to Atlanta and was mired in the demands attending any such transition. Suffice it to say that only in the past year have I been in a position to resume my actual work at a level resembling that at which I was operating prior to 2005.

Meanwhile, the process of being used by Those In Charge and their minions to illustrate the ongoing currency of Eugene V. Debs' 1918 observation that "it is extremely dangerous to exercise the constitutional right of free speech" in the U.S., a country then as now offering itself as the planetary exemplar of liberty while perpetually "fighting to make democracy safe in the world,"[2] has served the purpose of appreciably altering the priorities by which I'd have originally selected the line-up of essays contained herein. All things being equal, it would never have occurred to me to incorporate the blog-posted "*Some* People Push Back," for instance. As evidenced by its emergence as the ostensible catalyst of the "free speech firestorm" in which I found myself engulfed in early 2005,[3] however, what I'd written had clearly registered a solid hit upon those I view as being precisely the right parties. This in itself prompted me to reconsider the extent to which I'd previously discounted the piece.

In effect, both the nature and sheer volume of the collective whine emitted during "The Controversy," especially as manifested in demands that I retract—or, more accurately, recant—"the truth as I see it,"[4] simply ensured a diametrically opposite result. Embracing, as I did and do, Debs' principle that he'd "a thousand times over rather be a free soul in jail than a sycophant and coward on the streets," and his corresponding refusal "to say anything that I do not think,"[5] calls for my prosecution on charges of treason or sedition served mainly to confirm me in the view that I was obliged not only to include "*Some* People," albeit as an appendix, but to do so in annotated/amplified form.[6] My decision in this regard was strongly reinforced by threats that I'd be subject to what Mumia Abu-Jamal described as "the academic equivalent of a death sentence"[7]—or assassination of the more literal sort[8]—should I fail to "take it back."

This being so, also including "The Ghosts of 9–1–1," the much more thoroughly developed follow-up to "*Some* People," while it might—or might not—have secured a niche in *Wielding Words* as I first conceived it, now seems essential. So, too, the lengthy survey on U.S. war crimes and patterns of national self-exoneration/denial titled "'To Judge Them by the Standards of Their Time.'" Several others in this vein might well have been added, but doing so would place far too great an emphasis on only one of several interrelated themes pursued in my writing between 1995 and 2005. Even including the last essay mentioned has required that I significantly diminish the weight I originally intended to place on material addressing the eugenicist construction of identity imposed upon/internalized by American Indians under U.S. colonialism,[9] retaining only the newly postscripted "In the Spirit of Gunga Din" on that important topic.

Still, in selecting the contents of this volume, I've sought to provide a representative survey of my interests and resulting work during the period at issue, beginning with three essays—"Subverting the Law of Nations," "The United States and the Genocide Convention," and "Charades Anyone?"—focusing upon the ongoing refusal of the U.S. to comply with the rule of law whenever doing so might prove in any sense inconvenient. These might of course be rightly viewed as complements to "Some People," "Ghosts," and "'Standards,'" although "Charades" in particular delves into the question of internal colonialism and may thus be seen as linking up with "In the Spirit of Gunga Din" as well. The same can be said with regard to "Remembering Bob Thomas," my testimonial to the man who first applied an internal colonial framing to the situation of American Indians, and whom I was lucky enough to have been able to count among my mentors before his passing.

"Contours of Enlightenment" is also a testimonial, this one to the late Vine Deloria Jr., another mentor—and in his case, a longtime friend as well—whom I consider to have been among the leading intellects of his generation. There were any number of vectors of Vine's acumen—notably with respect to law, religion, and the music of Gene Autry—upon which I've drawn over the years, perhaps none more so than his

penetrating critiques of the array of mythologies bound up in anthropological and other canons of Western science. Hence, my inclusion
of "Science as Psychosis," not only on its own merits—which I believe
are more than sufficient to warrant a berth—but as a tribute to Vine's
influence, and because of the obvious relationship between the sort of
"scholarship" it dissects and popular misrepresentations of indigenous
people. The latter dovetails quite nicely with "American Indians in Film,"
a culminating exposition of ideas I've been exploring in successive iterations since the late 1970s with regard to the cinematic dimension of U.S.
colonialism on the "domestic" front.[10]

Casting Hollywood in this light of course ties my analysis of
Tinseltown's grotesquely distorted and dehumanizing depictions of
"Indians" to those in which I deal more directly with the issues of colonization and genocide (while offering a glimpse of my pedagogy as well).
As I said, the themes I pursue are invariably interrelated. This, to be sure,
is true of "Kizhiibaabinesik," a recounting of the life and death of my
late wife, Leah Renae Kelly, the only matter about which I experienced
a certain trepidation at taking up in the present context. In the end,
however, several people whose judgment I trust convinced me of the
importance not only of including something substantive to reflect the
work I've done on the genocidal effects of the Indian boarding schools—
or "residential schools," as they're known in Canada—but that the atypi-
cally personalized approach I'd taken in this essay might be especially
effective in rendering the costs of its ongoing perpetration more tangible.
Thus, despite my lingering queasiness at the self-revelation involved,
we'll see.

Finally, as was the case with From a Native Son, the volume of my
essays in indigenism selected from the decade 1985–1995, I've opted to
include a handful of book reviews—four, to be exact—and only partly
because I've long made a practice of publishing such items on a regular
basis. More compellingly, since I've always treated reviews as vehicles
upon which to address issues noticeably broader than the relative merits
of whatever book I might be assessing, their presence herein allows me
to at least partially fill several thematic holes—the disproportionate
rates at with American Indians are imprisoned in some areas of the
U.S., for example—in the range of material I've otherwise selected for
Wielding Words. (Besides, I've always appreciated referrals to useful books,
especially those that remain little-noticed, and to be cogently warned
against those that amount to no more than an additional layer of New
Age trash.)

A further reason for including a few reviews is to complete an illustrational continuum, showing how in this "minor" form, no less than in formal essays, words can and should serve as weapons. The key in this regard, as I see it, is simply to call things by their right names, without equivocation. To quote none other than U.S. Supreme Court justice Antonin Scalia, "Words have meaning. And their meaning doesn't change,"[11] or at least not into the veritable opposite of their original meaning. Hence, genocide is genocide, not "ethnocide," "ethnic cleansing," or any of the other euphemisms employed by "responsible" scholars to connote supposedly other and "lesser" crimes.[12] By the same token, colonialism is colonialism, not something else, and we'll not have arrived at "the postcolonial" until colonialism is actually abolished, everywhere and in all forms, and racism is racism, not mere "prejudice" or anything as innocuous-sounding as "bias."

This is to say, among many other things, that those who lend their proficiencies to the systematic immiseration of mostly darker-skinned Others for purposes of profit maximization/personal benefit are and will always be the psychological/moral equivalents of Adolf Eichmann. Arguments to the contrary, irrespective of their relative degrees of crudity or elegance, are, to borrow again from Justice Scalia, pure "interpretive jiggery-pokery,"[13] a mode of denial rendering the purveyors actively complicit in the perpetuation of genocide, colonialism, racism, and all the rest. This, by the way, most certainly includes Scalia himself, a flagrantly reactionary jackanape invested with endless streams of argle-bargle and rama-lama-dingdongery, a circumstance increasingly exacerbated by an apparent degeneration of his cognitive abilities (à la Alzheimer's).

While none bear responsibility for a single word I've written, and less still for the manner in which I've written it, a number of people have been influential in shaping the thinking inscribed in *Wielding Words*. Salient among them, for reasons already mentioned, were Vine Deloria Jr., Robert K. Thomas, and Leah Renae Kelly, all of whom are gone now. So, too, my elder brother, Russ Means, as well as my friend and co-conspirator, Bob Robideau, my stepfather, Henry Debo ("Bud," to those who knew him), his wife—my mother—Maralyn, and my great-aunt, Bonnie Favrot (née Allen). I miss them all, and will do so always and dearly, along with Sagye (Kenny Kane), Nilak Butler, Philip Deere, Bill Kunstler, George Manuel, Roberta Blackgoat, Mary Dann, Jack Forbes, John Mohawk, Ed Bernstick, Wallace Black Elk, Severt Young Bear, Aaron Two Elk, Fools Crow, and the Noble Red Man himself, Mathew King. The years have inevitably taken their toll, and the AIM circle of which I was part is now mostly a sometimes wistful memory. Yet, as it must, the struggle continues.

Among those continuing it to whom I owe various debts of gratitude for their intellectual inspiration and personal support, thanks goes especially to Barbara Alice Mann, and not only for the excellence of her foreword. Another round goes to my wife Natsu Taylor Saito, our daughter, Akilah, and her husband, Jed. Others include the Old Woman Bear (Sharon Venne), Michael Yellow Bird, Carrie Dann, Moana Jackson, Glenn Morris, Tink Tinker, Tony Belthem, Rob Williams, Jim Page, Jimmie Durham, Simon Ortiz, Chrystos, Haunani-Kay Trask and her sister, Mililani, David Stannard, Roland Chrisjohn, Waziyatawin (Angela Wilson), Ben Whitmer, Rob Chanate, Josh Dillabaugh, Annerika Whitebird, Irene Watson, Mike Ryan, and Jim Vander Wall. My appreciation as well to Ramsey, Steven, John, Gregory, and the other folks at PM Press for their enthusiasm, perseverance, and a job well done.

Ward Churchill
Atlanta, June 2015

Notes

1   For those who don't know—a cast of characters undoubtedly including his squads of impersonators at the University of Colorado—Roland Freisler headed the National Socialist People's Court from August 1942 until his death on February 3, 1944, and is deservedly notorious for conducting sham trials meant to lend a patina of "legality" to the nazis' transparently preordained verdicts. See generally H.W. Koch, *In the Name of the Volk: Political Justice in Hitler's Germany* (London: I.B. Tauris, 1989).

2   Debs was a leading socialist and among the founders of the IWW. The remark quoted was made at the beginning of a speech delivered in Canton, Ohio, on June 16, 1918, vociferously condemning U.S. participation in World War I. He was arrested two weeks later, charged with sedition. Convicted on September 12, he was sentenced to ten years in federal prison, ultimately serving a little over two and a half (April 13, 1919 to December 23, 1921). There are several more recent biographies, but my personal favorite remains McAlister Coleman's *Eugene V. Debs: A Man Unafraid* (New York: Greenberg, 1930).

3   See, e.g., Scott Smallwood, "Inside a Free Speech Firestorm: How a professor's 3-year-old essay sparked a national controversy," *Chronicle of Higher Education* (February. 18, 2005). Variations on the phrase quoted were endlessly repeated in the press, probably the most common formulation being "firestorm of controversy." That no controversy existed until the media announced it went all but universally unmentioned.

4   The phrase in quotes is adapted from a passage Laws of the Regents of the University of Colorado, Art. 5, Part D: Principles of Academic Freedom, to wit: "[A]cademic freedom is defined as the freedom to inquire, discover, publish, and teach truth as the faculty member sees it."

5   The passages quoted are from the speech cited in note 2.

6   On February 9, 2005, for example, FoxNoise bloviater-in-chief Bill O'Reilly, using a former officer in the naval Judge Advocate General's Corps named Greg Noone as a prop, sought to trigger a popular initiative to have me charged with treason or, alternatively, sedition.

7   Mumia Abu-Jamal, "The War Against Ward Churchill" (Prison Radio broadcast, August 4, 2007; transcript available at http://www.socialistviewpoint.org/sepoct_07/sepoct_07_20.html).

8   I received more than a few e-mailed death threats—and a handful by snail mail—during the spring of 2005, most of them sent either anonymously or under obvious pseudonyms. A number of the missives dared me to come to New York and repeat what I'd said in *"Some People."* I did so on several occasions, notably at the New School in December 2006, each time with ample advance publicity. The brave souls who'd been threatening dire consequences from a safe distance were conspicuous by their absence. This was entirely predictable, underscoring as it does the fact that those genuinely intent upon inflicting harm tend not to provide advance notice.

9   I initially envisioned including "The Nullification of Native America?," a lengthy analysis of the racial provisions embedded in the 1990 American Indian Arts and Craft Act, as well as an in-depth critique of Susan Miller's unspeakably racist and distortive "history" of the Seminoles, *Coacoochee's Bones,* originally solicited—and duly ignored—by the editors of its publisher, the University Press of Kansas. While "Nullification" is included in *Acts of Rebellion: The Ward Churchill Reader* (New York: Routledge, 2003), my critique of Miller's 2003 book will have wait for yet another day.

10 See, e.g., Ward Churchill, Mary Ann Hill, and Norbert S. Hill Jr., "Media Stereotyping and Native Response: An Historical Overview," *The Indian Historian,* Vol. 11, No. 4 (December 1978) pp. 45–56.

11 Jennifer Senior, "In Conversation: Antonin Scalia," *New York Magazine* (October 6, 2013).

12 Although there are other problems with the book, the terminological subterfuge involved with referring to "ethnic cleansing" as if it were something other than a particular modality of genocide is analyzed quite well in Martin Shaw's *What Is Genocide?* (Cambridge, UK: Polity Press, [2nd ed.] 2015) pp. 66–83. For a glaring example of how the term is employed as a means of minimization/denial, see Gary Clayton Anderson's *Ethnic Cleansing and the American Indian: The Crime that Should Haunt America* (Norman: University of Oklahoma Press, 2014).

13 The term, which dates back in English legal discourse to the mid-nineteenth century, was of course employed by Scalia in his dissent in *King v. Burwell* (2015). See Olivia Nuzzi, "Old Man Yells at Cloud: What Scalia's 'Jiggery-Pokery' Means," *Daily Beast* (June 25, 2015), available at http://www.thedailybeast.com/articles/2015/06/25/what-scalia-s-jiggery-pokery-meanso.html.

ONE

Remembering Bob Thomas

His Influence on the American Indian Liberation Struggle

> The Indian picture isn't any blacker than it always was. It is just that American Indians are trying to do something about their problems and injustices. They are speaking out more and making their wishes known. Maybe a new day is dawning for the Indian.
> —Robert K. Thomas, *Indian Voices*, 1966

Although Robert K. Thomas was known primarily as an ethnographer and cultural anthropologist of considerable stature, his interests and activities transcended all boundaries conventionally associated with those fields. Stan Steiner, for one, went to some lengths in recording Bob's involvement with organizations like the National Indian Youth Council during the 1960s,[1] and careful students will discover not a few explicitly political treatises published under his byline, mostly appearing in the American Indian activist venues of the day, papers like *Indian Voices* and *ABC: Americans Before Columbus*.[2] On the scholarly side of things, too, he was known to make such excursions into what has today come to be known as "applied" anthropology. His essay "Powerless Politics," for example, published in the Winter 1966–67 edition of *New University Thought*,[3] a small-circulation academic journal produced at the University of Chicago, is known to have had a significant impact upon the leadership of the fish-in protests of the Puget Sound in 1967,[4] occupation of Alcatraz Island in 1969,[5] and 1972 Trail of Broken Treaties.[6]

Originally published in Steve Palik, ed., *A Good Cherokee, A Good Anthropologist: Papers in Honor of Robert K. Thomas* (Los Angeles: UCLA American Indian Studies Center, 1998). It has been somewhat revised, expanded, and more heavily annotated for publication here. In almost all cases, the sources cited are those available when the essay was written.

It is one of the latter cluster of writings, also published in the 1966–67 issue of *New University Thought*, that I believe may turn out in the end to have been the most influential of all his many endeavors. The essay, entitled "Colonialism: Classic and Internal," was short, more a tentative probing of ideas than a finished piece of scholarship.[7] Yet for me, and for many of those with whom I've worked over the past two decades, it has assumed a decisive conceptual importance in terms of our understandings of ourselves and what it is we're about.[8] Perhaps predictably, perhaps ironically, many of those most affected by it at this point have forgotten—or were never really aware of—the article itself. By the same token, it is certain that Bob himself was, by the end of his life, both amazed and to a large extent perplexed by the directions in which some of us have taken his seminal perspective on the nature of the American Indian relationship to the United States. Most likely, he was also a bit frightened by certain of our prescriptions as to what should be done about it.

The Concept

What Bob Thomas accomplished in this one brief excursus was to redeem an entire classification of socioeconomic and political relations seemingly denied to analyses of the Indian condition in the U.S., one which appeared to have been permanently foreclosed by passage of the United Nations General Assembly Resolution 1541 (XV)—or "Blue Water Requirement," as it's often called—in 1960. According to the UN definition, a situation of colonialism can be properly (and legally) said to exist if, and *only* if, one nation directly and as a matter of policy dominates the social, economic and political life of another from which it is physically separated by an expanse of open water.[9] In such instances, the dominated nations are construed as being absolutely entitled to relief from their circumstances under international law, and, should their colonizers prove reluctant to comply with legal requirements in this regard, the colonized are accorded the right of pursuing decolonization and self-determination by any and all means available to them.[10]

In contrast, nations dominated by others to which they are contiguous, or within which they are encapsulated, are cast by Resolution 1541 not as colonies per se, but as "minority groups" domestic to the dominating power. While such populations are guaranteed (or conceded) a certain range of rights under international law,[11] both the type and extent of these rights, and the means by which they may be lawfully pursued, are very much constricted when compared to those acknowledged as inhering in "overseas" colonies.[12] This is to say that the self-determining rights of "national minorities," to borrow the vernacular of marxist-leninist discourse, are sharply circumscribed—if not foreclosed altogether—by an offsetting legal imperative of preserving "the territorial integrity of states" (irrespective of how this territory was obtained).[13]

Indirectly, and in the somewhat homey style that was his trademark, Bob pointed to the obvious. In effect, he argued that while the definition of colonialism at issue might be adequate to describe the traditional form marked by historical empires such as those of France, Spain and Great Britain—most of which had passed or were passing into oblivion by the late 1960s[14]—it plainly failed to address the realities underlying a number of other readily observable phenomena. Accepting the reasoning imbedded in Resolution 1541 would, for instance, force one to conclude that the Poles and French had been somehow transformed into "minority groups" by virtue of the World War II nazi conquest and occupation of Poland and France, both of which were/are contiguous to Germany.[15] Obviously, any such conclusion would be absurd, and is universally recognized as such; no one questions that France remained France, and Poland Poland, after the German invasion/occupation of each country; hence, no one questions the rights of the Poles and French to liberate themselves from German rule.[16]

Why then, Thomas asked by implication, should the situation be perceived as different for a host other nations—those of American Indians, for example—which can be readily shown to have suffered entirely similar processes of conquest and occupation of their homelands at the hands of contiguous aggressors? "If it walks like a duck, and talks like a duck," goes the old adage, "it's probably a duck." All evidence, Blue Water notwithstanding, combining to suggest that American Indians suffer exactly the same kinds of domination and exploitation as, say, the Algerians under French rule,[17] or Congolese peoples under the Belgians,[18] and for most of the same reasons, Bob concluded that the concept of colonization is as appropriate to describing the circumstances of indigenous nations within the U.S. as it is to describing those of the country's more easily recognizable colonies abroad: Hawai'i, the Philippines, Puerto Rico, Guam, "American" Samoa, the Marshall Islands, and the "U.S." Virgin Islands.[19]

To make his concept immediately comprehensible, he offered a formulation in which colonialism might be viewed as a system divided into two overarching types or categories: "classic" would be the descriptor used to designate those colonies separated from their colonizer by open ocean, "internal" the term used to define colonies appended to or incorporated directly into the territory claimed by the colonizing power as constituting its home turf. Arguably, the lineage of the formulation might trace to Antonio Gramsci's 1926 essay on the "Southern Question,"[20] although it's a virtual certainty that Bob was unfamiliar with it, and thus arrived at his position independently.[21]

It's also possible that he was in some sense influenced by the armed struggle mounted by Basque insurgents from the mid-1950s onward to liberate their homeland from its forced incorporation into Spain, although he neither said nor wrote anything suggesting that this was so.[22] A much better case can be made that Bob was aware that the thinking of black activists like Stokely Carmichael was following a trajectory similar to his own on the issue of colonialism, and that the effect was to some extent galvanizing.[23] Certainly, the indigenous intelligentsia of which Bob was part considered Carmichael's positions "significant," as was remarked by Vine Deloria Jr. in his landmark *Custer Died for Your Sins* in 1969,[24] and discussed more thoroughly in his *We Talk, You Listen* a year later.[25]

All that aside, Bob's notion of internal colonialism, applied as it was to the specific context of American Indians in the late twentieth century, has yielded a powerful analytical utility to those of us seeking to decipher the peculiarly convoluted relationship of the federal government to North America's native peoples, and how this relationship has caused Indians in "the land of the free"—despite our nominal retention of land and resources sufficient to make us the wealthiest single racial/ethnic population aggregate on the continent—to experience literal Third World levels of impoverishment.[26] By the mid-1970s, the idea of American Indian reservations as colonies had taken firm hold among a number of scholars exploring questions of Indian rights.[27] Even elements within the government itself had to some extent admitted the validity of the premise, with the U.S. Civil Rights Commission publishing a major study of conditions among the Diné (Navajos) titled *The Navajo Nation: An American Colony*.[28] A whole new understanding of Native North American context was beginning to evolve.

Applications

A perhaps even more significant effect could be found within the milieu of Indian political activism, of which Bob was himself a part, that had emerged in the wake of Afroamerican initiatives in the Deep South during the 1950s and '60s. Many were jolted by the implications of his argument away from of their tendency to struggle only for civil rights within the federal system, thus inadvertently reinforcing U.S. contentions that Indians and Indian Affairs should be properly understood as integral parts of itself.[29] By 1971, there was an increasingly militant trend—manifested mainly but not exclusively through the American Indian Movement (AIM)—to concentrate on rights obtaining under the proliferation of treaties with indigenous peoples by which the U.S. had acquired possession of the bulk of its continental landbase between 1778 and 1871.[30] Through their deemphasizing of civil rights in favor of treaty rights—which by both U.S. constitutional and international legal definition pertain *only* to nations, *never* to minority groups[31]—AIM and like-minded organizations, in common with many reservation traditionals, adopted a vision of Indian prerogatives falling well within the rubric of decolonization (or "national liberation," as it's often called) inherent to Bob's position.[32]

In substance, AIM, sometimes described as "the shock troops of Indian sovereignty,"[33] demanded that the treaty-implied rights of American Indian peoples to the status of nations completely separate and distinct from the U.S. be respected. This status, in turn, legally entitles native nations to reassert full control over their lands and other resources, determining for themselves the forms of their own political organization as well as the nature of their relationships to other nations, in a manner free from restriction or coercion by the U.S.[34] To the extent that exercise of these prerogatives by Indians was/is hampered or denied, AIM insisted, the United States stands in violation of international laws requiring decolonization as a universal norm, and provides native people with a legal footing upon which to pursue extraordinary methods of compelling U.S. compliance.[35]

AIM's stance, punctuated during the early-to-mid-1970s by instances of armed resistance to federal authority,[36] quickly linked American Indian rights issues to the well-recognized decolonization struggles of other peoples around the world. Consequently, 1974 saw the founding of the International Indian Treaty Council (IITC), often referred to as AIM's "diplomatic arm," created to handle liaisons with other national liberation movements and supportive governments on a global basis, and to take the matter of Indian treaties before the United Nations.[37] The latter objective was attained in 1977, when IITC was able to bring about a conference on native rights attended by representatives of some ninety-eight indigenous nations throughout the Americas and conducted at UN facilities in Geneva, Switzerland.[38]

By 1981, the results of this initial hearing had been translated into the establishment of a formal United Nations Working Group on Indigenous Populations, lodged under the UN Economic and Social Council (ECOSOC), and charged with conducting annual hearings and undertaking a comprehensive study of the conditions in which native peoples exist,[39] as well as a study of the nature, extent, and status of treaty relations between UN member states and indigenous peoples.[40] The Working Group's ultimate mandate was from the outset to collect the information necessary to predicate a "Universal Declaration of the Rights of Indigenous Peoples" by the General Assembly in 1992.[41][*]

In turn, all of this practical political ferment stimulated, rather naturally, a rapid expansion of the theoretical beachhead Bob had achieved by being the first to openly and coherently apply the concept of colonization to American Indians. In short order, other radical Indian intellectuals/scholars—John Mohawk, Roxanne Dunbar-Ortiz, Jack Forbes, Rob Williams, and Jimmie Durham among them[42]—began to explore ways of adapting the work of such major anticolonialist thinkers as Frantz Fanon and Albert Memmi to the Native American setting.[43] The door was thereby opened to utilization of related concepts such as the dependency theory articulated by Eduardo Galeano, and theories of underdevelopment deployed by Andre Gunder Frank and Walter Rodney, among others.[44]

This last has led to the forging of an understanding that the notion of internal colonialism must itself be subcategorized into two discrete domains or spheres if it is to adequately reflect the realities experienced by Indians and other indigenous peoples. One domain involves the subordination of many of the smaller nations within Europe itself—the Basques, Catalans, Scots, Welsh, Freislanders, Magyars, and a number of others—as part of a process of consolidating statist structures desired by the European subcontinent's dominant peoples. A particularly fruitful investigation in this connection was Michael Hector's in his 1975 book, Internal Colonialism,[45] and there have since been a number of useful contributions.[46]

---

[*] As it turned out, after endless obstruction by the U.S., Canada, Australia, and New Zealand, the much diluted United Nations Declaration on the Rights of Indigenous Peoples (U.N.G.A. Res. 61/295, U.N. Doc. A/61/L.67 and Add. 1) was not adopted until September 13, 2007. See generally my "A Travesty of a Mockery of a Sham: Colonialism as 'Self-Determination' in the UN Declaration on the Rights of Indigenous Peoples," *Griffith Law Review*, Vol. 20, No. 3 (Fall 2011) pp. 526–56.

The other sphere consists of a "settler state" variety of colonialism wherein populations exported from Europe first subordinate indigenous nations overseas, occupying the natives' land in behalf of one or another European state, then wrest their own national independence from that state (decolonizing themselves), a matter anchored in their continuing colonization of the native people whose land they occupy.[47] It is, of course, this "postcolonial" type of colonialism which afflicts American Indians and other indigenous peoples such as the Inuits and Kanaka Maoli (Native Hawaiians) in the U.S. and Canada. Settler state colonization is, moreover, the presiding form of domination suffered by numerous indigenous peoples elsewhere, notably in Northern Ireland, southern Africa,[48] Australia,[49] New Zealand,[50] most of Latin America,[51] and Palestine.[52]

Alternatively—as in the Soviet Union and China,[53] south and southeast Asia,[54] and much of Africa[55]—the substance of settler state colonialism is visited upon smaller indigenous nations by large and thoroughly europeanized regional peoples striving to replicate the forms of Western-style statist consolidation after the departure of the European colonizers themselves.[56] So pervasive was this circumstance that in a global survey undertaken during the late 1980s, cultural geographer Bernard Nietschmann determined that of 122 armed conflicts underway at that time, ninety-seven involved the efforts of one or more indigenous peoples to repel campaigns by states to place or maintain them in positions of internal colonial subjugation.[57]

While it goes without saying—or should—that a number of these conflicts were spawned by the presumptions of states embracing capitalism,[58] it should be emphasized that as many or more have resulted from attempts by régimes adhering to the principles of marxism-leninism, all of them purportedly anti-imperialist, to nullify the inherent rights of indigenous peoples within their domains under such rubrics as "internationalism" and "socialist unity."[59] Prominent examples include foreclosure upon the prospect of a Hmong free state by the People's Republic of Vietnam during the 1960s and early '70s, and the Sandinista attempt to forcibly "integrate" the Miskitu, Sumu, and Rama peoples of eastern Nicaragua—to say nothing of their lands and resources—into the country's "broader" (westernized) society and economy.[60]

In both cases—and many others—it was, as AIM leader Russell Means remarked, simply "the same old song" of eurosupremacist colonization of indigenous peoples,[61] or, to quote Bob with regard to the Sandinistas, "Colonialism's colonialism, no matter who's engaging in it."[62] Those truths duly recorded, it must be emphasized that the typology of colonialism Bob was instrumental in creating—that is, a schema delineating not only the classic overseas variety but the internal and settler modes as well—has proven essential to apprehending the phenomenon as it has actually existed, and as it *continues* to manifest itself, rather than in a manner convenient to "postcolonial theorists" and other obfuscators/defenders of the colonial status quo.[63]

Probably most significant in this regard is that Bob's (re)conceptualization of colonialism has provided those who struggle against the ongoing exploitation and oppression of indigenous nations a vernacular with which to give shape to their motives and aspirations in a manner more readily comprehensible—albeit not always especially palatable—to those steeped in the traditions of marxism, liberal progressivism, and other such thoroughly eurocentric "solutions."[64] Concomitantly, it has done much to foster a worldwide and growing sense of commonality and unity among indigenous peoples, a matter signified in part by establishment of the IITC in 1974, the World Council of Indigenous Peoples (WCIP) a year later,[65] the earlier-mentioned "Indian Summer in Geneva" in 1977,[66] and, to a somewhat lesser extent, the Fourth Russell Tribunal in 1980.[67]

By the early 1970s, this had already begun to congeal into a collective sense, in contradistinction to the schematic of "three worlds" popularized by the 1955 Bandung Conference,[68] of there being a "Fourth World," an underlying indigenous "Host World" atop which each of the others had been constructed.[69] Well before 1980, while terms like "irredentist" were often employed by our critics on both the left and the right, it was becoming increasingly common to describe those of us pursuing the liberation of indigenous nations as "indigenists," our outlook/agenda as "Fourth Worldism."[70]

A Legacy

Altogether, it could seem a bit much to suggest, as I may appear to have done, that alterations in thought and action as profound as those sketched above should have accrued from a single abbreviated essay published in an obscure journal in the United States. Indeed, any such "explanation" of what is described herein would be grotesquely simplistic. My point, then, is not that everything that has happened since is somehow directly attributable to a few pages of text produced by Robert K. Thomas. Instead, my thinking is that "Colonialism: Classic and Internal" represented what Herbert Marcuse once described as a "breach of false consciousness," an insight, the appropriateness and explanatory power of which "can provide the Archimedean point for a more comprehensive emancipation" of thought and action. Such breaches typically occur "on an infinitely small space," Marcuse concluded, "but the chance for change depends upon the widening of such small spaces."[71]

Before Bob wrote that little essay, Indians were by and large groping about for ways to make sense of what it was that had been happening to us throughout the twentieth century. After *New University Thought* published his piece, enough of us could put a name to it to find our voices, and thereby to begin moving in a constructive direction. A dynamic was unleashed which undoubtedly surpassed anything he might in his wildest imaginings have envisioned when he sat down to write what was on his mind in 1966. The small Archimedean space he crafted has been expanded beyond all recognition. Change has certainly occurred because of it, for better or worse, and it will inevitably continue to occur for some time. Quite possibly, things have gone in a direction very different from whatever it was he originally desired to see come of his work. That is often the fate of those who give birth to a new and different approach to understanding.

Indication that Thomas may not have been entirely comfortable with the conclusions reached by some of his politico-intellectual progeny was brought home to me one night in the mid-1980s when we sat together in a San Diego bar during a lull in the annual Western Social Science Association conference. He, ever the senior scholar, promptly broke the ice by inquiring into the nature my research. My response, and mention of the fact that his essay on colonialism had had an especially deep influence on me, provoked an outright interrogation. As I summed up, as succinctly as I could, what I'd been thinking and why, and what I was doing to try and put the ideas into practice, he fixed me with a somewhat baleful eye. "You'd have to dismantle the entire goddamn United States of America to make that work," he grumbled. I conceded that this was true. "Well, then," he said, glaring ferociously, "you're just about the most dismal son-of-a-bitch I ever met." Startled, I inquired as to why that might be. "Because," he replied, "if *that's* what it takes to win this thing, we're beat before we start, aren't we? You'd better think about what you're saying."[72] With that, he abruptly left me alone to do just that.

Still, as I was leaving for the airport the next morning, I saw him making a beeline for me across the hotel lobby. "I just wanted to say goodbye," he informed me, eyes now twinkling. "Take care of yourself. And, whatever else you do, give 'em hell for me." I told him he could count on it, and he laughed. "That's the spirit," he said, moving off to finish his breakfast.

Whatever the depth of his tension with his conceptual offspring, it always remained clear that he was unprepared to disavow us entirely. More likely, with the sharpness to which his rank as elder statesman entitled him, he remained committed to the end to pushing us all to ponder our propositions, to clarify and hone our postulations to the point they might see service in the way he knew we meant them. He could see that we were engaged in what he called "serious business," an involvement appropriate only if we took it seriously. And, figurative father of us all, he bothered himself whenever possible to see that we did.

So much has happened since Bob died that bears on his ideas, or at least what it is that has been done with them.[73] One can only wonder how the rapid disintegration of the world's other great superstate, the Soviet Union, and the reemergence of a host of long-suppressed nationalities as self-determining entities within its former territoriality, might have affected his skepticism that the U.S., too, might be ultimately dismembered, replaced in part by an archipelago of decolonized American Indian nations. Similarly, one would like to know his views on the ethnic strife which has broken out amid the rubble of what was once Yugoslavia. Would he see hope for the actualization of an independent Kurdistan? Nagaland? A Karen free state in Myanmar (Burma)? What would he think of the home rule arrangement achieved by the Inuits of Greenland vis-à-vis Denmark, or a self-governing territory carved out of northern Canada by those same circumpolar people? Would he see potential in the creation of an autonomous zone for the Maoris in Aoteoroa (New Zealand)? The "Aborigines" of Australia? There are scores of such queries one would wish to pose.

One can wish, but the man is gone. We must answer such questions for ourselves now. That he was instrumental in providing us the analytical tools with which to do so, whatever his personal hesitancies or misgivings about where it was all going to end up, is no small legacy. Ultimately, it's fair to say that Bob Thomas achieved a genuine breakthrough for American Indian people, setting out a much-needed conceptual beacon in the depths of a very dark night of ignorance and confusion. That is quite a lot for any one person to accomplish. It is now up to each of us to honor his accomplishment, using his beacon as a guide upon which to steer our liberatory project home, keeping in mind that only when we find ourselves in a Native America freed from every vestige of the plague of colonization, internal and otherwise, will we be able to say truthfully that we've at last arrived. Let that be our legacy to those who come after us.

Notes

1   Stan Steiner, *The New Indians* (New York: Delta Books, 1968) esp. pp. 45–46, 95, 257.

2   Bob stayed with it in this regard until the end. As examples of his later publications in such venues, see his "Who Is an Indian? An International Comparison, *Americans Before Columbus*, Vol. 9, No. 1 (1981); "The Taproot of Peoplehood," *Americans Before Columbus*, Vol. 10, No. 4 (1982); and "The Vanishing Indian," *Americans Before Columbus*, Vol. 14, No. 2 (1986).

3   Robert K. Thomas, "Powerless Politics," *New University Thought*, Vol. 4, No 4 (Winter 1966–67) pp. 44–53.

4   By the end of 1967, Janet McCloud, a principal leader of the Nisqually fish-ins, was essentially paraphrasing portions of Thomas' positions. See her "The Continuing Last Indian War," *The Humanist*, Vol. 27, Nos. 5–6 (September–December 1967) pp. 178–79. This is of course but one example. More generally, see American Friends Service Committee, *Uncommon Controversy: Fishing Rights of the Muckleshoot, Puyallup, and Nisqually Indians* (Seattle: University of Washington Press, 1970).

5   On the Alcatraz occupation, see Alvin M. Josephy Jr., *Now That the Buffalo's Gone: A Study of Today's Indians* (New York: Alfred A. Knopf, 1982) pp. 229–30. For personal accounts by participants, see Peter Blue Cloud, ed., *Alcatraz Is Not an Island* (Berkeley: Wingbow Press, 1972).

6   See Akwesasne Notes, BIA, *I'm Not Your Indian Anymore: The Trail of Broken Treaties* (Mohawk Nation via Rooseveltown, NY: Akwesasne Notes, 1973); Robert Burnette with John Koster, *The Road to Wounded Knee* (New York: Bantam Books, 1974) pp. 195–219; Vine Deloria Jr., *Behind the Trail of Broken Treaties: An Indian Declaration of Independence* (New York: Delacorte Press, 1974) esp. pp. 161–86.

7   Robert K. Thomas, "Colonialism: Classic and Internal," *New University Thought*, Vol. 4, No. 4 (Winter 1966–67) pp. 37–43.

8   Among the earliest to seize upon Thomas' application of the colonial paradigm to the situation of American Indians, and to begin to develop the idea was the radical Lenape historian Jack Forbes. See, as examples, his "Crisis in Indian Affairs," *Frontier*, Vol. 17, No. 8 (June 1966) p. 9; "Who Speaks for the Indian?," *The Humanist*, Vol. 27, Nos. 5–6 (September–December 1967) pp. 174–76; and "Do Tribes Have Rights? The Question of Self-Determination for Small Nations," *Journal of Human Relations*, Vol. 18, No. 1 (1970) pp. 670–79 (included in his *Tribes and Masses: Explorations in Red, White and Black* [Davis, CA: D-Q University Press, 1978] pp. 20–24, 30–37).

9   I've been told that it was originally envisioned that the expanse of "blue" or "salt" water at issue would be at least fifty miles wide, but that Great Britain insisted on thirty because of the proximity of Scotland to the British Ulster Colony (Northern Ireland). Although this is quite plausible, I've found nothing in the UN record attending Resolution 1541 specifying either distance. In any case, on how the resolution was effected, see Peter Thornberry, "Self-Determination, Minorities, Human Rights: A Review of International Instruments," *International Comparative Law Quarterly*, Vol. 38, No. 4 (October 1989) pp. 867–89. On its implications for American Indians in particular, e.g., see Roxanne Dunbar-Ortiz, "The Protection of American Indian Territories in the United States: The Applicability of International Law," in Imre Sutton, ed., *Irredeemable America: The Indians' Estate and Land Claims* (Albuquerque: University of New Mexico Press, 1985) esp. pp. 259–61.

10   Among other things, the legitimacy of "armed conflicts in which peoples are fighting against colonial domination and alien occupation and against racist régimes in

exercise of their right of self-determination" is explicitly affirmed in Article 1(4) of the Geneva Protocol I Additional to the Geneva Conventions of 12 August 1949 (1125 U.N.T.S. 3/1991 ATS No. 30/16 I.L.M. 1391(1977)). For cogent analyses, see Malcolm Shaw, "The International Status of National Liberation Movements," *Liverpool Law Review*, Vol. 5, No. 1 (1983) pp. 19–34. Heather Ann Wilson, *International Law and the Use of Force by National Liberation Movements* (Oxford, UK: Clarendon Press, 1988). For full text of the Protocol, see Adam Roberts and Richard Guelff, eds., *Documents on the Laws of War* (Oxford, UK: Clarendon Press, 1982) pp. 389–446, passage quoted at p. 390. For applications, see, e.g., the essays collected by Norman Miller and Roderick Aya, eds., *National Liberation: Revolution in the Third World* (New York: Free Press, 1971).

11   Most recently, these have been set forth in the United Nations Declaration on the Rights of Persons Belonging to National or Ethnic, Religious or Linguistic Minorities (U.N.G.A. Res. 47/135, December 18, 1992). Other elements of international law bearing most directly upon the circumstances of minorities are the Universal Declaration of Human Rights (U.N.G.A. Res. 217 A (III), U.N. Doc. A/810, at 71 (1948)), the International Convention on the Elimination of All Forms of Racial Discrimination (660 U.N.T.S. 195, reprinted in 5 I.L.M. 352 (1966)), the International Covenant on Economic, Social and Cultural Rights (U.N.G.A. Res. 2200 (XXI), 21 U.N. GAOR, Supp. (No. 16) 49, U.N.Doc. A/6316 (1967), reprinted in 6 I.L.M. 360 (1967)), and the International Covenant on Civil and Political Rights (U.N.G.A. Res. 2200 (XXI), 21 U.N. GAOR, Supp. (No. 16) 52, U.N.Doc. A/6316 (1967), reprinted in 6 I.L.M. 368 (1967)). For texts, see Burns H. Weston, Richard A. Falk, and Anthony D'Amato, *Basic Documents in International World Order* (St. Paul, MN: West, 1980) pp. 298–301, 364–68, 371–75, 376–85.

12   "According to UN practice, national liberation movements are only recognized in colonies [as defined in Resolution 1541], or in independent nations where it is alleged that the government are alien rulers (South Africa and Israel)." Moreover, "A colony has only one chance, according to UN practice, of 'national liberation.'" Once the "classic" colonizers from overseas have been expelled, national liberation has been presumptively attained, irrespective of the configuration of power relations among/between various peoples *within* the former colony. Continuation of armed struggle by given peoples to assert their self-determining rights in the latter context is correspondingly delegitimated. This formulation arose largely from the desire of the governments of newly independent Third World states, whose "frontiers were delineated by their colonizers" in a manner encompassing the territories of a number of indigenous peoples, to "avoid creating a foundation upon which successionist [sic] movements within their own [borders] could claim to be 'liberation movements'" in the much same sense that they themselves had often been before decolonization was achieved. Keith Sutter, *An International Law of Guerrilla Warfare* (New York: St. Martin's Press, 1984) pp. 159, 147–48.

13   Or "territorial integrity and political independence of any state," as the principle is posed in Chapter 1, Article 1(4) of the United Nations Charter (59 Stat. 1031, T.S. No. 993, 3 Bevans 1153, 1976 Y.B.U.N. 1043). Hence, "Any attempt aimed at the partial or total disruption of the national unity and the territorial integrity of a country is incompatible with the purposes of the [UN] Charter," according to Point 6 of the Declaration on the Granting of Independence to Colonial Countries and Peoples (U.N.G.A. Res. 1514 (XV), 15 U.N. GAOR, Supp. (No. 16) 66, U.N. Doc A/4684 (1961)). For text quoted, see Weston, Falk, and D'Amato, *Basic Documents*, pp. 12, 244.

14   See, e.g. Franz Ansprenger, *The Dissolution of Colonial Empires* (New York: Routledge, 1989). Also see the essays collected in Tony Smith, ed., *The End of European Empire: Decolonization after World War II* (Lexington, MA: DC Heath, 1975).

15   Not even the nazis were prepared to advance such an argument. Rather, as was observed by Aimé Césaire in his *Discourse on Colonialism* (New York: Monthly Review Press, 1972 trans. of 1955 French original), they simply did unto other Europeans what those same Europeans had long been doing—and were continuing to do—to darker-skinned Others overseas.

16   Indeed "liberation" was/is the standard term employed to describe the forcible repeal of German rule, e.g.: the 1944 "liberation of Paris," ostensibly by de Gaulle's "Free French" forces. See, e.g., Jean-Pierre Azema, *From Munich to Liberation, 1938–1944* (Cambridge, UK: Cambridge University Press, 1985).

17   It should be noted that France, like the U.S. vis-à-vis American Indian nations and its overseas colony of Hawai'i, declared Algeria to be an integral part of itself. See generally *France and Algeria: The Problem of Civil and Political Reform, 1870–1920* (Syracuse, NY: Syracuse University Press, 1966); Mahfoud Bennoune, *The Making of Contemporary Algeria, 1830–1987: Colonial Upheavals and Post-Independence Development* (Cambridge, UK: Cambridge University Press, 1988).

18   See generally Adam Hothschild, *King Leopold's Ghost: A Story of Greed, Terror, and Heroism in the Congo* (New York: Houghton Mifflin, 1998).

19   On the "fiftieth U.S. state," see Noel J. Kent, *Hawaii: Islands Under the Influence* (Honolulu: University of Hawaii Press, [2nd ed.] 1993). On the Philippines, see the material collected by Daniel B. Schirmer and Stephen Rosskamm Shalom in their coedited *The Philippines Reader: A History of Colonialism, Neocolonialism, Dictatorship, and Resistance* (Boston: South End Press, 1987). On the U.S. "commonwealth" territory of Puerto Rico, see Ronald Fernandez, *Prisoners of Colonialism: The Struggle for Justice in Puerto Rico* (Monroe, ME: Common Courage Press, 1994) and José Trías Monge, *Puerto Rico: The Trials of the Oldest Colony in the World* (New Haven, CT: Yale University Press, 1997). On the "unincorporated territories" of Guam, the Marshalls, and American Samoa, See generally Robert F. Rogers, *Destiny's Landfall: A History of Guam* (Honolulu: University of Hawaii Press, 1995); Francis X. Hezel, *Strangers in Their Own Land: A Century of Colonial Rule in the Caroline and Marshall Islands* (Honolulu: University of Hawaii Press, 1995); and George Herbert Ryden, *The Foreign Policy of the United States in Relation to Samoa* (New Haven, CT: Yale University Press, 1928) esp. pp. 570–76. Nothing useful was available on the Virgin Islands when this essay was originally written, but see E. Robert Statham, "The United States vs. the U.S. Virgin Islands: The Purchase of the Danish West Indies and Their Inhabitants," in his *Colonial Constitutionalism: The Tyranny of United States' Offshore Territorial Policy and Relations* (Lanham, MD: Lexington Books, 2002) pp. 51–64.

20   See "Some Aspects of the Southern Question," in Quintin Hoare, ed., *Antonio Gramsci: Selections from Political Writings, 1921–1926* (New York: International, 1978) pp. 441–62.

21   One firm indication is that while English-language translations of Gramsci's work began to appear in the UK as early as 1957, they were not generally available in the U.S. until the early-to-mid-1970s. Another is that when I mentioned Gramsci during a conversation during the mid-1980s, Bob initially looked blank, then pumped me for details after I'd sketched out his thinking on the Southern Question.

22   By and large, to the extent that anyone in North America outside the Basque immigrant communities of Idaho and Nevada was even aware of ETA during the 1950s

and '60s, they typically misconstrued the organization as an antifascist guerrilla force pitted against the Franco régime. Very few perceived its status as being that of a national liberation movement. For a useful corrective, see Robert P. Clark, *The Basque Insurgents: ETA, 1952–1980* (Madison: University of Wisconsin Press, 1984).

23 Although by 1966 Carmichael was routinely describing the situation of blacks in the U.S. as being "akin to that of a colony" in his lectures and speeches, his key articulation in this regard was undoubtedly made a year later, in his and Charles V. Hamilton's *Black Power*. And by the end of 1967, there were others, like Jack O'Dell. At that point, of course, Bob had already placed his own marker in *New University Thought*. An earlier written characterization of "the American Negro [as the] subject of colonization," was made by black radical Harold Cruse in 1962, but the essay was not widely available until the 1968 publication of his *Rebellion and Revolution*. There were of course others—by 1969, reference to "the black colony" in the U.S. was common, even in mostly white organizations like SDS—but they, too, were mostly after the fact. The most accurate framing is probably that, while the African American discourse on internal colonialism did not give rise to Bob's formulation, the high degree of resonance it attained during the late 1960s afforded his a degree of traction that would've been otherwise absent. See Stokely Carmichael and Charles V. Hamilton, *Black Power: The Politics of Liberation in America* (New York: Random House, 1967) pp. 2–32; J.H. O'Dell, "A Special Variety of Colonialism," *Freedomways*, Vol. 7, No. 1 (Winter 1967) pp. 7–15; Harold Cruse, "Revolutionary Nationalism and the Afro-American," *Studies on the Left*, Vol. 2, No. 3 (1962) pp. 12–25 (included in his *Rebellion and Revolution* [New York: William Morrow, 1968] pp. 74–96). As illustration of the ubiquitous reference by 1969 to a black colony in the U.S., see SDS, "The Black Panther Party: Towards the Liberation of the Colony," *New Left Notes* (April 4, 1969) pp. 1, 3.

24 Describing Carmichael as a "communications phenomenon," Deloria credited him with having "clarified the intellectual concepts which had kept [all too many] Indians and Mexicans confused and allowed the concept of self-determination suddenly to become valid" in their minds. "Indians understood when Carmichael talked about racial and national integrity"—precisely the same themes Bob pursued in *New University Thought*—and followed Carmichael's highly publicized 1966 demand for Black Power with a call "for *red power* in terms similar to what [he] was saying [emphasis in original]." Vine Deloria Jr., *Custer Died for Your Sins: An Indian Manifesto* (New York: Macmillan, 1969) p. 181. On Bob and Vine being of the same intellectual milieu during the period at issue, see Vine Deloria Jr., "Bob Thomas as Colleague," in Steve Pavlik, ed., *A Good Cherokee, A Good Anthropologist: Papers in Honor of Robert K. Thomas* (Los Angeles: UCLA American Indian Studies Center, 1998) pp. 27–38.

25 Deloria felt it important to give Carmichael's and Hamilton's analysis of the "classic formula of colonial co-optation" afflicting black communities "the careful and impartial reading it deserves," especially insofar as an identical "process [was] common to the experiences of . . . the Indian and Mexican communities." Vine Deloria Jr., *We Talk, You Listen: New Tribes, New Turf* (New York: Macmillan, 1970) pp. 100–113; language quoted at pp. 100–101.

26 Dividing the fifty million acres of remaining reservation land by the census count of Indians in the U.S. reveals Indians as the population with the most acreage on a per capita basis in North America. This acreage is the most mineral-rich on the continent, holding as much as two-thirds of U.S. uranium reserves, about a quarter of the low-sulfur coal, a fifth of the oil and natural gas, and abundances of copper, zeolites,

and other ores, all of it heavily mined over the past half-century. On paper, this computes to Indians being the wealthiest population aggregate in North America, on a per capita basis. Instead, according to the federal government's own data, we are the very poorest, experiencing, by a decisive margin, the lowest annual and lifetime incomes of any overall group. Correlated to this are all the statistical indices of dire poverty: highest infant mortality rate, highest rates of death by malnutrition, exposure and plague disease, shortest life expectancy. The factor reconciling this potential wealth on the one hand to the practical poverty evidenced on the other is the manner in which U.S. colonial domination of Indian Country has diverted profit from the development of indigenous resources to American corporations. See my "Indigenous Peoples of the U.S.: A Struggle Against Internal Colonialism," *Black Scholar*, Vol. 16, No. 1 (February 1985) pp. 29–35.

27 For a succinct overview, see Jack D. Forbes, "Colonialism as a Theme in American Indigenous Writing," in Pavlik, *A Good Cherokee, A Good Anthropologist*, pp. 241–59.

28 U.S. Department of Justice, Commission on Civil Rights, *The Navajo Nation: An American Colony* (Washington, DC: U.S. Government Printing Office, 1975).

29 A selection of essays and primary documents articulating the agenda of the civil rights phase of Indian activism will be found in Alvin Josephy, *Red Power: The American Indians' Fight for Freedom* (New York: American Heritage Press, 1971). Also see Deloria, *Custer Died for Your Sins*, p. 181; *We Talk, You Listen*, pp. 100–101.

30 For the texts of 369 ratified treaties, see Charles J. Kappler, ed., *Indian Treaties, 1778–1883* (New York: Interland, 1972). The texts of five additional ratified treaties, and a further eleven that are otherwise valid, are provided in Vine Deloria Jr. and Raymond J. DeMallie, *Documents of American Indian Diplomacy: Treaties, Agreements, and Conventions, 1775–1979*, 2 vols. (Norman: University of Oklahoma Press, 1999) Vol. 1, pp. 209–32. At page 203, the authors also reconcile the Kappler list of ratified treaties with that of the U.S. State Department, producing a total of 379. Adding the five ratified and eleven otherwise valid treaties they reproduce results in a total of 395 (excluding four treaties ratified in behalf of railroad corporations). For a detailed cartographic record of the process, see Charles C. Royce, *Indian Land Cessions in the United States*, 2 vols. (Washington, DC: Smithsonian Institution, Bureau of American Ethnology, 1899).

31 Under Article 1, Section 10, of the U.S. Constitution, this is necessarily so with respect to *any* entity with which the federal government enters into a treaty. Hence, a treaty effectively conveys formal U.S. recognition that the other party or parties is/ are sovereign nations. This is consistent with the understanding embodied in the 1969 Vienna Convention on the Law of Treaties (U.N. Treaty Series, Vol. 1155 at 331) that, apart from those with or between international organizations, treaties consist exclusively of compacts "between states" (i.e., "sovereign nations" or "peers"). While the Convention is itself nonretroactive, it's "generally agreed that most of [its] contents [are] merely expressive of rules that existed under customary international law" and thus applicable to U.S. treaties with American Indian nations. For constitutional interpretation, see Robert T. Coulter, "Contemporary Indian Sovereignty," in National Lawyers Guild, Committee on Native American Struggles, *Rethinking Indian Law* (New Haven, CT: Advocate Press, 1977) pp. 109–20. Also see my "A Question of Sovereignty: The International Implications of Treaty Relationships Between the United States and Various American Indian Nations," in Fremont Lyden and Lyman G. Letgers, eds., *Native Americans and Public Policy* (Pittsburgh: University of Pittsburgh Press, 1992) pp. 149–63. On the 1969 Convention, see Ian Sinclair, *The*

Vienna Convention on the Law of Treaties (Manchester, UK: Manchester University Press, [2nd ed.] 1984) pp. 6, 8; quoting at p. 8 the Swedish delegate Hans Blix, *Official Records, Second Session* (A/Conf.39/11 Add.1), 101st Meeting of the Committee as a Whole. On the number of U.S./Indian treaties, see note 30.

32   The transition is discussed in Vine Deloria Jr., *Behind the Trail of Broken Treaties: An Indian Declaration of Independence* (New York: Delta Books, 1974). On national liberation, see note 12.

33   Birgil Kills Straight, "The Meaning of AIM," *Rapid City Journal* (March 1973); reprinted in the *Idaho State Journal* (May 30, 1973) and included in Jim Willis, ed., *1960s Counterculture: Documents Decoded* (Santa Barbara, CA: ABC-CLIO, 2015) pp. 189–90.

34   This is simply a paraphrase of the language in Point 2 of UN Resolution 1514 and reiterated in Article 1 in both the International Covenant on Economic, Social and Cultural Rights and the International Covenant on Civil and Political Rights by which the right of self-determination is legally defined. For citations, see notes 11 and 13.

35   Such assertions were entirely consistent with a then-commonly held view of self-determining rights. See, as examples, Lee C. Buchheit's *Secession: The Legitimacy of Self-Determination* (New Haven, CT: Yale University Press, 1978), and his anonymously published "Note: The Logic of Secession," *Yale Law Journal*, Vol. 89, No. 4 (March 1980) pp. 802–24. On legitimate means of compelling compliance, see note 10.

36   See Robert Anderson, Joanna Brown, Jonny Lerner, and Barbara Lou Shafer, eds., *Voices from Wounded Knee, 1973: The People Are Standing Up* (Mohawk Nation via Roosevelt, NY: Akwesasne Notes, 1974); Bruce Johansen and Roberto Maestas, *Wasi'chu: The Continuing Indian Wars* (New York: Monthly Review Press, 1979); Rex Wyler, *Blood of the Land: The U.S. Government and Corporate War Against the American Indian Movement* (New York: Everest House, 1982); and Paul Chaat Smith and Robert Allen Warrior, *Like a Hurricane: The American Indian Movement from Alcatraz to Wounded Knee* (New York: New Press, 1996).

37   On the founding of IITC, see Roxanne Dunbar-Ortiz, *Indians of the America: Human Rights and Self-Determination* (London: Zed Press, 1984) pp. 33–35. On the legal dimension of IITC's original aspirations, see Glenn T. Morris, "In Support of the Right to Self-Determination for Indigenous Peoples Under International Law," *German Yearbook of International Law*, No. 29 (1986) pp. 277–316.

38   See Jimmie Durham, "The United Nations Conference on Indians," *IITC Reports* (April 1977), collected in his *A Certain Lack of Coherence: Writings on Art and Cultural Politics* (London: Kala Press, 1993) pp. 24–27. Also see Weyler, *Blood of the Land*, pp. 214–16; *A Basic Call to Consciousness: The Hau de no sau nee Address to the Western World—Geneva, Switzerland, Autumn 1977* (Mohawk Nation via Rooseveltown, NY: Akwesasne Notes, 1978). An excellent contemporaneous documentary, *Indian Summer in Geneva*, was also made by filmmaker David Hernandez Palmar (now available on YouTube).

39   The final report, titled *Study of the Problem of Discrimination Against Indigenous Populations*, was submitted by special rapporteur José R. Martinez Cobo in three parts—July 30, 1981 (E/CN.4/Sub.2/476/ Add.4), August 10, 1982 (E/CN.4/Sub.2/1982/2), and August 5, 1983 (E.CN.4/Sub.2/1983/21)—and published in three volumes by the UN in 1986.

40   This study was not initiated until September 2, 1987. The final report, titled *Study of Treaties, Agreements, and Other Constructive Arrangements Between States and Indigenous Populations*, was submitted by the special rapporteur, Cuban diplomat Miguel Alfonso Martinez, on June 22, 1997 (E/CN.4/ 1999/20). It was not published in book form.

41 See Gudmundur Alfredsson, "International Law, International Organizations, and Indigenous Peoples," *Journal of International Affairs*, Vol. 36, No. 1 (1982) pp. 113–25; Douglas Sanders, "The UN Working Group on Indigenous Populations," *Human Rights Quarterly*, Vol. 11, No. 3 (August 1989) pp. 406–33.

42 While he's published a number of short pieces under his own byline, some of the most important material produced by Mohawk, an editor of the trailblazing indigenist bimonthly *Akwesasne Notes*, has been anonymous, e.g.: the main text of *A Basic Call to Consciousness* (see note 38). Forbes' work has been cited in note 9, but also see his *Africans and Native Americans: The Language of Race and the Evolution of Red-Black Peoples* (Urbana: University of Illinois Press, 1994). Examples of Ortiz's work have also been cited in notes 10 and 38, to which should be added *The Great Sioux Nation: Sitting in Judgment on America* (San Francisco/New York: Moon Books/International Indian Treaty Council, 1975), one of several volumes she's edited. Williams has published several important articles on the conceptual relationship between European colonial doctrine and the formulation of federal Indian law, as well as the landmark *American Indian in Western Legal Thought: The Discourses of Conquest* (New York: Oxford University Press, 1990). Primarily a conceptual artist, Durham's written work includes *A Certain Lack of Coherence* and his earlier *Columbus Day* (Minneapolis: West End Press, 1983).

43 The most relevant works in this connection are of course Fanon's *The Wretched of the Earth* (New York: Grove Press, 1965) and Memmi's *The Colonizer and the Colonized* (Boston: Beacon Press, 1965).

44 Eduardo Galeano, *Open Veins of Latin America: Five Centuries of the Pillage of a Continent* (New York: Monthly Review Press, 1975); Andre Gunder Frank, *Capitalism and Underdevelopment in Latin America: Historical Studies of Chile and Brazil* (New York: Monthly Review Press, 1967); Walter Rodney, *How Capitalism Underdeveloped Africa* (Washington, DC: Howard University Press, 1974). A related but distinct framing is that developed by Samir Amin in his *Unequal Development: An Essay on the Social Formations of Peripheral Capitalism* (New York: Monthly Review Press, 1976). By far the most ambitious attempt at producing an historical synthesis based in these precepts was that initiated by Immanuel Wallerstein with his *The Modern World System* (New York: The Academic Press, 1974).

45 Michael Hector, *Internal Colonialism: The Celtic fringe in British national development, 1536–1966* (Berkeley: University of California Press, 1975).

46 See, e.g., the essays collected in Mikulás Teich and Roy Porter, eds., *The National Question in Europe in Historical Context* (Cambridge, UK: Cambridge University Press, 1993).

47 The seminal work on settler colonialism as a distinct phenomenon was A. Grenfell Price's *White Settlers in the Tropics* (New York: American Geographical Society, 1939), followed by his *White Settlers and Native Peoples: An Historical Study of Racial Contacts between English-speaking Whites and Aboriginal Peoples in the United States, Canada, Australia, and New Zealand* (Melbourne/Cambridge, UK: Georgian House/Cambridge University Press, 1950).

48 See J.H.P. Serfontein, *Brotherhood of Power: An Exposé of the Secret Afrikaner Broederbond* (Bloomington: Indiana University Press, 1978); John Ya-Otto, *Battlefront Namibia* (Westport, CT: Lawrence Hill, 1981); Ronald Weitzer, *Transforming Settler States: Communal Conflict and Internal Security in Northern Ireland and Zimbabwe* (Berkeley: University of California Press, 1992).

49   See Jan Roberts, *Massacres to Mining: The Colonization of Aboriginal Australia* (Victoria, Aus.: Dove Communications, 1981); Henry Reynolds, *Dispossession: Australian Aborigines and White Invaders* (St. Leonards, Aus.: Allen & Unwin, 1989); Ann McGrath, *Contested Ground: Australian Aborigines Under the British Crown* (St. Leonards, Aus.: Allen & Unwin, 1995).

50   See Mason Durie, *Te Mana, Te Kawanatanga: The Politics of Maori Self-Determination* (Auckland: Oxford University Press, 1998).

51   There was nothing in print offering an explicitly settler colonial framing of Latin America's "domestic affairs" when this essay was written, but see Richard Gott, "Latin America as a White Settler Society," *Bulletin of Latin American Research*, Vol. 26, No. 2 (2007) pp. 269–89.

52   See Maxime Rodinson, *Israel: A Colonial Settler State?* (New York: Pathfinder Press, 1973).

53   See Walker Connor, *The National Question in Marxist-Leninist Theory and Strategy* (Princeton, NJ: Princeton University Press, 1984) pp. 45–66, 67–100.

54   More than 380 peoples are indigenous to the subcontinental landmass known as India, many of whom never agreed to be subsumed within a unitary state patterned after the British Raj. The Nagas, for instance, have been waging an armed struggle to liberate themselves/their traditional territory from "India" since its 1947 inception. A similar situation prevails with regard to the Shanti Bahini of the Chittigong Hills Tracts of Bangladesh, while the Karens and other peoples indigenous to the former British colony of Burma have since 1948 been forced to fight protracted wars of resistance to being forcibly subsumed within the independent state of Myanmar, and the various "Montagnard" (or, more pejoratively, "Moi") peoples of the Annamese Cordillera have been subjugated by the lowland Vietnamese since Vietnam's liberation in 1975. These are only a handful among scores of possible examples. See IWGIA Staff, *The Naga Nation and Its Struggle Against Genocide: A Report Compiled by IWGIA* (Copenhagen: IWGIA Doc. 56, 1986); Wolfgang Mey, *Genocide in the Chittigong Hill Tracts* (Copenhagen: IWGIA Doc. 51, 1984); Independent Commission on International Humanitarian Issues, *Indigenous Peoples: A Global Quest for Justice* (London: Zed Press, 1987) pp. 28, 35–36, 54, 58–59, 81, 84; Conner, *National Question*, pp. 101–27.

55   Africa has been afflicted with an endless stream of bloody conflicts beginning with that centering upon Katanga's attempted secession from the Belgian-created and newly independent Congo, beginning in 1960, as one westernized régime after another has fought viciously to preserve their "territorial integrity" within boundaries demarcated by the colonial powers during the 1880s. Probably the ugliest example is that of Biafra, i.e.: Nigeria's genocidal repression of the Ibos' attempt to secede during the late 1960s. See Jules Gérard-Libois, *Katanga Secession* (Madison: University of Wisconsin Press, 1966); J.M. MacKenzie, *The Partition of Africa* (London: Metheun, 1983); Saadia Touval, *Boundary Politics in Independent Africa* (Cambridge, MA: Harvard University Press, 1972); Arthur A. Nwankwo and Samuel U. Ifejika, *Biafra: The Making of a Nation* (New York: Praeger, 1970); Alexander A. Madiebo, *The Nigerian Revolution and the Biafran War* (Enugu, Nigeria: Fourth Dimension, 1980).

56   The magnitude of the issue can be discerned in the fact that while there are fewer than 200 states, each asserting the right to exercise jurisdictional supremacy over all territory within its recognized borders, at least three *thousand* indigenous nations are situated therein. See Bernard Nietschmann, "The Fourth World: Nations versus States," in George J. Demko and William B. Wood, eds., *Reordering the World:*

Geopolitical Perspectives on the Twenty-first Century (Boulder, CO: Westview Press, 1994) pp. 225–42.

57 Bernard Nietschmann, "Militarization and Indigenous Peoples: The Third World War," *Cultural Survival Quarterly*, Vol. 11, No. 3 (1987) pp. 1–16.

58 This is certainly the case, and has generated continuous resistance by indigenous peoples, including armed struggles such as that marked by the uprising of the Zapatista Army of National Liberation (EZLN)—a primarily Mayan organization— in the Mexican province of Chiapas on New Year's Day, 1994. See John Ross, *Rebellion at the Grassroots: The Zapatista Uprising* (Monroe, ME: Common Courage Press, 1994). Also see my brief essay, "A North American Indigenist View," in Elaine Katzenberger, ed., *First World, Ha Ha Ha! The Zapatista Challenge* (San Francisco: City Lights, 1995) pp. 141–55.

59 The basis for this outcome—which has been quite consistent—resides in very core, not only of the marxist-leninist conception of history, but that of Marx and Engels themselves. The matter is far too complex to discuss here, but see Connor, *National Question*, pp. 5–42; Ronaldo Munck, *The Difficult Dialogue: Marxism and the National Question* (London: Zed Books, 1986).

60 Both examples are discussed at length in Glenn T. Morris and Ward Churchill, "Between a Rock and a Hard Place: Left-Wing Revolution, Right-Wing Reaction, and the Destruction of Indigenous Peoples," *Cultural Survival Quarterly*, Vol. 11, No. 3 (1987) pp. 17–24; included in my *Since Predator Came: Notes from the Struggle for American Indian Liberation* (Littleton, CO: Aigis, 1995) pp. 329–48. On the Sandinista example, also see Bernard Nietschmann, *The Unknown War: The Miskito Nation, Nicaragua, and the United States* (New York: Freedom House, 1989).

61 Russell Means, "The Same Old Song," in my *Marxism and Native Americans* (Boston: South End Press, 1983) pp. 19–34; reprinted as "For the World to Live, Europe Must Die" in Russell Means with Marvin J. Wolf, *Where White Men Fear to Tread: The Autobiography of Russell Means* (New York: St. Martin's Press, 1995) pp. 545–54.

62 Conversation during the Western Social Science Association (WSSA) annual conference in San Diego, 1984.

63 Simply put, the very term "postcolonial" indicates that colonialism is a thing of the past. That being so, it need not—indeed, *cannot*—be opposed in the present. A better defense of ongoing colonialism is difficult to imagine. The argument is made very well by Ella Shohat in her "Notes on the 'Post-Colonial,'" *Social Text*, Nos. 31/32 (1993) pp. 99–113. Also see Ann McClintock's "The Myth of Progress: Pitfalls of the Term Post-Colonialism" in the same issue at pp. 1–15.

64 For an emblematic—albeit especially virulent—reaction to indigenist thinking, see Revolutionary Communist Party, USA, "Searching for the Second Harvest," in my *Marxism and Native Americans*, pp. 35–58. For an incisive historical analysis of the attitudinal matrix underlying such responses, see J. Sakai, *Settlers: The Mythology of the White Proletariat* (Chicago: Morningstar Press, 1983).

65 The WCIP was founded in October 1975 during an international conference organized by Shuswap chief George Manuel, hosted by the Sheshaht Band of the Nuu-chah-nulth First Nation in what is now called British Columbia (Canada), and attended by 260 indigenous delegates from twenty countries (mostly from the Americas, but also including Australia and Aoteoroa [New Zealand]). It was dissolved in 1996. See Douglas E. Sanders, *The Formation of the World Council on Indigenous Peoples* (Copenhagen: IWGIA Doc. 29, 1977).

66 See note 38.

67 The tribunal was convened in Rotterdam in November 1980 to consider charges of genocide and "ethnocide" perpetrated by various states against indigenous peoples in the Americas. See, e.g., Ismaelillo and Robin Wright, eds., *Native Peoples in Struggle: Cases from the Fourth Russel Tribunal and Other International Forums* (Bombay/New York: E.R.I.N., 1982).

68 See Keith Buchanan, "The Third World," *New Left Review* Vol. 18, No. 1 (January–February 1963) pp. 5–23. For background on the conference itself, see the material collected by George McTurnan Kahin in *The Asian-African Conference: Bandung, Indonesia, April 1955* (Ithaca, NY: Cornell University Press, 1956). Also see Carlos Romulo, *The Meaning of Bandung* (Chapel Hill: University of North Carolina Press, 1956).

69 Although it was in use earlier, the term and its meaning were first afforded general visibility by publication of George Manuel's and Michael Posluns' *The Fourth World: An Indian Reality* (New York: The Free Press, 1974). For use of the term "Host World," see, e.g., Winona LaDuke, "Natural to Synthetic and Back Again," in my *Marxism and Native Americans*, p. vii.

70 See, e.g., my essay, "I Am Indigenist: Notes on the Ideology of the Fourth World," *Z Papers*, Vol. 1, No. 3 (1992); included in my *Struggle for the Land: Indigenous Resistance to Genocide, Ecocide, and Expropriation in Contemporary North America* (Monroe, ME: Common Courage Press, 1993) pp. 403–51.

71 Herbert Marcuse, "Repressive Tolerance," in Robert Paul Wolf, Barrington Moore Jr., and Herbert Marcuse, *A Critique of Pure Tolerance* (Boston: Beacon Press, 1965) p. 111.

72 See note 62.

73 Bob Thomas died quite unexpectedly on August 5, 1991.

TWO

Subverting the Law of Nations

American Indian Rights and U.S. Distortions of International Legality

> It's an old story, really. It's the story of a strategically unchallenged dominion, at the apogee of its power and influence, rewriting the global rules for how to manage its empire.
>
> —Phyllis Bennis, *Calling the Shots* (2001)

Anyone who has ever debated or negotiated with U.S. officials on matters concerning American Indian land rights can attest that the federal government's first position is invariably that its title to or authority over its territory was acquired incrementally. It obtained its holdings mostly through provisions of cession in some four hundred treaties with Indians ratified by the Senate between 1778 and 1871. When it is pointed out that the United States has violated the terms of every one of the treaties, thus voiding whatever title might otherwise have accrued therefrom, a few moments of thundering silence usually follows. The official U.S. position, publicly framed in 1999 by perennial "federal Indian expert" Leonard Garment, then shifts onto different ground: "If you don't accept the treaties as valid, we'll have to fall back on the Doctrine of Discovery and Rights of Conquest."[1] This rejoinder, to all appearances, is meant to crush, forestalling further discussion of a topic so obviously inconvenient to the status quo.

Although the idea that the United States obtained title to its "domestic sphere" by discovery and conquest has come to hold immense currency among North America's settler population, one finds that the international legal doctrines from which such notions derive are all but

Originally published in Donald A. Grinde Jr., ed., *Native Americans* (Washington, DC: CQ Press, 2002) with diminished annotation, now restored and slightly expanded.

unknown except among a few people. This small cadre of arguable exceptions has for the most part, however, not bothered to become acquainted
with the relevant concepts in their original or customary formulations.
Instead its members content themselves with reviewing the belated
and often transparently self-interested "interpretations" produced by
nineteenth-century American jurists, most notably Chief Justice John
Marshall. Overall, there seems not the least desire—or sense of obligation—to explore the matter further.

This situation is altogether curious, given Marshall's own bedrock
enunciation of the self-concept of the United States—the hallowed proposition that the United States should be viewed above all else as "a nation
governed by laws, not men."[2] Knowledge of or compliance with the law
is presupposed, of course, in any such construction of national image.
This is especially true with respect to the laws that, like those pertaining to discovery and conquest, form the core of the country's often and
loudly proclaimed contention that the acquisition and consolidation of
its transcontinental domain has all along been right, just, and therefore
lawful. Indeed, there can be no questions of legality more basic than
those concerning the integrity of the process by which the U.S. asserted
title to its territory and thereby purports to legitimate jurisdiction over it.

This essay addresses U.S. performance and the juridical logic attending it through the lens of contemporaneous international legal custom
and convention. It concludes with an exploration of the conceptual and
material conditions requisite to a reconciliation of rhetoric and reality
within the paradigm of explicitly U.S. legal (mis)understandings. Insofar
as much of this discourse devolves upon international law, and given the
emergence of the United States as "the world's only remaining superpower," the implications are not so much national as global.[3]

The Doctrine of Discovery

The concepts that were eventually systematized as doctrines of discovery
primarily originated in a series of bulls promulgated by Pope Innocent
IV during the late thirteenth century to elucidate material relations
between Christian crusaders and Islamic "infidels." Although the pon-
tiff's primary objective was to establish a legal framework compelling
Soldiers of the Cross to deliver the fruits of their pillage abroad to the
Vatican and Church-sanctioned heads of Europe's incipient states, the
Innocentian bull *Quod super his* embodied the first formal acknowledgment in Western law that non-Christians as well as Christians enjoyed
rights of property ownership.[4] In "justice," then, it followed that only

those ordained to rule by a Divine Right conferred by the One True God were imbued with a rightful prerogative to dispossess lesser mortals of their lands and other worldly holdings.[5]

The 1492 Columbian "discovery" of what proved to be an entire hemisphere, very much populated but of which most Europeans had been unaware, sparked a renewed focus on questions of whether and to what extent Christian sovereigns might declare proprietary interest in the assets of "heathens."[6] The first question, however, was whether the inhabitants of the so-called New World were endowed with souls, the criterion necessary for recognition of their essential humanity and, correspondingly, legal standing of any sort. This issue led to the famous 1550 debate in Valladolid between Frey Bartolomé de las Casas and Juan Ginés de Sepulveda, the outcome of which was papal recognition that American Indians were in fact human and therefore entitled to the exercise of at least rudimentary rights.[7]

Such Spanish legal theorists as Franciscus de Vitoria and Juan Matías de Paz were busily revising and expanding upon Innocent's canonical foundation as a means of delineating the property rights vested in those peoples "discovered" by Christian European powers as well as those rights presumably obtained in the process by their "discoverers."[8] In the first instance, Vitoria posited the principle that sovereigns acquired outright title to lands discovered by their subjects only when the territory involved was found to be ungoverned (terra nullius) or literally vacant of human occupants (vacuum domicilium).[9] Since almost none of the lands European explorers ever came across genuinely met this description, the premise of territorium res nullius was essentially moot from the outset. Regardless, the English—and the more so their North American offshoots—would later twist this concept to their own ends.[10]

For places found to be inhabited, international law, as interpreted by Vitoria, unequivocally acknowledged that native residents held inherent or "aboriginal" title to the land.[11] What the discoverer obtained was a monopolistic right vis-à-vis other powers to acquire the property from its native owners, in the event that they could be persuaded through peaceful means to alienate it. On balance, this formulation seems to have been devised as an attempt to order relations between European states in such a way as to prevent them from shredding one another in a mad scramble to glean the lion's share of the wealth all of them expected to flow from the Americas.[12]

Under the right of discovery, the first European nation to discover a land previously unknown to Europe had what is akin to an exclusive

European franchise to negotiate for the indigenous peoples' land within that area. The "law of nations," as it was known, forbade European powers from interfering with the diplomatic affairs each carried on with the indigenous nations within their respective "discovered" territories. The doctrine of discovery thus reduced friction and the possibility of warfare between competing European nations. That this principle of noninterference was well developed in international law and understood perfectly by the Founding Fathers of the United States is confirmed in an observation by no less luminous a figure than Thomas Jefferson:

> We consider it as established by the usage of different nations into a kind of jus gentium [natural or customary law of nations] for America, that a white nation settling down and declaring such and such are their limits, makes an invasion of those limits by any other white nation an act of war, but gives no right of soil against the native possessors . . . That is to say, [we hold simply] the sole and exclusive right of purchasing land from [indigenous peoples within our ostensible boundaries] whenever they should be willing to sell.[13]

The requirement that the consent of indigenous peoples was needed to legitimate cessions of their land was what prompted European states to begin entering into treaties with native peoples soon after the invasion of North America had commenced in earnest.[14] While treaties between European and indigenous nations comprise the fundamental real estate documents through which the disposition of land title on the continent must be assessed, they also served to convey formal recognition by each party that the other was its coequal in terms of legal stature or sovereignty.[15] To further quote Jefferson, "[T]he Indians [have] full, undivided and independent sovereignty as long as they choose to keep it, and . . . this might be forever."[16] As U.S. Attorney General William Wirt would put it in 1828,

> [Be it] once conceded, that the Indians are independent to the purpose of treating, their independence is to that purpose as absolute as any other nation. . . . Nor can it be conceded that their independence as a nation is a limited independence. Like all other nations, they have the absolute power of war and peace. Like any other nation, their territories are inviolable by any other sovereignty. . . . They are entirely self-governed, self-directed. They treat, or refuse to treat, at their pleasure; and there is no human power that can rightly control their discretion in this respect.[17]

From early on, the English had sought to create a loophole by which to exempt themselves in certain instances from the necessity of securing land title by treaty and to undermine the discovery rights of France, whose New World settlement patterns were vastly different from theirs. Termed the Norman Yoke, the theory was that an individual—or an entire people—could rightly claim only such property as they had converted from wilderness to a state of domestication, that is, turned into towns, placed in cultivation, and so forth.[18] Without regard for indigenous methods of land use, it was declared that any area remaining in an "undeveloped" condition could be declared *vacuum domicilium* by its discoverer and clear title thus claimed. By extension, a discovering power, such as France, that failed to pursue development of the sort evident in the English colonial model forfeited its discovery rights accordingly.

The Puritans of Plymouth Plantation and the Massachusetts Bay Colony experimented with this idea during the early seventeenth century, arguing that although native property rights might well be vested in their towns and fields, the remainder of their territory, since it was uncultivated, should be considered unoccupied, and thus not owned.[19] This precedent, however, never evolved into a more generalized English practice. Indeed, the Puritans themselves abandoned such presumption in 1629.[20]

Whatever theoretical disagreements existed concerning the nature of the respective ownership rights of Indians and Europeans to land in America, practical realities shaped legal relations between the natives and the colonists. The necessity of getting along with powerful indigenous peoples, who outnumbered the European settlers for several decades, dictated that as a matter of prudence the settlers buy lands that the Indians were willing to sell, rather than attempting to displace them by other methods. The result was that the English and Dutch colonial governments obtained most of their lands by purchase. For all practical purposes, the Indians were treated as sovereigns possessing full ownership of all the land of America.

So true was this that by 1750 England had dispatched a de facto ambassador to conduct diplomatic relations with the Haudenosaunee (the six nation Iroquois Confederacy)[21] and, in an effort to quell Indian unrest precipitated by his subjects' encroachments upon unceded lands, King George III issued a proclamation prohibiting English settlement west of the Allegheny Mountains in 1763.[22] This foreclosure upon the speculative interests in "western" lands, held by George Washington and other members of the settler élite, and coveted in the less grandiose aspirations to landed status by rank-and-file colonials, would prove a major cause of the American War of Independence.[23]

While it is popularly believed in the United States that the 1783 Treaty of Paris, through which England admitted defeat to the colonists, conveyed title to all lands east of the Mississippi River to the victorious insurgents, the reality is rather different. England merely relinquished its claim to the territory at issue. Hence, what the newly established republic actually acquired was title to such property as England owned— that is, the area of the original thirteen colonies situated east of the 1763 demarcation line, plus an exclusive right to acquire such property as native owners might be convinced to cede by treaty as far west as the Mississippi River.[24] The same principle pertained to the subsequent territorial acquisitions from European or euroderivative countries— for example, the 1803 Louisiana Purchase and the 1848 seizure of the northern half of Mexico through the Treaty of Guadalupe Hidalgo—from which the forty-eight contiguous states were eventually consolidated.[25]

As a concomitant to independence, moreover, the Continental Congress found itself presiding over a pariah state, defiance (much less forcible revocation) of Crown authority being among the worst offenses imaginable under European law. Unable to obtain recognition of its legitimacy in other quarters,[26] the federal government was compelled for nearly two decades to seek it through treaties of peace and friendship with indigenous nations—all of them recognized as legitimate sovereigns in prior treaties with the very European powers then shunning the United States—while going to extravagant rhetorical lengths to demonstrate that, far from being an outlaw state, it was really the most legally oriented of all.[27]

The fledgling U.S. could hardly peddle a strictly law-abiding image on the one hand while openly trampling upon the rights of indigenous peoples on the other. As a result, one of the earliest acts of Congress was to pass the Northwest Ordinance despite George Washington's having secretly and successfully recommended a diametrically opposing policy even before being sworn in as president.[28] In the ordinance, the United States solemnly pledged that "the utmost good faith shall always be observed towards the Indians; their lands and property shall never be taken without their consent; and, in their property, rights, and liberty, they shall never be invaded or disturbed."[29] For the most part, then, it was not until the United States had consolidated its diplomatic ties with France, and the demographic and military balance in the West had begun to shift decisively in its favor, that it began to make serious inroads on native lands.

The Marshall Opinions

The preliminary legal pretext for U.S. expansionism, set forth by Chief Justice Marshall in his *Fletcher v. Peck* opinion (1810),[30] amounted to little more than a recitation of Lockean theory, which was quite popular at the time with Jefferson and other leaders.[31] The proposition that significant portions of Indian territory amounted to *vacuum domicilium*, and was thus open to assertion of U.S. title without native agreement, was, however, contradicted by the country's policy of securing by treaty at least an appearance of indigenous consent to the relinquishment of each parcel brought under federal jurisdiction.[32] The presumption of underlying native land title in the doctrine of discovery thus remained the most vexing barrier to the fulfillment of U.S. territorial ambitions.

In the land claim case of *Johnson v. McIntosh* (1823), Marshall therefore proffered a major (re)interpretation of the doctrine itself.[33] While demonstrating a thorough mastery of the law as it had been previously articulated, and an undeniable ability to draw all the appropriate conclusions therefrom, the chief justice nonetheless inverted the law completely. Although Marshall readily conceded that title to the territories the United States occupied was vested in indigenous peoples, he denied that this afforded them supremacy within their respective domains. Rather, he argued, the self-assigned authority of discoverers to constrain the ability of indigenous people to alienate their property implied that supremacy inhered in the discovering power, not only with respect to other potential buyers but to the native owners themselves.[34]

Since the sovereign standing of discoverers—or derivatives, such as the United States—could in this sense be said to overarch that of those discovered, Marshall held that discovery also conveyed to the discoverer an absolute title, or eminent domain, underlying the aboriginal title possessed by indigenous peoples. The native right of possession was thereby reduced at the stroke of a pen to something enjoyed at the "sufferance of the discovering [superior] sovereign."[35]

> The principle was that discovery gave title to the government by whose subjects, or by whose authority, it was made, against all other European governments whose title might be consummated by possession. The exclusion of all other Europeans necessarily gave to the nation making the discovery the sole right of acquiring the soil from the natives, and establishing settlements upon it. . . . In the establishment of these relations, the rights of the original inhabitants were, in no instance, entirely disregarded;

but were, to a considerable extent, diminished. [T]heir rights to complete sovereignty, as independent nations, were necessarily diminished, and their power to dispose of the soil, at their own will, to whomever they pleased, was denied by the original fundamental principle, the discovery gave exclusive right to those who made it. . . . [T]he Indian inhabitants are [thus] to be considered merely as occupants.[36]

"However extravagant [my logic] might appear," Marshall summed up, "if the principle has been asserted in the first instance, and afterwards, sustained; if a country has been acquired and held under it; if the property of the great mass of the community originates in it, it cannot be questioned."[37] In other words, violations of law themselves become law if committed by those wielding enough power to get away with them. For all the elegant sophistry embodied in Johnson, its premise exemplifies the cliché that "might makes right." In this manner, Marshall not only integrated "the legacy of 1,000 years of European racism and colonialism directed against nonwestern peoples" into the canon of American law," but did so with a virulence unrivaled even by the European jurists upon whose precedents he professed his conclusions to be based.[38]

There were of course a few loose ends remaining, and Marshall assigned himself the task of tying them off in opinions rendered in the so-called Cherokee Cases: *Cherokee Nation v. Georgia* (1831) and *Worcester v. Georgia* (1832).[39] In his *Cherokee* opinion, the chief justice undertook to resolve questions concerning the standing to be accorded indigenous peoples. Since the United States had entered into numerous treaties with native peoples, it was bound by customary international law and Article 1, section 10, of the Constitution to treat them as coequal sovereigns. Marshall's verbiage in *Johnson* had plainly cast them in a very different light. Hence, in *Cherokee*, he conjured a whole new classification of politicolegal entity "marked by peculiar and cardinal distinctions which nowhere else exist,"[40] going on to assert that,

> [I]t may well be doubted whether those tribes which reside within the acknowledged boundaries of the United States can, with strict accuracy, be denominated foreign nations. They may, more correctly, perhaps, be denominated domestic dependent nations. They occupy a territory to which we assert a title independent of their will. . . . Their relation to the United States resembles that of a ward to his guardian.[41]

"The Indian territory is admitted to compose a part of the United States," he continued. "In all our maps, geographical treatises, histories, and laws, it is so considered. . . . [T]hey are [therefore] considered to be within the jurisdictional limits of the United States [and] acknowledge themselves to be under the protection of the United States."[42]

What Marshall described is a status virtually identical to that of a protectorate, yet as he himself would observe in *Worcester* a year later, "the settled doctrine of the law of nations is that a weaker power does not surrender its independence—its right of self-government—by associating with a stronger, and taking its protection. A weak state, in order to provide for its safety, may place itself under the protection of one more powerful, without stripping itself of the right of government, and ceasing to be a state."[43] It follows that a protectorate would also retain its land rights, unimpaired by its relationship with a stronger country.[44]

At another level, Marshall was describing a status similar to that of the states of the Union—subordinate to federal authority, while retaining a residue of sovereign prerogative. Yet he, better than most, was aware that if this were the case, the federal government would never have had a basis in either international or constitutional law to enter into treaties with indigenous peoples in the first place, a matter that would have invalidated any U.S. claim to land titles accruing therefrom. Small wonder, trapped as he was in the welter of his own contradictions, that Marshall eventually threw up his hands in frustration, unable or unwilling to further define Indians as either fish or fowl. In the end, he simply repeated his assertion that the U.S.-Indian relationship was "unique . . . perhaps unlike [that of] any two peoples in existence."[45]

Small wonder, too, all things considered, that the chief justice's *Cherokee* opinion was joined by only one other member of the high court.[46] The majority took exception, with Justices Henry Baldwin and William Johnson writing separate opinions,[47] and Smith Thompson and Joseph Story entering a strongly worded dissent that laid bare the only reasonable conclusions to be drawn from the (legal and historical) facts.[48]

> It is [the Indians'] political condition which determines their *foreign character,* and in that sense must the term *foreign* be understood as used in the Constitution. It can have no relation to local, geographical, or territorial position. It cannot mean a country beyond the sea. Mexico or Canada is certainly to be considered a foreign country, in reference to the United States. It is the political

relation in which one country stands to another, which constitutes it [as] foreign to the other.[49]

Nonetheless, Marshall's views prevailed, a circumstance allowing him to deploy his "domestic dependent nation" thesis against both the Cherokees and Georgia in *Worcester*.[50] First, he reserved on constitutional grounds relations with all "other nations" to the federal sphere, thereby dispensing with Georgia's contention that it possessed a state's right to exercise jurisdiction over a portion of the Cherokee nation falling within its boundaries.[51] Turning to the Cherokees, he reiterated his premise that they, and by implication all Indians within whatever borders the United States might eventually claim, occupied a nebulous quasi-sovereign status as "distinct, independent political communities" subject to federal authority.[52] In practical effect, Marshall cast indigenous nations as entities inherently endowed with a sufficient measure of sovereignty to alienate their territory by treaty when and wherever the United States desired they do so, but never with enough to refuse.[53]

As legal scholars Vine Deloria Jr. and David E. Wilkins have observed, the cumulative distortions of established law and historical reality in Marshall's Indian opinions created a very steep and slippery slope, with no bottom in sight:

> [T]he original assumption [was] that the federal government is authorized and empowered to protect American Indians in enjoyment of their lands. Once it is implied that this power also involves the ability of the federal government by itself to force a purchase of the lands, there is no way the implied power can be limited. If the government can force the disposal of lands, why can it not determine how the lands are to be used? And if it can determine how the lands are to be used, why can it not tell Indians how to live? And if it can tell Indians how to live, why can it not tell them how to behave and what to believe?[54]

By the end of the nineteenth century, less than seventy years after *Cherokee* and *Worcester*, the U.S. government would, indeed, determine land use, how Indians would live, how we should behave, and what we should believe. Within such territory as was by then reserved for indigenous use and occupancy, the traditional mode of collective land tenure had been supplanted by federal imposition of an allegedly more civilized form of individual title expressly intended to compel agricultural land usage.[55] Native spiritual practices were prohibited under penalty of law,[56] and entire generations of American Indian children were being shipped off, often forcibly, to boarding schools, where they were held for years on end, forbidden knowledge of their own languages and cultures while they were systematically indoctrinated with Christian beliefs and cultural values.[57] The overall policy of assimilation, under which these measures were implemented, readily conforms to the contemporary legal definition of cultural genocide.[58]

Meanwhile, American Indians had been reduced to utter destitution, dispossessed of approximately 97.5 percent of our original landholdings,[59] our remaining assets held in a perpetual and self-assigned trust by federal authorities wielding what Marshall's heirs on the Supreme Court described as an extraconstitutional, or plenary, power—that is, an unlimited, absolute, and judicially unchallengeable power—over our affairs.[60] Nothing in the doctrine of discovery empowered any country to impose itself on others in this way. On the contrary, the juridical reasoning evident in the Marshall opinions and their successors has much in common with, and in many respects prefigured, the now thoroughly repudiated body of law purported to legitimate the European imperialism of the first half of the twentieth century.[61]

Rights of Conquest

Rights of conquest in the New World accrued under the law of nations as a subset of the doctrine of discovery. An exception to the requirement that discoverers acquire land only through a voluntary alienation of title by native owners, it allowed those holding discovery rights under certain circumstances to seize land and other property through military force. This, however, was restricted to instance in which a discovering power was compelled to wage "Just War" (jus bellum iustum) against native peoples.[62] The United States clearly acknowledged this principle in the Northwest Ordinance, wherein it was solemnly pledged that indigenous nations would "never be invaded or disturbed, unless in just and lawful wars authorized by Congress."

The criteria for a Just War is defined quite narrowly in international law. As early as 1539, Vitoria asserted that there were only three: 1) when a native people refused to admit Christian missionaries among them, or 2) arbitrarily refused to engage in commerce with the discovering power, or 3) mounted an unprovoked physical attack against the power's representatives or subjects.[63] Absent at least one of these conditions, any war waged by a European state or its derivative would be "unjust"—the term was later changed to "aggressive"—and resulting claims to title illegitimate.[64] One can search in vain for an example in U.S. history in which any of these criteria might actually be viewed as applicable.

A more pragmatic problem confronting those claiming that the United States holds conquest rights to native lands is that although the federal government recognizes the existence of more than four hundred indigenous groups within its borders, its own count of the number of Indian wars it has fought is about forty.[65] Obviously, the United States cannot exercise conquest rights over the nations against which, by its own admission, it has never fought a war. Yet as is readily evident in *Tee-Hit-Ton v. U.S.* (1955), the Supreme Court has anchored U.S. land title in a pretense that exactly the opposite is true: "Every American schoolboy knows that the savage tribes of this continent were deprived of their ancestral ranges by force and that, even when the Indians ceded millions of acres by treaty in return for blankets, food and trinkets, it was not a sale but the conquerors' will that deprived them of their land."[66]

Chief Justice Marshall, particularly in his *Johnson v. McIntosh* opinion but also in *Cherokee*, sought to transcend this issue by treating discovery and conquest as if they were synonymous, a conflation evidencing even less legal merit than the flights of fancy in *Tee-Hit-Ton*. In fact, the high court was ultimately forced to distinguish between the two, acknowledging that the "English possessions in America were not claimed by right of conquest, but by right of discovery," and, therefore, that the "law which regulates, and ought to regulate in general, the relations between the conqueror and conquered, [is] incapable of application" by the U.S. to American Indians.[67]

A further complication is that by as early as 1672, such legal philosophers as Samuel Pufendorf had challenged the idea that territory seized in the course even of just wars might be permanently retained.[68] While Hugo Grotius, William Edward Hall, Emmerich de Vattel, John Westlake, and other theorists continued to aver the validity of conquest rights through the end of the nineteenth century,[69] by the 1920s a view similar to Pufendorf's had proven ascendant.[70]

Oddly, despite the U.S. stance concerning land cessions of American Indians, as well as the government's forcible acquisitions of Hawai'i, Puerto Rico, and the Philippines, the United States assumed a leading role in championing the unacceptability of seizing territory by force.[71] Although the Senate refused to allow the United States to join the League of Nations, President Woodrow Wilson was instrumental in creating the league, an organization intended "to substitute diplomacy for war in the resolution of international disputes."[72] In some ways, more important was the leadership role the U.S. assumed in fashioning the 1928 General Treaty on the Renunciation of War, also known as the Kellogg-Briand Pact or Pact of Paris.[73] In this treaty, the Great Powers and other states rejected the use of war as an instrument of national policy:

> By Article 1, "[T]he High Contracting Parties solemnly declare, in the names of their respective peoples, that they condemn war for the solution of international controversies, and renounce it as an instrument of national policy in their relations with one another." By Article 2, the Parties "agree that the settlement or solution of all disputes or conflicts, of whatever nature or of whatever origin they may be, which may arise among them, shall never be sought except by pacific means."[74]

In 1932 secretary of state Henry Stimson announced that the United States would no longer recognize as legitimate the title to territory acquired by force of arms.[75] This new dictum, shortly to be referred to as the Stimson Doctrine, was expressly designed to "effectively bar the legality hereafter of any title or right sought to be obtained by pressure or treaty violation, and which, as shown by history in the past, will eventually lead to the restoration to [vanquished nations] of rights and titles of which [they] have been unjustly deprived."[76]

By the time the Supreme Court penned its opinion in *Tee-Hit-Ton*, the Stimson Doctrine had served as a cornerstone in formulating the charges of planning and waging aggressive war against the primary nazi defendants at Nuremberg and their Japanese allies in Tokyo in tribunals instigated and organized mainly by the United States.[77] The doctrine was also a guiding principle in the U.S.-instigated establishment of the United Nations, the charter of which, like that of the ill-fated League of Nations before it, is devoted to the "the progressive codification of [international] law . . . for purposes of preventing war."[78] Indeed, Stimson's dictum found its most refined and affirmative expression in the UN Charter's proviso, reiterated almost as boilerplate in a host of subsequent UN resolutions, declarations, and conventions concerning the "equal rights and self-determination of all peoples."[79]

Contradictory as the *Tee-Hit-Ton* court's blatant conquest rhetoric was to the lofty posturing of the United States in the international arena, its position was even more contradictory with respect to a related subterfuge unfolding on the home front. By 1945 the U.S. was urgently seeking a means of distinguishing its own record of territorial expansion from that of the Germany whose nazi leaders it was preparing to hang for having undertaken very much the same course of action.[80] The workhorse employed in this effort was the so-called Indian Claims Commission (ICC), established to make retroactive payment to indigenous peoples whose property had been unlawfully taken over the years.[81] The purpose of the Commission was, as President Harry Truman explained upon signing the enabling legislation on August 14, 1946, to foster an impression that the United States had acquired *none* of its land by conquest.

> This bill makes perfectly clear what many men and women, here and abroad, have failed to recognize, that in our transactions with Indian tribes we have . . . set for ourselves the standard of fair and honorable dealings, pledging respect for all Indian property rights. Instead of confiscating Indian lands, we have purchased from the tribes that once owned this continent more than 90 percent of our public domain.[82]

The game was rigged from the outset, to be sure, since the ICC was not empowered to return land to native people even in cases where its review of the manner in which the United States had acquired it revealed the grossest illegalities. The terms of compensatory awards, moreover, were restricted to payment of the estimated value of the land at the time it was taken, often a century or more before, without such considerations as accrued interest or appreciation in land values during the intervening period.[83] Still, despite its self-serving and mostly cosmetic nature, the very existence of the ICC demonstrated quite clearly that, in terms of legality, U.S. assertions of title to or jurisdiction over Indian country could no more be viewed as based in conquest rights than in rights of discovery. All U.S. pretensions to legitimate ownership of property in North America must therefore be seen as treaty-based.

Through the Lens of the Law

When Congress established the ICC in 1946, it expected within five years to "resolve" all remaining land rights issues concerning American Indians.[84] The Commission was to identify and catalogue the basis in treaties, agreements, and statutes by which the United States had assumed lawful ownership of every disputed land parcel within its purported domain, awarding "just compensation" in each case where the propriety of the transaction(s) documented might otherwise be deemed inadequate.[85] By 1951, however, the 200-odd claims originally anticipated had swelled to 852.[86] The lifespan of the ICC was extended for five years, and then another five years, a process that was repeated until the third generation of commissioners gave up in exhaustion.[87]

By the time the Commission suspended operations on September 30, 1978, it had processed 547 of the 615 dockets into which the 852 claims had been consolidated, none in a manner satisfactory to the native claimants; nearly half the claims were simply dismissed.[88] Title to virtually the entire state of California, for instance, was supposedly "quieted" during the mid-1960s "settlement award" amounting to forty-seven cents per acre, despite the fact that the treaties by which the territory had ostensibly been ceded to the U.S. never been ratified.[89] Most important, the ICC in its final report acknowledged that after three decades of concerted effort, it had been unable to discern any legal basis for U.S. title assertion with respect to what the federal Public Lands Law Review Commission had described as "one third of the nation's land."[90]

> The fact is that about half the area of the country was purchased by treaty or agreement at an average price of less than a dollar per acre; another third of a [billion] acres, mainly in the West, was confiscated without compensation; another two-thirds of a [billion] acres was claimed by the United States without pretense of [even] a unilateral action extinguishing native title.[91]

There can be no serious question of the right of indigenous nations to recover property to which their title remains unclouded or that their right to recover lands seized without payment equals or exceeds that of the United States to preserve its territorial integrity by way of paltry and greatly belated compensatory awards.[92] Restitution rather than compensation is, after all, the guiding principle of international tort law.[93] Regarding the treaties or agreements through which the United States ostensibly acquired some areas, many of the instruments of cession are known to have been fraudulent or coerced. These must be considered invalid under Articles 48–53 of the Vienna Convention on the Law of Treaties.[94]

A classic illustration of fraud involves the 1861 Treaty of Fort Wise, in which federal commissioners forged the signatures of selected native leaders, several of whom were not even present during the "negotiations," and then the Senate altered many of the treaty's terms and provisions *after* it was supposedly signed and ratified, without so much as informing the Indians of the changes. On this basis, the United States claimed to have obtained the "consent" of the Cheyennes and Arapahos to its acquisition of the eastern half of what is now Colorado.[95] Comparable examples abound, including the earlier-mentioned "treaties of cession" in California.[96]

Examples of coercion are also legion, but none provides a better illustration than the 1876–1877 proceeding in which federal authorities suspended distribution of rations to the Lakotas—who at the time were directly subjugated by and therefore dependent upon the U.S. military for sustenance—and informed them that they would not be fed until their leaders had signed an agreement relinquishing title to the Black Hills region of present-day South Dakota.[97] Thus did the Congress contend that the 1851 and 1868 Treaties of Fort Laramie, in each of which the Black Hills were recognized as an integral part of the Lakota homeland, had been superseded and U.S. ownership of the area secured.[98]

Without doubt, North America's indigenous nations are entitled to recover lands expropriated through such travesties. Although it is currently impossible to offer a precise estimate of the acreage involved—to do so would require a contextual review of each U.S. treaty with American Indian nations and a parcel-by-parcel delineation of the title transfers accruing from invalid instruments—it is safe to suggest that adding it to the approximately 35 percent of the continental United States that was never ceded would place well more than half the present gross domestic territory of the United States at issue.

The United States holds the power to simply ignore the law in inconvenient situations such as these. Doing so, however, will never legitimate its comportment. It is through this lens that U.S. pronouncements and performance from Nuremberg to Vietnam must inevitably be evaluated, together with President George Herbert Walker Bush's rhetoric concerning the moral and legal obligation of the United States to end Iraq's forcible annexation of neighboring Kuwait.[99]

On the face of it, the reasonable conclusion to be drawn is that the racial and cultural arrogance, duplicity, and legal cynicism defining U.S. relations with indigenous nations from the outset have come long since to permeate U.S. relations with most other countries. How else to understand Bush's 1991 declaration that the display of U.S. military might he ordered against Iraq was intended more than anything else to put the entire world on notice that, henceforth, "what we say, goes"?[100] In what other manner can one explain the fact that although Bush claimed that the so-called New World Order that he was inaugurating would be marked by nothing so much as "the rule of law among nations,"[101] the United States was and remains unique in the consistency with which it has rejected the authority of international courts and any body of law other than its own?

For the past fifty years, federal policymakers have been increasingly adamant in their rejection of the proposition that the United States might be bound by customs or conventions that conflict with its sense of self-interest.[102] More recently, U.S. delegates to the United Nations have taken to arguing that new codifications of international law must be written in strict conformity to their country's constitutional requirements and that, for interpretive purposes, the existing law advanced by American jurists be considered preeminent.[103] In effect, the United States casts an aura of legitimacy over its ongoing subjugation of indigenous nations by engineering a normalization of such relations in universal legal terms.[104]

The implications of such maneuvering are by no means constrained to a foreclosure on the rights of native peoples. The broader result of U.S. unilateralism is that the United States is extrapolating its presumptive jurisdictional supremacy to worldwide proportions, just as it did with respect to North American Indian territories. This initiative is especially dangerous, given that the lopsided advantage held by the United States within the present balance of global military power closely resembles that which it enjoyed in relation to American Indians, Hawaiians, and Filipinos during the nineteenth century. The upshot is that if such trends are allowed to continue, the United States will have shortly converted most of the rest of the planet to Indian Country.

Notes

1   For background on Garment, see Paul Chaat Smith and Robert Allen Warrior, *Like a Hurricane: The American Indian Movement from Alcatraz to Wounded Knee* (New York: Free Press, 1996) pp. 164–65, 174.

2   Although I've repeated the wording usually attributed to Marshall, the passage actually reads "a *government* of laws, not men [emphasis added]." *Marbury v. Madison* (1 Cranch. (5 U.S.) 137 (1803)). For analysis, see Jean Edward Smith, *John Marshall: Definer of a Nation* (New York: Henry Holt, 1996) pp. 309–26; quote at p. 325.

3   Shortly after the dissolution of the Soviet Union in 1991, then-president George H.W. Bush announced in his annual State of the Union Address that the "world . . . now recognizes one sole and pre-eminent power," following up a year later with the observation, during a speech at West Point, that the U.S. was "the only remaining superpower." The country's militarily unrivaled position, remarked by Bush, has given rise to all manner of hubristic/imperialistic pronouncements by right-wing ideologues, especially those of the "neoconservative" variety. See "Transcript of President Bush's Address on the State of the Union," January 29, 1992 (available at http://www.nytimes.com/1992/01/29/us/state-union-transcript-president-bush-s-address-state-union.html); "Remarks by President George Bush at the United States Military Academy," January 5, 1993 (available at http://www.pbs.org/wgbh/pages/frontline/shows/military/force/bush.html); and the items collected in Andrew

Bracevich, ed., *The Imperial Tense: Prospects and Problems of American Empire* (Chicago: Ivan R. Dee, 2003).

4   Robert A. Williams Jr., *The American Indian in Western Legal Thought: The Discourses of Conquest* (New York: Oxford University Press, 1990) pp. 44–49, 64–65.

5   Ibid., pp. 70–71. Also see Mark Frank Lindley, *The Acquisition and Government of Backward Territory in International Law: A Treatise on the Law and Practice Relating to Colonial Expansion* (London: Longman, Green, 1929) pp. 24–29; Friedrich August Freiherr von der Heydte, "Discovery and Annexation in International Law," *American Journal of International Law*, Vol. 29, No. 1 (July 1935) pp. 448–51.

6   For a penetrating assessment of the "perplexities" instigated by the Columbian landfall, see Tzvetan Todorov, *The Conquest of America: The Question of the Other* (New York: Harper & Row, 1984); on proprietary interest, see pp. 146–67.

7   See Lewis Hanke, *All Mankind Is One: A Study in the Disputation Between Bartolomé de las Casas and Juan Ginés de Sepulveda on the Intellectual and Religious Capacity of American Indians* (DeKalb: Northern Illinois University Press, 1974).

8   Williams, *American Indian in Western Legal Thought*, pp. 89–90, 93–108. Also see Sharon Korman, *The Right of Conquest: The Acquisition of Territory by Force in International Law and Practice* (Oxford, UK: Clarendon Press, 1996) pp. 52–56.

9   Eventually, "land occupied by migratory or semi-sedentary peoples [was classified] as *terra nullius* or, perhaps more precisely, *vacuum domicilium*, in the phrasing of Massachusetts governor John Winthrop (1587/88–1647). In effect, these phrases meant that proprietary rights could only exist within a framework of law created by an organized state; the land of [nonstatist] people was therefore legally vacant." Olive P. Dickason, "Concepts of Sovereignty at the Time of First Contact," in L.C. Green and Olive P. Dickason, *The Law of Nations and the New World* (Edmonton: University of Alberta Press, 1989) p. 235. The notion of North America being a "vacant place" was most famously developed by John Locke in his *Second Treatise on Government* (1689). See Anthony Pagden, *Lords of All the World: Ideologies of Empire in Spain, Britain and France, c. 1500–c. 1800* (New Haven, CT: Yale University Press, 1995) p. 77. On the Puritan concept of *vacuum domicilium* more specifically, see Alden T. Vaughan, *New England Frontier: Puritans and Indians, 1620–1675* (Boston: Little, Brown, 1965) pp. 111–13.

10   England and its settler state derivatives were the worst, but by no means alone. Arguably, most of the expansionist European powers "applied the concept of *terra nullius* in the fifteenth and sixteenth centuries to any territory which did not belong to a Christian sovereign, and in the nineteenth century to any territory that did not belong to a 'civilized' state. Thus the concept of *terra nullius* . . . effectively constituted the spearhead of European powers." Korman, *Right of Conquest*, p. 42n5; citing the International Court of Justice, *ICJ Pleadings on Western Sahara* (1982) at pp. 452–94. It should be noted that in its "Advisory Opinion on Western Sahara," *ICJ Reports* (1975), the court had already concluded that invocation of the concept of *terra nullius* cannot in itself predicate valid title to or jurisdiction over the territories of nonstatist peoples (available at http://www.icj-cij.org/docket/index.php?sum=323&p1=3&p2=4&case=61&p3=5).

11   Emphasis should be placed upon the English common law doctrine of continuity. For discussion, see Kent McNeil, *Common Law Aboriginal Title* (New York: Oxford University Press, 1989) pp. 161–79. Also see Felix S. Cohen, "Original Indian Title," in Lucy Kramer Cohen, ed., *The Legal Conscience: Selected Papers of Felix S. Cohen* (New Haven, CT: Yale University Press, 1960) pp. 273–304; Howard Berman, "The Concept

of Aboriginal Rights in the Early Legal History of the United States," *Buffalo Law Review*, Vol. 27, No. 3 (Fall 1978) pp. 637–67.

12 "Under the right of discovery. The first European nation to discover American lands previously unknown to Europe had what is similar to an exclusive European franchise to negotiate for Indian land within the discovered [area]. International law forbade European nations from interfering with the diplomatic affairs each carried on with Indian nations within their respective 'discovered' territories. The doctrine thus reduced friction and the possibility of warfare between the competing European nations." Editors, "United States Denial of Indian Property Rights: A Study of Lawless Power and Racial Discrimination," in National Lawyers Guild, Committee on Native American Struggles, *Rethinking Indian Law* (New Haven, CT: Advocate Press, 1982) p. 16.

13 Paul Leicester Ford, ed., *The Works of Thomas Jefferson*, 10 vols. (New York: G.P. Putnam's Sons, 1904) Vol. 1, p. 225.

14 For a particularly astute analysis of how the Anglophone system of treatymaking ultimately worked, see Dorothy V. Jones, *License for Empire: Colonialism by Treaty in Early America* (Chicago: University of Chicago Press, 1982) esp. pp. 157–86. For texts, see Alden T. Vaughan, ed., *Early American Indian Documents: Treaties and Laws, 1607–1789*, 20 vols. (Washington, DC: University Publications of America, 1979).

15 The principle is enshrined in Article 1§10 of the U.S. Constitution, as well as the Vienna Convention on the Law of Treaties (U.N. Doc. A/CONF.39/27 at 289 (1969), 1155 U.N.T.S. 331, *reprinted in* 8 I.L.M. 679 (1969)), As formulated in the Convention, the word "treaty" refers to "an international arrangement between States [i.e., countries] in written form and enforceable under international law." Burns H. Weston, Richard A. Falk, and Anthony D'Amato, eds., *Basic Documents on International Law and World Order* (St. Paul, MN: West, 1990) p. 93; full text of the Vienna Convention at pp. 93–107. For further analysis, see Ian Sinclair, *The Vienna Convention on the Law of Treaties* (Manchester, UK: Manchester University Press, 1984) pp. 1–21. For an overview of the customary law codified in the Convention, see Samuel Benjamin Crandell, *Treaties: Their Making and Enforcement* (New York: Columbia University Press, 1916).

16 Quoted in Francis Paul Prucha, *American Indian Policy in the Formative Years: The Trade and Intercourse Acts, 1790–1834* (Lincoln: University of Nebraska Press, 1970) p. 141.

17 William Wirt, "Georgia and the Treaty of Indian Spring (July 28, 1828)," in *Official Opinions of the Attorney General of the United States*, Vol. II (Washington, DC: Robert Farnham, 1852) pp. 132–34.

18 See Robert A. Williams Jr., "Jefferson, the Norman Yoke, and American Indian Lands," *Arizona Law Review*, Vol. 29, No. 2 (Spring 1987) pp. 165–94.

19 See Roy Harvey Pierce, *Savagism and Civilization: A Study of the Indian and the American Mind* (Baltimore: Johns Hopkins University Press, 1967) pp. 20–22; citing, among other sources, Chester E. Eisinger, "The Puritans' Justification for Taking the Land," *Essex Institute Historical Collections*, LXXXIV (1948) pp. 131–43; and John Winthrop, "General Considerations for the Plantation in New-England [1629]," in Alexander Young, ed., *Chronicles of the First Planters of the Colony of Massachusetts Bay from 1623 to 1636* (Boston: Charles C. Little and James Brown, 1846) pp. 271–78.

20 See especially the letter from the Massachusetts Bay Company to Governor John Endicott, April 17, 1629, in N. Shurtleff, ed., *Records of the Governor and the Company of Massachusetts Bay in New England* (Boston: William White, 1853) p. 231. Also see Vaughan, *New England Frontier*, pp. 113–21; Rennard Strickland and Charles F.

Wilkinson, eds., *Felix S. Cohen's Handbook on Federal Indian Law* (Charlottesville, VA: Michie, 1982) p. 55.

21 For examples of the diplomacy practiced by England's "ambassador to the Iroquois," William Johnson, see Francis Jennings, *Empire of Fortune: Crowns, Colonies and Tribes in the Seven Years War in America* (New York: W.W, Norton, 1988) esp. pp. 75–79, 271–74, 434–37. On the man himself, see generally James Thomas Flexner, *Mohawk Baronet: Sir William Johnson of New York* (New York: Harper Bros., 1959).

22 On the Royal Proclamation of 1763 (RSC 1970, App. II, No. 1, at 127), see Pagden, *Lords of All the World*, pp. 83–86; Bruce Clark, *Native Liberty, Crown Sovereignty: The Existing Aboriginal Right to Self-Government in Canada* (Montréal: McGill-Queens University Press, 1990) pp. 134–46. The complete text is available at http://www. solon.org/Constitutions/Canada/English/PreConfederation/rp_1763.html.

23 See Williams, *American Indian in Western Legal Thought*, pp. 228–30, 249–80. Also see Thomas Perkins Abernethy, *Western Lands and the American Revolution* (New York: Appleton-Century, 1937).

24 The complete text of the Treaty of Paris (September 3, 1783) is included in Ruhl H. Bartlett, ed., *The Record of American Diplomacy: Documents and Readings in the History of U.S. Foreign Relations* (New York: Alfred A. Knopf, [4th ed.] 1964) pp. 39–42.

25 For the text of the Treaty Between the United States and France for the Cession of Louisiana, see Bartlett, *Record of American Diplomacy*, pp. 116–17. On similar acquisitions, see generally David M. Pelcher, *The Diplomacy of Annexation: Texas, Oregon, and the Mexican War* (Columbia: University of Missouri Press, 1973).

26 On the failure of U.S. diplomats to secure proper recognition even from France, which had supported its independence struggle against the British, see, e.g., Merrill D. Peterson, *Thomas Jefferson and the New Nation: A Biography* (New York: Oxford University Press, 1970) p. 300.

27 For an excellent framing, see Vine Deloria Jr., "Self-Determination and the Concept of Sovereignty," in Roxanne Dunbar-Ortiz and Larry Emerson, eds., *Economic Development in American Indian Reservations* (Albuquerque: University of New Mexico Native American Studies Ctr., 1979) pp. 22–28.

28 This concerns a written plan submitted to the Congress in which the "father of his country" recommended using treaties with Indians in much the same fashion Hitler would later employ them against his adversaries at Munich as elsewhere (i.e., to lull them into a false sense of security or complacency which placed them at a distinct disadvantage when it came time to subject them to wars of aggression). "Apart from the fact that it was immoral, unethical and actually criminal, this plan placed before Congress by Washington was so logical and well laid out that it was immediately accepted practically without opposition and immediately put into action. There might be—certainly *would* be—further strife with the Indians, new battles and new wars, but the end result was, with the adoption of Washington's plan, inevitable. Without [their] even realizing it had occurred, the fate of all the Indians was sealed. They had lost virtually everything [emphasis original]." Allan W. Eckert, *That Dark and Bloody River: Chronicles of the Ohio River Valley* (New York: Bantam Books, 1995) p. 440.

29 For the text of the Northwest Ordinance of July 26, 1787, see *Journals of the Continental Congress, 1774–1787*, 34 vols. (Washington, DC: Library of Congress, 1904–1937) Vol. 32, pp. 340–41. For context, see Francis Paul Prucha, *American Indian Policy in the Formative Years: The Trade and Intercourse Acts, 1790–1834* (Lincoln: University of Nebraska Press, 1970) pp. 26–40.

30 10 U.S. (6 Cranch.) 87 (1810). To all appearances the opinion was an expedient meant to facilitate redemption of scrip issued to troops and others during the American independence struggle in lieu of pay. The vouchers were to be exchanged for land parcels in Indian Country once victory had been achieved. Marshall and his father received instruments entitling them to 10,000 acres apiece in what is now the state of Kentucky. Smith, *John Marshall*, pp. 74–75. For further background, see C. Peter McGrath, *Yazoo: The Case of* Fletcher v. Peck (Providence, RI: Brown University Press, 1966).

31 See Williams, "Jefferson, the Norman Yoke, and American Indian Lands." Also see his *American Indian in Western Legal Thought*, pp. 249–56. In both treatments, Williams places particular emphasis on Jefferson's 1774 tract, published in pamphlet form, *A Summary View of the Rights of British America*, collected in Merrill Jensen, ed., *Tracts of the American Revolution, 1763–1776* (Indianapolis: Bobbs-Merrill, 1966) pp. 256–76.

32 See generally Reginald Horsman, *Expansion and American Indian Policy, 1783–1812* (Lansing: Michigan State University Press, 1967).

33 *Johnson & Graham's Lessee v. McIntosh* (22 U.S. (8 Wheat) 543 (1823)). For background, see Jill Norgren, *The Cherokee Cases: The Confrontation of Law and Politics* (New York: McGraw-Hill, 1996) pp. 92–95; David E, Wilkins, *American Indian Sovereignty and the Supreme Court* (Austin: University of Texas Press, 1997) pp. 27–35.

34 "The United States . . . maintain, as all others have maintained, that discovery gave an exclusive right to extinguish Indian title of occupancy, either by purchase or by conquest; and gave also a right to such degree of sovereignty as the circumstances of [the U.S. itself] allow [it] to exercise." *Johnson v. McIntosh* at 587.

35 "It has been contended that the Indian title amounted to nothing. Their right to possession has never been questioned. The claim of government extends, however, to the complete ultimate [or absolute] title. . . . An absolute [title] must be an exclusive title, a title that excludes all others not compatible with it. All our institutions recognize the absolute title of the crown [now held by the U.S.], subject only to the Indian right to occupancy, [a matter] incompatible with an absolute and complete title in the Indians." *Johnson v. McIntosh* at 588, 603.

36 *Johnson v. McIntosh* at 573, 587, 591.

37 Ibid., at 591.

38 Williams, *American Indian in Western Legal Thought*, p. 317. Also see Robert A. Williams Jr., "The Algebra of Federal Indian Law: The Hard Trail of Decolonizing the White Man's Jurisprudence," *Wisconsin Law Review*, Vol. 31, No. 1 (March–April 1986) pp. 219–99.

39 *Cherokee Nation v. The State of Georgia* (30 U.S. (5 Pet.) 1 (1831)) and *Worcester v. The State of Georgia* ((31 U.S. (6 Pet.) 551 (1832)). For background, se Norgren, *The Cherokee Cases*, pp. 98–111, 114–22.

40 *Cherokee v. Georgia* at 16.

41 Ibid., at 17.

42 Ibid.

43 *Worcester v. Georgia* at 16.

44 There are numerous examples of this being so. See Vine Deloria Jr., "The Size and Status of Nations," in Susan Lobo and Steve Talbot, eds., *Native American Voices: A Reader* (New York: Longman, 1998) pp. 457–65.

45 *Cherokee v. Georgia* at 16.

46 Joining Marshall was Justice John McLean. Norgren, *Cherokee Cases*, p. 100.

47 Ibid., pp. 106–7.

48　　Thompson wrote the dissent, endorsed by Story. See Joseph C. Burke, "The Cherokee Cases: A Study in Law, Politics, and Morality," *Stanford Law Review*, Vol. 21, No. 1 (February 1969) pp. 516–18.

49　　*Cherokee v. Georgia* at 55.

50　　Norgren, *Cherokee Cases*, pp. 117, 120–21.

51　　*Worcester v. Georgia* at 553–54.

52　　Ibid., 551–56.

53　　"Indian tribes are still recognized as sovereigns by the United States, but they are deprived of the one power all sovereigns must have to function effectively—the power to say 'no' to other sovereigns." Vine Deloria Jr. and David E. Wilkins, *Tribes, Treaties and Constitutional Tribulations* (Austin: University of Texas Press, 1999) p. 70.

54　　Ibid., p. 29.

55　　This was carried out under provision of the 1887 General Allotment Act (ch. 119, 24 Stat. 362, 385, now codified at 18 U.S.C. 331 *et seq.*). For historical overview, see Janet A. McDonnell, *The Dispossession of the American Indian, 1887–1934* (Bloomington: Indiana University Press, 1991). For legal background, see Sidney L. Harring, *Crow Dog's Case: American Indian Sovereignty, Tribal Law, and United States Law in the Nineteenth Century* (Cambridge, UK: Cambridge University Press, 1994) pp. 142–74.

56　　"The sun-dance [sic], and all other similar dances and so-called religious ceremonies are considered 'Indian offenses' under existing regulations, and corrective penalties are provided." U.S. Department of Interior, Office of Indian Affairs Circular 1665, April 16, 1921.

57　　See generally David Wallace Adams, *Education for Extinction: American Indians and the Boarding School Experience* (Lawrence: University Press of Kansas, 1995).

58　　Article II of the 1948 Convention on Prevention and Punishment of the Crime of Genocide (78 U.N.T.S. 277) outlaws as genocidal any policy leading to the "destruction . . . in whole or in part, [of] a national, ethnical, racial, or religious group, as such" (American Indians can of course be—indeed, have been and are—defined in a manner fitting *all four* criteria). More specifically, Article II(b) defines policies "causing serious . . . mental harm to members of the group" as genocide, while Article II(e) does the same with regard to policies involving the "forcibl[e] transferring children of the group to another group." For the text of the Convention, see Weston, Falk, and D'Amato, *Basic Documents on International Law and World Order*, pp. 297–301; language quoted at 297.

59　　For details, see Charles C. Royce, *Indian Land Cessions in the United States*, 2 vols. (Washington, DC: Bureau of American Ethnography, Smithsonian Institution, 1899)

60　　The implications of this term, first employed by the Marshall court in *Gibbons v. Ogden* (22 U.S. (9 Wheat.) 1 (1824)), were set forth more fully in *U.S. v. Kagama* (118 U.S. 375 (1886)), and finalized in *Lone Wolf v. Hitchcock* (187 U.S. 553 (1903)). In the latter case, Justice Edward D. White opined at 568 that, "Congress possesse[s] full power over Indian affairs, and the judiciary cannot question or inquire into its motives. . . . If injury [is] occasioned . . . by the use made by Congress of its power, relief must be sough from that body for redress and not from the courts." By 1942, the courts were even more blunt, quoting *Webster's New International Dictionary* to the effect that that Congress wielded "full, entire, complete, absolute, perfect, and unqualified" power over indigenous nations within its borders. *Mashunkashey v. Mashunkashey* (134 P.2d 976 (1942)) para. 19. For analyses, see Harring, *Crow Dog's Case*, pp. 142–74; Nell Jessup Newton, "Federal Power over Indians: Its Sources, Scope, and Limitations, *University of Pennsylvania Law Review*, Vol. 132, No. 2 (1984) pp. 195–288; Ann Laquer Estin, "*Lone Wolf v. Hitchcock*: The Long Shadow," in Sandra Cadwalader and Vine Deloria Jr., eds., *The Aggressions of Civilization: Federal Indian Policy since the 1880s* (Philadelphia: Temple University Press 1984) pp. 215–45; David E. Wilkins, "The Supreme Court's Explications of 'Federal Plenary Power': An Analysis of Case Law Affecting Tribal Sovereignty, 1886–1914," *American Indian Quarterly*, Vol. 18, No. 3 (Fall 1994) pp. 349–68; Blue Clark, Lone Wolf v. Hitchcock: *Treaty Rights and Indian Law at the End of the Nineteenth Century* (Lincoln: University of Nebraska Press, 1994).

61   Regarding the cases at issue, see, e.g., *American Journal of International Law*, No. 22 (1928), reporting on the *Island of Palmas* case (*U.S. v. Netherlands*, Perm. Ct. Arb. (1928)), in which it was held that a claim to territorial title based on discovery cannot prevail over title based in prior and unrelinquished sovereignty. On the body of colonial law, see, as examples, Lindley, *Acquisition and Government of Backward Territory*; Alpheus Snow, *The Question of Aborigines in the Law and Practice of Nations* (New York: Putnam's 1921). Also see A.P. Thornton, *Doctrines of Imperialism* (New York: John Wiley, 1964); Gerrit W. Gong, *The Standard of "Civilization" in International Society* (Oxford, UK: Clarendon Press, 1984); Martti Koskenniemi, *The Gentle Civilizer of Nations: The Rise* (Cambridge, UK: Cambridge University Press, 2001).

62   For a broad exploration of the concept, see Michael Walzer, *Just and Unjust Wars: A Moral Argument with Historical Illustrations* (New York: Basic Books, 1977). For specific application to U.S. comportment in Vietnam, see Paul Ramsey, *Just War: Force and Political Responsibility* (New York: Scribner's, 1968).

63   The constraint, derived from Augustinian theory, was formulated by Vitoria in his lecture, *De India Recenter Inventis* (1539). See Korman, *Right of Conquest*, pp. 52–56.

64   Williams, *American Indian in Western Legal Thought*, pp. 96–103; Korman, *Right of Conquest*, pp. 52–56; Matthew M. McMahon, *Conquest and Modern International Law: The Legal Limitations on Acquisition of Territory by Conquest* (Washington, DC: Catholic University of America Press, 1940) p. 35.

65   U.S. Department of Commerce, Bureau of the Census, *Report on Indians Taxed and Not Taxed, 1890* (Washington, DC: 53rd Cong., 3rd Sess., 1894) pp. 637–38. Many of the forty-odd wars are summarized in Alan Axelrod, *Chronicle of the Indian Wars from Colonial Times to Wounded Knee* (New York: Prentice Hall General Reference, 1993) pp. 101–256.

66   *Tee-Hit-Ton v. U.S.* (384 U.S. 273 (1955)) at 291. "The Alaska natives [who had pressed a land claim in *Tee-Hit-Ton*] had never fought a skirmish with Russia [which claimed their territories before the U.S.] or the United States. . . . To say that Alaska natives were subjugated by conquest stretches the imagination too far. The only sovereign act that can be said to have conquered the Alaska native was the *Tee-Hit-Ton* opinion itself." Nell Jessup Newton, "At the Whim of the Sovereign: Aboriginal Title Reconsidered," *Hastings Law Review*, Vol. 31, No. 4 (Winter 1979–80) p. 1244.

67   *Martin v. Waddell* (41 U.S. (6 Pet.) 367 (1842)) at 409; *Johnson v. McIntosh* at 591.

68   See esp. Samuel Pufendorf's *De Officio Hominis et Civis Juxta Legem Naturalem* (New York: Oxford University Press, 1927 trans. of 1682 original) Book II, Ch. 16, Sec. 16; and *De Jure Naturae et Gentium* (New York: Oxford University Press, 1934 trans. of 1688 original) Book VIII, Ch. 8, Sec. 1. On acknowledgement of Pufendorf's positions in early U.S. jurisprudence, see Williams, *American Indian in Western Legal Thought*, pp. 303, 309.

69   For a useful survey, see Korman, *Right of Conquest*, pp. 25–40.

70 "Many leading Continental authorities on the law of nations of the late nineteenth and early twentieth centuries—among whom may be cited Bonfils, Despagnet, Fiore, du Montluc, and Pradier-Fodéré—denied altogether that conquest rendered a legal title under international law." By 1923, it was openly asserted during an international conference that, "The right of conquest . . . has no validity in the present century." Korman, *Right of Conquest*, pp. 94, 157; quoting in the latter instance from "Records of Proceedings of the Lausanne Conference on Near Eastern Affairs, 1922–1923," Cmd. 1814 (1923) p. 347.

71 See generally Julius W. Pratt, *The Imperialists of 1898: The Acquisition of Hawaii and the Spanish Islands* (Baltimore: Johns Hopkins University Press, 1936); Stuart Creighton Miller, *"Benevolent Assimilation": The American Conquest of the Philippines, 1899–1903* (New Haven, CT: Yale University Press, 1982).

72 Francis Anthony Boyle, *Foundations of World Order: The Legalist Approach to International Relations, 1898–1922* (Durham, NC: Duke University Press, 1999) pp. 47–48, 53–54.

73 Treaty between the United States and other Powers providing for the renunciation of war as an instrument of national policy. Signed in Paris, August 27, 1928; ratified by the Senate, January 16, 1929 (U.S. Statutes at Large, Vol. 46, Pt. 2, p. 2343) (available at http://www.yale.edu/lawweb/avalon/imt/kbpact.htm).

74 Korman, *Right of Conquest*, p. 192.

75 Stimson's statement will be found in U.S. Department of State, *Documents on International Affairs* (Washington, DC: U.S. Government Printing Office 1932) p. 262. For discussion, see Robert Langer, *Seizure of Territory: The Stimson Doctrine and Related Principles in Legal Theory and Diplomatic Practice* (Princeton, NJ: Princeton University Press, 1947).

76 U.S. Department of State, Press Release No. 136 (May 7, 1932), quoted in Herbert W. Briggs, "Non-Recognition of Title by Conquest and Limitations of the Doctrine," *Proceedings of the American Society for International Law*, Vol. 34 (May 1940) p. 73.

77 See generally Bradley F. Smith, *The Road to Nuremberg* (New York: Basic books, 1981); Arnold C. Brackman, *The Other Nuremberg: The Untold Story of the Tokyo War Crimes Trials* (New York: Quill/Morrow, 1987).

78 On the U.S. role in founding the United Nations, see Phyllis Bennis, *Calling the Shots: How Washington Controls Today's U.N.* (New York: Olive Branch Press, [2nd ed.] 2000) pp. 1–12. On the League, see F.P. Walters, *A History of the League of Nations* (New York: Oxford University Press, 1960).

79 As stated in Article 1(1) and (2) of the UN Charter, "The purposes of the United Nations are [t]o maintain international peace and security [by] adjustment and settlement of international disputes or situations that might lead to a breach of the peace," mainly by developing "friendly relations among nations based on respect from the principle of equal rights and self-determination of people." Reference to "the principle of equal rights and self-determination of all peoples" is made in the 1960 Declaration on the Granting of Independence to Colonial Countries and Peoples (U.N.G.A. Res. 1514 (XV), 15 U.N. GAOR, Supp. (No. 16) 66, U.N. Doc. A/4684 (1961)), Article 1(1) of the International Covenant in Economic, Social and Cultural Rights (U.N.G.A. Res. 2200 (XXI), 21U.N. GAOR, Supp. (No. 16) 49, U.N. Doc. A/6316 (1967)), Article 1(1) of the Covenant on Civil and Political Rights (U.N.G.A. Res. 2200 (XXI), 21 U.N. GAOR, Supp. (No. 16) 52, U.N. Doc. A/6316 (1967)), and elsewhere. For texts, see Weston, Falk, and D'Amato, *Basic Documents on International Law and World Order*, pp. 16, 343, 371, 376.

80 Hitler, for one, was quite clear that the nazi *lebensraumpolitik* was based, theoretically, practically, and quite directly, on the U.S. realization of its "manifest destiny" vis-à-vis American Indians and others it deemed racial/cultural "inferiors." See Adolf Hitler, *Mein Kampf* (New York: Reynal and Hitchcock, 1939) pp. 403, 591; *Hitler's Secret Book* (New York: Grove Press, 1961) pp. 46–52; Frank Parella, *Lebensraum and Manifest Destiny: A Comparative Study in the Justification of Expansionism* (Washington, DC: MA thesis, School of International Relations, Georgetown University, 1950). Also see Norman Rich, *Hitler's War Aims: Ideology, the Nazi State, and the Course of Expansion* (New York: W.W. Norton, 1973) p. 8; John Toland, *Adolf Hitler* (New York: Doubleday, 1976) p. 802.

81 The most detailed study of the ICC is Harvey D. Rosenthal's *Their Day in Court: A History of the Indian Claims Commission* (New York: Garland, 1990).

82 *Public Papers of the Presidents of the United States, Harry S. Truman, 1946* (Washington, DC: U.S. Government Printing Office, 1962) p. 414.

83 All the ICC accomplished was to "clear out the underbrush" obscuring an accurate view of who actually owns what in the U.S. portion of North America. Vine Deloria Jr., *Behind the Trail of Broken Treaties: An Indian Declaration of Independence* (New York: Delacorte Press, 1974) p. 228.

84 U.S. House of Representatives, Committee on Indian Affairs, *Hearings on H.R. 1198 and 1341 to Create an Indian Claims Commission* (Washington, DC: 79th Cong., 1st Sess., March and June 1945) pp. 81–84.

85 See Thomas LeDuc, "The Work of the Indian Claims Commission Under the Act of 1946," *Pacific Historical Review*, Vol. 26, No. 1 (February 1957) pp. 1–16; John T. Vance, "The Congressional Mandate and the Indian Claims Commission," *North Dakota Law Review*, Vol. 45, No. 1 (Spring 1969) pp. 325–36; Wilcomb E. Washburn, "Land Claims in the Mainstream of Indian/White Relations," in Imre Sutton, ed., *Irredeemable America: The Indians' Estate and Land Claims* (Albuquerque: University of New Mexico Press, 1985) pp. 21–34.

86 U.S. House of Representatives, Subcommittee on Appropriations, *Hearings on Independent Office Appropriations for 1952* (Washington, DC: 82nd Cong., 1st Sess., 1951) pp. 28–37.

87 U.S. Senate, Committee on Interior and Insular Affairs, *Report 682: Amending the Indian Claims Commission Act of 1946 as Amended* (Washington, DC: 92nd Cong., 2nd Sess., March 2, 1972).

88 The remaining 68 dockets were turned over to the U.S. court of claims. See Russel Lawrence Barsh, "Behind Land Claims: Rationalizing Dispossession in Anglo-American Law," *Law and Anthropology*, Vol. 1, No. 1 (Spring 1986) pp. 15–50.

89 See generally Robert F. Heizer and Alfred L. Kroeber, "For Sale: California at 47¢ Per Acre," *Journal of California Anthropology*, Vol. 3, No. 2 (Winter 1976) pp. 38–65. Also see note 96, below.

90 Indian Claims Commission, *Final Report* (Washington, DC: 95th Cong., 2nd Sess., 1978); Public Lands Law Review Commission, *One Third of the Nation's Land* (Washington, DC: 91st Cong., 2nd Sess., 1970).

91 Russel Lawrence Barsh, "Indian Land Claims Policy in the United States," *North Dakota Law Review*, Vol. 58, No. 1 (January 1982) pp. 7–82.

92 The territorial integrity of states is guaranteed in Chapter I, Article 2(4) of the UN Charter. The guarantee presupposes, however, that there was a degree of basic legal integrity involved in the territorial acquisitions through which the states composed themselves in the first place. In cases where this is not so, the rights of peoples/

nations involuntarily incorporated into a given state's purported territorial corpus should in my view *always* be presumed to outweigh that state's interest in retaining their lands within its dominion. For discussion, see Lee C. Buchheit, *Secession: The Legitimacy of Self-Determination* (New Haven, CT: Yale University Press, 1978); Hurst Hannum, *Autonomy, Sovereignty, and Self-Determination: The Accommodation of Conflicting Rights* (Philadelphia: University of Pennsylvania Press, [rev. ed.] 1996) esp. pp. 471–77; B.C. Nirmal, *The Right to Self-Determination in International Law* (New Delhi: Deep & Deep, 1999) esp. pp. 165–85.

93   On international torts, see Eduardo Jimenez de Arechaga, "International Responsibility," in Max Sorenson, ed., *Manual of Public International Law* (New York: St. Martin's Press, 1968) pp. 564–72.

94   Treaty fraud, which is specifically prohibited under Article 49 of the Convention as a matter of *jus cogens*, has been defined by the International Law Commission (ILC) as including "any false statements, misrepresentations or deceitful proceedings by which [either party] is induced to give consent to a treaty which it would not otherwise have given." Coercion, which is prohibited under Articles 51 and 52, and as a matter of *jus cogens*, involves "acts or threats" directed by one nation involved in a treaty negotiation against another (or its representatives). The ILC has concluded that "the invalidity of a treaty procured by illegal threat or use of force is a principle which is *lex lata* in . . . international law." Sinclair, *Vienna Convention on the Law of Treaties*, pp. 14–16, 168–81.

95   Treaty with the Cheyennes and Arapahos (12 Stat. 1163, proc. December 5, 1861). For Text, see Charles J. Kappler, comp. and ed., *Indian Treaties, 1778–1883* (New York: Interland, 1972) pp. 807–11. For background, see Stan Hoig, *The Sand Creek Massacre* (Norman: University of Oklahoma Press, 1961) pp. 13–17.

96   "A glance at Royce's *Indian Land Cessions* [see note 59] shows several tracts of land, of not inconsiderable acreage [see note 91 and attendant text], that are listed as ceded to the United States that were not ratified," and are thus legally invalid. These include a "set of . . .21 treaties and 1 supplementary treaty with Indian nations" in California, negotiated in 1851 but never ratified by the Senate." Vine Deloria Jr. and Raymond J. DeMallie, eds., *Documents of American Indian Diplomacy: Treaties, Agreements, and Conventions, 1775–1979*, 2 vols. (Norman: University of Oklahoma Press, 1999) Vol. II, p. 747; treaty texts at pp. 801–45.

97   Treaty with the Sioux—Brulé, Oglala, Miniconjou, Yanktonai, Hunkpapa, Blackfeet, Cuthead, Two Kettle, Sans Arcs, and Santee—and Arapaho (15 Stat. 635, proc. February 24, 1869), otherwise known as the 1868 Fort Laramie Treaty. For text, see Kappler, *Indian Treaties*, pp. 998–1007. On the subsequent "negotiations" through which the Black Hills were "ceded," see the chapter titled "Sell or Starve" in Edward Lazarus, *Black Hills, White Justice: The Sioux Nation versus the United States, 1775 to the Present* (New York: HarperCollins, 1991) pp. 71–95.

98   U.S. title was formally asserted in an Act (19 Stat. 254) passed on February 28, 1877. It should be noted that while the express consent of three-quarters of all adult male Lakotas ("Sioux") was required under Article 12 of the 1868 treaty for any future alienations of land to be legal, that of only about 15 percent was obtained as "validation" of the Black Hills cession agreement.

99   Not least, of course, was his much publicized assertion that the U.S. was waging a "Just War" in the Persian Gulf, with all the moral baggage attending the term. See George H.W. Bush, "Remarks at the Annual Convention of National Religious

Broadcasters," January 28, 1991 (available at http://www.presidency.ucsb.edu/ws/?pid=19250).

100 See Noam Chomsky, "What We Say Goes: The Middle East in the New World Order," in Cynthia Peters, ed., *Collateral Damage: The New World Order at Home and Abroad* (Boston: South End Press, 1992) pp. 49–92.

101 Ibid., esp. pp. 82–88.

102 See generally Bennis, *Calling the Shots*; Nicole Deller, Arjun Makhijani, and John Burroughs, *Rule of Power or Rule of Law? An Assessment of U.S. Policies Regarding Security-Related Treaties* (New York: Apex Press, 2003); and the essays collected in Rosemary Foot, S. Neil MacFarlane, and Michael Mastanduno, eds., *US Hegemony and International Organizations* (New York: Oxford University Press, 2003).

103 An excellent overview is provided by Johan D. van der Vyver, "American Exceptionalism: Human Rights, International Criminal Justice, and National Self-Righteousness," *Emory Law Journal*, Vol. 50, No. 2 (Summer 2001) pp. 775–832. For a detailed study of an archetypal example, see Lawrence J. LeBlanc, *The United States and the Genocide Convention* (Durham, NC: Duke University Press, 1991). Also see Amnesty International, "International Criminal Court: US Efforts to Obtain Impunity for Genocide, Crimes Against Humanity and War Crimes," September 2002 (available at http://www.amnesty.org/en/documents/ior40/025/2002/en/).

104 Consider, for example, the efforts of the U.S. to render the United Nations Draft Declaration on the Rights of Indigenous Peoples "consistent with U.S. domestic law," i.e., by ensuring that it would not include the right of independence or permanent sovereignty over natural resources." National Security Council cable to the U.S, delegation to the World Conference on Racism (January 18, 2001), reproduced as Appendix D in my *Perversions of Justice: Indigenous Peoples and Angloamerican Law* (San Francisco: City Lights, 2003) pp. 427–32.

THREE

The United States and the Genocide Convention

A Half-Century of Obfuscation and Obstruction

> It is clear that the Genocide Convention is a moral document. It is a call for a higher standard of human conduct. It is not a panacea for injustice, [but it is] an important step toward civilizing the affairs of nations.
>
> —Senator William Proxmire (1977)

One of the earliest matters taken up by the United Nations after its 1945 founding convention in San Francisco was the sponsoring of an international legal instrument to punish and prevent the crime of genocide.[1] In General Assembly Resolution 96(1), passed unanimously and without debate on December 11, 1946, the UN made it clear that, although it may have been prompted to act with urgency because of what had been revealed during the recently concluded trial of the major nazi war criminals at Nuremberg, it was more broadly motivated in pursuing the issue: "*Many* instances of such crimes of genocide have occurred when racial, religious, political, and other groups have been destroyed, entirely or in part [emphasis added]."[2] The body's Economic and Social Council (ECOSOC) was mandated by the resolution to produce a draft of the desired convention for consideration at the next annual session of the General Assembly.[3]

ECOSOC immediately turned to the UN Secretariat for support in retaining a trio of experts on international law, notably including Raphaël Lemkin, an exiled Polish-Jewish jurist who had coined the term "genocide" in 1944, and who was thus considered the leading authority on the

Originally published in Daniel Egan and Levon A. Chorbanian, eds., *Power: A Critical Reader* (Upper Saddle River, NJ: Pearson/Prentice Hall, 2005).

topic.[4] The initial draft, authored primarily by Lemkin, was duly submitted to the Council on the Progressive Development of International Law and Its Codification in June 1947.[5] In July, however, the General Assembly, noting "important philosophical disagreements" among some member states with elements of the draft document, declined to put the matter to a vote. Instead, through Resolution 180(11), the assembly instructed ECOSOC to prepare another draft instrument for consideration the following year.[6]

An ad hoc committee, consisting of representatives of China, France, Lebanon, Poland, the United States, the USSR, and Venezuela, was then organized by the council to make the necessary revisions.[7] The new document was passed along to ECOSOC's Sixth (Legal) Committee, which made minor alterations, before submitting it to the General Assembly, which unanimously adopted it without further modification on December 9, 1948.[8] By January 12, 1951, a sufficient number of countries had ratified the Convention on Prevention and Punishment of the Crime of Genocide to afford it the status of binding international law (of both "customary" and "black letter" varieties).[9] As of 1990, more than a hundred UN member states had tendered valid ratifications.[10] The only significant exception was the United States of America.

The situation remains unchanged today, despite a pretense of ratification made at the behest of the Reagan administration in 1988, *forty years* after the convention first passed muster with the civilized countries of the world.[11] How and why this came to be are questions of no small significance, insofar as they shed a penetrating light on the true character and priorities of this "nation of laws," the self-professed "most humane and enlightened nation in the history of humanity."[12] They are no less important in that the United States, as the planet's only remaining superpower, is now in an unparalleled position to visit its version of "humanitarianism" upon virtually any sector of the species it chooses.[13]

Gutting the Convention

The United States assumed a leading role in formulating the application of international legal principle under which the nazi leadership was tried at Nuremberg, especially with regard to the somewhat nebulous category of "Crimes Against Humanity" under which the régime's most blatantly genocidal policies and practices were prosecuted.[14] Similarly, while engineering establishment of the United Nations in 1945—ostensibly as a barrier against the sort of "excesses" evidenced by nazism—it did much to promote the idea that each element of customary human rights law, including implicit prohibitions against genocide, should be codified in a "black letter" international legal instrument, formally embraced through a process of treaty ratifications by member states.[15]

When it came time for the drafting of an actual genocide convention, however, the United States conducted itself in what can only be described as a thoroughly subversive fashion. This began with its response to the initial draft instrument, a document which sought to frame the crime in a manner consistent with accepted definition.

> The draft aimed to protect "racial, national, linguistic, religious, or political groups." In sweeping terms it branded as criminal many physical and biological acts aimed at the destruction of such groups in whole or in part, or of "preventing [their] preservation or development." It specified that acts would be punishable, including attempt to commit genocide, participation in genocide, conspiracy to commit genocide, and engaging in a number of "preparatory" acts such as developing techniques of genocide and setting up installations. It called for punishment of "all forms of public propaganda tending by their systematic and hateful character to promote genocide, or tending to make it appear as a necessary, legitimate, or excusable act." It called for the creation of an international court to try offenders in cases when states were unwilling either to try them or extradite them to another country for trial.[16]

As the Saudi Arabian delegation observed at the time, the draft clearly articulated the nature of genocide as consisting not only in the systematic killing of members of a targeted population, but also in policies devoted to bringing about the "planned disintegration of the political, social, or economic structure of a group or nation" or the "systematic moral debasement of a group, people, or nation."[17] Things seemed to be moving in the right direction until U.S. representatives, often working through third parties such as Canada and Venezuela, went to work to scuttle what became known as the "Secretariat's Draft" on the grounds that its "net was cast much too wide[ly]" and, if approved as law, might therefore serve to "impair the sovereignty" of signatory states.[18]

The previously mentioned ad hoc committee, chaired by U.S. delegate John Maktos, was then assembled to produce a new draft, with attention focused on "the political as well as the legal dimensions" of the issue.[19] In short order, a quid pro quo was effected in which the Soviets were allowed to strike socioeconomic aggregates of the very sort they had been steadily obliterating since the early 1930s from the list of entities to receive protection under the law.[20] In exchange, the United States was able to remove an entire article delineating the criteria of cultural rather than physical or biological genocide, a maneuver serving to exempt a range of its own dirty linen from scrutiny. Davis and Zannis write in *The Genocide Machine in Canada*:

> The secretariat's draft [had gone] to considerable lengths to detail the specific conditions of the three forms of genocide. In the category of *physical*, it outlined mass extermination and "slow death" measures (i.e., subjection to conditions of life which, owing to lack of proper housing, clothing, food, hygiene and medical care or excessive work or physical exertion are likely to result in the debilitation or death of individuals; mutilations and biological experiments imposed for other than curative purposes; deprivation of all means of livelihood by confiscation of property; looting, curtailment of work, and the denial of housing and supplies otherwise available to the other inhabitants of the territory concerned. . . . The secretariat's draft took *biological* genocide to mean the restricting of births in the group. It named the methods of sterilization or compulsory abortion, segregation of the sexes and obstacles to marriage. . . . *Cultural* genocide was defined as the destruction of the specific characteristics of the group. Among the acts specified: forced transfer of children to another human group; forced and systematic exile of individuals representing the culture of a group; the prohibition of the use of the national language, or religious works, or the prohibition of new publications; systematic destruction of historical or religious monuments, or their diversion to alien uses; destruction or dispersion of documents and objects of historical, artistic, or religious value and of objects used in religious worship.[21]

In the Secretariat's Draft, one crime—genocide—was thus defined as having three distinct but interactive modes of perpetration. No effort was "made to distinguish the relative seriousness of the modes which are left to stand on par," with the deliberate eradication of cultural existence being treated with as much legal gravity as programs of outright physical annihilation.[22] By the time the United States had completed its overhaul of the text, over the heated objections of the Lebanese delegate, all that remained of the concept of cultural genocide was a provision prohibiting the forced transfer of children. Even the secretariat's proscription of genocidally oriented propaganda—a concept deployed by the U.S. in its prosecution of Julius Streicher at Nuremberg—had been scrapped in favor of a much more restrictive clause prohibiting "direct and public incitement."[23] In its final form, the key ingredients of the draft finally presented to the General Assembly had been reduced to the following:

> Article II. In the present Convention, genocide means any of the following acts committed to destroy, in whole or in part, a national, ethnical, racial or religious group, as such:
> (a) Killing members of the group;
> (b) Causing serious bodily or mental harm to members of the group;
> (c) Deliberately inflicting on members of the group conditions of life calculated to bring about its physical destruction in whole or in part;
> (d) Imposing measures intended to prevent births within the group;
> (e) Forcibly transferring children of the group to another group.
>
> Article III. The following acts shall be punishable:
> (a) Genocide;
> (b) Conspiracy to commit genocide;
> (c) Direct and public incitement to commit genocide;
> (d) Attempt to commit genocide;
> (e) Complicity in genocide.

It was this U.S.-designed and highly truncated instrument, not just diluting but effectively gutting Lemkin's original conception of genocide and the draft convention which arose from it, which was ultimately approved by the General Assembly. From there, it was an easy slide down the slippery slope of definitional erosion into a generalized misunderstanding that genocide occurs *only* within peculiarly focused incidents or processes of mass murder (à la Auschwitz and Babi Yar). For all practical intents and purposes, then, the United States had attained a diplomatic triumph of sorts, managing to void the very meaning of the crime in question while simultaneously appearing to stand at the forefront of those opposing it.

Nonratification

It appeared for a time that America might be able to have its cake and eat it too, at least on matters of international legality. At home, this liberal accomplishment—not only subversion of the Genocide Convention, but the forging of a position of primacy for the United States within the UN

itself had been masterminded by Truman-era State Department hold-
overs from the previous administration of Franklin Delano Roosevelt—
foundered on the shoals of extreme right-wing reaction.[24] The State
Department was a particular target of the Right during the entire period
of the Cold War,[25] especially its "communistic" notion of creating a
workable system of international problem resolution through nonmilitary means, embodied in the UN mandate to establish standards of comportment through the progressive codification of international law.[26]

While such forces never managed to fulfill their original objective of
bringing about an actual U.S. withdrawal from the United Nations—after
Korea, even the more thoughtful right-wingers could see the utility of
remaining within the organization—they were able to neutralize much
of what they found most objectionable about it by crafting an American
posture of refusing to ratify its promulgation of international legal instruments they perceived as constraining the latitude of U.S. policy options.
Among the more important elements of evolving human rights law which
the United States still refuses to accept are the International Covenant on
Civil and Political Rights (1966); the Covenant on Economic, Social and
Cultural Rights (1966); the Convention on the Elimination of All Forms
of Racial Discrimination (1966); and the American Declaration of the
Rights and Duties of Man (1965).[27] The same holds true concerning the
Laws of War, specifically the Declaration on the Prohibition of the Use of
Thermo-Nuclear Weapons (1961); the Resolution Regarding Weapons of
Mass Destruction in Outer Space (1964); the Resolution on the Non-Use
of Force in International Relations and Permanent Ban on the Use of
Nuclear Weapons (1972); the Resolution on the Definition of Aggression
(1974); Protocols Additional to the 1949 Geneva Conventions (1977); and
the Declaration on the Prohibition of Chemical Weapons (1989).[28]

By and large, the arguments advanced in the Senate against ratification of the treaties accepting each of these legal instruments has been
that to do so would "impair U.S. sovereignty" by conceding that there
was some body of law "standing at a level higher than that of our own
constitution."[29] This follows precisely the logic embodied in a cornerstone of the nazis' Nuremberg defense: insofar as the German government of which the defendants had been a part had never accepted most
of the international laws at issue, they had not been required to abide
by them.[30] Rather, the defense contended, they were bound only to
adhere to the legal code of the sovereign German state under which
authority they asserted legitimation of their various actions.[31] The tribunal rejected this line of reasoning out of hand, countering that the

defendants—indeed, the members of all governments—were bound under pain of criminal prosecution to conform to "higher laws" than those evidenced in their own domestic constitutions and statutory codes.[32] The UN member states, including the United States, went on to affirm this position in December 1946.[33]

Nonetheless, after conducting hearings on the matter in 1950—during which it became clear that many of its members were "profoundly skeptical about, and even hostile to, the notion of assuming an international legal obligation on genocide"[34]—the Senate Committee on Foreign Relations rejected the Genocide Convention.

Deeper Motives

Beneath the transparently invalid gloss of constitutional argument with which the Senate coated its rejection of the Genocide Convention lay deeper and more important motives.[35] These devolved upon the understanding that certain ongoing U.S. policies and practices abridged the meaning of the Convention, even in its most highly diluted form. In testimony brought before the Foreign Relations Committee, this was expressed in terms of the implications of the treatment accorded racial minorities in light of the Convention's provision that intent to destroy a target group "in part" was sufficient to predicate a charge of genocidal conduct.[36] Witness the following exchange between ABA representative Alfred Schweppe and the subcommittee chair, Connecticut Senator Brien McMahon, during the 1950 hearings:

> SCHWEPPE: The point is that the intent does not need to exist to destroy the whole group. It needs only to exist to destroy part of the group. Now whether we say part of the group could mean one person or whether we say a substantial part again requires us to inquire into the facts, as you often do in these cases, what is the group and how many were there?
> McMAHON: Part of the group—but because he is part of the group. Now let's take lynching for example. Let's assume that there is a lynching and a colored man is murdered in this fashion. Is it your contention that that could be construed as being within the confines of the definition; namely, with intent to destroy him as part of a group?
> SCHWEPPE: Well, Mr. Chairman, I don't want to answer that categorically. . . . Certainly, it doesn't mean if I want to drive five Chinamen out of town . . . that I must have the intent to destroy

all the 400,000,000 Chinese in the world or the 250,000 within the United States. It is part of a racial group, and if it is a group of 5, a group of 10, a group of 15, and I proceed after them with guns in some community solely because they belong to some racial group that the dictators don't like, I think you have a got a serious question. That's what bothers me.[37]

What was "bothering" both McMahon and Schweppe was not only the gratuitous violence habitually visited upon Chinese immigrants to the United States during the twentieth century, but the history of the lynchings of at least 2,505 black men and women in ten southern states between 1882 and 1930. That comes to an average of one such act of racially explicit lethal mob violence directed against African Americans each week for the entire forty-eight-year period, in an area encompassing only one-fifth of the country.[38] When the remaining 80 percent of the United States is added in, the actual number of "nonwhites" lynched was probably about double—more than 5,000—a racial murder rate markedly higher than that evidenced in Germany against Jews and Gypsies combined prior to 1939.[39] Tolnay and Beck write:

> As staggering as the lynching toll was, it vastly understates the total volume of violence aimed toward African-American citizens. . . . [The] lynching inventory does not count casualties of the urban race riots that erupted during those years, nor does it embrace victims of a single killer or pairs of assassins. Neither does it include the all-too-frequent beatings, whippings, verbal humiliations, threats, harangues, and other countless indignities suffered by the Black population [in much the same manner as they were undergone by target populations in Germany].[40]

The lynching of African Americans had not ended in 1930, of course. Indeed, with twenty-one reported fatalities in that year, it represented a high point for the period reported. In 1932, however, there were twenty-two documented lynchings of blacks in the South, another eighteen in 1933.[41] While the level of such violence would abate somewhat after 1935, it could hardly be said to have disappeared by 1950, and it would rise again sharply during the latter part of the decade and on through the mid-1960s.[42] There was, after all, a rather prominent organization, the Ku Klux Klan, which had been openly advocating not only the sort of atrocities at issue, but also the sordid racial doctrines underlying them. Not only had authorities at all levels declined to take decisive action to quell Klan-style activity, they had in many cases encouraged it, and in more than a few, were known to have actively participated in it.[43]

Unquestionably, it could be argued that such a pattern fell within the categories of state-sanctioned behavior prohibited by the Genocide Convention. It is therefore instructive that the immediate response of conservatives like Schweppe was not to embrace the law as a potentially powerful tool that might prove useful in an official drive to end the rampant and sustained racist violence plaguing the United States. Instead, it was the opposite: they denounced the Convention on the bizarre premise that such atrocities were somehow or another "constitutionally protected" under the mantle of U.S. sovereignty. Even more revealing in many ways is the fact that liberals agreed, albeit rather than rejecting the Convention outright, they sought to apply finesse by pretending it meant something other than what it said. Consider the following exchange between McMahon and then-deputy undersecretary of state Dean Rusk:

> RUSK: Genocide, as defined in Article II of the Convention, consists of the commission of certain specified acts, such as killing or causing serious bodily harm to individuals who are members of a national, ethnical, racial or religious group, with the intent to destroy that group. The legislative history of Article II shows that the United Nations negotiators felt that it should not be necessary that an entire human group be destroyed to constitute the crime of genocide, but rather that genocide meant the partial destruction of such a group with the intent to destroy the entire group concerned.
> McMAHON: That is important. They must have the intent to destroy the entire group.
> RUSK: That is correct.
> McMAHON: In other words, an action leveled against one or two of a race or religion would not be, as I understand it, the crime of genocide. They must have the intent to go through and kill them all.
> RUSK: That is correct. The Convention does not aim at the violent expression of prejudice which is directed against individual members of groups.[44]

This, to be sure, was nonsense, as Schweppe later emphatically—and quite correctly—pointed out to the committee.

> [Rusk] has undertaken in a gloss to say that basic to any charge of genocide must be the intent to destroy the entire group. Now that

is an exact negation of the text which is to be construed not only by [the Senate] but . . . by the International Court of Justice. Now, the International Court of Justice is not going to say intent to destroy a group in whole or in part means only to destroy a whole group . . . The Convention says you only need the intent to destroy part of a group; so there is a contradiction, gentlemen . . . which I suggest you very seriously consider.[45]

If the circumstances attending the lynching of blacks smacked of genocide, their targeting for involuntary sterilization was even worse. Already in 1950 there was considerable discussion in the African American community about this, and in December 1951, a 240-page petition, written by black attorney William L. Patterson for the American Civil Rights Congress (CRC) and entitled "We Charge Genocide," was deposited with the UN Secretariat in New York.[46] Although U.S. diplomats were able to prevent the document—which provided copious details on sterilization programs to which the Afroamerican community had been subjected—from being taken up by the UN's Commission on Human Rights, the submission sent lingering shock waves across the federal hierarchy.[47]

By 1970, when an updated version of the CRC petition was deposited with the secretariat, the situation was even more "sensitive." At that point, the government was not only continuing its "birth control efforts" with regard to poor blacks, it had secretly launched similar programs targeting American Indians and Puerto Ricans which eventually resulted in upward of 30 percent of the women of childbearing age in each group undergoing involuntary—and in many instances completely unwitting—sterilization.[48]

The only question in this regard which seemed to concern Idaho's liberal senator Frank Church during testimony provided by Assistant Attorney General (and future chief justice of the Supreme Court) William Rehnquist in hearings conducted the same year, was whether responsible officials could be "safeguarded" from meaningful prosecution, perchance charges were ever brought against them under the Genocide Convention.

> CHURCH: Another extreme criticism leveled at the Convention is that it would make birth control efforts among the poor blacks an act of genocide. How would you answer this allegation?
> REHNQUIST: I think that any birth control effort that might reasonably be contemplated in this country would certainly be

a voluntary one, and would likewise be directed towards all individuals rather than any particular race. I think it inconceivable
that any sort of birth control effort that would ever receive public
approval in this country would violate the provisions of this treaty.
CHURCH: Is it true that if any such effort were to be made, based
upon some compulsory method and directed toward some particular group, that the protections of the Constitution would be
fully applicable whether or not the United States had ratified and
become party to the Genocide Convention?
REHNQUIST: Certainly.[49]

Other aspects of U.S. domestic policy were coming into similar
focus at about the same time. There were, for instance, potential ram-
ifications to the maintenance of the apartheid structure of Jim Crow
segregation throughout much of the country for more than a hundred
years.[50] As ABA representative Eberhard Deutsch put it in his testimony
before the subcommittee in 1971, such a systematic pattern of statutory
racial discrimination could, at least in part, be seen as a violation of even
the most rigorous interpretation of the Convention's injunction against
visiting mental harm upon members of a target group.

> In Brown v. Board of Education, the leading desegregation case . . .
> the Supreme Court of the United States . . . held expressly that
> separation of Negro children . . . from others of similar age and
> qualifications solely because of their race, generates a feeling of
> inferiority as to their status in the community that affects their
> hearts and minds in a way unlikely ever to be undone . . . and has
> a tendency to retard their education and mental development. . . .
> In light of this holding by the Supreme Court, such an understand-
> ing as this committee has proposed . . . that mental harm is to be
> construed "to mean permanent impairment of mental faculties,"
> would hardly deter any tribunal from determining that any form
> of local segregation is within the definition of the international
> crime of genocide under the Convention.[51]

At no point during the subcommission's hearings was there serious
discussion of the implications of the Convention's prohibition against
the forced transfer of children in light of U.S. policy.[52] The reasons for
this are readily apparent. To have done so would have been to expose
the entire system of compulsory boarding schools long imposed by the
government upon American Indians to the kind of scrutiny it could ill

afford. Any such attention to Indian affairs would, moreover, all but inevitably raise the specter of the extermination campaigns waged against America's indigenous peoples in previous centuries.[53] From there, discussion would have led unerringly into the very sphere of consideration the United States had sought to evade when it arranged for deletion of the third article of the Secretariat's Draft: the broad range of culturally genocidal practices through which the Indians' final extinction was still being relentlessly pursued as a matter of policy. Rather, these genies were left in their bottles altogether, and the subjects of Indians and Indian policy never came up.[54]

Be that as it may, it is unquestionably a matter of record that it was with full knowledge that many of its own undertakings and positions were genocidal by legal definition—and with the stated intention of maintaining its own imagined "sovereign discretion" to continue in exactly the same vein—that the Senate of the United States, cheered on by the country's most representative body of jurists and attorneys, openly rejected the Genocide Convention for fully two generations.

"Ratification"

It was not until 1985, after the first signs of significant deterioration in the Soviet system signaled the potential for a decisive and potentially permanent shift in global power back to the United States, that a genuine senatorial interest in ratifying the Genocide Convention finally emerged.[55] By then, the Reagan administration had restored a certain "luster and authority" to America's martial image through the conquest of tiny Grenada, endorsement of Israel's invasion and partial occupation of neighboring Lebanon, support for Iraq's bloody attritional contest with Iran, initiation of a pair of substantial low-intensity wars in Nicaragua and El Salvador, and the repeated provocation of lopsided aerial combat over Libya's Gulf of Sidra, among numerous other things.[56] Moreover, the administration was in the process of repudiating the jurisdiction of the World Court to require U.S. adherence to even those relatively few standards of international legality it had formally embraced.[57]

Given that these developments dictated an increasing "unenforcability" of the Convention against the United States (to quote Reagan), it was decided that the time was finally ripe for America to reap whatever propaganda benefits might accrue from the "humanitarian gesture" of signing on to what had long since become customary law.[58] It was also discerned by more perceptive officials that, with the U.S. effectively self-exempted from abiding by provisions of this or any other element of international legality it might find inconvenient, endorsement of the relevant instruments might serve to forge useful new weapons for concrete rather than rhetorical utilization against America's enemies on certain occasions. A team of leading senatorial conservatives—Indiana's Richard Lugar, Orrin Hatch of Utah, and Jesse Helms—were therefore assembled to sell ratification to the Right.[59]

Together, the three crafted what they described as a "Sovereignty Package" containing two "reservations" and five "understandings" upon which U.S. "acceptance" of the Genocide Convention would be conditioned. These "clarifications" served to preclude any possibility that its provisions might actually be applied to America by reaffirming U.S. repudiation of the jurisdiction of international courts, asserting the primacy of the United States Constitution over international law, rejecting extradition of U.S. nationals for violation of the Convention (rather than the U.S. "interpretation" of it), and specifically absolving the effects of discriminatory domestic policies and external military actions from being classified as genocidal other than in cases where genocide was a stated intent.[60] As the package read in its final form:

> **Resolution of Ratification**
> **(Lugar-Helms-Hatch Sovereignty Package)**
> **Adopted February 19, 1986**
> *Resolved (two-thirds of the Senators present concurring therein),* That the Senate advise and consent to the ratification of the International Convention on the Prevention and Punishment of the Crime of Genocide, adopted unanimously by the General Assembly of the United Nations in Paris on December 9, 1948 (Executive 0, Eighty-first Congress, first session), *Provided that:*
>
> I. The Senate's advise and consent is subject to the following reservations:
>
> (1) That with reference to Article IX of the Convention, before any dispute to which the United States is a party may be submitted to the International Court of Justice under this article, the specific consent of the United States is required in each case.
>
> (2) That nothing in the Convention requires or authorizes legislation or other action by the United States prohibited by the Constitution of the United States as interpreted by the United States.

II. The Senate's advise and consent is subject to the following understandings, which shall apply to the obligations of the United States under this Convention:

(1) That the term "intent to destroy, in whole or in part, a national, ethnical, racial, or religious group as such" appearing in Article II means the *specific* intent to destroy, in whole or in *substantial* part, a national, ethnical, racial, or religious group as such by the acts specified in Article II [emphasis added].

(2) That the term "mental harm" in Article 11(b) means the permanent impairment of mental faculties through drugs, torture, or similar measures.

(3) That the pledge to grant extradition in accordance with a state's laws and treaties in force found in Article VII extends only to acts which are criminal under the laws of both the requesting and requested state and nothing in Article VII affects the right of any state to bring trial before its own tribunals any of its nationals for acts committed outside a state.

(4) That acts in the course of armed conflicts committed without the *specific* intent required by Article II are not sufficient to constitute genocide as defined by the Convention [emphasis added].

(5) That with regard to the reference to an international tribunal in Article VI of the Convention, the United States declares that it reserves the right to effect its participation in any such tribunal only by a treaty entered into specifically for that purpose with the advise and consent of the Senate.

III. The Senate's advise and consent is subject to the following declaration: That the President will not deposit the instrument of ratification until after the implementing legislation referred to in Article V has been enacted.[61]

With the force and implications of the instrument thus thoroughly negated, this "ratification" was affirmed by congressional passage of the Genocide Convention Implementation Act—also called the "Proxmire Act," a rather ironic reference to the senator who had been most prominent in advocating adoption of the law in its undiluted form—in October 1988.[62] The resulting documents, including the Lugar-Helms-Hatch package, were deposited by the Reagan administration with the United Nations a month later.[63] The Convention, in its congressionally approved form, became "binding" upon the United States in February 1989.

Long before the process was completed, however, some senators, notably Connecticut Democrat Christopher Dodd and Charles Mathias, a Maryland Republican, were warning that the U.S. claim to have ratified the Convention in this fashion would likely be rebuffed by the international community on grounds that the U.S. rejection of Article IX would completely undermine the [law's] effectiveness."[64] Dodd and Mathias were joined by several others when they argued that the *a priori* exoneration entered with respect to military action might have equally adverse effects.

> [A] question arises as to what the United States is really trying to accomplish by attaching this understanding. The language suggests the United States has something to hide. Moreover, the relatively imprecise definition of "armed conflict" in international law is an invitation to problems and will almost certainly draw adverse comments from other nations trying to figure out what the language is intended to do. To call attention to our fears of being brought to account for acts committed in armed conflicts is really an embarrassment to the United States and should have no place in our ratification of the Genocide Convention.[65]

As analyst Lawrence LeBlanc has observed, "There is much to commend this viewpoint, though it could be carried further. . . . [Other] provisions—for example, the understandings regarding intent and the meaning of mental harm—seem to carve out exceptions for the United States. . . . [They] could be understood by other parties as being reservations that are incompatible with the object and purpose of the Convention. The considerations that gave rise to these understandings— mainly domestic racial considerations—lend credibility to the viewpoint of those who object."[66]

LeBlanc's assessment is borne out in the fact that, by December 1989, nine European countries—Denmark, Finland, Ireland, Italy, the Netherlands, Norway, Spain, Sweden, and the United Kingdom—had entered formal objections to the "constitutional provision" of the U.S. Sovereignty Package with the UN Secretariat, describing it as a violation of international treaty law.[67] The United Kingdom and the Netherlands, joined by Australia, also objected to America's repudiation of World Court jurisdiction.[68] The Netherlands flatly declined to recognize U.S. ratification of the Convention as being valid until such time as these "problems" are corrected.[69] The other objecting governments were not so explicit in this regard, although the legal and diplomatic implications of their filing of objections is the same.[70] Hence, all pretensions to the

contrary notwithstanding, the United States remains—quite conspicuously—an outlaw state.

Costs and Consequences

The U.S. refusal to ratify even the ludicrously abbreviated conception of
genocide it had itself engineered, in effect undermined any attempt to apply
the Convention to prevent or punish perpetrators of the global proliferation of systematic mass murder programs which have been documented
after 1945. In *none* of the "episodes" occurring prior to 1990—encompassing processes of such magnitude as the U.S.-sponsored 1965 Indonesian
extermination of perhaps a million "communists,"[71] to the holocausts
in Burundi and Bangladesh in 1972[72] was the Genocide Convention
invoked by the United Nations.[73] Indeed, with the notable exception of
the Khmer Rouge "autogenocide" in Cambodia/Kampuchea—which was
showcased in the most propagandistic fashion, as a *post hoc* justification
for U.S. aggression there—none was ever characterized as genocidal by
mainstream journalists and commentators. It was not until the pretended
U.S. ratification of the Convention had gone into effect that it became
permissible for the UN to employ the term in serious fashion, and then
only with respect to *some* perpetrators in *certain* instances.

The most salient illustrations of this concern has been the
recent establishment of international tribunals—the first such since
Nuremberg—to prosecute a few of those responsible for bloodbaths in
Bosnia-Herzegovina and Rwanda on charges of genocide and related
crimes.[74] While this seems at first glance to be a positive development,
suggesting that the belated U.S. pretense of ratification, however illegitimate it may have been, is nonetheless serving constructive purposes,
closer scrutiny reveals a rather different picture.[75] Those slated to be
hauled into the defendants' dock are composed entirely of those who are
at most marginal to U.S. policy interests, and whose actions have offered
the prospect of disrupting the planetary order that policy is intended to
impose.[76]

To all appearances, the United States, now that it has finally "signed
on" to the Convention, has embarked upon a course of "claiming moral
high ground" by instigating show trials on charges of genocide against
those it considers essentially irrelevant—as it will undoubtedly do against
outright enemies whenever opportunity knocks—the better to immunize
itself and governments it deems useful from precisely the same charge.
The upshot is that after a half-century of blocking implementation of
the Genocide Convention, the U.S. has moved decisively to domesticate

it, harnessing international law entirely to the needs and dictates of American policy.[77] Universal condemnation of the crime of genocide is thus being co-opted to a point at which condemnation accrues only to genocides which, whether in form or in function, have failed to receive the sanction of the United States. Those which have not are to be punished. Those which have are to be reinforced, rewarded, defined as anything but what they are, even to the extent of describing them as "democratic."[78]

Notes

1   For the official record of how the resolution was formulated, see Prevention and Punishment of the Crime of Genocide: Historical Summary (UN Doc. E/621, January 1948) Sections I–V.

2   Quoted in Lawrence J. LeBlanc, *The United States and the Genocide Convention* (Durham, NC: Duke University Press, 1991) p. 23. While the term was used in the indictment, there was in fact no operant definition of genocide involved in the Nuremberg proceedings. Indeed, while it was certainly implied in what were termed "Crimes Against Humanity" in Article IV of the August 1945 London Charter authorizing formation of the International Military Tribunal before which ranking nazi leaders were tried, they were framed in a manner which was "both complex and confusing." Bradley F. Smith, *Reaching Judgment at Nuremberg* (New York: Basic Books, 1977) pp. 14–15, 60, 66–67. On use of the term "genocide" in the indictment, see Telford Taylor, *Anatomy of the Nuremberg Trials* (New York: Alfred A. Knopf, 1962) p. 103.

3   See Matthew Lippmann, "The Drafting of the 1948 Convention on the Punishment and Prevention of Genocide," *Boston University International Law Journal*, Vol. 3, No. 1 (Winter 1985) pp. 1–65.

4   For Lemkin's original definition of genocide, see his *Axis Rule in Occupied Europe: Laws of Occupation, Analysis of Government, Proposals for Redress* (Washington, DC: Carnegie Endowment for International Peace, 1944) pp. 79–94. ECOSOC's request to the Secretariat was made via Resolution 47(W), March 28, 1947.

5   U.N. Doc. A/362, June 14, 1947.

6   Nehemiah Robinson, *The Genocide Convention: A Commentary* (New York: Institute for Jewish Affairs, 1960) pp. 18–19.

7   *Report of the Ad Hoc Committee on Genocide* (3 U.N. ESCOR Supp. 6, U.N. Doc. E/794 (1948)).

8   Convention on the Punishment and Prevention of Genocide (U.S.T., T.I.A.S., 78 U.N.T.S. 277); done in New York, December 9, 1948; entered into force, January 12, 1951.

9   International Court of Justice, *Reports of Judgments, Advisory Opinions and Orders: Reservations to the Convention on Punishment and Prevention of the Crime of Genocide* (The Hague: ICJ, 1951) pp. 15–69.

10 *Multilateral Treaties Deposited with the Secretary General: Status as of 31 December 1989* (St/ Leg/Ser. E/8 97–98 (1990)).

11 LeBlanc, *The United States and the Genocide Convention*, p. 2.

12 Statement by President Ronald Reagan, as shown on CNN, March 14, 1981.

13 For a good sample of U.S. practice in this regard, see Noam Chomsky, *Deterring Democracy* (New York: Hill and Wang, 1992); Cynthia Peters, ed., *Collateral Damage: The "New World Order" At Home and Abroad* (Boston: South End Press, 1992).

14 Bradley F. Smith, *The Road to Nuremberg* (New York Basic Books, 1981) pp. 173–74, 236, 253. The same principles, though not an identical formulation, were employed in prosecuting the Japanese leadership a bit later. See generally Arnold C. Blackman, *The Other Nuremberg: The Untold Story of the Tokyo War Crimes Trials* (New York: William Morrow, 1987). For a more technical differentiation, see M. Cherif Bassiouni, *Crimes Against Humanity in International Law* (The Hague: Kluwer Law International, [2nd ed.] 1999) p. 530.

15 Edwin Tetlow, *The United Nations: The First 25 Years* (New York: Peter Owen, 1970).

16 LeBlanc, *The United States and the Genocide Convention*, pp. 26–27.

17 Quoted in Robert Davis and Mark Zannis, *The Genocide Machine in Canada: The Pacification of the North* (Montréal: Black Rose Books, 1973) p. 19.

18 3 U.N. ESCOR, Doc. E/447-623 (1948), esp. pp. 139–47.

19 See, e.g., the Brazilian intervention; ibid., p. 143.

20 On the Soviet policies at issue, see, e.g., Nikolai Dekker and Andrei Lebed, eds., *Genocide in the U.S.S.R: Studies in Group Destruction* (New York: Scarecrow Press, 1958); Robert Conquest, *The Nation Killers: The Soviet Deportation of Nationalities* (New York: Macmillan, 1970). The compromise was effected by Ernest Gross, U.S. delegate to ECOSOC's Sixth (Legal) Committee. See 3 U.N. GAOR C.6 (49th mtg.) at 407 (1948).

21 Davis and Zannis, *Genocide Machine*, pp. 19–20. The provision on cultural genocide, as well as Lemkin's original definition of the crime, would have taken in the virtual entirety of U.S. Indian policy from the 1880s onward. Officially entitled "Assimilation," the explicit goal of the policy was, as President Theodore Roosevelt put it in his 1901 State of the Union Address, to bring about the cultural eradication of every surviving indigenous society in the U.S. by creating "a mighty pulverizing engine to break up the tribal mass." While Roosevelt was specifically referring to the destruction of traditional modes of collective ownership though imposition of the Angloamerican system of individuated land titles under the 1887 General Allotment Act, he might as easily have emphasized the prohibition of traditional spiritual practices in full force by the 1890s, or the forced transfer of native children from their families and home communities to remote boarding schools for years on end.

The objective of the latter facilities was, according to the school system's overseer, army captain (later brigadier general) Richard Henry Pratt, to "kill the Indian" in every pupil. In 1934, under the Indian Reorganization Act, whatever remained of traditional modes of governance was supplanted by "tribal councils" operating under constitutions written by federal officials, androgen, during the decade following passage of House Concurrent Resolution 108 (1953), the U.S. "terminated" its recognition that 109 native peoples continued to exist. Meanwhile, pursuant to Public Law 959—the Indian Relocation Act of 1956—roughly half of all federally recognized American Indians had been dispersed from reservations to cities. See generally Wilcomb E. Washburn, *The Assault on Indian Tribalism: The General Allotment Law (Dawes Act) of 1887* (Malabar, FL: Robert E. Krieger, 1986); John Rhodes, "An American Tradition: The Religious Persecution of Native Americans," *Montana Law Review*, Vol. 52, No. 1 (January 1991) pp. 13–72; David Wallace Adams, *Education for Extinction: American Indians and the Boarding School Experience, 1875–1928* (Lawrence: University Press of Kansas, 1995); Graham D. Taylor, *The New Deal and American Indian Tribalism: The Administration of the Indian Reorganization Act, 1934–1945* (Lincoln: University of Nebraska Press, 1980); Donald L. Fixico, *Termination and Relocation: Federal Indian Policy, 1945–1960* (Albuquerque: University of New Mexico Press, 1986).

22 Davis and Zannis, *Genocide Machine*, p. 19.

23   On the Streicher prosecution, see Smith, *Reaching Judgment at Nuremberg*, pp. 200–203.

24   A good analysis, both of the composition of the U.S. diplomatic cadre at the UN and the duplicity imbedded in their agenda, is offered in Lloyd Garner's *Architects of Illusion: Men and Ideas in American Foreign Policy, 1941–49* (Chicago: Quadrangle, 1970). Also see Thomas M. Campbell, *Masquerade Peace: America's U.N. Policy, 1944–1945* (Tallahassee: Florida State University Press, 1973).

25   See, e.g., David Caute, *The Great Fear: The Anti-Communist Purge under Truman and Eisenhower* (New York: Simon and Schuster, 1978) pp. 303–24.

26   Caute, *The Great Fear*, pp. 325–38. Right-wing obstruction in this regard had been going on since at least as far back as the immediate aftermath of World War I, when reactionary "sovereigntists" like Henry Cabot Lodge managed to block U.S. entry into the League of Nations. See generally John Milton Cooper Jr., *Breaking the Heart of the World: Woodrow Wilson and the Fight for the League of Nations* (Cambridge, UK: Cambridge University Press, 2001).

27   For texts, see Burns H. Weston, Richard A. Falk, and Anthony D'Amato, *Basic Documents in International Law and World Order* (St. Paul, MN: West, [2nd ed.] 1990) pp. 371–75, 376–85, 364–68, 293–96; Ian Brownlie, ed., *Basic Documents on Human Rights* (Oxford: Clarendon Press, [3rd ed.] 1992) pp. 114–24, 125–43, 148–61, 488–94.

28   For texts, see Weston, Falk, and D'Amato, *Basic Documents in International Law*, pp. 10–91, 194, 218, 224, 230–52, 291–92; Adam Roberts and Richard Guelff, eds., *Documents on the Laws of War* (Oxford: Clarendon Press, 1984) pp. 387–464. For analysis of the U.S. nonratification of these and other important elements of international law, see Nicole Deller, Arjun Makhijani, and John Burrows, eds., *Rule of Power or Rule of Law? An Assessment of U.S. Policies and Actions Regarding Security-Related Treaties* (New York: Apex Press, 2003) esp. pp. xv–xxxviii, 1–18.

29   See, e.g., the remarks of Iowa Republican Bourke B. Hickenlooper during the 1950 Senate hearings: "[We] are in effect, in this Genocide Convention [and other elements of international law] dealing with the question of a certain area of the sovereignty of the United States which amounts to a surrender of that sovereignty." U.S. Senate, *Hearings on the Genocide Convention Before a Subcommittee of the Senate Committee on Foreign Relations* (Washington, DC: 81st Cong., 2nd Sess., 1950) p. 36. The Supreme Court sought a way out of this bind in *Reid v. Covert* (354 U.S. 1 (1957)) by holding that "any treaty provision that is inconsistent with the United States Constitution would simply be invalid under national law." Article 27 of the Vienna Convention on the Law of Treaties (U.N. Doc. A/CONF.39/27 at 289 (1969)) overrules this opinion, however, by stipulating that no party may "invoke the provisions of its internal law as justification for its failure to perform a treaty" obligation. See generally Ian Sinclair, *The Vienna Convention on the Law of Treaties* (Manchester: Manchester University Press, [2nd ed.] 1984).

30   The reference was in part to black letter instruments such as the 1928 Kellogg-Briand Pact (45 Stat. 2343, T.S. No. 796, 2 Bevans 732, L.N.T.S. 57)—to which Germany was in fact a signatory—outlawing aggressive wars for purposes of seizing territory. Much of what fell under the rubric of crimes against humanity had never been codified in black letter form, however. The defense therefore argued that no body of law existed prohibiting certain offenses at the time the defendants allegedly committed them, and that—under injunctions against application of *ex post facto* law—they could not thus be legitimately prosecuted. See Herbert Wechsler, "The Issues of the Nuremberg Trial," *Political Science Quarterly*, Vol. 62, No. 1 (March 1947) pp. 11–26. Some U.S. politicians, of course, agreed with the nazis. See, e.g., Sen. Robert A. Taft,

"Equal Justice Under the Law: The Heritage of English-Speaking Peoples and Their Responsibility," *Vital Speeches of the Day,* Vol. 13, No. 2 (November 1, 1946) pp. 44–48.

31 This position was actually perfectly in keeping with the formulations of German political philosophy, widely admired before the war. See, as examples of the sort of work engendering this response, Carl Schmitt, *Political Theology: Four Chapters on the Concept of Sovereignty* (Cambridge, MA: MIT Press, 1985 trans. of 1922 original) and *The Concept of the Political* (Chicago: University of Chicago Press, 1996 trans. of 1932 original). For recent assessments of Schmitt's thinking and its sociopolitical context, see Gopal Balakrishnan, *The Enemy: An Intellectual Portrait of Carl Schmitt* (London: Verso, 2000) and the contributions to Chantal Mouffe, ed., *The Challenge of Carl Schmitt* (London: Verso, 1999).

32 Quincy Wright, "The Law of the Nuremberg Trial," *American Journal of International Law,* Vol. 41, No. 1 (January 1947) pp. 38–72. For interpretation and application, see Richard Falk, *Human Rights and State Sovereignty* (New York: Holmes & Meier, 1981).

33 Affirmation of the Principles of International Law Recognized by the Charter of the Nuremberg Tribunal, adopted by the UN General Assembly, December 11, 1946 (U.N.GA. Res. 95(1), U.N. Doc. A/236 (1946) at 1144); for text, see Weston, Falk, and D'Amato, *Basic Documents in International Law,* p. 140. The Charter itself (59 Stat. 1544, 82 U.N.T.S. 279 (September 10, 1945)) appears at pp. 138–39.

34 LeBlanc, *The United States and the Genocide Convention,* p. 20.

35 Not least of these was entrenched racism/antisemitism and nativism. This was abundantly evident in the treatment accorded Raphaël Lemkin, who, despite the misgivings he must have felt concerning the U.S./Soviet dilution of the Secretariat's Draft, did his best to lobby the 1948 Convention through the Senate. In response, the subcommittee declined to call him as a witness in its hearings on the matter. According to New Jersey's Republican Senator H. Alexander Smith, this was because he and his colleagues were "irritated no end" by the idea that "a Jew . . . who comes from a foreign country [and] speaks broken English" should be the Convention's "biggest propagandist." Liberals like Brien McMahon (D-Conn.) and Theodore Francis Green (D-R.I.) appear to have substantially agreed, describing Lemkin's conspicuous Jewishness as "the biggest minus quality" of the entire ratification effort. Quoted in LeBlanc, *The United States and the Genocide Convention,* 20.

36 For a sampling of violence directed against one Asian American target group, see Charles J. McClain, *In Search of Equality: The Chinese Struggle Against Discrimination in the Nineteenth Century* (Berkeley: University of California Press, 1994) pp. 173–90.

37 *Hearings on the Genocide Convention (1950)* p. 205.

38 Stewart E. Tolnay and E.M. Beck, *A Festival of Violence: An Analysis of Southern Lynchings, 1882–1930* (Urbana: University of Illinois Press, 1995) p. 1. **2015 update:** Actually, the Tolnay-Beck figures were far too low. A recent study conducted by the Alabama-based Equal Justice Initiative documented 3,959 lynchings of African Americans in twelve southern states—Alabama, Arkansas, Florida, Georgia, Kentucky, Louisiana, Mississippi, North Carolina, South Carolina, Tennessee, Texas, and Virginia—between 1877 and 1950. This is roughly 700 more than the Tolnay's and Beck's total for the entire country over the same period. Another recent study, conducted by researchers William D. Carrigan and Clive Webb, documented the lynchings of 547 Mexicans and Mexican Americans, and the probable lynchings of at least 310 others, in five southwestern states—Arizona, California, Colorado, New Mexico, and Texas—over an eight decade period beginning in 1848. No comparable studies have as yet been completed with regard to American Indians or Asians/Asian

Americans. See Equal Justice Initiative, *Lynching in America: Confronting the Legacy of Racial Terror* (Montgomery, AL: EJI, 2015); William D. Carrigan and Clive Webb, *Forgotten Dead: Mob Violence against Mexicans in the United States, 1848–1928* (New York: Oxford University Press, 2013) pp. 5–6 and the two appendices.

39 For what may be the best survey of comparable prewar violence in Germany, see Raul Hilberg, *The Destruction of the European Jews*, 3 vols. (New York: Holmes & Meier, [2nd ed., rev. and expanded] 1985).

40 Tolnay and Beck, *Festival of Violence*. A detailed examination of lynching in a given region will be found in W. Fitzhugh Brundage, *Lynching in the New South, 1880–1930* (Urbana: University of Illinois Press, 1993).

41 Arthur F. Raper, *The Tragedy of Lynching* (Chapel Hill: University of North Carolina Press, 1933) pp. 469–72.

42 For case studies, see James Forman, *Sammy Younge, Jr.* (New York: Grove Press, 1968); Howard Smead, *Blood Justice: The Lynching of Charles Mack Parker* (New York: Oxford University Press, 1986); Stephen J. Whitfield, *A Death in the Delta: The Story of Emmett Till* (New York: Free Press, 1988).

43 See, e.g., Leon Friedman, ed., *Southern Justice* (New York: Pantheon, 1965); Robert Sherrill, *Gothic Politics in the Deep South: Stars of the New Confederacy* (New York: Grossman, 1968).

44 *Hearings on the Genocide Convention* (1950) p. 27.

45 U.S. Senate, *Hearings on the Genocide Convention Before a Subcommittee of the Senate Committee on Foreign Relations* (Washington, DC: 92nd Cong., 1st Sess., 1971) p. 189.

46 William L. Patterson, *The Man Who Cried Genocide: An Autobiography* (New York: International, 1971).

47 It seems U.S. delegates successfully argued that whatever was being done to poor blacks was being done to them as an economic aggregate rather than as a racial group. Hence, the victims were not subject to protection under the Genocide Convention—thanks to the *quid pro quo* these same delegates had effected with the Soviets during the ad hoc committee process in 1947—and any review of petitions in their behalf claiming otherwise would be "inappropriate." Meanwhile, right-wing senators and expert witnesses like the ABA's Alfred Schweppe were busily rejecting the Convention, partly because political and economic aggregates hadn't been retained among the protected groups, thereby "letting the Communists off the hook" for the genocidal aspects of stalinist and maoist collectivization policies. See U.S. Senate, *Hearings on the Genocide Convention Before a Subcommittee of the Senate Committee on Foreign Relations* (Washington, DC: 81st Cong., 2nd Sess., 1950); U.S. Senate, *Hearings on the Genocide Convention Before a Subcommittee of the Senate Committee on Foreign Relations* (Washington, DC: 92nd Cong., 1st Sess., 1971).

48 As concerns American Indian women, it was determined in 1976 that up to 42 percent were involuntarily sterilized in clinics run by the Indian Health Service, a component of the Interior Department's Bureau of Indian Affairs, between 1970 and 1975. In perhaps a quarter of these cases, the women had not only not consented, they had never been informed that a sterilization had been performed; Brint Dillingham, "Indian Women and IHS Sterilization Practices," *American Indian Journal*, Vol. 3, No. 1 (January 1977) pp. 27–28; Janet Larsen, "And Then There Were None: Is Federal Policy Endangering the American Indian 'Species'?," *Christian Century*, No. 94 (January 26, 1977) pp. 61–62; Women of All Red Nations, *American Indian Women* (New York: International Indian Treaty Council, 1978); Robin Jarrell, "Women and Children First: The Forced Sterilization of American Indian Women" (undergraduate

thesis, Wellesley College, 1978). With respect to Puertorriqueñas, the data were one-third of the women of childbearing age on the island of Puerto Rico, 44 percent of the same target population in New Haven, and 51 percent in Hartford, Connecticut. See Committee for Abortion Rights and Against Sterilization Abuse, *Women Under Attack: Abortion, Sterilization Abuse, and Reproductive Freedom* (New York: CARASA, 1979); Margarita Ostolaza, *Política Sexual y Socialización Política de la Mujer Puertorriqueña en la Consolidación del Bloque Histórico Colonial de Puerto Rico* (Río Piedras, PR: Ediciones Huracan, 1989).

49   U.S. Senate, *Hearings on the Genocide Convention Before a Subcommittee of the Committee on Foreign Relations* (Washington, DC: 91st Cong., 2nd Sess., 1970) pp. 148–49.

50   See generally C. Vann Woodward, *The Strange Career of Jim Crow* (New York: Oxford University Press, [3rd ed.] 1974).

51   *Hearings on the Genocide Convention (1971)* pp. 18–19. Deutsch was undoubtedly correct in his understanding, a matter which could have made the Convention a powerful weapon in any serious effort to abolish institutionalized racial/ethnical discrimination in the U.S. (a goal to which the ABA proclaimed itself "philosophically" committed). As with the earlier-discussed question of lynching however, it was this very potential effectiveness of the Convention in combating systemic discrimination which seems to have prompted the ABA to oppose its ratification.

52   Indeed, the only reference to the issue devolved upon an absurd query by segregationists as to whether the busing of schoolchildren to achieve integration in educational institutions might not qualify as "genocide." *Hearings on the Genocide Convention (1970)* pp. 138–39n11.

53   Although most of it is carefully framed in terms other than genocide, there is a vast literature on these historical processes of extermination. Two excellent works which call things by their right names are David Svaldi's *Sand Creek and the Rhetoric of Extermination: A Case Study in Indian-White Relations* (Washington, DC: University Press of America, 1989) and David E. Stannard's *American Holocaust: Columbus and the Conquest of the New World* (New York: Oxford University Press, 1992).

54   There is, for example, not a single reference to "American Indians" or "Native Americans"" in the index of LeBlanc's reasonably thorough study.

55   This followed Reagan's sudden endorsement of the Convention in a speech to the B'nai B'rith during his 1984 reelection campaign. The possibility of ratification was foreclosed that year through a filibuster by Jesse Helms. See LeBlanc, *The United States and the Genocide Convention*, pp. 142, 146.

56   As the editors of the *Wall Street Journal* put it on January 19, 1989, Reagan "restored the efficiency, and morale of the armed forces [and] demonstrated the will to use force in Grenada and Libya." For a thoroughly glorified account of the first of these travesties, see Major Mark Adkin, *Urgent Fury: The Battle for Grenada* (Lexington, MA: DC Heath, 1989). On the bloodbath in Lebanon, see Noam Chomsky, *The Fateful Triangle: The US., Israel and the Palestinians* (Boston: South End Press, 1983). On U.S. support to Iraq, see Rabab Hadi, "The Gulf Crisis: How We Got There," in Greg Bates, ed., *Mobilizing Democracy: Changing the US. Role in the Middle East* (Monroe: ME: Common Courage Press, 1991). On Nicaragua and El Salvador, see Holly Sklar, *Washington's War on Nicaragua* (Boston: South End Press, 1988). On Libya, see Jonathan Bearman, *Qadhafi's Libya* (London: Zed Books, 1986); Noam Chomsky, *Pirates and Emperors: International Terrorism in the Real World* (New York: Claremont, 1986) pp. 138–46. More broadly, see Chomsky, *Deterring Democracy*; Michael T. Klare, *Beyond the "Vietnam Syndrome": U.S. Interventionism in the 1980s* (Washington, DC: Institute for Policy Studies, 1981);

Michael T. Klare and Peter Kornbluh, eds., *Low Intensity Warfare: Counterinsurgency, Proinsurgency and Antiterrorism in the Eighties* (New York: Pantheon, 1989).

57   The action—renouncing America's voluntary 1946 acceptance of jurisdiction by the International Court of Justice (ICJ or "World Court")—was taken in response to the ICJ's October 1985 decision in the *Nicaragua v. United States* case, finding the covert U.S. war against the former country to be in violation of international law. See "U.S. Terminates Acceptance of ICJ Compulsory Jurisdiction," *Department of State Bulletin*, No. 86 (January 1986).

58   As Reagan described the situation, for the United States, the Convention had been reduced to a "mere symbol of opposition to genocide." U.S. Senate, *Executive Report No. 2* (Washington, DC: 99th Cong., 1st Sess., 1985) p. 4.

59   The three were apparently selected for this task, not simply on the basis of their individual credibility with various sectors of the Right, but because each had been prominent in opposing ratification on one or another grounds. Lugar and Hatch also chaired key bodies, the Foreign Affairs Committee and the Subcommittee on the Constitution of the Committee on the Judiciary, respectively. See Ben Whitaker, *Revised and Updated Report on the Punishment and Prevention of the Crime of Genocide* (U.N. Doc. E/CN.4/Sub.2/1985/6) pp. 42–44.

60   As further indication that the United States waited until the global balance of power shifted emphatically in its favor—thus effectively precluding the possibility that the Genocide Convention might be enforced against it—before ratifying the instrument, it should be noted that all the ingredients that eventually went into the Lugar-Helms-Hatch package was placed on the table at least as early as 1971. See *Hearings on the Genocide Convention* (1971).

61   U.S. Senate, *Senate Executive Report No. 2* (Washington, DC: 99th Cong., 1st Sess., 1985) pp. 26–27. It should be noted that at p. 23, mental harm accruing from the imposition of systematic discrimination against racial groups is specifically exempted from the American definition of genocide: "Psychological harm resulting from living conditions, differential treatment by government authorities and the like is excluded." No other country has ever tried to assert such a qualification. Similarly, no signatory has ever belabored the notion of specific intent in the manner evident in the Lugar-Helms-Hatch package. Nor has any country sought to require the destruction of a "substantial" part of a target group—whatever that means: ten percent? one-quarter? half? three-quarters? almost all?—as a qualification of genocide (apparently for the implicit purpose of removing the onus from the arbitrary destruction of some smaller portion of the group targeted). See LeBlanc, *The United States and the Genocide Convention*, pp. 52–53.

62   The Act was passed by voice vote—thus preventing a record of how many and which representatives voted for and against it—in the House on April 25, 1988; U.S. Senate, *Senate Report No. 333* (Washington, DC: 100th Cong., 2nd Sess., 1988) pp. 1–3. The same method was adopted in the Senate on October 13; *Congressional Record*, No. 134 (October 14, 1988) pp. S16107–17, S16266–9.

63   *Multilateral Treaties Deposited with the Secretary-General*, p. 101n2.

64   U.S. Senate, *Hearings on the Genocide Convention Before a Subcommittee of the Committee on Foreign Relations* (Washington, DC: 99th Cong., 1st Sess. (1985) pp. 24–25.

65   Aside from Dodd and Mathias, the signatories to the statement from which the quoted passage is excerpted were Claiborne Pell (D-RI), Joseph Biden Jr. (D-DL), Paul Sarbanes (D-MD), Alan Cranston (D-CA), Thomas Eagleton (D-MO) and John Kerry (D-MA); *Senate Executive Report No. 2*, p. 32.

THE UNITED STATES AND THE GENOCIDE CONVENTION

66 LeBlanc, *The United States and the Genocide Convention*, pp. 98, 240.

67 *Multilateral Treaties Deposited with the Secretary-General*, pp. 102–4.

68 This result was entirely predictable, given that the same three countries had already entered objections to attempts to avoid ICJ jurisdiction by Bulgaria, Poland, and Romania. See U.S. Senate, *Hearing on the Genocide Convention Before the Senate Committee on Foreign Relations* (Washington, DC: 98th Cong., 2nd. Sess., 1984) p. 63.

69 LeBlanc, *The United States and the Genocide Convention*, p. 12.

70 International Court of Justice, *Reports of Judgments, Advisory Opinions and Orders: Reservations to the Convention on the Prevention and Punishment of the Crime of Genocide* (The Hague: International Court of Justice) pp. 15–69. Also see Sinclair, *Vienna Convention*, pp. 47–69; Jean Kyongun Koh, "Reservations to Multilateral Treaties: How International Legal Doctrine Reflects World Vision," *Harvard International Law Journal*, Vol. 23, No. 1 (Summer 1982) pp. 71–116.

71 America provided crucial political, economic, and military assistance—including the training of the bulk of the officers corps—to the Indonesian army, which perpetrated the vast slaughter in the interests of the kind of "regional stability" demanded by U.S. policy. See generally Deirdre Griswold, *The Bloodbath That Was* (New York: World View, 1975).

72 The respective death tolls were about three million in Bangladesh, some 100,000 in Burundi. See Kalyan Chaudhuri, *Genocide in Bangladesh* (Bombay: Orient Longman, 1972); Rene Lemarchand and David Martin, *Selective Genocide in Burundi* (London: Minority Rights Group Report No. 20, 1974).

73 The "United Nations [refused] even to discuss the case" of Bangladesh, for example. Similarly, "the United States never publicly rebuked the Burundi government." Frank Chalk and Kurt Jonassohn, *History and Sociology of Genocide: Analyses and Case Studies* (New Haven, CT: Yale University Press, 1990) pp. 397, 391.

74 For examination of the groundwork upon which creation of the first of these tribunals was based, see Francis A. Boyle, *The Bosnian People Charge Genocide: Proceedings at the International Court of Justice Concerning Bosnia v. Serbia on the Prevention and Punishment of the Crime of Genocide* (Northampton, MA: Aletheia Press, 1996).

75 This is by no means to argue that the tribunals are in themselves inappropriate, or that those suspected of genocide in Africa and the Balkans should not be brought to trial. The principle of equal justice before the law should, however, apply as much to this level of jurisprudence as to any other. Thus, more than a few U.S. friends—Pol Pot, for example, there being no statute of limitations on the crime of genocide—should by rights be seated alongside the Serbian and Rwandan defendants. For that matter, there is still time to try a number of prominent American officials—from Robert McNamara to Ronald Wilson Reagan, George Herbert Walker Bush, and William Jefferson Clinton—for their multitudinous war crimes and implementation of genocidal policies at home and abroad.

76 No clearer indication of the marginality of the players involved is possible than that offered by U.S. State Department adviser (and former Democratic senator from Colorado) Tim Wirth when—after State Department official Peter Tarnoff admitted on April 28, 1993, that what was happening in Bosnia-Herzegovina amounted to genocide, and that the U.S. was therefore legally/morally obligated to intervene by all means necessary to stop it—he observed that such a move would be unpopular because America had "no vital interest" in the Balkans. Intervention stood to erode support for the Clinton administration among American citizens, Wirth argued, and "the survival of the fragile liberal [sic] coalition represented by this Presidency"

was more important than putting a stop to mere genocide. See Francis Anthony Boyle, *The Bosnian People Charge Genocide*, p. xix. The administration's performance vis-à-vis the slaughter in Rwanda was even more lackluster. It was only after the killing had run its course in both instances, and the perpetrators selected for prosecution were safely out of power, that the administration discovered the "resolve" to "do something." For further details, see David Rieff, *Slaughterhouse: Bosnia and the Failure of the West* (New York: Touchstone Books, 1995).

77   American demands that the codification of elements of international law be undertaken in conformity with the provisions of the U.S. Constitution (as interpreted by the U.S. Supreme Court)—thereby converting international law into little more than a global adjunct to the federal statutory code—have become endemic. The latest example is the assertion of the U.S. Department of State that it would block a draft Declaration on the Rights of Indigenous Peoples unless the instrument was written to such specifications. This maneuver, which would have enshrined the denial of the right to self-determination to native peoples as a matter of international as well as U.S. domestic law, precipitated a mass walkout by indigenous delegates from a meeting of the United Nations Working Group on Indigenous Populations on October 22, 1996.

78   Witness the example of Guatemala, which has slaughtered hundreds of thousands of indigenous Mayans since a CIA-sponsored coup in 1954, all the while being described as a "democratizing country" by the U.S. State Department. See Robert M. Carmack, ed., *Harvest of Violence: The Mayan Indians and the Guatemala Crisis* (Norman: University of Oklahoma Press, 1988). Another good illustration is Colombia. See Javier Giraldo, *Colombia: The Genocidal Democracy* (Monroe, ME: Common Courage Press, 1996). For a broader overview, see Noam Chomsky, *Deterring Democracy* (New York: Hill & Wang, 1992); Noam Chomsky and Edward S. Herman, *The Political Economy of Human Rights, Vol. 1: The Washington Connection and Third World Fascism* (Boston: South End Press, 1979).

FOUR

Charades, Anyone?

The Indian Claims Commission in Context

> For the nation, there is an unrequited account of sin and injustice
> that sooner or later will call for national retribution.
>
> —George Catlin, 1844

One of the more pernicious myths shrouding the realities of Indian/
white relations in the United States is that the U.S. has historically comported itself according to uniquely lofty legal and moral principles when
interacting with "its" indigenous peoples. The idea has been around
in the form of official rhetoric since at least as early as 1787, when the
Congress, already pursuing a practical policy going in exactly the opposite direction, used its enactment of the Northwest Ordinance as an
opportunity to pledge itself to conducting its Indian affairs in "utmost
good faith."[1] As President Harry S. Truman would put it 159 years later, it
should be "perfectly clear . . . that in our transactions with Indian tribes
we have . . . set for ourselves the standard of fair and honorable dealings,
pledging respect for all Indian property rights."[2]

In 1985, the late Wilcomb E. Washburn, then preeminent "American
Indianist" historian for the federal government's Smithsonian Institution,
waxed a bit more expansive when he observed that "[b]ecause U.S.
Indian policy is . . . supportive of Indian values and aspirations, questions that in other countries would not arise are the subject of intense
debate in the United States. . . . [Hence,] in broad, general perspective, one is impressed with the extraordinary recognition accorded to

Originally published in *American Indian Culture and Research Journal*, Vol. 24, No. 1 (Spring
2000). Subsequently included in my *Perversions of Justice: Indigenous Peoples and Angloamerican
Law* (San Francisco: City Lights, 2003).

the now-powerless Indian tribes of this country not only to maintain a secure trust-guaranteed and tax-free land base, but to exercise aspects of sovereignty that normally derive from the control of territory held by a powerful sovereign."[3]

Lest it be argued that views like Truman's and Washburn's represent little at this point beyond quaintly jingoistic anachronisms, note should be taken that the United States is presently engaged at the United Nations in pushing its own version of Indian law as the model upon which the UN's incipient Universal Declaration on the Rights of Indigenous Peoples should be based, its own Indian policy as that most worthy of emulation by the rest of the world. Conversely, the U.S. has threatened to block any codification of native rights in international law which fails to conform to its own purportedly exalted standards of enlightened humanitarianism.[4]

The expression of such sentiments is by no means a uniquely conservative vice. They are continually voiced by more moderate commentators. "Few great powers," observed liberal policy analyst Harvey D. Rosenthal in 1990, "have acknowledged such fundamental moral or legal debts, especially from a small, powerless minority in their midst," as has the United States with respect to American Indians.[5] Nor, by and large, will one encounter much of an alternative among what are ostensibly the more radical sectors of the euroamerican populace, a matter abundantly evidenced in the recent tirades of Bob Black and other prominent "antiauthoritarians" in the pages of *Anarchy* magazine.[6]

From start to finish, then, and irrespective of ideological cant, the U.S. settler society's interpretation of itself is all but invariably adorned in "that protective cloak of righteousness which is the inevitable garment of the Anglo-Philistine."[7] As Rosenthal himself admits, the resulting hegemony—that the U.S. has always been "well-intentioned" in its relations with Indians and that, while less than perfect, the process of interaction has ultimately "worked out for the best" for all concerned—is one "that [has] long comforted whites and afflicted Indians" in the most grotesque manner imaginable.[8]

This last is not difficult to discern, at least for anyone willing to look at the matter honestly. Despite Washburn's glowing description of Native North America's "trust-guaranteed and tax-free land base," the fact is that reservation-based American Indians are the poorest people on the continent, receiving by far the lowest annual and lifetime incomes of any census group. Unemployment on most reservations hovers around 60 percent, while on some it has been in the ninetieth percentile for decades.[9] The most impoverished area of the U.S. for the past forty years has been Shannon County, on the Pine Ridge Sioux Reservation, in South Dakota.[10] Overall, the indices of poverty in Indian Country are now, as they have been throughout the twentieth century, of a sort more commonly associated with Third World locales than with those inside the earth's mightiest economic superpower.

> The Indian health level is the lowest and the disease rate the highest of all major population groups in the United States. The incidence of tuberculosis is over 400 percent higher than the national average. Similar statistics show that the incidence of strep infections is 1,000 percent, meningitis is 2,000 percent higher, and dysentery is 10,000 percent higher. Death rates from disease are shocking when Indian and non-Indian populations are compared. Influenza and pneumonia are 300 percent greater killers among Indians. Diseases such as hepatitis are at epidemic proportions, with an 800 percent higher chance of death. Diabetes is almost a plague.[11]

Malnutrition claims American Indians at twelve times the U.S. national rate, while infant mortality runs as high as 1400 *percent* of the norm,[12] and "between fifty thousand and fifty-seven thousand Indian homes are [officially] considered uninhabitable. Many of these are beyond repair. For example, over 88 percent of the homes of the Sioux in Pine Ridge have been classified as substandard dwellings."[13] Consequently, Indians die from exposure at five times the national rate.[14] Under such conditions, despair is endemic, a circumstance engendering massive rates of alcoholism and other forms of substance abuse, as well as attendant social/familial violence, each of which takes its toll. The suicide rate among native teenagers is several times higher than that of non-Indian youth.[15]

All told, in a country where male life expectancy averages 71.8 years, a reservation-based American Indian man can expect to live less than forty-five. Although his female counterpart lives about thirty-six months longer than he, her general population sister has an average life expectancy of 78.8 years.[16] Thus, each time an American Indian dies—or is born—on a reservation in the United States, a third of a lifetime is lost. To put it another way, one-third of each succeeding generation of American Indians has been annihilated in a quiet holocaust which has continued unabated since the "Indian Wars" supposedly ended in 1890.

The reason underlying this altogether dismal situation is also strikingly apparent. It will be found in the very trust status—the locus of

Washburn's effusive profession of pride—in which indigenous property is held by the United States. Asserted most clearly in the Supreme Court's 1903 *Lone Wolf* opinion, the federal government's self-assigned and perpetual "fiduciary authority" over Indians has afforded it the "plenary power" to dispose of native assets in whatever manner it sees fit.[17] Hence, the abundance of minerals and other resources found on many reservations have been exploited with increasing intensity over the past half-century at prices deeply discounted to corporate "developers" by the secretary of interior (acting in his "trustee" capacity).[18] Both resources and profits have correspondingly flowed into the U.S. economy while Indians have been left destitute.

The term by which such relations between nations or peoples are customarily described is "colonialism," albeit in this case of a sort in which the colonized are encapsulated within the claimed domestic territoriality of the colonizer rather than of the more classical overseas variety.[19] Internal colonialism is colonialism nonetheless, and it has been prohibited under international law since the United Nations Charter was effected in 1945.[20] In no small part, this is because to be colonized, whether externally or internally, is to be denied that range of self-determining prerogatives which, as a matter of law, constitute the most fundamental rights of any nation.[21] Colonialism is thus the very obverse of the sovereignty Washburn and his colleagues contend is exercised by indigenous nations in the United States. Moreover, given the nature of its impact upon native people over the past hundred years, it is fair to say that the U.S. internal colonial model offers ample confirmation of Jean-Paul Sartre's famous equation of colonialism to genocide.[22]

Necessary Illusions

One would think that the astonishing gulf separating Washburnian descriptions of U.S. benevolence toward native peoples from the unremitting squalor to which those same peoples continue to be subjected at the hands of the United States might provoke what the sociologist C. Wright Mills once termed "cognitive dissonance" among the public at large.[23] This, in turn, might be expected to generate the sort of outrage that would compel a constructive alteration in the relationship between the U.S. and those indigenous nations upon whose traditional territories it has constituted itself.

As Vine Deloria Jr. long ago observed, however, it is a characteristic aspect of contemporary North American society that "no significant number of people will be stirred from their inertia to accomplish anything. They will not think. They will not question. And, most importantly, they will not object to whatever happens until it directly affects the manner in which they view their own personal survival."[24] More charitably, Imre Sutton has remarked that "other factors [also] inhibit our fullest perception of tribal grievances. Perhaps apathy or indifference prevails. Yet I am inclined to think that most Americans too readily believe that [American Indians have been] properly compensated" for whatever evils may have befallen us in the past, and that things really *are* "better" now.[25]

There are a number of reasons why this (mis)impression has come to be so deeply rooted in the mainstream American mind, beginning with the relentless drumbeat of official pronouncements such as Truman's and extending through the matrices of news packaging, media depiction and the spin so carefully put to truth by the myriad "responsible scholars" like Washburn and Rosenthal who infest the academic milieu.[26] The cornerstone upon which the whole proposition's credibility may be said to rest, however, assumes a much more concrete form, that of the federal government's Indian Claims Commission (ICC), an entity maintained from 1946 to 1978 for the express purpose of "resolving" outstanding grievances accumulated by native people against the United States during the course of the latter's expansion and consolidation over the preceding two centuries.[27]

The prevailing view is that the Commission represented not only "the greatest submission ever made by a sovereign state to moral and legal claims," as one federal jurist put it at the time,[28] but that its purpose was "to do justice for its own sake" where American Indians were/are concerned.[29] Over the past three generations, it has thus become a veritable truism among members of the dominant settler society that "no stronger motive than conscience has compelled this nation . . . to grant its indigenous minority the right to seek redress" through such a mechanism.[30] The most cursory examination of the record reveals the magnitude of untruth embedded in such postulations. Had the United States ever actually been motivated by its collective "conscience" to dispense justice to Indians, it might all along, or at any point, have simply elected to comply with the extant requirements of international law rather than ignoring them or seeking to pervert them to its own ends (a stance it still displays).[31]

Even within the framework of its own judicial structure, the U.S. might easily have provided the peoples whose land it was so systematically expropriating some measure of redress at least as early as 1855, when it created a special court to "hear and determine all claims founded upon any law of Congress, or upon any contract, express or implied, with the government of the United States."[32] Instead, in 1863, Indians were specifically denied access to the Court of Claims by an Act of Congress.[33]

> [Moreover, at] the same time the right to redress claims was being circumscribed *for* the Indian it was being expanded for the white man *against* the red man. The claims of whites for "depredations" committed against them by Indians under treaty were first recognized in an act of 1796. This act and ones following it in 1834 and 1859 provided for indemnification of losses from Indian depredations to be paid out of Indian annuities or "out of any money in the Treasury not otherwise appropriated." Thus, though the Indian could not sue the government, he could be "sued" by it (and denied counsel) in the name of its citizens and be subject to forced payment of claims from his treaty funds. By 1872 (the depredation legislation was renewed in 1870, 1872, 1885, 1886 and 1891) close to 300 claims were settled against the Indians for over $434,000. This amount was 55 percent of what was claimed.[34]

Indeed, although they were obviously considered human enough to convey land title by treaty and to compensate euroamericans for losses (real or invented), U.S. courts never formally conceded that Indians were actually "persons" capable of legal standing in their own right until the *Standing Bear* case of 1879.[35] This led, in 1881, to an act permitting native people to sue in the Court of Claims, but only in the event that they obtained specific legislative authorization whenever they sought to do so.[36] The expensive and time-consuming burden of acquiring a predicating Act of Congress each time they desired access to the claims court had the entirely predictable, and undoubtedly intended, effect of constraining Indians' ability to avail themselves of it. Hence, from 1881 to 1923, only thirty-nine claims were filed.[37]

A further complication was that in considering claims prior to authorizing them for adjudication, Congress was positioned to alter them substantially. This it did with consistent abandon, invariably rejecting attempts to recover unceded land on their face.[38] Legislators habitually deleted provisions for payment of interest, even on matters dating back a century or more.[39] And, with equal frequency, they introduced provisions requiring that judicial awards forthcoming to the native plaintiffs, if any, be subject to "gratuitous offsets" equal to whatever monies the government could be said to have already expended "in their behalf."[40]

The gratuitous offsets constituted an especially onerous imposition insofar as they placed Indians in the position of retroactively subsidizing "services" they'd never wanted and, in many cases, vociferously opposed. "Gratuities allowed," Rosenthal notes, "included the payment of [federal] Indian agents [and] police, judges, interpreters, maintenance and repair of agency buildings, teachers, and prorated expenses for education of Indian children at various institutions."[41] He concludes, with typical understatement, that most "of these 'gratuities' were more for the benefit of the government than the Indians."[42]

For its part, the U.S. Department of Justice devoted itself to delaying and otherwise obstructing Indian claims cases by all possible means. Years, often decades, passed while federal attorneys "prepared themselves," not to see to it that the government's self-assigned fiduciary responsibility to Indians was fulfilled, but to ensure that native claimants received nothing, or at least as little as possible, in court.[43] As was observed in 1940, it "cannot be shown that the [U.S. Attorneys] in a single case investigated the complaints . . . of the Indians with a view towards doing justice to them."[44]

On the contrary, the energy of Justice Department personnel was spent prodding the General Accounting Office (GAO) to dig up offsets with which to diminish or nullify awards expected to accrue from claims they knew to be valid (if offsets could be advanced in an amount equal to or exceeding the amount of the potential award in any case, the claims court could be expected to dismiss it out-of-hand).[45] The fruits of such tactics are altogether unsurprising.

> The Wichita of Oklahoma first gained the right to sue in an act of 1895 but were stalled until a jurisdictional act of 1924 led to a final dismissal in 1939. The Klamath in Oregon gained their act in 1920 [but] were dismissed in 1938. . . . The Northwestern Band of Shoshone of Utah and Idaho [having begun their efforts in 1879] received their act in 1926, and saw dismissal in 1942. The Osage of Oklahoma [after spending 48 years in the process] gained a jurisdictional act 1921, and were dismissed in 1928.[46]

And so it went. By the latter year, Senator Linn Frazier of North Dakota, a member of the Committee on Indian Affairs, was estimating that at the then current rate it would take another 172 years to wade through the eighty-six pending cases he believed would eventually go to trial.[47] In the sixteen instances where awards had actually been made at that point, the court had allowed a mere $13.6 million against claims totaling $346 million. Offsets amounting to $11 million were then deducted, leaving Indians with a paltry $2.65 million overall.[48]

All told, by 1946, the attorney general was able to report that Indians had been awarded only $49.4 million—well under 10 percent of the gross amount claimed in the cases involved—offset by $29.4 million in gratuity deductions.[49] This afforded those indigenous nations filing the suits an aggregate payout of only $20 million, from which they had to absorb legal costs, the expense of lobbying Congress to gain authorization, and so on. At best, the federal government's vaunted "due process" was for Indians essentially a break-even endeavor, while a number of people lost large chunks of their lives and appreciable sums attempting it.[50]

Truly, the U.S. proved itself an "unsympathetic foe" of indigenous nations, a "tough and clever opponent" when using its own courts to defend against the claims of its native "wards," no matter how legitimate.[51] It can be argued—and has been often enough—that this is exactly as it should be in an adversarial system of justice like that of the United States.[52] Perhaps, although the blatant systemic conflict of interest with which the process was riddled from top to bottom should really suggest something else.[53] In any event, the portrait thus presented is anything but that of a government/society committed by its conscience to doing the right thing, either morally or legally.

Footdragging in the First Degree

It's not that the government lacked alternatives to the courts in dealing with Indian land claims, even within its own politicojudicial structure and experience. During the nineteenth century, sixteen separate commissions were created by the United States under various treaties, conventions and agreements, to dispense settlements from foreign nations, and to resolve mutual claims.[54] The last of these, convened in 1901, had barely completed its work when, in 1910, former Indian Commissioner Francis E. Leupp recommended establishing something like a claims commission to expedite the processing of Indian claims cases.[55]

In 1913, Assistant Commissioner of Indian Affairs Edgar B. Merritt went further, testifying before the House of Representatives that an "investigatory commission . . . or comparable body" should be created to prepare reports and recommendations allowing Congress rather than the Court of Claims to "make some permanent disposition" of native claims. This approach, he argued, would not only be more "prompt and efficient" than the judicial process, but produce more "equitable" outcomes.[56] Such proposals were met with yawns by legislators, not least because Leupp and Merritt were both avid proponents of assimilation, a national policy then in full force and intended to bring about the disappearance of the last traces of indigenous culture within the U.S.[57] Since it was generally believed that the Indians that were left were rapidly "vanishing" anyway, and would likely "die off" long before their claims ever came to trial, there seemed no pressing need for improvement in the mechanisms for dealing with them.[58]

It was not until the 1920s, with the increasingly proliferate discovery of mineral deposits on Indian reservations, that attitudes began to change.[59] Loath to recreate the irrational squandering of resources that had occurred in Oklahoma when reservations were abolished and underlying oil deposits opened to the ravages of "free enterprise" at the turn of the century,[60] at least some policymakers began to cast about for ways of retaining these new finds under a central planning authority. The most logical route to this end resided in continuing the government's administration of the reservations "in trust" for an indefinite period, a matter requiring the abrupt abandonment of assimilation policy as it had been configured up till then.[61]

In 1928, the Meriam Commission, a body of one hundred prominent business and civic leaders assembled by Secretary of Interior Hubert Work to consider the "Indian Question," recommended exactly that.[62] The group, echoing Leupp's earlier suggestion, also urged that a "special commission" be created, separate from the courts, to investigate and draft legislation by which Congress could resolve whatever Indian claims were deemed "meritorious."[63] The idea was seconded a year later by Nathan R. Margold, a New York attorney specializing in Indian law and policy, who had been retained by the Institute for Government Research to assess the situation.[64]

Although Congress was relatively quick to "reorganize" the reservations for longterm existence, passing an act for this purpose in 1934, it consistently balked at addressing the claims issue.[65] To a significant extent, this was due to an outright hostility expressed by the Justice Department to any measure which might serve to accomplish such objectives. As Attorney General Francis Biddle eventually summed up the Department's position, it would cost "huge sums"—he estimated $3 billion or more—to achieve anything resembling an equitable and comprehensive disposition of native claims. Since it would be "inordinately expensive" for the United States to actually pay for what it had taken from Indians, he reasoned, it would be better to do nothing at all.[66]

Such thinking was restated, endlessly and with discernible vehemence, by legislators like Missouri's John J. Cochrane, who noted with pride in 1937 that he'd personally prevented "dozens" of native claims from being paid over the preceding three years. Congress, he said, could "disregard millions and think of billions if the Indian claims ever got in the hands of [a] commission" designed to treat such cases on their merits.[67] Thomas O'Malley of Wisconsin described the whole idea of native people being compensated for the taking of their property—or anything else, apparently—as "the biggest racket in the country."[68]

Others, plainly ignorant of, or choosing to ignore, the government's historical policy of denying Indians access to U.S. courts, now opined that native claims cases were too "ancient" to be considered. William M. Colmer of Mississippi argued that while "a great injury [had undoubtedly been] done to Indians in the past," it would be unfair to "some 130,000,000 American citizens who are taxpayers" to make any serious contemporary effort to set things right.[69] O'Malley chimed in that it was absolutely necessary for Congress to prevent "some shyster lawyer" from "dig[ging] up a descendant of some blanket Indian and make a million dollar claim against the government" over Manhattan Island.[70]

Perspectives of this sort, which were ubiquitous, received substantial reinforcement from the Supreme Court. As late as 1945, Justice Robert H. Jackson, writing for the majority in the *Northwestern Bands of Shoshone* case, held that the ongoing expropriation of native land was not compensable because any injuries done to Indians were "committed by our forefathers in the distant past against remote ancestors of the present claimants."[71] Moreover, Jackson asserted, such claims as a general rule should not be considered legally actionable, since Indians, unlike whites, had traditionally possessed "no true conception" of property ownership.[72]

In arriving at the latter conclusion—which, if applied consistently rather than being trotted out only when convenient to nullify a native claim, would have served to void the legitimacy of all transfers of property from indigenous peoples to the U.S. (leaving the United States without so much as a pretense of valid title to most of its purported territoriality)—Jackson and his colleagues resorted to what has been called "The Menagerie Theory." At base, this is the notion that Indians "are less than human and that their relations to their lands is not the human relation of ownership but rather something similar to the relation that animals bear to the areas in which they may be temporarily confined."[73]

President Franklin D. Roosevelt also made it clear on several occasions that he was "unsympathetic" to creation of a commission or comparable mechanism by which Indian claims might be resolved in an equitable manner. Purporting to be more preoccupied with the future than with the past, he announced in 1936 that he would be unlikely to sign any bill which might lead to the government's "paying out monies on account of wrongs done to the dead."[74]

Given the negative consensus dominant in all three branches of the federal government, proposals to establish a claims commission went nowhere for more than a third of a century after Francis Leupp's initial recommendation. From 1930 to 1945, at least seventeen bills offering variations on the theme were rejected by Congress, most of them dying in committee before they ever reached the floor of either the House or Senate.[75] On the other hand, legislation *was* passed in 1935 to further entrench the practice of deducting gratuitous offsets from awards achieved through the Court of Claims.[76]

In the Matter of Self-Interest

Recitation of its background raises the obvious question of why, the Senate having already done so on July 17, the U.S. House of Representatives unanimously approved creation of the ICC on August 2, 1946.[77] The answers here are two, neither of them having the least to do with "good conscience" or a legislative desire "to see justice done" to indigenous peoples encapsulated within the United States. Quite the opposite, Congress as a whole was demonstrably motivated by the crassest sort of national self-interest.

One track along which things moved concerned a U.S. ambition to assert itself as a planetary moral authority by way of organizing an international tribunal to oversee the punishment of Germany's nazi government in the aftermath of World War II.[78] First publicly articulated in 1944 over the strong objections of America's wartime allies, this precedential concept actually dated from 1943.[79] Eventually, U.S. diplomats were able to negotiate the London Charter of August 8, 1945, setting in motion the Nuremberg Trials.[80]

A problem for the Americans all along, however, resided in their intent to prosecute the nazi leadership for the waging of aggressive war(s) for purposes of acquiring lebensraum (living space) at the expense of peoples they considered untermenschen (subhumans) in eastern Europe.[81] The sticking point was that, from at least as early as the publication of Mein Kampf in 1925, Adolf Hitler himself had been at pains to explain that he was basing the nazi lebensraumpolitik (policy of territorial expansion) directly on the U.S. design of militarily expropriating American Indians

during the nineteenth century.[82] As historian Norman Rich has summarized the thesis openly proclaimed therein:

> Neither Spain nor Britain should be the models for German expan-
> sion, but the Nordics of North America, who had ruthlessly pushed
> aside an inferior race to win for themselves soil and territory for
> the future. To undertake this essential task, sometimes difficult,
> always cruel—this was Hitler's version of the White Man's Burden.[83]

So well-known were the parallels between U.S. and nazi expansionist policies by war's end that graduate students were embarking upon
studies of them.[84] Plainly, if it were to assume the moral high ground at
Nuremberg and appear to be dispensing anything more than mere "victor's justice," it was vital for the United States to do something concrete
to distinguish the contours of its own process of expansion from that
pursued by the men in the defendants' dock.[85] In essence, it was understood that the whole historical pattern of U.S. territorial growth needed
to be placed, *post hoc*, on a footing that could be projected as consisting
of "acquisition by purchase" rather than by conquest, and the sooner
the better.

Not coincidentally, in late 1943—at just the moment the United
States first became interested in staging a postwar trial of the nazi hierarchy—Congress quietly convened a select committee both to revive
the long dormant and much reviled idea of a claims commission, and
to hammer out the details of how it would work.[86] Over the next year
and a half, other sectors of the government were brought to accept that
establishment the ICC would be necessary to putting a proper gloss on
the U.S. image internationally.

Hence, by 1945 even Attorney General Biddle, preparing as he was to
don the judicial robes in which he would sit in judgment at Nuremberg,
entered a grudging endorsement of claims commission proposals (albeit,
he couldn't resist leaving behind suggestions as to how the final bill
might be prevented from compensating Indians too "liberally").[87] The
same can be said for Justice Jackson, the ink not yet dry on his description of Indians as a "menagerie" in *Northwestern Bands*, who was in the
process of temporarily reversing roles with Biddle by taking leave of the
Supreme Court to serve as chief U.S. prosecutor in the cases brought,
among others, against Julius Streicher, a nazi publisher charged with
depicting Jews as less than human.[88]

The extent to which Congress's belated creation of the ICC was
intended not just as a measure fulfilling U.S. domestic requirements,

but as a PR gesture meant to resonate favorably at Nuremberg and elsewhere within the international community, was quite evident in the way South Dakota Representative Karl Mundt introduced the bill authorizing it to the House. The Commission, he said, would stand as "an example for all the world to follow in its treatment of minorities."[89] Such posturing was amplified when President Truman, upon signing it, acquainted the public with the Indian Claims Commission Act on August 13, 1946. "This bill," he intoned with a straight face, "makes perfectly clear what many men and women, here *and abroad*, have failed to recognize, that . . . [i]nstead of confiscating Indian lands, we have purchased from the tribes that once owned this continent more than 90 percent of our public domain [emphasis added]."[90] No mention was made, of course, of which party it was that had set—and was continuing to set—the "sales" price, or whether the native owners had wanted to sell their homelands.

A Final Solution, American-Style

If the stench of hypocrisy can be said to have emanated from the first of the U.S. motivations in bringing the ICC into being, the second was even more malodorous. This had to do with a desire on the part of such unabashed foes of indigenous rights as Karl Mundt to impose what he called a "permanent solution to the Indian problem."[91] A "final settlement" of outstanding claims, it was argued, would position the government to terminate all further expenditures in behalf of Indians,[92] and to withdraw from its trust relationship with/recognition of the existence of selected peoples,[93] effectively bringing about their speedy dissolution and disappearance as identifiable human groups.[94]

The key for many legislators was how to accomplish the objective in the cheapest manner possible. "Our only real interest," said Representative, later Senator, Henry M. "Scoop" Jackson of Washington, "is to try and economize in this matter."[95] Given that Jackson chaired the House committee responsible for drafting the bill ultimately enacted as law, it is not difficult to discern the reasoning underlying a number of its principal elements. For instance, although the Act mandated the ICC to investigate and "resolve" all claims alleging "wrongful takings" of native land, under no circumstances were Indians permitted to recover their property.[96]

Nor were native people to be compensated at a rate equivalent to the contemporary value of what they'd lost, or, as a rule, allowed to collect interest against whatever amount the Commission concluded they should have received when their land was taken.[97] Moreover, the old practice of deducting gratuitous offsets from any monies awarded was carried over from the Court of Claims to the ICC.[98] With things thus stacked against them, as Oklahoma Senator Elmer Thomas had earlier remarked, Indians "would be lucky [if] in the final adjudication they should get [even] a few dollars."[99]

Cynical as it was, Thomas' insight was more than borne out when, after a full decade of its operational existence, Chief Commissioner Edgar E. Witt reported to Congress in 1956 that the ICC had by then awarded a payout of less than $10 million against aggregate claims exceeding $800 million.[100] A decade later, from the grand total of $194 million awarded by the ICC against nearly $2 billion in claims, "compromise settlements" had resulted in net payouts of only $87 million (including the $10 million reported by Witt).[101] Such puny awards were expressly construed under the 1946 Act as precluding "any further claims or demand against the United States."[102]

Unquestionably, "Congress could take some fiscal satisfaction [in having] got the better of the Indian once more," even as the ICC averred to have "cleared title" to millions of acres of contested territory.[103] But this was not the worst of it. Since "the goals of Termination and the Claims Commission were seen as parallel for the first twenty years,"[104] a native people's acceptance of even a pittance—which the Justice Department continued to insist was awarded only "as a matter of grace, not as a matter of right"[105]—often served as a pretext upon which it could be declared it "extinct."[106]

Nowhere was this "alliance of the Commission and termination legislation" more blatant than in the appointment of former Utah Senator Arthur V. Watkins as Chief Commissioner in 1959.[107] A proverbial architect of U.S. termination policy in the 1940s and early '50s, Watkins was responsible to a degree probably greater than any other individual for the formal nullification of more than a hundred targeted peoples over the following decade.[108] These ranged from the populous and relatively solvent Menominees and Klamaths in Wisconsin and Oregon to the tiny "Mission Bands" of southern California. They did not, however, include a single nation whose reserved land base was endowed with mineral deposits federal planners wished to retain in trust.[109]

As head of the ICC, Watkins' stated objective was, as it had been in the Senate, to "get the government out of the Indian business." His method was to accelerate the pace of awards to/termination of "superfluous" peoples as much as possible.[110] This, in a stunning Orwellianism, he described as "emancipation" (he himself was often referred to during the Eisenhower years as "The Great Emancipator").[111] In his *Red Man's Land, White Man's Law*, even Wilcomb Washburn was forced to choke on this one, outlining the whole minuet orchestrated by Watkins and his colleagues in terms of "Congress cloaking its own interests in a rhetoric of generosity toward the Indian."[112]

More to the point, while until the end of the Second World War native peoples "were thought of as defeated nations and were so treated and so held captive," after the war the resulting relationship "between prisoner and jailer" more frequently became that between condemned and executioner as many of them were liquidated altogether.[113] The ICC was created and maintained largely to mask this ugly reality, sometimes making it appear as the opposite of itself. But it did nothing to change it.

Charades, Anyone?

When Congress established the ICC in 1946, it anticipated that the new body would be responsible for handling perhaps two hundred cases—a figure roughly corresponding to the backlog piled up in the Court of Claims—and that the task could be accomplished in five years.[114] By the end of 1951, the number of claims had reached 852, "more than ever contemplated by anyone in the process."[115] The lifespan of the Commission was therefore extended for another five years, a procedure which would be repeated several times before the ICC was finally phased out in 1978.

The protracted nature of the proceedings were not due simply to the unexpectedly large number of claims filed. Nor, it should be noted in fairness to the Commission itself, were they typically a result of its own many faults. Rather, applying its usual perverse twist to the dictum that justice delayed is justice denied (always a desirable outcome in Indian claims cases), the Justice Department asked for not less than five thousand extensions of time in which to file its pleadings between 1951 and 1955 alone.[116] By 1960, Chief Commissioner Watkins—who, after all, wanted to speed things up for his own reasons—was complaining that U.S. Attorneys had received as many as thirty-five continuances in a single case.[117] A decade later, things were no better; in 1971, Watkins' successor, Jerome Kuykendall, observed that the Justice Department had requested some 6,451 days' worth of extensions in active cases over the preceding eighteen months.[118]

Thus, despite having outlived its original charter sixfold, and notwithstanding its increasingly strenuous efforts to do so as time wore on, the Commission was never able to complete its calendar. When it finally expired on September 30, 1978, the commissioners reported that the ICC had over three decades disposed of 547 of the 615 dockets into which the original 852 claims had been consolidated. The remaining 68 dockets were passed along, still unresolved, to the Court of Claims. Of the combined claims in which the ICC was said to have reached a final determination, about 45 percent had been dismissed without award.[119]

> The end result was that the Indian [nations] via a commission that cost the government only $15 million to operate for thirty-two years . . . paid $100 million in legal fees to pry loose some $800 million properly owed them. For thirty years most of this sum remained in the U.S. Treasury, interest free, at a benefit to the government.[120]

At the same time, the Department of Justice and its collaborators in the GAO expended approximately $200 million—an amount equal to one-quarter of total awards—on efforts to block or minimize each and every settlement.[121] So obstinately did they pursue these ends that when in 1955 the Otoes actually won a significant concession in legal principle from the ICC, federal attorneys stalled the resulting award for some months while lobbying Congress to rewrite the law in their favor.[122]

Such data cast in bold relief the contradictions inherent to the kind of subterfuge in which, as a matter of policy, any government sets out to play both (or several) ends against the middle. They do not, however, begin to address the real magnitude of the stakes involved in the ICC process. Aside from the sheer volume of claims that emerged, a development which seems to have genuinely taken all official parties by surprise, there is the matter of the scope of questions raised with respect to U.S. territorial legitimacy.[123]

As early as 1956, the Justice Department warned Congress that the country's legal ownership of about half the area of the lower forty-eight states was subject to serious challenge.[124] By the mid-1960s, based in large part on research undertaken by the ICC in its struggles to document the basis for U.S. assertion of title to each area within its putative domain, informed observers were reckoning that the United States had never acquired a valid proprietary interest in some 750 million acres.[125] In other words, "one third of the nation's land," as the Interior Department put it in 1970, still legally belonged—and belongs—to native people.[126]

If the ICC accomplished anything of positive utility, it was, according to Vine Deloria Jr., to "update the legal parity" of Indian land rights by "clear[ing] out the underbrush" which had obscured an accurate view of who actually owns which parts of the United States.[127] Thereby, it can be said to have set the stage for the resolution of title questions, but not in any defensible legal, moral, or ethical sense to have "settled" them.[128] As things stand, such monetary awards as were made by the ICC—or the Court of Claims, for that matter—serve only as payment against "back rent" accrued through usage of native property to which the United States has *never* held title.[129]

This has led many observers to conclude, along with American Indian Movement leader Russell Means, that the U.S. portion of Native North America continues to be "illegally occupied in exactly the same way France and Poland were illegally occupied by Germany during the Second World War." In Means' view, *post hoc* U.S. awards of cash compensation for the expropriation of native territory "no more puts things right than if the nazis had issued a check to the Vichy government in exchange for France after the fall of Paris." Anyone suggesting otherwise "is either ignorant of the facts, delusional, or playing an elaborate game of charades to try and hide the truth."[130]

Far from being unrepresentatively "extreme," Means' position, or something closely akin to it, has been repeatedly manifested in the reactions of indigenous nations to contentions that ICC awards might serve to "uncloud" title to their lands.[131]

> The Suquamish, Puyallup, and Stillaguamish refused their judgments on the grounds that their claims were never adjudicated, only those pushed upon them by their attorneys and the Commission. At a tribal council, the [Western Shoshones] voted to reject their settlement, claiming preference for land rather than money. The Oneida Indians of New York filed strong land claims for nearly six million acres of that state.[132]

Under the premise that the "Black Hills Are Not For Sale," Means' own Lakota people have adamantly refused to accept any part of an award which now totals well over $130 million, insisting that recovery of their treaty-guaranteed land base rather than monetary compensation is and always was the basis of their claim.[133] Hopi traditionals have taken an even harder line, observing that their land was already theirs "long before Columbus' great-great-grandmother was born" and that they'd never dignify an upstart entity like the ICC by petitioning it for "a piece of land that is already ours."[134]

It follows that even if the U.S. were to suddenly evince a willingness to pay something like a fair price for the native property upon which it has constituted, expanded, and consolidated itself—something it has never shown the least interest in doing—it is unlikely that title questions would be much affected. To borrow from Richard A. Nielson, "land, not money, is the *only* remedy" to many Indian claims.[135] As the sentiment was expressed in the Declaration of Purpose of the 1961 American Indian Chicago Conference:

> [E]ach remaining acre is a promise that we still be here tomorrow. Were we paid a thousand times the market value of our lost holdings, still the payment would not suffice. Money never mothered the Indian people, as the land has mothered them, nor has any people become more attached to the land, religiously or traditionally.[136]

The only real question is whether the "preposterous" idea of restoring unceded native land to its rightful owners is in any way feasible and, if so, to what extent.[137] With deadening predictability, naysayers argue that to attempt such restitution would require a concomitant, massive and wholly unwarranted dispossession of non-Indian property owners. Such notions, often advanced in highly sensationalized terms, have gone far toward keeping public opinion four-square against accommodation of indigenous land rights in any tangible form.[138]

The facts of the matter are, however, that, in addition to the roughly fifty million acres it presently "holds in trust" for Indians (about 2 percent of the "Lower 48"), the federal government possesses some seven hundred and seventy million acres of parklands, national forests, wildlife preserves, military reservations, and so on. Collectively, the individual states hold yet another seventy-eight million acres of unpopulated or sparsely populated land.[139] Clearly, it would be possible to return *all* the acreage indigenous peoples are now "short" from governmental holdings, without revoking title to the individual holdings of a single non-Indian.

Some native leaders have suggested that as little as fifty million acres—that is, a doubling of the existing reservation land base—might be enough to stabilize indigenous nations, providing them the resources needed to, among other things, alleviate the dire conditions sketched in the opening section of this essay.[140] Far from responding favorably to such invitations to compromise, however, the government has elected not only to ignore them but to continue whittling away at what little remains of Indian Country (during the first ten years of the ICC, the native land base was actually reduced from 54.6 million to 52.5 million acres).[141]

Merely putting a stop to this trend will not be enough. If the United States is ever to resemble in any fashion the resplendent characterizations of it put forth by its promoters and apologists, the attitudes and policies underlying the ongoing erosion of indigenous property rights must be reversed, native people afforded the sort of territorial restitution to which they are entitled under international law.[142]

This, in turn, could serve as the pivot from which to get at an entire range of claims—everything from damages accruing through the government's sustained and systematic suppression of native languages and religions to those resulting from the supplanting of traditional governments and economies—which the ICC refused even to consider.[143] Each of these is legally/morally compensable, and compensation might in such connections go a long way toward healing the gaping cultural and psychic wounds inflicted upon indigenous societies by the nature of U.S. Indian policy.[144]

In the alternative, if the travesty of justice embodied in the ICC continues to be employed as "proof" that the United States has conducted itself "in good conscience" and "in accordance with a standard of fair and honorable dealings" with Indians, or that native claims have been reasonably well "settled," Russ Means' harsh remarks about nazis, charades, and illegal occupations may come to be seen as restrained in comparison to what follows. "There are," as Harvey Rosenthal has acknowledged, "much harder payments to be made" before the debts the U.S. owes indigenous nations can ever honestly be marked "paid in full."[145]

Notes

1   1 Stat. 50 (1787). The more practical policy was suggested in a written plan submitted to the Continental Congress by George Washington, shortly before he became president. In it, the "Father of his Country" recommended using treaties with Indians in much the same fashion Adolf Hitler would employ them against his adversaries at Munich and elsewhere a century and a half later (i.e., to lull them into a false sense of security or complacency which placed them at a distinct military disadvantage when it came time to confront them with a war of aggression). "Apart from the fact that it was immoral, unethical and actually criminal, this plan placed before Congress by Washington was so logical and well laid out that it was immediately accepted practically without opposition and immediately put into action. There might be—certainly would be—further strife with the Indians, new battles and new wars, but the end result was, with the adoption of Washington's plan, inevitable: Without even realizing it had occurred, the fate of all the Indians in the country was sealed. They had lost virtually everything." Allan W. Eckert, *That Dark and Bloody River: Chronicles of the Ohio River Valley* (New York: Bantam, 1995) p. 440.

2   *Public Papers of the Presidents of the United States: Harry S. Truman, 1946* (Washington, DC: U.S. Government Printing Office, 1962) p. 414.

3   Wilcomb E. Washburn, "Land Claims in the Mainstream of Indian/White Relations," in Imre Sutton, ed., *Irredeemable America: The Indians' Estate and Land Claims* (Albuquerque: University of New Mexico Press, 1985) pp. 26, 30–31. One is left unsure exactly which "powerful sovereigns" Washburn considers "normal" in this instance. Certainly, the governments of such obviously weak states as Monaco, Liechtenstein, and San Marino enjoy a far greater degree of practical sovereignty than does any American Indian government in the U.S., even though the latter are often territorially larger and, in many cases, more resource-rich. See Vine Deloria Jr., "The Size and Status of Nations," in Susan Lobo and Steve Talbot, eds., *Native American Voices: A Reader* (New York: Longman, 1998) pp. 457–65.

4   Glenn T. Morris, "Further Motion by the State Department to Railroad Indigenous Rights," *Fourth World Bulletin*, No. 6 (Summer 1998) pp. 1–9.

5   H.D. Rosenthal, *Their Day in Court: A History of the Indian Claims Commission* (New York: Garland, 1990) pp. 49–50.

6   See Black's commentaries in the "Letters" section of *Anarchy*, 1997–99, inclusive.

7   William H. Harnell, *Man-Made Morals: Four Philosophies That Shaped America* (New York: Anchor Books, 1969) p. 238.

8   Rosenthal, *Their Day in Court*, p. 49.

9   See, e.g., U.S. Senate, Committee on Labor and Human Resources, Subcommittee on Employment and Productivity, *Guaranteed Job Opportunity Act: Hearing on S.777* (Washington, DC: 100th Cong., 1st Sess., 1980).

10   For a good profile midway through the period, see Cheryl McCall, "Life on Pine Ridge Bleak," *Colorado Daily* (May 16, 1975).

11   Rennard Strickland, *Tonto's Revenge: Reflections on American Indian Culture and Policy* (Albuquerque: University of New Mexico Press, 1998) p. 53.

12   See generally U.S. Department of Education, National Institute of Education, Office of Research and Improvement, *Conference on the Educational and Occupational Needs of American Indian Women* (Washington, DC: U.S. Government Printing Office, 1980).

13   Strickland, *Tonto's Revenge*, p. 53.

14   See generally U.S. Department of Health and Human Services, Indian Health Service, *Indian Health Service Chart Series Book* (Washington, DC: U.S. Government Printing Office, 1988).

15   Strickland, *Tonto's Revenge*, p. 53.

16   U.S. Dept. of Commerce, Bureau of the Census, *U.S. Census of the Population, 1990: General Population Characteristics* (Washington, DC: U.S. Government Printing Office, 1992) p. 3.

17   *Lone Wolf v. Hitchcock* (187 U.S. 553 (1903)). There have of course been modifications to the *Lone Wolf* doctrine over the years. Nevertheless, it continues to represent the essential framework within which U.S. Indian policy is formulated and implemented. See, e.g., Ann Laquer Estin, "*Lone Wolf v. Hitchcock*: The Long Shadow," in Sandra L. Cadwalader and Vine Deloria Jr., eds., *The Aggressions of Civilization: Federal Indian Policy Since the 1880s* (Philadelphia: Temple University Press, 1984) pp. 215–45.

18   Ronald L. Trosper, "Appendix I: Indian Minerals: Literature Search and Reform Proposals," in American Indian Policy Review Commission, *Task Force 7 Final Report: Reservation and Resource Development and Protection* (Washington, DC: U.S. Government Printing Office, 1977) pp. 136–47; U.S. Department of Interior, Bureau of Indian Affairs, *Indian Lands Map: Oil, Gas and Minerals on Indian Reservations* (Washington,

DC: U.S. Government Printing Office, 1978); Louis R. Moore, *Mineral Development on Indian Lands: Cooperation and Conflict* (Denver: Rocky Mountain Mineral Law Foundation, 1983); Presidential Commission on Indian Reservation Economies, *Report and Recommendation to the President of the United States* (Washington, DC: U.S. Government Printing Office, November 1984).

19 Robert K. Thomas, "Colonialism: Classic and Internal," *New University Thought*, Vol. 4, No. 4 (Winter 1966–67) pp. 44–53.

20 59 Stat. 1031, T.S. No. 993, 3 Bevans 1153, 1976 Y.B.U.N. 1043 (entered into force, October 24, 1945). For text, see Burns H. Weston, Richard A. Falk, and Anthony D'Amato, eds., *Basic Documents in International Law and World Order* (Minneapolis: West, [2nd ed.] 1990) pp. 16–32, esp. pp. 27–30.

21 "All peoples have the right to self-determination; by virtue of that right they freely determine their political status and freely pursue their economic, social and cultural development." United Nations Declaration on the Granting of Independence to Colonial Countries and Peoples (U.N.G.A. Res. 1514 (XV), 15 U.N. GAOR, Supp. (No. 16) 66, U.N. Doc. A/4684 (1961)), point 2. The position is reiterated as Article 1(1) of the International Covenant on Economic, Social and Cultural Rights (U.N.G.A. Res. 2200 (XXI), 21 U.N. GAOR, Supp. (No. 16) 49, U.N. Doc. A/6316 (1967; entered into force, January 3, 1976) and Article 1(1) of the International Covenant on Civil and Political Rights (U.N.G.A. Res. 2200 (XXI), 21 U.M. GAOR, Supp. (No. 16) 52, U.N. Doc. A/6316 (1967; entered into force, March 23, 1976). See Weston, Falk, and D'Amato, *Basic Documents*, pp. 344, 371, 376.

22 Jean-Paul Sartre, "On Genocide," *Ramparts* (February 1968) pp. 35–42. This, at least in part, may be why the U.S., virtually alone among UN member states, refused to ratify the 1948 Convention on Prevention and Punishment of the Crime of Genocide (U.N.T.S. 277; entered into force, January 12, 1951) for more forty years, and then attempted to do so by way of attaching a "sovereignty package" which would have allowed it to exempt itself from any and all provisions it might find inconvenient. See generally Lawrence J. LeBlanc, *The United States and the Genocide Convention* (Durham, NC: Duke University Press, 1991). For the relevant articles of the Convention itself, see Weston, Falk, and D'Amato, *Basic Documents*, p. 297. Full text will be found in Ian Brownlie, ed., *Basic Documents on Human Rights* (Oxford, UK: Clarendon Press, [3rd ed.] 1992) pp. 31–34.

23 Mills may have first touched upon the concept of cognitive dissonance in his "Situated Actions and Vocabularies of Motive," *American Sociological Review*, Vol. 5, No. 6 (1940) pp. 904–13. It is implicit throughout many of his later works, notably *The Sociological Imagination* (New York: Oxford University Press, 1959), although it was developed far more thoroughly in Leon Festinger's *A Theory of Cognitive Dissonance* (Stanford, CA: Stanford University Press, 1957).

24 Vine Deloria Jr., "Non-Violence in American Society," *Katallegete*, Vol. 5, No. 2 (1974) pp. 4–7; reprinted in James Treat, ed., *For This Land: Writings on Religion in America* (New York: Routledge, 1999) pp. 44–50, quote at p. 45.

25 Imre Sutton, "Prolegomena," in Sutton, *Irredeemable America*, p. 6.

26 This is hardly the only connection in which such things are true. For an useful analysis of the same process at work in other dimensions, see Noam Chomsky, *Necessary Illusions: Thought Control in Democratic Societies* (Boston: South End Press, 1989).

27 See generally John T. Vance, "The Congressional Mandate and the Indian Claims Commission," *North Dakota Law Review*, No. 45 (Spring 1969) pp. 325–36.

28   Quoted in John Kobler, "These Indians Struck It Rich: The Utes' Treaty Land," *Saturday Evening Post* (September 6, 1972) p. 132.

29   Rosenthal, *Their Day in Court*, p. 49.

30   Sutton, "Prolegomena," p. 5. Not least among the problems of such formulations is the unanswered question of exactly how American Indians, formally recognized by the United States through a lengthy series of eighteenth- and nineteenth-century treaties as constituting separate and distinct nations of people, have come to be construed as "a minority" group within the U.S. during the twentieth. Did the Indians at some point agree to such a radical and across-the-board alteration of their status? If so, when and by what means? The issue is fundamental, because, under international law, it has long been the case that a nation, having once recognized the sovereignty of another, has no legal authority whatsoever to unilaterally "demote" it at some later point. Alteration in the sovereign status of any nation legitimately occurs only on the basis of its voluntary consent to the change, See Lassa Oppenheim's *International Law: A Treatise* (London: Longman's, Green, [5th ed.] 1955) p. 120. Also see Robert T. Coulter, "Contemporary Indian Sovereignty," in National Lawyers Guild Committee on Native American Struggles, *Rethinking Indian Law* (New Haven, CT: Advocate Press, 1982) pp. 109–20, esp. p. 118.

31   See notes 4, 20, 21 and 22, above. Also see my essay, "Perversions of Justice: Examining the Doctrine of U.S. Rights to Occupancy in North America," in David S. Caudill and Steven Jay Gold, eds., *Radical Philosophy of Law: Contemporary Challenges to Mainstream Legal Theory and Practice* (Atlantic Highlands, NJ: Humanities Press, 1995) pp. 200–220.

32   10 Stat. 612 (February 24, 1855).

33   12 Stat. 765 (March 3, 1863). Section 9 specifies that the Court of Claims "shall not extend to or include any claim against the Government . . . growing out of or dependent on, any treaty stipulation entered into with . . . the Indian tribes."

34   Rosenthal, *Their Day in Court*, pp. 9–10.

35   *United States ex rel. Standing Bear v. Crook* (25 Fed. Cas. 695 (C.C.D. Nebraska, 1879)). For background, see Thomas Henry Tibbles, *The Ponca Chiefs: An Account of the Trial of Standing Bear* (Lincoln: University of Nebraska Press, 1972).

36   21 Stat. 504, Chap. 139 (March 3, 1881). For results, see E.B. Smith, *Indian Tribal Claims Decided in the U.S. Court of Claims, Briefed and Compiled June 30, 1947*, 2 vols. (New York: Praeger, 1976 reprint).

37   U.S. House of Representatives. Committee on Interior and Insular Affairs, *Indirect Services and Expenditures by the Federal Government for the American Indian* (Washington, DC: 86th Cong., 1st Sess., 1959) pp. 11–14.

38   Richard A. Nielson, "American Indian Land Claims: Land versus Money as a Remedy," *University of Florida Law Review*, Vol. 25, No. 3 (Winter 1973) p. 308. Also see Glen A. Wilkinson, "Indian Tribal Claims Before the Court of Claims," *Georgetown Law Journal*, Vol. 55, No. 4 (December 1966) pp. 511–28.

39   Howard Friedman, "Interest on Indian Land Claims: Judicial Protection of the Fisc," *Valparaiso University Law Review*, Vol. 5, No. 1 (Fall 1970) pp. 26–47. Also see Wilkinson, "Tribal Claims."

40   John R. White, "Barmecide Revisited: The Gratuitous Offset in Indian Claims Cases," *Ethnohistory*, Vol. 25, No. 2 (Spring 1978) pp. 179–92. Also see Wilkinson, "Tribal Claims."

41   Rosenthal, *Their Day in Court*, p. 30. For a useful overview of resistance to the government's imposition of compulsory schooling—to take but one example—see

David Wallace Adams, *Education for Extinction: American Indians and the Boarding School Experience, 1875–1928* (Lawrence: University Press of Kansas, 1995).

42 Rosenthal, *Their Day in Court*, pp. 30–31.

43 It was officially estimated during the mid-1930s that it took, on average, a full ten years from the time an Indian claims case was authorized by Congress at the point it actually came to trial; U.S. House of Representatives, Committee on Indian Affairs, *Hearing on H.R. 7838 to Create an Indian Claims Commission* (Washington, DC: 74th Cong., 1st Sess., 1935) p. 10.

44 U.S. Senate, Subcommittee of the Senate Committee on the Judiciary, *Hearing on S. 3083* (Washington, DC, 76th Cong., 3rd Sess., February 1940) p. 139.

45 "The General Accounting Office estimated, in 1935, that it had [by that point] spent one million dollars examining some 1.38 million 'claim instances' and over 83,000 accounts for reports" to U.S. Attorneys working on the nullification of Indian claims cases. Rosenthal, *Their Day in Court*, p. 30.

46 Ibid., p. 20.

47 Quoted in Walter Hart Blumenthal, *American Indians Dispossessed: Fraud in Land Cessions Forced Upon the Tribes* (Philadelphia: G.S. McManus, 1955) p. 174.

48 Rosenthal, *Their Day in Court*, p. 30.

49 *Hearings on S. 3083*, p. 20. On page 24 of *Their Day in Court*, Rosenthal contends that, "From 1881 to 1946, 219 claims were filed with the Court of Claims. Of these cases only thirty-five won awards which totaled $77.3 million or an average of $1.2 million per year in net recoveries."

50 The brunt of this of course fell on already impoverished native peoples, but it also included more than a few of the white attorneys who represented them. For example, Francis A. Goodwin, a lawyer in Washington state who took on the case of the Nez Perce, lost twelve years and $5,000 of his own funds in a losing effort. See generally U.S. House of Representatives, Committee on Indian Affairs, *Hearings on H.R. 1198 and 1341 to Create an Indian Claims Commission* (Washington, DC: 79th Cong., 1st Sess., March and June 1945) pp. 81–84.

51 Rosenthal, *Their Day in Court*, pp. 23, 32.

52 The position has been taken in any number of works by legal "scholars" who embrace the fundamentally colonialist premise that U.S.–Indian relations are properly subject to domestic rather than international law and jurisprudence. As but one example, see Charles F. Wilkinson, *American Indians, Time, and the Law* (New Haven, CT: Yale University Press, 1987).

53 Such bias is likely inherent to any process of this sort. For numerous examples leading to this conclusion, see Richard B. Lillich, *International Claims: Their Adjudication by National Commissions* (Syracuse, NY: Syracuse University Press, 1962).

54 Ibid., p. 6.

55 Francis E. Leupp, *The Indian and His Problem* (New York: Scribner's, 1910) pp. 194–96.

56 U.S. House of Representatives, Subcommittee of the Committee on Indian Affairs, *Hearings on the Appropriations Bill of 1914* (Washington, DC: 64th Cong., 2nd Sess., 1913) p. 99.

57 See generally Henry E. Fritz, *The Movement for Indian Assimilation, 1860–1890* (Philadelphia: University of Pennsylvania Press, 1963); Frederick E. Hoxie, *A Final Promise: The Campaign to Assimilate the Indians, 1880–1920* (Lincoln: University of Nebraska Press, 1984).

58   Overall, see Brian W. Dippie, *The Vanishing American: White Attitudes and U.S. Indian Policy* (Middletown, CT: Wesleyan University Press, 1982); Christopher M. Lyman, *The Vanishing Race and Other Illusions* (New York: Pantheon Books, 1982).

59   The kickoff came with Standard Oil's preliminary exploration of the Navajo Reservation in 1919–21, under provision of the 1918 Metalliferous Minerals Act. See Lorraine Turner Ruffing, "Navajo Mineral Development," *American Indian Journal*, Vol. 4, No. 9 (September 1978) pp. 2–16.

60   See generally Terry P. Wilson, *The Underground Reservation: Osage Oil* (Lincoln: University of Nebraska Press, 1985).

61   An interesting take on this is provided by Hollis Whitson and Martha Roberge in their "Moving Those Indians Into the Twentieth Century," *Technology Review*, No. 89 (July 1986) pp. 47–51.

62   Lewis Meriam, *The Problems of Indian Administration* (Baltimore: Johns Hopkins University Press, 1928).

63   Ibid., p. 48.

64   U.S. Senate, Subcommittee of the Committee on Indian Affairs, *Hearings on the Survey of Conditions of Indians in the United States* (Washington, DC: 70th–71st Cong., 1928–29) pp. 13670–7.

65   Indian Reorganization Act of 1934 (ch. 5776, 48 Stat. 948, now codified at 25 U.S.C. 461–279). For background, see Vine Deloria Jr. and Clifford M. Lytle, *The Nations Within: The Past and Future of American Indian Sovereignty* (New York: Pantheon, 1984).

66   U.S. House of Representatives, Committee on Indian Affairs, *Creating an Indian Claims Commission* (Washington, DC: 79th Cong., 1st Sess., 1945) p. 1466.

67   *Congressional Record* (June 21, 1937) p. 6058.

68   Ibid., p. 6246.

69   Ibid., p. 6241.

70   Ibid., p. 6261.

71   *Northwestern Bands of Shoshone Indians v. United States* (324 U.S. 335 (1945)). Quoted in Felix S. Cohen, *The Legal Conscience: Selected Papers* (New Haven, CT: Yale University Press, 1960) p. 264. The takings in question were only sixty-to-seventy years old at the time Jackson wrote, meaning that the "ancestors" involved were the parents and grandparents of the Shoshone claimants. How "remote" a degree of ancestry Jackson considered his own parents was left unstated.

72   Cohen, *Legal Conscience*, p. 302.

73   Ibid., p. 303.

74   For an overall description of Roosevelt's attitude, including the statement quoted, see John Collier, *From Every Zenith: A Memoir* (Denver: Sage Books, 1963) pp. 294–99.

75   These included H.R. 7963 (1930), which was never reported out of the House Judiciary Committee; S. 3444 (1934) and S. 1465 (1935), both of which died in committee; H.R. 6655 (1935), which suffered the same fate; S. 2731 (1935) and H.R. 7837 (1935), both of which were reported out—S. 2731 was actually approved by the full Senate—but passed over and tabled in the House until the congressional session expired; S.1902 (1937), which was again passed by the Senate, but, despite being considerably amended in committee, was voted down by the full house (176 to 73); S. 3083 (1939), which died in committee; S. 4206 (1940), killed in committee; S. 4234 (1940), killed in committee; S. 4349 (1940), on which the congressional session expired before a vote was taken; S. 1111 and H.R. 4693 (both 1941), which were hashed about interminably and then tabled; H.R. 4593 and H.R. 5569 (1944), both of which died in committee; H.R. 1198 and H.R. 1341 (both 1945), both of which

were killed before reaching the floor. These are summarized in Rosenthal, *Their Day in Court*, pp. 53–84.

76 Act of Aug, 12, 1935 (49 Stat. 596), also known as the "Gratuities Act."

77 Indian Claims Commission Act (60 Stat. 1049 (1946)).

78 For the best overview of U.S. insistence on this idea in the face of staunch allied opposition to it, see Bradley F. Smith, *The Road to Nuremberg* (New York: Basic Books, 1981) esp. chaps. 2–3.

79 Bradley F. Smith, *The American Road to Nuremberg: The Documentary Record* (Stanford, CA: Hoover Institution Press, 1982) p. 6.

80 Agreement for the Prosecution and Punishment of the Major War Criminals of the European Axis Powers and Charter of the International Military Tribunal (59 Stat. 1544, 82 U.N.T.S. 279 (August 8, 1945). For text, see Weston, Falk, and D'Amato, *Basic Documents*, pp. 138–39. On the ensuing prosecution of primary nazi leaders, see Eugene Davidson, *The Trial of the Germans, 1945–1946* (New York: Macmillan, 1966). On the subsequent series of prosecutions of lesser nazi defendants, see John Alan Appleman, *Military Tribunals and Military Crimes* (Westport, CT: Greenwood Press, 1954). With respect to related prosecutions of Japanese, see Arnold C. Brackman, *The Other Nuremberg: The Untold Story of the Tokyo War Crimes Trials* (New York: William Morrow, 1987).

81 As formulated in a July 25, 1945, "Memorandum to All Legal Personnel" prepared by Col. Murray C. Bernays, a key figure in U.S. war crimes policy development, the four overarching categories of activity for which the top nazis should be tried were "the 'Nazi master plan' (aggressive war conspiracy); 'preparatory measures' (preparations for aggression); 'occupying neighboring German areas'; and 'military conquest' (acts of aggression and war crimes, covering the period 1939–45)." In only slightly revised form, this was the schematic actually adopted for the Nuremberg prosecutions. See Bradley F. Smith, *Reaching Judgment at Nuremberg* (New York: Basic Books, 1977) p. 65.

82 Adolf Hitler, *Mein Kampf* (New York: Reynal and Hitchcock, 1939) pp. 403, 591; *Hitler's Secret Book* (New York: Grove Press, 1961) pp. 46–52. Another iteration will be found in a memorandum prepared by an aide, Col. Friedrich Hössbach, summarizing Hitler's statements during a high-level "Führer Conference" conducted shortly before Germany's 1939 invasion of Poland. The document is included in *Trial of the Major Nazi War Criminals Before the International Military Tribunal*, 42 vols. (Nuremberg: International Military Tribunal, 1947–49) Vol. 25, pp. 402–13.

83 Norman Rich, *Hitler's War Aims: Ideology, the Nazi State, and the Course of Expansion* (New York: W.W. Norton, 1973) p. 8. Also see John Toland, *Adolf Hitler* (Garden City, NY: Doubleday, 1976) p. 802.

84 See, e.g., Frank Parella, *Lebensraum and Manifest Destiny: A Comparative Study in the Justification of Expansionism* (Washington, DC: MA thesis, School of International Relations, Georgetown University, 1950).

85 Since it is now fashionable to view the U.S. wars against American Indians and the crimes of nazism as belonging to entirely different epochs, it is important to remember that the Wounded Knee Massacre—generally considered to be the last round of the former—occurred in 1890, and that the latter commenced when Hitler came to power only forty-two years later. Predictably, under the circumstances, claims of "victor's justice" being visited upon the nazis were raised rather forcefully by German defense counsel Hermann Jahrreiss in his opening statement to the Nuremberg Tribunal. Less expectedly, perhaps, they were also raised by

individuals like Senator Robert A. Taft in the United States itself. See Hermann Jahrreiss, "Statement Before the Nuremberg Tribunal," and Robert A. Taft, "Equal Justice Before the Law," both in Jay W. Baird, ed., *From Nuremberg to My Lai* (Lexington, MA: DC Heath, 1972) at pp. 84–90 and 107–13, respectively.

86 See U.S. House of Representatives, Select Committee of the Committee of Indian Affairs, *An Investigation to Determine Whether the Changed Status of the Indian Requires a Revision of the Laws and Regulations Affecting the Indian* (Washington, DC: 78th Cong., 2nd Sess., December 23, 1944).

87 The effect of the Justice Department's recommended changes to the Claims Commission Act would have been to "cut many 'identifiable groups' of Indians from the scope of the bill, to strike from the list of claims those based on fraud, duress, mistake and the taking of lands without compensation (the most common kind), to disallow the commission discretion on offsets, to ban transfer of suits from the Court of Claims, to remove the [commission's] investigation division, to limit the commission's access to records[,] to the judicial character of the commission, to prevent compromise settlements, to deny the [commission's] power of final decision, and to close the Court of Claims to post-1946 claims." Rosenthal, *Their Day in Court*, p. 87.

88 On the case against Streicher, see Davidson, *Trial of the Germans*, pp. 40–57; Smith, *Reaching Judgment at Nuremberg*, pp. 200–203. For implications, see the essay titled "In the Matter of Julius Streicher: Applying Nuremberg Standards to the United States," in my *From a Native Son: Selected Essays in Indigenism, 1985–1995* (Boston: South End Press, 1996) pp. 445–54.

89 *Congressional Record* (July 30, 1946) p. A. 4923.

90 Truman, *Papers*, p. 414.

91 *Congressional Record* (May 20, 1946) p. 5319.

92 U.S. Dept. of Interior report to the House, 1945. Quoted in Rosenthal, *Their Day in Court*, pp. 86–87.

93 U.S. withdrawal from its trust relations with indigenous nations would have been fine, had the move been attended by a simultaneous relinquishment of its claim to title and jurisdiction over their territories. Since it was not, however, it amounted to their final and illegal absorption into the U.S. territorial corpus. See, e.g., Eyal Benvenisti, *The International Law of Occupation* (Princeton, NJ: Princeton University Press, 1993) pp. 5–6.

94 See, e.g., the statement of Indian Commissioner William A. Brophy in U.S. Senate, Committee on Indian Affairs, *Hearings on H.R. 4497 to Create an Indian Claims Commission* (Washington, DC: 79th Cong., 2nd Sess., 1946) p. 15. It should be noted that such goals are entirely consistent with the definition of genocide advanced by Raphaël Lemkin when he coined the term in his *Axis Rule in Occupied Europe* (Washington, DC: Carnegie Endowment for the Promotion of World Peace, 1944) p. 79.

95 *Congressional Record* (May 20, 1946) p. 5312.

96 The sole exception was the case of *Pueblo de Taos v. U.S.* (Doc. No. 357, Ind. Cl. Comm. (1965)), in which 48,000 acres in the Blue Lake area were actually restored at the request of President Richard M. Nixon. This outcome was, however, explicitly predicated on a 1926 arrangement negotiated by the Pueblo Lands Board in which the Indians agreed to drop a suit for $300,000 in compensation for reserved land onto which the town of Taos, New Mexico, had been steadily expanding. The case was therefore defined as "unique," and found to hold no precedential value in other land claims settlements. See Nielson, "Land Claims," pp. 320–23.

97   The ICC rationalized its "judicial fiscal responsibility" in denying awards interest against unpaid principal in perfectly circular fashion. In the case of *Loyal Creeks v. U.S.* (1 Ind. Cl. Comm. 22 (1951)) it held that since the taking of Creek land during the 1830s had been extraconstitutional, it lacked a legal authority on which to award interest against unpaid principal. Of course, if the taking were extraconstitutional, principal should never have been at issue in the first place since no valid transfer of title to the U.S. had ever occurred. This meant that the land remained Creek property, subject to recovery. On this point, however, the commissioners argued that the 1946 Act itself afforded them a legal authority upon which to deny any such remedy. The juridical contradiction thus presented is discussed in Thomas LeDuc's "The Work of the Indian Claims Commission Under the Act of 1946," *Pacific Historical Review*, Vol. 26, No. 1 (February 1957) pp. 1–16.

98   Rosenthal, *Their Day in Court*, p. 138.

99   *Congressional Record* (July 29, 1935) p. 11975.

100 U.S. Senate, Subcommittee of the Committee on Appropriations, *Hearings on H.R. 9390 for Appropriations for Interior and Related Agencies for 1957* (Washington, DC: 84th Cong., 2nd Sess., 1956) pp. 552–58.

101 U.S. Senate, Subcommittee on Indian Affairs of the Committee on Interior and Insular Affairs, *Hearings on S. 307, A Bill to amend the Indian Claims Commission Act of 1946* (Washington, DC: 90th Cong., 1st Sess., 1967) p. 74.

102 General Rules of the Indian Claims Commission (ch. 3, 25 U.S.C. 503 (1968)).

103 Rosenthal, *Their Day in Court*, p. 123.

104 Ibid., p. 178.

105 *Hearing on S.* 4497, p. 16.

106 The 1958 Rancheria Act (72 Stat. 619), for example, authorized disbursement of checks compensating all identified members of forty-one federally recognized "Mission Bands" in southern California for loss of their historic homelands in the amount of 47¢ per acre (the rate was determined by the Court of Claims in 1944 to be applicable to all Indian lands in the state). As each check was cashed, the signature on it was tallied as a "vote for termination" of federal recognition (the only way an Indian could vote *not* to be terminated was thus to refuse his/her portion of the settlement). On this basis, it was claimed that their "extinction" was "voluntary." For history and effects, see Florence Connolly Shipeck, *Pushed into the Rocks: Southern California Indian Land Tenure, 1769–1986* (Lincoln: University of Nebraska Press, 1988). For a broader range of examples, see Bruce Granville Miller, *Invisible Indigenes: The Politics of Nonrecognition* (Lincoln: University of Nebraska Press, 2003). On "termination," see note 108.

107 Rosenthal, *Their Day in Court*, pp. 166, 178.

108 Pursuant to House Concurrent Resolution 108 (August 1, 1953) federal recognition of one hundred and nine peoples, or portions of peoples, was terminated under a series of specific statutes by 1962, the great bulk of them by 1958 (one group, the Poncas of Oklahoma, was terminated in 1966). A handful, such as the Menominees in Wisconsin and Siletz in Oregon, were "reinstated" during the 1970s, followed by a number of others, including several California Mission Bands (see note 106), during the 1980s and '90s. Many were stripped of considerable property in the process, however, and well over half of those terminated remain so at present. See generally American Indian Policy Review Commission (Task Force 10), *Final Report: Report on Terminated and Nonfederally Recognized Indians* (Washington, DC: U.S. Government Printing Office, 1976); Donald L. Fixico, *Termination and Relocation: Federal Indian Policy,*

1945–1960 (Albuquerque: University of New Mexico Press, 1986); R. Warren Metcalf, *Termination's Legacy: The Discarded Indians of Utah* (Lincoln: University of Nebraska Press, 2002).

109   For a rather self-congratulatory official assessment, see U.S. House of Representatives, *Present Relations of the Federal Government to the American Indians* (Washington, DC: 85th Cong., 2nd Sess., December 1958).

110   Rosenthal, *Their Day in Court*, pp. 175–98.

111   Richard Drinnon, *Keeper of Concentration Camps: Dillon S. Myer and American Racism* (Berkeley: University of California Press, 1987) pp. 208–9.

112   Wilcomb E. Washburn, *Red Man's Land, White Man's Law* (New York: Scribner's, 1971) pp. 81–86, 103–4.

113   Stan Steiner, *The New Indians* (New York: Harper & Row, 1967) p. 83.

114   Chief Claims Commissioner Witt estimated in early 1951 that the number might ultimately run as high as 300 by the time the filing period expired at the end of that year. See U.S. House of Representatives, Subcommittee of the Committee on Appropriations, *Hearings on the Independent Office Appropriations for 1952* (Washington, DC: 82nd Cong., 1st Sess., 1951) pp. 28–37.

115   Rosenthal, *Their Day in Court*, p. 115.

116   *Hearings on H.R. 9390*, pp. 552–58.

117   *Hearings on S. 307*, p. 20.

118   U.S. Senate, Committee on Appropriations, *Hearings on H.R. 9417 for Appropriations for the Department of Interior and Related Agencies for 1972* (Washington, DC: 92nd Cong., 1st Sess., 1971) pp. 1433–50. Also see Committee on Interior and Insular Affairs, *Amending the Indian Claims Commission Act of 1946 as Amended* (Washington, DC: 92nd Cong., 2nd Sess., Rpt. 682, March 2, 1972).

119   Indian Claims Commission, *Final Report* (Washington, DC: U.S. Government Printing Office, 1978). Through 1962—the termination era—there were 105 dismissals versus 37 awards. The ratio improved thereafter, although the average award amount obviously remained quite small.

120   Rosenthal, *Their Day in Court*, p. 255.

121   During the late 1950s, the ICC was funded at the level of $178,000 annually. At the same time, the Justice Department was expending upward of $600,000 and the GAO about $500,000 per year "defending" the United States from having to pay its debts; *Indirect Services and Expenditures 1959*, pp. 5–8. Also see U.S. Senate, Subcommittee of the Committee on Appropriations, *Hearings on H.R. 10802 on Appropriations for Interior Department and Related Agencies for 1963* (Washington, DC: 87th Cong., 2nd Sess., 1962) pp. 773–88.

122   *Otoe and Missouria Tribe of Indians v. United States* (131 Ct. Cl. 593 (1955)). The size of the award, which was small, was not itself at issue. Rather, it was the ICC's decision to base it on "aboriginal title" per se, rather than on some earlier recognition of that title. When the Court of Claims upheld the ICC position on appeal, and the Supreme Court declined to review the matter, the Justice Department set out to change the law itself, renewing Francis Biddle's absurd contention that it would cost taxpayers $3 billion in awards if Congress failed to comply with the attorney general's wishes. See U.S. Senate, *Terminating the Existence of the Indian Claims Commission* (Washington, DC: 84th Cong., 2nd Sess., Rpt. 1727, April 11, 1956). In the face of this—not to mention the pattern of behavior described in association with notes 116, 117, and 118—the contention advanced by Rosenthal (*Their Day in Court*, p. 197) that it would be "biased" to suggest the Justice Department was objectively "anti-Indian

and purposefully obstructionist" in its handling of Indian claims cases is simply laughable.

123   It is true that the United Nations Charter provides that exercise of the right of self-determination by all peoples be balanced against the need to preserve the territorial integrity of UN member states. It is presumptive, however, that the territory in question have been in some sense legitimately acquired. See Lee C. Buchheit, *Secession: The Legitimacy of Self-Determination* (New Haven, CT: Yale University Press, 1978). pp. 17, 92, 244–45;.Allen Buchanan, *Secession: The Morality of Political Divorce from Fort Sumter to Lithuania and Quebec* (Boulder, CO: Westview Press, 1991) pp. 22–23, 52–68.

124   Rosenthal, *Their Day in Court*, p. 151.

125   This includes land title "secured" by fraudulent treaties or agreements, lands appropriated by a unilateral Act of Congress, and lands confiscated without even the latter pretense of legal justification. These are issues entirely separate from that of lands for which some arguably legitimate form of native consent to cession was obtain, but for which they were uncompensated or uncompensated at the time. This last is all the ICC was authorized to adjudicate, although, as with the Western Shoshone Land Claim, it often attempted to "create title where none had previously existed" whenever it came upon any of the first three situations. See Jack D. Forbes, "The 'Public Domain' of Nevada and Its Relationship to Indian Property Rights," *Nevada State Bar Journal*, Vol. 30, No. 3 (July 1965) pp. 16–47; Russel L. Barsh, "Indian Land Claims Policy in the United States," *North Dakota Law Review*, Vol. 58, No, 1 (1982) pp. 7–82.

126   U.S. Department of Interior, Public Lands Law Review Commission, *One Third of the Nation's Land* (Washington, DC: U.S. Government Printing Office, 1970).

127   Vine Deloria Jr., *Behind the Trail of Broken Treaties: An Indian Declaration of Independence* (New York: Delacorte Press, 1974) p. 227.

128   Robert T. Coulter and Steven M. Tullburg, "Indian Land Rights," in Cadwalader and Deloria, *Aggressions of Civilization*, p. 204.

129   See the 1967 statement by National Indian Youth Council representative Hank Adams to the U.S. Senate, in *Hearings on S. 307*, p. 91.

130   Videotaped interview, April 1982.

131   The term accrues from Scoop Jackson's assertion, made during his advocacy of the Claims Commission Act in 1946, that failure to dispose of native claims would "perpetuate clouds upon white men's title that interfere with development of our public domain." *Congressional Record* (May 20, 1946) p. 5312.

132   Rosenthal, *Their Day in Court*, p. 250. On the Suquamish, Puyallup, and Stillaguamish, see U.S. Senate, Subcommittee on Indian Affairs of the Committee on Interior and Insular Affairs, *Hearing on S. 721, A Bill to Authorize Appropriations for the Indian Claims Commission for Fiscal Year 1974 and Other Purposes* (Washington, DC: 93d Cong., 1st Sess., February 16, 1973) p. 118. On the Shoshones, see Elmer R. Rusco, "Historic Change in Western Shoshone Country: The Establishment of the Western Shoshone National Council and Traditionalist Land Claims, *American Indian Quarterly*, Vol. 16, No. 3 (Summer 1992) pp. 337–60. On the Oneidas, see Arlinda Locklear, "The Oneida Land Claims: A Legal Overview," in Christopher Vecsey and William A. Starna, eds., *Iroquois Land Claims* (Syracuse, NY: Syracuse University Press, 1988) pp. 141–53.

133   At issue is the Black Hills area of South Dakota, guaranteed by the 1868 Fort Laramie Treaty but taken by the U.S. in 1877. The original award was for $17.5 million, interest free; *Sioux Nation v. U.S.* (220 Ct. Cl. 442, 601 F.2d 1157 (1975)). On appeal, the Supreme Court, deeming the matter compensable under the Fourth Amendment,

added 5 percent simple interest, making the gross amount awarded $122.5 million. By referendum, the Lakotas declined to accept; *Sioux Nation v. U.S.* (488 U.S. 371 (1980)). During the 1980s, New Jersey Senator Bill Bradley attempted to resolve the issue by introducing a bill in which the award would have been paid as an indemnity, certain lands would have been restored, and a split jurisdiction effected over the rest. The plan was opposed by South Dakota's congressional delegation and therefore withdrawn. See "The Black Hills Are Not For Sale: The Lakota Struggle for the 1868 Treaty Territory," in my *Struggle for the Land: Native North American Resistance to Genocide, Ecocide and Colonization* (San Francisco: City Lights, [2nd ed.] 2002) pp. 113–34.

134 Richard O. Clemmer, *Roads in the Sky: The Hopi Indians in a Century of Change* (Boulder: Westview Press, 1995) p. 187.

135 Nielson, "Indian Land Claims," p. 308.

136 Quoted in Fred Eggan, *The American Indian: Perspectives for the Study of Social Change* (Chicago: Aldine, 1966) p. 166.

137 As legal scholar Morton E. Price opined, "It was preposterous to recognize fully such extraordinary claims of a handful of poor people, even if they were based on legitimate entitlement." Quoted in Harold Fey and D'Arcy McNickle, *Indians and Other Americans: Two Ways of Life Meet* (New York: Harper & Row, 1970) p. 123. No indication is offered, of course, as to why it would've been—or be—any more "preposterous" to recognize these particular claims that to recognize the extraordinary claims of, say, the wealthiest one percent of Americans to ownership of or control over of more than a third of the country's assets.

138 See, e.g., the examples of such disinformation discussed by Paul Brodeur in his *Restitution: The Land Claims of the Mashpee, Passamaquoddy, and Penobscot Indians of New England* (Boston: Northeastern University Press, 1985). Also see the grotesque misrepresentations of reality advanced by Alan Van Gestel in "When Fictions Take Hostages," written for anthropologist James E. Clifton's *The Invented Indian: Cultural Fictions and Government Policies* (New Brunswick, NJ: Transaction Books, 1990) pp. 291–312.

139 For breakouts of this acreage, see *One Third of the Nation's Land*. For further analysis, see Barsh, "Land Claims Policy."

140 Rosenthal, *Their Day in Court*, p. 253.

141 Memo of the Chairman to the Committee on Interior and Insular Affairs, U.S. Senate, *An Analysis of the Problem and Effects of Our Diminishing Indian Land Base, 1948–1957* (Washington, DC: 85th Cong., 2nd Sess., December 1959) p. 101.

142 In international law, there are two fundamental principles of restitution: (a) "*restitutio integrum*" (restoration of the former legal situation) and, (b) "*restitutio in natura*" (returning of something wrongfully taken to its original owner). Acts of compensation or reparation are considered only if the former legal situation cannot be restored. István Vásárhelyi, *Restitution in International Law* (Budapest: Hungarian Academy of Sciences, 1964) p. 74.

143 Deloria, *Trail of Broken Treaties*, pp. 223–26.

144 Consider as analogs the compensation customarily awarded for such things as "mental anguish," "pain and suffering," and "discrimination" in U.S. civil law.

145 Rosenthal, *Their Day in Court*, p. 257.

FIVE

In the Spirit of Gunga Din

A Response to John LaVelle

> Those who have become so mentally conditioned by colonialism
> that they forget the very fact of their colonization must surely be
> the most colonized people of all.
>
> —Russell Means, 1992

The *American Indian Quarterly* recently published a grossly and I believe deliberately misleading "critique" by John LaVelle of my 1994 book, *Indians Are Us? Culture and Genocide in Native North America*, wherein I'm accused of everything from fabricating history and misquoting sources to being secretly "anti-Indian."[1] Since he elected to focus most heavily upon my open opposition to blood quantum standards and other federal manipulations of American Indian identity criteria—claiming that it undermines native sovereignty and self-determination—I'd like to begin my response to LaVelle's myriad distortions and inaccuracies by

---

I wrote this reply to John LaVelle's review essay shortly after it appeared in *American Indian Quarterly* during the winter of 1996, and duly submitted it to the journal's editor, University of Oklahoma anthropology professor Morris Foster, a few months later. After much back-and-forth, during which Foster insisted on his "right" to edit my piece, and my equally adamant refusal to allow him any such prerogative, he formally declined to publish it. At that point, I simply set the piece aside, figuring it would eventually see print. Were it not for events beginning in late-January 2005 that, among other effects, drew my time, energy, and attention away from publishing over an extended period, the present volume, including my response to LaVelle, would have appeared years ago. Given the nature and extent of LaVelle's role in the events in question, not least by way of his 1996 review, it seems more appropriate than ever that my response finally see the light of day. Other than correction of several typos, completion of a single endnote, and addition of another, it appears exactly as it was submitted to Foster. For reasons that will be obvious, I've also added a lengthy Postscript covering what has transpired since 2005.

quoting in its entirety Point 11 of the Twenty-Point Program submitted by the Trail of Broken Treaties caravan to the Nixon administration in November 1972.

> The Congress should enact measures fully in support of the doctrine that an Indian Nation has complete power to govern and control its own membership—by eradicating the extortive and coercive devices in federal policy and programming that have subverted and denied the natural human relationships and natural development of Indian communities, and committed countless injuries upon Indian families and individuals. The general prohibition against benefitting dually from federal assistances or tribal resources by having membership or maintaining relationships in more than one Indian Tribe has frequently resulted in denial of rights and benefits from any source. Blood quantum criteria, closed and restrictive enrollment, and "dual benefits prohibitions" have generated minimal problems for Indians having successive non-Indian parentage involved in their ancestry—while creating vast problems and complexities for full-blood or predominant-Indian blood persons, when ancestry or current relationships involve two separate Indian tribes, or more. Full-blood Indians can fail to qualify for membership in any of several tribes to which they may be directly related if quantum-relationships happen to be in the wrong configurations, or non-qualifying fractions. Families have been divided to be partly included upon enrollments, while some children of the same parents are wrongly (if there are to be enrollments at all) excluded. There should be a restoration of Indian and tribal rights to all individual Indians who have been victimized and deprived by the various forms of termination effected by forced choices between multiple-related tribes, abusive application of blood quantum criteria, and federally-engineered and federally-approved enrollments. The right of Indian persons to maintain, sever, or resume valid relations with several Indian Nations or communities unto which they are born, or acquire relationships through natural marriage relations or parenthood or other customary forms, must again be recognized under law and practice and also the right of Indian Nations to receive other Indian people into relations with them—or to maintain relations with all their own people, without regard to blood-quantum criteria and federal standards for exclusion or restrictions upon benefits. (It

may be recognized that the general Indian leadership has been conditioned to accept and give application to these forms of terminating rights, patterns which are an atrocious aberration from any concepts of Indian justice and sovereignty.)[2]

Although I wrote not a word of the above position—it was drafted by Assiniboine/Sioux legal scholar Hank Adams and ratified by hundreds of Trail participants, people who unquestionably stand among the late twentieth century's strongest champions of native rights—there is nothing I've ever written or said that is inconsistent with this "Indian Declaration of Independence."[3] Given that both Point 11 and my own writing lay the onus for "the abusive application of blood quantum" and related matters directly at the feet of the federal government rather than "the tribes," each corresponds quite well with the analyses offered by Russell Thornton and Patricia Nelson Limerick, scholars whose conclusions LaVelle asserts I've taken out of context and twisted beyond recognition.[4]

It's instructive that, despite my long sharing of a campus with Patty Limerick, she's never suggested anything of the sort. Nor has Thornton. The latter, however, might well have a few bones to pick with LaVelle for the manner in which he distorted the "optimistic" demographic projections in Thornton's *American Indian Holocaust and Survival*, given that they're predicated on an abandonment of the very methods of defining Indians by blood quantum that LaVelle is so bound and determined to defend.[5] Thornton's conclusions in this respect are dissimilar neither to my own nor to those reached by other native analysts, Jack Forbes, Lenore Stiffarm, and Phil Lane among them.[6]

Toeing the Federal Line

The Nixon administration did in fact to respond to the twenty points of the Trail of Broken Treaties, and it is worth quoting from the government's rejoinder to Point 11 before proceeding to analyze the underpinnings of LaVelle's assorted misrepresentations of reality.

> The Trail of Broken Treaties recognizes that their recommendation is contrary to the position taken by the members of tribes in their referendums adopting constitutions setting forth their membership requirements. The Trail of Broken Treaties argument is really with the tribes who prescribe their membership provisions pursuant to constitutions and by-laws that have been adopted.[7]

This interesting little exercise in buck-passing neglects to mention that the constitutions and by-laws at issue were drafted not by Indians, but by federal bureaucrats acting in pursuance of the 1934 Indian Reorganization Act (IRA). It also omits reference to the fact that the referenda by which such instruments were adopted—and this of course includes the "standards" applicable to enrollment—were administered not by tribal members, but by agents of the U.S. Interior Department's office of internal colonialism, the Bureau of Indian Affairs (BIA).[8] Moreover, it it completely glosses over the fact that in numerous instances—at Hopi, for example, and throughout the Sioux reservation complex—the polling was quite literally permeated with fraud (large numbers of dead people voting, abstentions counted as "aye" votes, and so on).[9]

To say, as I often have and will continue to do, that under such conditions the rules and structures attending the IRA were imposed over the strenuous objections of Indians—and thus constitute an egregious usurpation of indigenous sovereignty—is to say nothing that hasn't been said by a wide range of other commentators, from Oliver LaFarge, Rupert Costo, and Robert K. Thomas to Russell Means, Jeanette Henry, and Tim Coulter.[10] If I'm somehow "anti-tribe" because of my opposition to IRA governments, as LaVelle insists, then it follows that each of these six individuals must be as well, along with traditional leaders like the late Frank Fools Crow, Oren Lyons, Phillip Deere, and Thomas Banyacya, not to mention the entire membership of the American Indian Movement (AIM) circa 1972–73.[11]

LaVelle's subterfuge in seeking to discredit me as "anti-tribal" because of my criticism of existing reservation governments is hardly a new or novel propaganda technique. It is essentially the same as that employed by publicists of the Capone-era administration of Big Bill Thompson in Chicago, branding as "anti-Chicagoan" anyone who came out against the blatant corruption then flourishing in city government.[12] Nor is it different in either approach or intent from Parnell Thomas' and Joe McCarthy's campaigns to blacklist those critical of U.S. policy as "Un-Americans" during the 1940s and '50s.[13] The most accurate comparison, however— since we are dealing here with a situation in which one country has occupied and imposed its preferred mode of governance on others—would be to smearing Charles De Gaulle and Jean-Paul Sartre as "anti-French" because of their opposition to the collaborationist Vichy government installed by Germany in their homeland during the Second World War.[14]

The nazis, to be sure, were not shy about offering exactly such characterizations of the French resistance, nor were clients like Pierre Laval in the Vichy régime.[15] This same occupier/collaborator propaganda scheme was followed with some precision by the Nixon administration when, in the immediate aftermath of the Trail of Broken Treaties, it funded the appearance in Washington, DC, of a bevy of its IRA puppets to denounce Trail participants.[16] Leading this spectacle was Webster Two Hawk, head of the federally sponsored National Tribal Chairmen's Association (NTCA), who—resplendently attired in "an Indian suit that could only have come from a costume shop," his "close-cropped crew cut" covered by a turkey feather headdress—went on national television to contend that the Trail's leadership was "unrepresentative of Indian interests" and possessed "no constituency among Indian people."[17]

The validity of Two Hawk's much-publicized tirade is perhaps best judged by the fact that he was promptly unseated as Rosebud Sioux Tribal Chair by no less than the late Robert Burnette, a major Trail organizer and endorser of the Twenty-Point Program.[18] Thereafter, the vanquished "spokesman" slunk away to the American Indian Studies Program at that great bastion of indigenous rights activism, the University of South Dakota at Vermillion—possibly the only sizable institution of higher learning in the U.S. where no prominent AIM representative or other such "militant" was invited to speak during the 1970s and '80s—while the Nixonites and subsequent administrations continued to trumpet his paid pronouncements as if they were emblematic sentiments of a "legitimate" and "responsible" Indian leader.[19]

Blaming the Victims

Since a brief stint as a fellow at Two Hawk's home institution seems to provide the sole basis for John LaVelle's academic pretensions, it's unsurprising to find him quite comfortably treading in his mentor's federally funded ideological footsteps. Actually, he goes well beyond anything overtly attempted by Webster Two Hawk, or even Richard Nixon. Not content simply to follow their lead in substituting the federally devised and imposed IRA structure for Indian peoples themselves, he sets about taking the U.S. off the hook with respect to the methods and motives it evidenced while constructing tribal rolls after passage of the 1887 General Allotment Act.

This is done when, in an effort to discredit my observation that the blood quantum mode of Indian identification came into general usage as a result of the Dawes Act, as the allotment statute was also called, LaVelle makes the preposterous assertion that the criteria employed in determining eligibility for tribal enrollment, and thence to be allotted an individual land parcel, were simply "the laws and usages of the tribe."[20] This would undoubtedly come as a great surprise to the Act's framers, since a main purpose of allotment—its "civilizing mission," as it were— was specifically to negate these very laws and usages.[21] At another level, of course, it was expressly designed to create an appearance that much acreage within reservations was "surplus," thereby casting a legalistic veneer of propriety over the wholesale expropriation of native property. In order for the scheme to work, it was plainly necessary to low-count Indians to the extent possible, thereby minimizing the acreage bound up in their allotments.[22]

It is true, as LaVelle points out, that the Dawes Act itself contains no language defining the criteria for tribal enrollment, and that the regulatory language through which it was implemented is vague on this point. All this suggests, however, is that details of implementation such as enrollment criteria were delegated to federal agents presiding directly over each reservation.[23] These BIA employees were men who not only by and large subscribed to the more virulent doctrines of nineteenth-century scientific racism, but, as Vine Deloria Jr. and others have observed, exercised "near-dictatorial powers" through which to actualize their fantasies within their "quasi-feudal" domains.[24]

Even a most cursory examination of the manner in which the agents compiled tribal rolls after 1887 reveals a pervasive reliance upon half-blood quantum as a minimum standard of "racial" eligibility,[25] beyond which a range of other exclusionary rules were imposed (e.g., Cherokees who happened to reside in Arkansas, Missouri, Kansas, or Texas, rather than Oklahoma, were deemed ineligible, regardless of quantum).[26] Tribal membership was thus radically circumscribed, with the entirely predictable—indeed, predicted—result that native societies underwent a considerable acceleration in the process of fragmentation they were already suffering while approximately two-thirds of their aggregate landholdings "passed" into non-Indian hands.[27] Small wonder that in his 1901 Message to Congress, president Theodore Roosevelt described allotment as "a mighty pulverizing engine for breaking up the tribal mass."[28]

In LaVelle's rendering, there is none of this. Instead, we are expected to believe that typically interactive and inclusive indigenous peoples suddenly, en masse and of their own volition, reversed their traditions to demand of their hapless federal custodians that they be defined as arbitrarily and narrowly as possible, thereby reducing their own numbers to an absolute minimum, entrenching rampant factionalism and polarization as permanent facts of life within their once harmonious societies, and divesting themselves of some 86 million of their remaining 138 million acres of property into the bargain.[29] Unto me, giveth a break. This is neither scholarship, nor even common sense.

If it were meant as satire, LaVelle's altogether bizarre version of events might be seen as reinforcing a "Henny Youngblood" joke used by Oneida comic Charlie Hill to parody America's officially sanctioned historiography of conquest (Charlie always got laughs when he conjured the image of a smiling Indian greeting the invaders with the words, "Hey, thanks for coming. Here's my land. Take it, *please!*"). In the alternative, barring some incredible degree of ignorance which is not evident in his writing, LaVelle's deliberately distortive treatment of both fact and logic should be seen as propaganda of the most perniciously colonialist sort, a perfect complement to/extension of the Nixonian response to the Trail of Broken Treaties' assertion of indigenous rights.

Confirmation that this last is the case comes almost immediately, when, having carefully shifted blame for their victimization squarely onto Indians themselves, the author uses his invented scenario not just to absolve the U.S. of usurping native sovereignty in creating the Dawes Rolls, but to present the thrust of federal Indian identification policy in its virtual entirety as affirming rather than denying indigenous self-determination. In LaVelle's telling, "nearly all federal legislation in both historical and modern times . . . defers to tribal membership as the core criterion" in determining native identity.[30]

This formulation, with its casual merger of the federal postures evident before and after allotment, is truly worthy of Orwell (or Joseph Goebbels). No hint is offered of the tremendous difference between the implications of such federal deference in, say, 1820—when most indigenous peoples still functioned as autonomous nations—and 1890, after they had been thoroughly subordinated to the jurisdictional assertions of the United States.[31] In the latter context, to say that U.S. law "defers" to the criteria of tribal membership is only to say that it defers to itself, since indigenous laws and usages had been thoroughly supplanted, not just by the Allotment Act, but by the Major Crimes Act and a battery of other statutes and regulations).[32] It alters this fundamental equation not one whit that Indians themselves were later made responsible for enforcing federal identity criteria when the BIA codified it as an integral component of the lengthy series of "tribal constitutions and bylaws" imposed under the IRA.[33]

Other Distortions

The remainder of LaVelle's "critique" is delivered with a comparable degree of intellectual dishonesty. He accuses me, for instance, of the "considerable impropriety" of reprinting two public documents—"Alert Concerning the Abuse and Exploitation of Lakota Sacred Traditions" and "Declaration of War Against Exploiters of Lakota Spirituality"—both of which he claims to have drafted, without obtaining an okay from his Center for the SPIRIT in San Francisco.[34] Putting aside the facts that permission is hardly needed to disseminate materials expressly released for such purposes (reprinting constitutes a service in this connection), and that the "Declaration" was issued in the name of the Lakota/Nakota/Dakota people rather than the Center, there is something else left conspicuously unmentioned in LaVelle's account.

This is a note, prominently displayed at the conclusion of my reprinting of the "Alert," stating that the 1993 Center document is little more than an awkward paraphrase of my own essay, "Spiritual Hucksterism: The Rise of the Plastic Medicine Men," published in Z Magazine in 1990 and collected in my Fantasies of the Master Race in 1992 (earlier published versions date back as far as 1983).[35] In effect, LaVelle first seeks to claim credit for the content of my work—a habit which may go along way toward explaining his avid defense of fellow plagiarist Jack Weatherford[36]—and then exhibits the breathtaking audacity to publicly accuse me of "impropriety" for not having sought his permission to use it.

Meanwhile, having managed to "overlook" an entire block of text as important but personally inconvenient as the note, LaVelle spends nearly a full page belaboring my supposed removal of a single word from the text of the "Declaration." In fact, no such deletion occurred. The iteration of the document which was hurriedly faxed to me for the express purpose of my including it in Indians Are Us? (in press at the time)—apparently the Lakota elders were as unaware as I that they needed anyone's permission to disseminate their own document in whatever manner they saw fit—reads exactly as it appears in my book.[37] In any case, insertion of the word "imitation" before the word "tribe" is actually redundant, given that the latter word appears in quotes in all versions of the text, my own included. So much for the imagined implications of my alleged deletion: the phrasing means precisely the same thing, either way.

Another serious misrepresentation is embodied in LaVelle's allegation that I engage in "scurrilous name-calling" with regard to "prominent, widely respected . . . Indian rights activists and grassroots community organizers [like] American Indian Movement leaders Vernon

Bellecourt, Carole Standing Elk, and Fern Mathias."[38] In reality, none of these individuals are AIM members, much less leaders. Rather, they are board members of an entity called National American Indian Movement, Inc., a federally/corporately funded and Minnesota-chartered nonprofit corporation, the constituency of which may be measured by the fact that the location of its annual membership meeting is listed as being Vernon Bellecourt's living room.[39] Bellecourt himself, along with his brother Clyde, was permanently banished from AIM by an internally constituted tribunal of movement veterans in October 1994.[40]

Finally, there is the matter of how LaVelle seeks to finesse my analysis of the implications, legal and otherwise, of the federal government's semantic demotion of indigenous peoples from status as "nations" to that of "tribes" during the nineteenth century.[41] He offers up my opposition to this nomenclatural transformation as a sort of final proof of my supposed "antitribalism," a euphemism by which it should by now be clear he means to impart a sense of my being literally anti-Indian. Here again, he presents his case by resorting to the most tedious sort of obfuscation, going on at length about how I might have been equally offended by the connotations embodied in dictionary definitions of other words— "family" and "community," for instance—by which groups of Indians are conventionally described.

This, again, is technically true but utterly irrelevant since it ignores completely the facts that, unlike "tribe," terms like "family" and "community" have never been reserved exclusively for application to native peoples and are not used to convey impressions of "primitivism" or inferiority.[42] Nor, unlike "nation," do they correspond to a particular legal standing or evidence an historical shift in official usage. Moreover, LaVelle's argument begs entirely—and is perhaps intended to divert attention away from—the very serious topical question of why, if such issues were as trivial as he would have his readers believe, the UN delegates of both the United States and Canada have spent the past decade and more bitterly opposing international legal characterizations of indigenous peoples as *peoples* rather than as "populations."[43]

In the Spirit of Gunga Din
The first line of defense of any refined system of colonialism will never be found among the guns of the colonizers. Rather, it devolves upon its ability to proceed from a foundation of mere physical oppression to attainment of a matrix of domination over the consciousness of the colonized, confusing and thereby co-opting them into active collusion in

reinforcing the order of their own colonization. As anticolonial theorist Albert Memmi once observed in this connection:

> In order for the colonizer to be a complete master, it is not enough for him to be so in actual fact, but he must also believe in [the colonial system's] legitimacy. In order for that to be complete, it is not enough for the colonized to be a slave, he must also accept his role. The bond between colonizer and colonized is thus destructive and creative. It destroys and recreates the two partners in colonization into colonizer and colonized. One is disfigured into an oppressor, a partial, unpatriotic and treacherous being, worrying only about his privileges and their defense; the other, into an oppressed creature, whose development is broken and who compromises by his defeat.[44]

At issue is not the vulgar straw man of "conspiracy" between colonizer and colonized John LaVelle falsely attributes to my analysis in order to have something to rebut. The reality is that of a far deeper and more ubiquitous dynamic of psychointellectual domination and subordination long since illuminated by Memmi, Frantz Fanon, and their counterparts.[45] Or, to borrow a term from Antonio Gramsci, it goes to the construction of an ever more sophisticated and self-perpetuating imperial hegemony,[46] a process of systemically reinforcing the falsification in which LaVelle himself apparently longs to play some prideful part.

In the netherworld of disunderstanding thus deliberately created, lies, officially ordained and repeated often enough, take on the aura, first of "opinions," then of truth itself. Truth, subjected to continual and concerted denial, is diminished to the level of just another "point of view" before being dismissed as outright falsehood.[47] Eventually the structures of oppression are perceived as modes of liberation, capitulation as resistance, deculturation as tradition, degradation as honor and respect. Among native people, the symbolic descendants of those "good Indians" who pinned the arms of Crazy Horse while a soldier bayoneted him now lay claim to being the sole rightful heirs to his struggle, reviling as "irresponsible, self-styled renegades and revolutionaries" who "damage the cause of Indian people" the progeny of those who fought by his side.[48] Colonialism itself, its fact, form and function buried and forgotten under this growing mountain of prevarication, is thus embraced by the colonized as the essence of their sovereignty and self-determination, a matter relieving the colonizers of any requirement to defend the colonial order by resort to main force.

In 1892, Rudyard Kipling, that erstwhile literary lion of British imperialism, penned in epic verse a saga signifying the heart of the phenomenon at hand. This is the story of Gunga Din—proverbial archetype of all Good Indians—valued as such only by virtue of his willingness to sacrifice himself to save his colonizers from the liberatory wrath of his own people.[49] So it is with John LaVelle and his ilk, their pseudoscholarly noses thrust so long and so deeply into the colonial crevice that they have seemingly come to mistake the scent of excrement therein for that of roses. The putrefying polemics, rationalizations, and deformities of history they offer have nothing to with championing the rights of indigenous people. To the contrary, writing in the spirit of Gunga Din, they have everything to do with preserving and protecting the imperial status quo.

Postscript

Although the then-editor of *American Indian Quarterly*, Morris Foster, refused to publish my response, he apparently shared it with LaVelle. This prompted the latter to undertake a far more ambitious "debunking" of my observations concerning the BIA's imposition of a half-blood quantum standard for purposes of allotment pursuant to the 1887 Act, and the effects of this procedure in terms of American Indian land loss. While I'd never discussed the matter in any depth—my most extensive elaboration totaled three paragraphs[50]—LaVelle's new piece, titled "The General Allotment Act 'Eligibility' Hoax" and published in 1999, encumbered 51 oversized pages (including 111 endnotes).[51] This time, I didn't bother to formulate a response, and LaVelle's grand critique was to all appearances simply ignored.[52]

　　This changed rather abruptly in early 2005, when University of Colorado (UC) administrators, hoping to establish a legally defensible pretext for firing me, set about conjuring up the appearance that I'd engaged in scholarly fraud ("research misconduct," in the official vernacular).[53] David Getches, the now-deceased dean of the UC law school and part of a three-member ad hoc committee fielded by acting chancellor Phil DiStefano to find something upon which the desired charges might be predicated, recalled that LaVelle had given him a copy of his 1999 article shortly after its publication, verbally expressing considerable personal hostility toward me as he did so.[54] By his own account, Getches never deigned to read LaVelle's screed, but, sensing that it might prove useful in the context at hand, he phoned its author and requested a fresh copy.[55]

The actual purpose of this rather peculiar procedure—there was no need for Getches to call LaVelle to obtain the article, since it was readily available online—was for the dean to enlist LaVelle's services in soliciting others to lodge complaints about my work.[56] In any case, DiStefano shortly filed several allegations against me with the administration's Standing Committee on Research Misconduct (SCRM, pronounced "scrum"), one of which—that I'd "misrepresented a federal statute," to wit, the 1887 General Allotment Act—was based entirely on the contentions advanced in LaVelle's material.[57] Charges in hand, the SCRM assembled a special investigating committee, ostensibly composed of experts in each of the subject matters involved, to determine their validity and issue a report on their findings.

Procedurally, as has elsewhere been thoroughly detailed, the investigation was a farce from the outset.[58] The investigating committee, moreover, advanced such contrafactual arguments in finding me culpable with respect to virtually every charge in its final report that the members were themselves the target of several formal research misconduct complaints, a turn of events that forced the SCRM to hurriedly immunize them on grounds that they'd produced was an "administrative work product" rather than "a work of scholarship."[59] In this regard, LaVelle's assertions concerning my supposed misrepresentation of the 1887 Act proved especially problematic since even the administration's handpicked expert on federal Indian law—Arizona State University law professor Robert N. Clinton, hardly a flaming radical and certainly no friend of mine—found himself in the awkward position of being rather embarrassed by them.

Indeed, Clinton *began* his analysis by observing that, "The general thrust of Professor Churchill's underlying basic point (seemingly and surprisingly rejected by Professor LaVelle) is that late nineteenth-century racism by federal officials in implementing the General Allotment Act of 1887, rather than traditional Indian cultural practices based on community membership, better accounts for the predominance of current blood quantum requirements in tribal membership. That argument certainly has a firm historical basis."[60]

> Implementation of the *policy* of the General Allotment Act of 1887 clearly limited tribal eligibility for allotments to those of Indian blood. . . . Thus, [while] it was not literally the General Allotment Act of 1887 that *required* Indian blood as a precondition for allotment . . . that requirement constituted the general assumptions among federal legislative and executive officials in the late

nineteenth-century regarding who constituted an Indian [and] federal officials often refused to follow tribal definitions of their identity [emphasis in original].[61]

In Clinton's carefully understated estimation, "there is more truth to . . . Churchill's claim than Professor LaVelle is prepared to credit," that I'd certainly perpetrated "no general hoax of the type suggested by some of Professor LaVelle's broader claims, since the core of [Churchill's] point . . . is correct, or clearly arguable." In sum, "Churchill may have the stronger side of the debate with Professor LaVelle as to the origins of the blood quantum requirement in tribal membership rolls" because "Churchill is . . . more correct than Professor LaVelle in suggesting, as he does, that the requirement of Indian blood began with *federally-imposed* definitions of Indian status [emphasis in original]."[62]

Having thus dispensed with the reputational liability attending association with LaVelle's "scholarship," Clinton of course undertook to build his own case against me, primarily by denying the validity of my methodological approach to legal/historical interpretation.[63] His effort to discredit my three paragraphs on the 1887 Act spanned fourteen single-spaced pages but ultimately fared no better than LaVelle's. In May 2007, the UC faculty senate's Committee on Privilege and Tenure (P&T), after an extensive review, dismissed as unsustainable Clinton's findings that I'd transgressed scholarly propriety in the matter, and again in my depiction of the 1990 Indian Arts and Crafts Act.[64] UC President Hank Brown, hired for the explicit purpose of ridding the university of its highly politicized "Ward Churchill problem,"[65] quickly overrode the faculty by unilaterally reinstating both findings, which were then cited by the board of regents as part of its justification for firing me in July.[66]

This triggered a lawsuit on my part, the result of which was a four-week trial in March 2009 culminating in a verdict wherein the jurors unanimously concluded that the university, its experts subject to genuine cross-examination for the first time, had failed to show that I'd committed *any* of the scholarly offenses imputed to me by Clinton and his colleagues on the administration's investigating committee.[67] The university was saved from having to restore my professorship only by the unprecedented ruling of the trial judge, Larry Naves—a graduate of the UC law school which shortly thereafter bestowed upon him its highest alumnus service award—that the regents enjoy "quasi-judicial immunity" from liability in personnel matters, no matter how flagrant the constitutional violations embodied in their actions.[68]

This really did nothing to salvage Clinton's situation, however. In November 2011 the Colorado Council of the American Association of University Professors (AAUP) released a 136-page report setting forth the results of an exhaustive two-year investigation of my case. Therein, Clinton's various claims regarding my characterization of the 1887 Act were dismantled—"shredded" might be a better word—point by point, and he himself was shown to have indulged in a range of misrepresentations and outright fabrications.[69] These included his handling of the 1846 *Rogers* case,[70] as well as his assertions that "there was *never* a half-blood quantum requirement for eligibility for an allotment [emphasis in original],"[71] and that I'd falsely portrayed blood quantum requirements as a "eugenics code."[72] As concerns the latter:

> The final detail that Churchill got wrong, according to [Clinton], is his reference to [blood quantum standards] as a "eugenics code." In an expansive essay on his prosecution by the University of Colorado in the academic journal *Works and Days*, Churchill argues that Clinton, in claiming that [blood quantum] was not a eugenics code and finding Churchill factually incorrect for claiming that it *was*, offers no citation to support his assertion, is "contradicted by the standard literature on eugenics," and confuses the subset "negative eugenics." Churchill's opinion here cannot be seen as entirely disinterested, but Paul Lombardo, a law professor at Georgia State University and an expert on the history of eugenics, made the same point even more strongly in his testimony at the trial. Noting that no member of the I[nvestigating] C[ommittee] could be considered professionally knowledgeable about eugenics, Lombardo testified that, "[T]he definition [Clinton] gave was extremely limited. . . . It was focused in a way that excluded whole bodies of work," including, Lombardo added, his own.[73]

Cumulatively, such manipulations of the available data to arrive at a predetermined result were so consistent that the AAUP investigators were led to conclude that Clinton's behavior—which they describe as "intellectually dishonest"[74]—was more likely motivated by ideological than scholarly considerations.

> In our analysis of [the] portion of the IC Report attributed to Robert Clinton, we have made the case that Clinton, an eminent legal scholar, has disregarded or dismissed as irrational a methodology that, one must assume, he is aware is widely considered to be

reputable; that he has, according to other legal experts, confused legal code with case law; and that he has pretended to have an expertise in eugenics that he does not possess. . . . [T]he reason may be that . . . scholars in federal Indian law such as Clinton are uncomfortable with AIS scholars such as Churchill who apply critical race theory, the philosophy that interprets events through the lens of racism that provides much of the foundation for the field of American Indian Studies.[75]

Bob Clinton is far too senior, his status as a preeminent rationalizer of U.S. colonial law too valued by the status quo, for exposure of his fraudulent scholarship in the IC Report to have any more effect on his career than did publication of Norman Finkelstein's conclusive evidence of Harvard legal luminary *cum* zionist propagandist Alan Dershowitz's wanton plagiarism in his *The Case for Israel* of Joan Peters' *From Time Immemorial*,[76] Jon Weiner's detailed exploration of the myriad fabrications embedded in Georgetown historian Allen Weinstein's *Perjury* and *The Haunted Wood*,[77] or Noam Chomsky's demonstration of how Yale's John Lewis Gaddis, veritable dean of the right's Cold War historians, had systematically and often grossly misrepresented the sources cited in his *Surprise, Security, and the American Experience*,[78] on theirs. Which is to say, none at all. Or at least none of an adverse variety. Especially in Weinstein's case, the very opposite was true.[79]

But, what of Gunga Din himself, John LaVelle? He can hardly be seen as playing in the same league as those just mentioned, and, as a matter of record, he stands accused of scholarly fraud, not only by Clinton, but Cornell University professor Eric Cheyfitz, an acknowledged authority on the history of federal Indian law,[80] and others as well.[81] One might reasonably expect this to have sounded the professional death knell of one with so gossamer a publication record that it, even were it untainted, is a source of mirth.[82] Quite the contrary, however: LaVelle was promoted by the University of New Mexico law school even after his work was discredited and now "holds the title of Dickason Professor of Law and directs the Indian Law Program" at that backward bastion of "academic excellence."[83] Thus does the empire reward its spear-carriers.

Notes

1   John LaVelle, "Review Essay: Ward Churchill, *Indians Are Us? Culture and Genocide in Native North America*," *American Indian Quarterly*, Vol. 20, No. 1 (Winter 1996) pp. 109–18.

2   Editors, B.I.A., *I'm Not Your Indian Any More: Trail of Broken Treaties* (Mohawk Nation via Rooseveltown, NY: Akwesasne Notes, [3rd ed., rev.] 1976) p. 76.

3   The best account of the drafting of the Twenty-Point Program will be found in Vine Deloria Jr., *Behind the Trail of Broken Treaties: An Indian Declaration of Independence* (Austin: University of Texas Press, [2nd ed., rev.] 1984) pp. 48–53. For the full text of the Twenty Points, as well as federal responses to each point, see B.I.A., *I'm Not Your Indian Any More*, pp. 63–90.

4   In actuality, it's LaVelle who distorts Limerick's position. She uses the 1986 Reagan initiative to illustrate the broader sweep of federal Indian identification policy—and why it has always been antithetical to native interests—taking as a hopeful sign the willingness of at least some indigenous leaders to take a position repudiating rather than internalizing the legitimacy of blood quantum as a method of defining "Indianness." See Patricia Nelson Limerick, *The Legacy of Conquest: The Unbroken Past of the American West* (New York: W.W. Norton, 1987) p. 338. For strong articulations of the perspective she finds constructive, see Charles E. Dawes, "Tribal leaders see danger in use of blood quantum as eligibility standard," *Uset Calumet* (February–March 1986); Ron Martz, "Indians decry verification plan for federally-funded health care," *Cox News Service* (October 26, 1986).

5   Compare Thornton's assessment of the demographic implications of the non-quantum-based enrollment criteria developed by the Cherokee Nation of Oklahoma, to that attending maintenance of what I call "purely racial definitions." Plainly, his optimism is confined to the former. See Russell Thornton, *American Indian Holocaust and Survival: A Population History Since 1492* (Norman: University of Oklahoma Press, 1987) pp. 180, 199–200, 174–75, 236–37, 239.

6   Jack D. Forbes, "Undercounting Native Americans: The 1980 Census and Manipulation of Racial Identity in the United States," *Wicazo Sa Review*, Vol. VI, No. 1 (Spring 1990) pp. 2–26; Lenore Stiffarm and Phil Lane Jr., "The Demography of Native North America: A Question of American Indian Survival," in M. Annette Jaimes, ed., *The State of Native America: Genocide, Colonization and Resistance* (Boston: South End Press, 1992) pp. 40–46.

7   B.I.A., *I'm Not Your Indian Any More*, p. 76.

8   These facts are confirmed by virtually all analysts and commentators, including those rather favorably disposed to the IRA, e.g.: Vine Deloria Jr. and Clifford M. Lytle, *The Nations Within: The Past and Future of American Indian Sovereignty* (New York: Pantheon, 1984). With respect to the applicability of the term "internal colonialism" to the situation of American Indians, see Robert K. Thomas, "Colonialism: Classic and Internal," *New University Thought*, Vol. IV, No. 4 (Winter 1966–67) pp. 44–53; collected under the title "On an Indian Reservation: How Colonialism Works" in Shirley Hill Witt and Stan Steiner, eds., *The Way: An Anthology of American Indian Literature* (New York: Alfred A. Knopf, 1972) pp. 60–68.

9   On Hopi, see Charles Lummis, *Bullying the Hopi* (Prescott, AZ: Prescott College Press, 1968). On the Sioux complex, see Thomas Biolosi, *Organizing the Lakota: The Political Economy of the New Deal on the Pine Ridge and Rosebud Reservations* (Tucson: University of Arizona Press, 1992) esp. p. 78.

10   A good sampling of such opinion will be found in Kenneth R. Philp, ed., *Indian Self-Rule: First-Hand Accounts of Indian-White Relations from Roosevelt to Reagan* (Salt Lake City: Howe Brothers, 1986).

11   Deposing the IRA régime on Pine Ridge and restoring the traditional form of Oglala governance was a stated objective of grassroots reservation residents and their AIM

supporters at Wounded Knee in 1973. This was why Fools Crow, principal leader of the traditional Oglalas, proclaimed the reestablishment of an "Independent Oglala Nation" (ION) within the siege zone. Regarding the distinction to be drawn between the federally-created IRA government's reliance upon blood quantum as a determining criterion for tribal membership, and traditional (sovereign) Oglala practice in this regard, it should be noted that one of Fools Crow's first acts after announcing formation of the ION was to naturalize as full citizens seven white members of Vietnam Veterans Against the War who were assisting in the armed defense of Wounded Knee. See Rex Weyler, *Blood of the Land: The Government and Corporate War Against the American Indian Movement* (New York: Everest House, 1982) p. 83.

12 A really good examination of Thompsonite methods can be found in Lloyd Lewis and Henry Justin Smith, *Chicago: The History of Its Reputation* (New York: Harcourt, Brace, 1929). Also see John Kobler, *Capone: The Life and World of Al Capone* (New York: G.P. Putnam's Sons, 1971).

13 This is exhaustively detailed in David Caute's *The Great Fear: The Anti-Communist Purge Under Truman and Eisenhower* (New York: Simon and Schuster, 1978).

14 For background, see Robert Smith Thompson, *Pledge to Destiny: Charles De Gaulle and the Rise of the Free French* (New York: McGraw-Hill, 1974) and H.R. Kedward, *Resistance in Vichy France: A Study of Ideas and Motivations* (New York: Oxford University Press, 1978).

15 See generally Geoffrey Warner, *Pierre Laval and the Eclipse of France* (London: Macmillan, 1968).

16 For a selection of excerpts from the statements of tribal chairmen see B.I.A., *I'm Not Your Indian Any More*, pp. 22–24; on federal subsidy, see pp. 32–33. The implications of NTCA's performance were explained by Vine Deloria months before its press conference: "Already people suspected [the IRA chairmen] were tools of the BIA; this would be confirmed" by their denunciation of the Trail and its Twenty-Point Program. Quoted in Paul Chaat Smith and Robert Allen Warrior, *Like a Hurricane: The American Indian Movement from Alcatraz to Wounded Knee* (New York: New Press, 1996) p. 125. LaVelle apparently never got the message that the IRA structure of governance he tries to present as being synonymous with indigenous interests openly revealed itself as the opposite nearly a quarter-century ago.

17 Two Hawk, prefiguring LaVelle, also argued that the Twenty-Point Trail of Broken Treaties program would lead unerringly to an "undermining and breakdown of authority of the duly elected representatives of the various tribes," by which he meant the IRA régimes. In sum, the IRA form of governance was/is, even in Two Hawk's estimation, utterly incompatible with any genuine assertion of indigenous rights to self-determination. For the quote, see B.I.A., *I'm Not Your Indian Any More*, p. 32. For further background on Two Hawk, including the "monstrous parody" of his parading about in a "warbonnet," see Robert Burnette and John Koster, *The Road to Wounded Knee* (New York: Bantam, 1974) pp. 174–76, 195–96, 217, 269–70.

18 Burnette and Koster, *Road to Wounded Knee*, p. 270.

19 Two Hawk moved to Vermillion to accept the university position and was thereafter barred from running for tribal president on grounds that he no longer resided on the reservation. See *Webster Two Hawk v. Rosebud Sioux Tribe* (534 F.2d 101, 1976). That no AIM representative was ever asked to speak at the University of South Dakota after Two Hawk joined its American Indian Studies faculty was confirmed by Russell Means during an interview conducted on October 17, 1993.

20   Having made a major issue of my not quoting specific statutory language to support
     my understanding of how the rolls were compiled, I may perhaps be forgiven for
     finding it a bit odd that LaVelle fails to provide any point of reference for his alterna-
     tive interpretation. This is the more curious in that he's anything but specific about
     which peoples' traditional laws and usages supposedly included blood quantum as a
     formal criteria of membership. Surely, he's not referring to the Cherokees, a nation
     in which whites had been naturalized as citizens for nearly two centuries; nor the
     Mohawks, who had incorporated more than their own number of non-Mohawks
     into their polity—virtually all of the surviving Wyandots and Susquehannocks,
     as examples—by 1700; nor the Seminoles, whose composition from the outset
     included large numbers—perhaps a quarter of their whole society—of escaped
     African chattel slaves; nor the Crows, whose history includes Jim Beckwith, a
     black man accepted as a tribal leader during the early nineteenth century; nor the
     Comanches, with the saga of Cynthia Ann Parker and others to their credit; nor
     the Cheyennes, as is witnessed by the Bent family and others; nor the Lakotas, nor
     the Ojibwes, nor the Choctaws, nor the Chickasaws, nor the Muscogees, nor any
     of a half a hundred other peoples who spring readily to mind. While a case might
     be made for a kind of quantum standard applying among the Havasupai, certain
     Pueblos, etc., these peoples were not subjected to allotment. Hence, it seems fair to
     observe that LaVelle's bald assertion—hewing as it does to the line of self-serving
     federal "interpretation"—is on its face a complete and utter falsehood. For further
     background, see my "The Crucible of American Indian Identity: Native Tradition
     versus Colonial Imposition in Postconquest North America," *American Indian Culture
     and Research Journal*, Vol. 23, No. 1 (Spring 1999) pp. 39–67.

21   This is the standard interpretation, even among rather staid and establishmentar-
     ian scholars. See, as examples, Henry E. Fritz, *The Movement for Indian Assimilation,
     1860–1890* (Philadelphia: University of Pennsylvania Press, 1963) and Francis Paul
     Prucha, *Americanizing the American Indian: Writings of the "Friends of the Indian," 1800–1900*
     (Lincoln: University of Nebraska Press, 1973).

22   As the law was constructed, each Indian recognized as such by the federal govern-
     ment on a given reservation would be allotted a land parcel averaging 160 acres in
     size. Once each individual had been allotted his/her parcel, the balance of the land
     within the reservation would be declared surplus and opened to non-Indian home-
     steading, assigned to corporate usage (e.g., railroads), or assigned to national park,
     forest or other designated federal trust usage. Obviously, the purpose of the Act was
     in no small part to strip away native property. Equally obviously, the fewer Indians
     recognized as such, the greater the quantity of property available to be taken. For
     analyses delivered with different ideological cants but nonetheless supporting this
     conclusion, see D.S. Otis, *The Dawes Act and the Allotment of Indian Land* (Norman:
     University of Oklahoma Press, 1973); Kirk Kicking Bird and Karen Ducheneaux,
     One Hundred Million Acres (New York: Macmillan, 1973); Wilcomb E. Washburn, *The
     Assault on Indian Tribalism: The General Allotment (Dawes) Act of 1887* (Philadelphia: J.B.
     Lippincott, 1975); and Janet A. McDonnell, *The Dispossession of the American Indian,
     1887–1934* (Bloomington: Indiana University Press, 1991).

23   This would be consistent with Section III of the Act, which specifies that "allotments
     will be made by special agents appointed by the President for such purpose, and
     the agents in charge of the respective reservations on which the allotments are to
     be made, under such rules and regulations as the Secretary of Interior may from
     time to time prescribe." The text of the Act is included in Washburn, *Assault on Indian*

Tribalism, pp. 68–73; language quoted at pp. 69–70. The question thus becomes what "rule" was applied by the agents in determining which persons would be defined as Indians for purposes of enrollment/allotment. In that regard, see note 25, below.

24   Vine Deloria Jr. and Clifford M. Lytle, *American Indians, American Justice* (Austin: University of Texas Press, 1983) p. 10; Sidney L. Herring, *Crow Dog's Case: American Sovereignty, Tribal Law, and United States Law in the Nineteenth Century* (Cambridge, MA: Cambridge University Press, 1994) p. 206. Another strong indication of the explicitly racial orientation of the law's implementation was the manner in which land patents were issued to allottees. Those enrolled as mixed-bloods were provided with patents in fee simple while those designated fullbloods were issued trust patents under the presumption, common among eugenicists, that they were genetically incompetent to manage their own affairs. Since he leaves such matters entirely unmentioned, we are left to conclude on the basis of the rest of his argument that LaVelle must believe the practice derived, not from white racism, but from that same mysteriously unnamed body of indigenous law and usage that generated reliance upon blood quantum criteria more generally. For a detailed study of the nature and effects of the policy at issue in a specific reservation context, see Melissa L. Meyer, *The White Earth Tragedy: Ethnicity and Dispossession at a Minnesota Anishinaabe Reservation, 1889–1920* (Lincoln: University of Nebraska Press, 1994).

25   The BIA was heavily influenced by the "racial sciences" during the late nineteenth century, especially that of ethnology, and its personnel undoubtedly subscribed to the idea that "to be considered an Indian for ethnological purposes"—which is to say, to be considered Indian at all—a person would have to be of at least one-half degree Indian blood. On the racial theories of Lewis Henry Morgan, generally considered to have been the leading light of American ethnology during the period leading up to passage of the Allotment Act, see Robert E. Bieder, *Science Encounters the Indian, 1820–1880: The Early Years of American Ethnology* (Norman: University of Oklahoma Press, 1986) pp. 219–35. On the influence of Morgan's protégé John Wesley Powell, director of the American Bureau of Ethnology, on the formulators of federal Indian policy and Interior Department (BIA) officials during the years in which the Act was passed and implemented, see Frederick E. Hoxie, *A Final Promise: The Campaign to Assimilate the Indians, 1880–1920* (Lincoln: University of Nebraska Press, 1984) pp. 24, 28–29. For the language quoted in relation to the ethnological definition of an Indian, see Rennard Strickland, ed., *Felix S. Cohen's Handbook on Federal Indian Law* (Charlottesville, VA: Michie, 1982) p. 19.

26   Cherokee land was allotted under the 1898 Curtis Act, a derivative of the 1887 statute. Resistance to enrollment, especially among members of the traditionalist Keetoowahs—the "Nighthawks" or "Redbird Smith Movement," as they were also known—was so strong that federal marshals had to be imported by the Dawes Commission to enforce an choice between enrollment and imprisonment. See Robert K. Thomas, "The Redbird Smith Movement," in W.N. Fenton and John Gulick, eds., *Bureau of American Ethnology No. 180: Symposium of Cherokee and Iroquois Cultures* (Washington, DC: Bureau of American Ethnology, 1961) pp. 161–71; Albert L. Wahrhaftig and Robert K. Thomas, "Renaissance and Repression: The Oklahoma Cherokee," *Trans-action*, Vol. 6, No. 4 (February 1969) pp. 42–48. More broadly, see William E. Unrau, *Mixed Bloods and Tribal Dissolution: Charles Curtis and the Quest for Indian Identity* (Lawrence: University Press of Kansas, 1989) esp. pp. 1–8, 122–37.

27   See McDonnell, *Dispossession of the American Indian*, p. 121.

28 Theodore Roosevelt, "First Annual Message" (December 3, 1901), in James Richardson, ed., *A Compilation of Materials and Papers of the Presidents*, 15 vols. (Washington, DC: Bureau of National Literature and Art, 1917) Vol. 6, p. 672; quoted in Wilcomb Washburn, *Red Man's Land/White Man's Law: A Study of the Past and Present Status of the American Indian* (New York: Scribner's, 1971) p. 145. Roosevelt's sound bite was consistent with the broader objectives embodied in the Act, as summarized by Indian Commissioner Thomas J. Morton in 1890: "It has become the settled policy of the Government to break up the reservations, destroy tribal relations, settle Indians upon their own homesteads, incorporate them into the national life, and deal with them not as nations, tribes, or bands, but as individual citizens [of the U.S.]." Quoted in Harold E. Fey and D'Arcy McNickle, *Indians and Other Americans: Two Ways of Life Meet* (New York: Harper Bros., 1959) p. 67. It will be noted that Morton's formulation was itself consistent with Raphaël Lemkin's description of policies that should be considered genocidal, when he coined the term "genocide" in 1944: "Genocide has two phases: one, destruction of the national pattern of the oppressed group; the other, the imposition of the national pattern of the oppressor. This imposition, in turn, may be made upon the oppressed population which is allowed to remain, or upon the territory alone, after removal of the population and colonization of the area by the oppressor's own nationals." Raphaël Lemkin, *Axis Rule in Occupied Europe: Laws of Occupation, Analysis of Government, Proposals for Redress* (Washington, DC: Carnegie Endowment for International Peace, 1944) p. 79.

29 The figures have often been rounded off to 100 million of 150 million acres. The loss was as stated herein, however, with "38 million acres of surplus land ceded after allotment, 22 million acres of surplus land opened to white settlement, 23 million acres of fee patented land lost, and 3.4 million acres of original and heirship allotments sold" under duress. McDonnell, *Dispossessing the American Indian*, p. 121. For use of the round numbers, see, e.g., Kicking Bird and Ducheneaux, *One Hundred Million Acres*. On the so-called heirship problem regarding allotments, see Washburn, *Red Man's Land/White Man's Law*, pp. 150–52.

30 The one example LaVelle cites, the 1990 Act for the Protection of American Indian Arts and Crafts, is ludicrous. So far from conformity with indigenous law and usage was this statute making it a federal offense for any artist not formally enrolled in a governmentally recognized "tribe" to identify him/herself as an Indian—or for their representatives to thus identify them—that one of its first effects was to force closure of the Cherokee National Museum in Tahlequah, Oklahoma. The reason was that many well-known and respected Cherokee artists—including Willard Stone, carver of the Great Seal of the Cherokee Nation—had always refused, as a matter of sovereign principle, to enroll (or otherwise allow the U.S. to dictate the terms of their identity). Cherokee Principal Chief Wilma Mankiller, who did not applaud the Act, was forced, in order to reopen the museum, to violate the express preferences of such Cherokee patriots by posthumously enrolling them. As it is, numerous living Cherokee artists who refuse to abandon their ancestral tradition of resistance to enrollment—Burt Seaborne and Jimmie Durham, for instance, as well as Murv Jacobs and Willard Stone's granddaughter, Jean Walker Rorex—are proscribed under pain of ten years incarceration in a federal prison from identifying themselves as who they are. See Donna Hales, "Tribe Touts Unregistered Artists," *Muskogee Daily Phoenix* (September 3, 1990); Lyn Nichols, "New Art Regulations Shut Down Muskogee Museum," *San Francisco Examiner* (December 3, 1990); James J. Kirkpatrick, "Government Playing the Indian Game" (1992 syndicated column

distributed in xerox form by the Thomas Jefferson Center, Charlottesville, VA); Gail K. Sheffield, *The Arbitrary Indian: The Indian Arts and Crafts Act of 1990* (Norman: University of Oklahoma Press, 1997) pp. 102–20.

31 For a brief but excellent excursus on this transition, see Vine Deloria Jr., "Self-Determination and the Concept of Sovereignty," in Roxanne Dunbar-Ortiz and Larry Emerson, eds., *Economic Development in American Indian Reservations* (Albuquerque: University of New Mexico Native American Studies Center, 1979) pp. 22–28.

32 This was also the period when, through its *Kagama* (118 U.S. 375 (1886)) and *Lone Wolf* (187 U.S. 553 (1903)) opinions, the U.S. Supreme Court was perfecting the rationale for asserting federal "plenary power"—that is, absolute and unchallengeable authority—over every aspect of indigenous life. For analysis, see Sidney L. Harring, *Crow Dog's Case: American Indian Sovereignty, Tribal Law, and United States Law in the Nineteenth Century* (Cambridge, UK: Cambridge University Press, 1994) pp. 134–74; Blue Clark, *Lone Wolf v. Hitchcock: Treaty Rights and Indian Law at the End of the Nineteenth Century* (Lincoln: University of Nebraska Press, 1994) esp. pp. 71–72, 95–111. Also see Irene K. Harvey, "Congressional Plenary Power Over American Indian Affairs—A Doctrine Rooted in Prejudice," *American Indian Law Review*, No. 10 (1982) pp. 117–50; Ann Laquer Estin, "*Lone Wolf v. Hitchcock*: The Long Shadow," in Susan L. Cadwalader and Vine Deloria Jr., eds., *The Aggressions of Civilization: Federal Indian Policy Since the 1880s* (Philadelphia: Temple University Press, 1984) pp. 215–45.

33 The crystallization of this sort of statutory subterfuge came with passage of the Indian Self-Determination and Educational Assistance Act in 1975 (P.L. 93–638; 88 Stat. 2203, codified at 25 U.S.C. 450a, and elsewhere in Titles 25, 42 and 50, U.S.C.A.). Therein, the international legal definition of self-determination—in which colonized peoples exercise the unconstrained right to choose for themselves the nature of their political destinies—is subverted to signify the reverse of itself: a hiring preference extended to Indians in implementing policies and programs promulgated by the federal government. Far from embodying the principle of self-determination, the U.S. law reflects the standard administrative practice of colonial régimes everywhere. While myriad examples might be offered, that of the British Raj seems in some ways especially instructive. See Thomas R. Metcalf, *The New Cambridge History of India*, Vol. III.4: *Ideologies of the Raj* (Cambridge, UK: Cambridge University Press, 1995) esp. pp. 113–59.

34 "As co-founder and executive director of Center for the SPIRIT, I assumed the responsibility of drafting in their entirety both of [sic] the 'Declaration of War' and the 'Alert'. . . . Ward Churchill neither requested nor was granted Center for the SPIRIT's permission to reprint either the 'Declaration of War' or the 'Alert.'" LaVelle, "Review Essay," p. 114.

35 "Editor's Note: The thematics and much of the terminology in this alert are taken directly from Ward Churchill's 'Spirit Hucksterism: The Rise of the Plastic Medicine Men,' in his *Fantasies of the Master Race: Literature, Cinema, and the Colonization of American Indians* (Monroe, ME: Common Courage Press, 1992, pp. 215–22). The essay also appeared in *Z Magazine* [Vol. 3, No. 12] in December 1990" at pp. 94–98." *Indians Are Us?*, p. 281. Actually, the initial version of the piece was published in Denver's now defunct *Camp Crier* during the summer of 1983. I've long since mislaid my file copy of the relevant issue and thus cannot provide a proper citation. I can say, however, that in addition to what's mentioned in the "Editor's Note," the *Z Magazine* iteration was reprinted in *Indigenous Thought*, Vol. 1, Nos. 2–3 (1991).

36   LaVelle takes particular exception to my "'P' is for Plagiarism: A Closer Look at Jack
      Weatherford's *Indian Givers*," at pp. 167–72 of *Indians Are Us?*, which he summarily
      denounces as an "outlandish raid on [Weatherford's] reputation." Quite apart from
      the fact that I pointed out exactly how and where in his celebrated *Indian Givers: How
      the Indians of the Americas Transformed the World* (New York: Crown, 1988) Weatherford
      lifted material without attribution from the late Warren Lowes' unfinished, post-
      humously published, and relatively unknown *Indian Giver: A Legacy of North American
      Native Peoples* (Penticton, BC: Canadian Alliance in Solidarity with Native Peoples/
      Theytus Books, 1986), it should be noted that I've been publicly thanked by Theytus
      for having brought the matter to light. Since Theytus is one of the very few genu-
      inely native publishing houses in North America, LaVelle's reflexive alignment with
      Weatherford speaks volumes.

37   Copies on file.

38   Concerning the matter of respect, always a subjective consideration, the extent to
      which it may rightly be said to inhere among the group at issue might be perhaps
      best assessed in view of LaVelle associate Carole Standing Elk's remarkable record
      as self-proclaimed "head of the [racial] purity police" in the San Francisco Bay Area.
      During the single twelve-month period leading up to publication of *Indians Are Us?*
      she managed, among other singular accomplishments, to get herself evicted from
      Fools Crow's Sun Dance on Pine Ridge, legally enjoined from setting foot on the
      San Francisco State University campus by that institution's Native American Studies
      Program, barred from attending Parent Committee meetings of the San Francisco
      Public School District's Title-V Indian Education Program, and to disrupt virtu-
      ally every event or activity—from pow-wows, protests, and fundraisers to radio
      programming, shelters for the homeless, and AIDS counseling—undertaken in
      any quarter of the local Indian community over which she lacked direct control. A
      certain kind of notoriety ("prominence"?) undoubtedly attends such antics, but
      respect is—or certainly should be—another matter entirely. To describe such behav-
      ior as either "leadership" or "grassroots organizing" is at best absurd. My knowl-
      edge on this score derives in part from personal experiences with/observations of
      Standing Elk's behavior, in part from discussions of the situation with Betty Parent,
      director of the Native American Studies Program at San Francisco State, Bobby
      Castillo and George Martin of San Francisco's Autonomous AIM chapter, and a
      number of others.

39   According to its year-end report for 1993 (copy on file), the Minneapolis-based
      "National AIM, Inc." received approximately $4 million in federal and $3.3 million
      in corporate subsidies during that single year. Suffice it to say that AIM is *supposed*
      to be a liberation movement, and it is a given that neither the government nor
      Honeywell underwrites such endeavors. Hence, the "National AIM" clique, while
      still calling itself AIM, has obviously become something else altogether. No less
      obviously, it has done so in exchange for a regularized cash flow. I'm not sure what
      criteria LaVelle uses to define "sell-out," but such behavior certainly figures in mine.
      An interesting question in this connection might be the source of the funding with
      which LaVelle runs his own Center for the SPIRIT. For further background, see Bob
      Robideau, "An Open Letter to Paul DeMain," *Dark Night field notes* (Summer 1994;
      currently available at http://archive.is/bmDu).

40   The tribunal was convened first in San Rafael, California, in March 1994, and again
      in Rapid City, South Dakota, in October. For by far the most comprehensive back-
      ground/treatment of the evidence presented, see Faith Attaguile, "Why Do You Think

We Call It Struggle? An Essay on the Subversion of the American Indian Movement"
(currently available at http://kersplebedeb.com/posts/churchill_struggle-2/). Also
see Final Opinion and Statement of the Tribunal Panel, *Autonomous Chapters of AIM v.
Vernon and Clyde Bellecourt,* November 4, 1994 (reprinted in Barbara Nixon, *Mi' Taku'Ye-
Oyasin: Letters from Wounded Knee* [Bloomington, IN: Xlibris, 2012] pp. 456–61).

41   It might be noted that the essay in question, "Naming Our Destiny: Towards a
      Language of American Indian Liberation," which appears in *Indians Are Us?* at
      pp. 291–357, has elsewhere been characterized by native reviewers—e.g., Keith
      A. Winsell in *Canadian Journal of Native Studies,* Vol. 14, No. 1 (1994) pp. 1–5—as a
      "significant contribution" to the understanding of indigenous circumstance in con-
      temporary North America..

42   One can readily imagine the hue and cry that would be raised, and rightly so, if I
      were to begin referring to Indians as "primitives." Yet the word simply means "first"
      or "original" and is thus, by definition, far less potentially pejorative than "tribe."

43   "All *peoples* have the right to self-determination [emphasis added]," under several
      instruments of international law. "Populations," on the other hand—given that they
      are legally construed as being subparts of larger societies over which statist govern-
      ments like those of the U.S. and Canada exercise legitimate "domestic" author-
      ity—are imbued with no such right. See generally Glenn T. Morris, "In Support of
      the Right of Indigenous Peoples to Self-Determination under International Law,"
      German Yearbook of International Law, No. 29 (1986) pp. 277–316.

44   Albert Memmi, *Colonizer and Colonized* (Boston: Beacon Press, 1965) pp. 88–89.

45   Ibid. Also see Albert Memmi, *Dominated Man* (Boston: Beacon Press, 1969); Frantz
      Fanon, *Wretched of the Earth* (New York: Grove Press, 1965) and *Black Skin/White Masks:
      The Experiences of a Black Man in a White World* (New York: Grove Press, 1967). An inter-
      esting application of certain of these principles to the American Indian context will
      be found in Vine Deloria Jr., "Education and Imperialism," *Integrateducation,* Vol. 19,
      Nos. 1–2 (1982) pp. 58–63.

46   On the concept at issue, see Walter L. Adamson, *Hegemony and Revolution: A Study of
      Antonio Gramsci's Political and Cultural Theory* (Berkeley: University of California Press,
      1980) esp. pp. 170–79.

47   Chomsky provides superb analysis of these dynamics in his *Necessary Illusions: Thought
      Control in Democratic Societies* (Boston: South End Press, 1989) and elsewhere.

48   Characterization of the AIM leadership by Webster Two Hawk in the aftermath of
      the Trail of Broken Treaties, quoted in B.I.A., *I'm Not Your Indian Any More,* p. 32.

49   "Gunga Din" is collected in *Rudyard Kipling's Verse: Inclusive Edition, 1885–1918* (Garden
      City, NY: Doubleday, Page, 1922) at pp. 462–64.

50   See "Perversions of Justice: Examining U.S. Rights to Occupancy in North America,"
      in my *Struggle for the Land: Indigenous Resistance to Genocide, Ecocide, and Expropriation in
      Contemporary North America* (Monroe, ME: Common Courage Press, 1993) pp. 48–49.

51   John LaVelle, "The General Allotment Act 'Eligibility' Hoax: Distortions of Law,
      Policy and History in the Derogation of Indian Tribes," *Wicazo Sa Review,* Vol. 14,
      No. 1 (Spring 1999) pp. 251–302.

52   So far as I've been able to determine, the piece was cited only twice during the five
      years following its publication. This, despite LaVelle's passing out copies during
      at least one academic conference shortly after it appeared. One recipient, the late
      David Getches, a specialist in federal Indian law who became dean of the University
      of Colorado law school, later stated that while he was personally handed a copy by
      LaVelle in 1999, he never bothered to read it.

53   See Richard Delgado, "Shooting the Messenger," *American Indian Law Review*, Vol. 30, No. 2 (2005–06) pp. 477–94; Eric Cheyfitz, "Framing Ward Churchill: The Political Construction of Research Misconduct," *Works and Days*, Vols. 26–27 (2008–09) pp. 231–52.

54   Testimony of David Getches, *Churchill v. University of Colorado* (Case No. 06 CV 11479, District Court for the City and County of Denver, 2009) transcript at pp. 781–82.

55   Ibid., pp. 782–84, 787.

56   As one of the supposed complainants against me, Fay Cohen, stated in writing, she neither filed a complaint nor initiated contact with the university "at any point in time." Rather, "Contact was initiated in February 2005 by Dean Getches through John LaVelle." *Churchill v. University of Colorado*, transcript at pp. 794–95. There are several similar examples, both of LaVelle having solicited accusations by others on Getches' behalf, and of his otherwise serving as the dean's "consultant" on my case.

57   LaVelle himself never actually filed a formal complaint against me, as required by university rules for consideration/action by the SCRM. Testimony of David Getches, *Churchill v. University of Colorado*, transcript at p. 791. As it turned out, *none* of the charges submitted to the committee by acting chancellor DiStefano was attended by the lodging of a complaint. "[T]echnically, this made the chancellor the sole complainant." Cheyfitz, "Framing Ward Churchill," p. 249n6.

58   For the most comprehensive examination, see Don Eron, Suzanne Hudson, and Myron Hulen, *Report on the Termination of Ward Churchill* (Colorado Council of the American Association of University Professors, Committee to Protect Faculty Rights, November 1, 2011), published in *Journal of Academic Freedom*, No. 3 (2012) (available at http://www.aaup.org/reports-publications/journal-academic-freedom/volume-3; hereinafter cited as *AAUP Report*). Also see my "The Myth of Academic Freedom: Experiencing the Fraudulence of Liberal Principles in a Neoconservative Era," *Works and Days*, Vols. 26–27 (2008–09) pp. 139–230; abridged versions published in Anthony J. Nocella II, Steven Best, and Peter McLaren, eds., *Academic Repression: Reflections from the Academic Industrial Complex* (Oakland, CA: AK Press, 2010) pp. 179–99; Edward J. Carvalho and David B. Downing, eds., *Academic Freedom in the Post-9/11 Era* (New York: Palgrave Macmillan, 2010) pp. 65–113.

59   At least nine formal complaints were filed, detailing instances of plagiarism, misrepresentation of sources, factual falsification/fabrication, and other scholarly offenses in the IC's final report. See, e.g., Professors Vijay Gupta, Margaret LeCompte, Paul Levitt, Thomas Meyer, Emma Perez, Michael Yellow Bird, Eric Cheyfitz, Elisa Facio, Martin Walter, Leonard Baca, and Brenda Romero, "A Filing of Misconduct Charges Against the Churchill Investigating Committee," May 28, 2007; Professors James M. Craven, Ruth Hsu, David E. Stannard, and Haunani-Kay Trask, joined by attorneys Jennifer Harbury and Sharon H. Venne, "Research Misconduct Complaint Concerning Investigative Committee Report of May 9, 2006," May 28, 2007 (both available at http://www.wardchurchill.net). The university's official response, issued by business professor *cum* SCRM chair Joseph Rosse on July 18, 2007, was that, "complaints of scientific misconduct lodged against the committee which investigated Professor Churchill do not fall within the purview of the Standing Committee because the activities of the [IC] did not constitute research[;] rather, they were an administrative investigation and are therefore not scientific misconduct." Quoted in Jefferson Dodge, "Churchill, others had filed complaints against committee," *Silver & Gold Record* (July 26, 2007). For analysis, see the *Works and Days* version of my "Myth of Academic Freedom," pp. 197–98.

60   Marianne Wesson, Robert N. Clinton, José E. Limón, Marjory McIntosh, and Michael L. Radelet, *Report of the Investigative Committee of the Standing Committee on Research Misconduct of the University of Colorado at Boulder concerning Allegations of Academic Misconduct against Professor Ward Churchill* (May 9, 2006) p. 22 (available at http://www.colorado.edu/philosophy/vstenger/Briefs/Churchill%20Report.pdf; hereinafter cited as IC Report). The 105-page document is divided into sections, seven of which are devoted to specific allegations, each written by a committee member purportedly well-versed in the relevant subject matter. The section dealing with the 1887 Act, written by Clinton, is at pp. 13–27.

61   IC Report, pp. 16–17, 18. Note that Clinton neglects to mention the language in the Act quoted in note 24, assigning responsibility for determining "who constituted an Indian" to precisely the federal officials in question. Hence, the distinction he seeks to draw between the Act and its implementation is not only tedious but false. Imposition of blood quantum standards by said officials was authorized in the Act itself. Also see note 63, below.

62   IC Report, pp. 16, 22, 18.

63   "According to [Cornell University professor] Eric Cheyfitz, who is a legal scholar as well as an expert in [American Indian Studies], Churchill practices the standard approach to critical inquiry: '[I]t is normative to interpret acts of congress or any legal document . . . to include both their implementation and effects. . . . [Clinton] insists on violating this standard and confining the acts under investigation to their literal language. . . . [Clinton's] approach runs counter to the accepted practices of scholarly and critical interpretation, the purpose of which is to encourage a range of interpretations as long as plausible evidence can be produced in their support.'" AAUP Report, p. 64.

64   University of Colorado, Faculty Senate Committee on Privilege and Tenure, *Panel Report Regarding Dismissal for Cause of Ward Churchill and the Issue of Selective Enforcement* (April 11, 2007) pp. 38, 42 (available at https://web.archive.org/web/20101205114925/http://www.wardchurchill.net/files/PT_panel_report_041107.pdf; hereinafter cited as P&T Report).

65   Brown, a conservative Republican and former U.S. senator from Colorado, was a cofounder of Lynne Cheney's arch-reactionary American Council of Trustees and Alumni (ACTA), and remains quite involved with the organization to this day. For background on his hiring, see Rachel Burns, "Don't dismiss him: Scholars publish letter requesting reversal," *Colorado Daily*, April 12, 2007. The subtitle refers to a full-page letter signed by Derrick Bell, Noam Chomsky, Juan Cole, Drucilla Cornell, Richard Delgado, Richard Falk, Irene Gendzier, Rashid Khalidi, Mahmood Mamdani, Immanuel Wallerstein, and Howard Zinn, published in the *New York Review of Books* the same day.

66   AAUP Report, pp. 55–56. Also see Jeff Kass and Lynn Bartles, "CU president recommends firing of Churchill," *Rocky Mountain News* (May 29, 2007); Allison Sherry and Tom McGee, "Regents ax prof: Battle not yet settled," *Denver Post* (July 25, 2007); Berny Morson, "Churchill Fired: Next Shot in Court," *Rocky Mountain News* (July 25, 2007).

67   The jurors were told that if the university had been able to establish that I was in fact guilty of even one of the offenses listed in the IC Report, this would constitute legitimate cause for my firing. They found that it had failed to do so. Moreover, as was subsequently explained by juror Bethany Newill, the jury concluded that the university's procedures had been highly "biased" in my case, and that all of the university's witnesses—including Clinton—had been less than truthful at various points in

their testimony. Verdict, *Churchill v. University of Colorado*, transcript at pp. 4159–62; Affidavit of Bethany R. Newill, *Churchill v. University of Colorado*, July 17, 2009 (available at http://www.wardchurchill.net). Also see Michael Roberts, "Juror Bethany Newill talks about the Ward Churchill trial," *Westword*, April 3, 2009 (available at http://blogs.westword.com/latestword/2009/04/juror_bethany_newill_talks_abo.php).

68   "[I]n 2011, CU's Law School awarded Judge Larry Naves the William Lee Knous Award, the law school's highest award to an alumnus or alumna in recognition of outstanding achievement and sustained service to the Law School." *AAUP Report*, p. 58. On the ruling, see ACLU of Colorado, American Association of University Professors, and the National Coalition Against Censorship, Amicus Brief in *Churchill v. University of Colorado* (available at https://www.aclu.org/files/assets/amicus_brief_09-CA-1713.pdf).

69   *AAUP Report*, pp. 62–70. The same is done at pp. 71–75 with respect to the IC's analysis of my depiction of the 1990 Indian Arts and Crafts Act, officially attributed to University of Texas literature professor José Limón, but, as Clinton acknowledged during the P&T hearings, actually ghostwritten by him.

70   *IC Report*, pp. 18–19, arguing that the Supreme Court's opinion in *U.S. v. Rogers* (45 U.S. 567 (1846)) accomplished what I attributed to the General Allotment Act. "*Rogers* was a Supreme Court case. It wasn't a code. So, this implication of Professor Clinton . . . which says, Well, you're wrong because it was recognized in *Rogers*, there is a dramatic—and Clinton knows it—there is a dramatic difference between a decision based on federal common law by the Supreme Court and an entire legal apparatus which was constructed under the Allotment Act." Moreover, "[T]he interpretation of Robert Clinton on *U.S. v. Rogers* is wrong. . . . There's no mention of blood quantum in *U.S. v. Rogers* because it had not yet been developed into a formal paradigm. It did not get developed into a formal paradigm until the . . . time of allotment." *AAUP Report*, p. 66; quoting University of Arizona law Professor Robert A. Williams Jr., a leading authority on federal Indian law and well-grounded in critical race theory, and Eric Cheyfitz (see note 63), from their expert witness testimonies during the 2007 P&T hearings (transcript at pp. 1337–38 and 1550–51, respectively; hereinafter cited as *P&T Transcript*).

71   *IC Report*, p. 22. The AAUP investigators note only that Clinton "found Churchill factually wrong because 'there was never a half-blood quantum requirement for eligibility,'" but, in the same very sentence, "admits that Churchill is, in fact, right." *AAUP Report*, p. 66. During his testimony during the P&T testimony, Eric Cheyfitz observed that Clinton cited *nothing* in support of his bald assertion, and that, in any case, the only way it *could* be supported would be if the specific criteria employed in determining allotment eligibility/compiling tribal rolls on each reservation allotted was documented or otherwise ascertained to a reasonable degree of certainty. Suffice it to say that the project is daunting, and no one—including Clinton—has as yet undertaken it. As Cheyfitz concluded, "It may well be that a half-blood quantum *was* used," hence, LaVelle and Clinton "have accused [Churchill] of something for which they have no proof and for which [he] may well be right." *P&T Transcript* at pp. 1567–70. It should be noted that under these circumstances, applying the IC's own definition, Clinton's assertion constitutes "historical fabrication."

72   *IC Report*, p. 22.

73   *AAUP Report*, p. 66; citing the *Works and Days* version of my "Myth of Academic Freedom," p. 210; testimony of Paul Lombardo, *Churchill v. University of Colorado*, transcript at p. 1226.

74 Indeed, they describe the entire *IC Report* as such. *AAUP Report*, p. 122.

75 *AAUP Report*, p. 67.

76 Among other things, Finkelstein presents ten solid pages of side-by-side comparisons of text blocks in Dershowitz's book to counterparts in that by Peters, published nearly twenty years earlier. In each instance, the language is virtually identical. Dershowitz even replicated Peters' notational errors. See Norman G. Finkelstein, *Beyond Chutzpah: On the Misuse of Anti-Semitism and the Abuse of History* (Berkeley: University of California Press, 2005) pp. 229–54. The books compared are Alan Dershowitz, *The Case for Israel* (Hoboken, NJ: John Wiley & Sons, 2003) and Joan Peters, *From Time Immemorial: The Origins of the Arab-Jewish Conflict Over Palestine* (New York: Harper & Row, 1984). On the fraudulence of Peters' material, see Edward W. Said, "Conspiracy of Praise," and Norman G. Finkelstein, "Disinformation and the Palestine Question: The Not-So-Strange Case of Joan Peters's *From Time Immemorial*," both in Edward W. Said and Christopher Hitchens, eds., *Blaming the Victims: Spurious Scholarship and the Palestinian Question* (New York: Verso, [2nd ed.] 2001) pp. 23–32, 33–71. Also see Norman G. Finkelstein, *Image and Reality of the Israel-Palestine* Conflict (New York: Verso, [2nd ed.] 2003) pp. xxxi, 21–50.

77 For example, Weinstein has supported his conclusions, all which purportedly confirm right-wing contentions regarding Soviet espionage activities in the U.S. during the 1930s and '40s, with "quotes" from interviews with former American communist party members that several of the interviewees supposedly quoted insist were invented. Similarly, he "quoted" passages from KGB files to which he purchased exclusive access that his translator says appeared nowhere therein. Moreover, Weinstein has adamantly refused other scholars access to the interview tapes and the Soviet file material for purposes of verifying the accuracy of his quotations (as he's required to do under the American Historical Association's professional standards). See Jon Weiner, *Historians in Trouble: Plagiarism, Fraud and Politics in the Ivory Tower* (New York: New Press, 2005) pp. 31–57. The books at issue are Weinstein's *Perjury: The Hiss-Chambers Case* (New York: Alfred A. Knopf, 1978; reprinted by Random House in 1997 with an added "Note on Documentation") and *The Haunted Wood: Soviet Espionage in America—The Stalin Era* (New York: Random House, 1999).

78 Those whose work was most egregiously abused by Gaddis included eminent liberal historian William Earl Weeks and his lesser-known counterpart Thomas Hietala. See Noam Chomsky, *Failed States: The Abuse of Power and the Assault on Democracy* (New York: Metropolitan Books, 2006) pp. 89–94; citing Richard Immerman and Regina Gramer, "The Sources of American Conduct." *Passport: Newsletter of the Society for Historians of American Foreign Relations* (August 2005). The book critiqued is John Lewis Gaddis, *Surprise, Security, and the American Experience* (Cambridge, MA: Harvard University Press, 2004).

79 Despite his sustained and rather spectacular refusal to comply with basic professional standards in administering his own archival material (see note 77, above), Weinstein was appointed U.S. National Archivist—widely regarded as the top job for an American historian—in February 2005. See Herodotus Jr., "Archivist of the U.S.: Questionable Bush appointment slips under the radar," *The Daily Kos* (February 16, 2005; available at http://www.dailykos.com/story/2005/02/16/93147/-Archivist-of-the-U-S-Questionable-Bush-appointment-slips-under-the-radar#).

80 Clinton's accusation is not explicitly stated, but, as discussed, clearly implied in the *IC Report*. Cheyfitz's, however, is bluntly put: "I'm very disturbed by the LaVelle critique [of Churchill's work]. I think it's shoddy scholarship. . . . [T]he LaVelle review

essay, and then the longer essays [sic] based on it, strikes me as research misconduct. In the ways that Professor Churchill is being accused of research misconduct, I think the LaVelle essay participates in it. . . . So I find it an absolutely useless—and I say this without qualification—a useless piece of writing." *P&T Transcript* at pp. 1564–65.

81 In late 2001, for example, University of South Dakota law professor Robert B. Porter (Odawi), former attorney general for the Seneca Nation of Indians, advanced a blistering critique of LaVelle's "putting a happy face of colonialism" by systematically distorting both law and history. See Robert B. Porter—*Odawi*, "Two Kinds of Indians, Two Kinds of Indian Nation Sovereignty: A Surreply to Professor LaVelle," *Kansas Journal of Law and Public Policy*, Vol. 11, No. 1 (Spring 2002) pp. 629–56.

82 LaVelle's bibliography is posted on the official website of the University of New Mexico law school, where he currently teaches. It lists a total of ten publications—including the pair of tainted essays devoted to me—beginning in 1996. Only two of the items listed, a 1999 article in the *Arizona State Law Journal* and another in 2006, published in the *Connecticut Law Review*, would ordinarily carry much weight for promotion and tenure on a law faculty. He also lists coauthorship of the 2005 edition of *Cohen's Handbook of Federal Indian Law*, although the extent of his contribution is unspecified and the claim is in any case undermined by his *Connecticut Law Review* article, consisting as it does of material that did not make the editorial cut in *Cohen*. He appears to have published nary a word after 2006, although it is unclear whether this was a result of mounting criticism of his "scholarship," because it coincided with his promotion to full professor by UNM, or some combination. See University of New Mexico School of Law, *Professor John P. LaVelle: Publications* (available at http://lawschool.unm.edu/faculty/lavelle/index.php).

83 See University of New Mexico School of Law, *Professor John P. LaVelle: Profile* (available at http://lawschool.unm.edu/faculty/lavelle/index.php).

SIX

History in Service to Liberation

Ron Welburn's *Roanoke and Wampum*

It is typically the reviewer's lot to have to dig through a dozen numbing tracts in order to find a gem. Fortunately for me, Ron Welburn's *Roanoke and Wampum* was the first volume in my current pile. The book, consisting of thirteen exceedingly well-crafted essays using as a lens the frequently ignored literary/cultural terrain of that portion of Native North America situated east of the Mississippi, explores such topics as indigenous identity and continuity, literary theory, and the reclamation of historical reality. It is quite simply excellent in every respect, adding up to one of the better reads I've experienced in the past couple of years.

My personal favorite is a short chapter entitled "Who Are the Southeastern Blackfoot?" (pp. 9–24) in which the author thoroughly debunks the common misperception that persons of Afro-Indian descent who describe themselves in this fashion are erroneously (or falsely) asserting a genealogical connection to the Blackfeet Nation of present-day Montana and Alberta (i.e., the Blackfeet, Piegans, and Bloods). Rather, as Welburn argues on the basis of a number of historical, anthropological and linguistic markers, they are acknowledging their affinity to—by way of descent from—the Saponi, a supposedly extinct eastern Sioux people related to, but by no means interchangeable with, the western Sihasapa ("Blackfoot" or "Black Moccasin") Band of Lakota.

Another very good effort concerning red/black history and resulting issues of identity is "The Other Middle Passage: The Bermuda-Barbados Trade in Native American Slaves" (pp. 25–32), a rather dense little piece

Originally published in *American Indian Culture and Research Journal*, Vol. 26, No. 4 (Winter 2002). The book reviewed is Ron Welburn's *Roanoke and Wampum: Topics in Native American Heritage and Literatures* (New York: Peter Lang, 2001).

which fills in some of the gaps left by, and might thus best be read in con-junction with, Jack Forbes' groundbreaking *Africans and Native Americans*.[1] The same might be said, albeit in a somewhat different sense, with respect to Alan Gallay's recent study, *The Indian Slave Trade*.[2]

Very nearly as rewarding as the "Blackfoot" chapter, in my esti-mation, is "Amherst and the Indians: Then and Today" (pp. 35–50), in which Welburn painstakingly excavates the chronology—thus dispel-ling whatever ambiguities remained about who did what to whom and when—regarding Lord Jeffrey Amherst's notorious 1763 instruction that his subordinates distribute smallpox-infected blankets among the Indians of the Ohio River Valley. The appropriate conclusions are drawn with respect to the implications of Amherst's contemporary status as a revered figure throughout the Northeast, his name bestowed upon everything from cities, towns, and parks to institutions of higher educa-tion. If there is a quibble to be had with the author's treatment of this matter, it is in his depiction of Lord Jeff as engaging in "germ warfare" (pp. 35–37, 39) when, in fact, any policy explicitly intended to bring about the "extirpation" of a *race* must, by even the most restrictive definition, be considered genocidal (war and genocide are not synonyms, and should not be conflated).

Shifting to another front, Welburn makes a solid contribution in an essay entitled "Native American Literature Studies: Postcoloniality?/ Resistance/Ecocriticism?" (pp. 109–40) to rebutting the notion that faddish constructions like "postcolonialism" might be in any way properly or productively applied to active colonial contexts like North America. Here, one wishes he'd been clearer in delineating the distinc-tions between, as well as the commonalities uniting, the so-called classic, internal, and settler state modes of colonialism; reference to founda-tional works like Antonio Gramsci's "The Southern Question" (in *The Modern Prince and Other Writings*, International Publishers, 1957, pp. 28–51) and Michael Hector's *Internal Colonialism* (University of California Press, 1975) would have been helpful. Still, the essay offers compelling insights about the necessity of refusing the settler society's self-serving termino-logical/conceptual foreclosure upon the fact that the decolonization of Native North America remains an issue of paramount importance.

While I confess to being for the most part less interested in the chapters devoted to explicating the significance of particular American Indian authors/cultural figures, these too have much to commend them. Whether it is in retrieving the enigmatic native actor known as X-Brands from Trotsky's proverbial "dustbin of history" ("A Good

Word About X-Brands's Discourses in Sign," pp. 3–8) or accomplishing the same for the Appalachian writer Mildred Haun's observations on mixed-bloodedness ("*Hawk's Done Gone*: Mildred Haun's Vanishing Melungeons," pp. 167–83) as well as the remarkable Chippewa short prose writer Thomas S. Whitecloud's "Blue Winds Dancing" ("Going Home with Thomas Whitecloud," pp. 223–27) the quality of Welburn's accomplishment is substantial.

In this vein, though more topically, I found myself especially appreciative of his astute handling of contemporary Cherokee novelist Robert Conley ("The Indigenous Fiction of Joseph Bruchac and Robert J. Conley," pp. 187–222), lifting Conley from the bracket of being merely a writer of "young people's literature" to which he's been for too long and unfairly consigned, and presenting him as what he actually is: a principal medium through which his people's oral tradition is transformed into print (relatedly, see Welburn's "Life/Oral History Method: Three Nineteenth-Century Native American Prototypes," pp. 141–66). My only complaint, if it may be called such, is that Welburn failed to mention Cherokee painter Murv Jacobs, whose graphic work has sometimes accompanied Conley's texts.

All in all, I doubt that there's been a better or more useful collection of essays recently published than *Roanoke and Wampum*. It follows that I highly recommend it to anyone interested in the nuances of American Indian history and literary criticism.

Notes

1   Jack D. Forbes, *Africans and Native Americans: The Language of Race and the Evolution of Red-Black Peoples* (Urbana: University of Illinois Press, 1993).
2   Alan Gallay, *The Indian Slave Trade: The Rise of the English Empire in the American South, 1670–1717* (New Haven, CT: Yale University Press, 2002).

SEVEN

Broadening Our View of the Penal Colony

Luana Ross' *Inventing the Savage*

The United States currently incarcerates a greater proportion of its population than any other country. Prison construction, penal technologies, and the privatization of prison administration have all become significant growth industries in the U.S. since 1980. Increasingly, the vast inmate population—some two million and still growing by the mid-1990s—has itself come to be viewed in terms of profit potential, with corporations dipping ever more deeply into the reservoir of extraordinarily cheap labor embodied in the captive workforce.

Concern that this represents a return to an "American slave economy" has been voiced with mounting intensity over the past decade, a worry lent substance by the extent to which people of color are overrepresented among those behind bars. As things stand, one in four Afroamerican men is in prison, has been imprisoned, or will be locked up before age 26; young, black American males now suffer a greater probability of doing time than did their South African counterparts during the height of apartheid.

All of this has of course prompted a burgeoning literature analyzing the socioeconomic implications of imprisonment. While many useful contributions to understanding have been made, there have been deficiencies in the cumulative scope and focus of published material. Notably, these include a rather lopsided emphasis on men, and a pronounced tendency to ignore American Indians.

Fortunately, both issues are addressed in *Inventing the Savage*, a recent study by Luana Ross (Salish), associate professor of Native American

Originally published in *Contemporary Sociology*, Vol. 28, No. 3 (Spring 1999). The book reviewed is Luana Ross' *Inventing the Savage: The Social Construction of Native American Criminality* (Austin: University of Texas Press, 1998).

studies at University of California/Davis. Drawing "upon the life histories of imprisoned Native American women to demonstrate how race/
ethnicity, gender, and class contribute to the criminalizing of various
behaviors and subsequent incarceration rates" (jacket), Ross paints a
truly chilling portrait of what is being done to Indians and why.

> Native Americans are only 0.6 percent of the total population, yet
> they comprise 2.9 percent of federal and state prison populations.
> The disproportion of imprisoned Natives is more clearly seen at
> the state level, where they account for 33.2 percent of the total
> prisoner population in Alaska, 23.6 percent in South Dakota, 16.9
> percent in North Dakota, and 17.3 percent in Montana compared
> to approximately 15 percent, 7 percent, 4 percent and 6 percent of
> overall state populations, respectively (p. 89).

More specifically, "Although Native Americans in Montana make up
only about 6 percent of the total state population, Native men account
for approximately 20 percent of the total male prisoner population, and
Native women constitute approximately 25 percent of the total female
prisoner population. Nationwide, women make up 5.2 percent of the
total state prisoner population. Thus, Native women are more likely to be
imprisoned than Native men or white women, indicating [both] racism
and sexism in Montana's criminal justice system" (pp. 89–90).

The purpose served by such extravagant and doubly biased rates of
incarceration? Here, Ross is straightforward: The very existence of the
United States requires an ongoing internal colonization of the indigenous nations upon whose land it has constituted itself. Native societies
must therefore be perpetually subjugated. To this end, given the centrality of their role in maintaining cohesion/stability within traditional
societies, especially harsh treatment is visited upon indigenous women.
Overall, "Prisons, as employed by the Euro-American system, operate to
keep Native Americans in a colonial situation" (p. 89).

This is a performance worthy of Frantz Fanon, illuminating as it
does the very bedrock of U.S./Indian relations. In this sense, the lens
Ross provides is applicable, albeit with some adjustment, to other disproportionately imprisoned sectors of the U.S. population, whether
these are defined by race, ethnicity, sex, or income. Anyone seeking to
apprehend the real meanings underlying the proliferation of the U.S.
"prison industry" is well advised to examine this scholarly, readily accessible, and deeply troubling study.

EIGHT

Contours of Enlightenment

Reflections on Science, Theology, Law, and the Alternative Vision of Vine Deloria Jr.

> On the wings of synthesis one can fly to such a height that the blood turns to ice and the human body freezes, a height no flier has ever attained.
>
> —Valerian Maikov

It is a testament to the centrality of Vine Deloria Jr. to the thinking of my generation of native scholars, that many of us can scarcely recall a time when our opinions formed without reference to his, it is as if, for us, he has somehow *always* been there, a kind of institutional presence whose major purpose has been to test the verisimilitude of taken-for-granted propositions, challenging the pat assumptions and assertions of orthodoxy; calling inconsistencies, hypocrisies, and sheer banalities by their right names. Many a balloon of pretension, both academic and official, he has punctured on our behalf, leaving those who would preside as emperors over our minds standing naked and exposed, red-faced, spluttering and without adequate retort, the eventual objects of ridicule or revulsion rather than reverence.

Such exercises have won Deloria few admirers among those thus humbled, of course. On the contrary, the number of those now bearing him a degree of professional animus has grown to the proportions of a legion. There were surely more personally comfortable and convenient ways in which he might have proceeded. Yet the result has, on the whole, been quite empowering, licensing the rest of us to engage our

Originally published in Richard A. Grounds, George E. Tinker, and David E. Wilkins, eds., *Native Voices: American Indian Identity and Resistance* (Lawrence: University Press of Kansas, 2003).

own inquisitiveness and critical faculties, coming thereby to actually understand something of what we think we know. And this, to be sure, has been his intention all along. From the outset, Deloria's project has been an implicitly "counterhegemonic" one.[1] It follows that his posture has been that of a consistently and explicitly liberatory figure.

All this I know to be true, and still I am aware that my sense of remembrance bears the unmistakable signature of retrospective apostasy. We did not "grow up on Deloria."[2] He was *not* "always there." In my own case, there is nothing at all to recollect until his first book, *Custer Died for Your Sins*, came along in 1969.[3] By then I was twenty-two, working in a foundry while attending a community college, having already reached my "maturity" in the central highlands of Vietnam. Our "encounter," moreover, was no more direct than my reading of what he had written. For me, however, as with many of my peers, that experience alone prompted a resonance so profound as to cause our embrace of the author—or, rather, our imaginings of him—with all the presumptuous intimacy of those who believe they have found another speaking in their own voice and whom they therefore feel they've known forever.

It would be another decade and another half-dozen books before I actually met the man,[4] and in the event, there seemed nothing especially cerebral or intellectually portentous about our rendezvous. Although he was awaiting the release of his *Metaphysics of Modern Existence*,[5] and I was collaborating on several essays for a volume of the Smithsonian's *Handbook on North American Indians* he was editing (but which never appeared),[6] the fact is that I simply tagged along with Joe Bageant, a mutual friend and editor of the Boulder-based *Rocky Mountain Musical Express*, a pop periodical in which Deloria had recently published a short satire lampooning New Age filmmakers.[7]

Joe had it in mind to coax another such contribution, so we spent the afternoon chatting mostly about Vine's interactions with Marlon Brando,[8] the Denver Broncos' prospects for the coming season, and local country-western songwriter Michael Burton, whom we all knew and who'd just finished a tune entitled "The Cowboy's Lament." Since Vine was in the process of packing for his move to Tucson, where he'd recently accepted a professorship at the University of Arizona, no article for the *Express* was ever forthcoming. Bageant ended up putting together a riff about the Deloria-Brando connection himself,[9] and the Broncos, typically, had a miserable year. As for Mike Burton, Jerry Jeff Walker acquired the rights to his song, pronouncing it "the greatest piece of cowboy music ever written."[10]

For me, maybe it was because we both smoked the same brand of cigarette (and at about the same rate), or perhaps it was because I knew who played the Steve McQueen character's parents in *Junior Bonner*,[11] but for whatever reason, Vine took a liking to me. Thus began what would eventually add up to a close, fifteen-year relationship in which many an evening was spent watching NFL football and reruns of *Shane*. Others were passed in rambling discussions of everything from the influence of Gene Autry's 1930s recordings on the emergence of 1950s rock'n'roll to questions such as whether dinosaurs were warm-blooded or cold and the likelihood that the universe functions primarily on electromagnetic rather than thermonuclear principles.[12] Almost never did our far-ranging conversations land directly within the subject matters on which either of us was working at any given moment.

I recount such things not as an indulgence in the vice of personal reminiscence but to illustrate the nature, or at least certain facets, of what Raymond DeMallie has aptly described as Deloria's "disconcertingly brilliant intellect."[13] Like Theodor Adorno (whose approach to understanding Vine's often reminds me of), his gaze is at once probing and virtually all-encompassing in its perpetual labor to apprehend meaning in its most subtle, nuanced, and thoroughly contextualized essence. Although he would undoubtedly resist being saddled with the label, Deloria is, as was Adorno, a master dialectician, insisting that the sum and substance of anything can be ascertained only in its intrinsic relationality to others.[14] Hence the abiding preoccupation of both men with situating the concreta on which they've focused—politics, law, or whatever—within the vastly broader ferment of sociocultural expression—art, music, and so on—which both reflects and lends them their inherent shapes and trajectories.[15]

Unlike his counterpart's coldly ascetic preference for such rarified fare as Schoenberg's twelve-tone row,[16] however, Deloria's fascination has remained firmly ensconced within the framework of the very mass cultural idioms that Adorno's densely theoretical tracts were designed to critique (and, he hoped, eventually negate altogether).[17] Both the orientation and the expository style it compels have left Deloria's texts, and consequently the reasoning underlying them, vastly more accessible than those of Adorno, their author far less tormented and self-isolating.[18] Whereas Adorno can rightly be said to have cast himself as an exemplar of élitist obscuritanism, Deloria has proceeded along the same lines but in a precisely opposite direction. This, I think, accounts for much—though certainly not all—of the resonance his work has mustered over the years.[19]

The Politics

Like so many of my peers, I came to Deloria politically. The matter can be explained only in part by the explicitly political content of the criticisms of Congress, the Bureau of Indian Affairs (BIA), and other official institutions he advanced first in *Custer*, then in *We Talk, You Listen* (1970), and, most unequivocally, in *Behind the Trail of Broken Treaties* (1974).[20] His credibility, and thus his appeal, devolved in at least equal proportion from the sense that, although clearly an intellectual of the first order, he was also in some discernible sense an activist involved at least indirectly in such watershed processes and events as the 1969–71 occupation of Alcatraz Island,[21] the 1972 occupation of the BIA headquarters building in Washington, DC,[22] and the 1973 siege of Wounded Knee.[23]

While such ideas had been present in his work all along, it was especially in the latter connection that Vine set forth with greatest clarity his conception of American Indian peoples' aboriginal and treaty-based right to the status of nations, separate and distinct from the United States.[24] Most forcefully, he summarized the thrust of his arguments in testimony challenging U.S. jurisdiction over Lakota territory, and thus the Wounded Knee defendants, during the "Sioux Sovereignty Hearings" of 1974.[25] It would not be until 1979 that this radical fecundation of Native America's legal standing was finalized and available in essay form.[26] Meanwhile, it had galvanized a successful effort by the American Indian Movement (AIM) to establish a formal presence in the United Nations for purposes of (re)asserting indigenous rights through available international mechanisms.[27]

On some levels, these developments and the logic underlying them dovetailed quite well with the principle of decolonization enshrined in the UN Charter and actualized on a global scale since the end of World War II.[28] AIM's "diplomatic arm," the International Indian Treaty Council (IITC), originally headed by Russell Means and Jimmie Durham, pursued an agenda of forging what it hoped would be mutually supportive alliances with liberation movements and newly independent governments, most of them with a decidedly marxian orientation, throughout the so-called Third World of colonized or formerly colonized countries.[29] Among the other early accomplishments of this strategy was the formation of the Working Group on Indigenous Populations, a subpart of the UN Economic and Social Council mandated to review the conditions affecting native peoples around the world, assess the implications of their treaty relations with various UN member-states to which they were subordinated, recommend applications of extant international law where appropriate, and, ultimately, break new ground by preparing a draft Declaration on the Rights of Indigenous Peoples.[30]

Suffice it to say that the overt anti-imperialism of such ferment proved more than sufficient to draw me from the ranks of Vietnam Veterans Against the War and the mostly white Students for a Democratic Society, in which I'd become rather heavily involved after my stint in the army, and into AIM. From late 1972 onward, I was increasingly engaged with the latter, missing Wounded Knee altogether but winding up a decade later as codirector of the movement's Colorado chapter, a participant in the Yellow Thunder occupation in the Black Hills,[31] and an IITC delegate to Libya, Cuba, and the UN Working Group.

By 1983, the initial blush of optimism attending the admission of indigenous peoples to United Nations processes had waned considerably. The ascendant First World (capitalist) UN member-states had already begun to make it clear that they would defend themselves against our claims to the right of self-determination by invoking a clause in the charter guaranteeing the territorial integrity of all states as well as a General Assembly resolution defining a colony as being a country separated from its colonizer by at least thirty miles of open ocean.[32] Many of us set out to counter this "blue water thesis" by following the lead of Cherokee anthropologist Robert K. Thomas, who, during the mid-1960s, had undertaken to adapt the Gramscian theory of internal colonialism to the situation of American Indians.[33]

Despite the patent analytical and polemical utility of Gramsci's construction, our embrace of it served mainly to reveal the disjuncture between the objectives pursued by indigenous rights advocates and those acceptable to our marxist "allies," virtually all of whom were busily working out their own variations of statist order squarely atop the territories—and using the resources—of whatever indigenous peoples were situated within their purported boundaries.[34] While a number of examples might be cited, the nature of the problem was perhaps best illustrated by the campaign of Nicaragua's Sandinista régime during the 1980s to forcibly suppress the aspirations of the Miskito, Sumu, and Rama peoples to regain a genuinely self-determining status in a post-revolutionary context.[35]

The most noticeable outcome was the Sandinistas' failure to achieve the degree of stability necessary to fend off a U.S. low-intensity war waged to depose them. The dispute also led to the disintegration of AIM and IITC, as both groups split along the lines of those determined to align with anyone opposing the United States, regardless of other considerations, and those of us dedicated to supporting indigenous liberation struggles, irrespective of their oppressors' ideological persuasion.[36] The latter tendency has come to be referred to as "indigenism," and its adherents are known as "Fourth Worlders,"[37] those committed not to the revolutionary ideal of seizing state power but rather to dismantling the territorial and jurisdictional corpus of the state altogether.[38]

Although he contributed to the framing of our disavowal of marxism as a remedy to the oppression suffered by native people,[39] by the early 1980s, Deloria had already begun to look askance at the way things were shaping up. As he later explained, although conceding its descriptive accuracy, he had come to view the whole notion of internal colonialism as presenting at best a practical dead end in terms of realizing indigenous rights.[40] Consequently, his next two books, American Indians, American Justice and The Nations Within, both coauthored with Clifford M. Lytle, embodied a substantive departure from the explicit anticolonialism marking his earlier work.[41] Instead, he advocated a "progressive" approach, working within the parameters of colonial legality to achieve limited but nevertheless tangible improvements in the dire material circumstances afflicting most of Native America.[42]

This sort of pragmatism, manifested most recently in Tribes, Treaties, and Constitutional Tribulations, Vine's 1999 collaboration with his protégé David Wilkins,[43] has caused many to view him as an aging sellout (accommodationist).[44] In actuality, although my own persistence in exploring indigenist thematics has led to our increasing estrangement over the past decade, I believe this to be a profound misreading of both the man and the nature of his endeavor. If anything, it seems to me that he has harnessed himself to a task far more subversive in its implications than any conceivable brand of purely political praxis. Indeed, like Adorno, he long ago came to the realization that alterations in the political status quo, irrespective of their extremity, accomplish little in terms of correcting the core problems that confront us all, oppressed and oppressor alike.[45]

Beneath the web of extant political relations lies a much deeper matrix of ostensibly "apolitical" (mis)perceptions, (dis)understandings, and imputed values that foster the illusion that the relations themselves, or some discernably close approximation, are "natural" and therefore "inevitable." Thus, in Deloria's assessment, concentration on the superficialities of a mere political "fix" is at best diversionary. Worse, it tends to instill a false sense of resolution among those who accomplish it.[46] Absent an attendant reconsideration of the more fundamental aspects of consciousness that gave rise to the political conditions supposedly confronted and transformed, the confronters and transformers are doomed to replicate what they sought to oppose.[47]

The objective is therefore to engage in what Michel Foucault in a celebrated turn of the phrase, once referred to as the "archaeology of knowledge," apprehending the codes and symbologies of domination at their sources, and, to borrow a term from Jacques Derrida, "deconstruct" them from start to finish.[48] Only then, freed from the conceptual blinders imposed by what Jean-François Lyotard called "the master narrative,"[49] can one—or an entire culture—hope to (re)envision a truly liberatory reordering of the polity. Outlined today, nearly twenty years after postmodernism became intellectually fashionable, such ideas sound almost clichéd. In the late 1960s, however, when Deloria first began to delve into them, the opposite was true.

Vine, moreover, always wielded a decisive advantage over the great majority of postmodernists. Steeped during his upbringing in the traditional Lakota cosmology, yet formally trained in the canons of Western intellectualism (he was schooled in geology, theology, and law), he's been ideally positioned to assault paradigmatic eurocentrism from a perspective that is, to borrow the nomenclature of anthropology, simultaneously emic and etic.[50] In philosophical terms, his critique has been uniquely both "immanent" and "transcendent."[51] Additionally, his lifelong immersion in the vocabularies of popular culture has precluded his ever sliding into the deliberate opacity marking virtually all postmodernist discourse, including that offered by such native *poseurs* as Gerald Vizenor.[52]

Excavations

"Long before anyone in anthropology had heard of Michel Foucault or Pierre Bourdieu," Thomas Biolsi and Larry Zimmerman point out, "Deloria had put his finger on what would later be called discursive formations, symbolic capital, and the micropolitics of the academy."[53] Deloria's initial critique, advanced most forcefully in *Custer*, was openly political, assailing the sheer arrogance of anthropological practice and practitioners,[54] as well as the function of resulting theory in casting a patina of rationalism and objectivity over an otherwise glaring irrationality in the formation of U.S. Indian policy.[55] Here, he shared a conclusion shortly enunciated by Jean Baudrillard that "the deepest racist avatar is to think that an error about [other] societies is politically or theoretically less serious than a misinterpretation of [one's] own world. Just as a people that oppresses another cannot be free, so a culture that is mistaken about another must also be mistaken about itself."[56]

Among other methodological observations offered in *Custer*, Deloria noted that while conducting fieldwork and other sorts of research, anthropologists invariably seemed to have predetermined what they would find and what it would mean. Their purpose could thus be seen as little more than an exercise designed to create the appearance—but hardly the reality—that their preconceptions had been verified.[57] It follows that the whole procedural thrust of anthropology stems from a fundamental violation of the very "scientific method" on which the discipline has based its claim to being a mode of understanding more accurate than, and therefore superior to, the modes prevailing among the mostly nonwestern peoples it studies.[58]

In seeking to dig out the source of this dysfunction, Deloria unearthed a far broader and more disconcerting reality: although the colonially inspired enterprise of anthropology[59]—its brief history laden with such clear-cut illustrations of racist pseudoscience as craniometry, phrenology, eugenics,[60] social Darwinism,[61] and the Piltdown hoax[62]—represents a thoroughly sordid example, it is by no means unique in that regard. Everywhere he turned, in "hard" sciences such as physics, biology, and astronomy as much as among the pretenders of anthropology and the social sciences, Deloria encountered the same sorts of unscientific or even antiscientific claptrap passed off as the opposite of itself.[63]

As his excavations became deeper, he was more strongly drawn to the conclusion that the origins of Western science itself could be located *not* in an oppositional relationship to the mysticism of Judeo-Christian tradition—as the "scientific community" has been wont to insist—but in an obsessive and usually subliminal desire to fulfill the biblical enjoinder, set forth on the first page of Genesis, for humans to dominate nature.[64] As a consequence, the very notion of scientific objectivity can best be understood as a myth designed to mask the underlying and utterly subjective motivations of those claiming allegiance to it.[65] The result is that science has been transposed into scientism—that is, a religion-like belief structure—and its adherents have been transformed from scientists into beings more accurately categorized as "scientians." As a matter of practicality, scientism may be said not to have supplanted but to have subsumed Christianity as the "faith of choice" in Western societies.[66]

Significant evidence of this, Deloria argued in his 1973 *God Is Red*, may be found in the fact that the scientific establishment has incorporated the essentially theological charge of "heresy," once deployed by the church against scientists such as Galileo, as a weapon in the arsenal with which it defends its own dogmas.[67] To illustrate, he offered the case of Immanuel Velikovsky, an interdisciplinary scholar of undeniable stature who had the audacity to demonstrate that a profound rethinking would be necessary to rectify the many substantial inadequacies, inconsistencies, and full-fledged logical impossibilities embodied in orthodox geological and astronomical theory.[68]

Correlating the traditional histories of the Mideast and elsewhere with available physical data, Velikovsky set out in a 1950 book entitled *Worlds in Collision* to offer what he called a "catastrophist" alternative to conventional explanatory paradigms.[69] As Deloria recounts, he was thereupon subjected to a modern scientian equivalent of the medieval Inquisition: "*Worlds in Collision* was attacked by 'respectable' scientists even before it was published. A concentrated effort was begun to force the Macmillan Company, Velikovsky's publisher, to stop the presses. Scholars began a boycott of Macmillan's textbook division, its most vulnerable place. Macmillan could not withstand the concerted attack and transferred the book's rights to Doubleday. A conspiracy of silence dropped over discussion of Velikovsky's works. He subsequently published *Earth in Upheaval*, which was an embarrassing revelation of geological shortcomings."[70]

Although Velikovsky would remain an intellectual pariah for the remainder of his life, several of his supposedly "wild-eyed" theories have been borne out. Indeed, his contention that the sun is an electrically charged body, and that the solar system must therefore function as a large, gravitating electromagnet, has been appropriated without attribution by some of the very scientists who were most scornful in their dismissals when Velikovsky first advanced the idea.[71] Similarly: "Velikovsky suggested in a 1953 talk at Princeton that Jupiter was probably a dark star giving off radio signals. Less than two years later, two scientists discovered radio signals coming from Jupiter, and by 1965 Jupiter was declared a dark star. [He] also argued that Earth [exerted] a magnetosphere reaching as far as the moon. In 1958 the Van Allen belts were discovered, named after James Van Allen who had only measured them and not after Velikovsky who had predicted [their existence]."[72]

Deloria returned briefly to the "Velikovsky affair" in *The Metaphysics of Modern Existence*,[73] a 1979 book intended as the first in a trilogy of volumes devoted to exploring the problematic substitution of science for religion in the West. Opining that "Indians don't write books on philosophy," Harper & Row first tried to evade its contractual obligation to release it; then, failing that, it published only a small hardcover edition that was remaindered almost immediately.[74] Absent the other two volumes, fragments of which have appeared as commentaries and freestanding essays over the years,[75] Deloria was left with a somewhat unbalanced and largely unread critique of Heisenberg's physics and Jungian psychology, as well as the thinking of theologians such as Teilhard de Chardin and Paul Tillich.[76]

By then, having realized along with Paul Schmitt that the conception of sovereignty at issue in the indigenist liberation struggle amounted in important respects to a Christianesque expression of "political theology,"[77] he'd taken to calling for a refocusing of the movement's energy and attention. Our continuing investiture in the attainment of power in terms defined by the worldview of our oppressors, he reasoned, could, even if successful, serve only to complete their grip on our consciousness, thereby consummating rather than repealing our subordination.[78] The imperative, as Vine saw it, was to reclaim the insights and understandings lodged within our own nonwestern traditions, employing them first as a counter to the distortive outlooks imposed by the West and then as the basis on which to determine for ourselves the form and meaning of the relations we should pursue not just with other cultures but with the natural world in its totality.[79]

Deloria, for his part, more or less picked up where Velikovsky left off,[80] undertaking a protracted study in which he combined a broad selection of Native North American origin stories with elements of the same peoples' cosmologies and oral histories, comparing the resultant narrative overview with the continent's geological record. Additional comparisons to the fossil record completed the picture, allowing him to systematically demolish the factual/logical structures underpinning entire components of standard evolutionary theory and attendant chronologies, while validating much of what is contained in indigenous "lore" as the literal recapitulation of observed reality.[81]

Much of this was brought together in Red Earth, White Lies, a 1995 release subtitled Native Americans and the Myth of Scientific Fact.[82] Therein, it is demonstrated that the Hopi "legends" depicting a sequence of ages marked by fire, ice, and water might be interpreted as recountings of actual volcanic events, the last ice age, and the following period of glacial melt.[83] Similarly, it is shown that a traditional Klamath story perfectly describes the formation, violent eruption, and subsequent collapse of a volcanic cone. Other stories shared by the peoples of the Warm Springs Reservation account quite well for the formation of the mountains known as the "Three Sisters" in central Oregon.[84]

The "problem" with these and numerous other uncannily accurate native depictions of geological events is that, according to scientian orthodoxy, they occurred far too long ago for humans to have witnessed them. People, after all, are decreed to have first entered the hemisphere across the Bering Strait land bridge not more than 15,000 years ago (until 1950, the official "truth" was that the migration occurred only 3,000 years ago), with only heretics and other "irresponsible" types suggesting otherwise.[85] This constraint, in turn, is necessitated by the requirements of conventional evolutionary theory, which has modern humans—*Homo sapiens sapiens*, the only variety of hominid known to have resided in the Americas—emerging somewhere in Africa about 100,000 years ago and slowly spreading across the planet.[86]

Noting that there is virtually nothing in traditional indigenous accounts that suggests a traverse of the Bering Strait—a major exception, the so-called *Walam Olum* of the Leni Lenapes (Delawares), turned out to be an outright fabrication[87]—Deloria proceeds to make mincemeat of the whole proposition. Juxtaposing the elements of geography, geology, meteorology, biology, and anthropology that bear on the Beringian migration hypothesis, he points out how each tends to contradict the other. For openers, while anthropologists posit pursuit of America's "megafauna"—mammoths, giant rhinos, and the like—as being the motive for Paleolithic hunters to cross the strait from Siberia to Alaska during the last ice age, biologists account for the appearance of these same species in Asia at about the same time by having them migrate in the opposite direction.[88]

Actually, neither of these mutually nullifying scenarios is especially plausible, given the geological barriers involved; to get to the fabled land bridge from either direction would have required migrants to traverse several of the more formidable mountain ranges on the planet.[89] Nor does the meteorological record conform to the requirements of anthropological orthodoxy; an "ice-free corridor" along the Mackenzie River, through which migrant humans are supposed to have moved southward from Alaska into the U.S. portion of North America, could not have existed during the period indicated (if it ever existed at all).[90] Even the conventional explanation of the weather patterns precipitating an ice age—on which the existence of the Beringian land bridge itself depends—is found wanting.[91]

Other aspects of what passes for science fare no better. Even the technological "proofs" with which the discipline professes to have confirmed key elements of its theory are demonstrably faulty. With respect to the sophisticated potassium-argon tests that supposedly establish the dates of geological events with great precision. Deloria, following Cremo and Thompson, points out that "scientists have obtained dates ranging from 116 million to 2.96 billion years for Hawaiian lava flows that occurred in the year 1800."[92] Much the same pertains to radiocarbon dating, by which the antiquity of organic material is supposedly ascertained:

> In the *Atlantic Journal of the United States*, W. Dort wrote that freshly slaughtered seals, when subjected to radiocarbon analysis, were dated at 1,300 years old.

> In *Science*, M. Keith and G. Anderson wrote that shells of living mollusks were dated at 2,300 years old.

> In *The Physiology of Trees*, Bruno Haber wrote that wood from a growing tree was dated at 10,000 years old.[93]

Compounding such technological defects is the fact that "responsible" anthropologists have routinely suppressed radiocarbon datings that conflict with orthodoxy. Although test results from materials gathered at a number of sites as far south as Brazil have indicated human occupancy in the Americas for as long as forty millennia, they've been invariably dismissed—when they've been acknowledged at all—as "marred by serious questions of whether the material used for radiocarbon dating was contaminated by older carbon, or whether the dated material was really associated with human remains," and the like.[94]

Impossible standards have been assigned to the verification of evidence conflicting with the Bering Strait migration hypothesis, but the reverse does not hold true. Assessing the work of the late William Laughlin, Deloria observes that he provides "no evidence at all that any Paleo-Indians were within a thousand miles of Alaska during [the specified period]. No sites, trails, or signs of habitation are cited. . . . Laughlin is the acknowledged dean of American Bering Strait scholars, and yet he offered no concrete evidence whatsoever . . . in support of his theory."[95] Nonetheless, anthropologists all but invariably "begin with the *assumption* that the Bering Strait migration doctrine was proved a long time ago . . . and proceed without the slightest doubt" as to its validity, having "accepted the idea at face value on faith alone" and defending it ferociously against all challengers.[96]

A better illustration of how science has been diverted from its original purposes into service as "a secular but very powerful religion" would be hard to find.[97] Indeed, had he wished, Deloria could easily have demonstrated that the very notion of the Bering Strait crossing was given birth around 1580, not by scientists but by Jesuits eager to conjure up some means of reconciling the Christian version of how humanity was created with the recently discovered fact that there was an entire "New World" teeming with people who, to all appearances, could not have descended from Adam and Eve.[98] Since Judaism shares its origin story with Christianity, rabbinical scholars also had a stake in the issue. It is thus unsurprising that the next major contributor was a rabbi, Menasseh ben Isreal, who in 1650 published the thesis that people had found their way from the Old World to the New across what was then called the Strait of Anian, and tentatively identified the migrants as descendants of several "lost tribes" of Hebrews mentioned in the Bible.[99]

Mannasseh's speculation quickly took hold and was eventually adopted as an article of faith by the Church of Latter-Day Saints, which to this day maintains a lavishly funded New World Archaeological Foundation at Brigham Young University, the primary mission of which is to locate physical evidence supporting its sponsor's unabashedly theological agenda.[100] Nor has non-Mormon anthropology proved itself one whit less doctrinally biased. Although the idea that Indians are Jews has long since been abandoned, the anthropological establishment has, from at least the publication of Thomas Jefferson's 1781 *Notes on the State of Virginia,* harnessed itself with astonishing single-mindedness to the task of proving the Judeo-Christian Old World origin story correct in its essentials.[101] In the process, anthropology has as a discipline proved itself quite insistent on ignoring or suppressing countervailing evidence while busily cooking the books to make its preferred postulations seem vastly more solidly based than they actually are. Thereby, it has forfeited whatever claim to scientific integrity it might ever have possessed.[102]

Insofar as it reduces in the end to nothing more than an elaborate advocacy of a given origin story (however much revised), there is no *rational* reason why interpretations of the world advanced via the scientian edifice of anthropology should be privileged over belief systems arising in conjunction with any other such story. By extension, much the same can be said of the other sectors of what is typically referred to as "scientific knowledge."[103] To say that scientism presently possesses the *power* to impose itself on other traditions at their expense—a power acquired largely through the sustained subterfuge of pretending that science and scientism are synonymous—is not to concede that it enjoys any *right* to do so. The principle is identical to that enshrined in international law that precludes any people, no matter how powerful, from legitimately preempting the self-determining prerogatives of another.[104] Although usually subtler than its physical counterpart, intellectual imperialism is, after all, imperialism nonetheless.[105]

From this standpoint, Deloria's laying bare the religious roots of scientism, his tracing of their outgrowths and consequent debunking of contemporary scientian pretension, as well as his concomitant (re) assertion of the validity of indigenous knowledge, can only be seen as integrally related components within an overarching and steadily expanding intellectual anti-imperialism. His is, in substance, a veritable frontal assault on the entire conceptual structure by which the system of eurocentric global dominance has come to be rationalized, justified, and made to seem inevitable over the past five centuries. To this extent, if none other, the effects of his endeavor are potentially more radical and far-reaching than anything those of us locked into the trajectory of mere political activism ever aspired to achieve.[106]

Toward a New Synthesis of Understanding

For obvious reasons, none of this has gone unnoticed by the status quo. The response, predictably enough, has been a stream of invective from establishment attack dogs, branding Deloria everything from a "creationist" to an "ethnic pseudoscientist."[107] While much of the spew has issued from dolts like H. David Brumble, representing the most openly reactionary elements of anthropology (those who find continuing appeal in the long-discredited doctrines of nineteenth-century "scientific racism"),[108] a more sophisticated approach has been adopted by liberals such as David Hurst Thomas, who, while readily admitting that the bulk of Deloria's argument is well-founded, nevertheless manage to conclude that the solution to the problem he presents can be found *only* within the problem itself. Deloria's, Thomas sums up, is a "stridently anti-science position" that must ultimately be discounted on that basis alone.[109] Far more "constructive," he implies, are the contributions of Indians such as novelist N. Scott Momaday, who are willing to confirm scientian "understandings" through such mystical devices as "genetic memory,"[110] and those imbued with the smugly subaltern mentality of Roger Echo-Hawk, who are prepared to offer all the proper genuflections to the sanctity of scientism even as they purportedly inject it with their dubiously "Native" voices.[111]

Although this systematic conflation of science and scientism has been mirrored to some extent in Deloria's own formulations—apparently in the not unreasonable belief that to the degree scientists have avoided an outright disavowal of scientism, they deserve to be tarred with the brush of the latter's improprieties—such criticisms are grossly and in all likelihood deliberately misleading. Were Deloria's critique accepted for what it is, and the paradigms of "scientific understanding" correspondingly purged of their present scientian pretensions,[112] science itself might at last have a chance to fulfill the revelatory promise with which it has been invested since the days of the Enlightenment.[113] By the same token, obfuscatory rejections like those advanced by Brumble and Thomas exhibit every probability of foreclosing such potential, consigning "science," for all the narrowly technological proficiency its adherents have amassed over the past two centuries,[114] to the realm of the most vulgar form of ideological existence imaginable.[115]

Divesting science of scientian religiosity might also serve to detach it from the deep teleological linkages with Judeo-Christian values that have all along undermined its quest for objectivity. By demoting Christianity to its legitimate standing as merely one among many spiritual appreciations of the world, neither inferior nor superior to any other, either in its own right or in its relationship to scientific inquiry, the door would be opened for the literal content of myriad other traditions to inform and immeasurably broaden both the context and the process of empirical research.[116] The result could only be that humanity as a whole would be better positioned to realize the goal of understanding all we think we know, even as we come to know with increasing accuracy the limits of what it is we are inherently capable of understanding.[117] As Deloria put it as far back as 1979:

> [As] we seek to expand our knowledge of the world, the signposts point to a reconciliation of the [various] approaches to experience. Western science must now reintegrate human emotions and institutions into its interpretation of phenomena; Eastern peoples must confront the physical world and technology. We shall understand as these traditionally opposing views seek a unity that the world of historical experiences is far more mysterious and eventful than we had previously suspected. In the re-creation of metaphysics as a continuing search for meaning which incorporates all aspects of science and historical experience, we can hasten a time when we will come to an integrated conception of how our species came to be, what it has accomplished, and where it can expect to go in the millennia ahead. Our next immediate task is the unification of human knowledge.[118]

To paraphrase Chardin,[119] Deloria was and still is in effect calling for and sketching out the parameters of a "new synthesis of understanding" in which all the constituent components of knowledge are brought together on a level playing field for the first time, their presumptive efficaciousness constrained only by the requirement that they not be phenomenologically self-contradictory, and then joined on the basis of their interactive logical consistencies into an unprecedentedly panoramic whole. In this sense, his project can and should be seen as an effort to achieve not only an immanent completion of the "old" Enlightenment but also its transcendence, a tracing of the contours of what would, if pursued and refined, constitute an entirely new and overarching dimension of intellectual possibility.[120]

Like dominoes, the toppling of any one of scientism's more cherished "truths" necessitates a fundamental rearrangement of the entire "field of knowledge" that attends it, and rearranging a given field necessitates a concomitant rearrangement of related fields; at each step along the way, the inherent plausibility of alternative explanations offered by "primitive" and "dissident" traditions is underscored. Eliminating the fraudulent Bering Strait migration theory, for example, elevates the credibility of American Indian origin stories holding that indigenous people have "always" been here. This, in turn, requires a fundamental rethinking of human dispersal patterns across the planet and, ultimately, of prevailing notions concerning human evolution.[121] Equally, it renders implausible the scientian contention that the abrupt die-out of whole species of megafauna was precipitated by the initial influx of humans into North America some 12,000 to 15,000 years ago.[122]

If these so-called Pleistocene extinctions cannot be accounted for by an imaginary invasion of Paleolithic hunters, they must be explained in another, more reasonable fashion. Here, Velikovsky's theory of catastrophism, conforming as it does with the recollections of natural phenomena encompassed within the traditions of America's indigenous peoples, immediately presents itself as a viable candidate.[123] Any serious investigation of the meaning of such correlations would entail a foundational reassessment not only of the duration of human habitation in the New World but of its geological and meteorological chronologies as well.[124] Even the most tentative verification of the Velikovskian formulation would demand a reconsideration of the history and functioning of the solar system and, from there, of the universe as a whole.[125] The implications are, or should be, obvious.

Neither Deloria's deconstruction of the extant master narrative nor his efforts to forge a more tenable alternative has been confined to the masturbatory realm of petty postmodernist abstraction. Instead, he has been actively and consistently engaged in an attempt to communicate his alternative vision in terms of a viable grassroots pedagogy,[126] at least as concrete and potentially empowering as anything offered by Illich, Freire, Giroux, or McLaren.[127] If, as Martin Carnoy once famously observed, educational "mainstreaming" has served the purpose of cultural imperialism[128] then Deloria's must be appreciated as one of the more explicitly decolonizing strategies yet conceived. Paradoxical as it may seem, the "antiscientific" arguments contained in God Is Red, Metaphysics, and Red Earth, White Lies are revealed as one of the stronger attempts to salvage science from the ravages of its impersonators in recent years. Only thus can Deloria's desired "unification of human knowledge" be completed.

Though it's plainly true that there was life before Deloria, it's equally the case that things have not been—indeed, can never be—the same since his arrival on the intellectual scene. He's flown higher and farther on the wings of synthesis than anyone, or any three people, I can name. That he's dragged the rest of us along, despite our often strenuous kicks, screams, and general recalcitrance, is something for which we—his most bitter detractors above all—owe him an incalculable debt. If we as a species are to have a future, much less achieve liberation from the condition imposed by the collectivity of our blinders, it is because he's forced us to see things in new ways, equipping us with the minds to free ourselves from a fate that had come to seem preordained.

The conceptual seeds he's sown will undoubtedly continue to sprout decades hence, after the man himself and those of us who have been honored to know him personally are no longer present to savor the pleasures of their fruit. His, then, has been the bestowal of the gift of his very life on coming generations and, in perhaps greater denomination, the eternity of this land that is the mother of us all.[129] Irrespective of the cosmopolitanism that has marked his learning, he's remained first, foremost, and always an Indian, unshrinking from the responsibilities attending that identity, the pride of all who came before. He stands as the signpost of continuity between that which was, that which is, and that which may yet be (if only because he has done so much to make it so).

Notes

1   For explication of the concept, see Walter L. Adamson, *Hegemony and Revolution: A Study of Antonio Gramsci's Political and Cultural Theory* (Berkeley: University of California Press, 1980) esp. 170–79.

2   Elizabeth S. Grobsmith, "Growing up on Deloria: His Impact on a New Generation of Anthropologists," in Thomas Biolsi and Larry J. Zimmerman, eds., *Indians and Anthropologists: Vine Deloria, Jr., and the Critique of Anthropology* (Tucson: University of Arizona Press, 1997) pp. 35–49.

3   Vine Deloria Jr., *Custer Died for Your Sins: An Indian Manifesto* (New York: Macmillan, 1969).

4   Vine Deloria Jr., *We Talk, You Listen: New Tribes, New Turf* (New York: Macmillan, 1970); *Of Utmost Good Faith* (San Francisco: Straight Arrow Books, 1971); *God Is Red* (New York: Grosset and Dunlap, 1973); *Behind the Trail of Broken Treaties: An Indian Declaration of Independence* (New York: Delacorte Press, 1974); *The Indian Affair* (New York: Friendship Press, 1974); *The Indians of the Pacific Northwest: From the Coming of the White Man to the Present Day* (Garden City, NY: Doubleday, 1977).

5   Vine Deloria Jr., *The Metaphysics of Modern Existence* (New York: Harper & Row, 1979).

6   When the Smithsonian project derailed, Deloria arranged for my coauthors and me to publish our material in a now-defunct journal. See Ward Churchill, Mary Ann Hill, and Norbert S. Hill Jr., "Media Stereotyping and the Native Response: An Historical Overview," *Indian Historian*, Vol. 11, No. 4 (Winter 1978–1979) pp. 45–56; Ward Churchill and Norbert S. Hill Jr., "An Historical Survey of Tendencies in American Indian Education: Higher Education," *Indian Historian*, Vol. 12, No. 1 (Spring 1979) pp. 35–46; Ward Churchill, Norbert S. Hill Jr., and Mary Jo Barlow, "An Historical Survey of Twentieth Century Native American Athletes," *Indian Historian*, Vol. 12, No. 4 (Winter 1979–1980) pp. 22–32.

7   Vine Deloria Jr., "Why Me, Tonto?," *Rocky Mountain Musical Express* (March 1977).

8   Deloria himself has never written about his relationship with Brando. It is, however, mentioned in Peter Manso's *Brando: The Biography* (New York: Hyperion, 1994) at pp. 797, 804, 817, and 890.

9   Joe Bageant, "Cracks in the Bottom of the Brando Pool," *Denver Magazine* (September 1980).

10 The song is recorded on Walker's *Ridin' High* (MCA, 1975). Although he has never said so, Deloria may have played a key role in connecting the two men. In any event, he not only knew Burton but was familiar enough with Walker to have stood in on rhythm guitar with the Lost Gonzo Band during a 1977 concert at Red Rocks Amphitheater, outside Denver. A photo of him taken during that performance accompanies his interview in Studs Terkel's *American Dreams: Lost and Found* (New York: Pantheon, 1980).

11 Robert Preston and Ida Lupino. The 1972 film, directed by Sam Peckinpah, is one of Deloria's favorites.

12 As will be understood by anyone who has bothered to actually listen to Autry's bass lines, Deloria made his case. They are often identical to those utilized by rocker Bill Haley and his Comets. The point of departure for the dinosaur discourses was usually Adrian J. Desmond's *The Hot-Blooded Dinosaurs: A Revolution in Paleontology* (New York: Dial Press, 1976). The thrust of the electromagnetic/thermonuclear queries derived from Deloria's ongoing preoccupation with Velikovsky, discussed later.

13 The characterization was offered in a 1990 letter submitted in support of Deloria's application to join the Ethnic Studies faculty at the University of Colorado at Boulder.

14 Max Horkheimer and Theodor W. Adorno, *The Dialectic of Enlightenment* (New York: Continuum, 1972). For explication, see Martin Jay, *Adorno* (Cambridge: Harvard University Press, 1984), esp. pp. 51–54, 114–17, 150–52.

15   Theodor W. Adorno, *Prisms: Cultural Criticism and Society* (London: Neville Spearman, 1967). For methodological analysis, see the relevant sections in Fredric Jameson's *Marxism and Form: Twentieth-Century Dialectical Theories of Literature* (Princeton, NJ.: Princeton University Press, 1971).

16   Theodor W. Adorno, *Philosophy of Modern Music* (New York: Seabury Press, 1973) and *Introduction to the Sociology of Music* (New York: Seabury Press, 1976).

17   Anyone who has broken their teeth on Adorno's *Negative Dialectics* (New York: Seabury Press, 1979), as I have, will know what I mean by "densely theoretical tracts." For an excellent effort at decipherment, see Susan Buck-Morss, *The Origin of Negative Dialectics: Theodor W. Adorno, Walter Benjamin and the Frankfurt Institute* (Brighton, UK: Harvester Press, 1977).

18   Theodor W. Adorno, *Minima Moralia: Reflections from a Damaged Life* (London: New Left Books, 1974). For analyses, see Gillian Rose, *The Melancholy Science: An Introduction to the Thought of Theodor W. Adorno* (London: Macmillan, 1978) and Edward Said, "Intellectual Exile: Expatriates and Marginals," in his *Representations of the Intellectual* (New York: Pantheon, 1994) pp. 54–61.

19   Deloria once explained to me that he consciously restricts the vocabulary he uses in his writings for precisely this reason. As he articulated the trade-off, whatever might be sacrificed in terms of precision is more than recaptured by breadth of readership. "It doesn't matter how accurate you are," he contends, "if nobody is [or only a relatively few people are] able to understand what you're trying to say."

20   See note 4. Also of particular interest in this respect are Deloria's "Custer Died for Your Sins," *Playboy* (August 1969); "The War between the Redskins and the Feds," *New York Times Magazine* (December 7, 1969); "This Country Was a Lot Better off When the Indians Were Running It," *New York Times Magazine* (March 8, 1970); "Bureau of Indian Affairs: My Brother's Keeper," *Art in America* (July–August 1970); "It Is a Good Day to Die," *Katallagete*, Vol. 4, Nos. 2–3 (Winter 1972) pp. 62–65; "Old Indian Refrain: Treachery on the Potomac," *New York Times* (February 8, 1973); "Federal Policy Still Victimizes and Exploits," *Los Angeles Times* (August 17, 1975).

21   For the best overview, see Troy R. Johnson, *The Occupation of Alcatraz Island* (Urbana: University of Illinois Press, 1996). A more personal rendering, introduced by Deloria, is provided by a participant, Adam Fortunate Eagle (Nordwall), in his *Alcatraz! Alcatraz! The Indian Occupation of 1969–1971* (Berkeley, CA: Heyday Books, 1992).

22   The BIA takeover is probably best handled in Paul Chaat Smith and Robert Allen Warrior, *Like a Hurricane: The American Indian Movement from Alcatraz to Wounded Knee* (New York: New Press, 1996) pp. 149–68. Also see Deloria, *Trail of Broken Treaties*, and "The New Activism," *Dialogue*, Vol. 6, No. 2 (1973) pp. 3–12.

23   There is a raft of material available on Wounded Knee and its backdrop. Among the better efforts is Peter Matthiessen's *In the Spirit of Crazy Horse* (New York: Viking Press, [2nd ed.] 1991). Also see Smith and Warrior, *Like a Hurricane*; Vine Deloria Jr., "Wounded Knee," *Los Angeles Times* (April 2 1973); "Final Reflections on Wounded Knee," *Black Politician*, Vol. 4, No. 1 (Summer 1973); "Beyond Wounded Knee," *Akwesasne Notes*, Vol. 5, No. 4 (Late Summer 1973) p. 8; "From Wounded Knee to Wounded Knee," in Jules Billard, ed., *The World of the American Indian* (Washington, DC: National Geographic Society, 1974) pp. 355–83; "The Indian Movement: Out of a Wounded Past," *Ramparts*, Vol. 13, No. 6 (March 1975) pp. 28–32.

24   Deloria addressed not only the legal doctrines underlying such entitlement but also questions of the material viability of its exercise; see the chapter entitled "The Size and Status of Nations," in *Trail of Broken Treaties*, pp. 161–86. Also see Vine Deloria

Jr., "The Basis of Indian Law," *American Airlines Magazine* (April 1972); "The Question of the 1868 Sioux Treaty: A Crucial Element in the Wounded Knee Trials," *Akwesasne Notes*, Vol. 5, No. 2 (Spring 1973); "The Significance of the 1868 Treaty," *Medicine Root Magazine*, Vol. 1, No. 2 (1974) pp. 14–16; "Breaking the Treaty of Ruby Valley," *New Dimensions Magazine* (September 1975).

25 Two excerpts from Deloria's testimony, entitled "Sovereignty" and "The United States Has No Jurisdiction in Sioux Territory," are included in Roxanne Dunbar-Ortiz, ed., *The Great Sioux Nation: Sitting in Judgment on America* (New York: American Indian Treaty Council/Moon Books, 1977) pp. 16–18, 141–46.

26 Vine Deloria Jr., "Self-Determination and the Concept of Sovereignty," in Roxanne Dunbar-Ortiz, ed., *Economic Development in American Indian Reservations* (Albuquerque: Native American Studies Center, University of New Mexico, 1979) pp. 22–28. Relatedly, see "Sovereignty: Fact or Fiction? A Debate between Congressman Lloyd Meeds and Vine Deloria Jr.," *La Confluencia*, Vol. 2, Nos. 2–3 (October 1978; available online through ERIC).

27 For Deloria's thinking on this initiative, see the second edition of *Behind the Trail of Broken Treaties* (Austin: University of Texas Press, 1985) pp. 266–74.

28 The relevant portion of the charter can be found in Ian Brownlie, ed., *Basic Documents on Human Rights* (Oxford: Clarendon Press, [3rd ed.] 1992) pp. 9–10. Amplification and a certain degree of clarification of the principle are embodied in the UN General Assembly's subsequent Resolution 1514 (XV), usually referred to as the Declaration on the Granting of Independence to Colonial Countries and Peoples (1960); ibid., pp. 28–30. On the postwar trend toward decolonization itself, see Franz Ansprenger, *The Dissolution of Colonial Empires* (New York: Routledge, 1989).

29 For Means' recollections on this score, see his autobiographical collaboration with Marvin J. Wolf, *Where White Men Fear to Tread* (New York: St. Martin's Press, 1995) pp. 324–26, 356–57, 365. Durham has yet to produce so concise a recounting, although his views, or fragments of them, are scattered throughout *Columbus Day* (Minneapolis, MN: West End Press, 1983) and *A Certain Lack of Coherence: Writings on Art and Cultural Politics* (London: Kala Press, 1993). Probably the best, or at least broadest, overview will be found in Roxanne Dunbar-Ortiz, *Indians of the Americas: Human Rights and Self-Determination* (London: Zed Books, 1984).

30 Douglas Sanders, "The UN Working Group on Indigenous Populations," *Human Rights Quarterly*, No. 11 (1989) pp. 406–33. The global survey was completed early on; see José R. Martínez Cobo, *Study of the Problem of Discrimination against Indigenous Populations* (UN Doc. E/CN.4/Sub.2/1983/21/Add.83, September 1983). The treaty study has now been completed by working group special rapporteur Miguel Alfonso Martínez but [was not completed until after this essay was published]. The Draft Declaration has also been completed but remains stalemated by the United States, which insists that it must be revised in a manner legitimating U.S. violations of indigenous rights; see, e.g., Glenn T. Morris, "Commentary: Further Motion by State Department to Railroad Indigenous Rights," *Fourth World Bulletin*, No. 6 (1998) p. 9.

31 On Yellow Thunder, of which Deloria was an active supporter, see Means and Wolf, *White Men*, pp. 407–36. Also see Rex Weyler, *Blood of the Land: The US Government and Corporate War against the American Indian Movement* (Philadelphia: New Society, [2nd ed.] 1992) pp. 241–54.

32 Brownlie, *Basic Documents*, p. 4. For analysis of the "blue water" interpretation and its implications, see Roxanne Dunbar-Ortiz, "Protection of American Indian

Territories in the United States: The Applicability of International Law," in Imre Sutton, ed., *Irredeemable America: The Indians' Estate and Land Tenure* (Albuquerque: University of New Mexico Press, 1985) pp. 260–61.

33   The theory was originally formulated by Antonio Gramsci in his 1920 essay "The Southern Question," included in *The Modern Prince and Other Writings* (New York: International, 1957) pp. 28–51. For Thomas' adaptation, see his "Colonialism: Classic and Internal," *New University Thought*, Vol. 4, No. 4 (Winter 1966–1967) pp. 37–44. Whether Bob was actually familiar with Gramsci's work is open to question; the conceptual similarities may well have been unknowing on his part. In any case, for one of my own earlier attempts to apply the idea in a systematic way, see my "Indigenous Peoples of the U.S.: A Struggle against Internal Colonialism," *Black Scholar*, Vol. 16, No. 1 (February 1985) pp. 29–35.

34   For an excellent and relatively comprehensive survey and analysis, see Walker Conner, *The National Question in Marxist-Leninist Theory and Strategy* (Princeton, NJ: Princeton University Press, 1984).

35   See generally Glenn T. Morris and Ward Churchill, "Between a Rock and a Hard Place: Left-Wing Revolution, Right-Wing Reaction, and the Destruction of Indigenous Peoples," *Cultural Survival Quarterly*, Vol. 11, No. 3 (Fall 1988) pp. 17–24.

36   An overview is provided in Means and Wolf, *White Men*, pp. 459–88. To be fair, however, it should be noted that the split over Nicaragua represented a culmination rather than the precipitation of the process. Both AIM and IITC had been fragmenting for several years by that point. See, e.g., Jimmie Durham's 1979 "Open Letter on Recent Developments in the American Indian Movement/International Indian Treaty Council," in his *A Certain Lack of Coherence*, pp. 46–56.

37   The term *indigenist* derives from the Spanish *indigenista*, as employed by Guillermo Bonfil Batalla in his *Utopia y Revolución: El Pensamiento Político Contemporáneo de los Indios en América Latina* (Mexico City: Editorial Nueva Imagen, 1981). On the concept of an indigenous Fourth World underlying Mao Tse-tung's famous "three world" schematic, see George Manuel and Michael Posluns, *The Fourth World: An Indigenous Reality* (New York: Free Press, 1974); Weyler, *Blood of the Land*, pp. 212–40. Anishnaabe activist Winona LaDuke has also described indigenous peoples as making up a "Host World" atop which the other three have been erected. See her "Natural to Synthetic to Back Again," in my *Marxism and Native Americans* (Boston: South End Press, 1983) p. vi.

38   In this, indigenism shares certain obvious commonalities with anarchism. See, e.g., Ulrike Heider, *Anarchism: Left, Right, and Green* (San Francisco: City Lights, 1994).

39   See Vine Deloria Jr., "Circling the Same Old Rock: The Coming of the Materialist Missionaries," in my *Marxism and Native Americans*, pp. 113–36.

40   Vine Deloria Jr., "Bob Thomas as Colleague," in Steve Pavlik, ed., *A Good Cherokee, a Good Anthropologist: Papers in Honor of Robert K. Thomas* (Los Angeles: UCLA American Indian Studies Center, 1998) p. 31.

41   Vine Deloria Jr. and Clifford M. Lytle, *American Indians, American Justice* (Austin: University of Texas Press, 1983); *The Nations Within: The Past and Future of American Indian Sovereignty* (New York: Pantheon, 1984). Much the same can be said of *The Aggressions of Civilization; Federal Indian Policy since the 1880s* (Philadelphia: Temple University Press, 1984), coedited by Deloria and Sandra L. Cadwalader.

42   For a brief summary of these conditions, set forth in an argument not dissimilar to Deloria's own, see Rennard Strickland, "You Can't Rollerskate in a Buffalo Herd Even If You Have All the Medicine: American Indian Law and Policy," in his *Tonto's*

Revenge: Reflections on American Indian Culture and Policy (Albuquerque: University of New Mexico Press, 1997) pp. 53–54.

43　Vine Deloria Jr. and David E. Wilkins, *Tribes, Treaties, and Constitutional Tribulations* (Austin: University of Texas Press, 1999).

44　As Vine recently put it, with decided understatement, the shift resulted in his receiving "several bad book reviews." Deloria, "Bob Thomas," p. 31.

45　For Adorno, "reification was not merely a relationship among men, but also one entailing the domination of the otherness of the natural world. Through the kind of conceptual imperialism Adorno discerned in both positivism and idealism, the natural world was reified into fungible fields for human control and manipulation," a circumstance that, unless addressed at a foundational conceptual rather than political level, would result in the perpetuation of "a negative dialectics [that] played off nature against . . . society and vice versa chiasmically." Within this framework, reification of human relations would be unavoidable, regardless of political arrangements. Jay, *Adorno*, p. 69.

46　At issue here is essentially the conception of "false consciousness" first articulated by Georg Lukács in his 1930 essay collection *History and Class Consciousness: Studies in Marxist Dialectics* (Cambridge, MA: MIT Press, 1971), and much refined by Herbert Marcuse in *An Essay on Liberation* (Boston: Beacon Press, 1969) and elsewhere. See, generally, Joseph Gabel, *False Consciousness: An Essay on Reification* (New York: Harper Torchbooks, 1978).

47　Hence, as has been amply demonstrated throughout the Third World since 1960, "postcolonial" régimes have demonstrated an all but uniform proclivity not only to maintain themselves on the basis of the internal colonial dominion of indigenous peoples but also to submit themselves to the ravages of neocolonial subordination and exploitation. It should be noted that the recipe concocted by "scientific socialism" to combat the latter devolves upon an ever more virulent intensification of the former. See, e.g., Kwame Nkrumah, *Neo-Colonialism: The Last Stage of Imperialism* (New York: International Publishers, 1966); Elenga M'buyinga, *Pan Africanism or Neo-Colonialism: The Bankruptcy of the OAS* (London: Zed Books, 1982).

48　Michel Foucault, *The Archaeology of Knowledge* (New York: Pantheon, 1972); Jacques Derrida, *Of Grammatology* (Baltimore: Johns Hopkins University Press, 1974).

49　Jean-François Lyotard, *The Postmodern Condition: A Report on Knowledge* (Minneapolis: University of Minnesota Press, 1984).

50　*Emic* refers to the view of a culture arising from within it, while *etic* describes views arising from without. Born in 1933, Deloria spent his first sixteen years on the Pine Ridge Sioux Reservation, which afforded him a solid foundation in the conceptions of his own culture. However, his credentials include a diploma from the Kent School, an undergraduate education obtained at the Colorado School of Mines and Iowa State University, a graduate degree from the Lutheran Theological Seminary (1963), and a degree in law from the University of Colorado (1970). James Treat, "Introduction: An American View of Religion," in Vine Deloria Jr., *For This Land: Writings on Religion in America* (New York: Routledge, 1999) pp. 9–11.

51　"Immanent" critique is that which arises from within a philosophical tendency or tradition and is offered with the object of completing, perfecting, and thus surpassing it. "Transcendent" critique is usually advanced by those opposing the philosophy at issue and is intended to supplant it. See, generally, the chapter titled "The Transformation of Critique" in John Rajchman, *Michel Foucault: The Freedom of*

Philosophy (New York: Columbia University Press, 1985) pp. 7–95; Dick Howard, *The Politics of Critique* (Minneapolis: University of Minnesota Press, 1988) pp. 84–87.

52   See the chapter titled "The Jargon of Postmodernity" in Alex Callinicos, *Against Postmodernism: A Marxist Critique* (New York: St. Martin's Press, 1989) pp. 9–28. For samples of the pretentiously jargon-driven fare ladled up by Vizenor, see his *Manifest Manners: Postindian Warriors of Survivance* (Hanover, NJ: Wesleyan University Press, 1994); *Fugitive Poses: Native American Scenes of Absence and Presence* (Lincoln: University of Nebraska Press, 1998); and, with A. Robert Lee, *Postindian Conversations* (Lincoln: University of Nebraska Press, 1999).

53   Thomas Biolsi and Larry J. Zimmerman, "What's Changed, What Hasn't," in their *Indians and Anthropologists*, p. 4.

54   Deloria, "Anthropologists and Other Friends," in *Custer*, pp. 78–100. Also see Vine Deloria Jr., "Hobby Farm: On the Reservation," in Dotson Rader, ed., *Defiance #2: A Radical Review* (New York: Paperback Library, 1971) pp. 22–42; "Some Criticisms and a Number of Suggestions," in Jeanette Henry, ed., *Anthropology and the American Indian: Report of a Symposium* (San Francisco: Indian Historian Press, 1973) pp. 153–57.

55   See, e.g., the dissection of Peter Farb's egregious *Man's Rise to Civilization as Shown by the Indians of North America from Primeval Times to the Coming of the Industrial Age* (New York: E. P. Dutton, 1968) in Deloria, *Custer*, pp. 96–99.

56   Jean Baudrillard, *The Mirror of Production* (St. Louis: Telos Press, 1975) p. 107.

57   Deloria, *Custer*, p. 80.

58   In simplest terms, the scientific method requires that any hypothesis be subjected to empirical and logical interrogation designed to disprove it. The relative validity of the hypothesis is thus adduced by the extent to which it withstands such tests. Tailoring the tests to support the hypothesis nullifies the utility of the method itself. See, e.g., Karl Popper, *The Logic of Scientific Discovery* (New York: Science Editions, 1961 reprint of 1934 original); *Conjectures and Refutations: The Growth of Scientific Knowledge* (New York: Harper Torchbooks, [2nd ed.] 1968).

59   On the origins and development of anthropology, see Asad Talal, ed., *Anthropology and the Colonial Encounter* (London: Ithaca Press, 1973); Nicholas Thomas, *Colonialism's Culture: Anthropology, Travel, and Government* (Princeton, NJ: Princeton University Press, 1984).

60   For the best overview, see Stephen Jay Gould, *The Mismeasure of Man* (New York: W. W. Norton, 1981). Also see William Stanton, *The Leopard's Spots: Scientific Attitudes towards Race in America, 1815–1859* (Chicago: University of Chicago Press, 1960); Stefan Kuhn, *The Nazi Connection: Eugenics, American Racism, and German National Socialism* (New York: Oxford University Press, 1994).

61   The concept of "social evolution" articulated by Lewis Henry Morgan in his *Ancient Society* (New York: World, 1877) served as "the backbone of American anthropology" during the late nineteenth century. Together with an entirely similar theory laid out in John Lubbock's *Pre-historic Times, as Illustrated by Ancient Remains, and the Manners and Customs of Modern Savages* (London: Williams and Northgate, 1865), it has provided the foundation for the white supremacist doctrine known as "social Darwinism" right up to the present. See David Hurst Thomas, *Skull Wars: Kennewick Man, Archaeology, and the Battle for Native American Identity* (New York: Basic Books, 2000) pp. 44–51.

62   The Piltdown hoax began in 1912 with the purported discovery of a skull belonging to the "missing link" between man and ape in an English gravel quarry. It was actually a combination of a modern human cranium and an altered ape's jaw. Insofar as

the "find" supposedly proved that the first true humans were Europeans, it served as the ultimate scientific confirmation of white supremacist dogma. Validated by several curators of the British Museum and carefully shielded from public scrutiny, the fabrication continued to serve this useful purpose until it was finally exposed as a fraud during the mid-1950s. Frank Spencer, *Piltdown: A Scientific Forgery* (New York: Oxford University Press, 1990).

63 One of Deloria's better articulations of this theme is in "Comfortable Fictions and the Struggle for Turf," *American Indian Quarterly*, Vol. 16, No. 3 (Summer 1992) pp. 397–410.

64 The theological dimension is covered quite well in Deloria's "Christianity and Indigenous Religion: Friends or Enemies?" in David G. Burke, ed., *Creation and Culture: The Challenge of Indigenous Spirituality and Culture to Western Creation Thought* (New York: Lutheran World Ministries, 1987) pp. 31–43. It should be noted that, at least in terms of the secular enunciation of theological concepts, Deloria's point was acknowledged by Western scientists themselves until rather recently. See, e.g., E.A. Burtt, *The Metaphysical Foundations of Natural Science* (New York: Doubleday, 1954 reprint of 1924 original).

65 Vine Deloria Jr., "Myth and the Origin of Religion," *Pensée*, Vol. 4, No. 4 (Fall 1974) pp. 45–50.

66 For a materialist critique that arrives at remarkably similar conclusions, see Stanley Aronowitz, *Science as Power: Discourse and Ideology in Modern Society* (Minneapolis: University of Minnesota Press, 1988).

67 This theme is most fully developed in Deloria's "The Fascination of Heresy," *Katallegete*, Vol. 6, No. 4 (Spring 1977) pp. 47–50. On Galileo's experience at the hands of the Inquisition, see Georgio De Santillana, *The Crime of Galileo* (New York: Heinemann, 1958).

68 Deloria, *God Is Red*, pp. 123–34.

69 Immanuel Velikovsky, *Worlds in Collision* (Garden City, NY: Doubleday, 1950). The ideas therein were developed with greater precision in Velikovsky's second book, *Ages in Chaos* (Garden City, NY: Doubleday, 1952).

70 Deloria, *God Is Red*, pp. 117–28. The second reference is to Velikovsky's *Earth in Upheaval* (Garden City, NY: Doubleday, 1955).

71 Deloria, *God Is Red*, p. 129.

72 Ibid., pp. 129–30. For further details, see Alfred de Grazia, *The Velikovsky Affair: The War of Science and Scientism* (New Hyde Park, NY: University Books, 1966); Editors of *Pensée*, *Velikovsky Reconsidered* (Garden City, NY: Doubleday, 1976).

73 Deloria, *Metaphysics*, pp. 167–74.

74 These circumstances were summarized in my review, "A Critique of Vine Deloria Jr.'s *The Metaphysics of Modern Existence*," *American Indian Culture and Research Journal*, Vol. 5, No. 3 (Fall 1981) pp. 82–88.

75 See, as examples, Deloria's "The Traditional Western Answers Offer No Solution to Me," in Remmelt Hummelen and Ruth Hummelen, eds., *Stories of Survival: Conversations with Native North Americans* (New York: Friendship Press, 1985) pp. 13–15; "American Indian Metaphysics," *Winds of Change*, Vol. I, No. 2 (June 1986) pp. 2–3; "Ethnoscience and Indian Realities," *Winds Of Change*, Vol. 7, No. 3 (Summer 1992) pp. 12–18; "Relativity, Relatedness and Reality," *Winds of Change*, Vol. 7, No. 4 (Fall 1992) pp. 34–40; "If You Think About It, You Will See That It Is True," *Noetic Sciences Review*, No. 27 (Autumn 1993) pp. 62–71.

76   Harper & Row did not bother to have *Metaphysics* indexed. On Heisenberg, see esp. pp. 33–45; on Jung, pp. 90–101; on Chardin, pp. 52–69; on Tillich, pp. 25–32.

77   Deloria, "Self-Determination and the Concept of Sovereignty," p. 22; "Law and Theology III: The Theme," *Church and Society*, Vol. 79, No. 1 (September–October 1988) pp. 8–13; Carl Schmitt, *Political Theology: Four Chapters on the Concept of Sovereignty* (Cambridge, MA: MIT Press, 1985 trans. of 1922 German original). Interestingly, Schmitt emerges from the Hegelian philosophical tradition, which Deloria has by and large ignored in his interrogations.

78   See, e.g., "From Reservation to Global Society: American Culture, Liberation and the Native American—An Interview with Vine Deloria, Jr., by Michael McKale," *Radical Religion*, Vol. 2, No. 4 (Fall 1976) pp. 49–58; "A Native American Perspective on Liberation," *Occasional Bulletin of Missionary Research*, Vol. 1, No. 3 (July 1977) pp. 15–17.

79   Aside from the relevant sections of *God Is Red* and *Metaphysics*, the more important articulations offered during the period include "The Theological Dimension of the Indian Protest Movement," *Christian Century* (September 19, 1973) pp. 912–14; "Religion and Revolution among American Indians," *Worldview*, Vol. 17, No. 1 (January 1974) pp. 12–15; "Religion and the Modern American Indian," *Current History*, Vol. 67, No. 400 (December 1974) pp. 250–53; "1976: The Desperate Need for Understanding," *Cross Talk*, Vol. 3, No. 4 (February 1975); "God Is Also Red: An Interview with Vine Deloria by James R. McGraw," *Christianity and Crisis*, No. 35 (September 15, 1975) pp. 198–206; "Native American Spirituality," *Gamaliel*, Vol. 13, No. 1 (Spring 1977); "Kinship and the World," *Journal of Current Social Issues*, Vol. 15, No 3 (Fall 1978) pp. 19–21.

80   Velikovsky's last book, *Peoples of the Sea*, was published by Doubleday in 1977. Therein, he attempted a comprehensive restructuring of Mideastern historical chronology corresponding to the sequence of physical phenomena he had outlined in his earlier works. That Deloria was in some sense consciously adopting Velikovsky's task as his own is made clear in his essay "Catastrophism and Planetary History," *Kronos*, Vol. 3, No. 4 (1978) pp. 45–51.

81   Deloria has always evidenced a strong inclination in the latter direction. See, e.g., his "Revision and Reversion," in Calvin Martin, ed., *American Indians and the Problem of History* (New York: Oxford University Press, 1987) pp. 84–90.

82   Vine Deloria Jr., *Red Earth, White Lies: Native Americans and the Myth of Scientific Pact* (New York: Scribner, 1995).

83   Ibid., pp. 99, 184, 203–4. During the early 1980s, Deloria's interest in the Hopi origin story led him into a brief association with independent archaeologist Jeffrey Goodman, who attempted to confirm it by conducting a dig at the location indicated. Although the results were ambiguous, Goodman may have unearthed the oldest humanly inscribed stone yet recovered in North America. See Jeffrey Goodman, *American Genesis* (New York: Summit Books, 1981) pp. 193–216.

84   Deloria, *Red Earth, White Lies*, pp. 194–202.

85   The three-thousand-year limit, which makes no geological sense at all, was proclaimed and defended by Smithsonian curator Aleš Hrdlička throughout the first half of the twentieth century. In 1953 Alfred Kroeber, who succeeded Hrdlička as "dean" of Americanist anthropology, acknowledged the cumulative weight of evidence embodied in the discovery of Clovis culture, as well as the geological chronology of Beringia, by announcing that the limit had been revised to twelve thousand to fifteen thousand years. Presently, it appears that an accumulation of linguistic, genetic, and other evidence is on the verge of precipitating a revision

to about thirty thousand years, a dating that comes much closer to what native people have been saying all along. At each step along the way, however, archaeologists like the late George Carter, who have argued that the human occupancy of America was much older than what was admitted by anthropological orthodoxy, have been subjected to ridicule, marginalized, and often driven from the profession altogether. For a detailed examination of the record and its implications, see "About that Bering Strait Land Bridge: Let's Turn Those Footprints Around," in my *Since Predator Came: Notes From the Struggle for American Indian Liberation* (Littleton, CO: Aigis, 1995) pp. 265–97.

86   Rather instructively, this is referred to as the "Eve hypothesis." Deloria recommends William Fix's *The Bone Peddlers* (New York: Macmillan, 1984) as an effective antidote to the belief that it has been proven.

87   The forgery, first published in 1836, was put together by an amateur naturalist named Constantine Samuel de Rafinesque-Schmaltz (usually known simply as "Rafinesque"). Although it had long since been discredited as a fraud by linguists, its contents were supposedly "verified" by an archaeological team funded by the Lilly Foundation during the 1950s. As recently as 1987, it was still being cited by "reputable" scholars such as historian C.A. Weslager as corroborating the Bering Strait migration hypothesis. See generally David M. Ostreicher, "Unraveling the *Walam Olum*," *Natural History*, Vol. 105, No. 10 (October 1996) pp. 14–21.

88   Deloria, *Red Earth, White Lies*, pp. 86–90, 100–104. On animal migrations, he relies in large part on L. Taylor Hansen's *The Ancient Atlantic* (Amherst, WI: Amherst Press, 1969).

89   From a starting point on the Kolmya River in eastern Siberia, these would have included the daunting Khrebet Gydan and Chukotskoye ranges. To get to the strait from the American side would have entailed scaling the Kaiyuh, Kuskokwim, and Richardson ranges from the south or the Ogilvie, Mackenzie, and Franklin ranges from the southeast. Deloria, *Red Earth, White Lies*, p. 88.

90   Ibid., pp. 96–97. For the particulars of the meteorological data, see Reid Bryson, *Radiocarbon Isochromes of the Laurentian Tide Sheet* (Madison: University of Wisconsin Technical Report No. 35, 1967). For implications to anthropological theory, see Alan Bryan, "Early Man in the Late Pleistocene Chronology of Western Canada and Alaska," *Current Anthropology* 10, No. 4 (Fall 1969).

91   They would require a prevailing south-to-north wind direction, whereas east-west is the actual planetary norm. Deloria, *Red Earth, White Lies*, pp. 92–93.

92   Ibid., p. 203; quoting Michael Cremo and Richard Thompson, *Forbidden Archeology* (San Francisco: Bhaktivedanta Institute, 1993) p. 694.

93   Deloria, *Red Earth, White Lies*, p. 247; referencing Charles Cline, "Scientific Dating Methods in Ruins," *Velikovskian*, Vol. 2, No. 4 (1994) p. 53.

94   Deloria, *Red Earth, White Lies*, p. 250; quoting Jared Diamond, "America: A Mammoth Undertaking," *Discover*, Vol. 8, No. 6 (June 1987) p. 84. On the denial and suppression of inconvenient evidence, see Goodman, *American Genesis*, pp. 81–87. Also see George E. Carter, *Earlier than You Think: A Personal View of Man in America* (College Station: Texas A&M University Press, 1980).

95   Deloria, *Red Earth, While Lies*, p. 87. His reference is to William S. Laughlin, "Human Migration and Permanent Occupation in the Bering Sea Area," in David M. Hopkins, ed., *The Bering Land Bridge* (Stanford, CA: Stanford University Press, 1967) pp. 409–50. Although Deloria doesn't mention it, I can attest that no better evidence is assembled in the more recent and reputedly definitive collection of specialist essays edited

by Frederick Hadleigh West under the title *American Beginnings: The Prehistory and Paleontology of Beringia* (Chicago: University of Chicago Press, 1996).

96   Deloria, *Red Earth, White Lies*, pp. 84–85, 87.

97   Ibid., p. 87.

98   The first recorded articulation of the idea is attributed to Father Acosta, a Spanish priest. Carter, *Earlier than You Think*, p. 7. For further background, see Lee H. Huddleston, *Origins of the American Indians, European Concepts, 1492–1729* (Austin: University of Texas Press, 1969).

99   Ronald Sanders, *Lost Tribes and Promised Lands: The Origins of American Racism* (New York: HarperPerennial, [2nd ed.] 1992) p. 370.

100 In 1683 Quaker leader William Penn, for example, went on record asserting that he was "ready to believe [Indians] to be of the Jewish race—I mean stock of the ten tribes." Quoted in Goodman, *American Genesis*, p. 25. The Puritan leader Cotton Mather also professed such beliefs in his 1702 book, *Magnali Christiani Americana*. On Mormon beliefs, see Milton R. Hunter and Thomas Stuart Ferguson, *Ancient America and the Book of Mormon* (Oakland, CA: Kolob Books, 1950). On the New World Archaeological Foundation, see Goodman, *American Genesis*, p. 28.

101 Thomas Jefferson, *Notes on the State of Virginia* (Chapel Hill: University of North Carolina Press, 1982 reprint of 1781 original) p. 101. Actually, the inception of the "scientific" process should probably be dated from 1775, when amateur linguist James Adair first published a lengthy set of phonetic "proofs" that American Indian languages derive from ancient Hebrew. See James Adair, *The History of the American Indians* (London: E. and C. Dilly, 1775).

102 This has been at least as true, and in some ways more so, after Franz Boas' supposedly rigorous scientific footing during the first decade of the twentieth century as it was at any earlier point. On the Boasian "revolution"—sometimes referred to as a manifestation of anthropology's "physics envy"—see Thomas, *Skull Wars*, pp. 97–98.

103 A comparable, if entirely secular, conclusion is drawn in Aronowitz, *Science as Power*.

104 As the matter is framed in UN General Assembly Resolution 1514, it is a fundamental legal requirement that "the principle of equal rights and self-determination of all peoples" be respected. Brownlie, *Basic Documents*, p. 28.

105 See generally John Tomlinson, *Cultural Imperialism* (Baltimore: Johns Hopkins University Press, 1991). For an example of Deloria consciously working the same theme, see his "Education and Imperialism," *Integrateducation*, Vol. 19, Nos. 1–2 (January 1982) pp. 58–63.

106 The term *radical* is used here in accordance with its actual meaning—to "go to the root"—rather than its colloquially corrupted form of serving as a synonym for "extreme," "extremist," or "revolutionary."

107 H. David Brumble, "Vine Deloria, Jr., Creationism and Ethnic Pseudoscience," *American Literary History*, Vol. 10, No. 2 (Summer 1998) pp. 335–46. For Vine's reply, see pp. 347–49.

108 Alan Goodman, "Resurrecting Race: The Concept of Race in Physical Anthropology in the 1990s," in L.T. Reynolds and L. Lieberman, eds., *Race and Other Misadventures: Essays in Honor of Ashley Montague in His Ninetieth Year* (Dix Hills, NY: General Hall, 1996) pp. 174–86; Yolanda T. Moses, "An Idea Whose Time Has Come Again: Anthropology Reclaims 'Race,'" *Anthropology Newsletter*, Vol. 38, No. 7 (1998) pp. 1–4.

109 Thomas, *Skull Wars*, p. 251.

110 Momaday, a Kiowa, professes a vague "genetic recollection" of a time when his ancestors resided in Asia. N. Scott Momaday, "Disturbing the Spirits: The Bones

Must Stay in the Ground," *New York Times* (November 2, 1996). Deloria publicly demanded that Momaday provide some—any—form of material corroboration of his "memory." Vine Deloria Jr., "OK, Scott, Where's the Beef?," *News from Indian Country* (Late December 1996). Momaday declined to attempt such substantiation, but Thomas—a self-professed scientist—plainly sides with him, even to the extent of reproducing a photo to illustrate how "Asiatic" Momaday appeared as a child. Thomas, *Skull Wars*, pp. 256–57.

111 Like every good colonialist author since Kipling wrote "Gunga Din," Thomas makes a fetish of showcasing the statements of "right-thinking wogs" who are willing, in exchange for preferential treatment by their colonizers, to endorse colonialism as desirable. Echo-Hawk, a Pawnee, is a University of Colorado-trained anthropologist who has denounced *Red Earth, White Lies* as "fringe literature" while championing a "partnership ecology" between Indians and the archaeological establishment on which his livelihood and status depend. Thomas, *Skull Wars*, p. 252.

112 The idea here, although it is advanced in a far deeper and more sweeping fashion, is not altogether different from that put forth by Thomas Kuhn in his acclaimed but poorly understood *The Structure of Scientific Revolutions* (Chicago: University of Chicago Press, 1962).

113 For a good overview of the expectations at issue, see Ernst Cassirer, *The Philosophy of the Enlightenment* (Princeton, NJ: Princeton University Press, 1951). My own view is that Deloria's position shares much in common with Marcuse's contention that, although long derailed by its context, fulfillment of the more hopeful aspects of the Enlightenment remained a "possibility" in the late twentieth century. See Herbert Marcuse, *One Dimensional Man* (Boston: Beacon Press, 1964) pp. 234–35.

114 One indication of the degree to which scientism has supplanted science is the ubiquitous belief that technology and science are synonymous, the former being simply the "application" of the latter. For a powerful and insightful delineation of the reasons why science, to be science, must function in a manner that is entirely autonomous from considerations of technological applicability, see David Landes, *Unbounded Prometheus: Technological Change and Industrial Development in Western Europe from 1750 to the Present* (Cambridge, UK: Cambridge University Press, 1969). Also see Jacques Ellul, *The Technological Bluff* (Grand Rapids, MI: Wm. B. Eerdmans, 1990).

115 See, e.g., Alvin W. Gouldner, *The Dialectic of Ideology and Technology: Origins, Grammar, and Future of Ideology* (New York: Continuum, 1976). Related arguments can be found in Jacques Ellul, *The Technological Society* (New York: Alfred A. Knopf, 1964); J. C. Merquoir, *The Veil and the Mask: Essays on Culture and Ideology* (London; Routledge and Keegan Paul, 1979); Jürgen Habermas, "Technology and Science as Ideology," in his *Towards a Rational Society* (Boston: Beacon Press, 1970) pp. 81–84.

116 For a somewhat garbled enunciation of a similar thesis, see Jerry Mander, *In the Absence of the Sacred: The Failure of Technology and the Survival of the Indian Nations* (San Francisco: Sierra Club, 1991). The book's main strength is its survey of Western theories whose thinking is taking them in the same direction.

117 Vine Deloria Jr., "Knowing and Understanding: Traditional Education in the Modern World," *Winds of Change*, Vol. 5, No. 1 (Winter 1990) pp. 12–18. For a much denser but nonetheless comparable Western articulation, see Noam Chomsky's discussions of accessible and inaccessible knowledge in the chapters entitled "A Philosophy of Language?" and "Empiricism and Rationalism," in *Language and Responsibility: Based on Conversations with Mitsou Ronat* (New York: Pantheon, 1977) pp. 63–80 and 81–99, respectively.

118 Deloria, *Metaphysics*, pp. 212–13.

119 Teilhard de Chardin, *A New Synthesis of Evolution* (Glen Rock, NJ: Deus Books, 1964).

120 This is again not inconsistent with the dynamic described by Horkheimer and Adorno in *The Dialectic of Enlightenment*. Taken from a somewhat different angle, it dovetails quite neatly with the thinking of Jürgen Habermas, perhaps especially in his essay "Modernism—An Incomplete Project," in Hal Foster, ed., *Postmodern Culture* (London: Routledge, 1985) pp. 3–16.

121 For elaboration, see Nelson Eldredge and Ian Tattersal, *The Myths of Human Evolution* (New York: Columbia University Press, 1982).

122 The idea is that small groups of Paleolithic hunters rapidly exterminated the woolly mammoth and other similarly daunting types of prey, apparently by alternately beating them to death with sticks or somehow driving them off cliffs in huge numbers; Diamond, "American Blitzkrieg." More comprehensively, see the collections of essays in Paul S. Martin and H. E. Wright, eds., *Pleistocene Extinctions: The Search for a Cause* (New Haven, CT: Yale University Press, 1967); Paul S. Martin and Richard G. Klein, eds., *Quaternary Extinctions* (Tucson: University of Arizona Press, 1984). An even more absurdist variation on the theme was offered by Shepard Krech in *The Ecological Indian: Myth and History* (New York: W. W. Norton, 1999), wherein Indians are depicted as doing essentially the same thing with the buffalo during the nineteenth century.

123 For what may be the best overview of the evolution of Velikovskian thinking over the past twenty years, see Derek Ager, *The New Catastrophism* (Cambridge, UK: Cambridge University Press, 1993).

124 Deloria's thesis, expressed most compellingly in *Red Earth, White Lies*, is that while the chronology of human occupancy in the Americas has been arbitrarily rendered in far too shallow a manner, the geological chronology has been rendered in a manner that is in many cases far too deep. For elaboration on the problems attending the scientian depiction of geological chronology, see Derek Ager, *The Nature of the Stratigraphic Record* (New York: John Wiley and Sons, 1973).

125 Vine Deloria Jr., "Conclusion: Anthros, Indians, and Planetary Reality," in Biolsi and Zimmerman, *Indians and Anthropologists*, pp. 209–21.

126 See Vine Deloria Jr., "The Rise and Fall of Ethnic Studies," in Steven A. Margaritis, ed., *In Search of a Future for Education: Readings in Foundations* (Columbus, OH: Charles E. Merritt 1973) pp. 153–57; "Integrity before Education," *Integrateducation*, Vol. 7, No. 3 (May–June 1974) pp. 22–28; "The Place of Indians in Contemporary Education," *American Indian Journal*, Vol. 2, No. 2 (February 1976) pp. 2–9; "Token Indian, Token Education," *Four Winds*, No. 1 (Winter 1980); "Out of Chaos," *Parabola*, Vol. 10, No. 2 (Spring 1985) pp. 14–22; "Indian Studies: The Orphan of Academia," *Wicazo Sa Review*, Vol. 2, No. 2 (Summer 1986) pp. 1–7; "Transitional Education," *Winds of Change*, Vol. 5, No. 3 (Summer 1990) pp. 10–15; "Research, Redskins and Reality," *American Indian Quarterly*, Vol. 15, No. 4 (Fall 1991) pp. 457–68; "Tribal Colleges and Traditional Knowledge," *Tribal College*, Vol. 5, No. 2 (Autumn 1993) pp. 31–32; "Redefining the Path of Indian Education," *The Circle*, Vol. 16, No. 9 (September 1995) p. 16. Also see the entire section titled "Education" in Barbara Deloria, Kristen Foehner, and Sam Scinta, eds., *Spirit and Reason: The Vine Deloria, Jr., Reader* (Golden, CO: Fulcrum, 1999) pp. 129–86.

127 Ivan Illich, *Deschooling Society* (New York: Harper & Row, 1970); Paulo Freire, *Pedagogy of the Oppressed* (New York: Herder and Herder, 1970) and *Education for Critical Consciousness* (New York: Continuum, 1983); Paulo Freire and Antonio Faundez,

Learning to Question: A Pedagogy of Liberation (New York: Continuum, 1989); Henry A. Giroux, *Ideology, Culture and the Process of Schooling* (Philadelphia: Temple University Press 1981); Henry A. Giroux and Peter McLaren, eds., *Critical Pedagogy, the State and Cultural Struggle* (Albany: SUNY Press, 1989).

128 Martin Carnoy, *Education as Cultural Imperialism* (New York: David McKay, 1974). Deloria's interpretation and application of the same theme will be found in his "Education and Imperialism."

129 The connection is hardly lost on Deloria. See his *For This Land: Writings on Religion in America* (New York: Routledge, 1999).

Science as Psychosis

An American Corollary to Germany's Blood Libel of the Jews

These islands are inhabited by Canabilli, a wild, unconquered race which feeds on human flesh. I would be right to call them anthropophagi. They wage unceasing wars against gentle and timid Indians to supply flesh; this is their booty and what they hunt. They ravage, despoil, and terrorize the Indians ruthlessly.

—Guillermo Coma, November 3, 1493

Thus did a Columbian lieutenant during the second voyage describe those his commander habitually referred to as "*Canibales*," "*Canibas*" or, most commonly, "*Caribas*," a people with whom, we have it on good authority, neither man ever once interacted and of whose supposedly rapacious consumption of human flesh there is not a single reliable account dating from theirs or any other era. At its core, as later historians would discover, the whole notion of the "Caribs" as a race of man-eaters "was never more than a bogey, born of [Columbus'] own paranoia or stubborn ferocity and spread to his comrades, to the chroniclers of Europe, and to history."[1]

Even at the time, there were those such as the Franciscan priest Bartolomé de las Casas who struggled valiantly to rebut such (mis)characterizations with more factual renderings,[2] but all for naught. The derogatory appellation applied by Columbus to the Kalinas and Kalinagos, as the "Island-Caribs" called themselves, not only stuck but evolved into the word "cannibal," a descriptor now universally applied to any human who eats humans.[3] Indeed, the very water surrounding their erstwhile island domain has become known to the world as the "Caribbean Sea" (literally translated, "Sea of Cannibals").

Originally published in *North American Archaeologist*, Vol. 21, No. 3 (2000).

Nor were the hapless Caribs alone in their fate. While there is virtually no mention of it in Spanish chronicles written during the campaign itself,[4] highly sensationalized depictions of Aztec (Mexíca) cannibalism also began to assume an ever increasing prominence in accounts published in the aftermath of Hernán Cortés' conquest of Mexico.[5] Taken in combination with claims that the vanquished Indians were avid sodomites, and that they engaged in human sacrifice on a truly massive scale,[6] such stories seem more than anything to have been originally advanced as a sort of counterpropaganda offsetting the "Black Legend" of Spanish brutality in the Americas then being circulated by the English and Spain's other European rivals.[7] In any event, there has never been the least credible evidence offered to support them.

The closest things came in this respect was the "historical memoir" of an obscure military figure, Bernal Díaz del Castillo, written nearly a half-century after his participation in the conquest.[8] Although he often waxes eloquent on the topic, a close reading of the text reveals that even the most detailed accounts are offered at second-hand; Díaz never once claims to have seen tangible evidence of cannibalism, much less to have witnessed the practice itself. On the matter of human sacrifice, about which the author becomes still more rhetorically extravagant, we find that everything hinges upon a single incident in which Díaz claimed to have viewed the ritual killing of several captured Spaniards at the Templo Mayor, in the Aztec capital of Tenochtitlán (now Mexico City).[9] Not usually remarked upon is the fact that he claimed to have witnessed the scene from what turns out to be a distance of three to four miles, unassisted by a telescope.[10]

To this may be added the translations of native texts performed by the priests Diego Durán and, much more extensively, Bernardo de Sahagún.[11] Both men were demonstrably committed to the "fact" of Aztec cannibalism before they began their task, however, and proceeded to interpret the materials accordingly. Ultimately, there is nothing in the texts which is necessarily more suggestive that the Aztecs consumed actual human flesh than are descriptions of the Christian communion ceremony that Durán and Sahagún themselves were literal rather than merely symbolic cannibals.[12] Their translations were "corroborated" by surviving Aztec priests, of course, but such testimonies invariably amounted to little more than "confessions" extracted under the worst forms of inquisitional torture, or threat of it, and are thus extremely suspect.[13]

Nonetheless, without further proof, but with ever more embellishment, tales of Carib and Aztec cannibalism entered the scientific and philosophical literature of the West,[14] coming by the twentieth century to be considered matters of "ethnographic fact."[15] Along the way, similar allegations had been extended against many other peoples: the Iroquois of North America,[16] for example, as well as the Tupi-Guaranis and Amahuacas of the South.[17] An elaborate analytical superstructure had also been developed to explore such esoteric concerns as whether particular groups of natives were supposed to have cooked their victims or eaten them raw,[18] whether they practiced "endocannibalism" (eating one another), "exocannibalism" (eating outsiders) or even "autocannibalism" (eating pieces of themselves),[19] and whether their these practices fulfilled spiritual needs, nutritional requirements, or both.[20]

So refined, entrenched, and apparently compelling were these ideas by the mid-1970s that, somewhat paradoxically, popularizers like Gary Hogg and Eli Sagan were beginning to complain that "insufficient attention" had been paid by anthropologists to the "obvious centrality" of anthropophagy in the understanding of indigenous cultures, that of the Aztecs in particular.[21] Responding for the discipline, at least in his own mind, a young anthro named Michael Harner thereupon advanced what may be taken as the crowning scientian articulation in this regard.[22] Working from the usual set of vacuous assumptions, and inflating them with noticeable abandon as he went along, he contrived a superficially impressive mathematical formulation with which he purported to demonstrate that the consumption of human flesh had been not only a key to Aztec spirituality but an essential protein source in the daily diet of the native élite.[23]

Given its sheer methodological transparency, Harner plainly overreached in the claims he attached to his "model." While a few established figures like his mentor, Marvin Harris, applauded his findings,[24] the field as a whole exhibited an altogether appropriate sense of professional embarrassment. While the most typical stance was an uncomfortable silence, several competent reviewers—Bernard Montellano, Barbara J. Price, and George Pierre Castile among them—responded by literally and quite publicly demolishing Harner's argument, root and branch.[25] Even Marshall Sahlins, otherwise a firm believer in the equation of "primitivism" to cannibalism, wrote an article for the *New York Review of Books* wherein he outlined the ethnocentrism and statistical absurdity with which Harner's pronouncements abounded.[26]

The Harner controversy prompted a number scholars, most of them for the first time, to finally undertake a serious and in some cases systematic probing of the evidentiary underpinnings of long-held beliefs about the culinary practices, not just of the Aztecs and Caribs but among a host of other native peoples around the world.[27] This flurry of critical inquiry resulted, most pointedly, in William Arens' 1979 book, The Man-Eating Myth, in which it was revealed that for all anecdotes and opinionating on the topic which had littered Western letters since Herodotus first broached it in the fifth century A.D., "only the fleeting quality of the documentation remains constant."[28]

Arens, in fact, professed himself unable to find direct evidence of "the actual existence of this act as an accepted practice for any time or place [or] as a custom in any form for any society [emphasis added]."[29] Ultimately, he likened the very concept of the anthropophagi to that of the "Amazons," "Wild Men," "Monstrous Races," and similar European fables of the dangerously exotic nonwestern Other.[30]

> In the deft hands and fertile imaginations of anthropologists, former or contemporary anthropophagists have multiplied with the advance of [Western] civilization and fieldwork in formerly unstudied areas. The existence of man-eating peoples just beyond the pale of civilization is a common ethnographic suggestion. While the Mediterranean was the center of the European cultural universe, Herodotus assumed that the custom flourished in Eastern Europe, while Strabo had the same fear about the barbarians on the western fringe. Thus, in good company and classic form, a current encyclopedia of anthropology for today's generation of students reports that cannibalism "is practiced today only in the remotest parts of New Guinea and South America."[31]

In other words, as archaeologist Paul Bahn put it in the much more recent Cambridge Encyclopedia of Human Evolution, "the extreme scarcity of cannibalism in historic times" has rendered its "very existence in prehistory [increasingly] hard to swallow."[32] Or, citing the current edition of the Encyclopedia of Anthropology, the notion that autochthonous native societies are or ever were cannibalistic has never amounted to more than a matter of "our own surmise."[33] "The fantasy lay on the surface of the minds of the explorers from Europe, from centuries of myth-making, an expression of deep desire and passions and terrors," noted Marina Warner in a 1995 assessment completed by Marianna Torgovnick's observation that "cannibalism, human sacrifice and head-hunting apparently did not and do not exist within . . . indigenous cultures."[34]

In sum, the appearance of a vast array of anthropophagic peoples was, to quote Kirkpatrick Sale, simply "invented by those who had need of them" for whatever reasons, and "served their multiple purposes for . . . several centuries."[35] Even if such falsehoods might be to some extent "understandable in the context of sixteenth century missionary reporting," as Arens suggests, his follow-up assertion that they "deserve no place in the record of contemporary archaeology" and related endeavors must be considered equally valid.[36] Unfortunately, as Warner concluded, the cannibal myth "has survived and still influences attitudes today."[37] The question thus becomes not so much how the fiction was originally fostered as why it has been perpetuated with such remarkable intensity in the modern era, and by those supposedly best equipped to know better.

The Perverse Persistence of "Canibales"

Such queries might be of mere academic interest, perhaps as grist for the mills of postmodernist analysis, had the preoccupation with cannibalism previously exhibited by anthropologists ended, or at least significantly abated, after publication of The Man-Eating Myth. But, to be sure, it didn't. By 1982, cultural anthropologists with a vested interest in rebutting Arens' "anticannibalism thesis" had assembled a special panel to air their views during the American Anthropological Association's annual meeting, and self-published the collected ripostes as an anthology a year later. While most of the material contained therein served more to illustrate than to counter Arens' thinking, the editors nevertheless announced that it demonstrated the extent to which he'd reached his conclusions "erroneously."[38]

Marshall Sahlins, meanwhile, capped a lengthy polemic laced with ad hominem arguments by branding Arens' book a "scandal," its author a counterpart to the neonazi Holocaust deniers.[39] This smear, despite the logical inversion it so blatantly displays,[40] has been repeated with regularity, first by Thomas Riley, later by Pierre Vidal-Naquet, and most recently by Michael Palencia-Roth.[41] Mary Douglas, a woman notable mainly for her spirited defense of Carlos Castaneda and his fraudulent "Don Juan" texts a few years earlier,[42] denounced The Man-Eating Myth as "a slur upon ethnography."[43] Peter Rivière warned that it was "dangerous,"[44] while Shirley Lindenbaum classified Arens himself as a cannibal.[45] Others entering comparable invective included Edmund Leach, Charles Leroux, James Weiner, Marvin Harris, and Donald Forsyth.[46]

A very different tack was taken by physical anthropologists. Readily conceding the evidentiary deficiencies attending many of the interpretations extrapolated by their colleagues in cultural anthropology, archaeologists nonetheless expressed the consensus view that it would be "premature" to either confirm or foreclose upon the existence of institutionalized cannibalism in precontact indigenous societies. Only the most rigorous and comprehensive application of forensic science, they maintained, would be sufficient to make such determinations.[47]

Imminently reasonable on its surface, this argument is actually far more slippery than anything embodied in the vituperations of Sahlins and his cohorts. Nothing was said, for example, about how Arens or anyone else is supposed to go about proving a negative. No matter how many specific allegations of anthropophagy are refuted, it will always and by definition remain "premature" to conclude that the practice has not prevailed at some other time, in some other place, among some other people. Hence, "suspicions" of native cannibalism can be extended into infinity, always on the pretext that, since they can never be absolutely disproven, "scientific proof" is, or at least might be, just around the corner (or at the next dig site).[48]

Although there have been myriad statements to this effect, one of the more straightforward was recently offered by University of Colorado paleontologist Peter Robinson during an interview for the academic publication *Lingua Franca*. Notwithstanding the paucity of physical evidence forthcoming from well over a century's digging and analysis, Robinson asserted, "It's only a matter of time before the buildup of a critical mass of irrefutable evidence from the archaeological record . . . settles the debate" in favor of those subscribing to the idea that cannibalism "must have" existed in indigenous societies.[49] Exactly how, absent a crystal ball, Robinson and his colleagues might already know what will be found "in time" is left as mysterious as what it is they might wish to hold out as "irrefutable proof."

Clearly, this was not the statement of a "neutral and objective practitioner of the scientific method" basing his opinions in empirical fact. Quite the reverse. By positing the outcome of research before the research itself has been completed—or, more accurately, in a manner so completely at odds with those results the investigation has thus far yielded—Robinson revealed himself to be much more a proponent of scientism than of science. In effect, the approach he describes is one of repeating the same failed experiment endlessly, always confident that it will eventually produce the desired result. Suffice it to say that no medieval alchemist seeking to convert lead into gold might have put it better.[50]

A more tangible problem for physical anthropologists during the early 1980s was that, all posturing aside, they'd never really mastered the forensic procedures they claimed would distinguish their findings from the vagaries of cultural anthropology. They were only just then beginning to employ such rudimentary techniques as microscopic analysis in their examinations of artifacts and human remains.[51] Nonetheless, for nearly a century, they'd been generating ostensibly scientific reports in which they claimed that the results of one or another site investigation had proven what, as of 1997, even true believers like Peter Robinson were tacitly admitting has yet to be proven.

As concerns U.S. territory, the first of these was a rather exuberant article on his findings in northern Arizona published by Smithsonian archaeologist Walter Hough in 1902.[52] Thereafter, similar claims began to accumulate at a fairly steady rate, as when, in 1919, Frederick Webb Hodge, an archaeologist with the American Bureau of Ethnology, announced that he'd found "solid evidence" at the Hawikuh site, about fifteen miles southwest of the Zuni Pueblo, in New Mexico.[53] In 1920, George H. Pepper, an archaeologist working for the American Museum of Natural History, reported much the same thing with respect to human remains found at the Peñasco Blanco and Pueblo Bonito sites in Chaco Canyon, New Mexico.[54] This was followed, in 1929, with a report by American Museum archaeologists Earl H. and Ann Axtell Morris that they'd uncovered comparable evidence at Battle Cave, in the Canyon de Chelly, Arizona.[55] A decade later, Earl Morris, by then working for the Carnegie Institution, claimed to have found further proof of prehistoric anthropophagy at a pair of sites along the La Plata River, in southwestern Colorado.[56]

Although each of these studies was highly touted in its time, none passed scientific muster in the first comprehensive survey of the literature, performed by National Park Service archaeologist Erik Reed in 1949.[57] On the other hand, Reed confirmed reports by a colleague, Gordon C. Baldwin, that he'd uncovered unassailable evidence of cannibalism in at least two unspecified sites in the Grand Canyon during the summer of 1947.[58] In 1952, Watson Smith added a claim for the "House of Tragedy," near the Wupatki Pueblo, in northeastern Arizona.[59] Three years after that, Reed and Marie Wormington, an archaeologist with the Denver Museum of Natural History, reported further such evidence at the Turner-Look site, in east-central Utah.[60] Smithsonian archaeologist Frank H.H. Roberts Jr. followed up by reporting in 1957 that he'd uncovered evidence of cannibalism about thirty years earlier at the "Small House" site, near Pueblo Bonito.[61]

During the 1960s, there was a tentative finding of cannibalism submitted by Christy G. Turner II with respect to the remains of the so-called

"Coombs Woman," discovered in southern Utah,[62] and a much splashier claim turned in by an Arizona State University team that had been excavating at the Sambrito Village site, in northwestern New Mexico.[63] By 1970, all of the post–World War II reports were being discounted on the basis of their dubious scientific merit, but only to be replaced by far more sensational reports emanating from the Polacca Wash site, in northern Arizona.[64] The latter was joined over the next few years by reports from the Leroux Wash,[65] Mancos Canyon,[66] Burnt Mesa,[67] the Herfano Mesa/ Llaves-Alkali Springs sites,[68] the Largo-Gallina Towers ("Nogales Cliff House"),[69] and elsewhere in the Four Corners region of Arizona, New Mexico, Colorado, and Utah.[70]

These last findings, it is now admitted, were as deeply "flawed in both method and theory" as their predecessors,[71] but, just as with the Hough report at the beginning of the century, each was trumpeted with considerable fanfare as constituting the epitome of "hard" scientific evidence that cannibalism was a fact of precolumbian native life.[72] They served, moreover, as the veritable launching pad for a raft of new claims, all of them advanced in light of the relatively more sophisticated methods of taphonomic analysis and other forensic techniques which began making their appearance on the archaeological scene during the early 1980s.[73]

The first of these came in 1982 and involved the reexamination of skeletal materials collected in 1979 by archaeologist Paul R. Nickens at the Grinnell site, in southwestern Colorado.[74] The same year, a report of cannibalism was submitted with respect to a suspected Kayenta Anasazi site in the Monument Valley of southern Utah.[75] A year later, Christy Turner reported a similar find along Ash Creek, in central Arizona.[76] It seems that 1988 established something of a benchmark, as separate finds were announced by Turner at the Marshview Hamlet, near Delores, Colorado;[77] Tim D. White, in Utah's Cottonwood Wash;[78] and Shane A. Baker, at the Rattlesnake Ruin, also in southern Utah.[79] An equally impressive record was set in 1989, however, as Turner weighed in yet again, this time regarding the Teec Nos Pos site, in northeastern Arizona.[80] His report was attended by those of Sharon S. Grant vis-à-vis the Fence Lake site in northwestern New Mexico,[81] and Nancy J. Malville concerning the series of Yellow Jacket sites in southwestern Colorado.[82]

The pace actually increased somewhat during the early 1990s, as Turner, by then working with his wife Jacqueline, reported forensic evidence of cannibalism at the Aztec Wash sites in southeastern Colorado (1992),[83] the "Midsummer," Barker Arroyo, and Salmon Ruin sites in northwestern New Mexico (1993),[84] the Coyote Village and St. Christopher's Mission sites in southeastern Colorado (1993),[85] the San Juan River site in southern Utah (1993),[86] and the Houck K site in northeastern Arizona.[87] While several of these reports involved analysis of skeletal materials exhumed in earlier digs, new finds were reported by a team excavating the Ram Mesa kiva and pithouse in northwestern New Mexico (1993)[88] and another excavating the Hanson Pueblo site in southwestern Colorado (1993).[89] Truly, as it was put in a 1997 issue of *Science*, archaeologists had "rediscovered" cannibalism in the American Southwest.[90]

The centerpiece of this whole "new wave" was University of California archaeologist Tim White's book-length 1992 study, *Prehistoric Cannibalism at Mancos*.[91] Displaying "dazzling subtlety" while "raising the sophistication of statistical and analytic tools of physical anthropology to unprecedented levels," White reported employing an electron microscope in his exhaustive examination of percussion marks, burn traces, disarticulation, breakages and what he termed "pot polish" on some 2,106 bone fragments accruing from the skeletons of thirty individuals earlier exhumed from the Colorado site.[92] His conclusion was "sustained and unequivocal: Mancos contained the remains of a cannibal meal comprising seventeen adults and twelve children, the heads cooked whole and then broken open with heavy implements."[93]

Initial responses were quite favorable, largely, it seems, because White had sent his galleys out for early review by a select group of cannibalogists like SUNY Oswego's Ivan Brady, who then grandly proclaimed the book to be "the best scientific work ever done on cannibalism by anyone."[94] In short order, however, more critical reviews began to appear, as when Paul Bahn took to the pages of *New Scientist* to point out a range of interpretive precedents White appeared to have deliberately overlooked in the process of formulating his own conclusions.[95] As William Arens subsequently explained, in certain mortuary rituals, mourners "bury the dead, leave them in the ground, [sometimes] for months, and then . . . dig them up . . . put them in pots [and] boil them . . . remove the flesh . . . then rebury or keep the bones. This is going to look like cannibalism, [but] it's never quite clear if the people are paying respect to the dead or eating their dead."[96]

The defects in White's interpretive design were further underscored by Peter Bullock, a researcher at the Museum of New Mexico. "Human action that is the result of human motivation cannot be studied through the use of a methodology that systematically excludes motivation," he observed in a critique published in *Man*.[97] On the face of it, Bullock elsewhere concluded, "violence and mutilation are as likely a correct interpretation as cannibalism" with respect to the bulk of White's evidence.[98] Indeed, for all the intricate charts, tables, and jargon with which White salted his book, there is not even a scientifically precise means of distinguishing the effects of human action on the one hand from the sorts of degradation of skeletal materials caused by animal digestion on the other.[99]

As Arens summed up, even while setting out to expose the fraudulent nature of a series of photos purportedly "documenting" contemporary anthropophagy among the indigenous Fore of Papua New Guinea,[100] White appears to have been effectively "seduced by the idea of cannibalism. It was inevitable that he concluded the people were cannibals. There wouldn't be any news if he concluded they were *not* [emphasis in original]."[101] White, for his part, bitterly compared his detractors to "creationists," thus replicating the logical inversion performed by Marshall Sahlins more than a decade earlier.[102] Announcing that the discipline was "turning its back on science" altogether, he angrily removed himself from Berkeley's anthropology department, taking up a new station in biology.[103]

The years immediately following the "Mancos Debate" were marked by an apparent sense of caution among cannibalogists. Even the Turners, who had advanced far and away the greatest number of claims by the end of 1993, suddenly evidenced a new circumspection, pronouncing the evidentiary value of skeletal remains exhumed at Colorado's Mesa Verde 875 site,[104] the Guadalupe Ruin in northern New Mexico,[105] and the Moenkopi Wash site in northeastern Arizona[106] to be either "problematic" or "uncertain." A tentative confidence was restored in November 1998, when University of North Carolina archaeologist Brian Billman reported myoglobin in coprolites recovered from a "charnel house" at the 1001-0 site in southwestern Colorado,[107] but began to dissipate after it was pointed out that the protein might be found in nonhuman tissue.

Then, in 1999 came publication of the Turners' lengthy volume, *Man Corn*, the title of which the authors tell us is their own translation into English of a Nahuatl word, *tlacatlaolli*, meaning the Aztec élite's "invariable meal of sacrificed human meat, cooked with corn."[108] As to contents, 359 of 484 pages in the main text are devoted to summaries and technical analyses of seventy-six archaeological sites in the Four Corners region—another dozen are dealt with more briefly, under the heading "Other Cases"—in what can only be described as by far the most comprehensive and detailed such assessment ever undertaken.[109] The authors are quite explicit in their intent: It is their desire that the matter of prehistoric Southwestern cannibalism, which they assert has been proven by their data array, at last be "understood."[110]

"Man Corn"

The misleading nature of Man Corn becomes evident before one has finished reading its subtitle. Although the focus of their study is plainly on anthropophagy, captioning it Cannibalism and Violence in the Southwest allows them to include every instance in which indications of some form of violence may be present in the archaeological record, thereby creating an appearance that presumptive evidence of cannibalism in the Four Corners area is far more extensive than even the most devout cannibalogist has claimed to date. This none-too-subtle conflation of cannibalism and violence in the book's packaging has led to predictable popular misimpressions, as when it was erroneously reported by the New York Times in 1998 that consumption of human flesh had been confirmed at a total of "72 [sic] 'charnel houses' identified by Turner on historic Anasazi territory."[111]

Even the most cursory examination of the sites upon which the authors concentrate reveals something entirely different, however. Of the seventy-six, nearly a third (23), involve finds in which there have never been contentions of cannibalism. Another pair are listed as being "problematic," still another pair as "uncertain." Three others include a question mark after the word "cannibalism" in their headings, and should thus have been included in the "uncertain" category.[112] We are thus left with a total of forty-five sites which seem at first glance to be offered as proof of anthropophagy. A closer reading, however, reveals that even this is not the case.

Regarding those instances in which claims of cannibalism have been made by the excavators or subsequent analysts, the Turners conclude a half-dozen times that the evidence actually indicates something else.[113] With respect to a further seven, they opine that either the evidence or initial analyses of it are insufficient to sustain the allegation.[114] Subtracting these thirteen sites from the tally leaves a mere thirty-two, well under half the original list. And what of these? How well do they bear up to scrutiny?

Let it be said, first of all, that in ten cases, neither Christy nor Jacqueline Turner bothered to inspect the osteological material for themselves before confirming it as evidence of anthropophagy.[115] This is more than passingly peculiar, since at least three of the reports were submitted as long as sixty years before the taphonomic methods upon which the Turners ostensibly base the scientific integrity of their findings came into use.[116] In one instance, moreover, the skeletal material upon which the original report was based has long since and rather mysteriously disappeared, presumably as the result of "some sort of housekeeping event . . . at the Peabody Museum."[117] Here, the authors note that they opted to simply "accept [the] cannibalism interpretation" at face value "because burning, breakage, and good bone preservation are identified." Other criteria aren't mentioned in the report, they say, but "*may* have been met also [emphasis added]."[118]

To describe such evidence as underwhelming is to put it mildly, a matter which should lead a careful observer to deduct all three pre-1982 findings from the roster of confirmed sites. The validity of the Turners' confirmation of the seven reports dated 1982 or later is of course contingent on their own reliability in terms of interpreting textual rather than physical materials. A hint as to their integrity in this respect is offered in the very first sentence of the book, when they observe that the "word *cannibal* comes from the Carib Indian tribal name [emphasis in original],"[119] which, to be sure, it does not.[120]

Similar distortions abound. Having duly noted the strong exception entered by Arens, for example, the authors nonetheless announce that it is "*without question* [whether] cannibalism occurred . . . in Mexico [emphasis added]," that there is "*no doubt* that violence and cannibalism . . . were common features of the [Mesoamerican] sociopolitical landscape, especially in central Mexico [emphasis added]" and that "Aztec feasting on sacrificed enemy captives was permitted . . . although supposedly only by members of the upper class."[121] Flatly ignoring the fact that Paul Bahn, Peter Hassler, and a number of others have arrived at conclusions virtually identical to Arens', moreover, they assert that of all indigenous peoples, "the Aztecs are *universally regarded* as having been the most bloodstained and violent, performing sacrificial killings, victim mutilation, and cannibalism on a scale known nowhere else in America [emphasis added]."[122]

Given their obvious propensity to twist these aspects of the written record into conformity with their own desires, it must be adduced that the Turners are likely to have been equally untrustworthy when it came to summarizing the contents and implications of otherwise unexamined archaeological reports. This leaves a grand total of twenty-two sites, skeletal materials from which the authors claim they personally inspected and upon which they might therefore legitimately attempt to base their claim that anthropophagy had become a relative commonplace in the Southwest by 900 AD and remained so for the next four hundred years.[123]

The problem is that not only is their sample far too meager to sustain such sweeping contentions, there is nothing involved in the Turners' forensic methods which goes beyond those employed by Tim White in *Prehistoric Cannibalism at Mancos*. Indeed, they cite him as a primary authority upon whom they based their own approach to apprehending taphonomic evidence of cannibalism.[124] To put it bluntly, all they've done is take his techniques, treat them as if they weren't already discredited in terms of supporting the conclusions at issue, and then applied them far more broadly.

Undoubtedly aware that their data base was far too thin to withstand close scrutiny in its own right, the authors set about larding it with the very sort of ethnological speculations their reputedly superior laboratory approach was supposed to supplant. In a chapter entitled "Cannibalism and Human Body Processing in Mexico,"[125] which they say is meant to contextualize their own findings, they trot out virtually every fable about the Aztecs from Sahagún and Durán to Bernal Díaz, usually filtered through contemporary commentators like David Carrasco (a professor of religious studies whom they erroneously refer to as a historian).[126]

Not only were the Aztecs anthropophagi, the Turners conclude, but pathologically so. Quoting Richard Adams, they observe that the "Aztec state . . . [by the late 1400s] had become a mad world of bloody terrorism based on the cynical, psychopathic politics of the high imperial rulers. Coronation ceremonies of the later kings were accompanied by the offering of fantastic quantities of human victims to the gods."[127] A goodly portion of these victims, it is implied, were then eaten after being prepared in accordance with the recipe for cooking up batches of *tlacatlaolli*.

From there, the authors look first to the east, noting similar claims made with respect to the Tlaxcalans,[128] and then northward, placing particular emphasis on the "masterful synthesis of the warfare-religion-sacrifice complex" contained in an archaic ethnography of northern Mexico published by Ralph Beals in 1932.[129] By the time they've completed their tour, the Turners have concluded that virtually every native people in the U.S./Mexican border region, from the Tarahumara to the Acaxee and Xixime, to the Cáhita, to the Yavapai and Karankawa, were all regular consumers of human flesh.[130] The only reason there's as yet no evidence that the Hohokams too were cannibals, they opine, is because nobody has bothered to look for it.[131]

Little of what is cited in this connection adds up to more than passing comments in the literature, most of them deriving from sources like Fray Vicente de Santa María's eighteenth-century *Relación histórica de la colonia del Nuevo Santander*.[132] Unmistakably, these are tracts in which, as with Bernal Díaz, all manner of tall tales and unsubstantiated rumors about the culinary habits of local natives were first committed to print, then recapitulated at face value by succeeding generations of "scholars" until, by way of continuous repetition and reciprocal citation among believers, they have become enshrined as "settled facts." The Turners' latest reiteration falls squarely within this tradition.[133]

Having set out their markers in this fashion, the authors quickly switch back to their effort to shore up their case with physical evidence. In a section headed "The Archaeological Record,"[134] they run through an inventory of everything of consequence available to support anthropology's grandiose extrapolations about the nature of Mesoamerican societies. Launching their survey with the preaztecan city-state of Teotihuacan,[135] they also review studies of the Toltecs,[136] Olmecs,[137] and peoples of Michoacán,[138] in addition to the Aztecs.[139] Tellingly, almost nothing is brought forth with respect to the cultures of northern Mexico for the simple reason that "little [is] known about the archaeology of the region and even less about the physical anthropology."[140]

In terms of taphonomy, special attention is paid to the work of a graduate student named Carmen María Pijoan Aguadé, whom the Turners initially laud has having "definitely identified cannibalism" in association with skeletal remains excavated from the Aztec ceremonial center of Tlatelolco, in Mexico City.[141] A few pages later, however, they reverse themselves completely on the validity of Pijoan's forensics, stating that after they themselves examined 136 of 170 skulls she and her colleagues subjected to taphonomic analysis, they concluded the site might best serve as an example of how to go about "ruling cannibalism *out* [their emphasis]."[142] The net result is that they end up presenting no physical substantiation of any sort for the ethnographic proposition that Aztec society was endemically anthropophagistic.

Osteological evidence accruing from only four other sites in all of Mexico is afforded detailed exposition. The remains exhumed in one of these, the Coxcatlan Cave, in the Tehuacán Valley of Puebla, dates from 5200 BC, and involves the cranium of a single child.[143] Another, at Tlatecomila, in the federal district, involves six adults and dates from about 700 BC (Zacantenco culture).[144] At the 1,650-year-old "Electra" site, about forty miles south of San Luis Potosí, the remains of nine individuals are at issue.[145] Then there are several sets of skeletal remains exhumed at Alta Vista, a site in the state of Zacatecas which was abandoned at least a thousand years ago.[146]

Rather self-evidently, with the exception of Alta Vista—at which it is admitted that no one, including the Turners, has been able to distinguish the "osteological signature of cannibalism" from the signature of ossuary rituals known to have been practiced by the inhabitants[147]—each of the four sites is far too old to shed any real light on the "classical" era of Mesoamerica. Assuming even that evidence of anthropophagy does obtain from the other sites, which is anything but clear, the fates of twenty-odd individuals cannibalized in three widely separated locations over a span of six millennia are hardly sufficient to warrant contentions that cannibalism was an institutionalized commonplace—"ubiquitous" and "irrefutable," as the Turners would have it[148]—at any point in the prehistory of Mexico.

Aside from a few mutterings about how "some type of Tarahumara Indian ceremonial or culinary activity might account for the condition of bones" at one site,[149] and how remains found at another suggest "possible . . . human sacrifice . . . ancestor worship, and cannibalism,"[150] no osteological indicators at all are deployed vis-à-vis any Mexican locale north of Durango. One would do well to wonder, given this utter absence of supporting evidence, why the authors were so insistent upon raising the matter of border region ethnography in the first place. Ultimately, their concern in this regard appears to have been purely speculative, having nothing in the least to do with anything so banal as mere factuality. More precisely, they were motivated by little aside from a desire to promote their own theory of how and why cannibalism supposedly prevailed among the peoples indigenous to the Southwestern United States.[151]

More precisely still, Christy Turner in particular seems to have learned a hard lesson from the experience of Tim White, one of whose mistakes lay in his attribution of cannibalism to the Anasazis, a pre-puebloan Four Corners people generally believed to have been composed of peaceful agriculturists.[152] Turner, of course, held much the same view as White on the Anasazis' propensity to anthropophagy—he was still articulating it as recently as 1994[153]—and published polemics in White's defense.[154] At the same time, however, he seems to have been casting about for ways to avoid incurring the same response.[155] For all practical intents and purposes, it appears that what Turner took as the means to this end was provided by Hopi cultural preservation officer Leigh Jenkins, when he asserted that his "main point of contention" was not necessarily whether cannibalism had occurred within the Anasazi domain, but how anyone might know that it resulted from "Puebloans cannibalizing Puebloans? Couldn't it have been some other people doing this?"[156]

Seeing his opening, Turner moved rapidly, reshaping his version of who did what to whom in a manner exempting the Anasazis themselves from "culpability."[157] In short order, he—the major responsibility for this must logically fall upon Christy Turner, given that Jacqueline died in early 1996 and that, in the book, he continuously refers to himself as the "primary author" of *Man Corn*—had concocted a theory which had a "psychotic gang" of cannibalistic Toltec "warrior-cultists" moving northward out of central Mexico at some point around 900 AD, spreading anthropophagy as they went, until they eventually encountered and subordinated the Anasazis, ensconcing themselves for the next four centuries as rulers of a new empire centered around Chaco Canyon.[158]

> Specifically, we think some of these immigrants might have been warrior-cultists dedicated to gods of the Tezcatlipoca-Xipe Totec complex, with its human sacrifice and cannibalism. We propose that in the Chaco area, some such group of Mexicans was able to use these practices for social control, terrorizing the local populace into submission and developing the hierarchical social system we see reflected in the region's architecture.[159]

A dozen pages are then expended summarizing the "Mesoamerican influences" on Chacoan architecture and, similarly, upon the culture's art, spiritual belief system, and so on.[160] Not only is much of this quite speculative, as Turner himself admits, but, even if correct, can be readily accounted for by interactions produced through the extensive trade relations which are believed to have existed between the Toltecs and such northerly peoples as the Anasazis.[161] The only osteological evidence upon which he rests his notion that Toltec "cannibal-warriors" might have conquered and ruled the Chacoans for four hundred years comes down to the 1954 discovery by archaeologist Neil Judd of a single skull in Room 330 of Pueblo Bonito, the teeth of which were "intentionally chipped" in a Toltec-like manner.[162]

It seems likely that Turner is correct in his contention that the teeth are chipped in distinctively Toltec style and that the skull should be presumed that of a Toltec.[163] This in itself might be considered indicative only of a fatality among traders coming in and out of the area, however, or that some random refugee died after finding sanctuary among the Chacoan Anasazi. All told, fewer than a dozen Toltec skulls, identified as such by their "dental disfigurement," have turned up in the Southwest.[164] Taken together, they hardly amount to persuasive underpinning for Turner's contention that a substantial body of Toltecs invaded and exercised a protracted dominion in the region. The mere fact of a "Toltec presence," moreover, can in no event be considered evidence of anthropophagy, given that two of the finds have been made at Hohokam sites where there has never been a hint that cannibalism occurred.[165] Nonetheless, Turner concludes not by tempering but rather by amplifying his thesis.

> The Chacoans apparently had different values regarding the consumption of humans from those prevailing before, and elsewhere at the same time, in the prehistoric Southwest. The interregional contrast in Southwestern cannibalism seems to fit the idea of an actual Mexican Indian presence stimulating or even directing the Chaco phenomenon. We propose that these southerners were practitioners of Xipe Totec (or Maasaw) and the Tezcatlipoca-Quetzalcoatl (plumed serpent) cults. They entered the San Juan basin about A.D. 900 and found a suspicious but pliant population whom they terrorized into reproducing the theocratic lifestyle they had previously known in Mesoamerica. This involved heavy payments of tribute, constructing the Chaco system of great houses and roads, and providing victims for ceremonial sacrifice. The Mexicans advanced their objectives through the use of warfare, violent example, and terrifying cult ceremonies that included human sacrifice and cannibalism.[166]

The otherwise curious propensity of the authors to highlight unsupported ethnographic depictions of border region peoples like the Tarahumara thus stands revealed for what it is. Geoculturally, they are intended to serve as a figurative but essential "missing link" between the mythically bloodthirsty Toltecs of the Mesoamerican south and the reputedly much gentler Anasazis far to the north. It is difficult to conceive a better example of the symbiotic relationship between physical and cultural anthropology, how, all polemics to the contrary notwithstanding, each serves mainly to reinforce and complete the other, interacting in such a way as to create illusions of substance where there is none worth mentioning.[167]

Hence, despite the intricacy of its surface texturing, *Man Corn*, like its predecessors, is a hollow shell. More appropriately, it might be compared to an onion. Peeling off one translucent layer simply reveals the next, layer after layer, until at last one arrives at the core. Unlike a real onion, however, the "core" is in this case a vacuum. Since nature and readerships alike abhor all such emptinesses, however, the void is one the authors strive continuously to backfill with a blend of their own prejudices and consequent predispositions. Distilled to its purest form, their endeavor may in the end may be perceived as an exercise in sheer subterfuge, a perfect illustration of the impulse captured so aptly in the prattlings of scientians like Peter Robinson.

"Science" as Psychosis

"In attempting to understand Southwestern cannibalism," the Turners wrote in their introduction, "it is certainly not our intent to shame, ridicule, or belittle any prehistoric American Indian people—the great majority of whom were given careful, considerate burials—or their possible living descendants."[168] Theirs, they maintain, is simply "one of a number of studies that need to be conducted if cannibalism is ever to be understood as a human phenomenon," part of a noble "quest for truth" in a strictly scientific sense.[169] As we have seen, however, this last is itself rather far from the truth.[170] Even were it otherwise, William Arens' recent observation that there are surely "more constructive" research venues available to anthropology would remain entirely on point.[171] The lie is thus put to the Turners' assertion of benign intent.

There can be no reasonable evaluation of *Man Corn* but that it was/is meant precisely to shame, ridicule, and belittle native people, past *and* present. The descriptive vernacular its authors assign to those cultures they portray as "unquestionably" anthropophagistic, and the value judgments inhering in these characterizations, are more than sufficient to demonstrate that this is so. How else, after all, is one to construe depictions of all Mesoamerican and certain Puebloan societies as "bloodthirsty" and "psychopathic" collectivities, explicitly comparable in their configuration and dynamics to those evident among Charlie Manson's lethally deranged "family"?[172] How else, the highly distortive exclusiveness with which Christy Turner links the very act of cannibalism to such virulent pathologies as those displayed by contemporary "monsters" like Albert Fish, Edmund Kemper, and Jeffrey Dahmer?[173]

As was noted earlier, the question is not whether an intent to defame and degrade native people "might" be bound up in all this—plainly, it is— but why this is so. Arens, Hugh Trevor-Roper, and others have offered important insights in this connection, showing how anthropology's ongoing perpetuation of the man-eating myth parallels not only the historical response of Spain to the Black Legend and the inquisitional persecution of European "witches,"[174] but to such far more contemporary phenomena as the "Blood Libel," a fable wherein it was posited as fact that Jews routinely engaged in the sacrifice of Christian victims, especially children, and "mixed the blood with their ritual foods at Passover."[175]

> These accusations were so numerous, widespread and persistent that in [the early twentieth] century a non-Jewish scholar who wrote on this phenomenon actually entitled one chapter of his book "Is the Use of Christian Blood Required or Allowed for Any Rite Whatsoever of the Jewish Religion?" This is followed by a sober assessment of Jewish dietary strictures, including the prohibition on the use of animal blood, which the author contends would also hold for the vital fluid of Christians.[176]

Despite such efforts to debunk it, the Blood Libel, often cloaked in "scientific" garb,[177] was put to considerable use by nazi propagandists like Julius Streicher in their drive to exacerbate German antisemitism to a degree that outright genocide might be condoned by the general public.[178] A similar mythology concerning the Gypsies' supposed "relish for human flesh" was utilized to accomplish very much the same thing.[179] As is extraordinarily well-documented, these ubiquitous falsehoods, taken together with such fabricated evidence as the notorious *Protocols of the Elders of Zion*, achieved the desired result.[180] It may well be true, as Arens contends, that, concerning Jews at least, such abominable tripe has by now been "banished from our consciousness."[181] But, quite obviously, the precise opposite holds true for the native peoples of this hemisphere (and elsewhere, for that matter).

For most contemporary American Indians, of course, physical genocide of the sort that threatened European Jews and Gypsies during the 1930s is not an incipient danger.[182] Instead, it is a consummate historical reality.[183] The function of a blood libel is therefore somewhat different in a modern euroamerican country like the U.S. than it was in nazi Germany. In the latter, the object was to whip the dominant population up to commit genocide; in the U.S., it is to condition the transplanted New World counterparts of nazism's "Good Germans" to feel virtuous about—or at least comfortable with—the fact that their currently privileged position in the hemisphere depends upon genocide having already been committed against its indigenous inhabitants. This last is all the more true, given that the impact has left the surviving residue of natives in a condition of chronically genocidal dispossession and destitution.[184]

To be sure, a pervasive and neonazi-like denial that American Indians have ever suffered "true" genocide forms the first line of conceptual defense for the euroamerican status quo.[185] Whenever the first is breached, however, a second line immediately presents itself: the mode of existence manifested in preinvasion Native America was so hideous, it is argued, that things have "worked out for the best," irrespective of what may have been done, or continues to be done, by the European invaders and their descendants.[186] In this, the blood libel of indigenous cannibalism and ritual sacrifice forms a key—perhaps *the* key—component. The myth cannot be relinquished if euroamerica's hegemonic self-justification of its ascendancy is to be sustained.[187]

Such doctrinal needs undoubtedly explain in large part why first the European and then the euroamerican intelligentsia, no matter how nebulous the allegations involved or how thorough their rebuttal, has always returned to the "issue" of indigenous anthropophagy like flies buzzing around a pile of dung.[188] Yet, even this incentive does not seem entirely adequate to explicate a certain obsessive quality which has discernibly imbued the attitudes and behavior of many or perhaps most cannibalogists over the years. It is impossible to avoid the uncomfortable feeling that, as a group, they have been motivated by a compulsion far deeper than anything which might be prompted by a rational if unsavory desire to affirm the extant hegemony with which their own privileged station is secured.

Their culture is, after all, one in which a core ritual practice has for nearly two millennia been "communion" with the Christ/messiah through a symbolic but nonetheless regularized eating of his flesh and drinking of his blood.[189] Even in pre-Christian times, the ancient Greeks evinced a similarly peculiar spiritual preoccupation with anthropophagy, including among their pantheon the god Cronus, who, it was said, ate his offspring.[190] Eighteen hundred years later, the same god, endowed with a more Romanesque name, was still being depicted by Church-sponsored high Renaissance painters like Peter Paul Rubens in his "Saturn Devouring His Children" (1523), and, three centuries later yet, by Francisco de Goya in his famous black fresco on the walls of the Quinta del Sordo.[191]

From Greek mythology to the fairy tales of Charles Perrault and the brothers Grimm,[192] from Shakespeare's *Titus Andronicus* to Bram Stoker's *Dracula* and Joseph Conrad's *Heart of Darkness*, up to the present moment, with Thomas Harris' *Silence of the Lambs* and Malcolm Bradbury's *Eating People Is Wrong*, the literary constructions of the West reveal an emic fixation on cannibalism far more pervasive and sustained than has been evidenced in any other cultural setting.[193] Even more, the cinematic output of the late twentieth century.

> [S]ince the 1960s the cannibal has become a modern mythical figure—appearing in films ranging from Romero's cult *Living Dead* series, through other fringe hits such as *Soylent Green*, *The Texas Chainsaw Massacre*, *Eating Raoul*, *Parents*, *Eat the Rich*, [*Consuming Passions*,] *Big Meat Eater*, *CHUD*, and more recently breaking into art films: Greenaway's *The Cook, the Thief, His Wife and Her Lover*, *Delicatessen*, *Cronos* [and, more lately, *Ravenous*]. Even more tellingly, perhaps, it has moved into the Hollywood mainstream, through *Fried Green Tomatoes* and *Silence of the Lambs*, which sent a cannibal to the academy awards.[194]

At another level, both the formal and popular discourses of European/euroamerican cultures are literally permeated with metaphorical signifiers of anthropophagy, as in Karl Marx's mid-nineteenth-century portrayal of capitalism's "unquenchable thirst [and] werewolf-like hunger . . . for the living blood of labor,"[195] or more contemporary descriptions of individuals being "swallowed up" by corporate entities and of corporations themselves "cannibalizing" one another in the course of the West's ongoing drive for economic consolidation and globalization.[196] Indeed, serious analysts have suggested that the entire "consumerist" pathos presently and increasingly afflicting Western societies is nothing so much as a vast analogue to cannibalism, not only of the endo- and exo- varieties, but auto- as well.[197]

So unavoidably abundant are these indicators of a sublimated but nevertheless literal "cannibalistic impulse" residing beneath the surface aggregate of Western consciousness that the problem has drawn the attention of psychosocial theoreticians as diverse as Sigmund Freud, Carl Jung, R.D. Laing, Gilles Deleuze, Félix Guattari, and Jacques Derrida.[198] Freud, with singular clarity, perceived the repression of powerful anthropophagistic and incestuous desires as a motive force in the origin and evolution of Western civilization itself.[199] The resulting subconscious battle between attraction and revulsion served, however, to foster a sense of primal self-loathing among those involved.[200] This, in turn, dovetailed rather well with an already abiding sense of cultural inadequacy afflicting incipient "Europeans."[201]

It is a well understood tenet of psychology that those suffering such an "inferiority complex," especially one so virulent as that manifested among early Europeans, will all but invariably seek to compensate for their often imaginary deficiencies in various ways.[202] One of the more prominent is a tendency to employ physical force—the more severe the neurosis, the more extreme the violence employed—in a chronic effort to impose themselves upon those they perceive as "betters" (which, in some cases, can be almost everyone).[203] A second is to project those aspects of their own makeup of which they are most ashamed, or which they believe to be most defective, upon those they victimize.[204]

The pathology bound up in this combination of ingredients, amplified to culturally normative proportions, has been dubbed the "*wétiko* Disease" by indigenous scholar Jack Forbes,[205] and analyzed brilliantly by Joel Kovel, among others.[206] Put most straightforwardly, it is this psychological malady which accounts for the genocidal fury with which Europe has propelled itself to a position of planetary ascendancy over the past several centuries.[207] It also accounts for why, even as it appropriated their assets and intellectual attainments, the West set out so compulsively to misrepresent and defile those it overran and subordinated, imbuing them unerringly with what it secretly feared was the true nature of itself, eventually conjuring up the enterprise of anthropology as a means of systematizing the whole charade.[208] This, in turn, has served as the predicating rationalization of an endless series of ego-deficient assertions of eurosupremacism (or "white supremacy," as it is more usually known).[209]

Physical anthropology has been especially guilty in this respect, having produced, always in the name of "science," such preposterous offshoots as craniometry, craniology, and phrenology, to say nothing of eugenics.[210] And, of course, there was the Piltdown fraud, the fabricated set of cranial remains supposedly establishing the "fact" that the missing evolutionary link between man and ape had resided in England, and that the first true humans were therefore European rather than African. Verified as authentic by the most eminent paleontologists of the British Museum, the bones and their ostensible implications were embraced by a lopsided majority within the discipline from 1912 to 1953.[211] Similar examples are abundant, albeit most are of far lesser magnitude.

Witness *Man Corn*. The Turners' book could not fall more squarely within this squalid tradition if they had set out, malice aforethought, to craft it that way. And in a way they almost certainly did, for reasons of the kind of crass self-interest elsewhere described as a "possessive investment in whiteness."[212] Even had they elected to do otherwise, however, it is supremely unlikely that they could have succeeded, no more than Tim White, say, or lesser cannibalogists like Lawrence Goldman, who are now seeking to ride the momentum created by the Turners' endeavor into positions of mainstream academic status and security.[213] The insurmountable barrier confronting each of them is, as it has been for a host of their predecessors, well-intentioned and ill-, the intensity of the psychointellectual imbalance they've incurred through their acceptance of eurosupremacy as a natural and inevitable condi-tion.[214] In this sense, they are as utterly helpless as any other group of psychotics to behave differently than they do.

Thus have the lunatics taken charge of the asylum, so to speak. Under such circumstances, pretensions to scientific demeanor are no more than—nay, *can be* no more than—the rank subterfuge of scientism. Science is not science, but "science," a manipulative, deceptive and ulti-mately irredeemable outward manifestation of the intractable psychosis shared by its proponents and practitioners. Whether those beset by the derangement can be cured remains uncertain. It would prerequire that inveterate scientians like Christy Turner acknowledge their collective disorder and seek help (rather than dispensing further triumphalist dec-larations of its/their own transcendent "virtues").[215] Unfortunately, we seem a very long distance from the probability that any such change in outlook might occur.

For the rest of us, the prospects are in many ways equally murky.[216] We are, after all, the figurative asylum-keepers overrun by inmates, most of whom have been diagnosed as homicidally insane. Exactly how we go about saving ourselves is a matter for experimentation and debate. Nonetheless, on one point we can surely all agree: to get anywhere at all, we must refuse as a first and overarching priority to allow the loonies the liberty of defining for us the realities of our past and present situations, or our future possibilities. This implies that, whatever else we might aspire to accomplish, we will have to rely upon our own critical faculties and understandings deriving from nonwestern contexts to guide us.

Notes

1   Kirkpatrick Sale, *The Conquest of Paradise: Christopher Columbus and the Columbian Legacy* (New York: Alfred A. Knopf, 1990) p. 131. Among the earlier and more comprehen-sive investigators of the evidence supporting Columbus' depictions of the "Caribs" was the historian William Sheldon, who concluded that it was nonexistent; William Sheldon, "Brief Account of the Caribs, Who Inhabited the Antilles," *Transactions and*

Collections of the American Antiquarian Society, Vol. 1 (Worcester, MA: William Manning, 1820) pp. 366–433. Also see Peter Hulme, *Colonial Encounters: Europe and the Native Caribbean, 1492–1797* (London: Metheun, 1986).

2 Bartolomé de las Casas, *Destruction of the Indies* (New York: Harper & Row, 1971) and *In Defense of the Indians* (DeKalb: Northern Illinois University Press, 1974).

3 The matter is simply treated as a foregone conclusion. As recently as 1992, a senior anthropologist specializing in the area's indigenous peoples felt it unnecessary to bother citing references or any other form of evidence in the process of asserting that the Island Caribs "ate bits of the flesh of opposing warriors in order to acquire the latter's prowess." Irving Rouse, *The Tainos: Rise and Decline of the People Who Greeted Columbus* (New Haven, CT: Yale University Press, 1992) p. 22. Also see Robert A. Myers, "Island Carib Cannibalism," *New West Indian Guide,* Vol. 58, Nos. 3–4 (1984) pp. 147–84.

4 The bulk of the primary literature, such as the reports of Alvarado and other Spanish officers, make no mention at all of native cannibalism, e.g.: "Two Letters of Pedro de Alvarado," in Patricia de Fuentes, ed., *The Conquistadors* (New York: Orion Press, 1963) pp. 165–81. There seem to have been only two exceptions. The first was a report by one of his subordinates, mentioned but not confirmed by Cortés in his own dispatches, that the Aztecs were storing "roasted babies" as a food supply; "The Third Letter of Hernan Cortés," in Fuentes, *Conquistadors,* p. 107. The other, which Cortés also declined to confirm, concerns the fate of a group of Spanish captives who were supposedly executed and eaten. See Hernando Cortés, *Five Letters, 1519–1526* (New York: W.W. Norton, 1962) p. 199.

5 The first such effort seems to have been Francisco López de Gómara's postconquest *Cortés: The Life of the Conqueror by His Secretary* (Berkeley: University of California Press, 1964). It is worth noting that Gómara himself was not a witness to what he recounted and made no claim that either Cortés or other Spanish principals had seen it. He had, however, been commissioned by Cortés' family to produce what amounted to "readable and flamboyant" adventure story for purposes of enhancing his subject's fame and popularity. While he undoubtedly succeeded in that respect, his account constitutes a rather less than reliable history or ethnography. See W. Arens, *The Man-Eating Myth: Anthropology and Anthropophagy* (New York: Oxford University Press, 1979) pp. 60–61.

6 These sorts of "recollections" did not begin to make their appearance until about forty years after the fact. See, as examples, "The Chronicle of Fray Francisco de Aguilar" and "The Chronicle of an Anonymous Conquistador," both in Fuentes, *Conquistadors,* pp. 134–64, 165–81.

7 While accounts of Spanish New World atrocities were undoubtedly pumped up for effect by the English and others, they seem to have been largely based in the accounts of Bartolomé de las Casas, and were thus rather more factually based than was much of what the Spanish consequently attributed to the Aztecs. See, e.g., Michael Palencia-Roth, "Cannibalism and the New Man in Latin America," *Comparative Civilizations Review,* No. 12 (Spring 1985) pp. 1–27; Gregory Cerio, "The Black Legend: Were the Spaniards That Cruel?" *Newsweek: Special Issue on Columbus* (Fall/Winter 1992) pp. 48–51.

8 Bernal Díaz del Castillo, *The Discovery and Conquest of Mexico* (New York: Octagon Books, 1970).

9 This utterly implausible tale is all but invariably cited by contemporary writers as the foundational "proof" upon which everything else they wish to say is based; see,

e.g., David Carrasco, "Myth, Cosmic Terror, and the Templo Mayor," in J. Broda, D. Carrasco, and E. Matos Moctezuma, eds., *The Great Temple of Tenochtitlan: Center and Periphery of the Aztec World* (Berkeley: University of California Press, 1987) p. 124.

10   Peter Hassler, "Cutting Through the Myth of Human Sacrifice: Lies of the Conquistadors," *World Press Review*, Vol. 39, No. 12 (December 1992) pp. 28–29.

11   Fray Diego Durán, *Book of the Gods and the Ancient Calendar* (Norman: University of Oklahoma Press, 1971); Fray Bernardo de Sahagún, *The Florentine Codex*, 13 vols. (Santa Fe, NM: School of American Research, 1950–1959).

12   George Pierre Castile, for one, has done an excellent job of challenging the accuracy and integrity of the Durán and Sahagún translations in his "Purple People Eaters? A Comment on Aztec Elite Class Cannibalism à la Harris-Harner," *American Anthropologist*, Vol. 88, No. 2 (June 1980) pp. 389–91.

13   Hassler, "Lies of the Conquistadors."

14   For what may be the earliest truly philosophical consideration of anthropophagy, see Michel de Montaigne's 1580 treatise, "Of Cannibals," in *Essays*, ed. John M. Cohen (New York: Penguin, 1958) pp. 105–8.

15   One need only skim the pages of Marvin Harris' *Cannibals and Kings: The Origins of Culture* (New York: Random House, 1971), especially the chapter on the Aztecs entitled "The Cannibal Kingdom" (pp. 97–110), to discern the extent to which this is true. For a good survey, see Benjamin Keen, *The Aztec Image in Western Thought* (New Brunswick, NJ: Rutgers University Press, 1971). More broadly, see Ray Tannahill, *Flesh and Blood: A History of Cannibalism* (New York: Stein and Day, 1975).

16   In what should be by now a familiar pattern, modern anthropological/historical interpretations of Iroquois cannibalism are anchored in a series of seventeenth-century reports of priests along the St. Lawrence River, not one of which includes an eyewitness account. See Ralph Thwaites, ed., *The Jesuit Relations and Allied Documents*, Vol. 5 (New York: Pageant Books, 1959). As to archaeological evidence, "Iroquoianists" must content themselves with the remains of a single individual exhumed at the "Bloody Hill" site, near Syracuse. See James A. Tuck, "The Iroquois Confederacy," in E.B.W. Zubrow, ed., *New World Archaeology* (San Francisco: W.H. Freeman, 1974) pp. 192–95. Even assuming the individual in question was actually cannibalized—and this is at best ambiguous—that fact in itself might reasonably serve as proof only of an anomalous incident, not the "cultural pattern" so often and sweepingly asserted. For a prime example of the latter, see Thomas S. Abler, "Iroquois Cannibalism: Fact Not Fiction," *Ethnohistory*, Vol. 27, No. 4 (1980) pp. 309–16.

17   The key text upon which the legend of Tupi-Guarani cannibalism has been constructed was "true" story of a German adventurer named Hans Staden, supposedly held captive—but obviously not eaten—by the "man-eating" Tupinambas of Brazil, before "escaping" in 1557. Originally published as *Hans Staden: The True History of a Country of Savages, a Naked and Terrible People, Eaters of Men's Flesh, Who Dwell in the New World Called America*, his lavishly illustrated book was a bestseller at the time and has seen regular reprintings since. It also formed the basis for A. Métraux's ostensibly "scholarly" entry, "The Tupi Namba," in Julian Steward, ed., *Handbook of South American Indians*, 3 vols. (New York: Cooper Square Press, 1948) Vol. 3, pp. 69–94. From there, it's found its way into such works as Peggy Reeves Sanday's *Divine Hunger: Cannibalism as a Cultural System* (New York: Cambridge University Press, 1986). More technically, see, e.g., Gertrude Dole, "Endocannibalism among the Amahuaca

Indians," *Transactions of the New York Academy of Science* (Series II), Vol. 24, No. 5 (March 1962) pp. 567–73.

18 See, e.g., Claude Lévi-Strauss, *The Raw and the Cooked* (New York: Harper & Row, 1969).

19 In all seriousness, this is actually discussed by Claude Lévi-Strauss in "The Culinary Triangle," *Partisan Review*, No. 33 (1966) pp. 586–96.

20 For arguments along this line, see Dole, "Endocannibalism"; S.M. Garn and W.D. Block, "The Limited Nutritional Value of Cannibalism," *American Anthropologist*, Vol. 72, No. 1 (1970) p. 106; M.D. Dornstreich and G.E.B. Morren, "Does New Guinea Cannibalism Have Nutritional Value?" *Human Ecology*, Vol. 2, No. 1 (January 1974) pp. 1–12.

21 Gary Hogg, *Cannibalism and Human Sacrifice* (London: Pan Books, 1973); Eli Sagan, *Cannibalism: Human Aggression and Cultural Form* (New York: Harper & Row, 1974).

22 Michael Harner, "The Ecological Basis for Aztec Sacrifice," *American Ethnologist*, Vol. 4, No. 1 (October 1977) pp. 117–35; "The Enigma of Aztec Sacrifice," *Natural History*, Vol. 86, No. 4 (April 1977) pp. 46–51.

23 Harner anchors his argument in a crucial set of assumptions. The first is that the Aztecs actually performed human sacrifices; secondly, that every Aztec temple served as a site for such activities; third, that the rate of sacrifice could be "reasonably averaged" at ten people per-temple-per-day, making the aggregate number of humans sacrificed annually about a quarter-million; and, finally, that those killed were then eaten, the whole process being essentially a matter of "large-scale cannibalism, disguised as human sacrifice" ("Ecological Basis," p. 118). Since he offers not the least substantiation to any of this, the whole of his resulting model resembles nothing so much as a castle built on air.

24 Harris, *Cannibals and Kings*, p. 108.

25 Bernard R. Ortiz de Montellano, "Aztec Sacrifice: An Ecological Necessity?" *Science*, Vol. 200, No. 4342 (May 12, 1978) pp. 611–17; Barbara J. Price, "Demystification, Enriddlement, and Aztec Cannibalism: A Materialist Rejoinder to Harner, *American Ethnologist*, Vol. 5, No. 1 (February 1978) pp. 98–115; Castile, "Purple People Eaters?"

26 Marshall Sahlins, "Culture as Protein and Profit," *New York Review of Books* (November 23, 1978) pp. 45–53.

27 One of the earlier forays along this line was Ashley Montagu's "A Brief Excursion into Cannibalism" (*Science*, Vol. 86 [1937] pp. 56–57; collected in his *Man in Progress* [New York: New American Library, 1961] pp. 85–86). Montagu renewed his efforts in his efforts three decades later with "The Fallacy of the Primitive," a short essay with which he introduced his edited collection, *The Concept of the Primitive* (New York: Free Press, 1986, pp. 1–6), and amplified his thinking in *The Nature of Human Aggression* (New York: Oxford University Press, 1976, esp. p. 111).

28 Arens, *Man-Eating Myth*, p. 165; referencing Henry Cary's *Herodotus: A New and Literal Version* (London: George Bell & Sons, 1879) pp. 272–73.

29 Arens, *Man-Eating Myth*, pp. 9, 21.

30 See generally Richard Bernheimer, *Wild Men in the Middle Ages* (Cambridge, MA: Harvard University Press, 1952); Clements R. Markham, *Expeditions into the Valley of the Amazons* (New York: Burt Franklin, 1964); A. Malefijt, "Homo Monstrousus," *Scientific American*, Vol. 219, No. 4 (October 1968) pp. 113–18; John Block Friedman, *The Monstrous Races in Medieval Art and Thought* (Cambridge, MA: Harvard University Press, 1981); Olive Dickason, *The Myth of the Savage* (Edmonton: University of Alberta Press, 1984). More specific to the Aztecs and Caribs, see Tzvetan Todorov, *The*

Conquest of America: The Question of the Other (New York: HarperPerennial, 1984) esp. pp. 185–201.

31 Arens, *Man-Eating Myth*, pp. 165–66; referencing H.L. Jones' *The Geography of Strabo, Book 4* (London: William Heinemann, 1939) esp. p. 261; Klaus-Friedrich Koch, "Cannibalism," in D.E. Hunter and P. Whitten, *Encyclopedia of Anthropology* (New York: Harper & Row, 1976) p. 66.

32 Paul Bahn, "Cannibalism or Ritual Dismemberment?" in Steve Jones, Robert Martin and David Pilbeam, eds., *Cambridge Encyclopedia of Human Evolution* (New York: Cambridge University Press, 1992) p. 330.

33 Quoted in Lawrence Osborne, "Does Man Eat Man? Inside the Great Cannibalism Controversy," *Lingua Franca*, Vol. 7, No. 4 (1997) at p. 31. It should be noted that a number of the current reference works, such as Tim Ingold's *Companion Encyclopedia of Anthropology* (New York: Routledge, 1994) make no reference to cannibalism whatsoever.

34 Marina Warner, *Managing Monsters: Six Myths of Our Time* (London: Vintage, 1994) p. 100; Marianna Torgovnick, *Primitive Passions: Men, Women, and the Quest for Ecstasy* (New York: Alfred A. Knopf, 1996) p. 6.

35 Sale, *Conquest of Paradise*, p. 135.

36 Arens, *Man-Eating Myth*, p. 129.

37 Warner, *Managing Monsters*, p. 100.

38 Paula Brown and Donald Tuzin, eds., *The Ethnography of Cannibalism* (Washington, DC: Society for Psychological Anthropology, 1983) p. 3.

39 Marshall Sahlins, "Cannibalism: An Exchange," *New York Review of Books* (March 22, 1979) pp. 45–47.

40 As has been noted elsewhere, for Arens' position to conform with that of the neo-nazis, he would have had to have questioned whether Europe's colonizing legions—the analogy's nazi counterparts—had ever "really" perpetrated the sort of geno-cidal violence usually attributed to them, not whether their victims had displayed "savage behaviors" serving to mitigate or even justify such crimes. Hence, to be logically consistent in his allegation against Arens, Sahlins would be required to take a comparable position vis-à-vis Norman Cohn and others who have debunked nazi mythologies about "Jewish blood rites." See, e.g., Peter Hulme, "Introduction: The Cannibal Scene," in Francis Barker, Peter Hulme, and Margaret Iverson, eds., *Cannibalism and the Colonial World* (New York: Cambridge University Press, 1998) pp. 10–16.

41 Thomas Riley, "The Existence of Cannibalism," *Science*, Vol. 233, 4767 (August 29, 1986) p. 926; Pierre Vidal-Naquet, *Assassins of Memory: Essays on Denial of the Holocaust* (New York: Columbia University Press, 1992) pp. 17–20; Michael Palencia-Roth, "The Cannibalism Law of 1503," in Jerry M. Williams and Robert E. Lewis, eds., *Early Images of America: Transfer and Invention* (Tucson: University of Arizona Press, 1993) p. 22. It's worth noting that Vidal-Naquet appears never to have so much as bothered reading *The Man-Eating Myth* before defaming Arens in this manner. He offers no quotations, references no page references, and seems content merely to paraphrase Rodney Needham's review of Arens' book published under the title "Chewing on Cannibals," *Times Literary Supplement* (January 25, 1980) pp. 75–76.

42 Mary Douglas, "The Authenticity of Castaneda," in her *Implicit Meanings* (London: Routledge and Kegan Paul, 1975). Also see her "Torn Between Two Realities," pub-lished in the *Times Higher Education Supplement* on June 15, 1973, where she extols Castaneda's blatant fraud as "a significant pedagogical breakthrough." For the most

detailed examination(s) of "the greatest anthropological hoax since Piltdown Man," see Richard de Mille's *Castaneda's Journey: The Power and the Allegory* (Santa Barbara, CA: Capra Press, 1976) and *The Don Juan Papers: Further Castaneda Controversies* (Santa Barbara, CA: Ross-Erikson, 1980).

43　Mary Douglas, "The Hotel Kwilu: A Model of Models," *American Anthropologist*, Vol. 91, No. 4 (December 1989) p. 856.

44　Peter Rivière, "Review of *The Man-Eating Myth*," *Man*, Vol. 15, No. 1 (January 1980) pp. 203–5.

45　Shirley Lindebaum, "Review of *The Man-Eating Myth*," *Ethnohistory*, Vol. 29, No. 1 (Winter 1982) pp. 58–60.

46　Edmund Leach, "Long Pig, Tall Story: A Review of *The Man-Eating Myth*," *New Society*, No. 49 (August 30, 1979) p. 467; Charles Leroux, "The Professor Who Was Consumed by Cannibalism," *Chicago Tribune* (April 13, 1982); James Weiner, "Cannibalism: Why Not?" *Australian Natural History*, No. 22 (1987) pp. 172–73; Marvin Harris, *Cultural Anthropology* (New York: Harper & Row, 1995 ed.) p. 214; Donald W. Forsyth, "The Beginnings of Brazilian Anthropology: The Jesuits and Tupinamba Cannibalism," *Journal of Anthropological Research*, Vol. 39, No. 1 (Spring 1983) pp. 147–78; "Three Cheers for Hans Staden: The Case for Brazilian Cannibalism," *Ethnohistory*, Vol. 32, No. 1 (Winter 1985) pp. 17–36.

47　The argument was probably best formulated by Lewis R. Binford in his *Bones: Ancient Men and Modern Myths* (New York: Academic Press, 1981).

48　For the record, this is the same polemical technique employed by cryptozoologists, ufologists, and other "paranaturalists" whose stock-in-trade includes such matters as extraterrestrial visitation, the Loch Ness Monster, dinosaur survivals in the Congo Basin and the Abominable Snowman. For a surprisingly good overview, see Jerome Clark, *Unexplained! Strange Sightings, Incredible Occurrences & Puzzling Physical Phenomena* (Farmington Hills, MI: Visible Ink Press, [2nd ed.] 1999).

49　Quoted in Osborne, "Does Man Eat Man?" at pp. 36–37.

50　For a succinct overview of this pseudoscientific tradition, see Allen G. Debus, "Alchemy," in Philip P. Wiener, ed., *Dictionary of the History of Ideas*, 5 vols. (New York: Scribner's, 1973) Vol. 1, pp. 27–34.

51　Christy G. Turner II, "Taphonomic Reconstructions of Human Violence and Cannibalism Based on Mass Burials in the American Southwest," in G.M. LeMoine and A.S. MacEachern, eds., *Carnivores, Human Scavengers, and Predators: A Question of Bone Technology* (Calgary: Archaeological Association and the University of Calgary, 1983) pp. 219–40.

52　Walter Hough, "Ancient Peoples of the Petrified Forest of Arizona," *Harper's Monthly*, Vol. 105 (November 1902) pp. 897–901. The article dovetailed nicely with Jesse Walter Fewkes' earlier "Ah-wá-to-bi: An Archaeological Verification of a Tusayan Legend" (*American Anthropologist*, Vol. 6, No. 4 [1893] pp. 363–75), in which, although cannibalism as such is never mentioned, the focus is on a large-scale massacre. For an interesting overview, see Christy G. Turner II and Jacqueline A. Turner, "The First Claim for Cannibalism in the Southwest: Walter Hough's 1901 Discovery at Canyon Butte Ruin 3, Northeastern Arizona," *American Antiquity*, Vol. 57, No. 4 (October 1992) pp. 661–82.

53　Watson Smith, Richard B. Woodbury, Natalie F.S. Woodbury and Ross G. Montgomery, *The Excavation of Hawikuh by Frederick Webb Hodge: Report of the Hendricks-Hodge Expedition, 1917–1923* (New York: Museum of the American Indian/Heye Foundation No. 20, 1966).

54   George H. Pepper, *Pueblo Bonito* (New York: Anthropological Papers of the Museum of Natural History No. 27, 1920).

55   Like Hough, Earl Morris was a bit prone to hyperbole, a characterization readily evident in the very title of his "Exploring in the Canyon of Death" (*National Geographic*, Vol. 48, No. 3 [1925] pp. 263–300), written years before he claimed to have validated his nomenclature. Tellingly, the undated technical report of the Battle Cave find, entitled "Field Notes: Canyon del Muerto," carries exactly the same designation, albeit in Spanish. For further information, see Ann Axtell Morris, *Digging in the Southwest* (Chicago: Cadmus Books, 1933); Elizabeth Ann Morris, "A Biography of Earl H. Morris," *Southwestern Lore*, Vol. 22, No. 3 (1956) pp. 40–43.

56   Earl H. Morris, *Archaeological Studies in the La Plata District, Southwestern Colorado and Northwestern New Mexico* (Washington, DC: Carnegie Institution of Washington, Pub. 519, 1939).

57   Erik K. Reed, "Fractional Burials, Trophy Skulls, and Cannibalism," *National Park Service Region 3 Anthropology Notes*, No. 79 (1949).

58   Ibid. Also see Gordon C. Baldwin, *Lake Mead Recreational Area: Archaeological Surveys and Excavations at the Davis Dam Reservoir Area* (unpublished 1948 manuscript on file in the Harold S. Coulton Library, Northern Arizona University).

59   Watson Smith, *Excavations in the Big Hawk Valley, Wupatki National Monument, Arizona* (Flagstaff: Museum of Northern Arizona Bull. 24, 1952). All-in-all, Smith seems to have been something of a cannibal fetishist. See his "One Man's Archaeology," *Kiva*, Vol. 57, No. 2 (Spring 1992) pp. 99–191.

60   See Erik K. Reed, "Human Skeletal Remains from the Turner-Look Site," in H. Marie Wormington, *A Reappraisal of the Fremont Culture, with a Summary of the Archaeology of the Northern Periphery* (Denver: Denver Museum of Natural History Proceedings No. 1, 1955) pp. 38–43.

61   Roberts apparently never made a formal report of his supposed 1926 discovery. Rather, he recounted it in a personal letter written to anthropologist Frank McNitt in 1957. McNitt then included reference to it in his *Richard Wetherill-Anasazi: Pioneer Explorer of Southwestern Ruins* (Albuquerque: University of New Mexico Press, [2nd ed.] 1966).

62   Christy G. Turner II, "Appendix II, Human Skeletons from the Coombs Site: Skeletal and Dental Aspects," in R.H. Lister and F.C. Lister, *The Coombs Site, Pt. 3: Summary and Conclusions* (Salt Lake City: Anthropological Papers No. 41 (Glen Canyon Series), University of Utah Press, 1961) esp. p. 118.

63   A.E. Dittert Jr., F.W. Eddy, and B.L. Dickey, "LA 4195: Sambrito Village," in F.W. Eddy, ed., *Prehistory in the Navajo Reservoir District, Northwestern New Mexico* (Santa Fe: Museum of New Mexico Papers in Anthropology No. 15, Pt. 1, 1966) pp. 230–54. Also see K. Bennett, "Appendix B: Analysis of Prehistoric Human Skeletal Remains from the Navajo Reservoir District," in the same volume, pp. 523–46.

64   Alan P. Olson, "A Mass Secondary Burial from Northern Arizona," *American Antiquity*, Vol. 31, No. 6 (1966) pp. 822–26; Christy G. Turner II and Nancy T. Morris, "A Massacre at Hopi," *American Antiquity*, Vol. 35, No. 3 (1970) pp. 320–31. The site is the same one described by Fewkes in 1893 (see note 53), and pertains to the apparent killing of the residents of the Hopi village of Awatovi during an intratribal conflict.

65   Peter J. Pilles, "The Leroux Wash Excavation," a report presented at the Pecos Conference, Mesa Verde National Park, 1974.

66   Larry V. Nordby, *The Excavation of Sites 5MTUMR 2343, 5MTUMR 2345 and 5MTUMR 2346, Mancos Canyon, Ute Mountain, Ute Homelands, Colorado* (Washington, DC:

Bureau of Indian Affairs Contract Rpt. No. MOOC14201337, 1974); Paul R. Nickens, "Prehistoric Cannibalism in the Mancos Canyon, Southwestern Colorado," *Kiva*, Vol. 40, No. 4 (Summer 1975) pp. 283–93.

67   Linn Flynn, Christy G. Turner II, and Alan Brew, "Additional Evidence for Cannibalism in the Southwest: The Case of LA4528," *American Antiquity*, Vol. 41, No. 3 (1976) pp. 308–18.

68   James E. Chase, "Deviance in the Gallina: A Report on a Small Series of Gallina Human Skeletal Remains," in H.W. Dick, ed., *Archaeological Excavations in the Llaves Area, Santa Fe National Forest, New Mexico, 1972–1974* (Albuquerque: USDA Forest Service, Southwest Region, Archaeological Report No. 13, 1976) pp. 67–106.

69   James Mackey and R.C. Green, "The Largo-Gallina Towers: An Explanation," *American Antiquity*, Vol. 44, No. 1 (1979) pp. 144–54.

70   Dana Hartman, "Preliminary Assessment of Mass Burials in the Southwest," *American Journal of Physical Anthropology*, Vol. 42, No. 2 (1975) pp. 305–6.

71   Christy G. Turner II and Jacqueline A. Turner, *Man Corn: Cannibalism and Violence in the Prehistoric American Southwest* (Salt Lake City: University of Utah Press, 1999) p. 6.

72   See, e.g., George Alexander, "New Discoveries Indicate Widespread Cannibalism in Early Pueblos," *Los Angeles Times* (September 15, 1974).

73   The term "taphonomy" was coined by a Soviet paleontologist in 1940 to describe the process of analyzing skeletal materials exhumed during archaeological investigations. See I.A. Efremov, "Taphonomy: A New Branch of Paleontology," *Pan-American Geologist*, Vol. 74, No. 2 (1940) pp. 81–93. As was remarked earlier, the techniques involved didn't really begin to see systematic application in American archaeology until the early 1980s (see note 52), but then evolved steadily throughout the decade. See generally Richard E. Morlan, "Archaeology as Paleobiology," *Transactions of the Royal Society of Canada*, Series 5, Vol. 2 (1987) pp. 117–24; Christopher P. Koch, *Taphonomy: A Bibliographic Guide to the Literature* (Orono, ME: Center for the Study of the First Americans, 1989); Tim D. White and Peter Arend Folkens, *Human Osteology* (San Diego: Academic Press, 1991).

74   Ralph A. Luebben and Paul R. Nickens, "A Mass Internment in an Early Pueblo III Kiva in Southwestern Colorado," *Journal of Intermountain Archaeology*, No. 1 (1982) pp. 66–79; Ralph A. Luebben, "The Grinnell Site: A Small Ceremonial Center near Yucca House, Colorado," *Journal of Intermountain Archaeology*, No. 2 (1983) pp. 1–26.

75   G. Gilesa Nass and Nicholas F. Bellantoni, "A Prehistoric Multiple Burial from Monument Valley Evidencing Trauma and Possible Cannibalism," *Kiva*, Vol. 47, No. 4 (Summer 1982) pp. 257–71.

76   Turner, "Taphonomic Reconstructions"; Everett J. Bassett and Karen A. Atwell, "Osteological Data on the Ash Creek Population," in G. Rice, ed., *Studies in the Hohokam and Salado of the Tonto Basin* (Tempe: Arizona State University, Office of Cultural Resource Management Report No. 6, 1985) pp. 221–36.

77   Christy G. Turner II, "Another Prehistoric Southwest Mass Human Burial Suggesting Violence and Cannibalism: Marshview Hamlet, Colorado," Ann Lucy Wiener, "Human Remains from Marshview Hamlet," and Richard H. Wilshusen, "Excavations at Marshview Hamlet (Site 5MT2235)," all in G.T. Gross and A.E. Kane, eds., *Dolores Archaeological Program: Aceramic and Late Occupations at Dolores* (Denver: U.S. Dept. of Interior, Bureau of Reclamation, Engineering and Research Center, 1988) pp. 81–83, 71–72, 15–53.

78   Tim D. White, "Cottonwood Wash, Southeastern Utah: The Human Osteology of Feature 3, FS#27, Site 42SA12209," in J. Fetterman, L. Honeycutt, and K. Kuckelman,

eds., *Salvage Excavations* (Yellow Jacket, CO: Woods Canyon Archaeological Consultants, 1988) pp. 1–7.

79   Shane A. Baker, "Rattlesnake Ruin and Anasazi Cannibalism," *Newsletter of BYU Anthropology and Archaeology*, Vol. 4, No. 1 (1988); "Rattlesnake Ruin: The Question of Cannibalism and Violence in Anasazi Culture," *Canyon Legacy*, No. 17 (1993) pp. 2–11; "The Question of Cannibalism and Violence in Anasazi Culture: A Case Study from San Juan County, Utah," *Blue Mountain Shadows*, No. 13 (1994) pp. 30–41.

80   Christy G. Turner II, "Teec Nos Pos: More Possible Cannibalism in Northeastern Arizona," *Kiva*, Vol. 54, No. 2 (1989) pp. 147–52.

81   Sharon S. Grant, "Secondary Burial or Cannibalism? An Example from New Mexico," *American Journal of Physical Anthropology*, No. 78 (1989) pp. 230–31.

82   Nancy J. Malville, "Two Fragmented Human Bone Assemblages from Yellow Jacket, Southwestern Colorado," *Kiva*, Vol. 55, No. 1 (1989) pp. 3–22.

83   Michael H. Dice, "Disarticulated Human Remains from Reach III of the Towaoc Canal, Ute Mountain Reservation, Montezuma County, Colorado" (unpublished report by Complete Archaeological Services to the U.S. Bureau of Reclamation regional office, Salt Lake City, 1993) pp. 3–14. Christy G. Turner II, Jacqueline A. Turner, and Roger C. Green, "Taphonomic Analysis of Anasazi Skeletal Remains from the Largo-Gallina Sites in Northwestern New Mexico," *Journal of Anthropological Research*, Vol. 49, No. 2 (1993) pp. 83–110; Mary M. Errickson et al., *Prehistoric Archaeological Investigations on Reach III of the Towaoc Canal, Ute Mountain Reservation, Montezuma County, Colorado* (Cortez, CO: Complete Archaeological Services, 1993).

84   Turner, Turner, and Green, "Taphonomic Analysis." Also see Jeff H. Shipman, "Human Skeletal Remains from the Salmon Ruin (LA 8846)," in C. Irwin-Williams and P.H. Shelly, eds., *Investigations at the Salmon Ruins: The Structure of Chacoan Society in the Northern Southwest*, Vol. 4 (Portales: Eastern New Mexico University Press, 1980) pp. 47–78.

85   Turner, Turner, and Green, "Taphonomic Analysis."

86   Ibid. For background, see Alexander J. Lindsey Jr., Christy G. Turner II, and Paul V. Long Jr., "Excavations along the Lower San Juan River, Utah, 1958–1960" (unpublished 1961 report on file at the Harold S. Colton Library, Northern Arizona University).

87   For background, see George J. Gumerman and Alan P. Olson, "Prehistory in the Puerco Valley, Eastern Arizona," *Plateau*, Vol. 40, No. 4 (1968) pp. 113–27.

88   Nicholas P. Herrmann, Marsha D. Ogilvie, Charles E. Hilton, and Kenneth L. Brown, *Across the Colorado Plateau: Anthropological Studies for the Transwestern Pipeline Project, Vol. 18: Human Remains and Burial Goods* (Albuquerque: University of New Mexico, Office of Contract Archaeology and the Maxwell Museum of Anthropology, 1993) pp. 11–75, 153–57.

89   James N. Morris, Linda Honeycutt, and Jerry Fetterman, *Preliminary Report on 1990–1991 Excavations at Hanson Pueblo Site 5MT3876* (Yellow Jacket, CO: Woods Canyon Archaeological Associates, Indian Camp Ranch Archaeological Report No. 12, 1993); Michael H. Dice, "Disarticulated Human Remains from the Hanson Pueblo, 5MT3876, Cortez, Colorado" (unpublished 1993 report on file with Woods Canyon Archaeological Associates).

90   Ann Gibbons, "Archaeologists Rediscover Cannibals," *Science*, Vol. 277, No. 5326 (August 1, 1997) pp. 635–37.

91   Tim D. White, *Prehistoric Cannibalism at Mancos 5MTUMR-2346* (Princeton, NJ: Princeton University Press, 1992).

92 Osborne, "Does Man Eat Man?" pp. 33–34.

93 Ibid., p. 34.

94 Quoted in ibid., p. 34. Brady, a presumed expert on Polynesian cannibalism, had made the virulence of his opinions known during the early 1980s in polemics directed against William Arens. See Ivan Brady, "The Myth-Eating Man," *American Anthropologist*, No. 841 (1982) pp. 595–610.

95 Paul Bahn, "Is Cannibalism Too Much to Swallow?" *New Scientist*, Vol. 130, No. 1766 (April 1991) pp. 38–40; "Ancestral Cannibalism Gives Us Food for Thought: A Review of Prehistoric Cannibalism by T.D. White," *New Scientist*, Vol. 134, No. 1816 (April 1992) pp. 40–41. Bahn drew particular attention to White's failure to acknowledge Australian archaeologist Michael Pickering's recent finding that funerary practices among certain aboriginal groups involve the cracking of long bones and extraction of marrow, leaving skeletal damage virtually identical to that White discovered among the Mancos remains. In other such rituals, the brain is removed.

96 William Arens, interview included as part of a 1994 documentary released by The Learning Channel (TLC) under the title, *Archaeology*.

97 Quoted in Osborne, "Does Man Eat Man?" p. 34.

98 Peter Y. Bullock, "A Return to the Question of Anasazi Cannibalism," *Kiva*, Vol. 58, No. 2 (1992) p. 204. Also see his "A Reappraisal of Anasazi Cannibalism," *Kiva*, Vol. 57, No. 1 (1991) pp. 147–52.

99 "Unfortunately for archaeologists, the stomach of a hyena is 50 percent hydrochloric acid and can leave smooth holes in digested bones which resemble the supposed traces of cannibalism." Osborne, "Does Man Eat Man?" p. 36.

100 The photos were originally deployed in a rather misleading manner by D. Carleton Gajdusek to accompany his Nobel Prize–winning research on the mysterious and invariably lethal kuru sickness among the Fore; D. Carleton Gajdusek, "Unconventional Viruses and the Origin and Disappearance of Kuru: Nobel Lecture, December 13, 1976," in W. Oldenberg, ed., *Les Prix Nobel* (Stockholm: Nobel Foundation, 1977) pp. 160–216; subsequently published as "Unconventional Viruses and the Origin and Disappearance of Kuru," *Science*, Vol. 197, No. 4307 (September 2, 1977) pp. 943–60. Although he alluded to the possibility, Gajdusek never actually attributed the spread of kuru to cannibalism. Rather, he surmised that infection was most likely incurred through cuts and abrasions suffered during funerary rituals in which the brain was removed. Nonetheless, he included in his sequence a photo which, its placement suggested, showed a group of Fore men dining on the flesh of a kuru victim. More than a decade later, Vincent Zigas, who had taken the photo, published it in his *Laughing Death: The Untold Story of Kuru* (Clifton, NJ: Humana Press, 1990), clearly indicating in his caption that men were eating nothing more sinister than roast pork. Gajdusek's photographic fraud rivals another perpetrated by Robert Glasse and Shirley Lindenbaum, anthropologists who take the more extreme position that kuru could "only" have been transmitted through cannibalism. While discussing alleged Fore cannibalism in their *Essays on Kuru* (Faringdon, UK: E.W. Classey, 1976), Glasse and Lindenbaum accompanied their text with a photo of a group of men tending an earth oven. The implication was/is clear, although the caption was ambiguous. Lindenbaum has since admitted that the scene had nothing to do with cannibalism and argues, rather implausibly, that neither she nor her coauthor ever intended to suggest that it did. See William Arens, "Rethinking Anthropophagy," in Barker, Hulme, and Iverson, *Cannibalism and the Colonial World*, pp. 56–62. For what is probably the soundest assessment of kuru—that it was

actually a pathogen introduced by European interlopers—see L.B. Steadman and C.E. Merbs, "Kuru and Cannibalism?" *American Anthropologist*, Vol. 84, No. 3 (June 1982) pp. 611–27.

101   TLC interview.

102   Quoted in Osborne, "Does Man Eat Man?" p. 36. As with Sahlins' characterization of Arens as the equivalent of a "holocaust denier" (note 39), White's comparison of doubters with "creationists" seems exactly backwards. It is, after all, those who insist upon the myth of the anthropophagi who compose the ranks of true believers in this instance. Skeptics like Arens, who demand unassailable evidence, obviously fall within the tradition of science.

103   Osborne, "Does Man Eat Man?" p. 36.

104   For background, see Robert H. Lister, *Contributions to Mesa Verde Archaeology II: Site 875, Mesa Verde National Park, Colorado* (Boulder: University of Colorado Press, Anthropology Series No. 11, 1965). For the state of current taphonomic analysis, see Turner and Turner, *Man Corn*, pp. 365–66.

105   For background, see Lonnie C. Pippin, Prehistory and Paleoecology of the Guadalupe Ruin, New Mexico (Salt Lake City: Utah Anthropology Paper 112, University of Utah Press, 1987). For the state of current taphonomic analysis, see Turner and Turner, *Man Corn*, pp. 363–64.

106   For background, see Clifton W. Sink, Douglas M. Davu, A. Trinkle Jones, Laura Michalik, and Diane Pitz, "Arizona D:7:262," in P.P. Andrews et al., eds., *Excavations on Black Mesa, 1980: A Descriptive Report* (Carbondale: Southern Illinois University Center for Archaeological Investigations, 1982) pp. 86–108. For the state of current taphonomic analysis, see Turner and Turner, *Man Corn*, pp. 395–97.

107   Coprolites are the fossilized remains of human feces. Myoglobin is a protein which, in humans, is found only in the heart muscle; "Cannibalism find shakes U.S. legends: An ancient dwelling in Colorado points to evidence that some North American Indians practiced ritual cannibalism," *New York Times* (November 28, 1998). It has by no means been determined that myoglobin is found only in humans, however.

108   Turner and Turner, *Man Corn*, p. 417. The Turners make no claim to speak or read Nahuatl. Rather, their method is to translate into English the Spanish translations of Aztec words performed by Adela Fernández in her *Diccionario ritual de voces nahuas: Definiciones de palabras que expresan el pensamiento mítico y religioso de los Nahuas prehispánicos* (México, D.F.: Panorama Editorial, 1992).

109   The overall section runs from page 55 through page 414, while the "Other Cases" subsection takes up pages 397–404. Another chapter, consuming 44 pages (pp. 10–54) is devoted to explaining the authors' taphonomic, ethnographic, and archaeological methods. The remaining 69 pages of the 484-page main text is consumed by a comparative chapter (pp. 415–58) and another purporting to "explain Southwestern cannibalism" (pp. 459–84).

110   Turner and Turner, *Man Corn*, pp. 8–9.

111   "Cannibalism find shakes U.S. legends."

112   The Turners list all seventy-six sites in the chronological order by which they were reported. The damaged to skeletal remains recovered at sites 1, 2, 3, 4, 10, 11, 12, 15, 16, 19, 23, 38, 40, 42, 43, 45, 53, 68, 69, 70, 73, and 75 are all categorized as indicative of noncannibalistic "Violence." Sites 71 and 72 are categorized as "Problematic," sites 54 and 55 as "Uncertain," sites 58, 63, and 64 as "Cannibalism?" Turner and Turner, *Man Corn*, pp. 56–57.

113 The Turners disagree with a "Cannibalism" classification vis-à-vis sites 22, 27, 35, 36, 37, and 38. Ibid. p. 56.

114 Sites 6, 17, 20, 30, 31, 32, and 33. Ibid.

115 Sites 8, 14, 28, 39, 41, 48, 50, 51, 58, and 59. Ibid., pp. 56–57.

116 Sites 8 (1920), 14 (1939), and 39 (1979). Ibid., p. 56.

117 Ibid., p. 151.

118 Ibid., p. 152. At issue is the report submitted by Earl H. Morris concerning the La Plata 41 site. See note 57 and accompanying text.

119 Turner and Turner, *Man Corn*, p. 1.

120 See notes 1 and 3, with accompanying text.

121 Turner and Turner, *Man Corn*, pp. 1–2, 8, 415, 1.

122 Ibid., p. 415. Given the comprehensiveness of their bibliography—it spans 29 pages (507–36)—it seems unlikely that the Turners were unaware of or simply overlooked the positions taken by Bahn, Hassler, Sale, Torgovnick, Warner, and a number of others cited herein. Indeed, in another connection, they reference two of the articles in which Bahn explicitly rejects the view of Aztec society to which they subscribe (see note 96). The appearance is thus that they quite deliberately avoid mention of countervailing opinions in order to create the (mis)impression that they are part of a scholarly "consensus" where Aztec cannibalism is concerned.

123 Turner and Turner, *Man Corn*, pp. 2, 469. Actually, the most recent instance of cannibalism the Turners purport to have confirmed—at Polacca Wash—is associated the destruction of the Hopi village of Awatovi, and would thus have occurred around 1580. Ibid., pp. 168–200. On the Awatovi Massacre, see Harold Courlander, *The Fourth World of the Hopi* (Greenwich, CT: Fawcett, 1971) pp. 217–19; Harry C. James, *Pages from Hopi History* (Tucson: University of Arizona Press, 1974) pp. 62–64; Ekkehart Malotki, Michael Lomatuway'ma, Lorena Lomatuway'ma, and Sidney Naminha Jr., *Kikötutuwutsi: Hopi Ruin Legends* (Flagstaff/Lincoln: Northern Arizona University Press and University of Nebraska Press, 1993) pp. 399–403.

124 Turner and Turner, *Man Corn*, p. 24. They also cite two others: the methods employed by graduate student Michael Dice at Leroux Wash during the early 1990s, and that described by paleontologist Paola Villa in his "Cannibalism in Prehistoric Europe," *Evolutionary Anthropology*, Vol. 1, No. 3 (1992) pp. 93–104. Christy Turner's own earlier work is also referenced, of course, but none of this serves to alter the situation: All the techniques are fundamentally the same as those employed by White.

125 Turner and Turner, *Man Corn*, pp. 415–58.

126 Ibid., p. 417. The references are to Carrasco, "Myth, Cosmic Terror, and the Templo Mayor"; *Quetzalcoatl and the Irony of Empire: Myths and Prophesies in the Aztec Tradition* (Chicago: University of Chicago Press, 1982). Aside from the Sahagún, Durán, and Bernal Díaz texts themselves (see notes 8 and 11), other "authorities" cited in this section include Zelia Nuttall's *The Book of the Life of the Ancient Mexicans Containing an Account of Their Rites and Superstitions*, Pt. 1 (Berkeley: University of California Press, 1903); Charles E. Dibble's *Codex Hall: An Ancient Mexican Hieroglyphic Picture Manuscript* (Albuquerque: University of New Mexico Press, 1947); Christopher L. Moser's *Human Decapitation in Ancient Mesoamerica* (Washington, DC: Studies in Precolumbian Art and History No. 11, Trustees of Harvard University, 1973); as well as Gisele Díaz's and Alan Rodgers' *Codex Borgia: A Full-Color Restoration of the Ancient Mexican Manuscript* (New York: Dover, 1993).

127 Turner and Turner, *Man Corn*, p. 421; quoting Richard E.W. Adams, *Prehistoric Mesoamerica* (Norman: University of Oklahoma Press, 1991) p. 401.

128 Turner and Turner, *Man Corn*, p. 419; citing mainly Hugh Thomas, *The Conquest of Mexico* (London: Hutchinson, 1993) p. 240; Eduard Seler, *Collected Works of Mesoamerican Linguistics and Archaeology, Vol. 4* (Culver City, CA: Labyrinthos, 1993) pp. 24–25, 44; and Moser, Human Decapitation, p. 7.

129 Turner and Turner, *Man Corn*, pp. 420–21; quoting Ralph L. Beals, *The Comparative Ethnology of Northern Mexico before 1750* (Berkeley: Ibero-Americana No. 2, University of California, 1932) pp. 114, 129–30.

130 Turner and Turner, *Man Corn*, pp. 419–20. Their reference on the Tarahumaras is Wendell C. Bennett and Robert M. Zingg, *The Tarahumara: An Indian Tribe of Northern Mexico* (Chicago: University of Chicago Press, 1935) p. 288. On the Acaxee and Xixime, they rely upon Thomas B. Hinton, "Southwest Periphery: West," and William B. Griffin, "Southwest Periphery: East," both in Alfonso Ortiz, ed., *Handbook of North American Indians, Vol. 10: Southwest* (Washington, DC: Smithsonian Institution Press, 1983) pp. 315–28, 329–42, passages quoted at 323, 335–36; and Beals, *Comparative Ethnology*, p. 130. On the Cáhita, they quote Ralph L. Beals, *The Aboriginal Culture of the Cáhita Indians* (Berkeley: Ibero-America No. 19, University of California, 1943) pp. 40–43; on the Yavapai and Karankawa, Beals, *Comparative Ethnology*, p. 130.

131 Turner and Turner, *Man Corn*, p. 4.

132 Fray Vicente de Santa María, *Relación histórica de la colonia del Nuevo Santander* (México, DF: Instituto de Investiganciones Bibliográficas, Universidad Nacional Autónoma de México, 1973). At no point does Santa María purport to have firsthand knowledge or direct evidence of the indigenous anthropophagy he so consistently reports.

133 The authors themselves confirm this interpretation fairly openly, stating at the outset that their intention, irrespective of the evidence, is to "simply assert [their] acceptance that the act of cannibalism has been practiced on men, women, and children all over the world for a very long time." Turner and Turner, *Man Corn*, p. 2.

134 Ibid., pp. 421–28.

135 Here, the Turners rely upon Adams, *Prehistoric Mesoamerica*, p. 224; Rubén Cabrera Castro, "Human Sacrifice at the Temple of the Feathered Serpent: Recent Discoveries at Teotihuacan," and Carlos Serrano Sánchez, "Funerary Practices and Human Sacrifice in Teotihuacan Burials," both in K. Berrin and E. Pasztory, eds., *Teotihuacan: Art from the City of the Gods* (New York: Thames and Hudson, 1993) pp. 101–7, 108–15; and, especially, Rebecca Storey's *Life and Death in the Ancient City of Teotihuacan: A Modern Paleodemographic Synthesis* (Tuscaloosa: University of Alabama Press, 1992).

136 In advancing their claims about the Toltecs, the authors rely primarily upon Richard A. Diehl's *Tula: The Toltec Capital of Ancient Mexico* (London: Thames and Hudson, 1983) as well as a single undated report of faunal remains. On the other hand, quoting Mexican anthropologists Josephina Mansilla and José Antonio Pompa, they concede that most of the skeletal material upon which their conclusions are based have been "lost." Turner and Turner, *Man Corn*, p. 426.

137 On the Olmecs, the Turners' sole source seems to be Michael A. Coe's and Richard A. Diehl's *In the Land of the Olmec, Vol. 1: The Archaeology of San Lorenzo Tenochtitlán* (Austin: University of Texas Press, 1980).

138 With respect to Michoacán, the authors deploy no citations at all, contenting themselves with three photographs of ornamental objects they say were crafted from human bones in to support their value judgment that the precolumbian indigenous societies of the region exhibited an "ignoble, if not socially pathological, attitude toward the use and treatment of people [consistent with] ritual sacrifice and cannibalism." Turner and Turner, *Man Corn*, pp. 426–27.

139 Despite their inflated rhetoric on the topic, the Turners' roster of what they apparently consider credible archaeological studies concerning the Aztecs' mass sacrifices and cannibalism reduce to four, all involving a single site and the same grad students/authors: Carmen María Pijoan Aguadé and Alejandro Pastrana, "Evidencias de antropofagia y sacrificio humano en restos óseos," *Avances en Antropología Física*, No. 2 (1985) pp. 37–45; Carmen María Pijoan Aguadé, Alejandro Pastrana, and Consuelo Maquivar, "El tzompantli de Tlatelolco: Una evidencia de sacrificio humano," *Estudios de Antropología Biológica, 4: Coloquio de Antropología Física Juan Comas, 1986, 1989*, pp. 561–83; Carmen María Pijoan Aguadé, Josephina Mansilla, and Alejandro Pastrana, "Un caso de desmembramiento, Tlatelolco, D.F.," *Estudios de Antropología Biológica*, No. 5 (1995) pp. 89–100; and Carmen María Pijoan Aguadé, *Evidencia de sacrificio humano y canibalismo en restos óseos: El caso del entierro número 14 de Tlatelolco, D.F.* (México, D.F.: doctoral dissertation in anthropology, Universidad Nacional Autónoma de México, 1997).

140 Turner and Turner, *Man Corn*, p. 426; quoting Robert B. Pickering and Michael S. Foster, "A Survey of Prehistoric Disease and Trauma in Northwest and West Mexico," *Proceedings of the Denver Museum of Natural History*, Vol. 3, No. 7 (1994) p. 14.

141 Turner and Turner, *Man Corn*, p. 424. For citations, see note 140.

142 Ibid., pp. 451–53.

143 Remains from the Coxcatlan Cave site were exhumed in 1962 and the disarticulated skulls of three children offered as evidence of "possible cannibalism." See Richard S. MacNeish, *Second Annual Report of the Tehuacán Archaeological-Botanical Project* (Andover, MA: Peabody Foundation for Archaeology, Phillips Academy, 1962); Melvin L. Fowler and Richard S. MacNeish, "Excavations at the Coxcatlan Locality in the Alluvial Slopes," in R.S. MacNeish, et al., eds., *Prehistory of the Tehuacán Valley, Vol. 5: Excavations and Reconnaissance* (Austin: University of Texas Press, 1972) pp. 219–340. In their own undated taphonomic examination, the Turners somewhat tentatively concur that one of the skulls represents "a strange candidate for the oldest known case of sacrifice and cannibalism in the Americas." Turner and Turner, *Man Corn*, p. 429. Also see James E. Anderson, "Human Skeletons of Tehuacán," *Science*, Vol. 148, No. 3669 (1965) pp. 496–97; "The Human Skeletons," in D.S. Byers, *The Prehistory of the Tehuacán Valley, Vol. 1: Environment and Subsistence* (Austin: University of Texas Press, 1967) pp. 91–113.

144 Carmen María Pijoan Aguadé and Alejandro Pastrada, "Método para registro de marcas de corte en huesos humanos: El caso Tlatelcomila, Tetelpan, D.F.," *Estudios de Antropología Biológia*, No. 3 (1987) pp. 561–83; "Evidencias de actividades rituales en restos óseos humanos en Tlatelcomila, D.F.: El Preclasico o Formativo," *Avances y Perspectivas* (1989) pp. 287–307. The Turners, after examining the skeletal materials in 1993, concurred that they "exhibit the taphonomic signature of cannibalism without ambiguity." Turner and Turner, *Man Corn*, p. 439.

145 Carmen María Pijoan Aguadé and Josephina Mansilla Lory, "Prácticas rituales en el norte de Mesoamerica: Evidencias en Electra, Villa de Reyes, San Luis Potosí," *Arqueologia*, No. 4 (1990) pp. 87–96; "Evidencias rituales en restos humanos del norte de Mesoamerica," in F. Sodi Miranda, ed., *Mesoamerica y Norte de México, Siglo IX–XII* (México, D.F.: Museo Nacional de Antropología e Historia, 1990) pp. 467–78. After their own examination of the osteological materials, the Turners professed, rather ambiguously, that they were "inclined to agree with Pijoan and Mansilla that some cooking of one or more Electra individuals probably took place." Turner and Turner, *Man Corn*, p. 445.

146   Ellen A. Kelly, "The Temple Skulls at Alta Vista, Chalchihuites," in Carroll L. Riley
      and Basel C. Hedrick, eds., *Across the Chichimec Sea: Papers in Honor of J. Charles Kelly*
      (Carbondale: Southern Illinois University Press, 1978) pp. 102–26. This is a classic
      case of modern archaeological conclusions being shaped by the nebulous "eth-
      nography" of early European chronicles: "Kelly concluded that cannibalism had
      occurred at Alta Vista, because it had been associated by the Spaniards with the
      saving of skulls and bones of enemies in ceremonial houses." Turner and Turner,
      Man Corn, p. 446.

147   Robert B. Pickering, "Human Osteological Remains from Alta Vista, Zacatecas: An
      Analysis of the Isolated Bone," in M.S. Foster and P.C. Weigand, eds., *The Archaeology
      of the West and Northwest Mesoamerica* (Boulder, CO: Westview Press, 1985) pp. 289–325.
      As the Turners conclude, there is "no firm evidence of cannibalism" at Alta Vista,
      "though it remains a strong possibility." Ever hopeful, they suggest that "it would be
      surprising if excavations in refuse areas away from the ceremonial complex failed
      to turn up human remains with the taphonomic signature of cannibalism." Turner
      and Turner, *Man Corn*, pp. 445, 451.

148   Ibid., p. 439.

149   Ibid., p. 428. The authors are following Sheilagh T. Brooks and Richard H. Brooks,
      "Skeletal Remains from La Cueva de Dos Chuchillos, San Francisco de Borja,
      Chihuahua, Mexico," in L. Lara Tapia, ed., *Para conocer al hombre: Homenaje a Santiago
      Genoves a los 33 años como investigador en la UNAM* (México, D.F.: Universidad Nacional
      Autónoma México, 1990) pp. 261–71.

150   Turner and Turner, *Man Corn*, p. 428; following Pickering and Foster, "Survey," p. 4;
      Pickering, "Osteological Remains," p. 323.

151   As Zuni tribal archaeologist Kurt Dongoske put it as far back as 1988, Christy
      "Turner's using cannibalism as a sensational way to promote his own [status]."
      Quoted in David Roberts, *In Search of the Old Ones: Exploring the Anasazi World of the
      American Southwest* (New York: Simon and Schuster, 1996) p. 159.

152   For an archetypal expression of the standard view, see Thomas Y. Canby, "The
      Anasazi: Riddles in the Ruins," *National Geographic*, No. 162 (November 1982)
      pp. 554–92.

153   Quoted in Roberts, *Old Ones*, p. 159.

154   See, as examples, Christy G. Turner II, "Anasazi Cannibalism: Review of Tim
      White's *Prehistoric Cannibalism at Mancos 5MTUMR-2346*," *Review of Archaeology*, Vol. 13,
      No. 2 (Summer 1992) pp. 7–13; Christy G. Turner II and Jacqueline A. Turner, "On
      Peter Y. Bullock's 'A Reappraisal of Anasazi Cannibalism,'" *Kiva*, Vol. 58, No. 2 (1992)
      pp. 189–201.

155   Actually, Turner had direct experience with such responses in his own right. "Posters
      announcing his lectures have been torn down, and at the 1988 Pecos Conference,
      a symposium on cannibalism [in which he was to participate] was canceled after
      protests by Native American groups." Roberts, *Old Ones*, p. 159.

156   Quoted in ibid., p. 162.

157   The word "culpability" is used advisedly, euroamerican pop writers being almost
      invariably prone to the casting of smug value judgments upon such things as
      anthropophagy. Such telltale semantic biases literally infest the mainstream litera-
      ture. Even so "sympathetic" a commentator as David Roberts, a self-proclaimed
      "cultural relativist," feels obliged to explain that cannibalism—of which he believes
      the Anasazis "guilty"—is "hard to continence in any form." Roberts, it should be
      noted, also refers to "the skeletal remains of eleven *murdered* persons [emphasis

added]" exhumed by archaeologists at Burnt Mesa, as if he/they were somehow able to distinguish the remains of those who died as a result of a criminal act from those who were killed in warfare or self-defense, or perhaps executed as the result of having themselves perpetrated some crime. See Roberts, *Old Ones*, p. 216.

158 This is outlined in a section captioned "A Proximate Explanation for Anasazi Cannibalism" (pp. 462–64), and embellished over the next twenty pages of the chapter entitled "Explaining Southwestern Cannibalism" (pp. 459–84). The idea of groups of Toltecs fleeing northward as their own culture disintegrated during the period 800–1000 AD is credited to Bertha Dutton, "Mesoamerican Culture Traits which Appear in the American Southwest," *Proceedings of the Thirty-fifth Congress of Americanists, 1962, Vol. 1* (México, D.F.: Instituto Nacional de Antropología e Historia, 1964) pp. 481–92.

159 Turner and Turner, *Man Corn*, p. 463. The only citation offered anywhere in the book to support the authors' horrific assessment of "the Xipe Totec cult," which comes at p. 217, is a thinly documented three-page span of Charles C. Di Peso's *Casas Grandes, a Fallen Trading Center of the Gran Chichimeca, Vol. 1: Medio Period* (Flagstaff, AZ: Northland Press, 1974) pp. 562–64. None at all is offered with respect to the Tezcatlipoca.

160 Turner and Turner, *Man Corn*, pp. 464–71. On architectural correspondences, the authors cite Dutton, "Mesoamerican Culture Traits," p. 485; Adams, *Prehistoric Mesoamerica*, p. 285; Erik K. Reed, "The Greater Southwest," in J.D. Jennings and E. Norbeck, eds., *Prehistoric Man in the New World* (Chicago: University of Chicago Press, 1964) pp. 183–84; Robert H. Lister and Florence C. Lister, *Chaco Canyon: Archaeology and Archaeologists* (Albuquerque: University of New Mexico Press, 1981) pp. 174–75. On correspondences in spiritual belief systems and symbologies, they rely heavily on such archaic fare as Jesse Walter Fewkes' "The Sacrificial Element in Hopi Worship," *Journal of American Folklore*, Vol. 10, No. 38 (1897) pp. 187–201; "Archaeology of the Lower Mimbres Valley, New Mexico," *Smithsonian Miscellaneous Collections*, Vol. 63, No. 10 (1914) pp. 1–47; and "Sun Worship of the Hopi Indians," *Smithsonian Report for 1918* (Washington, DC: Smithsonian Pub. 2571, 1920) pp. 493–526. Citation of more current material seems rather hit-or-miss, but includes Randall McGuire's "The Mesoamerican Connection in the Southwest," *Kiva*, Vol. 46, Nos. 1–2 (1980) pp. 3–38; J.J. Brody's *Mimbres Pottery: Ancient Art of the American Southwest* (New York: Hudson Hills Press, 1983) p. 115; and Carol J. Riley's *The Frontier People: The Greater Southwest in the Protohistoric Period* (Albuquerque: University of New Mexico Press, 1987) p. 322.

161 "Objections have repeatedly been raised against the hypothesis of a strong Mesoamerican influence on the development of the Chaco system." Turner and Turner, *Man Corn*, p. 470. On dissemination of limited influences via trade relations, they quote Edwin J. Ferdon, *A Trial Survey of Mexican-Southwestern Architectural Parallels* (Santa Fe: Monographs of the School of American Research and Museum of New Mexico, No. 21, 1955) pp. 24–25. Reference is also made to Arthur J. Jelinik's "Mimbres Warfare?" *Kiva*, Vol. 27, No. 2 (1961) pp. 28–30; and Steven A. LeBlanc's "Cultural Dynamics in the Southern Mogollon Area," in L.S. Cordell and G.J. Gumerman, eds., *Dynamics of Southwestern Prehistory* (Washington, DC: Smithsonian Institution Press, 1989) pp. 179–207.

162 Turner and Turner, *Man Corn*, p. 473.

163 Ibid. See esp. the comparative photos on pp. 474–75.

164 Turner and Turner, *Man Corn*, p. 473. Also see T.D. Campbell, "Dental Condition of a Skull from the Sikyatki Site, Arizona," *Washington Academy of Sciences*, Vol. 34, No. 10

(1944) pp. 317–21; Marcia H. Regan, Christy G. Turner II, and Joel D. Irish, "Physical Anthropology of the Schoolhouse Point Mound, U:8:24/13A," in O. Lindauer with P.H. McCartney et al., eds., *The Place of the Storehouses, Roosevelt Platform Mound Study: Report on the Schoolhouse Point Mound, Pinto Creek Complex, Pt. 2* (Tempe: Dept. of Anthropology Monograph Series 6, Arizona State University, 1996) pp. 787–840; S.E. Burnett, "Dental Mutilation at Pecos Pueblo, New Mexico: Two Cases Dating from 1400–1600 A.D.," *American Journal of Physical Anthropology*, Supp. 24 (1997) pp. 84–85.

165   Turner and Turner, *Man Corn*, p. 473. Also see their "Cannibalism in the Prehistoric American Southwest: Occurrence, Taphonomy, Explanation, and Suggestions for a Standardized World Definition," *Anthropological Science*, Vol. 103, No. 1. (1995) pp. 1–22.

166   Turner and Turner, *Man Corn*, pp. 482–83.

167   Reinforcing this interface, with physical anthropology of course in the driver's seat, was in fact one of the explicitly stated goals of White's *Prehistoric Cannibalism at Mancos*. See the quote in Osborne, "Does Man Eat Man?" p. 34.

168   Turner and Turner, *Man Corn*, p. 8.

169   Ibid.

170   Suffice it to say that the dynamic represents an obverse of the general procedures indicated in Karl Popper's *The Logic of Scientific Discovery* (New York: Science Editions, 1961 reprint of 1934 original), or, by extension, Thomas Kuhn's *The Structure of Scientific Revolutions* (Chicago: University of Chicago Press, 1962). Indeed, it clearly falls within the realm of what Popper later described as constituting unscientific or even antiscientific—that is, "metaphysical"—understanding in his *Conjectures and Refutations: The Growth of Scientific Knowledge* (New York: Harper Torchbooks, 1968 ed. of 1962 original). For further commentary, see notes 48 and 50, with accompanying text; E.A. Burtt's superb but little-remembered book, *The Metaphysical Foundations of Modern Science* (New York: Doubleday, 1954 reprint of 1924 original); and the essays collected in Roy Wallis, ed., *On the Margins of Science* (Keele, UK: University of Keele Press, 1979).

171   Arens, TLC interview.

172   Turner and Turner, *Man Corn*, p. 481; citing Ed Sanders, *The Family: The Story of Charles Manson's Dune Buggy Attack Battalion* (New York: E.P. Dutton, 1971).

173   Turner and Turner, *Man Corn*, p. 478; citing Fredric Wertham, *The Show of Violence* (Garden City, NY: Doubleday, 1949); Donald T. Lunde, *Murder and Madness* (San Francisco: Portable Library, 1976); Robert T. Ressler and Tom Schachtman, *Whoever Fights Monsters* (New York: St. Martin's Press, 1992). Turner conspicuously avoids mentioning such equally well-known but radically different examples as Alferd Packer, "the gentle cannibal," and Ed Gein, who evidenced a primarily necrophilic rather than homicidal orientation. See James E. Banks, *Alferd Packer's Wilderness Cookbook: The Story of Colorado's Cannibal* (Palmer Lake, CO: Filter Press, 1998) and Paul Anthony Woods, *Ed Gein: Psycho* (New York: St. Martin's Press, 1995). It is thus accurate to observe that he distorts the already biased "cannibalism as pathology" model he sets forth, apparently to render it even more prejudicial than it might otherwise be.

174   On the Black Legend, see note 7. On the "witches," see Hugh Trevor-Roper, *The European Witch Craze of the Sixteenth and Seventeenth Centuries and Other Essays* (New York: Harper & Row, 1969).

175   John Weiss, *Ideology of Death: Why the Holocaust Happened in Nazi Germany* (Chicago: Ivan R. Dee, 1996) pp. 18–19. More comprehensively, see Alan Dundes, *The Blood*

Libel Legend: A Casebook in Anti-Semitic Folklore (Madison: University of Wisconsin Press, 1991).

176 Arens, *Man-Eating Myth*, p. 19; citing Herman L. Strack, *The Jew and Human Sacrifice* (New York: Block, 1909). Strack grapples with a list of nearly 120 instances in which it was claimed there was "proof" that European Jews had performed ritual murders and cannibalism during the late nineteenth and early twentieth centuries. Such charges had been regularly advanced, always on the basis of supposed "hard evidence," since the twelfth century. See Dundes, *Blood Libel Legend*; Joshua Trachtenberg, *The Devil and the Jews: The Medieval Conception of the Jews and Its Connection to Modern Anti-Semitism* (New Haven, CT: Yale University Press, 1946) and R. Po-Chia Hsia, *The Myth of Ritual Murder: Jews and Magic in Reformation Germany* (New Haven, CT: Yale University Press, 1988).

177 Benjamin W. Segal, *A Lie and a Libel: The History of the Protocols of the Elders of Zion* (Lincoln: University of Nebraska Press, 1995) pp. 69–70, 124.

178 See, e.g., the first page of the "Special Edition on Jewish Ritual Murder" released by Streicher's *Dur Stürmer* in May 1934, reproduced as Figure 16 in Randall L. Bytwerk's *Julius Streicher: The Man Who Persuaded a Nation to Hate Jews* (New York: Dorset Press, 1983). More broadly, see C.C. Aronsfeld, *The Text of the Holocaust: A Study of the Nazi Extermination Propaganda, 1919–1945* (Marblehead, MA: Micah, 1985).

179 Isabel Fonseca, *Bury Me Standing: The Gypsies and Their Journey* (New York: Vintage, 1995) p. 88; Donald Kendrick and Donald Paxon, *Gypsies Under the Swastika* (Hertfordshire, UK: University of Hertfordshire Press, 1995) pp. 11–12.

180 On the Protocols, see Segal, *A Lie and a Libel*, and Norman Cohn, *Warrant for Genocide: The Myth of the Jewish World Conspiracy and the Protocols of the Elders of Zion* (London: Serif, [2nd ed.] 1996). On the effectiveness of such conditioning, see, e.g., Daniel Jonah Goldhagen, *Hitler's Willing Executioners: Ordinary Germans and the Holocaust* (New York: Alfred A. Knopf, 1996).

181 Arens, *Man-Eating Myth*, p. 19.

182 There are, to be sure, exceptions to this rule, mainly in South America. On the outright butchery of the Aché people of Paraguay during the early 1970s, for example, see Richard Arens, ed., *Genocide in Paraguay* (Philadelphia: Temple University Press, 1976). For a much broader survey, see *Report of the Fourth Russell Tribunal on the Rights of the Indians of the Americas* (Nottingham, UK: Bertrand Russell Foundation, 1980); Ismaelillo and Robin Wright, eds., *Native Peoples in Struggle: Cases from the Fourth Russell Tribunal and Other International Forums* (Bombay/New York: E.R.I.N., 1982).

183 Probably the most comprehensive and best-documented overviews will be found in David E. Stannard's *American Holocaust: Columbus and the Conquest of the New World* (New York: Oxford University Press, 1992) and my *A Little Matter of Genocide: Holocaust and Denial in the Americas, 1492 to the Present* (San Francisco: City Lights, 1997).

184 For a succinct overview, see Rennard Strickland, *Tonto's Revenge: Reflections on American Indian Culture and Policy* (Albuquerque: University of New Mexico Press, 1997) p. 53.

185 For a devastating analysis, see David E. Stannard, "The Politics of Holocaust Scholarship: Uniqueness as Denial," in Alan S. Rosenbaum, ed., *Is the Holocaust Unique? Perspectives in Comparative Genocide* (Boulder, CO: Westview Press, 1996) pp. 163–208.

186 Variations on the theme were advanced from literally every point on the ideological continuum during the run-up to the 1992 Columbian quincentenary. On the right, see, e.g., Jeffrey Hart, "Discovering Columbus," *National Review* (October 15, 1990) pp. 56–57. On the left, see, e.g., Christopher Hitchens' "Minority Report" in the

October 19, 1992 installment of *The Nation* (p. 422). Representing the center, see, e.g., the entire special issue on Columbus released by *Newsweek* during the fall/winter of 1991. The points made/sentiments expressed are virtually interchangeable.

187   For the sense in which the term "hegemonic" is intended here, see Walter L. Adamson, *Hegemony and Revolution: A Study of Antonio Gramsci's Political and Cultural Theory* (Berkeley: University of California Press, 1980) pp. 170–79.

188   American Indian Movement leader Russell Means has made a similar analogy, comparing "anthros [to] a cloud of gnats. . . . You swat at 'em, they scatter for a few seconds, and then they're back, swarming around your head as if nothing had happened." Personal conversation, June 1988.

189   Interestingly, and in no small part because of the communion ceremony, early Christians were accused by the Romans of drinking human blood in "mysterious secret rites." Arens, *Man-Eating Myth*, p. 19. Much more broadly, see Maggie Kilgour, *From Communion to Cannibalism: An Anatomy of the Metaphors of Incorporation* (Princeton, NJ: Princeton University Press, 1990).

190   Marina Warner, "Fee fie fo fum: children in the jaws of history," in Barker, Hulme and Iverson, *Cannibalism and the Colonial World*, p. 168–72; citing Hesiod, *Theogony* (Harmondsworth, UK: Penguin, 1982) pp. 38–39.

191   Warner, "Fee fie fo fum." See esp. the plates at pp. 170–71.

192   There is in fact an entire genre dubbed "swallow tales" because of the sheer rate at which human flesh is consumed therein. See Iona Opie and Peter Opie, eds., *The Classic Fairy Tales* (New York: Oxford University Press, 1974) p. 55.

193   Shakespeare also surfaces themes of cannibalism or its approximation in both *The Tempest* and *The Merchant of Venice*. For context, see Fredson Bowers, *Elizabethan Revenge Tragedy* (Princeton, NJ: Princeton University Press, 1940). For more extensive surveys, see Claude Rawson, "Cannibalism and Fiction: Reflections on Narrative Form and 'Extreme' Situations, Part 1: Satire and the Novel (Swift, Flaubert and Others)," *Genre*, Vol. 10 (Winter 1977) pp. 667–711; "Narrative and the Proscribed Act: Homer, Euripides and the Literature of Cannibalism" in Joseph P. Strelka, ed., *Literary Theory and Criticism: Festschrift Presented to René Welleck in Honor of His Eightieth Birthday* (Bern: Peter Lang, 1984) pp. 159–87. More broadly, see Frederic Jameson, *The Political Unconscious: The Narrative as a Socially Symbolic Act* (London: Metheun, 1983).

194   Maggie Kilgour, "The Function of Cannibalism at the Present Time," in Barker, Hulme and Iverson, *Cannibalism and the Colonial World*, pp. 240–41. To the list might be added such vampire fare as *Nosferatu*, *Lost Boys*, *Bram Stoker's Dracula*, and *Interview with the Vampire*, all of which display obviously anthropophagic thematics. There is an entire section devoted to "Cannibalism" in *VideoHound's Golden Movie Retriever* for 1995, listing nearly a hundred titles.

195   Karl Marx, *Capital*, Vol. 1 (New York: Penguin, 1990) pp. 367, 353.

196   See generally David Harvey, *The Condition of Postmodernity* (Cambridge, MA: Blackwell, 1990).

197   See Crystal Bartolovich, "Consumerism, or, the Cultural Logic of Late Cannibalism," in Barker, Hulme and Iverson, *Cannibalism and the Colonial World*, pp. 204–37. Bartolovich is of course providing her own twist to the title of Frederic Jameson's *Postmodernism, or, the Cultural Logic of Late Capitalism* (Durham, NC: Duke University Press, 1991).

198   See, as examples, Sigmund Freud, *Totem and Taboo* (London: Ark Paperbacks, 1983); C.G. Jung, *Mysterium Conjunctions: An Inquiry into the Separation and Synthesis of Psychic*

Opposites in Alchemy (Princeton, NJ: Princeton University Press, 1970); Gilles Deleuze and Félix Guattari, *Anti-Oedipus: Capitalism and Schizophrenia* (New York: Viking, 1977); Jacques Derrida, "Eating Well . . .," in Eduardo Cadava, Peter Connor and Jean-Luc Nancy, eds., *Who Comes After the Subject?* (London: Routledge, 1991) pp. 96–119. Laing approaches the topic obliquely, inviting comparison to the Aztecs' alleged mass sacrifice of human beings with his observation that in European and euroderivative societies, "Normal men have killed perhaps 100,000,000 of their fellow normal men in the past fifty years." R.D. Laing, *The Politics of Experience* (New York: Ballantine, 1967) p. 28.

199 Kilgour, "The function of cannibalism," p. 244; citing Freud, *Totem and Taboo.* Whether or not the prehistoric inhabitants of the European subcontinent were actually anthropophagistic is a matter of the usual conjecture. An interesting assessment of the probabilities and implications will be found in Norman Cohn, *Europe's Inner Demons* (London: Chatto Heinemann for Sussex University, 1975). Also see Villa, "Cannibalism in Prehistoric Europe"; Paola Villa, Claude Bouville and Jean Courtin, "Cannibalism in the Neolithic," *Science*, Vol. 233, No. 4 (July 1986) pp. 431–37.

200 See the essay "Repression" in *Sigmund Freud: Collected Papers*, 5 Vols. (New York: Basic Books, 1959) Vol. 4 pp. 84–97. Also see Wilhelm Reich, *The Invasion of Compulsory Sex Morality* (New York: Farrar, Straus & Giroux, 1971) esp. pp. 112–42.

201 As has been noted, "An observer looking at the world in 800 A.D. would barely have taken note of the European peninsula." Eric R. Wolf, *Europe and the People Without History* (Berkeley: University of California Press, 1982) p. 101. So much for Europe's self-concept at the moment of its inception. Also see Richard Hodges and David Whitehouse, *Mohammed, Charlemagne and the Origins of Europe* (Ithaca, NY: Cornell University Press, 1983) and Robert Reynolds, *Europe Emerges* (Madison: University of Wisconsin Press, 1961).

202 The term "inferiority complex" is used here in the sense described by Wilhelm Reich in his *Character Analysis* (New York: Farrar, Straus & Giroux, 1972) p. 323.

203 In an individuated sense, this dynamic was explored quite well by Donald T. Lunde in his *Murder and Madness* (San Francisco: San Francisco Book Co., 1976). At the sociocultural level, see Wilhelm Reich, *The Mass Psychology of Fascism* (New York: Farrar, Straus & Giroux, 1970), esp. pp. 24–33.

204 A useful examination of this tendency will be found in the chapter entitled "The Savage Art of Discovery: How to Blame the Victim," in William Ryan's *Blaming the Victim* (New York: Vintage Books, 1971) pp. 3–29.

205 Jack D. Forbes, *Columbus and Other Cannibals: The Wetiko Disease of Exploitation, Imperialism, and Terrorism* (New York: Autonomedia/Semiotext(e), 1992).

206 Joel Kovel, *White Racism: A Psychohistory* (New York: Columbia University Press, [2nd ed.] 1984). Another useful reading in this connection is Albert Memmi's *The Colonizer and the Colonized* (Boston: Beacon Press, 1967).

207 See my *Little Matter of Genocide*; Stannard, *American Holocaust*; Sven Lindquist, *"Exterminate All the Brutes": One Man's Journey Into the Heart of Darkness and the Origins of Modern Genocide* (New York: New Press, 1996).

208 For insights into the creation, development of anthropology, see, e.g., Kathleen Gough, "Anthropology: and Imperialism," *Monthly Review*, Vol. 19, No. 11 (April 1968) pp. 12–27; Talal Asad, ed., *Anthropology and the Colonial Encounter* (London: Ithaca Press, 1973); Johannes Fabian, *Time and the Other: How Anthropology Makes Its Object* (New York: Columbia University Press, 1983); Nicholas Thomas, *Colonialism's Culture: Anthropology, Travel and Government* (Princeton, NJ: Princeton University Press,

1984). Taking the process at issue more broadly, see Edward Said's *Orientalism* (New York: Pantheon, 1978) and Anne McClintock's *Imperial Leather: Race, Gender and Sexuality in the Colonial Contest* (New York: Routledge, 1995).

209   Léon Poliakov, *The Aryan Myth: A History of Racist and Nationalist Ideas in Europe* (New York: Barnes & Noble, 1971); Albert Memmi, *Racism* (Minneapolis: University of Minnesota Press, 2000).

210   Historically, see William Stanton, *The Leopard's Spots: Scientific Attitudes Towards Race in America, 1815–1859* (Chicago: University of Chicago, 1960); Stephen Jay Gould, *The Mismeasure of Man* (New York: W.W. Norton, 1981); Stefan Kühl, *The Nazi Connection: Eugenics, American Racism, and German National Socialism* (New York: Oxford University Press, 1994). More currently, see Troy Duster, *Backdoor to Eugenics* (New York: Routledge, 1990); William H. Tucker, *The Science and Politics of Racial Research* (Urbana: University of Illinois Press, 1994); Russell Jacoby and Naomi Glauberman, eds., *The Bell Curve Debate: History, Documents, Opinions* (New York: Times Books, 1995).

211   J.S. Weiner, *The Piltdown Forgery* (London: Oxford University Press, 1955); Ronald Millar, *The Piltdown Men* (New York: St. Martin's Press, 1972).

212   George Lipsitz, *The Possessive Investment in Whiteness: How White People Profit from Identity Politics* (Philadelphia: Temple University Press, 1998).

213   See Lawrence C. Goldman, *The Anthropology of Cannibalism* (Westport, CT: Bergin & Garvey, 1999).

214   For useful analyses following two distinct trajectories, see Samir Amin, *Eurocentrism* (New York: Monthly Review Press, 1989) and Vassilis Lambropoulos, *The Rise of Eurocentrism: Anatomy of Interpretation* (Princeton, NJ: Princeton University Press, 1994).

215   This is a consensus view among all variants of therapy from the most establishmentarian to the most alternative-oriented, and even those describing themselves as "antitheraputic." See, e.g., Jerome Agel and the Radical Therapy Collective, *The Radical Therapist: Therapy Means Change, Not Adjustment* (New York: Ballantine, 1971); Jeffrey Moussaieff Masson, *Against Therapy: Emotional Tyranny and the Myth of Psychological Healing* (Monroe, ME: Common Courage Press, 1994).

216   By "the rest of us," I do not mean to imply people of color, per se. The fact of the matter is that, whether one takes as a focus the United States or the world as a whole, an untold proportion of nonwhites have been co-opted by or coercively assimilated into the paradigm of eurocentrism. Conversely, an appreciable number of whites have opted out, both conceptually and materially. The latter would be part of the "us" at issue, the former not. For explication, see David Roediger, *Towards the Abolition of Whiteness* (London: Verso, 1994); Noel Ignatiev and John Garvey, eds., *Race Traitor* (New York: Routledge, 1996).

TEN

American Indians in Film
Thematic Contours of Cinematic Colonization

> Politics is the ability to define a phenomenon and cause it to act
> in a desired manner.
>
> —Huey P. Newton (1967)

The peoples indigenous to North America have occupied a position of centrality in North American cinema since the moment of its inception. This was certainly true of two of the very first experimental flickers—*Buck Dancer* and *Serving Rations to the Indians*—in 1898, and no less so of the first significant narrative film crafted by a euroamerican, D.W. Griffith's *The Battle of Elderbush Gulch*, in 1913.[1] As well, the first docudrama, an epic entitled *The Indian Wars Refought*, produced by the Colonel W.F. (Buffalo Bill) Cody Historical Motion Picture Company a year later.[2] All told, the North American film industry—usually, and rather inaccurately, referred to as "Hollywood"—has ground out more than 2,000 movies and perhaps 10,000 television segments on Indians and Indian themes during the past century.[3]

To be sure, the sheer vastness of output bespeaks the extent to which both the industry and its audience(s) appreciate, whether at a conscious level or more subliminally, the elemental nature of their relationship with/to the first peoples of this land.[4] Nothing, after all, is, or could be, more foundationally important to all that is now pronounced "American" than the verity that every square centimeter of territory from which "America" has been constructed, and every nickel's worth of the

Originally published in Jun Xing and Lane Ryo Hirabayashi, eds., *Reversing the Lens: Ethnicity, Race, Gender, and Sexuality Through Film* (Boulder: University Press of Colorado, 2003). It was and remains dedicated to Leah Renae Kelly, film student extraordinaire.

"domestic" resources upon which it subsists, have been extracted directly from us.[5] How this came to be, and how we ourselves came to "vanish" in the process, are pivotal questions, the answers to which are definitive of the American Story and thence the American Character.

Unfortunately for those whose task it is to tell it, the story is one a federal judge, when confronted with a fragment of the factual record, proclaimed sufficient to prompt persons of average sensibility to "wretch at the recollection."[6] The implications of this truth to the country's image, self-concept, and self-esteem are so obviously negative, at least from the perspective of those benefiting most tangibly from its creation and consolidation, that it must be veiled, deformed beyond recognition—better yet, completely expunged—through all available means. As Cherokee analyst Jimmie Durham has remarked, "the relationship between Americans and American Indians [is therefore] the most invisible and lied about" of any on the continent.[7]

In this endeavor, literature, the press and institutions of "responsible scholarship" have each played a hefty role.[8] Given the extraordinary and much-remarked potency of cinema/television in shaping consciousness,[9] however, it was perhaps predictable that moving pictures would serve as a disinformational workhorse, beginning by some point in the mid-1930s.[10] Indeed, no overstatement is embodied in observations that film and video have long since become the key media for articulating the master narrative with which North America's élites "explain" their history—and thus themselves—to the world.[11]

It comes as no surprise, then, to discover that, virtually without exception, Hollywood's massive spew of "Cowboy and Indian" movies has been devoted to misrepresenting the actualities of native cultures, as well as those of the emphatically euroderivative settler societies that have taken root and flourished here over the past several centuries, continuously rationalizing, sanitizing, inverting—in other words, systematically falsifying—the nature of the process by which the latter have come to all but completely decimate, dispossess, and dominate the former.[12] Such sins of commission are, moreover, compounded by and completed through the omissions embedded in hundreds, perhaps thousands, of additional films in which Indians are simply deleted from contexts and settings to which we rightly belong.[13] As Durham puts it:

> A false history is [thus] supplied as an alibi to cover up the truth, and this alibi in turn informs [American] culture in ways that serve to reinforce its control. . . . The lies are not simply a denial; they

constitute a new world, the world in which American culture is located. . . . By invasion, murder, theft, complex denial, alibi, and insignification, American culture gains tremendous (if pathological) psychological power and energy, which draw their strength almost exclusively from their own falseness.[14]

The hegemonic function served by Tinseltown's celluloid fabrications is unmistakable.[15] The dominant society—that is to say, that of the euroamerican settlers—is led thereby to believe, as it desires to do anyway, that realization of its self-anointed "Manifest Destiny" to subjugate all it encounters was/is not only natural, inevitable, and therefore right, but, by easy extension, heroic, even noble.[16] In this triumphalist script, native people, who by virtue of our very existence stood in the way of the settlers' mythic evocations of "progress" and "civilization," can only be construed as obstacles, inferior beings consigned by the savagery—or, with more supposed charity, the "tragedy"—of our inherent "backwardness" to the fate of being supplanted and ultimately extinguished by our euroderivative "betters."[17]

There are consequently few signs of dis-eased conscience among those who have always chosen to believe themselves entitled to replace us on our lands, no more need to mourn our "passing" than to regret the draining of a malarial swamp in making way for another "golfing community" in the south of Florida. To the contrary, such "developments" are typically couched, when they are discussed at all, as a cause for smugness, sanctimony, and celebration.[18] In a still more refined iteration, reality is reshaped, repackaged, and re-presented to the "viewing"—or "reading" or "voting"—public as if neither we nor the swamp had ever "truly" been here in the first place.[19] That which never really was, of course, need never be accounted for, either psychically or materially.

Freed almost entirely by this construction from the potential of instability-inducing cognitive dissonance that any candid acknowledgment of historical factuality might unleash within the body politic, élite sectors of the settler populace—and this, to be sure, includes the upper echelons of the conglomerates producing the great bulk of North America's cinematic fare—have positioned themselves to pursue their peculiarly expansionist vision in an especially efficient and all-encompassing manner.[20] To this, there can be little better testimony than the fact that over the past century their presumed dominion has transcended first the continent, then the hemisphere, by now becoming unabashedly planetary.[21]

Reversing the Lens

Proceeding from the premises that the juxtaposition of euro- to Native North America constitutes the bedrock sociopolitical and economic relationship(s) of the continent, and that movies and television have become the ingredient most indispensable to masking/denying the character of those relations,[22] it stands to reason that certain modes of cinematic analysis offer unparalleled opportunities to forge a genuinely counterhegemonic discourse and resultant liberatory consciousness. It is in fact possible at this juncture to craft an entire pedagogy in which film critique forms the curricular core.[23]

By this, I don't mean an orthodox film studies approach, devoted to the instilling of "visual literacy" and exploration of cinemagraphic technique—although such things are undeniably interesting and can at times be useful in their own right—but rather the kinds of interrogation/(re)interpretation of factual/thematic content increasingly evident over the past twenty years or so by bell hooks, Jun Xing, S. Elizabeth Bird, Ed Guerrero, Gina Marchette, Ella Shohat, Robert Stam, Jacqueline Kilpatrick, Ralph and Natasha Friar, Richard Slotkin, and others.[24] The objective of such scholarship remains what it's been since its inception: a reversal of the lens, scrutinizing and unraveling the codes of disunderstanding embedded in simulations of sign and signifier in such ways as to transform them from "reel to real."[25]

For this to happen—with respect to portrayals of Native North America no less than of other Others[26]—the films selected for viewing must be subjected to a process of immanent critique. That is, as Horkheimer once put it, "to confront the existent, in its historical context, with the claim of its historical principles, in order to realize the relationship between the two and transcend them."[27] Taking the films viewed as "the existent," and "the claim [of their] historical principles" as being explication of the phenomena depicted, apprehension of "historical context" can be seen as the methodological crux upon which attainment of transcendent (liberatory) understanding (consciousness) is contingent.[28]

Initially, the questions posed must concern the degree to which a given depiction embodies an accurate historicization of its subject matter, and, to the degree that it may be discernibly inaccurate, the nature of the inaccuracies involved. The latter aspect must be approached comprehensively and with a great deal of precision, thereby forming a basis upon which the question of what interests are served by presentation of specific factual misrepresentations in the films. This, in turn, sets the stage for the question of whether the treatments under consideration are in some sense anomalous, or are instead emblematic of a broader stream of films incorporating similar or even identical distortions (as in, "How many anomalies are required to make a norm?").[29]

The more consistently the latter can be shown to be the case, the less plausible established apologetics about "inadvertency" and "literary license" begin to appear, and the more acute the question about service of interest becomes.[30] The answer, ultimately and rather self-evidently, can emerge only from the kind of careful probing of the current socio-economic/political order to which many people, especially but by no means exclusively those of "mainstream" (settler) background, are highly resistant in other contexts.[31] The perception of linkages between the historical and the topical is thereby facilitated at a highly concrete level of cognizance (i.e., the "reel" starts to become "real").

Such things cannot be accomplished, of course, simply by watching and discussing the technical and aesthetic merits of movies. The successful deconstruction of any hegemonic discourse demands a (re)construction among listeners/readers/viewers of a knowledge-base adequate to the purpose. As concerns assessment of the biases and inadequacies ingrained in Hollywood's Cowboy/Indian fantasy, it is thus required that those engaged in critique be (or become) functionally conversant with the subject matters depicted. Considerable textual investigation of the historical events and personalities ostensibly portrayed on screen is therefore essential.[32] The same can be said of related areas of inquiry—law, for example[33]—by which the relevant historical circumstances are informed. This is where some truly serious work comes in.

As students who have participated in my "American Indians in Film" classes will undoubtedly attest, it often takes a half-dozen hours or more to plow through the contextual material assigned in preparation for the viewing of a single movie. In addition, recommendations for still further reading are all but invariably generated by way of dispelling ongoing confusions/misperceptions revealed during postscreening discussion. Almost none of what I assign or recommend focuses on film, per se. In my experience teaching the course mostly to undergraduates over more than a decade, students, although frequently startled and occasionally disgruntled at the outset by my approach, usually end up finding that it afforded them an overwhelmingly positive learning experience.[34]

Establishing an Analytical Framework

The sheer volume of primary material upon which one might base a course on American Indians in film seems in many respects daunting, even overwhelming. It would in principle be possible to teach it every semester for a century, screening a different work during every class session, without exhausting the presently available inventory of titles. This in itself can be used to advantage in framing the ongoing significance of native people to the American self-concept, both in terms of the gross emphasis which has so obviously been placed upon us in the country's cinematic discourse, and by way of the fact that the gigantic corpus of material all but inevitably subdivides itself into an array of overlapping but discrete thematic packages (stereotypes and tropes), ceaselessly reiterated.

The implications of this latter characteristic of the genre can be readily discerned in Hitler's famous dictum that the more regularly a lie is repeated, the more plausible it is likely to appear.[35] On the other hand, as "postcolonial" theorist Homi Bhabha has noted, the very compulsiveness with which certain lies are repeated can serve to reveal not only the degree of their falsity but the extent to which their authors understand them to be false.[36]

> "The Other Question" begins by observing the dependence of colonial discourse on concepts of "fixity" in its representation of the unchanging identity of subject peoples (as examples, the stereotypes of the "lustful Turk" or the "noble savage" . . . the "wily Oriental" or the "untrustworthy servant"). However, for Bhabha there is a curiously contradictory effect in the economy of stereotype, insofar as what is supposedly already known must be endlessly reconfirmed through repetition. For Bhabha, this suggests that the "already known" is not as securely established as the currency and the rhetorical power of the stereotype might imply.[37]

Hitler's and Bhabha's points alike are illustrated and confirmed by Hollywood's avalanche of Cowboy/Indian movies. In this, it is entirely unnecessary—or undesirable, in that doing so opens one to accusations of setting up a straw man—to dwell upon the thousands of serials and otherwise indisputably shoddy epics with which most studio inventories are laden, although it is sometimes useful to screen a B-movie or two as a means of exploring the ways in which the worst merely reflect the "best."[38] Selecting primarily—or only—the aesthetically finest fare the genre has to offer and grouping the films both chronologically and thematically, it is easily possible to demonstrate that, irrespective of the steadily evolving artistic/technical proficiency with which the films are constructed, they're designed and intended to convey more or less precisely the same "messages" now as did their far cruder counterparts at the outset. The effect is to show that "the better they get," aesthetically, "the worse they are" in terms of their capacity to implant and sustain untruths of the most fundamental and calculated sort.

The question of intentionality bound up in the last sentence tends to generate considerable and times vociferous debate among students. Here, the focal points of controversy emerge as being whether much or even most of the disinformation at issue hasn't resulted from some majestic and essentially uniform "ignorance" on the parts of several generations of euroamerican filmmakers and, thus, whether the apparent thematic homogeneity of the films isn't really a matter of "accident" rather than conscious design.[39] Once again, the movies themselves can be allowed to carry the weight in resolving such issues.

As concerns ignorance—here, used for all practical intents and purposes as a synonym for "innocence"—there are a number of approaches to clarification. An obvious choice concerns elaboration of John Ford's long record of acknowledgments that he was fully aware that he was deforming both historical fact and popular impression by staging all of his "Indian" films in Monument Valley.[40] This couples rather well with King Vidor's admission during an interview conducted for the PBS series Images of Indians that he'd deliberately distorted history in the making of Northwest Passage (1940).[41] Shifting to the current moment, there is the matter of the much-celebrated "exhaustive historical research" conducted by Bruce Beresford in the making of Black Robe (1991), a film which nonetheless perpetuates virtually every imaginable stereotype.[42] A capstone can, I've found, be placed upon the whole by juxtaposing Michael Apted's documentary, Incident at Oglala (1992), to his commercial depiction of exactly the same subject matter in Thunderheart (1992); in the documentary, which was shot first but released belatedly and with the expectation that it would be viewed by a relatively restricted audience, he presents the facts quite accurately;[43] in the commercial release, meant for mass viewership, he presents them in an altogether different fashion.

Usually, the idea of directorial ignorance—or innocence—has been thoroughly dispensed with by this point. Interestingly, the notion that the films' thematic unities result from accident or "coincidence" rather than conscious design is simultaneously abated, most often without the need for direct discussion. To reinforce this newfound consensus of understanding among students, however, it is nonetheless helpful to briefly examine the economics and attendant management/oversight procedures entailed in studio production, with an emphasis on how little is actually left to chance in the corporatized mode of filmmaking that has increasingly prevailed since the early 1930s.[44]

As icing on the proverbial cake, the laws of probability can be deployed to devastatingly good effect: if mere happenstance explained anything with respect to the topic at hand, one could be confidant to a mathematical certainty that at least one of the thousands of films on the Hollywood roster would have had to have reversed the polarities of value imbedded in orthodox cinematic depictions of natives and settlers. The offer of an "A" grade for the course to any student who can find any such film has invariably proved sufficient to lay the matter to rest, once and for all (there has yet to be a taker).[45]

Thus denied the convenience of dismissing—or even mitigating—the situation as something that in reality it isn't, students are instead placed in the position of having to decide whether they approve or disapprove of what in fact it is. While I've personally encountered none prepared to attempt a defense on outright ideological grounds, a distinct minority have sought to evade the implications of their own conclusion(s) by resort to a line of argument—essentially a verbatim regurgitation of the studios' own tired prevarication on such matters—peculiarly circular in its logic. The first half of this contortion assigns a purely economic motive to the phenomenon, this being that "no one would want to watch" movies offering "alternative" interpretations of native/settler relations, thereby rendering them box office flops.[46] The second half holds that the studios produce what they do in response to popular demand, because "that's what people want to see."

Inquiring as to which people—Indians, for example?—generally brings such polemics to abrupt halt. The question of how, since none have ever been placed in distribution, the studios—much less student polemicists—could possibly know whether "people" would pay to see genuinely alternative interpretations of American history is met with silence.[47] Equally unanswered go queries as to how "what the public wants" might have been determined, since "the public" has never really been offered the least choice in the matter. (It is one thing to note that Cowboy/Indian movies affirm the settler populace in what it already wishes to believe about itself and its Others, quite another to claim that it's unwilling/incapable of entertaining other outlooks.)[48]

This leaves things at the level of debates concerning those prerogatives supposedly attending an "artistic license" enjoyed by filmmakers. Here, arguments typically devolve upon propositions that "everyone knows" movies are fictions—dramatic fantasies, to be precise—and that it's therefore "unfair" to assess films in the same sense that one assesses works of ostensible nonfiction.[49] The subtext to such contentions is, of course, that anyone taking cinema to be a conveyer of literal fact is at best "a fool," themselves responsible for whatever misperceptions—or delusions—they incur.

Such premises begin to break down the moment someone introduces the fact that generations of children, none of whom might reasonably be expected to exercise the sort of critical discernment at issue, have by now grown up on movies and TV segments, much of it of a variety especially developed for their consumption.[50] This opens the door to examining how the tropes and stereotypes evident in such "kiddie films" as Walt Disney's *Tonka* (1958) and *Pocahontas* (1995) parallel—or prefigure—those embodied in "adult" cinema, thus insidiously conditioning child viewers in ways manifest in their receptivity to essentially identical conflations of fact and fantasy as/after they reach maturity.[51]

From there, it is easy enough to demonstrate how Hollywood's fetishizing of "authenticity"—Beresford's going to extravagant lengths to ensure the exact correctitude of nailheads visible on the walls of a reconstructed French settlement appearing in the opening scenes of *Black Robe* presents a salient recent illustration[52]—is implicitly designed to consolidate such confusion among preconditioned adults. An even better example, at least to the extent that it is blatantly explicit, concerns director Elliot Silverstein's enlisting no less than the Smithsonian Institution, that quasi-official arbiter of all things historically/anthropologically "true" in the United States, to provide a scroll at the beginning of *A Man Called Horse* (1970) in which the film is endorsed as being "the most accurate and authentic ever made."[53]

Add to this the prideful declamations of numerous directors on how they believe their work to have surpassed the traditional theatrical goal of leading audiences into a temporary "suspension of disbelief," instead imparting to viewers a lasting sense of having witnessed—or vicariously experienced—"history as it really was."[54] In substance, the "history" served up in the Cowboy/Indian movies is intended, expressly so, to be received as something vastly more "real" than history itself. Conversely, the objective, long since avowedly achieved, has been to convert popular conceptions of history into fantasy. Whichever way it is viewed, the magical line reputedly dividing art from its antithesis has been purposefully dissolved by the "artists" themselves, and with it has gone their pretensions to enjoy the license thereof.[55]

It follows as an unavoidable conclusion that Hollywood's filmmakers should in every respect be as much subject to the methods of assessment—and as accountable to concomitant standards of factuality—as are the historians, anthropologists and other more "scholarly" types whose material they've so enthusiastically assimilated, reformulated, and to a noticeable extent supplanted in the public mind.[56] Arguing to the contrary under the circumstances described in this section—or brought out in corresponding class discussions—is to be actively complicit in a sophistry the film industry has been allowed to perpetrate for far too long already.

Thematic Contours

With the analytical underbrush thus cleared away, it's possible to proceed fairly rapidly in tracing the contours of the thematic packages in which Hollywood has consistently delivered its misrepresentations of American Indians to the settler population thereby misrepresenting both the settlers and the countries they've crafted to the settlers themselves.[57] As with the number of available films, the range of potential emphases/orientations is far too broad to be encompassed within the constraints of a single course (or this essay). Fortunately, focusing upon only a handful of the major thematic elements has proven sufficient to achieve the desired results, allowing students time not only to delve into both the mechanics and the implications involved at an appreciable depth, but to explore—and thereby hopefully avoid—a few of the theoretical pitfalls that have lately resulted from "progressive" attempts to explain the meaning of it all.[58]

What follows is a sampling of the topics framed and investigated in my own course—drawn for the most part from the earlier-mentioned PBS series, *Images of Indians*, which I use as a kickoff to each semester—and a synthesis of the perspectives elicited therefrom. In each case, the films employed for illustrative purposes are specified, and the readings assigned or recommended included in my annotation.

Those Bloodthirsty Hordes

Probably the most enduring myth of Americana concerns attacks by "hordes" of "Bloodthirsty Savages" bent upon the "Massacre" of "Peaceful Settlers" (always white). Sometimes the savages succeed, albeit temporarily. In other variations, "The Army" arrives at the last and most desperate moment to save the day. In still others, the army is deployed as a substitute for the settlers, some portion of it being defeated—and, thus, by definition, "massacred"—in the course of "Civilization's" final, inevitable and triumphant victory over "Savagism," allowing the beginning of a "New and Better Day for All Mankind."[59] Regardless of its particulars, the unfolding plot invariably requires that the audience receive the deaths of settlers or their military surrogates with solemnity, a sense of loss, even grief, while the eventual vanquishment—"vanishment," really—of the savage "Red Men" is greeted with jubilation.[60]

The "historical" scenario is, to be sure, utterly dehistoricized. It is as if the settlers had always been here, struggling valiantly to "Tame" a "Vacant Wilderness" and the natives were brutally alien interlopers—or a peculiarly vicious form of wildlife—whose sole existential purpose is to obstruct "Progress"—that is, the settlers' attainment of "That Which is Rightfully Theirs" (a phrase used to signify "all" and "everything")—in almost inconceivably horrific ways.[61] Thus constructed, the settlers' actions, no matter how extreme, are invariably justified and therefore heroic. Correspondingly, the fate of the natives is, because of their innate and immutable "Cruelty" and "Aggression," deserved; "They brought it on themselves," as the saying goes.[62] The Indians receiving their "Just Desserts" can—or must—be seen from this contrived viewpoint as cause, if not to openly celebrate, then at least to experience a deep feeling of smug satisfaction that "Things Worked Out for the Best."[63]

Casting templates for cinematic iterations of this diametrical reversal of victim and victimizer appears to have been one of filmdom's very first priorities, given that they materialize in both Griffith's The Battle at Elderbush Gulch and the Cody Company's Indian Wars Refought. In Elderbush Gulch, we find an archetype of the "Friendly Settler Family" besieged in their cabin by an equally archetypal band of mindless—or, in this case, seemingly drug-crazed[64]—savages, only to be saved at the last instant by arrival of the third archetype, a troop of cavalry in full charge. To signal both the imminence and the magnitude of the peril faced by settlers in the moments before the soldiers' timely appearance, Griffith also established another trope—"You Know What They Do to White Women, Don't You?" (discussed below)—by having the brother of heroine Lillian Gish prepare to use his last bullet to spare her "A Fate Worse Than Death" at the hands of their attackers.[65]

For its part, Indian Wars—which purported to be a literal reenactment of the 1890 "Battle" of Wounded Knee, where the 7th U.S. Cavalry Regiment used Hotchkiss machine guns and pointblank execution methods to slaughter some 350 defenseless Lakota prisoners: infants, children, women, and mostly elderly men[66]—portrayed the

"Well-Intentioned" soldiers as being attacked without provocation and nearly overwhelmed by an inexplicably but nonetheless homicidally enraged mass of howling "Warriors." To authenticate this putrid bilge—worthy of comparison to the very worst material produced by the nazi propaganda ministry a generation later[67]—the Cody Company enlisted an endorsement of its accuracy from a much-acclaimed real-life "Indian Fighter," General Nelson A. Miles.[68]

There is no difficulty at all in demonstrating an unbroken pattern of equally breathtaking historical distortions employed by Hollywood right up into the present moment, all of them plainly intended to valorize the settlers—especially soldiers—while demonizing their hopelessly outnumbered and outgunned victims.[69] Very useful illustrations will be found in John Ford's classic "Cavalry Trilogy"—*Fort Apache* (1948), *She Wore a Yellow Ribbon* (1949), and *Rio Grande* (1950)—as when, in *She Wore a Yellow Ribbon*, "Hollywood's Old Master" invented a vast military alliance of literally every indigenous people of the Great Plains and Southwest regions in order to make the Indians seem properly "menacing," their executioners possessed of the requisite heroicism.[70]

In many ways, the crystallization of what Hollywood had so consistently in mind can be apprehended in its mythic treatment of Lt. Colonel George Armstrong Custer, a brevet major general who insisted subordinates address him by his honorary rather than actual rank, described by his most reputable biographer as "a vainglorious . . . self-serving . . . unscrupulous . . . glory-seeking thug . . . all too willing to sacrifice his men, the truth or whatever else came to hand in furthering his own ambitions."[71] Although Custer's solitary significant "victory" over native people was the slaughter of a villageful of noncombatant Cheyennes along the Washita River in November 1868,[72] and his only claim to lasting fame came through a sensational blunder that cost him and some 250 men under his command their lives at the Little Bighorn in June 1876,[73] Tinseltown unhesitatingly enshrined him as a "Cavalier in Buckskin."[74]

Although there were several earlier films devoted this purpose, the epitome was Raoul Walsh's *They Died with Their Boots On* (1941), starring the handsomely dashing Errol Flynn—angelically backlit in several scenes—as Custer (the real man, for all his posturing, was a big-nosed, balding, chinless wonder). Lending his hero a needed aura of moral fiber necessitated the director's deforming history far more drastically than in mere cosmetics, of course. "The General" is presented as "a soldier's soldier," with no hint he was court-martialed and temporarily cashiered in 1867 for deserting his command in the field.[75] He is made out to be a champion of the Lakotas' treaty rights to the Black Hills, when he was in fact the officer most immediately responsible for violating them.[76] He is portrayed as trying desperately to prevent an "Indian War" in 1876, while the record plainly shows him to have been among its most eager advocates.[77]

Finally, Walsh depicts Custer, the war he'd sought so strenuously to avoid nonetheless thrust upon him, nobly—and knowingly—sacrificing himself and his beloved troopers to save "The Frontier" from desolation at the hands of the usual bloodthirsty horde of savages. In actuality, Custer willfully disobeyed orders in a mad scramble to engage in what he erroneously believed would be a "turkey-shoot" sort of butchery akin to that in which he'd indulged at the Washita. The motive underpinning his disastrous insubordination appears to have been sheer self-interest: a belief that another such "single-handed triumph" would propel him into the White House.[78]

Were *They Died with Their Boots On* the culmination of an early Hollywood trend, or in any way anomalous, it might in itself be unworthy of the attention paid herein. There were, however, dozens of movies subsequently taking exactly the same tack. These were by no means confined to the 1940–1960 "Heyday of the Western."[79] Even Hollywood's so-called Protest Era during the late 1960s and early '70s saw release of Robert Siodmak's big-budget extravaganza *Custer of the West* (1967), a film adding up to little more than a poorly edited rehash of Walsh's by then quarter-century-old "classic." A 1991 made-for-TV production, *Son of the Morning Star*, was Custerania's most recent cinematic repesentative.[80]

So central had the Custer figure become in cinematic efforts to nourish and sustain the thematic ingredients of *The Indian Wars Refought* that, by 1970, the "revisionist" (or "protest") westerns making their initial appearance in that year featured it with similar prominence. In these films—notably Arthur Penn's *Little Big Man* and Ralph Nelson's *Soldier Blue*—he was used to the same effect in an opposite fashion.[81] While movies like Walsh's and Siodmak's were openly celebratory of the processes their "Custers" were intended to reflect, the traumatic effects upon public consciousness of America's then ongoing butchery in Southeast Asia—analogous in all too many respects to the "Indian Wars"[82]—made it necessary for filmmakers like Penn and Nelson to utilize their own versions of "The General" to let everyone else off the figurative hook.

Consequently, in both *Little Big Man* and *Soldier Blue*, "Custer"[83] is portrayed in psychopathic terms—that is, as being decisively deviant from the sociopsychological norm—a manipulation allowing the norm itself to be represented as a stark contrast. The latter is accomplished through introduction of a "Good Settler"[84]—Dustin Hoffman's "Jack Crabbe" character in *Little Big Man*, Peter Strauss' "Honus Gant" and Candice Bergen's "Cresta Lee" in *Soldier Blue*—to impute far more palatable attributes to euroamerican society as a whole. In that manner, the ugliness of things which could by the late '60s no longer be either denied or ennobled—My Lai, for instance, and the earlier massacres at places like the Washita (which is reenacted with considerable accuracy in *Little Big Man*) and Sand Creek (reenacted in *Soldier Blue*)[85]—is simultaneously acknowledged and assigned status as phenomena unreflective of euroamerica's "real" values and social mores.

In effect, "['explaining'] genocide by attributing it to the whims of a few unbalanced people, i.e., General Custer" serves to exonerate the settler state system of responsibility for the very processes upon which its founding and expansion have been most absolutely dependent.[86] Concerning the "morale" of the settlers in a more individuated sense, they are led to feel righteously "appalled" by the carefully fragmented and thoroughly decontextualized glimpses of holocaustal reality appearing on screen, and thereby absolved of it as well. After all, insofar as they "disapprove"—that's the sole requirement—they are empowered to imagine themselves signified by the "alternative" embodied in the equally imaginary Crabbe and Gant and Cresta Lee. This in itself positions them in their own minds to assume a place among "The Innocent" vis-à-vis what has occurred—and is thus *occurring*—even as they wallow in the benefits accruing from it.[87]

Since the revisionist flicks of thirty years ago, the thematic modifications pioneered therein have been steadily refined in such epics as Kevin Costner's *Dances with Wolves* (1990) and Michael Mann's subtly radical revamping of *Last of the Mohicans* (1992).[88] A still wider and more sustained audience has been attracted to television series like *Dr. Quinn, Medicine Woman*—the top-rated TV program of the 1992–93 season—advancing very much the same formulation.[89] By the time *Black Robe* was released, it had become possible to replace Errol Flynn's Custer with a missionary priest played by an equally appealing Lothaire Bluteau, and for reviewers to resultantly adduce that, whatever its "wrongheadedness," the sweep of European conquest in North America was ultimately prompted by "love [of humanity], nothing else," adding up—of course!—to "nothing less than sheer nobility."[90]

The more things seem to change, the more the appearance is sometimes designed merely to disguise the fact that they've never changed at all. Lending just the right touch of symbological consistency to the movies throughout this somewhat protracted transformation in the codes of settler valorization have been those fabled hordes of howling savages, still as bloodthirsty today as they were a hundred years ago: in *Dances with Wolves*, there is the perpetually scowling Cherokee actor Wes Studi with his gaggle of mindlessly malevolent "Pawnees"; in *Last of the Mohicans*, Studi returns, scowl and all, this time to head up a herd of demonic "Hurons"; *Black Robe*, for its part, offers up an exquisitely sadistic—one is tempted to say "Inquisitional"—swarm of "Mohawk" torturers to imperil Bluteau's heroic Father LaForge.[91]

All told, it's enough—as it was always meant to be—to make even the most "wrongheaded" and otherwise flawed settlers seem, if not of uniform saintliness, then at least always "understandable" in contrast to the incomprehensibly merciless inhumanity of the Others they are compelled by circumstance to confront. In the end, the settlers have "no choice" but to "defend themselves," sometimes, admittedly and regrettably, to the sort of "excess" born of their inherent "human frailties." Indians must thus be seen—as much now as through the lens of the Cody Company in 1914—to have precipitated our own fate(s), if not always by our actions, then surely by the inexcusable brutishness of our very "nature(s)."[92]

The Unspeakable Other

As should by now be apparent, a simple substitution of victims for victimizers has not been adequate in itself to "explain" the near-total eradication of Native North Americans by 1890.[93] Pleas of "self-defense" hardly seem plausible when it comes to butchering babies, after all. It has therefore been essential, not only that the indigenous victims of settler aggression be recast as aggressors—à la *The Indian Wars Refought*—but completely dehumanized in the bargain. Not infrequently, the process has been extended to the point of depicting Indians as a form of vermin—or insect life—characterizations identical in every respect to SS potentate Heinrich Himmler's notorious comparison of the nazis' extermination of Jews and Gypsies to "delousing."[94]

Most (in)famously, the euroamerican correlate to Himmler's pronouncement came on November 28, 1864, when Colonel John M. Chivington instructed his 3rd Colorado Volunteer Cavalry Regiment to systematically slaughter native infants at Sand Creek on the premise that "nits make lice."[95] The expression of such sentiments was anything but isolated, however, comparable statements being recorded as far back as 1677[96] and attributable to many of the most distinguished "humanitarians" in American settler history.[97] It is worth noting as well that, at one point or another, it was the policy of every state among the U.S. "Lower 48," and the eastern provinces of Canada, to pay a bounty similar to that offered on wolves and other such "predatory beasts" for the scalps of American Indians of any age and either sex.[98]

For what are undoubtedly obvious reasons, Hollywood has encountered considerable difficulty in finding a satisfactory method of visualizing native people at sufficiently degraded level. One of the more effective solutions was that developed by John Ford for his benchmark western, *Stagecoach* (1939), wherein "Apaches" are always lurking somewhere just over the horizon, never to be glimpsed until very late in the film. By carefully orchestrating settler dialogue, and relying upon the imaginations of viewers to take over from there—filling in the visual blanks far more convincingly than his cameras ever could—Ford was able to inculcate an astonishing sense of dread among his audiences long before a darkly shadowed, grim-visaged, and altogether silent "Geronimo" finally makes his momentary appearance.[99]

Although often employed with respect to Indians, the technique has seen its broadest application by the makers of sci-fi and horror movies, where the "monsters" are routinely withheld from view until the final few minutes, and sometimes never seen at all.[100] At other times, the "Indian/Monster" equation was established via the expedient of simply casting a famous cinematic movie monster as an Indian: *Dracula's* Bela Lugosi, for example, in the 1920 German version of *The Last of the Mohicans*, or *Frankenstein's* Boris Karloff in Cecil B. DeMille's *The Unconquered* (1947).[101] "Wolfman" Lon Chaney Jr. was similarly cast for several B-movies as well a late-1950s TV series called *Hawkeye and the Last of the Mohicans*.[102]

Probably the simultaneously most refined and concerted iteration of Hollywood's dehumanizing vernacular came in *The Stalking Moon* (1968), when director Robert Mulligan defined Indians in terms of a single "Apache" bestowed with the name "Salvaje"—literally "Savage" in Spanish—who, in keeping with Ford's *Stagecoach* formula, is withheld from view for almost the whole film. The requisite air of supernatural inhumanity is lent this unseen presence by tracing his route across Arizona and New Mexico—he is supposedly stalking the movie's stars, Gregory Peck and Eva Marie Sainte, the whole time—along the astonishingly large trail of corpses he singlehandedly leaves in his wake. When the "killing machine" is at last "revealed," it is only—but repeatedly—as a shadowy, faceless shape, cloaked in a bearskin, stunning in its relentless ferocity.[103]

At its most blatant, as in John Huston's *The Unforgiven* (1960), the recipe leads to descriptions of Indians—or, more accurately, Indian "blood"—as "filth." In such framing, there is an absolute clarity to the Manichean distinction drawn between "men" on the one hand and Indians—or "red niggers," as we are more often called in the Alan Le May novel upon which Huston based his film[104]—on the other. This, in turn, imbues even the most frankly genocidal utterances of the movie's settler characters—e.g., "I say to you, they must be cleansed from the face of this earth! Where one drop of their blood is found, it must be destroyed! For that is man's most sacred trust, before Almighty God!"—with an aura of implicit reasonability.[105]

Although the implications attending the cinematic trope of Indians as "Unspeakable Others" tend in many ways to speak for themselves, it is nonetheless worthwhile to hammer home the point that they are by no means unique within the context of settler consciousness. This can be accomplished in part by a brief survey of the dehumanizing and exterminatory thematics bound up in Anglophile literary depictions of Native North Americans since at least as early as John Smith's 1612 tract, *A Map of Virginia*.[106] Further insight can be gleaned from examining instances where the sensibilities reflected in such material have "bled" into euroamerica's collective fantasies concerning an array of non-Indian racial Others.[107]

In this last connection, it is often sufficient to focus upon the contents and immense popularity of the "Yellow Peril" literature of the late nineteenth and early twentieth centuries, exemplified in Jack London's "The Unparalleled Invasion," a 1910 short story in which the author openly dreams of establishing an "Aryan utopia" by eradicating in its entirety the "swarming" population of China. The means selected to achieve this lofty goal consist of first introducing among them "scores of plagues . . . every infectious form of death," then summarily executing "all survivors . . . wherever found."[108] An interesting cinematic corollary will be found in D.W. Griffith's *The Flying Torpedo* (1916) in which then-futuristic weapons are used to destroy vast legions of "yellow men from the East." At this juncture, there is usually no need to offer further comparisons to nazi rhetoric and ideology.[109] Any lingering doubts as to whether a "Genocidal Mentality" is involved have been thoroughly retired.[110]

You Know What They Do to White Women, Don't You?

As was mentioned earlier, one of the most dramatic moments in the seminal *Battle at Elderbush Gulch* was attained when Griffith directed that one of his celluloid settler-heroes prepare to put his last bullet through the head of the film's white heroine lest she fall alive into the hands of a group of Indians about to overrun the settlers' beleaguered cabin.[111] More than three decades later, John Ford would use an identical plot device in his much-celebrated *Stagecoach*—indeed, it was virtually the same scene—to even more sensational effect. A decade later still, in *Winchester '73* (1950), at a moment when the pair are surrounded by Indians and running short on ammunition, director Anthony Mann had his own white heroine explain to the movie's settler-hero how she understood "about the last bullet."[112] In *Fort Massacre* (1958), the settler-hero's wife actually follows through, killing not only herself but her two children in the face of capture by the dread "Apaches."

The motive, although left delicately unstated in each of these films— and hundreds of others—was voiced in a question put by another trooper to Honus Gant during the opening scenes of *Soldier Blue*: "You know what Indians do to women, don't you?" The matter is further clarified in *Chato's Land* (1972), when the movie's settler-hero restates the query: "Did you ever see what Indians do when they get a white woman?" Perchance anyone missed the point, Candice Bergen, playing Cresta Lee in *Soldier Blue*, informs a horrified Gant after they've been captured by "hostiles" that she will, as a consequence, be raped. Indeed, as a cavalry officer matter-of-factly explains in *The Gatling Gun* (1971), all any female settler taken captive by Indians has "to look forward to is rape and murder."[113]

Punctuation to this "truth" was provided by director Robert Aldrich in his *Ulzana's Raid* (1972), through portrayal of a white woman as having been raped into a state of drooling insanity by the usual horde of marauding "Apaches." Actually, the victim was "lucky," according to the movie's settler-hero, a veteran scout played by Burt Lancaster, because, he confides to the audience, such captives "are usually raped to death."[114] Given such circumstances, there can be little wonder why filmdom's gentle settler sex is forever putting a gun to its head—or having stronger male counterparts do the deed for them[115]—whenever a random Indian man wanders near.

A model for the overwhelming traumatic effects supposedly suffered by fair-haired females subjected to "ravages by savages"[116] had already been established by the inimitable John Ford in his Academy Award-nominated 1956 "masterpiece," *The Searchers*, perhaps the most grotesquely twisted depiction ever made of the psychosexual dynamics marking native/settler interaction. In this "landmark of the genre," Ford has his settler-hero, played by John Wayne—who'd also starred in

Stagecoach and all three films of the Cavalry Trilogy—spend virtually his entire stint on screen—a period ostensibly covering about fifteen years—relentlessly tracking a band of Comanches who'd abducted his niece (a child at the outset).[117]

After a while, as the little girl may be assumed to have reached maturity, it becomes clear that Wayne's purpose has evolved from simply wreaking vengeance on the Indians to also killing the niece, thus freeing her from the unutterable indignities she's suffered by being mated to "Red Vermin" (the effects of which are insinuated quite graphically during a scene in which he encounters a pair of female captives "recovered" by the army; both have been driven to stark madness by their experience, a matter prompting Wayne to proclaim them no longer "white").[118] At the last moment, however, the hero reveals the true depth of his nobility by sparing the young woman, "reclaiming" her despite her spoliation and thus, it is implied, empowering her to live happily ever after.[119]

The Searchers—both Ford's cinematic iteration and the Alan Le May novel upon which the film was based[120]—concern themselves with "reinterpreting" the famous case of Cynthia Ann Parker, a nine-year-old taken during an 1836 raid by Quahadi Comanches against encroaching settlers in West Texas. The real Cynthia Ann was raised as a Comanche and eventually married Pina Nacona, a noted Quahadi leader, mothering by him a daughter and two sons (including a major leader of Comanche resistance known as Quannah Parker).[121] After being "freed" by a group of Texans including her uncles in 1860—Pina was killed in the process—she repeatedly ran away, seeking to rejoin the Quahadis. Finally, confined to her room to prevent further such escape attempts, she "wasted away [and] died of a broken heart" (that is, starved herself to death rather than live among settlers).[122]

The Parker example is in many respects emblematic of a much larger whole. No less than Benjamin Franklin is known to have lamented during the 1750s that "when white persons of either sex have been taken prisoners by the Indians, and lived a while among them, tho' ransomed by their Friends, and treated with all imaginable tenderness to prevail with them to stay among the English, yet in a Short time they become disgusted with our manner of life . . . and take the first good Opportunity of escaping again into the Woods, from thence there is no reclaiming them."[123] Overall, as even James Axtell concedes:

> Although most of the returned captives did not try to escape, the
> emotional torment caused by separation from their adopted

families deeply impressed the colonists . . . . "Some, who could not make their escape, clung to their savage acquaintance at parting, and continued many days in bitter lamentations, even refusing sustenance." Children "cried as if they would die when they were presented to [their self-described 'rescuers']." With only small exaggeration an observer . . . could report that "every captive left the Indians with regret."[124]

The principle certainly applied as much to adult females as to men and children. Even the more celebrated "captive narratives" produced by women such as Mary Rowlandson (1682) flatly denied that threats to their "chastity" had occurred,[125] while less acclaimed tracts—that of Isabella McCoy (1747), for instance—went so far as to assert that the treatment accorded the authors by settler society was far worse than anything they'd experienced at the hands of Indians.[126] Ultimately, as Richard Drinnon, Richard Slotkin, and others have noted, it was left for "Puritan Fathers" like Cotton Mather to invent the "violence pornography" of native rapists finalized during the mid-twentieth century by Hollywood "masculinists" of the Ford/Aldrich school,[127] and subsequently adapted as an element of the "groundbreaking feminist scholarship" practiced by Susan Brownmiller.[128]

Tellingly, while there is a paucity of evidence suggesting that rape was common among any Native North American people[129]—by all indications, it was virtually nonexistent among the strikingly "prudish" Apaches[130]—there is a veritable mountain of documentation concerning the ubiquitous historical reality of settlers raping *indigenous* women.[131] Indeed, as was lately demonstrated in revelations of the endemic and sustained sexual predation suffered by the roughly half of all native children consigned to Canadian residential schools after 1900—and undoubtedly those lodged in U.S. facilities as well—the ugly pattern extended well into the 1980s.[132] Suffice it to observe that Hollywood has yet to release a single film devoted to the topic of wholesale rape of native women captured by settlers, much less the institutionalized molestation of American Indian youngsters of both sexes as recently as twenty years ago.[133]

Nor, for that matter, have Brownmiller's mainstream (i.e., "Western" or "euro-") feminist heirs had appreciably better to offer. To the contrary, following their mentor's astonishing conversion of Eldridge Cleaver's emphatic repudiation of the supposed liberatory signification embodied in transracial rape into an "advocacy" or "glorification" of it,[134] many eurofeminists have embraced the mythic sexual aggression assigned men of color in the colonial master narrative as if it were an historical given.[135] Seizing upon the contemporary panorama of psychosexual dysfunctions inculcated among American Indians by such traumas as the residential school experience—rather than upon the nature and predictable effects of the experience itself[136]—they've consistently "read it back" in time as if such maladies had always been integral to native societies.[137] This, in turn, has positioned them to advance a theoretical foreclosure upon the "nationalist" efforts of indigenous people to resume a self-determining existence on the basis that these would be inherently "phallocentric" and thus "do violence to women."[138]

From there, eurofeminism, in subscribing to such notions, entitles itself to speak for the Others incarnated in its darker sisters by denouncing the "sexism" with which it imbues its simulations of traditional nonwestern cultures,[139] its adherents thus replacing their masculinist counterparts in revitalizing a cornerstone rationalization of eurosupremacy: the hallowed "civilizing" narrative of a "moral imperative" upon which basis, as Gayatri Spivak describes it, "white [wo]men [are forever] saving brown women from brown men."[140] This, to be sure, is but a short step from a final occlusion in which eurofeminists substitute themselves for the oppressed altogether; that is, in imagining themselves as objects of the modes of rape delineated above, they reconfigure "herstory" in terms of their having been perpetual victims of the very racially/culturally Othered males most heavily damaged by processes of colonialism and racial subjugation in which white women are historically/currently complicit.[141]

The circle is thus both seamless and complete. The fervor with which settlers of every stripe cling to the fable of "Indians as Rapists" forces them into an overarching conceptual compact which dissolves the ideological divisions normally distinguishing those of the left from their right-wing opponents: anarchists from yuppies, say, or the Jerry Falwell/ Pat Robertson school of reactionary clergymen from radical feminists like Robin Morgan. One is hard-pressed to account for this other than as a need, desperate to the point of neurosis and often deeply sublimated, manifested by those buying in to secure at least some semblance of justification for the prevailing socioeconomic and political order (i.e., "The Patriarchy," "The Hierarchy," or whatever else it might more fashionably be called).[142]

To the extent that this is so, the otherwise bizarre consensus can—indeed, must—be viewed as an integral component of what George

Lipsitz has denominated "the possessive investment in whiteness," a process functioning both to the material advantage of investors, and, in some ways far more decisively, to afford them the delusional psychic luxury of believing themselves to be not only "part of the group in charge," but "naturally" entitled to such exalted standing.[143] For all the theoretical sophistry with which it has been recently adorned, the story is as old and as unsavory as eurosupremacism—which is to say, European and euroderivative forms of imperial domination—itself.[144]

Still more explicitly, it can be seen, especially when combined with the tropes discussed in the subsections above, as serving essentially the same purpose in contemporary North American settler society as did the myths of "Jewish Blood Rituals" and The Protocols of the Elders of Zion in Germany during the interwar period.[145] If there's a major functional distinction to be drawn, it's that the nazis deployed their monstrous fiction(s) to engender acceptance of incipient genocide among Germans while the North American equivalents are peddled to quell potential qualms among a populace in whose name genocide has already been perpetrated. Subtextually, the messages are identical: The victims, by some especially egregious victimization of their victimizers, got—or are getting, or will surely get—"what's coming to them," so, "under the circumstances," there's really "nothing to feel guilty about."[146]

In the Spirit of Gunga Din

With this groundwork laid, it would be quite possible to rapidly investigate several other constructions—characterizations of homosexuality within indigenous cultures, for instance,[147] or the Pocahontas-like attraction to white men allegedly evinced by all native women,[148] or the evils supposedly accruing through miscegenation[149]—clustered within the thematic package devolving upon questions of gender and sexuality. As was mentioned earlier, however, time constraints tend to preclude thorough consideration of more than one per course, and so it is best that we move along to another topic.

A question always arising, often repetitively and long before analysis of the first three packages has been completed, is whether cinematic depictions of American Indians have really been so monolithically negative as our focus has made it appear. The answer is that they have not, but this in itself opens to scrutiny the elements from which a "Good Indian" is composed by Hollywood, and the nature of the image implanted thereby in the public consciousness. Here, one might well be tempted to simply repeat the (in)famous 1869 declaration of General Phil Sheridan to the effect that "the only good Indian is a dead one"[150] while pointing out how many scores of thousands of native people have been slaughtered on screen over the years.[151] This in itself would be true enough, but the matter is nonetheless a bit more complicated.

The template for another sort of Good Indian was established by novelist James Fenimore Cooper in his "Leatherstocking Tales"— *The Pioneers, The Last of the Mohicans, The Deerslayer, The Prairie,* and *The Pathfinder*—during the first half of the nineteenth century.[152] This took the form of a character dubbed "Chingachgook," supposedly the last surviving member of his people,[153] who, in the words of Cherokee analyst Rayna Green, "acts as a friend to the white man, offering . . . aid, rescue and spiritual and physical comfort even at the cost of his own life or status and comfort in his own [nation] to do so. He saves white men from 'bad' Indians and thus becomes a 'good' Indian."[154]

Or, to follow Canadian author Daniel Francis, Cooper's notion of a "Good Indian is one who stands shoulder to shoulder" with whites in their "settlement" of North America, serving as "loyal friends and allies" to the invaders.[155] It is, concludes Robert S. Tilton, "their antiquated, stoic acceptance" of their own presumed inferiority to the settlers and, consequently, of "their individual fate and the ultimate demise of their people[s] that endeared these noble savages to whites."[156] In other words, the Cooperian concoction was/is designed to foster an emotionally satisfying sense among settlers that an indigenous seal of approval had been affixed upon the obliteration of Native North America.

So great has been the contemporary resonance of this formula that *The Last of the Mohicans* alone has been produced as a feature film on three occasions (precursors to the earlier-mentioned 1992 version were made in 1920 and 1936). *The Pathfinder* hit the big screen twice (1952 and 1996), while *The Deerslayer* has seen production both as a feature film (1957) and as a television series (1957–58).[157] In addition, certain of the archetypal characters deployed in Cooper's novels—not only the Good Indian represented by Chingachgook, but his settler "brother," the "Man Who Knows Indians" embodied in Natty Bumppo (otherwise known as "Hawkeye" to whites, "The Deerslayer" to native people)[158]—have been adapted to countless other skits on both big screen and small.

Undoubtedly the figures most indelibly imprinted on the American consciousness in this respect remain the Lone Ranger and "Tonto, his faithful Indian companion" ("Tonto" is a Spanish word meaning "dunce," "fool," or "dolt"). Created in Zane Grey's bestselling 1915 novel, *The Lone Ranger: A Romance of the Border,* the dynamic duo inhabited an extremely popular radio program broadcast weekly from 1933 onward. By 1938, they were also appearing regularly in movie theaters, as Hollywood serialized them in Saturday matinée fare. Their first feature film was released under the title *Hi-Yo Silver* in 1940, followed by such epics as *The Lone Ranger* (1956, remade in 1981 as *The Legend of the Lone Ranger*) and *The Lone Ranger and the Lost City of Gold* (1958). Meanwhile, beginning in 1948, the concept had been developed into a longrunning ABC-TV series.[159] There have been myriad mutations all along, the most recent variation to be found in the characters of Sully and Cloud Dancing in the pop-feminist CBS-TV series *Dr. Quinn, Medicine Woman*.[160]

At this point, it is useful to hammer home the nature of euroamerica's Good Indian stereotype by setting it side by side with that found in the literature of classic colonialism. The best-known example to draw upon is probably that of "Gunga Din," an East Indian invented by Rudyard Kipling during the late nineteenth century in an epic poem of the same name.[161] In Hollywood's version, *Gunga Din* (1939), the subaltern "ennobles" himself by blowing a bugle at the crucial moment, thereby warning a company of British lancers who've "adopted" him that they're riding into a trap set by his kinsmen. In thus saving his lancer "friends" from their fate—in other words, their defeat—Din sacrifices his own life along with those of his relatives, consigning his nation to a century of British imperial rule. He therefore signifies not just goodness but "heroism" of a sort, not to his own people—they have every reason to consider him a traitor of the worst kind—but to those who subjugate them.[162]

"Good" is, of course, always and most dramatically defined not in terms of idealist affirmation, but in opposition to "bad." Hence, in establishing the presence of the Good Indian, who, whether embodied as Gunga Din, Chingachgook, Tonto, or Cloud Dancing—or, for that matter, as Pocahontas or Sacajawea—is invariably constructed as an "exceptional" individual, colonialist mythmakers, both literary and cinematic, position themselves quite handily to amplify "the rule" against which such exceptions are posed. It follows that, as S. Elizabeth Bird has observed: "the brutal savage is still present" in the colonizers' Good Indian fables, most often "in the recurrent image of the renegade."[163]

> These ["bad"] Indians have not accepted White control, refuse to stay on the reservation, and use violent means to combat White people, raiding farms and destroying White property. Although occasional lip service is paid to the justness of their anger, the message is clear that these warriors are misguided. [Enlightened

settlers] are frequently seen trying to persuade the friendly Indians to curb the ["Hostiles'"] excesses. The renegades are clearly defined as deviant, out of control, and a challenge to the [Good Indian] who suffers all indignities with a stoic smile and acknowledgment that there are really many good, kind White people who wish this had never happened.[164]

As a consequence, the literary/cinematic contrivance of Good Indians must be seen mainly as an expedient in completing/consolidating the overwhelmingly negative characterization of native people more generally—and thus the goodness of settlers—as discussed in the preceding three sections (witness a recent episode of Dr. Quinn in which Cloud Dancing's son wins eternal Good Indian status by sacrificing himself to save a white female captive from being gang-raped by a group of renegade Cheyenne Dog Soldiers).

Understanding among students can be sharpened by asking them to consider the hypothetical of how, had they been victorious in World War II, the nazis might have been inclined to represent different factions among the peoples they'd conquered: the collaborationist Vichy French, for instance, vis-à-vis the French Resistance.[165] Little controversy attends a prognosis that figures like Vichy leader Pierre Laval would undoubtedly have been offered up as symbols of "The Good Frenchman" by postwar nazi filmmakers while Charles de Gaulle and his Free French forces, especially the Maquis ("Partisan") guerrillas, would with equal certainty have been depicted as "renegades," sinister, deviant, and violently "out of control." Thus the polarities of French patriotism and treason have been completely reversed, not by the French themselves, but by their German occupiers/colonizers (in reality, de Gaulle was treated as a hero by the vast majority of his countrymen and elected president of the postwar French Republic, while the Vichy collaborators were deeply reviled, many of them executed or imprisoned).[166]

It can be, and sometimes is, argued that the comparison is misleading since it concerns the portrayal of actual historical personalities, while the Good Indians heretofore discussed, whether Kipling's or Cooper's, have been fictional. The validity of the point can be readily conceded, if only as a basis upon which to pivot into an examination of the ways in which Hollywood has gone about characterizing certain real indigenous leaders as "good," others as "bad." In this connection, a key will be found in Delmer Daves' much-acclaimed 1950 "sympathy" film, Broken Arrow.[167] It takes no time at all to demonstrate how Cochise, a very significant figure in Chiricahua Apache history,[168] is first misrepresented as having been a veritable Tonto (or Gunga Din, or Pierre Laval)—thus to render him appealing to settler audiences—in no small part by contrasting him to a viciously irrational "Geronimo" (symbolizing the already thoroughly demonized Apache resistance).[169] So well was *Broken Arrow* received that it was quickly developed into a highly rated TV series that lasted several seasons.

The same pattern can easily be shown to have prevailed as recently as the 1994 *Squanto*, the formula applied to even the most substantial pillars of native resistance. Probably the most glaring example of the latter comes with *The White Buffalo* (1977), wherein none other than the legendary Oglala Lakota patriot, Crazy Horse,[170] is portrayed as teaming up with settler-hero Wild Bill Hickok to save humanity from the beast featured in the film's title. Since the white buffalo is actually a prime symbol of Lakota spirituality, the filmmaker's co-optive design is readily apparent: Crazy Horse (de Gaulle) is shown as being a man dedicated to nothing so much as subversion of his own tradition (Laval), thereby converting treason into a figuration of its opposite.

On the basis of all that has been digested up till now, it is appropriate to explore the implications of the fact that native as well as settler children are, and have long been, subject to continuous and increasing bombardment with the kinds of imagery and thematics we've discussed.[171] Since the impacts of such things upon the formation of self-concept among American Indian youth is obviously no less germane than those pertaining to mainstream kids, the matter can be reframed: What kind of self-esteem is manifested when native youngsters burst out into cheers whenever a cinematic bugle call signals that the cavalry will soon arrive on screen to symbolically slaughter their own forebears?[172]

There is no need for abstraction in this connection. Suicide is presently the leading cause of death among Native North American teenagers, standing at about 1,400 percent of the rate for the same age group among the general population.[173] In northern Manitoba, to offer but one exceedingly well-documented illustration, it has been estimated that some 70 percent of indigenous youngsters from six to sixteen have resorted to habitually sniffing gasoline and solvents in a desperate effort to utterly and in all too many cases permanently blot out their consciousness.[174] The grim toll could be recounted at far greater length, but there should be no need.

It would, to be sure, be grossly inaccurate to name cinema as the only culprit generating such ghastly results—apart from the conditions of material degradation which have for generations marked the quality of life in the great majority of native communities,[175] there are myriad psychological instigators, ranging from a proliferation of demeaning "Indian" sports team mascots[176] to routine use of the word "squaw" in both official and popular settler discourse[177]—it must, by virtue of its undisputed potency as an instrument of perceptual shaping, be regarded as a primary offender. That any society could subject another to such ongoing misery by indulging in a subterfuge designed solely to enable its own constituents to nonetheless "feel good about themselves" serves to reaffirm our earlier conclusion that a genocidal mentality is at work among North American settlers, although this time with respect to con-temporary rather than merely historical circumstances.[178]

On Terra Nullius

By now it should be apparent that, however intricate the route, all roads lead to the same destination where Hollywood's portrayal of American Indians is concerned. Along the way, it was perhaps inevitable—or at least far simpler—that, as people, we'd be reduced by and large to dehu-manized caricatures, the magnificent sweep of our histories constrained to a brief interlude in which we do combat with or provide assistance to the settlers who are overrunning us. Possessed of neither pasts nor futures, we are imbued with meaning only by Them,[179] the rich diversity and complexity of our cultures confined to a single dimension of inter-changeability: "Seen one Indian, seen 'em all," or so the saying goes.

"You'd think," as Cherokee law professor cum media critic Rennard Strickland has noted, "if you relied on Indian films, there were no [indig-enous peoples] east of the Mississippi, none but the Plains Indians [and Apaches], except possibly the Mohawks, and that the continent was unoccupied throughout the entire Great Lakes and Central region except for an occasional savage remnant, perhaps a stray Yaqui or two who wandered in from the Southwest. We almost never see a Chippewa or a Winnebago or a . . . Hopi or even a Navajo on screen."[180]

In "the early days"—that is to say, until well into the 1950s—almost all Cowboy/Indian flicks were filmed in southern California, a financial/logistical convenience convincing generations of children situated in other locales—myself included—that Kansas looked like area around Los Angeles, and utterly annihilating the concept that there might be the least relationship between the Plains cultures ostensibly depicted and the environments in which they actually evolved and flourished (by the 1930s, of course, John Ford had come along to "fix" all that by relocating his cinematic Cheyennes and Kiowas into Monument Valley).[181] The level of deformity in understanding conveyed was tantamount to representing life in Sicily by setting it in Sweden, but who cared? There were "aesthetic" concerns involved, and mere Indians were being misrepresented.

Even after the country's geography teachers conspired to compel filmmakers to more or less clean up their act in topographical terms,[182] the cultural emulsification of native people continued unabated. The Smithsonian-vetted *A Man Called Horse*, to offer one of the sorrier illustrations, creates a visual hodgepodge of Crow, Mandan, Assiniboine, and Comanche attributes, intermixes a variety of nonexistent "customs," and ladles the whole mess up as a representation of "The Sioux."[183] Equally egregious examples abound, from "Everglades-dwelling Seminoles wearing Plains feathered warbonnets and battling blue-coated cavalry on desert buttes" in *Seminole Uprising* (1955) to the eagle-feather-wearing "half-Choctaw" played by Billy Bob Thornton in *Pushing Tin* (1999).[184]

One can only imagine the reaction among settlers were some studio to release a cinematic extravaganza, purportedly "the most accurate rendering ever" of ancient Greece or Rome, in which the actors were dressed in a combination of kilts and ballroom attire, conversed in "authentic Spanglish," worshipped Odin, dined mostly on spaghetti and sauerkraut (with or without truffles and chocolate malts), and seemed to spend the bulk of their time galloping wildly across the steppes before retiring each night to harem-filled Irish fishing villages where, backdropped by the Matterhorn, they performed perfect ritual impersonations of the Marquis de Sade. The scenario is no more absurd than that imposed upon American Indians as a matter of course.[185]

Ultimately, as critic Richard Maltby has acknowledged, "in the Hollywood western, there are no 'real' Indians" at all, "only Hollywood Indians with different names," props serving as the backdrop to unending tables of Noble White Men.[186] Making a transition from this stance to having whites supplant Indians altogether is a matter of only minor adjustment. Actually, in a literal sense, there was no adjustment to make, because filmmakers have insisted upon casting whites as Indians from the outset (one of the first was Mary Pickford as the title character in a 1912 ditty called *Iola's Promise*).[187] The results have often been sublime, as when Chuck Connors—a six-foot-five, blonde-haired, blue-eyed Viking—was selected to play the five-foot-three, swarthy Geronimo in the 1962 film of the same title.[188] Meanwhile, native actors have been turned away in droves, usually on the pretext that they'd be "unconvincing" if allowed to portray native characters on screen.[189]

Figuratively, and in many respects more insidiously, there is often a settler-hero who comes off "more Indian than the Indians."[190] As has been observed with respect to Dr. Quinn, "Sully's role is to stand in for the Cheyenne, so that their culture is represented, while they as people can be pushed into the background. After all, he is a better Indian than the Cheyenne, as is made abundantly clear in the opening scene of one episode, when he beats Cloud Dancing in a tomahawk-throwing contest."[191] In this, Sully has everything in common with Cooper's Natty Bumppo, Walt Disney's *Davy Crockett, King of the Wild Frontier* (1955),[192] Robert Redford's title character in *Jeremiah Johnson* (1972), or any of a thousand other illusionary scouts and frontiersmen with which the silver screen has been set alight.

While there are many contenders, probably the most preposterous characterization(s) of all are those evident in *A Man Called Horse* where it becomes necessary for a captive English aristocrat played by Richard Harris to teach "The Sioux" how to defend themselves from other Indians with bows and arrows, thereupon becoming their leader.[193] So well was this absurd plot device received by mainstream audiences that *The Return of a Man Called Horse*, a sequel to the original movie, was released in 1976, and a rehash of the bow and arrow scene—this time using firearms— included in the hugely popular *Dances with Wolves* as recently as 1990.

Even when things are not pushed to such extremes, the "Indian side of the story" is forever being told, not by Indians, but by some "sympathetic" settler character: Jimmy Stewart's "Tom Jeffords" in *Broken Arrow*, for instance, or the white schoolmarm John Ford has bouncing along on a buckboard beside the fleeing savages in *Cheyenne Autumn* (1964),[194] or Dustin Hoffman's character in *Little Big Man*, or Matt Damon's "Britton Davis" in the 1993 version of *Geronimo*,[195] or the gravel-voiced bartender in *Last of the Dogmen* (1995).[196] As Jimmie Durham has pointed out, no Indian, "neither Queequeg in *Moby Dick*, nor Tonto, nor the Indian in Ken Kesey's *One Flew Over the Cuckoo's Nest*" has ever really been allowed to portray him/herself, less to articulate the perspective of his/her people, and still less to the voice of authority assigning the meaning to Indian/ white interactions.[197]

With Native Americans effectively eclipsed by whites even in the most "Indian-oriented" movies, it has been possible for filmmakers to simply erase us from the landscape whenever we've not been useful as an element of set décor. "In the last great wave of Hollywood westerns— *Shane* [1953], *High Noon* [1952], et al.," Durham observes, "the settlers are all by themselves on the endless prairies. They cannot remember when they last had to kill 'Indians.'"[198] The same might be said of such far more recent films as Clint Eastwood's Academy Award–winning *Unforgiven* (1992), George Cosmatos' *Tombstone* (1993), and Lawrence Kasdan's *Wyatt Earp* (1994), but the point remains unchanged:

> At some point late at night by the campfire, presumably, the Lone Ranger ate Tonto. By the time Alan Ladd becomes the Lone Ranger in *Shane* he has consumed his Indian companion. Now the Lone Ranger is himself the stoic, silent, Noble Savage, so much neater and more satisfactory at the job.[199]

All appearances to the contrary notwithstanding, this final cinematic conjuring—that of a complete and utter native absence—is not something innovative and new. Rather, it harkens back to the very earliest European fantasies of the New World, the mythic claim that the Americas, or at least appreciable portions of them, were composed of "*terra nullius*" (often, though somewhat inaccurately, translated as "vacant land," that is, devoid of human inhabitants and therefore free for the taking by any Old World settler who wished to grab a chunk).[200] As we've seen, much of Hollywood's (re)presentation of North America's indigenous population has been designed to dehumanize us sufficiently as to make the notion of *terra nullius* resonate as symbolic truth, even today. A still "neater and more satisfactory" outcome would be if the concept were to be seen as describing that which was—and thus remains—literally true.[201]

Blind Alleys

Yet, self-evidently, Indians were not only here when a lost Italian seaman "discovered" us by washing up on a Caribbean beach half-a-world away from where he thought he was—thus becoming known to posterity as "The Great Navigator"[202]—after all the centuries of ensuing horror, we're still here. With equal certainty, it can be asserted that, as a whole—regardless of the twists, turns and convolutions by which they've sought and still seek to avoid coming to grips with the knowledge—the settler populace is quite aware of this.[203] They are, moreover, aware that we exist today as the poorest of the poor in North America, stripped at gunpoint of the bulk of our property, the residues of our homelands subordinated to settler state control, disemployed, our remaining resources siphoned off to fuel the settler economy, even the pittance we are ostensibly paid in exchange impounded and often stolen by settler state authorities.[204] As Sartre put it:

You begin by occupying the country, then you take the land and exploit the former owners at starvation rates. Then, with mechanization, this cheap labor is still too expensive; you finish up taking from the natives their very right to work. All that is left for [them] to do, in their own land, at a time of great prosperity, is to die of starvation.[205]

On this basis it can be stated without hesitancy or equivocation that we exhibit all the attributes of being colonized nations.[206] That is to say, we are presently subjected to a political status prohibited under international law since the United Nations Charter was ratified in 1945 (whatever confusion attended the Charter's language was dispelled in 1960, with the passage of UN Resolution 1514, otherwise known as the "Declaration on the Granting of Independence to Colonial Countries and Peoples").[207] Although the implications for both of the extant North American settler states are readily apparent—this is true of the U.S. in particular, given the pride it professes in being "a nation of laws, not men"[208]—the issue is customarily greeted with a thundering silence within even the most purportedly progressive sectors of settler society.[209]

"If 'Indians' are not to be considered victims of colonial aggression," Jimmie Durham has asked, "how are we to be considered?" So urgent is the question, given the dire conditions prevailing throughout Native North America, that Durham pronounces himself "tempted to write the question twice, for emphasis." The first "implies a second question, however: why are we not considered as colonized? For any 'Indian' person, the questions are subjective and quotidian: 'How might I exist?'"[210] Or, following Sartre once again, the question might be reframed as "whether and for how long may I be permitted the option of existing at all."[211]

The crux of the all but monolithic refusal on the part of euroamericans of all political postures to acknowledge the fundamental illegitimacy of the internal colonial structures prevailing in both the U.S. and Canada, Durham reflects, seems bound up in their awareness of the legal/moral obligation to decolonize that would attend any such admission, and what this might mean in terms of a diminishment in the relatively privileged socioeconomic positions they are accustomed to occupying.[212]

The state called "France" is connected to something like a country, also called "France." The state called "America" is connected to an independent settler colony. At the end of its "empire" Great Britain could return to that island in Europe. The economic power of the

US is losing its grip in much of the world, but at the end, to where might it return? It is only a state, only a political entity [without a land base].[213]

"If someone imagines otherwise," Durham sums up, "at the end of America's 'external' empire it follows that there is a country called America. Would my country [the Cherokee Nation] become free of the US? If so, where is America?"[214] He recounts having explained "'American Indian' legal rights [to self-determination] and the consequent demands of the American Indian Movement" to a supposedly radical euroamerican scholar/activist employed by the staunchly anti-imperialist Institute for Policy Studies. His listener was aghast, sputtering in mortified astonishment that decolonization of Native North America "would mean the break up of the United States."[215]

Exactly so. And with it would go the system of White Skin Privilege upon which the vast majority of settlers, "radicals" no less than others, depend for the "quality of life" to which they believe themselves innately entitled.[216] Reactionaries like Allan Bloom and Arthur Schlesinger Jr. have been reasonably straightforward in their defense of the status quo, of course,[217] but their opponents can hardly afford to be. Hence, the latter have increasingly resorted to theoretical obfuscation and deception as methods of protecting their standing as "oppositionists," even as they endeavor to preclude emergence of the sort of consciousness requisite to seriously disrupting the colonial order.[218]

One such "ludic" subterfuge, found in eurofeminism's clever substitution of white women for black and other men of color as an historically oppressed group, has already been to some extent addressed.[219] The feminist example is by no means unique. A comparable but much older scam will be apprehended in marxism's insistent subsuming of racial, ethnic, and national distinctions under the rubric of a totalizing kind of "democratic class solidarity" where white workers inevitably end up the largest component, thereby ensuring that "liberation" will be defined more or less exclusively in terms of a "redistribution of social product" derived from the preservation rather than dissolution of existing state territorialities.[220]

It should be noted, moreover, that Karl Marx himself—in common with the worst of Europe's nineteenth-century imperialists—openly advocated colonialism as exerting a "civilizing influence" upon non-western peoples.[221] Attitudes have changed little among euromarxists during the century and a half since Marx's death. Indeed, "Sartre was the first (and last) European Marxist theorist to develop a theory of history in which colonialism, and the endemic violence of the colonial regime, was a major component, and which gave a significant role to anti-colonialist resistance."[222] In point of fact, however, there seem to be substantial questions among marxists, euro- and otherwise, as to whether Sartre can rightly be categorized as such.

A far slipperier innovation will be found in the recent emergence of "postcolonial theory," a concoction assigning primacy to many of the destructive effects of colonialism that euromarxism denies, but—as its very name implies—by way of placing it quite arbitrarily in the "bad old days" of the past tense.[223] As Anne McClintock has noted, having embraced a set of assumptions "organized around a binary axis of time rather than power," proponents are guilty of "obscuring the continuities . . . of colonial and imperial power."[224]

> The term "post-colonial" is, in many cases, prematurely cele-
> bratory. Ireland may, at a pinch, be "post-colonial," but for the
> inhabitants of British-occupied Northern Ireland, not to mention
> the Palestinian occupants of the Israeli Occupied Territories and
> the West Bank, there [is] nothing "post" about colonialism at
> all. Is [New Zealand] "post-colonial"? [Canada?] Australia? By
> what historical amnesia can the United States of America, in par-
> ticular, qualify as "post-colonial"—a term which can only be a
> monumental affront to the Native peoples currently [encapsulated
> therein]?[225]

The question of whether Canada—and, by extension, New Zealand, Australia, and the U.S.—are to be considered "postcolonial" has been answered in the affirmative, emphatically so, by such eurocanadian academics as Diana Brydon, who has written that anyone "truly interested in post-colonial . . . perspectives will come to us."[226] By "us," she means North America's settler population, which has assumed independent or "Commonwealth" status vis-à-vis the old British imperial center (as have those resident to Australia and New Zealand).[227] Thus do colonizers substitute themselves for colonized in the "postcolonial" equation, a sleight of hand entirely reminiscent of—but far more sweeping than—that earlier performed by eurofeminism.[228] In any event, postcolonialism's obscuring of native circumstance—even of native existence—is as thoroughgoing as anything ever dreamed up by Hollywood.

Beyond the domain of "postcoloniality," one encounters the more rarefied dominions of "poststructuralism" and "postmodernity"—one expects, upon entering this preciously self-referential netherworld, to be confronted at any moment with the ascendancy of Post Toasties as a "predominating mode of discourse"[229]—preoccupied with the supposedly "ahistorical operation of signs and tropes."[230] Devoted to "deconstructing" what they see as the "totalization" inherent to all "universalizing narratives"[231]—especially those harnessed to "hierarchy" (a term proponents often appear to confuse, alternately, with "structural oppression" and "élitism"),[232] "essentialism" (by which they seem to mean, alternately, "reification" and "meaning" itself),[233] "teleology" (frequently conflated with "sense of purpose"),[234] and "rationality" (that is, all claims that there is, or even could be, an inherent order to the universe)[235]—postmodernism posits as an alternative the conception of an infinite "plurality" of "decentered selves," each exercising the "free agency" of defining its own "identity" within a "permeable" arena subsisting upon equal quantities of "irony" and "contingency."[236]

At their most ludic—or "spectral," to borrow a term from Christopher Lasch[237]—postmodernists like Jean Baudrillard have argued that "history [is to be] had right now, in culture, discourse, sex and shopping mall, in the mobility of the contemporary subject or the multiplicities of social life," thereby offering "a false utopianism [that] projects the future into the present, thus selling the future short and imprisoning the present within itself."[238] All that is left to those discontented with this strange new best of all possible worlds are vacuous acts of "mimicry" or "trickster-like forms of parody."[239]

Even at its most constructively engaged, the individuation—sociopolitical atomization, really—inherent to the postmodernist vision precludes any possibility of a viable transformative politics, reducing both "opposition" and "resistance" to purely textual pursuits.[240] Indeed, having first adopted Foucault's premise that "the relations of discourse are of the nature of warfare,"[241] the highly influential theorist Homi Bhabha—an eclectic thinker whose work dissolves many of the boundaries separating postcoloniality from postmodernism[242]—has delighted in an "exorbitation of discourse,"[243] consciously "inflat[ing] the critic's role at the expense of the obviously much more critical role played by both armed resistance and conventional forms of political organization in ending the system of formal imperialism and challenging the current system of neocolonialism."[244]

For all its pontifications about its own "extremity," then, postmodernism "has the look of a sheepish liberalism in wolf's clothing," the "privileged view" of a subset within the settler intelligentsia—and among its compradors—whose function is diversionary; it is carefully designed to appear "politically oppositional," even as it functions in a manner "economically [and otherwise] complicit" with the status quo.[245] Taken as a whole, Terry Eagleton observes,

> [Postmodernism] is just another depressing instance of the way that much radical academia in the United States has managed to translate urgent political issues into its own blandly professional terms, so that conflicts beyond the campuses become transposed in unseemly fashion into tussles over defending academic patches, fighting off radical competitors in the academic marketplace, securing funds for this or that avant-garde enterprise.[246]

This is not to say that nothing useful can be learned, either from the "discourses of post-ality" or from their (neo)marxist/feminist counterparts.[247] Whatever utility they may yield is, however, entirely dependent upon recognizing from the outset the ultimate vestiture of their interest(s) in preserving the hegemony of eurosupremacism.[248] Adopting any or some combination of the "posts" as an analytical paradigm can therefore lead only to a disjunctural blind alley in terms of apprehending either the existence or the significance of the realms of factuality discussed in the present essay. Instead, educators will unerringly place themselves, intentionally or not, in the position of legitimating many—or all—of the interrelated streams of distortion and denial explored above.[249]

To See Things Clearly

What is needed is a theoretical/analytical framework such as that employed herein, harnessed to and equipped first and foremost for the nomenclatural task of assigning things their right names, hedging no bets in the process. Colonialism remains colonialism in this schema—not an ambiguous something qualified through addition of the prefix "neo,"[250] or foreclosed by addition of "post"—and, as Sartre observed in 1967, is inseparable from genocide.[251] Viewed with this degree of precision, no room obtains for the usual sorts of equivocation: there are no "good colonizers" to be counterposed against "bad colonizers" (no more than there could be good nazis); there are only those whose first commitment is to destroying colonialism, root-and-branch, and those whose sense of self-interest/entitlement dictates its preservation (whether by their direct and knowing participation in its imposition, or through the more mealymouthed acceptance embodied in their ignoring, discounting, relativizing, or otherwise trying to explain away its geno-cidal effects).[252]

Such explication compels all concerned to undertake an often painfully subjective process of personal values clarification—Ngugi wa Thiong'o has described it as being one of "decolonizing the mind"[253]—determining the side on which they wish to stand.[254] From there, pace postmodernist contentions, it is not only possible but quite desirable to attain a truly centered sense of self in which agency is manifested not simply by rejection of the existing master narrative(s) but through an embrace of counternarratives both redefining history and revealing its liberatory potentials for the future.[255] This, in turn—and alone—forms the basis for (the resumption of) exactly the sort of effective transforma-tive politics that proponents of postality have renounced.

There are, to be sure, precedents for the conceptualization at issue, most of them deriving from the period when imperialism was still called imperialism rather than "globalization."[256] These can be located to some extent in the explicitly anti-imperialist conception of "conscien-cism" propounded by Kwame Nkrumah and refined by Amílcar Cabral, among others,[257] reaching what was probably its greatest degree of ful-fillment in the works of Frantz Fanon and Albert Memmi.[258] Overall, the perspective was once known as "Third Worldism,"[259] although it has subsequently undergone profound challenges/revisions because of its failure to accommodate the reality/rights of an underlying "Fourth World" composed of indigenous peoples.[260] The resulting reconfiguration is sometimes referred to as "indigenism."[261]

In any event, resuming our focus upon North America, it can be observed that the explicitly anti-imperialist gaze of consciencism is most appropriate to apprehending the racially constructed internal col-onization not only of indigenous people, but of African Americans,[262] Latinos,[263] and even sectors of the settler underclass itself.[264] Freed of absurdist allegations of such sins as "inherent phallocentrism,"[265] "reverse racism"[266] and "totalization,"[267] a revitalization of the Third Worldist orientation, albeit in a much evolved form,[268] establishes the foundation upon which a "Fanonist pedagogy" leading to a genuinely "revolutionary multiculturalism" can be achieved.[269]

In this way, and perhaps only in this way, can we at last move "beyond pedagogies of protest," developing "a praxis that gives encouragement to those who, instead of being content with visiting history as curators or custodians of memory, choose to live in the furnace of history where memory is molten and can be bent into the contours of a dream and perhaps even acquire the force of a vision."[270] The point of any such exercise is, paraphrasing Marx, not simply an empowerment of students to interpret the world more accurately, but to change it.[271] That both the vision and the change must center upon repealing the colonization of Native North America—and, as a concomitant, the structural oppression of others made possible by the colonial arrangement on this continent— should by now seem utterly unremarkable. In the alternative, we're by all appearances destined to live out Hollywood's dreams of genocide in grotesque and endless repetition.[272] Surely, we owe ourselves—and more, our posterity—something infinitely better.

Notes

1   Scott Simmon, *The Films of D.W. Griffith* (Cambridge, UK: Cambridge University Press, 1993) p. 9. It's worth noting that, while it's often credited as such, *Elderbush Gulch* wasn't actually the first piece of coherent narrative cinema created by a euroamerican. It was preceded by such otherwise unremarkable fare as *Apache Gold* (1910), *The Curse of the Red Man* (1911), *On the Warpath* (1912) and *A Prisoner of the Apaches* (1913).

2   Rennard Strickland, "Tonto's Revenge, or, Who Is That Seminole in the Warbonnet?" in his *Tonto's Revenge: Reflections on American Indian Culture and Policy* (Albuquerque: University of New Mexico Press, 1997) p. 33.

3   The numbers accrue from *Images of Indians*, a five-part PBS series produced by Phil Lucas and narrated by Creek actor Will Sampson in 1980. For the best filmographies, neither of them complete, see Michael Hilger, *The American Indian in Film* (Metuchen, NJ: Scarecrow Press, 1986); Elizabeth Weatherford and Emelia Seubert, eds., *Native Americans in Film and Video*, 2 vols. (New York: Museum of the American Indian, 1981, 1988).

4   See Vine Deloria Jr., "Foreword: American Fantasy," in Gretchen Bataille and Charles L.P. Silet, eds., *The Pretend Indians: Images of Native Americans in Film* (Ames: Iowa State University Press, 1981) pp. xv–xvi.

5   A good overview is provided in Imre Sutton, ed., *Irredeemable America: The Indians' Estate and Land Tenure* (Albuquerque: University of New Mexico Press, 1985). Also see my *Struggle for the Land: Native North American Resistance to Genocide, Ecocide and Colonization* (Winnipeg: Arbeiter Ring, [2nd ed.] 1999).

6   Judge Warren Urbom, *U.S. v. Consolidated Wounded Knee Cases*, 389 F.Supp. 235 (1974) pp. 238–39.

7   Jimmie Durham, "This Ground Has Been Covered," in his *A Certain Lack of Coherence: Writings on Art and Cultural Politics* (London: Kala Press, 1993) p. 138.

8   For penetrating structural analyses, albeit deployed in analogous contexts rather than that specifically at hand, see Jacques Ellul, *Propaganda: The Formation of Men's Attitudes* (New York: Alfred A. Knopf, 1965) and Noam Chomsky, *Necessary Illusions: Thought Control in Democratic Societies* (Boston: South End Press, 1989). More targeted readings with respect to literature will be found in Robert F. Berkhofer's *The White Man's Indian: Images of the Indian from Columbus to the Present* (New York: Alfred A. Knopf, 1978), Raymond William Stedman's *Shadows of the Indian: Stereotypes in American Culture* (Norman: University of Oklahoma Press, 1982); and Richard Slotkin's *Regeneration*

Through Violence: The Mythology of the American Frontier (Middletown, CT: Wesleyan University Press, 1990). On academia, see, e.g., David Hurst Thomas' *Skull Wars: Kennewick Man, Archaeology, and the Battle for Native American Identity* (New York: Basic Books, 2000). An excellent historical survey of press performance is contained in David Svaldi's *Sand Creek and the Rhetoric of Extermination: A Case Study in Indian-White Relations* (Lanham, MD: University Press of America, 1989).

9   The benchmark work in this connection remains, in my estimation, Marshall McLuhan's *Understanding Media* (New York: McGraw-Hill, 1964). Also see Andrew Tudor, *Image and Influence: Studies in the Sociology of Film* (New York: St. Martin's Press, 1975).

10   This point was made early and well by Ralph and Natasha A. Friar in their *"The Only Good Indian . . .": The Hollywood Gospel* (New York: Drama Books, 1972).

11   On the concept of "Master Narratives"—also known as "Great" or "Grand" Narratives, as well as "metanarratives"—see Fredric Jameson, *Political Unconscious: Narrative as Socially Symbolic Act* (Ithaca, NY: Cornell University Press, 1981). As applied specifically to American Indians, see Jimmie Durham, "Cowboys and . . ." in his *Lack of Coherence*, esp. pp. 173–75.

12   For an exhaustive discussion, see Richard Slotkin, *Gunfighter Nation: The Myth of the Frontier in Twentieth-Century America* (Norman: University of Oklahoma Press, [2nd ed.] 1998).

13   I address this in the title essay of my *Fantasies of the Master Race: Literature, Cinema and the Colonization of American Indians* (San Francisco: City Lights, [2nd ed.] 1998) pp. 168–72. Also see Durham, "Cowboys and . . ." p. 176.

14   Durham, "This Ground Has Been Covered," p. 138.

15   For explication of the term in the sense intended here, see Walter L. Adamson, *Hegemony and Revolution: A Study of Antonio Gramsci's Political and Cultural Theory* (Berkeley: University of California Press, 1980) pp. 170–79.

16   See Frederick Merk, *Manifest Destiny and Mission in American History: A Reinterpretation* (New York: Alfred A. Knopf, 1963); Rita Parks, *The Western Hero in Film and Television: Mass Media Mythology* (Ann Arbor: University of Michigan Research Press, 1982); Slotkin, *Gunfighter Nation*.

17   Superb tracings of this thematic cluster will be found in Roy Harvey Pierce's *Savagism and Civilization: A Study of the American Indian in the American Mind* (Baltimore: Johns Hopkins University Press, 1953), Richard Drinnon's *Facing West: The Metaphysics of Indian-Hating and Empire-Building* (Minneapolis: University of Minnesota Press, 1980) and Reginald Horsman's *Race and Manifest Destiny: The Origins of American Racial Anglo-Saxonism* (Cambridge, MA: Harvard University Press, 1981). More broadly, see Robert Young's *White Mythologies: Writing, History and the West* (New York: Routledge, 1990) and the essays collected in Mick Gidley, ed., *Representing Others: White Views of Indigenous Peoples* (Exeter, UK: Exeter University Press, 1994).

18   Worthwhile readings on the topic are collected in John Ewell, Chris Dodge, and Jan DeSirey, eds., *Confronting Columbus: An Anthology* (Jefferson, NC: McFarland, 1992).

19   A classic illustration of this mentality at work will be found in Allan van Gestel's "When Fictions Take Hostages," in James A. Clifton, ed., *The Invented Indian: Cultural Fictions and Government Policies* (New Brunswick, NJ: Transaction Books, 1990) pp. 291–312.

20   Chomsky, *Necessary Illusions*. Also see Edward S. Herman and Noam Chomsky, *Manufacturing Consent: The Political Economy of the Mass Media* (New York: Pantheon, 1988).

21 A good tracing of the trajectory will be found in Noam Chomsky's *Year 501: The Conquest Continues* (Boston: South End Press, 1993). Also see Frank Furedi, *The New Ideology of Imperialism: Renewing the Moral Imperative* (London: Pluto Press, 1994).

22 This is as true within the classroom as without. See, e.g., the essays collected in Elizabeth Ellsworth and Marianne H. Whatley, eds., *The Ideology of Images in Educational Media: Hidden Curriculums in the Classroom* (New York: Teachers College Press, 1990). Also see David Trend, "Nationalities, Pedagogies, and the Media," in Henry A. Giroux and Peter McLaren, eds., *Between Borders: Pedagogy and the Politics of Cultural Studies* (New York: Routledge, 1994) pp. 225–41.

23 For the broad outlines of what I have in mind, see bell hooks, *Teaching to Transgress: Education as the Practice of Freedom* (New York: Routledge, 1994) and *Outlaw Culture: Resisting Representation* (New York: Routledge, 1994). At a more rarefied level, rather better suited to graduate students, see Gayatri Chakravorty Spivak, *Outside in the Teaching Machine* (New York: Routledge, 1993).

24 Exemplars of the scholarship at issue include bell hooks, *Black Looks: Race and Representation* (Boston: South End Press, 1994); Jun Xing, *Asian America Through the Lens: History, Representations and Reality* (Walnut Creek, CA: AltaMira Press, 1995); S. Elizabeth Bird, ed., *Dressing in Feathers: The Construction of the American Indian in Popular Culture* (Boulder, CO: Westview Press, 1996); Ed Guerrero, *Framing Blackness: The African American Image in Film* (Philadelphia: Temple University Press, 1993); Gina Marchette, *Romance and the Yellow Peril: Race, Sex and Discursive Strategies in Hollywood Fiction* (Berkeley: University of California Press, 1991); Ella Shohat and Robert Stam, *Unthinking Eurocentrism: Multiculturalism and the Media* (New York: Routledge, 1994); Jacqueline Kilpatrick, *Celluloid Indians: Native Americans and Film* (Lincoln: University of Nebraska Press, 1999). Also see Friar and Friar, "*The Only Good Indian . . .*"; Durham, *Lack of Coherence*; Slotkin, *Gunfighter Nation*; Churchill, *Fantasies of the Master Race*.

25 bell hooks, *Reel to Real: Race, Sex and Class at the Movies* (New York: Routledge, 1996).

26 The distinction between "other" and "Other" intended here follows that delineated by Homi K. Bhabha in "The other question: Stereotype, discrimination and colonial discourse," in his *The Location of Culture* (New York: Routledge, 1990) pp. 66–84. Also see Tzvetan Todorov, *The Conquest of America: The Question of the Other* (New York: Harper & Row, 1984).

27 Max Horkheimer, *The Eclipse of Reason*, quoted in Paul Z. Simmons, "Afterword: Commentary on Form and Content in *Elements of Refusal*," in John Zerzan, *Elements of Refusal* (New York: C.A.L. Press/Paleo Editions, [2nd ed.] 1999) p. 266.

28 This conforms generally to the approach advocated in other analytical arenas by Linda Tuhiwai Smith in her *Decolonizing Methodologies: Research and Indigenous Peoples* (London/Dunedin: Zed Books/University of Otago Press, 1999).

29 Overall, the strategy is not dissimilar to that described by Paulo Freire in his *Education for Critical Consciousness* (New York: Continuum, 1982). Also see Barbie Zelzier, "Reading the Past Against the Grain: The Shape of Memory Studies," *Critical Studies in Mass Communications* (1995) pp. 214–39.

30 For transparent iterations of such apologetics with regard to the handling of American Indians in commercial cinema, see Jack Nachbar, *Focus on the Western* (New York: Prentice-Hall, 1974) and John H. Lenihan, *Showdown: Confronting Modern America in the Western Film* (Urbana: University of Illinois Press, 1980). As one astute analyst has summarized the more recent of these tracts, "A book such as Lenihan's, which was considered sufficiently well-researched to earn a Ph.D. . . . actually does little more than extend the propaganda contained in the films themselves." John

Tuska, *The American West in Film: Critical Approaches to the Western* (Lincoln: University of Nebraska Press, 1988) p. 251.

31 The resistance to probing such things is formed quite differently within the two groups involved. Concerning so-called mainstreamers, see Stuart Hall, "The West and the Rest: Discourse and Power," in his and Bram Gieben's coedited volume, *The Formations of Modernity* (Oxford, UK: Polity Press/Open University, 1992) pp. 276–320. On those of other than mainstream backgrounds, see Ashis Nandy, *The Intimate Enemy: The Loss and Recovery of Self Under Colonialism* (New York: Oxford University Press, 1989).

32 Again, I'm following Freire, this time his *Literacy: Reading the Word and the World* (London: Routledge & Kegan Paul, 1987), as well as *Education for Critical Consciousness*.

33 See, e.g., John Denvir, ed., *Legal Reelism: Movies as Legal Texts* (Urbana: University of Illinois Press, 1996).

34 This is true at least insofar as students' (anonymous) end-of-semester evaluations are concerned, "American Indians in Film" never having been assessed at an aggregate rating lower than the top tenth percentile of all courses offered on campus during the semesters it's been taught.

35 In *Mein Kampf*, Hitler famously observed both that people "more easily fall victim to a big lie than to a little one," and that for propaganda purposes the key was to "repeat them over and over again." Under the direction of Joseph Goebbels, these principles were applied quite effectively, with the result that nazi "propaganda was able to make the lie a precise and systematic instrument, designed to transform [or solidify] certain values [and] provoke psychological twists in the individual. The lie was the essential instrument for that, but this was not just the falsification of some figure or fact.... [I]t was falsehood in depth." Ellul, *Propaganda*, p. 60. For the "big lie" and repetition quotes, see Adolf Hitler, *Mein Kampf* (Boston/Cambridge, MA: Houghton Mifflin/Riverside Press Sentry Editions, 1962) pp. 231, 184.

36 Bhabha, "The other question," esp. p. 69.

37 Bart Moore-Gilbert, *Postcolonial Theory: Contexts, Practices, Politics* (London: Verso, 1997) p. 117.

38 It is quite useful, however—if only to illustrate the scope and sustained nature of the effort to condition public sensibilities involved—to provide students with lists of lesser films represented in terms of message by the "classics" screened and analyzed more directly. The Friars provided an invaluable service in compiling just such a thematic itemization at the back of *"The Only Good Indian . . ."* (only minor updating is required). This, among other things, empowers skeptics to make a trip to their local video rental outlet and "see for themselves."

39 This is a variation on the charade of "American Innocence" dissected quite well by Stuart Creighton Miller in his *"Benevolent Assimilation": The American Conquest of the Philippines, 1899–1903* (New Haven, CT: Yale University Press, 1982) pp. 1–2, 253–67.

40 See, e.g., Richard Maltby, "A Better Sense of History: John Ford and the Indians," in Ian Cameron and Douglas Pye, eds., *The Book of Westerns* (New York: Continuum, 1996) pp. 34–49.

41 The interview is contained in Pt. 3.

42 See "And They Did It Like Dogs in the Dirt: An Indigenist Analysis of *Black Robe*," in my *Fantasies of the Master Race*, pp. 225–42. It should be noted here, however, that *Black Robe*, having been made in Canada by an Australian director, is not in the conventional sense a "Hollywood movie."

43   Apted seems to have shot the documentary mainly as a strategy to attain acceptance by, credibility among—and thence cooperation from—Oglala Lakotas resident to the Pine Ridge Reservation, where the events portrayed in *Thunderheart* had recently occurred. This enabled him to market the "authenticity" of his having set his distortive fiction in the actual locations where the events transpired, even including in some scenes a sampling of actual participants. Overall, there is a strong appearance that he never really planned to complete the documentary, doing so only after several of the Indians he'd conned threatened to undo much of his effort at authentication by venting their sense of betrayal in a very public fashion.

44   For what, despite its rather unfortunate subtitle, proves to be a very insightful study of the development, politics, and priorities inherent to the studio system, see Neal Gabler, *An Empire of Their Own: How the Jews Invented Hollywood* (New York: Anchor, 1989).

45   Actually, there are a few, in my opinion, albeit most of them are Canadian and therefore do not technically qualify as "Hollywood" productions. Notably, they include Donald Shabib's *Fish Hawk* (1980), with Will Sampson in the title role, Richard Bugajski's *Clearcut* (1991), featuring the Oneida actor Graham Green, and Jim Jarmusch's 1996 *Dead Man*, costarring Gary Farmer (Cayuga). See Leah Renae Kelly, "A Waltz of Violence and Counterviolence: Reflections on *Clearcut*," in her *In My Own Voice: Explorations in the Sociopolitical Context of Art and Cinema* (Winnipeg: Arbeiter Ring, 2001) pp. 119–22; Jonathan Rosenbaum, "A Gun Up Your Ass: An Interview with Jim Jarmusch," *Cineaste*, Vol. 22, No. 2, 1996) pp. 20–23; Kilpatrick, *Celluloid Indians*, pp. 169–76.

46   This is quite simply false, as is readily demonstrated by the spectacular success garnered by films like *Little Big Man* and *Soldier Blue*—or, for that matter, *Easy Rider*—explicitly, if rather misleadingly, marketed as "alternative" fare during the early 1970s. See, e.g., Margo Kasdan and Susan Tavernetti, "Native Americans in a Revisionist Western: *Little Big Man*," in Peter C. Rollins and John E. O'Connor, eds., *Hollywood's Indian: The Portrayal of Native Americans in Film* (Lexington: University Press of Kentucky, 1998) pp. 121–36.

47   Again, the argument is dubious on its face. While it was until recently advanced in almost identical terms as a rebuttal to demands for a relatively autonomous black cinema, the subsequently successful career of African American director Spike Lee alone offers ample testimony to the dimension of its falsity.

48   Herman and Chomsky offer a magnificent explication of this point in *Manufacturing Consent*.

49   This line of argument is ably rebutted in Peter C. Rollins' *Hollywood as Historian: American Film in a Cultural Context* (Lexington: University Press of Kentucky, 1983). Also see Robert A. Rosenstone, *Visions of the Past: The Challenge of Film to Our Idea of History* (Cambridge, MA: Harvard University Press, 1995).

50   An interesting analysis is contained in Theodore S. Jojola's "Moo Mesa: Some Thoughts on Stereotypes and Image Appropriation," in Bird, *Dressing in Feathers*, pp. 263–79.

51   See generally Pauline Turner Strong, "Playing Indian in the 1990s: *Pocahontas* and *The Indian in the Cupboard*," in Rollins and O'Connor, *Hollywood's Indian*, pp. 187–205.

52   Andrew L. Urban, "Black Robe," *Cinema Papers*, May 1991, pp. 6–12. At p. 10, Beresford's production designer, Herb Pinter, is quoted as estimating that in material terms—costuming, props and sets—about "99 percent of what you see [in the film] is accurate."

53 Jacqueline Kilpatrick, *Celluloid Indians*, pp. 179–84; my "Fantasies of the Master Race," pp. 172–73.

54 Or, to borrow from Princeton professor *cum* U.S. president Woodrow Wilson, upon viewing *Birth of a Nation*, D.W. Griffith's 1915 celluloid celebration of the Ku Klux Klan, "history written in lightning." Quoted in Wyn Craig Wade, *The Fiery Cross: The Ku Klux Klan in America* (New York: Oxford University Press, [2nd ed.] 1998) p. 126.

55 We arrive thus at a fairly comprehensive validation of our earlier assertion that the Gramscian notion of hegemony is applicable to the context we are exploring (see note 15 and accompanying text). More precisely. we have staked out our terrain as being the domain of hegemonic "colonial discourse" described by Edward Said in *Orientalism* (New York: Pantheon, 1978). Therein, "the arts"—especially literature (and, presumably, cinema)—are seen as being inseparable and in many respects virtually indistinguishable from purportedly nonfictive or "scientific" modes of explanation. In Said's schema, all of them function in a contributory and mutually supporting/completing manner, forming the master narrative (see note 11) by which the dominant/subordinate relationship between Europe and its Others is rationalized.

56 Although it is never set forth in straightforward fashion, this idea appears to be a motive force underlying Ted Jojola's "Absurd Reality II: Hollywood Goes to the Indians," in Rollins and O'Connor, *Hollywood's Indian*, pp. 12–26. It would also seem to inform much of what is written in Rollins' *Hollywood as Historian*.

57 Since Indians as well as settlers attend movies and watch TV these days, we are also systematically misrepresented to ourselves. Although the negative effects are somewhat wide of the scope of this essay, they are substantial and discussed in, among other sources, Strickland's "Tonto's Revenge."

58 This, as will be seen, applies primarily to certain strains of feminism, marxism, "postmodernism" and, perhaps most explicitly, "postcolonialism," each of which has "challenged" the prevailing order in ways that reinforce its cohesion. These will be addressed in due course.

59 For analysis of the myth, see Harvey Pearce, *Savagism and Civilization* and Berkhofer, *The White Man's Indian*. A classic, if somewhat sentimental, rendering of the mythic theme in a supposedly nonfictional format will be found in Jay P. Kinney's *A Continent Lost—A Civilization Won: Indian Land Tenure in America* (Baltimore: Johns Hopkins University Press, 1937).

60 See Brian W. Dippie, *The Vanishing American: White Attitudes and U.S. Indian Policy* (Middletown, CT: Wesleyan University Press, 1982); Christopher M. Lyman, *The Vanishing Race and Other Illusions* (New York: Pantheon, 1982).

61 Drinnon does a wonderful job of unraveling these codes of sign and signifier in the opening chapters of *Facing West*. One aspect he does not discuss, however, is the construction of savages as interlopers. The concept—or, more accurately, the phobia—appears to find its origins in the deepest recesses of the European mind, accruing from the trauma of such things as the repetitive sacking of Rome by "barbarians" during the fifth century AD and the thirteenth-century Mongol invasion. See Roger Bartra, *Wild Men in the Looking Glass: The Mythic Origins of European Otherness* (Ann Arbor: University of Michigan Press, 1994).

62 The correspondence at issue was at times formalized as a matter of European/euroamerican law. See, e.g., Robert A. Williams Jr., *The American Indian in Western Legal Thought: The Discourses of Conquest* (New York: Oxford University Press, 1990).

63 Lest anyone deceive themselves into believing that such attitudes are either consignable to "The Past," or to only the more retrograde segments of contemporary settler society, see "progressive" commentator Christopher Hitchens' celebration of Columbus and the Columbian legacy in *The Nation* (October 19, 1992) p. 442.

64 In a truly bizarre twist, Griffith has his "Indians" cook and eat a puppy, the flesh of which animal he seems to have believed are imbued with psychedelic properties. In any event, those who ingest it shortly begin to exhibit clear signs of hallucinogenic intoxication.

65 For the moment, simply refer to the section titled "Ravages by Savages" in my "Fantasies of the Master Race," pp. 190–95. Alternately, see Tuska, *American West in Film*, pp. 248–56.

66 Ralph K. Andrist, *The Long Death: The Last Days of the Plains Indian* (New York: Macmillan, 1964) pp. 351–52; Dee Brown, *Bury My Heart at Wounded Knee: An Indian History of the American West* (New York: Holt, Rinehart and Winston, 1970) pp. 164–66, 401–2.

67 In fairness, the comparison should be reversed. There is no record of nazi propagandists having produced a film claiming to "reenact" a similarly ferocious assault on SS personnel in an effort to transform the slaughter of Jewish infants into a heroic act of self-defense. Nor, for that matter, is there a record of the nazi régime awarding decorations for gallantry to members of the SS for their service in the extermination squads. The U.S. Army, on the other hand, bestowed upward of thirty Medals of Honor upon troops participating at Wounded Knee. The massacre site was also formally designated a "battlefield"—the massacre itself a "battle"—until 1975. There is no record of the Germans ever making analogous references to, say, "The Battle of Babi Yar."

68 Strickland, "Tonto's Revenge," p. 33.

69 Alternatively, extermination is sometimes employed as an object of humor. Witness Bob Hope's "comedy classic," *Son of Paleface* (1952), wherein the comic draws laughs by slaughtering a dozen Indians—two with a single bullet from his sixgun—all but one of whom fall in a neat pile. The wounded "recalcitrant," who staggers about for a few moments, is finally dispatched by Hope's hitting him in the head and adding his corpse to the stack. The sequence is included in *Images of Indians*. After viewing, it is good to pose the question of the likely response were the Germans to offer comparably "funny" movies depicting their elimination of Jews during the 1940s.

70 See Leah Renae Kelly, "The Auteurism of John Ford's 'Indian Films': A Brief Analysis," in her *In My Own Voice*, pp. 98–103; Ken Nolley, "The Representation of Conquest: John Ford and the Hollywood Indian (1938–1964)," in Rollins and O'Connor, *Hollywood's Indian*, pp. 73–88. For the quote, see Donald L. Davis, *John Ford: Hollywood's Old Master* (Norman: University of Oklahoma Press, 1995) p. 118.

71 Frederick F. Van de Water, *Glory Hunter: A Life of General Custer* (New York: Bobbs-Merrill, 1934).

72 Stan Hoig, *The Battle of the Washita* (Garden City, NY: Doubleday, 1976). As Hoig points out in his introduction, the word "battle" is used in his title only on "the basis of official convention" (i.e., to avoid confusing potential readers as to whether some different event is discussed therein). He is quite clear in the introduction, and more so in the body of his book, that what actually happened at the Washita was a massacre.

73 See Brian Dippie, *Custer's Last Stand: The Anatomy of an American Myth* (Missoula: University of Montana Press, 1976); W.A. Graham, *The Custer Myth: A Sourcebook of Custerania* (Lincoln: University of Nebraska Press, 1986 reprint of 1953 original).

74 For a "scholarly" rendering of this ludicrous characterization, see Robert M. Utley, *Cavalier in Buckskin: George Armstrong Custer and the Western Military Frontier* (Norman: University of Oklahoma Press, 1988).

75 Van de Water, *Glory Hunter*, pp. 168–77.

76 See Donald Jackson, *Custer's Gold: The United States Cavalry Expedition of 1874* (Lincoln: University of Nebraska Press, 1966).

77 See John E. Gray, *The Centennial Campaign: The Sioux War of 1876* (Norman: University of Oklahoma Press, 1988).

78 There is a range of interpretation concerning Custer's presidential ambitions. For a representative sampling, see Utley, *Cavalier in Buckskin*, pp. 163–64; David Humphreys Miller, *Custer's Fall: The Native American Side of the Story* (New York: Penguin, 1992 reprint of 1953 original) p. 37; Steven E. Ambrose, *Crazy Horse and Custer: The Parallel Lives of Two American Warriors* (Garden City, NY: Doubleday, 1975) pp. 368–69; James Welch with Paul Stekler, *Killing Custer: The Battle of the Little Big Horn and the Fate of the Plains Indians* (New York: Penguin, 1995) p. 302, It is also worth noting that, far from being "the last man standing"—as not only by Walsh's but in every other euroamerican depiction has framed the scene—Custer was in all likelihood the very first of his immediate command felled during his "Last Stand." Humphreys Miller, *Custer's Fall*, pp. 129, 133.

79 It has been estimated that nearly 3,000 westerns were churned out between 1930 and 1960. Nachbar, *Focus on the Western*, p. 9. Comparing this total to that offered in the text accompanying note 3 demonstrates the emphasis Hollywood has placed upon depictions of "How the West Was Won."

80 The film—a TV miniseries, actually—was adapted from Evan S. Connell's bestselling biography, *Son of the Morning Star: Custer and the Little Big Horn* (San Francisco: North Point Press, 1984). The success of book and movie alike attest to the extent of the Custer myth's ongoing attraction.

81 See generally Kasdan and Tavernetti, "Revisionist Western."

82 The comparison is in no sense rhetorically intended. The parallels are so close that U.S. ambassador to Vietnam Maxwell Taylor referred to his own country's military operations there as an "Indian War" (quoted in Drinnon, *Facing West*, p. 369), while American troops routinely referred to areas not under their immediate control as "Indian Country." See, e.g., Noam Chomsky, *For Reasons of State* (New York: Pantheon, 1975) p. 120.

83 Actually, the "Colonel Iverson" character deployed in *Soldier Blue* more nearly resembles Col. John Chivington, perpetrator of the 1864 Sand Creek Massacre in Colorado. See Kilpatrick, *Celluloid Indians*, pp. 77–79.

84 Such characters of course invite comparison to the "Good German" figure so prominent in that country's post-nazi mythology. It was an exactly similar wriggling in a different but distinctly related context that led Sartre to remark that "there are neither good nor bad colonists: there are colonists." Jean-Paul Sartre. "Introduction to Albert Memmi's *The Colonizer and the Colonized*," in his *Colonialism and Neocolonialism* (New York: Routledge, 2001) p. 51.

85 Stan Hoig, *The Sand Creek Massacre* (Norman: University of Oklahoma Press, 1961).

86 Friar and Friar, "*The Only Good Indian . . .*" p. 213.

87   As Sartre observed in a related connection, many "among them reject their objective reality: carried along by the colonial apparatus, they do each day, in deed, what they condemn in their dreams, and each of their acts contributes to the maintaining of oppression. They will change nothing, be of no use to anyone, and find their moral comfort in their malaise, that is all." Sartre, "Introduction to Albert Memmi's *The Colonizer and the Colonized*," p. 51.

88   To be accurate, neither Penn nor Nelson created the model. They, and certainly Costner, patterned their rather clumsier efforts after those of English director David Lean, who developed and perfected the formula in his 1962 *Lawrence of Arabia*. See my "Lawrence of South Dakota," in *Fantasies of the Master Race*, pp. 239–42. Also see Robert Baird's "Going Indian: *Dances with Wolves*," and Jeffrey Walker's "Deconstructing an American Myth: *Last of the Mohicans*," both in Rollins and O'Connor, *Hollywood's Indian*, pp. 153–69, 170–86.

89   See S. Elizabeth Bird's "Not My Fantasy: The Persistence of Indian Imagery in *Dr. Quinn, Medicine Woman*," in her *Dressing in Feathers*, pp. 245–62.

90   Antoinette Bosco, "Remembering Heaven-Bent Men Wearing Black Robes," *Litchfield County Times*, February 14, 1992. On the actual roles played by missionaries during the invasion of North America, see George E. Tinker, *Missionary Conquest: The Gospel and Native American Cultural Genocide* (Minneapolis: Fortress Press, 1993).

91   Although they are never actually depicted, the horrors of "Iroquoian torture" compose a sinister subtext throughout the first two-thirds of *Black Robe*, ultimately informing a dramatic sequence that is a cruxpoint of the film. Tellingly, although it is set in the early seventeenth century, its hero a representative of Roman Catholicism, there is no whisper of the ubiquitous instrumentation of torture—the rack, body saws, and much worse—attending the Church's centuries-long and then-still lingering Inquisition. See Hoffman Nickerson, *The Inquisition: A Political and Military History of Its Establishment* (Port Washington, NY: Kennikat Press, 1968 reprint of 1932 original); Jean Guiraud, *The Medieval Inquisition* (New York: AMS Press, 1979).

92   Todorov explores this construction very thoroughly in *Conquest of America*, as does Drinnon in the early-to-mid chapters of *Facing West*. Probably the best overview of the impacts attending the rationalization will be found in David E. Stannard's *American Holocaust: Columbus and the Conquest of the New World* (New York: Oxford University Press, 1992). Also see the essay entitled "'Nits Make Lice': The Extermination of North American Indians, 1607–1996," in my *A Little Matter of Genocide: Holocaust and Denial in the Americas, 1492 to the Present* (San Francisco: City Lights, 1997) pp. 129–288.

93   The indigenous population of North America has been credibly estimated to have numbered as many as 18.5 million in 1500. By 1890, it was less than a quarter-million, a 99th percentile reduction. For the estimate of preinvasion population size cited here, see Henry F. Dobyns, *Their Number Become Thinned: Native American Population Dynamics in Eastern North America* (Knoxville: University of Tennessee Press, 1983) pp. 42, 343.

94   Quoted in Robert Jay Lifton, *The Nazi Doctors: Medical Killing and the Psychology of Genocide* (New York: Basic Books, 1986) p. 477. For context, see James M. Glass, *"Life Unworthy of Life": Racial Phobia and Mass Murder in Hitler's Germany* (New York: Basic Books, 1997).

95   See generally Hoig, *Sand Creek Massacre*. It is noteworthy that Chivington was paraphrasing H.L. Hall, a prominent California "Indian fighter," who'd already expressed the much-publicized view that native babies should be killed whenever possible because "a knit [sic] would make a louse." Quoted in Lynwood Carranco and

Estle Beard, *Genocide and Vendetta: The Round Valley Wars of Northern California* (Norman: University of Oklahoma Press, 1981) p. 63.

96   Witness the clever little jingle, popular in the Massachusetts Colony in that year, written in celebration of the colonists' recent "extirpation" of the Narragansetts: "A swarm of flies, they may arise/a Nation to annoy/Yea Rats and Mice or Swarms of Lice/a Nation may destroy." Reproduced in Drinnon, *Facing West*, p. 54.

97   These include everyone from Thomas Jefferson to Abraham Lincoln; see the quotations in Svaldi, *Rhetoric of Extermination*, throughout.

98   For a fairly comprehensive overview, see the section titled "The Most Savage of Practices" in my "'Nits Make Lice,'" pp. 178–88.

99   Nolley, "Representation of Conquest," p. 83. Also see the relevant discussions in William Darby's *John Ford's Westerns: A Thematic Analysis with Filmography* (Jefferson, NC: McFarland, 1996).

100 See Carlos Clarens, *An Illustrated History of Horror and Science-Fiction Films: The Classic Era, 1895–1967* (New York: Da Capo Press, 1997).

101 Friar and Friar, "The Only Good Indian . . ." p. 134.

102 Ibid., p. 215.

103 Stedman, *Shadows of the Indian*, p. 116.

104 Alan Le May, *The Unforgiven* (New York: Harper & Bros., 1957).

105 In *Images of Indians*, Will Sampson describes *Unforgiven* as "the most racist movie about Indians ever made." For additional analysis, see Stedman, *Shadows of the Indian*, pp. 124–25.

106 Capt. John Smith, *A Map of Virginia, with a description of the Country, the Commodities, People, Government and Religion* (1612). For an overview of this literary stream, see my "Literature and the Colonization of American Indians," in *Fantasies of the Master Race*, pp. 1–18; Berkhofer, *White Man's Indian*; Stedman, *Shadows of the Indian*.

107 For framing, see the essays collected by Gidley in *Representing Others*. Also see Francis Barker, Peter Hume, Margaret Iverson, and Diana Loxley, eds., *Europe and Its Others: Proceedings of the Essex Conference on the Sociology of Literature, July 1984*, 2 vols. (Essex, UK: Essex University Press, 1985).

108 Published in *McClure's* magazine in 1910, London's short story is representative in every respect of its genre. See Richard Austin Thompson, *The Yellow Peril, 1890–1924* (New York: Arno Books, 1978); William F. Wu, *The Yellow Peril: Chinese Americans in American Fiction, 1850–1940* (Hamden, CT: Archon Books, 1982).

109 For analysis, see H. Bruce Franklin's *War Stars: The Superweapon and the American Imagination* (New York: Oxford University Press, 1988) pp. 101–2.

110 The phrase in quotes is taken from Robert Jay Lifton and Eric Markusen, *The Genocidal Mentality: Nazi Holocaust and Nuclear Threat* (New York: Basic Books, 1988).

111 Griffith himself seems to have lifted the scene whole from David Belasco's 1893 Broadway play, *The Girl I Left Behind Me*. See Stedman, *Shadows of the Indian*, p. 109.

112 Tuska, *American West in Film*, p. 239.

113 For these and other relevant quotes, see Stedman, *Shadows of the Indian*, p. 105; Tuska, *American West in Film*, pp. 246, 250. Also see Jimmie Durham's "Savage Attacks on White Women, as Usual," in his *Lack of Coherence*, pp. 120–25.

114 Jack Nachbar, "Ulzana's Raid," in William T. Pilkington and Don Graham, eds., *Western Movies* (Albuquerque: University of New Mexico Press, 1979) pp. 139–47.

115 Perhaps the most straightforward of all articulations of this theme will be found in Burt Kennedy's *The Deserter* (1971), when the settler-hero's wife is captured, gang-raped, then skinned alive and left for him to kill. Tuska, *American West in Film*, p. 250.

116 The phrase is borrowed from Oneida comedian Charlie Hill.

117 This theme runs deep in the euroamerican psyche. The bloodthirsty "Ethan Edwards" portrayed by Wayne shares much in common with the revenge-crazed "Nathan Slaughter" constructed by Robert Montgomery Bird in his acclaimed 1837 novel, Nick of the Woods (adapted by Louisa H. Medina for production as a stage play in 1838). See Curtis Dahl, Robert Montgomery Bird (New York: Twayne, 1963) esp. p. 97.

118 For a glimpse of the lengths to which mainstream critics have been willing to go in seeking to protect The Searchers—and Ford himself—from being categorized as racist, see Peter Lehman, "Looking at Look's Missing Reverse Shot: Psychoanalysis and Style in John Ford's The Searchers," in Jim Kitses and Gregg Rickman, eds., The Western Reader (New York: Limelight Editions, 1998) pp. 259–68.

119 This outcome can be usefully contrasted to that obtaining in Unforgiven, where Natalie Wood, portraying a young "mixed-breed" woman "taken in" as a child by "kindly" white raiders, is scripted to prove her "virtue"—and, more importantly, that she's "at heart, really more white than not"—by killing her Kiowa half-brother when he comes to retrieve her.

120 Alan Le May, The Searchers (New York: Harper & Row, 1954).

121 See, e.g., Zoe A. Tilghman, Quannah: Eagle of the Comanches (Oklahoma City: Harlow, 1958).

122 See generally Cynthia Schmidt Hacker, Cynthia Ann Parker: The Life and the Legend (El Paso: Texas Western Press, 1990). Also see Jimmie Durham, "Cowboy S-M," in his Lack of Coherence, pp. 187–90.

123 Benjamin Franklin, letter to Peter Collinson, May 9, 1753, in Leonard W. Larabee et al., eds., The Papers of Benjamin Franklin, 12 vols. (New Haven, CT: Yale University Press, 1959–1963) Vol. 4, pp. 481–82.

124 James Axtell, "The White Indians of Colonial America," in his The European and the Indian: Essays on the Ethnohistory of North America (New York: Oxford University Press, 1981) p. 177; quoting from William Smith, D.D., Historical Account of Colonel Bouquet's Expedition Against the Ohio Indians, 1764 (Philadelphia, 1765) pp. 390–91; "Provincial Correspondence, 1750–1765," Register of Pennsylvania, No. 4, 1839, p. 500; "Relation of Frederick Post of Conversation with Indians, 1760," Pennsylvania Archive, No. 3, 1853. Hundreds—perhaps thousands—of similar observations might be quoted. See my "The Crucible of American Indian Identity: Native Tradition versus Colonial Imposition in Postconquest North America," American Indian Culture and Research Journal, Vol. 23, No. 1 (1999) pp. 39–67.

125 Mary Rowlandson, The Narrative of the Captivity and Restoration of Mrs. Mary Rowlandson (Boston: Houghton-Mifflin, 1930 reprint of 1682 original).

126 Isabella McCoy, "The Captivity of Isabella McCoy," in Colin G. Galloway, ed., North Country Captives: Selected Narratives of Indian Captivity from Vermont and New Hampshire (Hanover, NH: University Press of New England, 1992) pp. 17–21.

127 Drinnon, Facing West, p. 61; Slotkin, Regeneration, p. 357. More broadly, see Jenny Sharpe, "The Unspeakable Limits of Rape: Colonial Violence and Counter-Insurgency," in Patrick Williams and Laura Chrisman, eds., Colonial Discourse and Post-Colonial Theory: A Reader (New York: Columbia University Press, 1995) pp. 221–43.

128 In order to arrive at her desired conclusion—that men of all cultures are consistently disposed to rape—it was often necessary for Brownmiller to wildly distort the available evidence. With respect to the captivity narratives, for example, she is not only sweeping in her dismissal of native sources but also in discounting the accounts of the "victims" themselves. Meanwhile, the libidinal fantasies filling Mather's

third-hand propaganda tracts are treated as credible sources. One can only wonder why she didn't follow through by citing the stories published during the 1930s in Julius Streicher's *Der Stürmer* as "evidence" that Jews habitually ravaged fair Aryan maidens. See Susan Brownmiller, *Against Our Will: Men, Women and Rape* (New York: Simon and Schuster, 1975) pp. 140–45.

129 "Isabella McCoy," in Frederick Drimmer, ed., *Scalps and Tomahawks: Narratives of Indian Captivity* (New York: Howard-McCann, 1961) p. 13.

130 Morris Edward Opler, *An Apache Life-Way: The Economic, Social, and Religious Institutions of the Chiricahua Indians* (Chicago: University of Chicago Press, 1941) p. 228.

131 See the chapter titled "Sex, Race and Holy War" in Stannard, *American Holocaust*, pp. 195–246. Also see Leslie Feidler, *Return of the Vanishing American* (New York: Stein & Day, 1968) pp. 45–46.

132 The literature in this connection is burgeoning. See, as examples, Agnes Grant, *No End of Grief: Indian Residential Schools in Canada* (Winnipeg: Pemmican Press, 1996); Suzanne Fournier and Ernie Grey, *Stolen from Our Embrace: The Abduction of First Nations Children and the Restoration of Aboriginal Communities* (Vancouver, BC: Douglas & McIntyre, 1997); Roland Chrisjohn and Sherri Young with Michael Maraun, *The Circle Game: Shadows and Substance in the Indian Residential School Experience in Canada* (Penticton, BC: Theytus Books, 1997); John S. Milloy, *A National Crime: The Canadian Government and the Residential School System, 1879–1986* (Winnipeg: University of Manitoba Press, 1999).

133 The few films touching upon the effects of Indian boarding schools in the U.S.—e.g., *Jim Thorpe, All American* (1951) and *Running Brave* (1981)—have been frankly celebratory. Even the somewhat more accurate depiction offered in *The Education of Little Tree* (1997) avoids any hint of sexual predation by the school's staff.

134 Cleaver's astute analysis of rapist psychology—offered through the lens of self-understanding attained by his own earlier affliction with it—was offered in his *Soul on Ice* (New York: Ramparts Books/McGraw-Hill, 1968); see esp. pp. 16–17. For Brownmiller's incredibly distortive "interpretation"—it amounts to a complete inversion of Cleaver's argument—see *Against Our Will*, pp. 248–52. The most recent regurgitation I'm aware of is Judy "Gumbo" Albert's comment in an interview that "it's true that Eldridge Cleaver glorified rape as an insurrectionary act in his book, *Soul on Ice*." See "Thoughts on Subversion from Two Yippie Elders," *Green Anarchy*, No. 6 (Summer 2001) p. 8. For a solid rejoinder to all such nonsense, see Angela Y. Davis' "Rape, Racism, and the Myth of the Black Rapist," in her *Women, Race, and Class* (New York: Random House, 1981) pp. 172–201.

135 There are, of course, exceptions, albeit of a rather peculiar sort. In her recent *Cartographies of Desire: Captivity, Race, and Sex in the Shaping of the American Nation* (Norman: University of Oklahoma Press, 1999), Rebecca Blevins Faery, to offer a prime example, follows both Cleaver and the facts to conclude that red on white rape has been mostly nonexistent. To explain the virulent mythology that has nonetheless attended issues of red/white sexuality, she also "borrows," intact and in its entirety, the quadrilateral typology of interracial sexual archetypes Cleaver set forth quite brilliantly in his essay "The Primeval Mitosis" (*Soul on Ice*, pp. 176–90). Having thus dredged Cleaver for his undeniable explanatory utility, Faery repays her debt by making absolutely no reference to him. *Cartographies*, which is in my opinion an otherwise admirable work, must therefore be seen as a classic illustration of intellectual imperialism.

136 I say "predictable," since such results have long been known to attend acute psycho-
     logical trauma, most especially that of a recurrent, sustained variety, inaugurated
     at an early age. For an excellent overview—which nonetheless neglects all mention
     of the residential/boarding school context in North America—see Judith Herman,
     Trauma and Recovery (New York: Basic Books, [2nd ed.] 1997).

137 A stunning example is Mary Daly's *Gyn/Ecology: The Metaethic of Radical Feminism*
     (Boston: Beacon Press, 1978).

138 The eurofeminist equation of nationalism to "masculinist dominance" commenced
     at least as early as Barbara Burris' "The Fourth World Manifesto," in Anne Koedt,
     ed., *Radical Feminism* ([New York: Quadrangle Books, 1973] pp. 322–57), and has
     seen continued refinement in essays such as those collected by Miranda Davis
     in her *Third World/Second Sex: Women's Struggles and National Liberation* (London: Zed
     Books, 1983); those collected by Roberta Hamilton and Michèle Barrett, eds., *The
     Politics of Diversity: Feminism, Marxism and Nationalism* (London: Verso, 1987), and, most
     recently, attempts to discredit the work of anticolonial theorists like Frantz Fanon
     spearheaded by mainstreamers such as Diana Fuss (see, e.g., her "Interior Colonies:
     Frantz Fanon and the Politics of Identification," in Nigel C. Gibson, ed., *Rethinking
     Fanon: The Continuing Dialogue* [Amherst, NY: Humanity Books, 1999] pp. 294–328).
     A firm rejoinder will be found in Gayatri Chakravorty Spivak's "Feminism in
     Decolonization," *Differences*, Vol. 3, No. 3 (1991) pp. 139–70.

139 For explication, see Gayatri Chakravorty Spivak, "French Feminism in an
     International Frame," in her *In Other Worlds: Essays on Cultural Politics* (New York:
     Metheun, 1987) pp. 134–53; Linda Alcolff, "The Problem of Speaking for Others,"
     Cultural Critique, No. 20 (1991–92) pp. 5–32; Chandra Talpade Mohanty, "Under
     Western Eyes: Feminist Scholarship and Colonial Discourses," in Williams and
     Chrisman, *Colonial Discourse and Post-Colonial Theory*, pp. 196–220.

140 Gayatri Chakravorty Spivak, "Can the Subaltern Speak?" in Carey Nelson and
     Lawrence Grossberg, eds., *Marxism and the Interpretation of Culture* (Urbana: University
     of Illinois Press, 1988) p. 297.

141 The issue of white women's complicity in racism and colonialism is of course a
     matter of considerable inconvenience to eurofeminist pretensions of victim status.
     This perhaps explains the recent spate of works seeking to separate women from
     the imperial project by setting forth the ways in which their "travel writing about
     the non-Western world," for example, "was markedly different from men's in form,
     thematic preoccupations and political positionality," thus allegedly posing "a
     subtle challenge to the dominant masculinist discourse of imperialism by 'helping
     to build a reservoir of mutual understanding' between the races, which was to
     smooth the way for decolonization." See Moore-Gilbert, *Postcolonial Theory*, p. 214,
     citing Helen Callaway, *Gender, Culture and Empire* (Urbana: University of Illinois Press,
     1987); Mary Louise Pratt, *Imperial Eyes: Travel Writing and Transculturation* (London:
     Routledge, 1992); Sara Mills, *Discourses of Difference: An Analysis of Women's Travel Writing
     and Colonialism* (London: Routledge, 1993); Lisa Lowe, *French and British Orientalisms*
     (Ithaca, NY: Cornell University Press, 1991). One need only undertake the most
     cursory comparison of men's writing during the classical colonial era—Kipling's
     to Melville's, for instance, or Sartre's to Graham Greene's—to apprehend equal or
     greater "differences in form, thematic preoccupation and political positionality."
     For analysis of the transparency entailed in eurofeminism's "'common oppression'
     rhetoric and . . . attempts to deny white women's privilege in an antiblack culture,"
     see T. Deneane Sharply-Whiting, "Fanon's Feminist Consciousness and Algerian

Women's Liberation: Colonialism, Nationalism and Fundamentalism," in Gibson, *Rethinking Fanon*, esp. pp. 350–1.

142　See Joel Kovel, *White Racism: A Psychohistory* (New York: Columbia University Press, 1984).

143　George Lipsitz, *The Possessive Investment in Whiteness: How White People Profit from Identity Politics* (Philadelphia: Temple University Press, 1998). Relatedly, see David Roediger, *The Wages of Whiteness: Race and the Making of the American Working Class* (London: Verso, 1991) and the sources cited below in notes 216 and 220.

144　For background, see, e.g., Eric Wolf, *Europe and the People Without History* (Berkeley: University of California Press, 1982) and Vassilis Lambropoulis, *The Rise of Eurocentrism: Anatomy of Interpretation* (Princeton, NJ: Princeton University Press, 1993).

145　See Norman Cohn, *Warrant for Genocide: The Myth of the Jewish World Conspiracy and the Protocols of the Elders of Zion* (London: Serrit, [2nd ed.] 1996). Also see the reproduction of the first page of the "Special Edition on Jewish Ritual Murder" put forth by *Der Stürmer* in May 1934, reproduced in Randall L. Bytwerk, *Julius Streicher: The Man Who Persuaded a Nation to Hate Jews* (New York: Dorset Press, 1983) Figure 16.

146　A dated but still very useful examination of this script will be found in the chapter titled "The Savage Art of Discovery: How to Blame the Victim," in William Ryan's *Blaming the Victim* (New York: Vintage Books, 1971) pp. 3–29.

147　Probably the best known example is that of "Little Horse," a lispingly stereotyped *heemaneh* portrayed by Lakota actor Robert Little Star in *Little Big Man*. See Kasdan and Tavernetti, "Revisionist Western," p. 131. Unpacking this trope can be difficult, given the misperceptions of native homosexuality engendered by such pop treatments as Paula Gunn Allen's *The Sacred Hoop: Recovering the Feminine in American Indian Cultures* (Boston: Beacon Press, 1986) and Walter L. Williams' *The Spirit and the Flesh: Sexual Diversity Among Native Americans* (Boston: Beacon Press, 1986). The most straightforward indicator of the sorts of problems riddling both books will be found in the juxtaposition of Gunn Allen's initial (and entirely accurate) representation of homosexuality as being uncommon to the point of uniqueness—and therefore "special"—in most indigenous societies to her later insinuation that it was so common as to constitute a normative orientation. Obviously, the matter can't be had both ways. Either something is common (banal) or special (unique). Thus, far from offering an accurate rendering of the facet of traditional native life she purports to depict, the author plays to the crowd, deliberately distorting her subject matter in a manner greatly appealing to a contemporary school of mostly non-Indian gay rights activists who demand that their constituencies be treated as if they were both special *and* "normal." Such posturing may well make for good politics, but it's lousy scholarship.

148　Probably the first two movies to pursue this theme were *An Indian Maiden's Choice* and *The Indian Girl's Romance* (both 1910), and they've continued in a torrent ever since; see my "Fantasies of the Master Race," pp. 193–96. The matter is handled in more depth—and rather well—by Faery, in *Cartographies of Desire*. Also see Robert S. Tilton, *Pocahontas: The Evolution of an American Narrative* (Cambridge, UK: Cambridge University Press, 1994).

149　This is brought out in an endless stream of films about the "problems of mixed-bloodedness," e.g., *The Halfbreed* (1916, remade as *The Half Breed* in 1922, and as *The Half-Breed* in 1952), *The Dumb Half-Breed's Defense* (1910), *The Half-Breed's Way* and *The Half-Breed's Sacrifice* (both 1912) *The Barrier of Blood*, *The Half-Breed Parson*, and *The*

Half-Breed Sheriff (all 1913), Indian Blood (1914), The Ancient Blood and The Quarter Breed (both 1916), One-Eighth Apache (1922), Call Her Savage (1932), and on, and on. In their "The Only Good Indian . . ." (pp. 300–1), the Friars list 108 films devolving upon such themes by 1970.

150 Sheridan's actual statement was that "the only good Indians I ever saw were dead." Quoted in Paul Andrew Hutton, Phil Sheridan and His Army (Lincoln: University of Nebraska Press, 1985) p. 180.

151 An excellent montage sequence including dozens of such scenes is included in Images of Indians.

152 Arguably, Cooper himself found a model for his Good Indian character in that of "Friday," the faithful native constructed by Daniel Defoe in Robinson Crusoe. See Stedman, Shadows of the Indian, pp. 52–54, 179, 260. Also see William P. Kelly, Plotting America's Past: Fenimore Cooper and the Leatherstocking Tales (Carbondale: Southern Illinois University Press, 1983).

153 Be it noted that the Mohicans still exist. Lumped together with several other small eastern peoples under the heading "Stockbridge-Munsee Indians," they reside on a small reservation near Green Bay, Wisconsin. See Patrick Frazier, The Mohicans of Stockbridge (Lincoln: University of Nebraska Press, 1992).

154 Rayna Green, The Only Good Indian: Images of Indians in American Vernacular Culture (Bloomington: PhD dissertation, Indiana University, 1974) p. 382.

155 Daniel Francis, The Imaginary Indian: The Image of the Indian in Canadian Culture (Vancouver, BC: Arsenal Pulp Press, 1992) p. 167.

156 Tilton, Pocahontas, p. 56.

157 Walker, "Deconstructing an American Myth."

158 On the concept of "The Man Who Knows Indians," see Slotkin, Gunfighter Nation, p. 47.

159 See generally James Van Hise, Who Was That Masked Man? The Story of the Lone Ranger (Las Vegas: Pioneer Books, 1990).

160 Bird, "Not My Fantasy." Also see Richard Zoglin, "Frontier Feminist," Time Magazine (March 1, 1993) p. 64; and the chapter titled "The Other Side of Postfeminism: Maternal Feminism in Dr. Quinn, Medicine Woman," in Bonnie J. Dow's Prime Time Feminism: Television, Media Culture, and the Women's Movement Since 1970 (Philadelphia: University of Pennsylvania Press, 1996) pp. 164–202.

161 Rudyard Kipling, Gunga Din and Other Favorite Poems (New York: Dover, 1991).

162 For exploration of levels of colonialist virulence in Kipling often ignored even by radical critics, see Patrick Williams, "Kim and Orientalism," in Williams and Chrisman, Colonial Discourse and Post-Colonial Theory, pp. 480–89. Also see Zoreh T. Sullivan, Narratives of Empire: The Fiction of Rudyard Kipling (Cambridge, UK: Cambridge University Press, 1993).

163 Bird, "Not My Fantasy," p. 249.

164 Ibid.

165 A hint of how the Vichy and Free French were juxtaposed in contemporaneous American cinema will be found in Michael Curtiz's 1942 classic, Casablanca.

166 See generally Geoffrey Warner, Pierre Laval and the Eclipse of France (London: Macmillan, 1968).

167 A good analysis will be found in Frank Manchel's "Cultural Confusion: Broken Arrow (1950)," in Rollins and O'Connor, Hollywood's Indian, pp. 91–106.

168 See generally. Edwin R. Sweeny, Cochise: Chiricahua Chief (Norman: University of Oklahoma Press, 1991).

169 For a relatively accurate view of "Geronimo" (Golthlay), see Britton Davis, *The Truth About Geronimo* (Chicago: Lakeside Press, 1951 reprint of 1929 original).

170 See, e.g., Mari Sandoz, *Crazy Horse: Strange Man of the Oglalas* (New York: Alfred A. Knopf, 1942). It can be worthwhile to have students read this fine biography, then view what director George Sherman did with it in his 1955 *Chief Crazy Horse*.

171 With respect to such exposure being "increasing," consider the program recently inaugurated by the Canadian government—which never seems to have funds available to meet its actual treaty obligations in terms of providing adequate housing, medical service and the like in exchange for its claimed land base—to install a satellite dish in every remote northern village so the kids therein will share the "opportunity" of reruns of John Ford movies. See Jerry Mander, *In the Absence of the Sacred: The Failure of Technology and the Survival of Indian Nations* (San Francisco: Sierra Club Books, 1992) pp. 97–119.

172 Strickland, "Tonto's Revenge," p. 18.

173 Strickland, "You Can't Rollerskate in a Buffalo Herd, Even If You Have All the Medicine: American Indian Law and Politics," in his *Tonto's Revenge*, p. 53. On Canada, see *Choosing Life: Special Report on Suicide Among Aboriginal People* (Ottawa: Canada Communication Group, 1994).

174 See Geoffrey York, *The Dispossessed: Life and Death in Native Canada* (Toronto: McArthur & Co., [2nd ed.] 1999) pp. 1–21; Gary Remington and Brian Hoffman, "Gas Sniffing as a Form of Substance Abuse," *Canadian Journal of Psychiatry*, Vol. 29, No. 1 (1984) pp. 31–35; Fournier and Grey, *Stolen from Our Embrace*, pp. 115–17.

175 See Leah Renae Kelly, "The Open Veins of Native North America," in her *In My Own Voice*, pp. 112–15.

176 The issue is covered in the essays entitled "Let's Spread the 'Fun' Around: The Issue of Sports Team Names and Mascots" and "In the Matter of Julius Streicher: Applying Nuremberg Standards in the United States," in my *From a Native Son: Selected Essays in Indigenism, 1985–1995* (Boston: South End Press, 1996) pp. 439–44, 445–54. Also see Carol Spindel, *Dancing at Halftime: Sports and the Controversy over American Indian Mascots* (New York: New York University Press, 2000); C. Richard King and Charles Frueling Springwood, eds., *Team Spirits: The Native American Mascots Controversy* (Lincoln: University of Nebraska Press, 2001).

177 "Squaw" is a corruption of the Mohawk word for female genitalia, analogous, when used as slang, to the term "cunt." See Barbara Alice Mann, *Iroquoian Women: The Gantowisas* (New York: Peter Lang, 2000) p. 364. The pervasiveness of this descriptor in settler discourse is to some extent evident in the titles of scores of potboiler films like *The Squaw Man* (1913, 1918, 1938) and *The Fate of the Squaw* (1914). Even more striking is the fact that in North America there are about a thousand officially-designated place names including the word: "Squaw Valley," "Squaw Peak," "Squaw Creek," and so on. The effect on native women—not to mention six-year-old little girls—of being referred to in this fashion is anything but "harmless." See Rayna Green, "The Pocahontas Perplex: The Image of Indian Women in American Culture," *Massachusetts Review*, Vol. 16, No. 4 (Autumn 1975) pp. 698–714.

178 The relationship between denial of genocides past and the perpetration of genocides present/future is bought out very well by Roger W. Smith, Eric Markusen, and Robert Jay Lifton in their "Professional Ethics and the Denial of the Armenian Genocide," *Holocaust and Genocide Studies*, Vol. 9, No. 1 (Spring 1995) pp. 1–22.

179 The implications are brought out well in Wolf, *Europe and the People Without History*.

180 Strickland, "Tonto's Revenge," p. 20.

181 The matter is discussed at several points in Allan L. Wald's and Randall H. Miller's *Ethics and Racial Images in American Film and Television: Historical Essays and Bibliography* (New York: Garland, 1987). On Ford's peculiar fixation on Monument Valley, see Maltby, "A Better Sense of History."

182 The largely Hollywood-induced deficit in geographical understanding suffered by American school children had become something of a scandal by the late 1960s. But, then, might one have expected of a culture that believes the European subcontinent not only to be a continent in its own right, but "The Continent"? See Kenneth C. Davis, *Don't Know Much about Geography: Everything You Need to Know about the World but Never Learned* (New York: William Morrow, 1992) p. 129.

183 This sort of thing, which was/is rampant, was addressed by Dan Georgakas in an article titled "They Have Not Spoken: American Indians in Film," Film Quarterly, Vol. 25, No. 3 (Spring 1972) pp. 26–32. Also see Ralph E. Friar and Natasha A. Friar, "White Man Speak with Split Tongue, Forked Tongue, Tongue of Snake," in Bataille and Silet, *Pretend Indians*, pp. 92–97.

184 Strickland, "Tonto's Revenge," p. 20.

185 Indigenous people are not alone in having protested this. As early as 1914, Alanson Skinner, curator of anthropology at the American Museum of Natural History, decried in a *New York Times* guest editorial the "ethnographically grotesque farces" embodied in such cinematic travesties as "Delawares dressed as Sioux" and "the Indians of Manhattan . . . dwelling in tipis" (quoted in Strickland, "Tonto's Revenge," p. 32). In view of this and many subsequent criticisms of the same sort, it's simply untenable to argue—as have apologists like Lenihan and Nachbar—that Hollywood's systematic misrepresentation of native culture has been in any sense "unintentional" or "unwitting."

186 Maltby, "A Better Sense of History," p. 35.

187 In their "*The Only Good Indian . . .*" (pp. 281–83), Ralph and Natasha Friar provide a list of some 350 noteworthy white actors, both male and female, who appeared in redface between 1910 and 1970. Suffice it to say that the list of Indians cast as whites is a bit shorter.

188 The effect, as Charlie Hill has put it, was "like casting Wilt Chamberlain as J. Edgar Hoover." Connor discusses his role without discernible embarrassment in *Images of Indians*.

189 Aside from the Mohawk Jay Silverheels, who found steady work playing Tonto in the *Lone Ranger* epics, the last overtly native actor before the 1990s to win name recognition in movie theaters was the Cherokee Will Rogers, during the 1930s. See my and Leah Renae Kelly's "*Smoke Signals* in Context: An Historical Overview," in her *In My Own Voice*, esp. pp. 123–25.

190 In this, there is a striking parallel to the arrogant assertion made by many "American Indianist" anthropologists—and undoubtedly harbored as an unstated belief by most others—that they "know more about Indians than the Indians themselves." See Wendy Rose, "The Great Pretenders: Further Reflections on White Shamanism," in M. Annette Jaimes, ed., *The State of Native America: Genocide, Colonization and Resistance* (Boston: South End Press, 1992) pp. 403–22.

191 Bird, "Not My Fantasy," p. 251.

192 The 1955 movie was a sequel to *Davy Crockett, Indian Scout* (1950), and fashioned from segments run on Disney's popular Sunday-night TV series. A third film, *Davy Crockett and the River Pirates*, was released in 1956. The package was such a hit that for a while it seemed that every grade-school-aged boy in the U.S. was running around

in a coonskin cap resembling that worn by Fess Parker in the title role. See Slotkin, *Gunfighter Nation*, p. 516. More fully, see Margaret J. King, "The Recycled Hero: Walt Disney's Davy Crockett," in Michael J. Lofaro, ed., *Davy Crockett: The Man, the Legend, the Legacy, 1786–1986* (Nashville: University of Tennessee Press, 1986) pp. 137–58.

193 An unnamed critic observed in *Film Quarterly* at the time of its release that, "Stripped of its pretensions, *Horse* parades the standard myth that a white man can do everything better than an Indian. Give him a little time and he will marry the best-looking girl (a princess, of course) and will end up chief." Quoted in Kilpatrick, *Celluloid Indians*, p. 82.

194 On *Cheyenne Autumn*—another devastating corruption of a fine book by Mari Sandoz—see Kilpatrick, *Celluloid Indians*, pp. 67–70; Noley, "Representations of Conquest," esp. pp. 79–82; and V.F. Perkins, "Cheyenne Autumn," in Bataille and Silet, *Pretend Indians*, esp. p. 153.

195 Loosely based on the book cited in note 169, the movie should really have been titled "The Britton Davis Story." In any event, see Kilpatrick, *Celluloid Indians*, pp. 143–48.

196 Ibid., pp. 154–56.

197 Durham, "Cowboys and . . ." p. 176. His entirely appropriate inclusion of Queequeg and Kesey's "Bromden" ("Chief Broom") character along with Tonto is instructive, insofar as both Melville's and Kesey's work have been considered counterhegemonic by most analysts. See, e.g., H. Bruce Franklin, "From Empire to Empire: Billy Budd, Sailor," in A. Robert Lee, ed., *Herman Melville: Reassessments* (London/Totowa, NJ: Vision Press/Barnes & Noble, 1984) pp. 199–216.

198 Durham, "Cowboys and . . ." p. 176.

199 Ibid. There is a deliberate irony imbedded in Durham's metaphor devolving upon a curious insistence among anthropologists—despite a total of evidence—that American Indians were in preinvasion times anthropophagi. This "scientific" assertion serves much the same "blood libel" purpose earlier discussed with respect to rape. See my "Science as Psychosis: An American Corollary to Germany's Blood Libel of the Jews," in this volume.

200 Europe even developed a legal principle—*territorium res nullius*—as a subset of its doctrine of discovery to accommodate the notion of "vacant land." See the essay entitled "The Tragedy and the Travesty: The Subversion of Indigenous Sovereignty in North America," in my *Struggle for the Land*, esp. pp. 43–50. For a good survey of the sorts of effects that attend application of this construction in the "real world," see Boyce Richardson, *The People of Terra Nullius: Betrayal and Rebirth in Aboriginal Canada* (Seattle/Vancouver: University of Washington Press/Douglas McIntire, 1993).

201 Once again, there is a clear interface between myth and "science" in the public consciousness. The standard estimate put forth by the Smithsonian Institution for most of the twentieth century has been that there were only about a million indigenous people residing in North America when the European invasion commenced. Over the past thirty years, it's been conclusively established that, beginning in the early nineteenth century, generations of settler academics deliberately falsified their data in order to make the preinvasion native population appear far smaller than it actually was (thereby making the continent appear to have been relatively uninhabited)., See the chapter entitled "Widowed Land" in Francis Jennings, *The Invasion of America: Indians, Colonialism, and the Cant of Conquest* (Chapel Hill: University of North Carolina Press, 1975) pp. 15–31.

202 See the essay titled "Deconstructing the Columbus Myth: Was the 'Great Discoverer' Italian or Spanish, Nazi or Jew?" in my *A Little Matter of Genocide*, pp. 81–96.

203   As Deloria has aptly observed, "the white man is haunted by the knowledge that he can never be alone" on the land of North America; "American Fantasy," p. xvi.

204   Such information—including the fact that self-anointed federal "trustees" have "misplaced" at least $40 billion in funds belonging to destitute Indians over the years, plowing the money into programs benefiting the settler populace—is readily available in the mass media. See, e.g., Peter Maas, "The Broken Promise," *Parade* (September 9, 2001). Overall, see Kelly, "Open Veins," and my "The Indigenous Peoples of North America: A Struggle Against Internal Colonialism," in *Struggle for the Land*, pp. 15–36.

205   Sartre, "Colonialism Is a System," in *Colonialism and Neocolonialism*, p. 39.

206   The standard rejoinder to this is that we didn't or don't "really" constitute nations and thus cannot be colonies in the sense contended. In response it can be pointed out that under both customary law and Article 1, Section 10 of its own constitution, the U.S. government has never been empowered to enter into treaty relationships with any entity but another nation. On record, the federal government has entered into and duly ratified some 400 treaties with indigenous American peoples, each of which conveys formal legal recognition that the other parties were/are separate nations. See Vine Deloria Jr. and Raymond J. DeMallie, *Documents of American Indian Diplomacy: Treaties, Agreements and Conventions, 1775–1979*, 2 vols. (Norman: University of Oklahoma Press, 1999). The same principle applies to Canada; see *Canada: Indian Treaties and Surrenders from 1680 to 1890*, 3 vols. (Ottawa: Queen's Printer, 1891; reprinted by Fifth House [Saskatoon], 1992). Overall, see Ian Sinclair, *The Vienna Convention on the Law of Treaties* (Manchester, UK: Manchester University Press, 1984).

207   For the relevant texts, see Burns H. Weston, Richard A. Falk, and Anthony D'Amato, *Basic Documents in International Law and World Order* (St. Paul, MN: West, [2nd ed.] 1990). For elaboration of principles, see John Howard Clinebell and Jim Thompson, "Sovereignty and Self-Determination: The Rights of Native Americans Under International Law," *Buffalo Law Review*, Vol. 27, No. 4 (Fall 1978) pp. 669–714.

208   The phrase was actually "a *government* of laws, not men [emphasis added]," but has been altered over time in popular usage. In any case, it first uttered by Chief Justice of the Supreme Court John Marshall in his 1803 *Marbury* opinion (1 Cranch. (5 U.S.) 137). For analysis, see the chapter titled "It's the Law" in Rodolfo Acuña's *Sometimes There Is No Other Side: Chicanos and the Myth of Equality* (Notre Dame, IN: Notre Dame University Press, 1998) pp. 33–56.

209   This seems to pertain not just in North America but to all comparable contexts. See Ronald Weitzer, *Transforming Settler States: Communal Conflict and Internal Security in Northern Ireland and Zimbabwe* (Berkeley: University of California Press, 1992).

210   Durham, "Cowboys and . . ." pp. 174–75. The final query plainly ties back to the suicide and gasoline sniffing epidemics afflicting native youth, mentioned in conjunction with notes 173 and 174.

211   "Conquest was achieved by violence; exploitation and oppression demand the maintenance of violence . . . Colonialism [thus necessarily] denies human rights to people it subjugates by violence, and whom it keeps in poverty and ignorance by force." Sartre, "Introduction to Memmi," p. 50.

212   Neither the idea of internal colonialism, nor its applicability to North America, is unique to Durham. Actually, the concept seems to have originated with Antonio Gramsci in his 1920 essay, "The Southern Question" (included in his *The Modern Prince and Other Writings* [New York: International, 1957] pp. 28–51). It was adapted by Cherokee anthropologist Robert K. Thomas to describe the situation of American

Indians in his "Colonialism: Classic and Internal" (*New University Thought*, Vol. 4, No. 4, Winter 1966–67) pp. 37–44. Since then, it has been employed by numerous scholars, including me, working on indigenous issues (both in North America and globally). Rodolfo Acuña, among others, has also used it to good effect in analyzing the circumstances Mexican Americans in the Southwestern U.S. See note 263.

213 Durham, "Cowboys and . . ." p. 175.

214 Ibid.

215 Ibid., p. 174.

216 For early elaborations of the concept of white skin privilege, see Noel Ignatin, (Ignatiev) and Ted Allen, "The White Blind Spot," and Ted Allen, "Can White Radicals Be Radicalized?," printed repeatedly between the late 1960s and mid-1970s and more recently included as "The White Blindspot Documents" in Carl Davidson, ed., *Revolutionary Youth and the New Working Class: The Praxis Papers, the Port Authority Statement, the RYM Documents and Other Lost Writings of SDS* (Pittsburgh: Changemaker, 2011) pp. 141–81.

217 See, e.g., Allan Bloom, *The Closing of the American Mind* (New York: Touchstone Books, 1988); Arthur M. Schlesinger Jr., *The Disuniting of America: Reflections on a Multicultural Society* (New York: W.W. Norton, [rev. ed.] 1998).

218 For especially telling comments in this connection, see Tuhiwai Smith, *Decolonizing Theory*, p. 98; Aijaz Ahmad, *In Theory: Classes, Nations, Literatures* (London: Verso, 1992) p. 7.

219 Although the term "ludic" is typically employed to signify "playfulness," I use it in the sense of meaning "ludicrous." For further explication, see Teresa Ebert, *Ludic Feminism and After: Postmodernism, Desire, and Labor in Late Capitalism* (Ann Arbor: University of Michigan Press, 1996).

220 A devastating critique of this tendency will be found in J. Sakai, *Settlers: The Myth of the White Proletariat* (Chicago: Morningstar, 1983). Also see Ignatin and Allen, "White Blind Spot"; Allen, "White Radicals"; Roediger, *Wages of Whiteness*; Lipsitz, *Investment in Whiteness*.

221 For abundant quotations to this effect, see the opening chapter of Walker Connor's *The National Question in Marxist-Leninist Theory and Strategy* (Princeton, NJ: Princeton University Press, 1984). For the best overall critiques of marxian ethnocentrism at the level of high theory, see Jean Baudrillard, *The Mirror of Production* (St. Louis: Telos Press, 1975). Still, one finds echoes of Marx's outlook on "the benefits of colonialism" in the unlikeliest of places. See, e.g., Gayatri Chakravorty Spivak, "Bonding in Difference: Interview with Alfred Arteaga," in Donna Landry and Gerald MacLean, eds., *The Spivak Reader* (New York: Routledge, 1996) esp. p. 19.

222 Robert J.C. Young, "Sartre: The 'African Philosopher,'" preface to Sartre, *Colonialism and Neocolonialism*, p. xix. For greater detail, see Young, *White Mythologies*, pp. 28–47.

223 See Vijay Mishra and Bob Hodge, "What is Post(-)colonialism?" in Williams and Chrisman, *Colonial Discourse and Post-Colonial Theory*, pp. 276–90; Stephen Slemon, "The Scramble for Theory," in Bill Ashcroft, Gareth Griffiths and Helen Tiffin, eds., *The Post-Colonial Studies Reader* (New York: Routledge, 1995) pp. 45–52.

224 Anne McClintock, "The Angel of Progress: Pitfalls of the Term 'Post-colonialism,'" in Williams and Chrisman, *Colonial Discourse and Post-Colonial Theory*, p. 294. Stuart Hall also does an excellent job of debunking "postcolonialist" temporality in his "When Was 'the Post-colonial'? Thinking at the Limits," in Iain Chambers and Lidia Curti, eds., *The Post-Colonial Question: Common Skies, Divided Horizons* (New York: Routledge, 1996) pp. 242–60.

225 McClintock, "Angel of Progress," p. 294.

226 Diana Brydon, "New Approaches to the New Literatures in English," in Hena Maes-Jelinek, Kristen Holst Peterson, and Anna Rutherford, eds., A Shaping of Connections: Commonwealth Studies, Then and Now (Mundelstrup, Denmark: Dangaroo Press, 1989) p. 95.

227 See R.S. Mathews, "The Canadian Problem," in John Press, ed., Commonwealth Literature: Unity and Diversity in a Common Culture (London: Heineman, 1965) pp. 157–67. Also see Deepika Bahri, "Once More with Feeling: What Is Postcolonialism?" Ariel, Vol. 26, No. 1 (1995) pp. 51–82.

228 Arif Dirlik explores these issues rather thoroughly in his The Postcolonial Aura: Third World Criticism in the Era of Global Capitalism (Boulder, CO: Westview Press, 1997). For what is probably the strongest debunking to date of the whole notion of "postcoloniality," see Gayatri Chakravorty Spivak, A Critique of Postcolonial Reason: Toward a History of the Vanishing Present (Cambridge, MA: Harvard University Press, 1999).

229 In addition to the various "posts" discussed herein, we find an intellectual terrain littered with outgrowths of "postmarxism" and "postfeminism," even "posthistory," a landscape of overall "postality" inhabited in part by—you guessed it—"postindians." See, as examples, Stuart Sim, Post-Marxism: An Intellectual History (New York: Routledge, 2001); Imelda Wheleman, Modern Feminist Thought: From the Second Wave to "Post-Feminism" (New York: New York University Press, 1995); Ken Harper, The Third Millennium: Living in the Posthistoric World (San Francisco: Harper, 1996); Mas'ud Zavarzadeh, Post-Ality: Marxism and Postmodernism (Washington, DC: Maisonneuve Press, 1995); Gerald Vizenor, Manifest Manners: Postindian Warriors of Survivance (Middletown, CT: Wesleyan University Press, 1994).

230 Teresa Ebert, "Political Semiosis in/of American Cultural Studies," American Journal of Semiotics, Vol. 8, Nos. 1–2 (1991) p. 117.

231 For what may be the key exposition on the issue of narrative totalization, see Jean-François Lyotard, The Postmodern Condition: A Report on Knowledge (Minneapolis: University of Minnesota Press, 1985). Also see Manfred Frank, What Is Neostructuralism? (Minneapolis: University of Minnesota Press, 1989); Derek Attridge and Robert Young, eds., Post-Structuralism and the Question of History (Cambridge, UK: Cambridge University Press, 1989).

232 "It is a mistake to confuse hierarchy with elitism. . . . 'Hierarchy,' a term which originally denoted the three categories of angels, has come to mean any kind of graduated structure. In its broadest sense, it refers to something like an order of priorities. In this broad sense of the word, everyone is a hierarchist, whereas not everyone is an elitist. Indeed you may object to elites because they offend your order of priorities." Terry Eagleton, The Illusions of Postmodernism (Oxford, UK: Blackwell, 1996) pp. 93–94.

233 Essentialism reduces, essentially, to the proposition that "things are made up of certain properties, and that some of these properties are actually constitutive of them, such that if they were removed or radically transformed the thing in question would become some other thing, or nothing at all." Eagleton, Illusions of Postmodernism, p. 97. This is rather different than the doctrine holding that there are "core properties, or clusters of properties, present, necessarily, in all and only those things which bear the common name" assailed by Wittgenstein. Garth L. Hallett, Essentialism: A Wittgensteinian Critique (New York: State University of New York Press, 1991) p. 2.

234 In simplest terms, "teleology" means only "the assumption that there is some potential in the present which could result in a particular sort of future." This is very different from the typical postmodernist contention that it implies "the belief that the world is moving purposively toward some predetermined goal which is immanent within it even now, and which provides the dynamic of this inexorable unfurling." Eagleton, *Illusions of Postmodernism*, pp. 108, 45.

235 The antirationalist impulse is discussed at length in Horace L. Fairlamb's *Critical Conditions: Postmodernity and the Question of Foundations* (Cambridge, UK: Cambridge University Press, 1994).

236 See, as examples, Barbara Hernstein Smith, *Contingencies of Value* (Cambridge, MA: Harvard University Press. 1988); Richard Rorty, *Contingency, Irony, Solidarity* (Cambridge, UK: Cambridge University Press, 1989); and Zygmunt Bauman, *Postmodern Ethics* (Oxford, UK: Blackwell, 1993).

237 Christopher Lasch, "Learning from Leipzig . . . or Politics in the Semiotic Society," *Theory, Culture and Society*, Vol. 7, No. 4 (1990) pp. 145–58.

238 Eagleton, *Illusions of Postmodernism*, p. 64. For a dose of the real thing, see Jean Baudrillard, *Simulacra and Simulation* (Ann Arbor: University of Michigan Press, 1995).

239 Gerald Vizenor, *The Trickster of Liberty: Tribal Heirs to a Wild Baronage* (Minneapolis: University of Minnesota Press, 1988) p. 3. Also see Homi K. Bhabha, "Of mimicry and man: The ambivalence of colonial discourse," in his *Location of Culture*, pp. 85–92.

240 See, e.g., Gayatri Chakravorty Spivak, "The Post-modern Condition: The End of Politics?" in her *The Post-Colonial Critic: Interviews, Strategies, Dialogues* (New York: Routledge, 1990) pp. 17–34. Also see the essays collected in Andrew Ross, ed., *Universal Abandon? The Politics of Postmodernism* (Minneapolis: University of Minnesota Press, 1988). The implications are brought out rather sharply in Terry Eagleton's observation that the "belief that values are constructed, inherently variable and inherently revisable has much to recommend it, though it fares rather better with Gorky than it does with genocide." Eagleton, *Illusions of Postmodernism*, p. 97.

241 Homi K. Bhabha, "DissimiNation: Time, narrative and the margins of the modern nation," in his *Location of Culture*, p. 145.

242 See, e.g., Homi K. Bhabha, "The postcolonial and the postmodern: The question of agency," in *Location of Culture*, pp. 171–97.

243 Ahmad, *In Theory*, pp. 68–69. Benita Parry makes much the same point in her "Signs of Our Times: A Discussion of Homi Bhabha's *The Location of Culture*," *Third Text*, Nos. 28–29 (1994) pp. 5–24.

244 Moore-Gilbert, *Postcolonial Theory*, p. 138. The assessment pertains directly to Bhabha's (mis)reading of Frantz Fanon, most notably in his "Interrogating identity: Frantz Fanon and the postcolonial prerogative" (*Location of Culture*, pp. 40–65) and "Remembering Fanon: Self, Psyche, and the Colonial Condition" (in Gibson, *Rethinking Fanon*, pp. 179–98). For further critique, see Neil Lazarus, "Disavowing Decolonization: Fanon, Nationalism, and the Problematic of Representation in Current Theories of Colonial Discourse," *Research in African Literatures*, Vol. 24, No. 2 (1993) pp. 69–97; Quadric Robinson, "The Appropriation of Frantz Fanon," *Race and Class*, Vol. 35, No. 1 (1993) pp. 79–91.

245 Eagleton, *Illusions of Postmodernism*, pp. 105, 120, 132. Very similar characterizations are advanced with respect to postcolonialism in Ahmad's *In Theory*, Dirlik's *Postcolonial Aura*, Spivak's *Critique of Postcolonial Reason*, and Abdul R. JanMohamed's "Worldliness-without-World, Homelessness-as-Home: Toward a Definition of the

Specular Border Intellectual," in Michael Sprinker, ed., *Edward Said: A Critical Reader* (London: Blackwell, 1992) pp. 96–120.

246 Eagleton, *Illusions of Postmodernism*, p. 122. Much the same criticism is advanced by Vicki Coppock, Deena Hayon, and Ingrid Richter in their *The Illusions of Post-Feminism: New Women/Old Myths* (London: Taylor and Francis, 1995).

247 The phrase is of course taken from Zavarzadeh's *Post-Ality*.

248 The confluence is exemplified in Slavoj Žižek's essay "Class Struggle or Postmodernism? Yes, please!" in Judith Butler, Ernesto Laclau, and Slavoj Žižek, *Contingency, Hegemony, Universality: Contemporary Dialogues on the Left* (London: Verso, 2000) pp. 90–135.

249 This is said despite the best efforts of Stanley Aronowitz, Henry Giroux, Peter McLaren and others to achieve an "organic" or "grassroots" version of postmodernism which might lend itself to genuinely liberatory pursuits. See, as examples, Stanley Aronowitz and Henry Giroux, *Postmodern Education* (Minneapolis: University of Minnesota Press, 1991); Peter McLaren, *Critical Pedagogy and Predatory Culture: Oppositional Politics in a Postmodern Era* (New York: Routledge, 1995); Gustavo Esteva and Madhu Suri Prakash, *Grassroots Postmodernism: Remaking the Soil of Cultures* (London: Zed Books, 1998).

250 This is not to argue that neocolonialism does not exist, or that it is unworthy of study/address, but simply that conflating it with the ongoing internal colonization of indigenous peoples—as postcolonialists habitually do—is deforming of both concepts. See, e.g., Moore-Gilbert, *Postcolonial Theory*. pp. 30–31. On the distinction which should be drawn between "neo" and internal colonial modes, see Kwame Nkrumah, *Neo-Colonialism: The Highest Stage of Imperialism* (New York: Monthly Review Press, 1967); Michael Hector, *Internal Colonialism: The Celtic Fringe in British National Development, 1536–1966* (Berkeley: University of California Press, 1975).

251 Jean-Paul Sartre, "On Genocide," in John Duffett, ed., *Against the Crime of Silence: Proceedings of the Russell International War Crimes Tribunal* (New York: O'Hare Books, 1968) pp. 612–26; reprinted in Jean-Paul Sartre and Arlette El Kaim-Sartre, *On Genocide and a Summary of the Evidence and Judgments of the International War Crimes Tribunal* (Boston: Beacon Press, 1968) pp. 57–85.

252 See Sartre, "Introduction to Memmi," p. 51.

253 Ngugi wa Thiong'o, *Decolonising the Mind: The Politics of Language in African Literature* (Oxford, UK: James Curry, 1986).

254 See, e.g., Julian Henriques, Wendy Holloway, Cathy Urwin, Couze Venn, and Valerie Walkerdine, *Changing the Subject: Psychology, Social Regulation and Subjectivity* (London: Routledge, [2nd ed.] 1998).

255 "It is interesting to note that at the very moment when celebrated Euro-American cultural theorists have pronounced the collapse of 'grand narratives' the expressive culture of [the] black poor is dominated by the need to construct them as narratives of redemption and emancipation." Paul Gilroy, "One Nation Under the Groove: The Cultural Politics of 'Race' and Representation in Britain," in David Theo Goldberg, ed., *Anatomy of Racism* (Minneapolis: University of Minnesota Press, 1990) p. 278. On the idea that grand narratives can serve liberatory as well as hegemonic purposes, see Patrick Taylor, *The Narrative of Liberation: Perspectives on Afro-Caribbean Literature, Popular Culture, and Politics* (Ithaca, NY: Cornell University Press, 1989); Mario Sáenz, "Memory, Enchantment and Salvation: Latin American Philosophies of Liberation and Salvation," *Philosophy and Social Criticism*, Vol. 17, No. 2 (1991) pp. 149–73.

256   To appreciate the depth of the relationship between the two, it is useful to juxtapose major contemporaneous texts describing each, e.g.: Albert Szymanski's *The Logic of Imperialism* (New York: Praeger, 1981) to Richard Falk's *Predatory Globalization: A Critique* (Cambridge, UK: Polity Press, 1999).

257   Kwame Nkrumah, *Consciencism: Philosophy and Ideology for Decolonization* (New York: Monthly Review Press, 1970); Amílcar Cabral, *Revolution in Guinea* (New York: Monthly Review Press, 1969). Also see Julius K. Nyerere, *Freedom and Unity: Uhuru Na Umoja* (Washington, DC: Africa House, 1973).

258   Frantz Fanon, *The Wretched of the Earth* (New York: Grove Press, 1963); *A Dying Colonialism* (New York: Grove Press, 1965); *Black Skin, White Masks* (New York: Grove Press, 1965); *Toward the African Revolution* (New York: Grove Press, 1967). Albert Memmi, *The Colonizer and the Colonized* (New York: Orion, 1965); *Dominated Man* (New York: Orion, 1968).

259   Peter Worsley, *The Third World* (London: Weidenfeld & Nicholson, [2nd. ed.] 1967); Heydar Reghaby, ed., *Philosophy of the Third World* (Davis, CA: D-Q University Press, 1974).

260   George Manuel and Michael Posluns, *The Fourth World: An Indian Reality* (New York: Free Press, 1974). On the fundamental nature of these conflicts, see Glenn T. Morris' and my essay, "Between a Rock and a Hard Place: Left-Wing Revolution, Right-Wing Reaction, and the Destruction of Indigenous Peoples," in my *Since Predator Came: Notes on the Struggle for American Indian Liberation* (Littleton, CO: Aigis, 1995) pp. 329–48; Bernard Neitschmann, "The Fourth World: Nations versus States," in George J. Demko and William B. Wood, eds., *Reordering the World: Geopolitical Perspectives on the Twenty-First Century* (Boulder, CO: Westview Press, 1994) pp. 225–42.

261   See the essay entitled "I Am Indigenist: Notes on the Ideology of the Fourth World," in my *Struggle for the Land*, pp. 367–402. Also see Guillermo Bonfil Batalla, *Utopia y Revolución: El Pensamiento Político Contemporáneo de los Indios en América Latina* (Mexico City: Editorial Nueva Imagen, 1981).

262   The Gramscian concept of internal colonialism was adapted by at least some members of the CPUSA during the 1930s to describe the situation of rural blacks in the Deep South, although the Party was largely resistant to the framing and repudiated it altogether after World War II. The idea was, however, forcefully revived by black liberationists like Stokely Carmichael during the mid-1960s, and formed the analytical bedrock of the Black Panther Party by the end of the decade. It may be, however, that James Boggs should be credited with the clearest and most comprehensive articulation of the idea in relation to peoples of color in the U.S. See Harry Haywood, *Black Bolshevik: The Autobiography of an Afro-American Communist* (Chicago: Liberator Press, 1978) pp. 322–23, 551–54; Stokely Carmichael and Charles V. Hamilton, *Black Power: The Politics of Liberation in America* (New York: Random House, 1967) pp. 2–32; Huey P. Newton, "Speech Delivered at Boston College, November 18, 1970," in *To Die for the People: The Writings of Huey P. Newton* (New York: Random House, 1972) pp. 20–38; James Boggs, *Racism and Class Struggle: Further Pages from a Black Worker's Notebook* (New York: Monthly Review Press, 1971).

263   See, e.g., Rodolfo Acuña, *Occupied America: The Chicano's Struggle Toward Liberation* (San Francisco: Canfield Press, 1972) esp. pp. 3–5, 222–77. Also see Mario Barrera, Carlos Muñoz, and Charles Ornelas, "The Barrio as an Internal Colony," *Urban Affairs Annual Reviews*, Vol. 6 (1972) pp. 565–98 (also included in Harlan Hahn, ed., *People and Politics in Urban Society* [Beverly Hills, CA: Sage, 1972] pp. 465–78; F. Chris Garcia, ed., *La Causa Política: A Chicano Politics Reader* [Notre Dame, IN: Notre Dame

University Press, 1974] pp. 281–301); and Guillermo Flores, "Race and Culture in the Internal Colony: Keeping the Chicano in His Place," in Frank Bonilla and Robert Girling, eds., *Structures of Dependency* (Palo Alto, CA: Stanford University Press, 1973) pp. 189–95.

264 It should be remembered that degraded socioeconomic status was once assigned certain groups within the settler populace itself, largely on the basis of their being perceived by the Angloamerican racial élite as "colored." See Noel Ignatiev, *How the Irish Became White* (New York: Routledge, 1995) and Matthew Frye Jacobson, *Whiteness of a Different Color: European Immigrants and the Alchemy of Race* (Cambridge, MA: Harvard University Press, 1998). The result, especially for those such as the Irish and Scots-Irish colonized at home, the result has been outright colonization in the New World as well. See Helen M. Lewis, Linda Johnson, and Donald Askins, eds., *Colonialism in Modern America: The Appalachian Case* (Boone, NC: Appalachian Consortium Press, 1978); Ada F. Haynes, *Poverty in Appalachia: Underdevelopment and Exploitation* (New York: Garland, 1996).

265 "The idea of a master narrative's 'phallic trajectory' into the telos of historical destiny needs to be discredited, yet the idea of totality as a heterogeneous and not homogeneous temporality must be recuperated." Peter McLaren, "Multiculturalism and the Postmodern Critique: Towards a Pedagogy of Resistance and Transformation," in Giroux and McLaren, *Between Borders*, p. 210.

266 See, e.g., David Horowitz, *Hating Whitey and Other Progressive Causes* (Los Angeles: Spense, 2000).

267 "The flip side of the tyranny of the whole is the tyranny of the fragment . . . [W]ithout some positive and normative concept of totality to counter-balance the poststructuralist/postmodern emphasis on difference and discontinuity, we are abandoned to the seriality of pluralist individualism and the supremacy of [those capitalist] competitive values" that have begotten the world we now inhabit. Steven Best, "Jameson, Totality and Post-Structuralist Critique," in Doug Kellner, ed., *Postmodernism/Jameson/ Critique* (Washington, DC: Maisonneuve, 1989) p. 361.

268 There has been a veritable torrent of drivel over the past twenty years—that is, since the success of Third Worldism in vanquishing the classic form of European imperialism—about how "inappropriate" the ideology was, and how its supposed defects have led to the "historic defeat of socialism." Such criticisms have ranged from contentions that the "sexism" inherent to the Third Worldist perspective paved the way for the rise of Islamic fundamentalism in the newly decolonized states to claims that decolonization leads inevitably to outbreaks of industrial capitalism and similar maladies. The questions always evaded in these critiques is, to quote Terry Eagleton, "what if this 'defeat' never happened in the first place? What if [the appearance to the contrary results mainly from] a gradual failure of nerve, a creeping paralysis" preventing those who now condemn Third Worldism—especially self-interested First World critics—from following through its liberatory potentials; Eagleton, *Illusions of Postmodernism*, p. 19. For representative critiques, see Nigel Harris, *The End of the Third World: Newly Industrializing Countries and the Decline of an Ideology* (New York: New Amsterdam Books, 1990) and Robert Malley, *The Call from Algeria: Third Worldism, Revolution, and the Return to Islam* (Berkeley: University of California Press, 1996).

269 On the conception of a "Fanonist pedagogy"—an idea entirely consistent with those referenced in notes 23, 29, and 32—see Kenneth Mostern, "Decolonization

as Learning: Practice and Pedagogy in Frantz Fanon's Revolutionary Narrative," in Giroux and McLaren, *Between Borders*, pp. 251–71

270 McLaren, "Multiculturalism and Postmodern Critique," p. 218. This would seem quite commensurate with Catherine Clément's staid but much better-known axiom that one must first "change the imaginary in order to act on the real." Quoted in Spivak, "French Feminism," p. 145.

271 Karl Marx, *The German Ideology* (New York: New World, 1963) p. 197.

272 "But what if the [colonized] asserts himself as a [human being], as the colonist's equal? Well, then, the colonist is wounded in his very being; he feels diminished, devalued: he not only sees the economic consequences of the accession of 'wogs' to the world of human beings, he also loathes it because of his personal decline. In his rage, he sometimes dreams of genocide." Jean-Paul Sartre, "A Victory," in his *Colonialism and Neocolonialism*, pp. 75–76.

ELEVEN

Distorted Images and Literary Appropriations

Gretchen Bataille's *Native American Representations*

That colonizing societies invariably produce self-serving (mis)representations of the "Others" they colonize has long been a theoretical commonplace. That such deliberate distortions of reality serve to dehumanize the colonially subjugated, rationalizing thereby the system of colonial domination and licensing the colonizers—in their own minds, at least—to indulge in whatever range of exploitative practices they desire, without regard to the well-being—or even survival—of the colonized, is by now equally well understood. Indeed, it has been pointed out that imposition of colonial order quite literally *requires* demolition of autochthonous existence among the colonized. Thus do we encounter Sartre's 1967 equation of colonialism to genocide.[1]

While a great deal of work has been done since publication of Edward Said's *Orientalism* with respect to the psychointellectual/literary "othering" at work within classic imperial processes,[2] these have been undertaken from an all but exclusively "postcolonialist" perspective and have therefore focused upon the Third World contexts of Africa, Asia, and, to a significantly lesser extent, Iberoamerica. Comparatively little emphasis has been placed on North America—or places like Australia and New Zealand—in this connection, and almost none upon the planetary array of indigenous peoples composing what has been aptly referred to as a "Fourth" or "Host" World.[3]

Originally published in *Pacific Historical Review*, Vol. 79, No. 4 (Winter 2002). The book reviewed is Gretchen M. Bataille, ed., *Native American Representations: First Encounters, Distorted Images, and Literary Appropriations* (Lincoln: University of Nebraska Press, 2001). Annotation has been added.

The latter term seems especially appropriate insofar as each of the other three "worlds" have of necessity constructed themselves squarely atop the fourth. It follows that worlds one-through-three can be sustained only through exercise of a perpetual and "internal" sort of colonial dominion over the native peoples they've subsumed. This is the bedrock sociopolitical/economic arrangement defining not only settler states like the U.S. and Canada,[4] but also such ostensibly decolonized Third World countries as India, Nigeria, and Brazil, each of whose borders were originally fixed by Europe's imperial powers, and whose ongoing territorial integrity is entirely contingent upon usurpation/dispossession of the indigenous nations situated therein.[5] The same can be said of nominally "anti-imperialist" Second World configurations like Vietnam and the People's Republic of China.[6]

In substance, while decolonization has yet to be seriously attempted in any First World settler state, it remains for the most part dramatically incomplete throughout the second and third worlds, where colonialism did not so much "end" as it *changed form* because of the multitudinous "national liberation struggles" carried out from 1945 to 1975.[7] Viewed from this perspective, notions of "postcoloniality" are truly insidious. In consigning colonialism itself to the past tense—that is, of denying its contemporary existence and consequent relevance—"postcolonial discourse" is not simply misguided or inappropriate (much less, "liberatory"). Rather, its function is hegemonic, reinforcing the conceptual apparatus by which colonialism in its present form(s) is naturalized and thus legitimated.[8]

The implications of all this in terms of representation are profound. Fortunately, a relative handful of activist/scholars—most but by no means all of whom are themselves "Fourth Worlders"—have lately begun to confront the matter head on. One of the better and more recent contributions to this emergent genre is *Native American Representations*, a slim and well-edited volume, put together by Gretchen Bataille and collecting ten papers prepared for a 1997 symposium in France. Although all the material assembled therein is solid and well worth reading, the book's cardinal virtue is its inclusion of Louis Owens' "As If an Indian Were Really an Indian: Native Voices and Postcolonial Theory" (pp. 11–24), a brief but extraordinarily impactful essay which seems likely to place its author's eventual influence alongside that of Fanon and the early Memmi.[9]

A word of advice should be extended by way of conclusion. The field in which *Native American Representations* finds its place is new, the attendant background scholarship requisite to appreciating certain of its nuances correspondingly little-known. Those ungrounded in its subject matter would thus do well not to expect it to stand on its own. "Beginners" might best approach the book in conjunction with several others, notably Jimmie Durham's *A Certain Lack of Coherence* (Kala, 1993), Arif Dirlik's *The Postcolonial Aura* (Westview, 1997), my own *Fantasies of the Master Race* (City Lights, 1998), and Linda Tuhiwai Smith's *Decolonizing Methodologies* (Zed, 2001). That said, *Native American Representations* is wholeheartedly recommended.

Notes

1 Published as "On Genocide" in John Duffett, ed., *Against the Crime of Silence: Proceedings of the Russell International War Crimes Tribunal* (New York: O'Hare Books, 1968) pp. 612–26.

2 Edward Said, *Orientalism* (New York: Macmillan, 1978).

3 For use of the terms in quotes, see George Manuel with Michael Posluns, *The Fourth World: An Indian Reality* (New York: Macmillan, 1974) and Winona LaDuke, "Natural to Synthetic and Back Again," in Ward Churchill, ed., *Marxism and Native Americans* (Boston: South End Press, 1983) p. vii.

4 See, e.g., "The Indigenous Peoples of North America: A Struggle Against Internal Colonialism," the introductory essay in my *Struggle for the Land: Native North American Resistance to Genocide, Ecocide and Colonization* (San Francisco: City Lights, [2nd ed.] 2002) pp. 15–33.

5 For an excellent survey, see International Commission on International Humanitarian Issues, *Indigenous Peoples: A Global Quest for Justice* (London: Zed Books, 1987). Also see Bernard Nietschmann, "The Fourth World: Nations versus States," in George J. Demko and William B. Wood, eds., *Reordering the World: Geopolitical Perspectives for the 21st Century* (Boulder, CO: Westview Press, 1994) pp. 225–42.

6 See Walker Connor, *The National Question in Marxist-Leninist Theory and Strategy* (Princeton, NJ: Princeton University Press, 1984); on China, see pp. 67–100, 322–29, 407–30.

7 One will search in vain for anything resembling an acknowledgement of indigenous rights in such influential collections of the period as Norman Miller's and Roderick Aya's coedited *National Liberation: Revolution in the Third World* (New York: Free Press, 1971) and John Gerassi's *The Coming of the New International: A Revolutionary Anthology* (New York: World, 1971).

8 For a concise but blistering critique, see Ella Shohat, "Notes on the Post-Colonial," in Padmini Mongia, ed., *Contemporary Postcolonial Theory: A Reader* (London/New York: Arnold/Oxford University Press, 1997) pp. 321–34.

9 Tragically, Owens' immense potential was foreclosed almost before this was written. Increasingly depressed by a concerted effort to discredit his Choctaw/Cherokee identity undertaken by an array of essentialist "Nickel Indians" like Elizabeth Cook-Lynn, he committed suicide on July 25, 2002.

TWELVE

Finding a "Middle Place"?

Not in Joni Adamson's *American Indian Literature, Environmental Justice, and Ecocriticism*

This book promises much, but, in the end, delivers very little of value. This seems due, at least in large part, to the fact that its author, Arizona State University assistant professor Joni Adamson, doesn't appear to be especially conversant with—or is unwilling to honestly confront—either the literary or the activist contexts she purports to address. In either event, her focus in terms of literature is so constricted as to be distortive, all but nonexistent where the realities of activism are concerned. Overall, it seems as if she's done nothing so much as polish up the notes she uses to teach her precollegiate/lower division undergraduate literature and writing courses, added a few anecdotal observations about the teaching experience (e.g., pp. 89–93), then topped things off with a few observations contrasting the beauty of purple owl clover to the malignant townhouse sprawl of Tucson (e.g., pp. 5–6).

The result is confused, confusing, often trite, and always a very long way from the comprehensive examination of "how mainstream conceptions of 'wilderness' and 'nature' create blind spots in the environmental movement" Adamson says at the outset she'll deliver (p. xix). Less does she produce anything resembling a coherent articulation of how environmentalism might reconceptualize itself by assimilating American Indian understandings and priorities—a process she repeatedly refers to as establishing a "middle place" (e.g., p. xvii)—in order to foster "concrete social and environmental change" (p. xix). The scope of her textual analyses is so circumscribed that she fails as well in her stated goal of providing an "orientation to a literature that is more theoretically,

Originally published in *American Indian Culture and Research Journal*, Vol. 27, No. 1 (2003).

multiculturally, and ecologically informed" than that currently holding sway in mainstream circles (p. xx).

It's not that there are no bright spots. Adamson develops a decidedly partial but nonetheless rather well-honed description of the arrogance and flagrant racism infecting the outlook of the late Edward Abbey (see esp. p. 45). As an alternative—antidote?—she offers the vision of Acoma poet Simon J. Ortiz, presenting it with a wonderful blend of insight and sensitivity (pp. 51–76).[1] Yet it is in her juxtaposition of Abbey's work to that of Ortiz, where the biases and deficiencies with which Adamson's analytical approach is riddled can first be discerned. For starters, consideration of Abbey's writerly output does not go beyond the essays collected in *Desert Solitaire*—the man published two dozen other books, after all[2]—while a much broader range of Ortiz's material is referenced. And, while pains are taken to situate Ortiz's holistic thinking on the relationality of humans and nature squarely within his own people's spiritual tradition, that of Abbey is treated much more ambiguously, in a manner concerned with his attitudes rather than their source.

The disparity seems initially quite peculiar, since the archetype upon which Abbey bases his perception of the separation of humanity from nature is hardly obscure. On the contrary, it will be found on the very first page of Genesis and is shared to one or another extent by virtually everyone raised in a Judeo-Christian society. This last perhaps accounts for Adamson's unbalanced handling of the two writers. Acknowledging the true magnitude, character, and sociocultural implications of the conceptual gulf dividing Abbey's standpoint from Ortiz's would have in a sense been self-defeating for her, devoted as she is to an "I'm OK, you're OK" sort of multiculturalism in which all points of view can be reconciled merely by "communicating," adopting "appropriate reading strategies," and attaining thereby an "intercultural understanding" that converts "contested terrain [into] common ground" (pp. xvii–xviii, xix).

Small wonder the author omits mentioning the markedly different conclusions reached by American Indian Movement leader Russell Means in his much-reprinted essay "For the World to Live, Europe Must Die: Fighting Words on the Future of Mother Earth" (appended to his autobiographical *Where White Men Fear to Tread*).[3] The fact is that AIM itself is mentioned nowhere in Adamson's book. Nor, despite their obvious centrality to her topic, is any other American Indian activist group aside from the Dineh Alliance (pp. 32, 52, 74, 76–77, 129). Instead, readers are offered lengthy elaborations upon the fictionalized hypotheses advanced by several nonactivist native authors about how social and environmental movements "should" be organized—crossculturally, of course—as if they'd thereby invented the political equivalent of a wheel (see, e.g., pp. 85, 175–77).

Utterly eclipsed in Adamson's rendering is the fact that a number of important indigenous activist/writers—Means, not least, but also the poet/recording artist John Trudell, activist poet/essayist/conceptual artist Jimmie Durham, and a score of others—have struggled valiantly to translate such ideas into practice, thus equipping themselves with a far greater wealth of insight and experience in these matters than any of the writers the author selected to represent Native North America (the sole exception is Winona LaDuke, mentioned in passing on p. 129).

There is either a woeful ignorance of indigenous politics at work here, or Adamson's is an exercise in deliberate obfuscation. A clear indication as to which can be gleaned from her tendency to deal with environmental activism in much the same way she does the Indian variety. On this front, only organizations like the Sierra Club and the Environmental Defense Fund are mentioned (pp. 25, 77). Although both groups certainly qualify as "mainstream," they share little in common with the brand of radicalism inspired by Adamson's exemplar of environmentalist literature, Edward Abbey. Here, the motive underlying the author's narrowness of focus is again obvious. Had she cast even a sidelong glance at Abbey's other books—far and away the most influential of which is The Monkey Wrench Gang[4]—reference to Earth First!, whose "rednecks for the wilderness" unquestionably comprise the most "Abbeyist" of all environmentalist groups, would have been unavoidable.[5]

Bringing up Earth First!, however, would have necessitated Adamson's departing from the sharply constricted—sanitized?—literary axis by which she represents environmentalism—a line running from John James Audubon through John Muir and ending in the Abbey of Desert Solitaire—to deal with the likes of Dave Foreman and "Miss Anthropy" himself, Christopher Manes.[6] This, in turn, would have compelled her to confront the implications of Abbeyism, not merely in terms of its instigator's personally privileged arrogance, but in its more significant relationship to what Janet Biehl and Peter Staudenmaier have called "ecofascism."[7] On that basis, Adamson might have positioned herself to accord their proper meanings to such virulent Abbeyist manifestations of anti-Indianism as former Greenpeace hanger-on Paul Watson's ongoing campaign against the resumption of traditional Makah whaling.[8]

As with the earlier-mentioned "man in nature vs. man apart from nature" dichotomy, fascism and antifascism form a far more deep-set and intractable polarity than Adamson is willing to admit, since it is not in the least susceptible to being "reconciled" through a process of "communication," intercultural or otherwise (Watson, in fact, can lay claim to being something of a media expert). In such circumstances, as Means' neglected essay points out, "healing" can begin only when the negative pole has been eliminated. Adamson's response to this inconvenient reality is consistent: she simply ignores it, leaving the Abbeyist variant of Earth First! as unmentioned as she did AIM.

Indeed, her depiction of environmental politics is so vacuous that it misses altogether the ascendance within Earth First! itself, beginning in the late 1980s, of a faction associated with the late Judi Bari which ultimately supplanted hardline Abbeyism in favor of something more nearly resembling the multiculturalist stance the author advocates. At a more purely textual level, Adamson bandies about terms like "environmental racism" (pp. xv–xvi, 76, 132, 168, 175) without ever referencing such cornerstone works on the topic as Robert D. Bullard's *Confronting Environmental Racism* and Al Gedicks' *The New Resource Wars*,[9] or key thinkers like Vandana Shiva and Kirkpatrick Sale.[10]

On the whole, the sheer detachment of Adamson's book from the movement it purports to inform militates strongly against its utility in instructional settings. This includes the localized contexts she—without so much as a hint that the late Paulo Freire, among others, made the same case more than thirty years ago[11]—quite correctly insists are most appropriate to learning (pp. 93–97, 112–15). Similarly, the intercultural methodology she calls for (pp. 97–101), has been described elsewhere, and far more thoroughly, by educational theorists like Henry Giroux and Peter McLaren.[12] Moreover, the not infrequent shots Adamson aims at the vanities of scientism are taken with no reference to writers like Vine Deloria Jr., who refined the very critique she deploys.[13] Without seeking to "valorize academicism" (pp. 93, 96), it seems fair to observe that attribution is not the least important obligation attending scholarship.

A fundamental problem with her material is that even when Adamson is doing what she presumably does best—literary criticism—the bulk of her effort is bound up in explaining what the native writers she treats have already explained by virtue of writing their poems and novels. If "ecocritism" is to serve a useful purpose, it will be in connecting the views expressed through fiction to those articulated in nonfiction and, more importantly, to tangible political phenomena Adamson conspicuously avoids. In fact, she resolutely refuses even to get the first part right. By inserting herself into the native fictive discourse in the hallowed role of "interpreter"—otherwise known as the "Great White Expert"—she substitutes her own voice for those of the authors she "analyzes," thus duplicating a transgression she rightly ascribes to Edward Abbey (p. 45).

The outcome, given all that has been said above, is predictable. While claiming to gaze, along with Muscogee poet Joy Harjo, into "the terrifying abyss of genocide and loss" (pp. 124–27, 165), for example, Adamson somehow manages to conclude—as Harjo neither would nor could— that a viable resistance strategy may be discerned in training Navajo teenagers to work for the Peabody Coal Company (pp. 49–50).[14] That this is roughly the equivalent of arguing that an appropriate response to the nazi genocide might have been for Jews to seek employment with I.G. Farben seems not to have occurred to her,[15] a matter demonstrating rather graphically the extent to which she is often divorced from the meaning of her own words.

A still more egregious abuse of her sources will be found in Adamson's spending two full chapters "embracing" Leslie Marmon Silko's *Almanac of the Dead* (pp. 128–79),[16] with all its elaborate explication of the theme that armed insurrection is increasingly a liberatory imperative, only to conclude that the appearance of "gun control [as] a 'hot-button' issue" in American electoral politics is one of the most "promising" developments in recent memory (pp. 178–79). This, after a section wherein the virtues of the continuing struggle waged by the EZLN in Chiapas have been extolled at length, albeit, and tellingly, Adamson endeavors to assign the Zapatistas' success more or less strictly to their innovative use of communications technology rather than weaponry (pp. 126–38). Suffice it here to observe—as is made clear in every study of the Chiapas uprising published to date, *none* of them cited by Adamson—that without their initial resort to arms, the subsequent dexterity with which the Zapatistas have availed themselves of the internet would be irrelevant.[17]

American Indian Literature, Environmental Justice, and Ecocriticism is studded with comparable inversions of both fact and indigenous sensibility. Adamson's performance reeks of the NIMBY mentality—a perverse form of American exceptionalism manifested through insistence that the harsh requirements of revolutionary social change are applicable everywhere but here, in the proverbial belly of the beast— for which liberal euroamericans have been long and deservedly notorious. Ultimately, the transparently co-optive nature of her "interpretive" process, if it may be called that, is intellectually integral to the "neocolonial alchemy" Eduardo Galeano once described in its more material dimension as embodying a figurative transformation of "gold into scrap metal."[18] Her book thus fulfills a function diametrically opposed to its author's pretensions, reinforcing and in palpable ways completing the hegemony it ostensibly rejects.

A volume of the sort Joni Adamson says in her introduction she's written is very much needed. Hopefully, someone adequate to the task will shortly undertake to write it. If so, they can use hers as a classic model of how *not* to proceed.

Notes

1   For an excellent sample of Ortiz's work, see his *Woven Stone* (Tucson: University of Arizona Press, 1992), which collects three earlier volumes of his poetry.

2   Edward Abbey, *Desert Solitaire: A Season in the Wilderness* (New York: McGraw-Hill, 1968). For background on the man and his writing, see James M. Calahan, *Edward Abbey: A Life* (Tucson: University of Arizona Press, 2003)

3   Russell Means with Marvin J. Wolf, *Where White Men Fear to Tread: The Autobiography of Russell Means* (New York: St. Martin's Press, 1995) pp. 545–54.

4   Edward Abbey, *The Monkey Wrench Gang* (New York: Avon Books, 1976).

5   See Susan Zakin, *Coyotes and Town Dogs: Earth First! and the Environmental Movement* (New York: Viking Press, 1993).

6   See, e.g., Dave Foreman, *Confessions of an Eco-Warrior* (New York: Harmony Books, 1991); Christopher Manes, *Green Rage: Radical Environmentalism and the Unmaking of Civilization* (Boston: Little. Brown, 1990).

7   Janet Biehl and Peter Staudenmaier, *Ecofascism: Lessons from the German Experience* (Oakland: AK Press, 1995).

8   See, e.g., Jim Page, "Captain Misanthrope and the Great White Supremacist," *Dark Night Press* (September 25, 2000; available at http://www.darknightpress.org/).

9   Robert D. Bullard, ed., *Confronting Environmental Racism: Voices from the Grassroots* (Cambridge, MA: South End Press, 1999); Al Gedicks, *The New Resource Wars* (Montréal: Black Rose Books, 1994).

10   For specific examples of what I had in mind, see Vandana Shiva, *Monocultures of the Mind: Perspectives on Biodiversity and Biotechnology* (London: Zed Books, 1993); Kirkpatrick Sale, *Dwellers in the Land: The Bioregional Vision* (New York: Random House, 1985).

11   I was specifically thinking of Freire's celebrated *Pedagogy of the Oppressed* (New York: Continuum, 1970), but was also influenced by the broader assessments offered by the essays included in Peter McLaren's and Colin Lankshire's coedited *Politics of Liberation: Paths from Freire* (New York: Routledge, 1994) and Peter Mayos' *Gramsci, Freire and Adult Education: Possibilities for Transformative Action* (London: Zed Books, 1999).

12   I was undoubtedly thinking of Giroux's *Border Crossings: Cultural Workers and the Politics of Education* (New York: Routledge, 1992) and McLaren's *Critical Pedagogy and Predatory Culture* (New York: Routledge, 1995), as well as their coedited *Between Borders: Pedagogy and the Politics of Cultural Studies* (New York: Routledge, 1993).

13   See my essay, "Contours of Enlightenment," included herein.

14   Peabody's desire to greatly expand its Kayenta coal stripping operation on Black Mesa was the precipitating factor in the forced removal of more than 13,000

traditional Diné (Navajos) from the Big Mountain area of the so-called Navajo-Hopi Joint Use Area in northern Arizona during the 1980s and '90s. See "Genocide in Arizona: The 'Navajo-Hopi Land Dispute' in Perspective," in my *Struggle for the Land: Native North American Resistance to Genocide, Ecocide, and Colonization* (San Francisco: City Lights, [2nd ed.] 2002) pp. 135–72. Also see Thayer Scudder, *No Place to Go: Effects of Compulsory Relocation on Navajos* (Philadelphia: Institute for the Study of Human Issues, 1982).

15   Among other things, the I.G. Farben chemical cartel manufactured the Zyklon B pesticide used in the gas chambers at Auschwitz-Birkenau, Sobibór, Treblinka, Chelmno, and other nazi extermination facilities, and employed more than 80,000 slave laborers in its Buna Werke, a massive factory producing synthetic oil and rubber at the Auschwitz III-Monowitz concentration camp. See generally Joseph Borkin, *The Crime and Punishment of I.G. Farben* (New York: Free Press, 1978).

16   Leslie Marmon Silko, *Almanac of the Dead* (New York: Simon and Schuster, 1991).

17   See John Ross, *Rebellion from the Roots: Indian Uprising in Chiapas* (Monroe, ME: Common Courage Press, 1994) and *The War Against Oblivion: The Zapatista Chronicles* (Monroe, ME: Common Courage Press, 2002).

18   Eduardo Galeano, *Open Veins of Latin America: Five Centuries of the Pillage of a Continent* (New York: Monthly Review Press, 1973) p. 12.

THIRTEEN

Kizhiibaabinesik

A Bright Star, Burning Briefly

> For this loss I could not speak,
> The tongue lay idle in a great darkness,
> The heart was strangely open,
> The moon had gone,
> And it was then
> When I said, "She is no longer here,"
> That the night put its arms around me
> And all the white stars turned bitter with grief.
> —David Whyte

Let it be said, first of all, that I don't write on personal themes. It's not a form to which I'm accustomed, to which I've aspired, with which I've ever been the least comfortable. This is all the more true in the present instance, devolving as it does on the destruction and death of my wife, my chosen one, the person who, in her very presence, afforded me a sense of direction, fulfillment, and completeness I'd neither known nor believed possible. She was my lover, yes, in every nuance of the term, my best friend, my partner, my ally, my teacher, my student, the only woman to whom I'd ever been entirely faithful, the confidant with whom alone I shared my innermost hopes, dreams, and fears. Her passing, and perhaps more particularly the manner in which it occurred, left a crater in my soul a million miles wide and infinitely deep.

I've long since come to realize that there are no words with which to truly describe the barren place in which it left me, or at least none that I

Originally published as the preface to Leah Renae Kelly, *In My Own Voice: Explorations in the Sociopolitical Context of Art and Cinema* (Winnipeg: Arbeiter Ring, 2001).

possess. The facts of my pain are too immense, too close, to be conveyed by vernacular expressions of shock, emptiness, and grieving. To say that I mourn her, will *always* mourn her, is to speak the truth. Yet, speaking thus is at most levels a mere indulgence, saying nothing of consequence or value. Whatever the scale of my anguish, its real measure can never be found within me. What was lost was, after all, vastly more decisive for her than me, no matter how tightly I was and will always remain bound to her. In ways both tangible and not, moreover, hers is a loss shared by everyone, without exception, irrespective of whether they know or are willing to admit it. Anything I might have to offer will come only in an effort to explain, however clumsily and imperfectly, why the latter is so.

Leah Renae Kelly was not simply an "inebriated pedestrian killed by [a] car," as the local newspaper so casually remarked on the date she died. There were reasons why that young, beautiful, incredibly promising, and catastrophically drunk Ojibwe woman was running barefooted down the middle of the road that night. Whether she thought she was running away from something, toward something else, or whether she was capable of thinking anything at all in that moment, are things beyond my power of knowing. In a larger sense, however, I do know why she was drunk, why she *was* a drunk, and therefore why things ended for her as they did. From there, I cannot avoid the meaning of it all. Leah's is the quintessential story of contemporary North America. It is thus ours, each of us, to the extent that we live on this continent. From this, squirm as one might, there is, can be, no escape.

The essential elements of Leah's story emerge from the realities of her identity as an American Indian and, consequently, the nature of her life and sense of self. Inevitably, these take shape only within the framework of such considerations for Native North Americans more generally. And, with equal certainty, this cannot be understood apart from the structural relationship presently existing between the continent's immigrant (settler) society and the peoples indigenous to what many of us call Turtle Island. It follows that an honest accounting must be made of the flows of impact and benefit involved, as well as an unequivocal repudiation of the elaborate veils of evasion and denial behind which such unpleasantries are habitually concealed.

What Leah desired most—aside, perhaps, from the fleeting moments of happiness we spent together—was to "be somebody," to "count for something" beyond the immediacy of herself. This, she told me often, and with a yearning that quite literally broke my heart. No matter that she *was* in fact somebody, somebody very special, and that to me she counted for absolutely everything, I knew what she meant and why she meant it that way. To the extent that her suffering can now serve to illustrate and reveal the grinding horror that destroyed her, she will have in some way succeeded in her desire, claiming the dignity she was due all along from the very indignity forced upon her at the instant of her birth.

Would that Leah herself were still here to speak, firmly, in that fine voice she fought so hard to find, and which she was so well along in harnessing to the task she saw before her. Would that she were here, but she's not and can never be again. Hence, I must allow her to speak through me, or with me, in ways and words of which she might approve. Aware as I am of my limitations, I have ample reason for anxiety concerning my ability to do her story justice. Still, I know that I'm obliged to try. She would certainly expect it of me, and she is forever entitled to demand no less.

Nobody Loves a Drunken Indian

It should surprise no one that Leah might have ended her days an alcoholic. Liquor and other intoxicants, after all, replaced Gatling guns and smallpox as the greatest killers of native people during the twentieth century.[1] Long before the dawn of the new millennium, upward of half the continent's indigenous people were known to be suffering or recovering from the effects of acute alcoholism, while on some Canadian reserves—Alkali Lake, Grassy Narrows, Cross Lake, Norway House, and others—the tally included every adult.[2] Children, too, are afflicted, although their chosen substances run more toward gasoline, spray paint, and nail polish remover. Seventy percent of the youngsters in northern Manitoba were found to be addicted to such toxics by the mid-1980s. In some villages, it had become necessary to post guards outside implement buildings to prevent nine-year-olds from breaking in and sniffing gas or solvents, deliberately and permanently blotting out their consciousness through the resulting brain damage or death.[3]

The toll is everywhere apparent, evidenced not only along the skid rows of most North American cities but also in the disintegration of indigenous family structures and communities, sometimes whole societies.[4] Alcohol-related patterns of domestic violence, spousal abandonment, and child neglect or abuse, unheard of in traditional settings, have become endemic facts of contemporary native life.[5] Deaths from accidents and exposure, the great majority involving inebriation, have remained at catastrophic levels for decades.[6] So, too, deaths resulting from cirrhosis and other degenerative illnesses associated with chronic alcoholism.[7] Fetal alcohol syndrome (FAS), a condition permanently impairing the offspring of alcoholic mothers, embodies yet another crisis for native people.[8]

Physical debilitation accruing from chronic alcoholism also figures prominently in the abysmal picture painted by American Indian health data overall.[9] American Indians die from readily survivable maladies like flu and pneumonia at a rate three times the norm in both Canada and the U.S.[10] Nutrition-related illnesses, often associated with binge drinking, abound. Diabetes is "almost a plague," afflicting upward of half of native adults.[11] Death from tuberculosis occurs among Indians at a rate four times that of the general population;[12] hepatitis, eight times; strep infections, ten times; infant mortality, up to fourteen times; meningitis, twenty times; dysentery, a hundred times.[13] Rounding out the picture, "the suicide rate for Indian youths ranges from 1,000 to 10,000 [percent] higher than for non-Indian youths."[14]

The bottom line is that reservation-based aboriginal men experienced a life expectancy of less than 45 years, their female counterparts only three years longer in 1990. This, in the world's most advanced industrial countries, where "mainstream" women outstripped the 71.8 year average lifespans of males by nearly a decade.[15] Viewed from this standpoint, it can be asserted with an undeniable degree of accuracy that every time an Indian dies on a reservation, one-third of a lifetime has been lost. And, since the pattern is intergenerational, having lasted now for more than a century, the observation can be inverted with equal precision: each baby born on a reserve represents a third of a lifetime that will remain unlived. Nor, for our part, do urbanized natives fare appreciably better.[16]

So ubiquitous are the effects of alcohol among native people that a whole mythology of "drunken Indians" has been contrived by the interloping euroderivative settler society.[17] The centerpiece of this complex of fables, promoted by everyone from the "scientific community" to pseudoreligious "self-help groups" like Alcoholics Anonymous,[18] and internalized as an article of faith by many native people,[19] is the claim that "aboriginals" are "congenitally predisposed" to suffer the "disease" of alcoholism. No one bothers to explain why, if this were so, we'd suffer it at rates virtually identical to those evident among the Irish,[20] say, or the Scotch-Irish "hillbillies" of Appalachia, inner-city blacks, and the poorer sectors of the Angloamerican mainstream itself.[21] All told, there are some twenty million alcoholics in the United States, only a half-million of them native, and a similar proportionality prevails in Canada.[22]

In truth, there's never been a shred of credible evidence to support claims that alcoholism is "hereditary" or in any physiological sense a "disease."[23] On the contrary, there is every indication that such addictions are "normal" concomitants of poverty and feelings of powerlessness, irrespective of the racial/cultural pedigree of those afflicted.[24] Frantz Fanon, Albert Memmi, and others have further demonstrated that self-destructive pathologies like alcoholism correlate to conditions of colonial domination.[25] Such conclusions are validated by the fact that while "drunken Indians" and "drunken Irish" share virtually nothing in terms of peculiarities in our DNA, we have everything in common when it comes to experiencing the ravages of centuries-long colonization.

For Indians, this translates into dispossession of some 98 percent of our lands,[26] the balance—and the astonishing abundance of resources with which it is endowed—administered in a unilaterally imposed and permanent "trust status" by Canada and the United States.[27] Exercise of this self-assigned "plenary power" has enabled the settler governments to siphon the residual assets of native peoples into their own economies—paying less than a dime on the dollar of market royalty rates for minerals extracted, to offer but one example[28]—while leaving native peoples increasingly destitute. The upshot is that Indians, still in nominal possession of the largest per capita landholdings of any sector of the North American population, and thus potentially the wealthiest of all groups on an individual basis, experience the practical reality of being far and away the poorest.[29]

As the remnants of traditional subsistence economies have been ever more thoroughly undermined, the very survival of native people has been rendered increasingly dependent upon our ability to participate in the settlers' wage/cash system. Yet, so complete has our marginalization been in this respect that our overall unemployment rate has hovered in the mid-sixtieth percentile for the past half-century. On some reservations, more than 90 percent of the workforce has remained jobless during the same period.[30] Per capita annual income in many communities barely exceeds $2,000 (U.S.), while it has been officially estimated that, in places, over 85 percent of the housing units are unfit for human habitation.[31] On balance, it is fair to say that the situation shows no sign of improvement. Indeed, there are indicators that it may actually be worsening.[32]

In and of themselves, such conditions contribute substantially to the grim health and longevity statistics recited above. More to the point, they combine to create among those perpetually burdened with them a sense of such utter disempowerment, despair, and hopelessness as to make the oblivion of chronic intoxication seem an attractive alternative to conscious awareness of one's circumstances. That the compulsion to opt for such figurative self-nullification, or the literal variety attainable through outright suicide, has by now become pronounced among aboriginal grade-schoolers bespeaks as little else can the depth of the misery the settler society has imposed upon native people.[33]

Others have evidenced strikingly similar patterns of response. German Jews, for example, when subjected to a harsh régime of discrimination, dispossession and disemployment by the nazis during the 1930s, shortly came to evidence a suicide rate some three times that of the German public as a whole. During the early 1940s, as they were being relocated to Poland and concentrated there in reservations and urban ghettos—they were not yet aware of being slated for outright extermination—the Jewish suicide rate rose to a level approximately fifty times higher than that of non-Jews.[34] The response of the Sinti and Romani (Gypsies) to nazi persecution was much the same, if somewhat less pronounced.[35] For that matter, the suicide rate among *Germans* rose steeply during the first years of occupation following their defeat in World War II.[36]

It follows that, were the North American settler population subjected to circumstances comparable to those imposed upon native people, it would soon come to exhibit many of the same "negative group characteristics" as do Indians (or Jews, Gypsies, Irishmen, and inner-city blacks). Just as clearly, holding Indians in a state of perpetual subordination/ destitution is a prerequisite to maintaining the relatively lavish level of comfort enjoyed by the settlers and collectively announced as their own entitlement. The implications of this cause/effect relationship are ready-made to instill a sense of guilt among beneficiaries, especially those so prideful of their self-proclaimed "humanitarian enlightenment" as the settlers. Since guilty feelings are at best an uncomfortable sensation, the implications—or the nature of the relationship itself—must be denied.

Better still that the victims themselves should be "held accountable"—that is, blamed—for the very fact of their victimization.[37] Vacuous assertions that American Indians are "innately endowed predisposed" toward alcoholism or suicide serve this purpose quite nicely, as do oft expressed "concerns" that there may be some mysterious set of "factors" at work in native cultures producing much the same effect.[38] Thus handily self-absolved of responsibility for what the system underpinning their privilege has wrought, the settler beneficiaries free themselves to enjoy its fruits absent the least discomfiting pangs of conscience.[39]

Indeed, they position themselves thereby to adopt a lofty air of "moral superiority" vis-à-vis those whose relentless agony pays the tab.[40] The mentality at issue is not dissimilar from that of the twisted little boys known to delight in torturing cats, its effect in exacerbating the pain of the victims self-evident.

"To Educate the Indian Out of Them"

If all this were not enough, still worse will be found in the legacy of a comprehensive system of residential "Indian Schools" established during the early 1880s and maintained for a century thereafter. A linchpin of "assimilationist" policies through which the U.S. and Canada alike sought to eradicate the last traces of indigenous culture in North America, the schools were meant to serve, in the words of U.S. president Theodore Roosevelt, as "a great pulverizing engine for breaking down the tribal mass."[41] In Ottawa, Minister of Aboriginal Affairs Duncan Campbell Scott was clearer and more blunt, observing that the "objective is to continue until there is not a single Indian in Canada" culturally identifiable as such.[42]

Such sentiments permeated the settler society. The goal of residential schooling, as articulated by the editors of the *Calgary Herald* in 1892, was nothing less than to "wipe out the whole Indian establishment."[43] At about the same time, U.S. Superintendent of Indian Schools Richard Henry Pratt—an army captain whose main qualification for the job seems to have been that he'd earlier presided over a military prison in Florida to which Geronimo and other "recalcitrant" native adults were sent to be broken—explained to wide applause that his object was to "kill the Indian, spare the man" in every pupil.[44] In Canada, the formulation was to "educate the Indian out of" each student.[45] Statements of this sort were legion, and made right into the 1980s.[46]

The techniques employed in such endeavors were as brutal as they were straightforward. Aboriginal children as young as five were "caught" by government agents and forcibly removed to facilities "located away from reserves so that parental influence would be reduced to a minimum."[47] Thus isolated from all that was familiar, the youngsters were shorn of their hair, outfitted in "proper" euroamerican/eurocanadian attire, their personal effects impounded or destroyed. Thereafter, they were subject to military/penal-style regimentation.[48] Crowded into barracks-like living quarters where disease often ran rampant,[49] they were fed on about one-third the officially estimated minimum cost of providing adequate nutrition to children their age.[50]

Severe corporal punishment—whippings, solitary confinement, restriction to bread and water rations—was routinely employed to prevent students speaking their own languages, practicing or in many cases even knowing about their spiritual traditions or anything else associated with the autochthonous functioning of their cultures.[51] Not infrequently, this harsh "discipline" was transmuted into outright torture, as when children were chained to walls or posts for days, sometimes weeks on end, burned or scalded, had needles run through their tongues, were forced to eat their own vomit, subjected to electrical shocks, and were denied medical attention.[52] Sadism was often conjoined by the sexual predations of staff members, a pattern of abuse now proven to have been pervasive in many institutions (and covered up by responsible officials).[53] Under such conditions, death rates among students were extraordinarily high.[54]

Those who survived were held for an average of ten years, living in a state of perpetual anxiety—or abject terror—as they were systematically "deculturated" through a process elsewhere described as "education for extinction."[55] In actuality, the entire procedure in many ways resembled the hideous "depatterning" techniques developed for the CIA by McGill University psychiatrist Ewen Cameron during the agency's notorious MK-ULTRA Project of the early 1960s.[56] More appropriate still, given Captain Pratt's seminal role, it might be seem as prefiguring the methods currently employed in super-high-security penal units to force ideological conversion upon politicized inmates, or, failing that, to reduce them to "psychological jelly."[57]

The form of conversion demanded of residential school students is not especially mysterious. Operating under government authority, the schools were administered mainly by the Anglican, Catholic, and other Christian churches.[58] It follows that, as their own spiritual beliefs were expunged, students were subjected to intensive indoctrination in "the true faith," spending about twice the time each day undergoing religious training as they did receiving academic instruction.[59] As recently as 1993, the Anglicans were still prepared to defend this "civilizing mission" in terms of the unabashed white supremacism it entailed.

> Canada . . . must increasingly become . . . a country of white men rooted and grounded in those fundamental scriptural conceptions of the individual, of society [and] of the state . . . as the same have been conceived and found expression through the struggles and conquests of the several peoples of British blood and tradition. The church felt it had a Christian responsibility to assist the

Aboriginal people in this transition. Assimilation, like medicine, might be intrusive and unpleasant, might even hurt a great deal, but in the long run it was for the people's own good . . . .[60]

In other words, the idea was to infect students at the most primal level with a perception of Indians corresponding to the emphatically negative views embraced by their colonizers.[61] Thus conditioned to see themselves and their heritage as consigned by god to a state of "natural inferiority"—if not as things "evil" or "satanic"[62]—students suffered profound and permanent psychological/emotional damage. Probably without exception, they left the residential schools with a deformed self-concept, their senses of self-esteem and -confidence severely undermined. In the majority of cases, active self-loathing appears to be at issue.[63]

Meanwhile, in a rather close parallel to what the nazis planned for a residue of Slavs after conquering eastern Europe,[64] initiatives were undertaken to "fit [students] into the lower echelons of the new economic order" in North America.[65] To this end, many residential facilities were configured as "industrial schools" providing "vocational training to prepare their pupils to fill certain limited occupations."[66] In practice, this meant the children typically worked more hours per day than they spent in the classroom, the bulk of their wages impounded to offset the "expense of their education."[67] Thereby reduced to de facto slave status, it was drummed into them, year after year, that their "place" would be forever to toil as manual laborers and domestics serving the needs of their racial "betters" at discount rates.[68]

In the end, of course, the racial biases of the settlers were such that there were precious few jobs for graduates, even of these demeaning varieties. Thus "disemployed," they were mostly forced into a posture of seemingly immutable material dependency upon those who most despised them. What the residential schools in effect produced were successive generations of increasingly desperate and dysfunctional human beings, incapable of valuing themselves as Indians and neither assimilated nor assimilable into the dominant society which had rendered them thus. Given the sheer impossibility of their situation, the self-negating pathologies evidenced by residential school graduates are, or should have been, perfectly predictable.[69]

Although it was originally intended that every aboriginal child between the ages of five and fifteen would be processed through the schools, attendance ultimately peaked at somewhere around half the youngsters in successive generations.[70] The correlation between this proportion of the indigenous population and the percentage now suffering alcoholism is obvious. One suspects that were a list of native alcoholics compared to a list of those who endured the residential schools—along with their sons and daughters—a well-nigh perfect match would result.

Worlds of Pain

While the diagnosis has been rather scrupulously avoided by psychoanalysts and therapeutic practitioners over the years, the core of the devastation inflicted upon those incarcerated in the residential schools was a magnitude of psychological trauma most commonly associated with men suffering the aftereffects of heavy combat.[71] "Emotional numbing," "incomplete mourning," and a range of other symptoms of acute trauma afflicting survivors of the nazi genocide, the Hiroshima/Nagasaki bombings, and comparable phenomena are equally apparent.[72] So too a confluence with the pathologies typically exhibited by hostages, rape victims, and the victims of political repression/state terrorism.[73]

The early age at which residential school victims typically incurred their traumas has also tended to amplify the impacts to a greater extent than those evident among the mostly adult counterpart groups noted above. In this sense, the pattern of ensuing pathologies more nearly resembles that displayed by victims of severe child abuse.[74] This is especially true with respect to children suffering not a single traumatic incident (or cluster of incidents), but upon whom abuse has been visited in a chronic and protracted fashion.[75] Thus layered and reinforced over a period of years, the result is not so much the classic "posttraumatic stress disorder" (PTSD) with which so many combat veterans and rape victims are afflicted as it is a sort of "Complex PTSD" described by Harvard psychiatry professor Judith Herman.[76]

Even Herman's is an inadequate characterization of the "Residential School Syndrome" (RSS), however.[77] For a condition to be accurately depicted as "posttraumatic," it is of course necessary that the circumstance(s) generating the trauma first be eliminated. A rape victim, for example, is not experiencing "posttraumatic stress," no matter how "complex," while the rape is occurring. S/he is instead undergoing the trauma itself. By the same token, there can be no reasonable expectation that a child might be "cured" of the psychological ravages of abuse before s/he is removed from the abusive setting, or a Gypsy victim of the nazi genocide during his/her confinement in Neuengamme or Auschwitz.

Effective therapeutic strategies for those suffering trauma-induced pathologies, moreover, invariably devolve upon some form of generalized and tangible withdrawal of social sanction from those who perpetrated the trauma-inducing acts or processes.[78] "Regular" rapists, child abusers and mass murderers are all viewed as criminals in a socially normative sense. They are not celebrated by the great majority of people in North America, nor are apologetics usually offered in their behalf, asserting that, however "misguided" they may have been in what they did, they acted on the basis of "the best of intentions."[79] Still less are their victims subjected to a broad and continuous bombardment of public scorn, ridicule, and trivialization.

Where a supportive environment exists, "healing" the effects of severe trauma is extraordinarily difficult.[80] Where it does not, as is to a noticeable extent the case with Vietnam combat veterans, and much more so with the victims of political repression, it is largely impossible. Vietnam vets continued to suffer disproportionately high rates of alcoholism, drug usage, incarceration, and suicide until those who'd borne the brunt of ground combat were largely and quite prematurely dead.[81] Although far less research has been done with respect to those suffering the aftershocks of state terrorism, there are indications that they manifest the same pattern in a still more pronounced form.[82]

For survivors of the residential schools, *none* of the criteria requisite to psychological "recovery" apply. Although the facilities themselves have by and large been phased out, the material incentives prompting the settler society to establish them in the first place—that is, the comprehensive dispossession/disempowerment of native people—were fulfilled long since. The results remain very much in effect and are treated as a "natural entitlement" by the perpetrator population. Other than those judicially proven to have engaged in specific acts of sexual predation, even the persons most directly involved—those who worked in and presided over the schools—are *not* normatively viewed as criminals.[83] Indeed, while the Canadian government has lately offered a tepid "expression of regret" for a carefully limited range of "negative impacts," it has formally declined to so much as apologize for the criminality inherent to the residential school system as a whole.[84] The U.S. has yet to rise even to this token level of acknowledgement.[85]

Meanwhile, the iconography of settler triumphalism is everywhere and always apparent, from annual celebrations of "Thanksgiving" and "Columbus Day" to the enshrinement of patently genocidal personages like Andrew Jackson and Theodore Roosevelt on national currencies, from the exalted statuary littering public spaces to the names bestowed upon the places themselves. And then, to be sure, there is the haughty supremacist aura with which the settlers have imbued their culture—and by extension themselves—in the canons of their literature and cinema[86] and the academic (mis)representations which continue to be imposed upon native youth with more force and sophistication today than ever before.[87]

The flip side of the triumphalist coin concerns a proliferate iconography of degradation and outright dehumanization where aboriginal people are concerned. This will be found in the same literary and academic texts through which the settler society lends a false burnish to the contrivances of its own image, in the 2,000-odd westerns released by Hollywood over the past century, in some 10,000 television segments produced between 1950 and 1990,[88] in "Tumbleweeds" cartoons and product names like Jeep "Cherokee" and "Winnebago" recreational vehicles, in sports team names and mascots like those of the Washington "Redskins," Cleveland "Indians," Atlanta "Braves," University of Illinois "Fighting Illini" and Florida State University "Seminoles,"[89] in the wooden Indian caricatures adorning tobacco shops across the continent, and in the more than a thousand North American place names presently featuring the word "squaw."[90]

In effect, the consciousness of residential school survivors continues to be inundated with the "lessons" imparted in those institutions, every waking moment of their lives (and perhaps in their dreams as well). The primal source of their psychic wounding thus remains hyperactive at all times, ripping away emotional scabs before they've had the least opportunity to form. Exacerbating the victims' situation still further is a grotesque and increasingly aggressive posture of denial on the part of the settlers that anything is being done to them at all.[91] While some survivors have obviously found means of coping with these circumstances,[92] theirs remains—how could it be otherwise?—an unremitting world of pain.

By Any Other Name

My use of terms like "criminal" to describe the actions and attitudes of the settler society is neither rhetorical nor a mere "matter of personal conjecture or opinion." A rather vast range of black letter law has been systematically violated, and in most cases continues to be violated, in the course of creating the situation sketched out in preceding sections.[93] Not least is the 1948 Convention on Prevention and Punishment of the Crime of Genocide, an element of international customary law making it a crime against humanity to undertake any policy intended "to destroy, in whole or in part, a national, ethnical, racial or religious group, as such" (Indians, of course, fit all four classifications).[94]

Among the categories of policy/action specifically delineated as genocidal in the convention's second article are those "causing serious bodily or mental harm to members of the group[,] deliberately inflicting on the group conditions of life calculated to bring about its physical destruction in whole or in part[, and] forcibly transferring children of the group to another group."[95] Unmistakably, the conditions imposed upon native people in both Canada and the U.S. fall well within the parameters of these criteria, so much so that they tend to validate Jean-Paul Sartre's "controversial" observation, made on entirely functionalist grounds, that colonialism equals genocide.[96]

Under the convention's third article, it is made clear that, aside from direct involvement in the perpetration of the crime, one is guilty of genocide if one participates in planning or conspiring to commit it, inciting it or is otherwise complicit in the process.[97] This last has been construed to mean simply ignoring or acquiescing in others' commission of the crime. In effect, where genocide is concerned, virtually every member of a perpetrator society not actively engaged in opposing it is, by definition, legally guilty of it. Obfuscation and denial are thus to be seen as part and parcel of the crime itself.[98]

The complaint is usually heard at this juncture, always from those benefiting quite tangibly from the ongoing genocide of American Indians, and in the aggrieved tone invariably adopted by all such offenders, that such framing of legal obligation is "unreasonable." That the opposite holds true is also a matter of black letter law. As the matter was put by U.S. Supreme Court Justice Robert H. Jackson during the trial of the nazi leadership at Nuremberg in 1945, responsibility for ensuring that its government adheres to the rule of law resides first, foremost, and by all available means in the citizenry of each country.[99] Default upon this responsibility by any citizen is a matter of legal culpability. There can be nothing "apolitical," no "bystanders" or "innocents" among beneficiaries of the "incomparable crime."[100] It follows that North America's "Good Settlers" are no less guilty than were the "Good Germans" of the Third Reich.[101]

This is the law to which all parties endorsing or participating in the Nuremberg proceedings bound themselves and their constituents. As Justice Jackson put it, "We are not prepared to lay down a rule of criminal conduct against others which we are not willing to have invoked against us."[102] His assertion was then enshrined in the 1946 "Affirmation of the Principles of International Law Recognized by the Charter of the Nuremberg Tribunal," a covenant to which both Canada and the United States are signatories.[103] Further, neither the Nuremberg Doctrine nor customary law more generally affords either country a legitimate recourse but to comply with the principles, whether or not they've formally subscribed to or even agree with them.[104]

Officially—and this speaks volumes to the extent of their mutual awareness that they are in violation of it—both governments have done their utmost to mask the implications of The Law. For its part, having taken the lead in formulating the noble principles espoused at Nuremberg,[105] the United States has adopted the naziesque posture of refusing the jurisdiction of any international judicial body.[106] Similarly, having been instrumental in shaping the content of the Genocide Convention, it declined to ratify it for forty years, purporting to do so in 1988 only after attaching a "sovereignty package" through which it claims a unique "right" to exempt itself from compliance whenever it finds an interest in doing so.[107] A list of international human rights laws the U.S. has treated in similar fashion over the past half-century would be exceedingly long.[108]

Canada's path to the same end has been more slippery. Although it claims to have ratified the Genocide Convention in 1952, it did so in a tellingly circumscribed fashion. After much discussion, the parliament simply deleted from the statute defining the crime in Canadian jurisprudence those criteria—causing serious bodily or mental harm to members of a target group, and the forced transfer of their children—describing the policies in which Canada was most clearly engaged with respect to native peoples.[109] In 1985, the statute was further "revised" to remove yet another criterion (imposing measures intended to prevent births within a target group).[110] Where the 1948 Convention lists five discrete categories of genocidal policy, the Canadian legal code now acknowledges but two.

In 1998, an Ontario judge, James MacPherson, went still further, disregarding black letter law and expert witnesses alike to rule that abridged dictionary definitions would henceforth be considered binding in Canadian courts.[111] This juridical absurdity, which has prompted no correction from the country's higher tribunals, had the effect of constraining Canada's "legal understanding" of genocide to a single criterion: engagement in nazi-style mass extermination programs. Absent incontrovertible evidence that such actions are being undertaken as a

matter of state policy, the judge opined, allegations of genocide constitute "an enormous injustice . . . bordering on the grotesque . . . cavalier
and grossly unfair" to perpetrators.[112] He concluded with a gag order
seeking to constrain anyone, especially the victims of Canada's most
genocidal policies, from saying otherwise.[113]

This, in a country where public denial of "the" Holocaust—by which
is meant the fate of the Jews at the hands of the nazis, and exclusively
so—has long been a criminal offense.[114] The significance of the disparity is by no means lost upon native people, residential school survivors
perhaps most of all. MacPherson's performance, emblematic as it is of
the overall settler sensibility, was precisely what one might have expected
of a nazi jurist/intellectual a couple of generations after a German victory
in World War II. Therein lies the distinction separating the nazis from
North America's settler élite: the former, unlike "the Nordics of North
America" they consciously emulated,[115] were losers in their drive to
assert dominion on a continental scale. The mentality involved is neither
more nor less genocidal, win or lose.[116] And genocide denied, or by any
other name,[117] remains genocide.

Down through Generations

Even had the full range of genocidal policies reflected in the residential
schools been terminated when the schools themselves were phased out,
and the mentality of the perpetrating society magically transformed into
a complete opposite of itself, it would be unreasonable to expect that
everything might suddenly have become "okay" for the victims or those
in close proximity to them. While trauma is no more hereditary or a
disease than its "symptoms," alcoholism and suicide included, its effects
are often extremely long-lasting.[118] It is also not especially uncommon
for traumatic wounding to work along the lines of a time-delayed bomb,
its effects (re)appearing, often quite suddenly, after extended periods
of apparent dormancy.[119] Such characteristics mark the malady even in
cases where trauma has been induced by natural disaster rather than the
malevolence of human agency.[120]

Given the nature of its effects, as well as their duration and some-
time recurrence, they can be transmitted in an almost epidemiological
fashion. This is to say that, unaddressed, "trauma begets trauma." People
suffering complex traumatic stress are apt—and in some circumstances
all but guaranteed—to traumatize others, especially those closest to
and most dependent on them. In this sense, the spouses, and more
particularly the children, of trauma victims are those most vulnerable

to being traumatized by them. There is no reason to expect this to be less true among residential school survivors than among other victim groups: survivors of the nazi genocide, for instance, or former POWs and combat veterans.[121] Quite the contrary, given the sources of ongoing wounding described above, it might be reasonably anticipated that it would be more so.

Such suspicions have been amply confirmed in a number of recent studies,[122] the findings of which were partially—and rather politely—summarized in a 1992 report by the Health Commission of Canada's Assembly of First Nations.

> The survivors of the Indian residential school system have . . . continued to have their lives shaped by their experiences in those schools. Persons who attended the schools continue to struggle with their identity after years of being taught to hate themselves and their culture. The residential school led to a disruption in the transference of parenting skills from one generation to the next. Without these skills, many survivors have difficulty in raising their own children. In residential schools, they learned that adults often exert power and control through abuse. The lessons learned in childhood are often repeated in adulthood with the result that many survivors of the residential school system often inflict abuse on their own children. These [victims] in turn use the same tools on their children.[123]

Much more is involved than nontransference of appropriate parenting skills, or the transference of inappropriate ones, of course. Even where residential school survivors both understand the requirements of good parenting and genuinely desire to be good parents—and this in all probability encompasses most cases—the dysfunctions with which they've been saddled by their trauma are likely to render them incapable of following through. The question is how, exactly, people burdened with a symptomology including somatism, dissociation, depression, fragmented personality structure, intense anxiety, hypersensitivity to slights ("paranoia"), inability to form stable or sustainable emotional bonds, panic attacks, nightmares and chronic insomnia, as well as a high degree of irritability, might be expected comport themselves as good parents irrespective of what they know or don't know about the techniques of proper parenting.[124]

Add to their incapacity to meet the emotional needs of their children—or spouses—a systemically imposed inability to meet their material responsibilities faced by the preponderance of residential school survivors, and you've a perfect recipe for disaster. Ever-deepening feelings of personal inadequacy, guilt, frustration, and, ultimately, uncontrollable rage blend with the already volatile stew simmering in the survivor psyche.[125] Unsurprisingly, especially but by no means exclusively among men, sometimes quickly, sometimes over a longer period, the process culminates in an explosion, a blind lashing out at whomever is unfortunate enough to be at hand.[126] Assuming the victims are family members, which is most frequently the case, an even greater sense of guilt and unworthiness ensues. At this point, if not before, attempts at self-nullification via alcohol, other substances, or suicide typically set in, most often in conjunction with an escalating rate of externalized violence.[127]

For children caught up in this hideous cycle, the impact is in many ways far greater than that of the residential schools upon their parents. In the schools, those by whom youngsters were victimized could at least be seen as alien "others." Such buffers are obviously removed when the victimizer is one's own father, mother, or both. Also, within the family setting, the pattern of abuse may well commence at an even earlier age than in the schools, sometimes at birth.[128] Even in the relatively rare instances where domestic violence is not present, but where one or both parents are serious alcoholics, the depth of the traumatic effects upon children are very well-documented.[129]

> The abused child's existential task is . . . formidable. Though she perceives herself as abandoned to a power without mercy, she must find a way to preserve hope and meaning. The alternative is utter despair, something no child can bear. To preserve her faith in her parents, she must reject the first and most obvious conclusion that something is terribly wrong with them. She will go to all lengths to construct an explanation for her fate that absolves her parents of all blame and responsibility.[130]

In simplest terms, such "adaptations serve the fundamental purpose of preserving her primary attachment to her parents in the face of daily evidence of their malice, helplessness or indifference. . . . Unable to alter the unbearable reality in fact, the child alters it in her mind."[131]

> When it is impossible to avoid the reality of the abuse, the child must construct some system of meaning that justifies it. Inevitably the child concludes that her innate badness is the cause. The child seizes upon this explanation early and clings to it tenaciously, for

it enables her to preserve a sense of meaning, hope, and power. If she is bad, then her parents are good. If, somehow, she has brought this fate upon herself, then somehow she has the power to change it. If she has driven her parents to mistreat her, then, if only she tries hard enough, she may someday earn their forgiveness and finally win the protection and care she so desperately needs.[132]

When this strategy also fails, as it all but inevitably must, the self-negation of gasoline sniffing or outright suicide often results. The disintegration of family/community structures in some quarters of Native North America has by now reached such a pass that parents traumatized in the residential schools have become desperate enough to request intervention by the very authorities who victimized them. Their premise, which holds a disquieting measure of undeniability, is that the youngsters probably stand a better prospect of physical survival in residential institutions than they do at home.[133] Even in better-case settings, the emotional damage already displayed by preschoolers is often staggering. Thus maimed before they begin, and trapped within an overall social construction in which they will be consistently denigrated, often openly reviled, and forever dispossessed of their birthright, they are forced with increasing frequency to hear sermons from their oppressors about how they should "stop whining and get over it," that they're now "as free as anyone else to become whoever or whatever they want."[134]

Kizhiibaabinesik

It was in this nightmarish environment that Leah spent her formative years. A Lynx Clan Ojibwe, her name in her own language was Kizhiibaabinesik (roughly translated, "Being Who Circles with the Birds"). She entered the world on February 19, 1970, in Thunder Bay, Ontario, the youngest of six siblings born in rapid succession.[135] Her father, John Peter Kelly, is from Sabaskong Bay, a reserve of the Onigaming Ojibwe First Nation located near the Ontario town of Kenora. Her mother, Barbara, is from the nearby Couchiching Reserve, outside Fort Frances, where she, John, their parents, and most of their relatives in their own generation, attended Roman Catholic residential school.[136]

At the point Leah arrived, the family was living crammed eight-deep in a small trailer house, struggling to make ends meet while John pursued an MA in educational administration. The first in his Band to complete an undergraduate degree, much less to take up graduate studies, his internalization of mainstream ideals led him to an angry repudiation of Ojibwe tradition and a period of self-imposed isolation from his people. A dark-complected fullblood, however, he was shortly forced to face the harsh reality that his skin tone was in itself sufficient to prevent either his acceptance among the eurocanadians he'd been conditioned to model himself after or employment in the sorts of positions to which he correspondingly aspired.[137]

The situation was complicated considerably by the devout Catholicism, a faith noted for its preclusion of birth control, into which Barbara had been indoctrinated at Fort Frances. The demands, both material and emotional, attending the resulting—and, for a time, seemingly endless—avalanche of children became overwhelming, magnifying John's already substantial sense of powerlessness and personal inadequacy. By the time Barbara became pregnant with Leah, he'd already commenced what would become a seventeen-year descent into what he now calls "the bottomless pit of alcoholism and despair." It did not end until his children were scattered to the winds.[138]

One of Leah's earliest recollections was that of being told that she'd been "unplanned for," a "mistake," observations the little girl easily translated to mean "unwanted." It was a feeling she would never escape,[139] along with an abiding sense of guilt that things might have worked out differently for her father, if only she'd never been born.[140] Other memories centered mainly on John's stumbling in, blind drunk, night after night, and of the violence that often ensued. For the most part, Leah was a witness, although, somewhere along the line, she was herself on the receiving end.[141] Barbara, battered, emotionally and otherwise, depressed and in a state of perpetual exhaustion, could offer little comfort or protection.

Verbal abuse was also endemic, often manifested in vituperative denunciations of the children's "stupidity," their "laziness" and supposed lack of hygiene.[142] More insidious still were John's expressions of resentment toward the lighter-complected among his offspring— Barbara is half-white, her coloration reflected in three of the children— including Leah. Glass was regularly ground into this wound when she was greeted with much the same disparagement by potential playmates during summers spent visiting her grandparents at Couchiching.[143] By the time she was four, she'd been thoroughly infected with the idea that there was something dreadfully wrong with the way she looked, a debilitating misperception that would stay with her the rest of her life.[144]

As John's alcoholism progressed, the family underwent periods of outright disintegration. The children were sent to live for varying intervals with relatives, themselves active or recovering alcoholics.[145] At other times, they would sleep whenever possible at the homes of friends. It was on one of these overnights, when she was perhaps twelve, that Leah was first sexually molested. The man was apparently the father of her best and perhaps only real chum, a figure of trust whom she'd embraced as an "uncle." Again, there is no clear indication whether the abuse was repetitive or, if so, whether more than a single predator was involved.[146]

Meanwhile, the Kellys had relocated to the Southdale area of Winnipeg, a predominantly white suburban sprawl largely devoid of anything resembling redeeming value. For Leah, however, it initially represented something of a new start. Twenty-odd years later, she'd recount how, having been consistently rebuffed as "too white" by her hoped-for friends on the reserves, she'd trotted off to school her first day, fully expecting to be accepted, eager for someone—anyone—to like her. Instead, she was chased all the way home by a rabid pack of little settler kids taunting her as a "squaw" and a "wagon burner."[147] As she put it, "I tried and tried, but I never really fit in with anybody, anywhere, ever."

At fifteen, desperate to escape the effects of her home life and the "mindlessly racist climate" of Southdale, Leah struck out on her own. Supporting herself as a waiter in Winnipeg proper, she managed to enroll at The Collegiate, a highly touted local prep school. She did quite well academically but, finding the attitudes of students and faculty to be "pretty much the same as [she'd] already experienced, only more so," she left before graduating. Relying upon her raw test scores, she then gained early admittance to Laval University, in Québec. A year later, having mastered conversational French,[148] she was back in Winnipeg, waiting tables at an upscale restaurant in the city's fashionable Cordon district.

For a while, it seemed enough. Having acquired for the first time a small circle of friends,[149] her first live-in lover, and earning enough money to indulge in clothes, a car, and other accouterments of what she then saw as "class," she appears to have briefly reveled in the sheer novelty of it all. Making the rounds of Winnipeg's surprisingly vibrant music and café scenes, she quickly built a reputation as something of a hipster, and the ingredients of an affirmative identity began at last to congeal. Soon, however, the relationship with her boyfriend soured and she found herself both pregnant and alone. An abortion followed,[150] and from there the world she'd been constructing for herself crumbled very rapidly.

The situation was more complex than it may sound. Although she would later insist things were otherwise, Leah confided in friends—before informing her partner that she was with child—that she would keep the baby and be married. That she rendered herself thus vulnerable bespoke the depth of her longing to create the kind of idealized family environment she'd craved all her life. His response upon receiving what she hoped would be glad tidings, that he wanted no part of either marriage or fatherhood, played directly into the already profound sense of unworthiness and rejection she harbored. It also destroyed at a single stroke the most important of the redemptive fantasies she'd been nurturing. His dropping her at a clinic and leaving her to find her own way home—she walked—was merely a cruel redundancy to how she must by then have felt.

Suddenly confronted not only with abandonment, but, having dared to dream aloud, what she believed to be the humiliation of public exposure, she berated herself endlessly in her diary, worrying that she'd "once again become a laughingstock," feeling the image of herself she'd so carefully crafted slipping away. For weeks she actively contemplated suicide.[151] Instead, she bolted, divesting herself of her worldly possessions[152] and setting out on what is still and sometimes fondly remembered by those who knew her as "Leah's grand adventure." In retrospect, it might better and more accurately be recalled as the trek of a hurt and terribly frightened young woman, trapped in a blind alley but running for her life.

Little Girl Lost (and Found?)

By the time we were introduced by northern California AIM leader Bobby Castillo at the San Francisco airport in November of 1993, Leah had completely circumnavigated the globe. Traveling for the most part alone, she'd journeyed first to Thailand, then to India, where she spent several months. There, she met and began a relationship with a German man, agreeing to live with him in his country after a stint in Nepal. He introduced her to hashish, then opium, adding heroin and the occasional psychedelic after they took up residence in one of Berlin's teeming squats. Finding work refurbishing apartments and moonlighting as a bar maid, she played rhythm guitar in an all-woman machine band, undertook side trips to Poland, France, and Denmark, spent a month alone in Egypt, and became increasingly strung out on smack.

It was a year after she arrived in Berlin that Bobby met her there. She'd come up to him after a speech he'd given at Humboldt University, saying she felt misplaced among the Germans and had grown homesick for North America. They talked further, he invited her to join him in the City by the Bay,[153] she accepted and a month later was again in Winnipeg, waiting tables in Cordon, saving money to underwrite yet another new start.[154] A couple months after that, she was sharing a house a block from Haight Street with another gaggle of dopers, beginning a brief but torrid interlude with cultural personality John Trudell,[155] another with a Mexican serigrapher named Chucho, and working at Ti Couz, then a hot new crepery, just off Valencia, in the Mission. The affairs faded fast, if not the job, and San Francisco shortly began to seem as cold and empty a place as any she'd ever been.

I knew nothing of Leah's background, and cared less, when we met. Further still from my awareness was the fact that I'd come upon a person whose lifelong sense of lonely futility had returned, settling in like the chill of a North Beach fog, leading her late in the night to wanderings along the Golden Gate, seeking whatever might precipitate a final plunge into the murky depths below, or that her diary brimmed once again with passages declaiming "how nice it would be to just lie down in the snow, go to sleep, and never wake up." No, I had no idea then of the demons dogging her every step. Such things she kept buried somewhere far from view. Had I known, had I *seen*, I can honestly say it would not have deterred me in the least. In the seeing, nonetheless, I might well have helped her more.

What I did see—in fact *all* I saw—stepping off the plane, was a remarkably beautiful young woman—I'd not be told *how* young for another six months—distinguished by nothing so much as a palpable aura of shyness, but endowed all the same with the brightest eyes I'd ever encountered and a smile, when sparked, lending a fresh meaning to the tired old saw about lighting up a room. She was radiant. I was dazzled. Packed like sardines into the cab of Bobby's old and undersized Toyota pickup, we ventured north to Willits, en route to a talk I was giving as a fundraiser for Judi Bari.[156] Long before we'd made our way back to the city, I was utterly smitten. Bobby, I think, was amused.

Still, she had her life and I had mine, including the death-throes of a bad marriage, to contend with. She was in California, I in Colorado—or, more accurately, in airports scattered across three continents—and we saw one another infrequently during the spring of '94, never sexually in those months, but whenever I'd hit town. In May, she told me she was moving into an apartment on Geary with a woman friend, then going off to Ireland for several weeks. I, for my part, was heading out on an extended drive, having no particular destination, schedule, or agenda, one of the best means I've found to gain respite from the pace I otherwise maintained, clearing and recharging my mind. We agreed that, upon her return, I'd stop in and visit for a "couple of weeks," maybe driving her up along the coast for a few days camping in the redwoods.

Cutting to the chase, once I arrived in early July I never left. We spent time in the redwoods, true, and in the vineyards of Simi Valley, in the forests below Mount Shasta, along beaches watching sunsets as far north as Coos Bay. Most of our time, however, was spent in the city, she working, me prowling bookstores or coffeehouses, chain-smoking as I read the postmodernists from Baudrillard to Lyotard, waiting every night in the Dalva, a bar across the street from Ti Couz, to share glasses of cider at the end of her shift. Her off hours we spent constantly together, probing, exploring, laughing, holding hands, or she my arm, as we strolled the streets. Common tastes were discovered in food and films, literature and music, art and much else. She displayed her knowledge of wines, refined through years of serving others. I showed off my talents as a gourmet cook, making her a batch of cioppino. In restaurants, she'd order for us both and I found myself delighted when she did so.

By then, I knew she was only 24. I was 46, working hard on 47. It mattered to neither of us, or so it seemed at the time. We'd gone, willy-nilly, from infatuation through mutual astonishment to what was a ripening of genuine love for one another. In late August, as I was preparing to go home for the start of another school year—I'd pushed my departure back to the last possible hour of the last possible day, driving straight through and pulling into town as new students were undergoing orientation—we conducted something of a summit conference, trying to decide what should come next. She, fearing me, as I now realize, to be just another in her lengthening skein of intense but ultimately transient unions, flashed visible signs of distress.

Surprised by the level of anxiety she displayed, unsure of its source, I sought to reassure her, saying that nothing between us need change, I'd take a year's leave from my job and simply stay on in San Francisco, finding permanent employment there if need be. She mulled my gestures for only a moment before dismissing them with an irritated wave of the hand, as if they were ridiculous—actually, they were—while herself posing no better alternative. We seemed at the point of stalemate. As she grew steadily more agitated, there seemed little I might say or do to calm her. Things were sliding downhill in a hurry.

At some point, though, I queried her as to what it was she really wanted to do, not just with me, or over the next months, but with her life. A cloud of indecipherable wistfulness passed across her face, her voice filling with a kind of yearning I'd not heard from her before. She'd been spinning her wheels for years, she said, going nowhere, but always meaning to finish college, to "get to know things," becoming an artist, a painter, a photographer, and above all, a maker of films. Her words rushed forth as if of their own volition, at once pensive and excited, seemingly propelled by some force altogether disconnected from her will.

Then, quite abruptly, she caught herself. Like the slamming of a door, a resigned and guarded look displaced her eager hopefulness. Canceling her previous torrent with a none-too-subtle hint of bitterness, she offered a curt endgame observation that "none of it will ever happen, of course."

"Why not?" I replied. "It sounds doable enough to me."

She appeared confused, unsure of whether she should be startled, happy, or simply baffled by my response. I'd definitely captured her attention.

"Really?" she asked, a bit incredulously.

"Sure," I said. "What's the problem?"

An hour later, we had a plan. I'd base myself in San Francisco during the fall semester, commuting to and from Denver to teach my three days per week's worth of classes. Then, in December, Leah would move to Boulder and I'd arrange her admission at the University of Colorado (where I was then a professor). We'd live together in my house outside of town and I'd provide her living expenses while she completed her undergraduate degree.[157] Thereafter, she'd take a job in some aspect of cinema or attend grad school. As she established herself in her field, I'd begin to phase out of mine, turning an increasing share of our financial burden over to her.[158] Perhaps I'd take early retirement and devote myself to writing, maybe even start painting again.[159] Perhaps I'd secure an end-of-career position at a university in or near Winnipeg. In either event, we'd eventually move there. She'd be our primary breadwinner making movies or something similar, we'd buy a big house in an older neighborhood, possibly raise a kid or two. We were in for the long haul.

Bright Star Rising

It's fair to say that Leah excelled intellectually. Already well-read, she ingested books with a gusto and seriousness that left me sometimes astonished, always impressed, preparing lists of questions for evening discussion, seeking recommendations of additional material with which to expand her apprehension of some of the more complex issues she raised. Soon my already ample library, focusing as it does on history, philosophy, and social theory, was complemented by her own growing collections on art, photography, and film criticism. She demonstrated powerful abilities not only to retain what she consumed but, more significantly, to synthesize it with increasing intricacy, combining Adorno with Robert Stam, Gramsci with David Caute and Vandana Shiva, to form patterns of understanding and explanation uniquely her own.

Having greeted the new year in Spain amid what might be described as a premature honeymoon, we spent the summer of '95 touring the U.S. eastern seaboard, driving first to Oklahoma to visit friends among my Keetoowah Band, thence to Natchez, Vicksburg and New Orleans. From there, it was Savannah, then Charleston, a week on the Outer Banks, another in Maine, and on to Québec, where she privied me to the domain of her time at Laval. Our route then meandered through Montréal to Ottawa, along the north shore of Lake Superior to Thunder Bay, then Lake of the Woods, stopping off at both Couchiching and Onigaming, and finally to Winnipeg. Returning to Boulder, we were married that August in a simple ceremony at the local courthouse, making a short trip to Mexico City by way of celebration.

In the fall, Leah's life as a student commenced in earnest,[160] and we outfitted a sizable building behind our house as a studio/study. Her painting began then, as did her photography, and a darkroom was shortly added. Eventually, when her film work started, a Bolex camera became part of her equipage. Frequent visits to art cinema houses in Denver and occasional excursions to New York to view key exhibitions—the 1997 Jasper Johns retrospective at MoMA, for instance—rounded out the package. The tools were in her hands and she used them well, staying not infrequently till dawn in her studio, moving paint, making collage, listening to the Velvet Underground and Townes Van Zandt.

Her work was strong, and not just in my opinion. The first of Leah's photos was published by the time she finished her second year in school,[161] and there would be many more to come. The small number of canvases she would complete yielded sufficient promise to attract gallery interest, her first participation in a group exhibit occurring just weeks before she died.[162] Her final filmmaking project, an ethnographic study of a working-class euroamerican couple undertaken from an indigenous viewpoint, so thoroughly reversed the genre's usual frame-of-reference that it stole the show the night it opened.[163] Having interned and then interviewed for a junior editing position with Encore Productions, she ended up at the top of their list of candidates. They phoned with their offer two months early. Her dream was coming true. But by then she was gone.

Leah never really conceived of herself as a writer,[164] perhaps in part because she considered it my turf, or at least because everyone said it was. As the essays collected in her own posthumously published volume readily attest, however, this was both unfortunate and in a very real sense unfair. She evidenced a potential in this respect at least as great as those centering in her preferred mode(s) of visual expression. Had her voice been allowed to reach its full maturity, aged and refined in its own way and at its own pace, one can readily imagine her achieving a truly inter-active repertoire of articulation, juxtaposing or combining cinematic, graphic, and literary forms in a personal synthesis wherein each was compelled to function as a marked enhancement of the others.[165]

Her published writings were "formal," at least to the extent that all but one, which we coauthored for publication, were prepared to fulfill the requirements of particular undergraduate courses. They are in that regard also to be considered "finished." Yet, in that each of them was quite plainly intended to transcend the limitations of length and content so arbitrarily assigned it, each must also be viewed as something more on the order of a "probe," a preliminary exploration by its author of the means through which she might subvert the sanctioned parameters of discourse to attain something far more meaningful, even liberatory, than the symbology of mere academic success. They are fragments of an immensely larger process of cognition, one which at the point of its termination remained very far from being either finished or complete.

In and of themselves, it's probably fair to say that these papers were relatively inconsequential to Leah. As she said quite frequently, they rep-resented no more than an expedient method of organizing her thoughts around given points or "dots" of information in such a way as to connect them, or at least render them connectable, to other such dots, ultimately revealing a whole much greater than the sum of its parts. It was only after attaining this broad base of understanding, and upon the foundation it provided, that she meant to begin offering statements for public con-sumption. She was, in effect, preparing herself, with utmost seriousness and quite systematically, to speak on her own terms, in her own voice, about things she knew should matter.

While the bulk of her intellectual energy was expended upon subject areas conventionally associated with aesthetics, and despite the fact that she was plainly interested in conceptions of beauty, honing her own artistic sensibilities to an exceedingly fine edge, Leah's major concerns never really fell within such parameters. Her abiding preoccupation was always more with apprehending the sociopolitical contexts within which aesthetic phenomena arise, searching for commonalities of motive and source, unmasking the signifiers of their popular acclaim for what they might secretly imply. Thus, her emphasis on exploring the cultural land-scape of nazism,[166] her comparisons of such terrain to that of Nordic North America, and her horrified fascination with the nihilistic sterility she attributed to both. As I said, she was busily connecting dots, actively seeking a means by which to transcend the ugly panorama of what she'd found.

The Unraveling

There were, of course, always signs that all was not well with her. Even in San Francisco, she'd whimper in her sleep, or awaken, trembling and terrified, unwilling or unable to name her terror.[167] And there were the rages, sudden and equally inexplicable, as when on my birthday that fall she celebrated first by treating me to dinner at a favorite seafood restaurant, then, shortly thereafter, by blindsiding me for no appar-ent reason with a looping right that split my lip so badly I was spitting blood two days later.[168] In the morning she tearfully apologized, saying she'd imbibed a bit too much of the wine we'd shared, lashing out in her confusion at someone or some thing from another time, another place, but not disclosing who or what or why. I hugged her, told her to forget it, asking no questions, glad only to believe her hostility had been directed at someone or something other than me.

Although it sounds otherwise, her drinking was not a problem then. Many nights, we'd savor a glass, sometimes two, selecting most often an elegant Shiraz, a red Zinfandel, on occasion a Merlot or Pinot Noir, as accompaniments to our meals or conversations. In the first two and a half years we were together, we drank with regularity—as I've said, she prided herself on her knowledge of wines—but seldom to excess. I remember her being drunk only thrice in all those months. Her control was clear,[169] punctuated by bitter asides concerning the toll alcoholism had taken among her family and how happy she was to be free of the same "curse." And I, be it said, was glad for her.

Looking back, I can see the undercurrents of what would happen surfacing mainly in the tension of her relationship with her father, the force of her need to bond with him, and he with her, the efforts both expended to make it happen, and their mutual inability to get wher-ever it was they needed so badly to go.[170] To me, she would defend him fiercely against things I'd never said or thought, or was even yet to realize, loving him in ways fathomable only in herself, struggling with all her might to absolve this small, remorse-ridden man of sins long forgotten, or perhaps never known at all, even by him.[171] In some ways, her attempts to accomplish this seem to have entailed displacing onto me the feelings of angry hurt he invoked, making of me his surrogate in this crucial sense, reserving for him only the tenderness that formed the other dimension of their compact.

Be that as it may, from our first day in Boulder her rages would spike almost daily in what at first I took to be a youthful and unfettered jealousy of the fact that I'd had a wife, or perhaps a life, before her.[172] I mustered all I had with which to offer reassurance, to demonstrate the depth of my love, my commitment, the degree to which I respected and esteemed her, continuing to spend virtually all my time with her, lavishing her with clothes, with shoes and boots and other such "finery"—her term—of the sorts she'd never had. Our house was overhauled to Leah's specifications, from antique chests to Persian rugs, its wood-paneled walls refinished from end to end.[173] We shopped for stained glass, browsed through prints and paintings. A new Ranger pick-up and later an Explorer were purchased for her to drive. I brought home flowers, a gesture so thoroughly out of character it filled my friends with wonder. We even had our hair cut together, she and I, in an upscale salon (another first for me).

Still, month after month, she'd turn on me, without warning, often in the midst of something nice, disparaging me, my family,[174] coming at me like a fury, clawing, kicking, biting, jerking out clumps of hair.[175] I covered up as best I could, doing clumsy rope-a-dope impersonations of Muhammad Ali, waiting out her anger, embarrassed when all too frequently I appeared before my classes wearing fresh scratches on my face, my neck, the backs of my hands. Things continued that way until early 1996, when, having arrived at some indefinable snapping point, I finally responded by slamming her backward against our bedroom wall, informing her that if she kept it up she'd be apt to land in a hospital. The look on her face told me I'd confirmed some secret dread far surpassing anything I'd meant to say or do, but she never raised a hand to me again.[176]

Our lives seemed to level out for a while thereafter, reclaiming more than a hint of the richness which had been ours that first summer by the Bay. "Candles, concerts and cuddles," she called us then. Late that spring, however, a combination of things—among them a miscarriage[177] and her erroneous belief that I'd been carrying on "an affair"[178]—put an end to all that. Our solution was to "give each other a break." I drove her north so she could spend her summer taking Ojibwe language and experimental film courses at the University of Manitoba, leaving her with the pick-up and flying back to finish a book and tend my garden. Before my departure, we agreed that in August I'd fly up to Winnipeg and we'd drive home together, leisurely, stopping off for a few days in the Black Hills along the way. Meanwhile, we'd talk regularly on the phone, sorting ourselves out.

I finished my book that summer, and she her courses.[179] She also began for the first time to pound the pow-wow circuit, running the guts out of her poor little four-cylinder Ranger in blazing nocturnal jaunts from Winnipeg to Bemidji and White Earth and Leech Lake, feasting on fry bread and fresh fish, dreaming to become a jingle-dress dancer, fashioning an affair with a man much younger than I, a Chippewa and would-be famous novelist, trying once again, as always, to "fit in." I knew of her romance and accepted it—indeed, I funded it by way of the truck and transfusions of cash used mostly for gas money getting to and from his place—figuring her as seeking somehow to even the score with me for what she misperceived as my betrayal, hoping she might at last square whatever fictive accounts she felt were in need of squaring.[180] She said that she had,[181] but really she hadn't, and she was gnawing at me for imaginary infidelities before we were well clear of Canada. By then, I knew something much more serious than jealousy was at issue.

Her drinking began in the fall, abruptly, with full force, like something undertaken by conscious design. And, in the beginning, I think there *was* a design to it, an intent, however forlorn and misguided, to accomplish something constructive. It was as if in her eternal struggle to come to grips with the meanings of her father and her childhood she'd decided to do in the most literal way possible what it was *he'd* done, to feel as he'd felt, to *know* firsthand the mire in which he'd been caught. Thus, she must have thought—or prayed—she might come finally and truly to understand him, to love him all the more or the better for it, and thereby herself as well. Too, I believe she was trying, ever so desperately, to show me, to help me *feel*, concretely, in the sheer misery of it, how it had been for her, why, at some level defying her every attempt to explain in words, she was the way she was. In this as well I think she hoped—again, praying may have entered in—to instill some greater understanding, and, thence, to empower a stronger, better love (this one mine, or maybe ours).

Had things worked as it seems she envisioned them, and surely they couldn't have, she might perhaps have found the salvation she sought, her "happily ever after." Instead, jumbled as she was already between the signs and signifiers of her life, alcohol triggered not clarity but implosion, quickly eroding the feeble network of defenses she'd erected, stripping her of the coping skills she'd fought so hard to gain. By the new year of 1997, there were nights when the look of a frightened doe would define her eyes, her mouth contorting into a Munch-like o-ring of horror, her soundless screams—for help? for mercy?—piercing my mind like rusty spikes. She'd found her own much worse version of that awful place where John had been. Thus was I confronted with a semblance of what had been suffered by that hideously maimed little girl still hiding within the person I valued above all others.

During the first months of her unraveling, I ran an emotional gamut, passing from irritation to anger, through frustration to confusion, arriving in a state of bewilderment before moving onward once again, entering a realm of perpetual fearfulness, the kind that nibbles constantly, like a rat, along the edges of one's soul. It happened with such swiftness and kaleidoscopic complexity that I was never quite able to catch up with myself, regaining the balance or perspective that alone might have enabled me to grasp the magnitude of what was happening. Nearly fifty when she began to crumble in earnest, thinking myself something of a tough guy to boot, I found myself completely unequipped with either the tools or the toughness necessary to retrieve her, or even hold myself together. Trying very hard on both counts, the best I knew how, I floundered under the intermingling of her pain and mine, overwhelmed by an increasing sense of my own helplessness.

Regressing some nights to a childlike state, I'd put her to bed when she passed out, later finding myself sitting alone in darkness, swaying back and forth on a chair as I hugged myself, weeping uncontrollably, mourning the lost comfort I'd encountered only as a three-year-old in the warmth of my mother's protecting embrace. Having been there as a full-grown man, battle-weary and seasoned, I know where she'd been in ways otherwise impossible. Nonetheless, it bears repeating that I was fully matured when I went. How Leah, or any child, might possibly have survived it is something far exceeding my power to comprehend. She did so for far longer than I could have. And she was right in the end: having gone there, even as an adult, I can now feel the why of her (and love her all the more for it).

Dis-integration

That which is usually referred to as "consciousness" does not come pre-assembled. It is delivered along with each newborn in pieces, or, more properly stated, in a cluster of flows or streams, each related to but operating more or less independently of the others.[182] A foundational phase of both cognitive and emotional development in younger children concerns the integration of these discrete streams, bringing about a unified and internally coherent perception of the child's self and of the external world with which that self must interact. Things like viable self-concept and personality formation are entirely dependent upon this process occurring in an orderly fashion. Should it be significantly disrupted, psychoemotional chaos can result, with one or more non-integrated streams of consciousness competing and often conflicting with the others.[183] The effect, which can be permanent, is that the child incurs multiple personalities or personality fragments and, thus, multiple perceptions of reality.[184]

Early childhood trauma is a major—probably *the* major—cause of such disruption.[185] Predictably, the pattern holds true particularly in cases where traumatic experience(s) is/are, chronic or prolonged.[186] This, to an all but absolute certainty, is what happened to Leah. Almost from the start, she made mention of hearing "voices," telling me of "others" who sometimes spoke to her and asking whether the same was so for me. At first, thinking she meant it in a traditional way, that this was her manner of informing me that she paid heed to messages conveyed by the spirits, I responded affirmatively, sometimes jokingly, saying "yes, but only when I take the time to listen." She'd laugh, but also look relieved, seemingly glad to hear she was not the only one.

Later, neither of us was laughing. I'd find her in the kitchen, standing at the sink, muttering, apparently to herself. If I inquired as to whom she was talking, she'd react with a start, as if jolted from a trance. "Them," she'd say, and that would be that. As time passed, and her condition deteriorated, "they" became far more threatening. Eyes wild, trembling with terror, she'd argue frantically with unseen others, gesticulating, pointing to corners where she imagined them to be.[187] My attempts to calm her, to wrap her in my arms, would be greeted with a horrified recoil, she cowering, assuming a near-fetal position, arms up as if to ward off blows, pleading in a disembodied little girl's voice: "Oh, please, please, please! Don't do that to *me!*"[188]

There was worse, much worse, most of which I cannot bring myself to go into here. I will recount only that she would occasionally reach a completely inchoate state, nonverbal, lying curled upon the floor, hands to face, shuddering, bringing up moans, sounds of such primal intensity and from somewhere so deep within her that I'd be temporarily stunned, my own eyes wide and staring, mind numb, frozen upon a single question:

"My god, where is this *coming* from?"[189]

Then it would pass. Gradually, she'd allow herself to be convinced that I meant her no harm, that I wished only to tuck her in. On such nights, I'd often sit with her a long while, stroking her hair, sometimes singing to her in my flat-toned croak, and she'd smile, childishly contented, before drifting off to sleep. Perhaps in those moments I served in some way as a surrogate for her mother,[190] or perhaps I emerged as some altogether other "alter,"[191] but I doubt I was ever simply me. I'll never be sure just who she may have thought I was, or who it was she feared.[192]

For the most part, I tried, as I'd been taught, to attribute Leah's "problems" to her massive infusions of alcohol, insistently conflating symptoms and causes.[193] Not that the symptoms weren't in themselves worthy of attention. Smallish like her father, Leah would regularly drink an entire quart of vodka—or scotch, cognac, anything handy—at a single sitting.[194] She drank rapidly, for effect, eventually demonstrating an ability to chug hard liquor in the manner of Nicolas Cage in *Leaving Las Vegas*. She drank not to get high but for oblivion, to black out, during her last year sometimes consuming so much that hospitalization was required.[195]

From early 1997 onward, our lives were ever more firmly defined by the orbit of her alcoholism. We couldn't go to a concert or a movie without Leah getting sloshed, often becoming so drunk I'd have to carry her to the car.[196] If we went out to dinner, she'd shortly excuse herself to "wash her hands," stop at the bar and get plowed. At public events—openings, for example—she'd invariably humiliate us both, sometimes others as well.[197] If we had guests, she'd make it a point to announce she was not imbibing, then slip off by herself, thoroughly smashed when she returned.[198] We'd make plans in the morning to have a lovely dinner, just the two of us, as we used to do; I'd cook, but more often than not she'd come staggering in late, the food cold and candles melted, pawing at the meal with her fingers.

After a while, a pall of fatigue settled over us, emotionally and physically, to be broken only intermittently, transiently, by reappearances of the one I loved. In the evenings, we sought refuge in the somnambulism of television, sometimes sharing a silent cigarette, sometimes not. Leah needed friends, and so did I. She reached out on occasion, usually courting women of some mutual taste, sensibility, or ambition, and there were takers, to be sure. Yet, craving them as she did, she'd turn, suddenly and often viciously, as she had with me, succeeding with a heartrending consistency in driving them away.[199] And I, as she isolated herself ever further, sealed myself in with her, trying to afford her some point of solidity despite it all, hoping she might find solace in my loyalty, the knowledge that I, if no one else, would always be there for her. This, she accepted, and I think she felt, but it had become truly an endurance test for us both.

Her work, to finish school and to do well at it, became her grail, infused with an importance far beyond itself. For her—and, in truth, for me—it took on an almost mystical significance, as if, somehow, assuming only that she might still accomplish it, everything could yet turn out as we'd dreamed. I marveled then, and do so now, at the determination she brought to bear, arising most mornings with a hangover bad enough to have daunted Hemingway, haggard and vomiting, she'd somehow focus on Foucault, on a film, a painting, signing on for credit-hour overloads, acing them all, or nearly all, fall, winter, and summer, seldom missing class. The respect Leah garnered, she earned.

Nowhere to Turn

Nonetheless, and for what should be obvious reasons, by mid-1998, we were both aware we were into something way over our heads. None of my behavioral, "token system" sorts of gimmicks had seemed to make a dent.[200] I'd taken her on some especially bad nights to Boulder County's so-called "Alcohol Recovery Center" with even less effect.[201] She'd already tried AA and would continue right up until the end to cast about for a group or sponsor to whom she could relate.[202] That summer, she asked whether I'd be willing to underwrite some more professional sort of intervention. Although generally skeptical of "the therapy racket"[203]— and opposed to psychiatry as a matter of moral principle[204]—I had nothing better to offer. I told her to go ahead, absolutely, to try *anything* she thought might work, and never mind the cost.[205]

The upshot, initially, was that one of Boulder's more prominent psychiatric hacks, after a brief "consultation," informed her she was afflicted with "Bipolar Disorder"[206] and prescribed Depakote, a drug he said would "stabilize her mood swings." His diagnosis had nothing to do with anything—Leah wasn't bipolar—and the drug caused her hair to fall out by the handful, thereby complicating immensely her long-festering deficits in self-concept and -esteem, but in subsequent visits his only substantive reaction to her "lack of responsiveness to treatment" was to try to increase her dosage. Appalled, she ditched the guy in short order.

There followed a parade of equally inept practitioners, one of them suggesting she undertake something called "rebirthing therapy,"[207] another offering to waive her fees if Leah would spend a few hours telling her all about Indians, still another recommending a four-week, $7,000 "alcoholism retreat" ("no guarantees, of course"). It was not until the spring of 2000, nearly two *years* after she'd begun to seek help and barely two months before her death, that she was finally and properly diagnosed as suffering a severe case of borderline personality disorder (BPD), "suicidally ideated" to a dangerous degree. Offered immediate inpatient placement—which she declined—she was placed on an accelerated outpatient schedule, as well as a strict régime of Antabuse to halt her alcohol consumption, and given a pager number accessing round-the-clock emergency intervention services.

It is doubtful whether anyone could've done much for Leah in the time remaining to her. BPD is "notorious" among therapists and clinicians for its virulence and apparent intractability, a the very term striking "terror into the heart of a middle-aged comfort-seeking psychiatrist."[208] Exhibiting a "bewildering array of symptoms," overlapping heavily with both multiple personality disorder and somatization disorder,[209] patients afflicted with, or at least diagnoses of, BPD tend to be avoided like the plague by many "caregivers." So much so that it is a standing joke among practitioners that the best means of treating Borderline cases is to "refer them to someone else."[210] Small wonder it took so long for any of the "experts" she sought out to be willing to call her problem by its right name. Had one of them been prepared to do so earlier, perhaps things could have worked out differently.

Or maybe not. Even the Charter Centennial Peaks Adult Recovery Program, whose therapists finally did so, refuses, along with the vast majority of its peers, to recognize the source of BPD for what it is, and thus to treat it effectively. Preoccupied all but exclusively with the "proximate causes" of stress—that is, things in their patients' immediate environment[211]—and with the search for "organic triggers"[212] or "genetic causes,"[213] they habitually evade the obvious prospect that deep, acute, and complex patterns of trauma could be at issue.

> The role of actual parental abuse in the development of this disorder has never been systematically investigated. Occasional case examples that include severe physical or sexual abuse in the background of borderline patients are found throughout the literature; generally these are reported without any impact of the trauma. In the main, the idea that borderline patients may have been severely abused tends to be discounted or dismissed. Gunderson, for example, writes: "It is common place for the borderline patients

to see themselves as having been repeatedly victimized and mis-
treated through a long series of relationships, often beginning
with their parents." The possibility that this perception might have
some validity is not considered.[214]

Studies in which such queries have been not only posed but pursued
reveal that between 75 and 90 percent of all patients diagnosed as
"borders" suffer the lingering trauma of child abuse.[215] Where therapists have been willing to acknowledge this, and treated their patients
accordingly, the "intractability" so commonly associated with BPD tends
to evaporate rather quickly.

> PTSD is often undiagnosed in cases where secrecy or stigma
> prevent recognition of the traumatic origins of [borderline per-
> sonality disorder]. Such patients often improve dramatically when
> the connection between symptoms and trauma is instituted. . . .
> The negative therapeutic reactions so frequently observed in bor-
> derline patients might be avoided by early and appropriate recogni-
> tion of the relationship between the patient's current symptoma-
> tology and its origins in a traumatic history.[216]

It has been argued, in fact, that for these patients, "integration of the
trauma is a *precondition* for development of improved affect tolerance,
impulse control, and defensive organization; the validation of trauma
is a *precondition* for a restoration of any integrated self-identity and the
capacity for appropriate relationships with others [emphasis added]."[217]
In the alternative, "treatment" strategies often tend to compound rather
than alleviate, much less "fix," the problem.

This being so, the question presents itself as to why the bulk of
"caregivers," even those willing to correctly diagnose BPD, remain so
resistant to seeing the malady for what it is and thus to providing those
who come to them in desperate need of help with the only kind of therapy
known to be effective. Unerringly, an answer emerges from the fact that
they are institutionally integral to the maintenance and functioning of
the status quo. The overriding objective of "the therapeutic state" is and
has been since its inception to rationalize the psychological ravages of
business as usual, convincing its victims that their well-being is ultimately contingent upon acceptance of things as they are, that they must
devise ways to "adjust," to "cope," accommodating themselves to whatever élite-defined psychosocial "norms" are most useful to the system
at any given moment.[218]

While this hegemonic enterprise has for the most part proven spectacularly successful, it breaks down where trauma is concerned. No therapist, irrespective of his/her ability to dissemble, can be expected to persuade a rape victim, for example, that what s/he suffered is a structurally justified phenomenon, the inherent legitimacy of which s/he is bound to accept. Nor can responsibility be conveniently dumped upon the victim him/herself, whether as a "genetic flaw" or as some form of "character defect." In such cases, the source of trauma be neither denied nor effectively equivocated. It must therefore be acknowledged and condemned. In this, however, it is imperative that they be restricted to those which can readily defined as "deviant" or "anomalous," and thus either correctable within the parameters of the extant system (e.g., rape) or outside it altogether (e.g., the Holocaust).[219] Both diagnoses of trauma and attribution of its sources are thereby constrained to very narrow limits, susceptible to individuated responses. Consequently, the institutional posture is one devoted only marginally to "healing," emphatically to minimization and containment.

In cases like Leah's, where peeling the onion inevitably reveals systemic sources of trauma in "50–60 percent of psychiatric inpatients and 40–60 percent of outpatients,"[220] as well as untold numbers of people who've never been diagnosed or treated at all, obfuscation is very much the rule. For the real nature of their malady to be admitted would be to condemn the system itself, pointing thereby to the urgency with which fundamental change in the existing social/political/economic order is required. An outcome more diametrically opposed to the mission embraced by the "caregiving" establishment is inconceivable. Of structural necessity, then, as well as the perceived self-interests of practitioners, patients, en masse and systematically, are simply herded, misled and deliberately confused, onto a conveyer belt into the oblivion of expendability.

Thus was Leah consigned, quite cynically, by those who knew better, or had reason to, to wander about in the living hell of her "splitting," her "good" self seeking frantically to excel, to please, to be well, to be happy even, while her "bad" self or selves waged what was for her a literal auditory and frequently visible campaign to subvert her every thought, move, and gesture, transforming them into ghastly mirror images of themselves.[221] The question is not why she drank to the point of undoing so much of what she might have been and said and done. The wonder is—and it truly is a wonder—that she was able to accomplish anything at all.

Losing Leah

Leah spent May 31, 2000, the last day of her life, in her studio, pronouncing finished a large, painterly canvas she'd been working at off and on for nearly a year.[222] It was one of a series she'd approached, slowly, rather deliberately, in preparation for a show at a Denver gallery she hoped to mount in the fall. I stayed mostly in my study, reading, writing letters, reviewing a manuscript. We'd planned that morning, over coffee, to spend our evening quietly, grilling lamb and green peppers to accompany some rice, watching a video of *Ulee's Gold* and maybe ending up with a late night ride on the motorcycle I'd bought her for her graduation just two weeks before. A good day, all in all.

A sort of softness had settled upon us that May, as if like weary boxers we'd retired to our respective corners at the end of some long bout, awaiting the magical decision of judges who were never there. Exhaustion, yes, a flatness even, but also something more. Leah had planted herbs just days earlier, as she always did, in a small plot I'd long ago shown her how to prepare. Then, for the first time, she'd quietly joined me in planting vegetables, laying in rows of corn and tomatoes, asking where to place the squash. And flowers, too, which she'd never done, in pots and the beds that surrounded our house. It had felt good to me, as if, perhaps, some unseen corner had at last been turned, a timid hope daring once again to well.

We were resting up, gaining space, taking our time, regrouping for what came next. Leah had done well in her interview with Encore, as well she knew—she'd been told—and had applied to Canada's Aboriginal Television Network in the bargain. There was talk of her signing on to learn Avid video editing at the Vancouver Film School, or perhaps in Toronto. One morning she'd awakened to ask me would I marry her again, renewing my vows. Embracing her so tightly she was startled, I'd said yes, oh yes, and this time by the Pipe, in a traditional way, taking tobacco to her Uncle Peter for the ceremony.[223] She'd glowed then, briefly, showing me in that moment a glimpse of the radiance I'd neither seen nor felt for far too long.

Her new program had helped a bit, or so it seemed, the counseling engaging her more, the Antabuse slamming a lid down hard upon her drinking. Still, there were undercurrents always leading in the opposite direction, as when, doubting despite all indications to the contrary that she'd be hired within the field of her training and desire, she told me she was thinking of taking a job waiting tables in a nearby Italian restaurant. There was a sense of deflation about it, a peculiarly world-weary sadness, as if, rather than something triumphant, her graduation had marked merely the end of an illusion, a silly pretense, that she'd now resume her place in the life from whence she'd come.

When her painting was done that last day, she came inside, showered and sat a while at a table, working on her Ojibwe language, using tapes and flash cards she'd made to help her form the words. I went out to start the coals, then to buy the meat. At about seven, I went in to ask whether I should start to cook. She was on the phone, smiling, glassy-eyed, voice thickening, a nearly empty glass of dark beer on the floor by her foot. "Oops," she said to whomever she was talking, "I gotta go now." Then, hanging up, to me, the beginnings of belligerence in her tone: "What's the problem, buddy?"

"You don't know?" I replied.

And she, suddenly meek, "Yes. I do."

She'd taken Antabuse that morning, and, knowing that drinking against the drug could make her violently ill,[224] I told her, as she'd said I should, to call her pager number. Without a word, she did. Fifteen minutes later, she called again. A few minutes after that, still again. She was starting to feel queasy, her face flushed, so I called, twice more. An hour after she'd first phoned, I asked her whether she was sure we were using the right number. She handed me a slip of paper on which was scribbled, in her counselor's handwriting, that "for emergency intervention, day or night" she should ring the sequence we'd been dialing. By then, my frustration was showing, and she, having talked up Centennial Peaks for weeks on end, was looking not only sick but embarrassed.[225] She said she needed to walk a bit, and, since she wasn't really drunk, I told her to go ahead, get some air, I'd wait where I was for someone to call.

It dawned on me about five minutes later that I might've made a wrong move, a liquor store having recently opened less than a quarter-mile away. Walking to the corner, trying to spot her, I saw she was nowhere in view. Returning to the house, I hopped on the motorcycle, thinking to find her, get her on the back, take her for a ride, reassure her that things would be all right. No luck. After a while, I went back to the house, parked the bike, and sat down on the porch to wait. About twenty minutes later—by then, it was fully dark—I saw her beneath a streetlamp, reeling along toward me. Meeting her in the driveway, I said, "Well, did you manage to get good and drunk?"

"You bet," she answered.[226]

"Happy?" I asked.

"Nope."

I took her by the arm and led her to a chair on the porch, got her situated, and lit her a cigarette, one of the filterless Pall Malls she liked so much, settling into a chair next to her for what looked to be another long night. I expected she'd throw up at any moment, unsure what to do if convulsions set in. Instead, after a few minutes of muttering to herself and dropping her cigarette on the floor, her head began to loll and she passed out. She was breathing regularly, so I decided to let things ride.

About 10 p.m.—some two and a half hours after we'd first started calling for an intervention—the phone finally rang. I went inside to answer, the counselor, Margie, explaining how she'd gone out for a movie and "forgotten" to take her pager along.[227] After absorbing the initial blast of my anger, she asked that I outline the situation in more detail. When I'd finished, she sounded worried, telling me I should bring Leah to the clinic immediately and that she'd meet me there. In all, the conversation had lasted less than ten minutes. I was still receiving directions when I walked back out onto the porch, intending simply to pick Leah up bodily, plop her in my truck, and head for town. The problem was, however, that Leah was gone.

It was then that I saw the blue strobes flashing two blocks away, on Arapahoe Road.

Dropping the phone, I ran toward the corner, seeing people gathering around, emergency vehicles now arriving in droves, a hollow, sinking sensation in the pit of my stomach, hoping against hope.

But there she lay, on the centerline of the road, like some broken little bird.[228]

As they loaded Leah into an ambulance, I trotted back to the house to get my truck and follow, stopping long enough only to fetch an eagle feather and a small bag of white sage and cedar, kept for times of need. At the small local hospital to which we went, they told me in solemn voices that a flight-for-life helicopter was already en route, that she'd be taken to St. Joseph's, a much larger facility in Denver, and that I should stay close at hand as I'd soon be taken into the emergency room.

Knowing even then that she'd be lost, that loved ones are never ushered into such settings unless no other time remains, I went outside and squatted, back against a wall, as I had in Vietnam,[229] sightless, mind empty, chain-smoking, awaiting what I could not change.

There were no tears just then. I was not yet ready, and neither, I think, was she.

A cop stopped, asking if I was all right. "No problem," I told him, and he looked at me oddly, as if to say more, but, thinking better of it, moved awkwardly away.

After that, I was in the room, knowing then just how really hurt she was, witnessing the terrible damage for the first time close up, her broken knees and shattered hands, the missing teeth, her tongue bitten through, hearing her struggle for every breath against the blood as, all the while, it was explained how the worst was what could not be seen, her shattered pelvis, and her skull, brain bruised and swelling against the fragments.[230]

"You should talk to her," a nurse said to me, and, knowing it was true, I knelt, taking one of Leah's hands in both my own, speaking gently in her ear, telling her for the last time how very much I loved her, my pride in being with her, a rare privilege even to have known her, how destitute I'd be in her absence. Then, having first to turn away in search of strength and calm, I let her go.

"Be at peace, my angel," I whispered. "You've suffered much too much."

They'd not allow me in the helicopter, of course, worried that she'd die in transit and that I might then lose control, becoming dangerous to everyone within that small, unstable space. So I followed once more in my pickup, driving alone those thirty-five miles, knowing she was lost to me forever, howling my despair. There were forms to sign, and waiting, still an hour before the coroner had finished and I was allowed to see but not to touch her, prevented even from placing a kiss upon her cheek, kneeling once more beside the gurney on which she laid, so quiet now, so pale and still, praying for the safety of her journey, offering a smudge, my feather, trying with all my heart to sing an honoring song. The tears came then, suddenly, against my will, driving me, impotent in my voicelessness, to the floor.

Aftermath

I remember only the barest snatches of my drive back to the house that cold predawn, and of the hours then spent trying unsuccessfully to reach someone to tell, with whom I might talk before calling her mother. Mostly I sat staring vacantly, in disbelief, feeling the sun rise, vaguely aware of things, her things, just as she'd left them, the little notepad lists of things to do, a book she'd been reading, a towel she'd tossed upon the bed. Walking to the porch, I found the sandals she'd been wearing, arranged neatly before the chair in which I'd left her. With that, I broke down for real, weeping as I'd not since I was eight or ten, no longer trying to hold back, but afraid I might never stop.

At a little after seven, thinking myself steadier, but really not, I called Barbara. Her screams were still echoing in my ears when, around nine that morning, people, those to whose machines I'd spoken, began to arrive. My AIM brothers rallied quickly, staying for days, taking charge, allowing me my grief.[231] Many others came as well, humbling me with their kindness.[232]

The next afternoon, a conference of sorts was conducted with the family by phone, John's brother, Fred, speaking for them all, asking what I wished to do. My reply, that I meant to bring her home, was well enough received. The answer to his query on whether Leah had left instructions—that she'd wished to be cremated, her ashes divided between Lake of the Woods and Rainy Lake—was not. Barb felt the need for burial, in consecrated ground, and I, knowing how little Leah would have wished to cause more pain, accepted her mother's wishes, saying it would be so.

A day later still, John, Barb, and the eldest sister, Rhonda, arrived by plane. With their approval, I chose a plain but dignified casket of poplar, a wood associated with the Lynx Clan.[233] Three local women prepared her then in a traditional way, using sage and the eagle feather bestowed at her naming, dressing her in garments I knew to hold special meaning: her clan shirt and the beaded moccasins her grandmother had made her, a fringed jacket of which she'd been quite proud, the blue beret she'd found in Spain, a purple-stoned bracelet I'd once offered in honor of her efforts at sobriety, silver earrings and a necklace from her father. With her we placed sweetgrass, a bundle sent by Zuni elders, a poster from her art show. Then we sent her north.

At Onigaming, the wake and funeral were held, Fred conducting a ceremony so exquisite, and sending with her a song so haunting in its beauty that he won my eternal gratitude.[234] Peter held a long sweat for us on the night of her wake, bringing into the lodge Leah's *doodam*, Tommy White, the head of her clan, to speak with her, his assistant to talk with me.[235] Then we drove her to Couchiching, assembling in the cemetery where her grandparents rested, committing her to earth close by. When we left, it was in the Ojibwe way. None of us looked back.[236]

In Denver, shortly thereafter, a memorial was held, hundreds of those who'd known her filling the Four Winds Center, paying their respects.[237] I was, meanwhile, undergoing a sequence of healing sweats, four in as many days, trying to regain some pretense of balance.[238] Those completed, I began my wandering, driving first in a long arc through

South Dakota to Illinois and on to the Carolinas, back across Arkansas and Kansas to Montana, then north to the Great Slave Lake, southward into Saskatchewan, out to San Francisco, where there were too many ghosts and I left in a hurry, passing through Colorado from time to time, eventually ending up in Winnipeg again, before finally landing in the empty desolation that had been our home.

More than 25,000 miles were put on my truck in those short months. I stopped often for ceremonies, visiting occasionally and always briefly with friends or relatives, traveling mostly alone, sometimes not, but talking all the while to Leah, cataloguing the beauty of places to which we could no longer go, seeing her everywhere, along a windswept beach, in wraithlike clouds and the embers of my evening fires, among great circling birds of prey, in the gait of a young woman walking alone in a park, running her through my mind in endless loops of remembrance, sifting the rubble of our lives, trying to fit together a mosaic, a puzzle to which I'd always been too close and far too overwhelmed ever to confront as it really was.

She helped as best she could, of course, coming to me at times in dreams so vivid I'd awaken with the scent of her hair fresh in my nostrils, her taste upon my tongue, having warmed me with her smile, touching my face softly, quietly, then speaking to me sometimes in her lilting English, sometimes in Ojibwe, imparting to me a new name—Kizhiinaabe, the Kind-Hearted Man[239]—guiding me thereby to the knowledge that I'd have to reach some other, deeper sense of things, learning to hear and feel and speak in ways previously alien to me if, truly, I wished to understand.

I taught little over the next year, only one seminar per semester, a single day per week. Motion remained necessary to my sanity, or even its possibility, and I pursued it relentlessly, my life a blur of airports, motel rooms, and lecture halls, running, like her, always at the bare edge of exhaustion. Yet, the very constancy of my movement allowed me to retain a certain edge, a focus, to follow ceaselessly and hard upon insights gained during the fasts and sweats and along the hot pavements of summer, expanding, filling blanks, immersing myself in thoughts and literatures I'd for far too long evaded. And gradually, excruciatingly, like the pulling of a badly rotted tooth, the picture began to emerge. The result is what has come above.

She Burned Too Briefly

Notwithstanding my earlier disclaimer, this essay has been written as it has, partly from my personal need to express the profundity of the sorrow I've incurred in the destruction of Leah. It follows that I've sought somehow to draw readers into sharing some facet of my sense of loss, to find and feel it for themselves, ultimately and inescapably embracing it as their own. For this, I make no apology. None at all. Misery, as they say, loves company (or perhaps demands it). As was noted at the outset, moreover, my motive has been broader than the offering of mere testimonial, or a pallid indulgence in self-pity. This is so because my loss really *was* everyone's. Had she lived, had she even been whole, the measure of what she might have contributed is incalculable.

This, certainly, is easy enough to realize and concede. I might well have needed to say nothing at all in making the point. My task, then, has been to avert the probability that such easy realization will be converted into the equally comfortable conclusion that her life and death added up to no more than an individual "tragedy." What happened to Leah was indeed tragic, but it was no tragedy. To the contrary, it was a crime, an offense against humanity remarkable not in its singularity but because it is so common, conveniently and all but universally ignored, hushed up, pushed far from the most peripheral vision of polite society.

Give the crime its name. Call it, as I have, colonialism. Or, as I also have, call it genocide. Better still, join in my communion with Sartre, observing that the two, while not identical, are inseparable, constituting only different dimensions of the same process.[240] Whichever descriptor is preferred, that which is described remains the most bedrock feature of business as usual in contemporary North America. It will be found in the relationship imposed by the continent's settler population upon the peoples native to this land, a sociopolitical and economic structuration without which neither Canada nor the United States would or could ever have come to exist.

I, along with many others,[241] have tried to address this reality in various ways, resorting mostly to the language and pretensions of "objective scholarship," deploying our graphs and charts, our proportionalities and other statistics, our historiographical, sociological, and legal definitions. In this, despite our best intentions, we have in many respects, perhaps most, served mainly to consummate the very crime we purport to oppose, objectifying and thus dehumanizing its victims, making the nature and magnitude of their suffering appear sterile, academic, as lifeless and inconsequential as even the most vile of perpetrators might wish them to be. There is a distinctly repugnant aroma of detachment, of distance and unreality about it all, as if what were at issue amounted only to grist for study groups and parlor debates.[242]

Yet, undeniably, the victims *are* real. They were *always* real. They are *not* objects, and never were. Each of them was, and continues to be, a human being, an historico-sociological *subject*, imbued with and therefore entitled to exercise the agency of such. This holds true both in their individuality and within the collectivities of group nomenclature and processing to which they have been rendered increasingly subjacent. How then to (re)humanize them, to restore their agency, according them their own meaning, redeeming their stolen lives from the stultifying realm of "scholarly" abstraction, or, worse still, the sanitizing soundbites of "news" commentary and "analysis"?[243]

Inverted, the question becomes one of visibility: How best to compel those fancying themselves outside the crime's functioning, most especially the more smugly complacent strata of settler society, to confront full-force the human costs of the colonial order from which they benefit, apprehending the actuality of business as usual not in the facile illusions of shopping malls and the Dow Jones Average, but in the faces of terrified three-year-olds, gaunt with privation, already trembling with the despair of being devalued and discarded? How to force such realities upon people who've made an art form of equivocating and avoiding them? How to overcome the genocidal mentality?

Such queries do not readily admit to answers. The route to a solution, however partial or otherwise imperfect, can nonetheless be discerned in focusing attention upon accounts of certain victims—that is, of individual *people*—in such a way as to inform the whole. The story of a single nine-year-old gasoline sniffer, properly told, can be used to illuminate the horror of gasoline sniffing in general and in ways impossible through even the most sensitive and studied recitation of data. The same can be said with respect to native alcoholism and all the rest. A key, however, resides in the words "properly told." Such stories, if they are to serve the desired purpose, cannot be recounted in the reductionist fashion of so much biographical/personal narrative.[244] They must be contextualized, deeply and quite explicitly so, the articulation of clearly defined objective conditions explicating the character, actions and experience of the subject, the emotions elicited by the subject bringing home the import of objective conditions, subject and object interacting in a complex manner precipitating a synthesis of understanding unattainable by focusing upon either at the expense of the other.[245]

When I observed that Leah's is "the quintessential North American story," I meant the statement in precisely this way. Not because she was so special or unique—although she was by any reasonable estimation among the "best and brightest" of her generation, and would thus surely qualify as both—but because her experience so clearly resonates with that undergone by so many others. Best, worst, brightest, dumbest, it makes no difference. If you're native, the settler system evinces no qualms in devouring you, your life, those you love, your very soul, indiscriminately, without regard to attributes. Yes, Leah was special, but this merely exemplifies the situation. *Every* victim was special—is special— each in their way. In their individuation, their uniqueness, they are united in the commonality of their destruction, finding solidarity in their dance of degeneration and death.[246] Leah's is thus the story of her people. Through her, *with* her, I've sought to tell it, to make it come alive.

To do so, it has been essential that I try and make *her* real to those who never knew her, and perhaps a few who thought they did, depicting her not simply in terms of her courage, her promise and nobility, but as she was in the abyss, her inherent beauty degraded and deformed. I've found it exceedingly difficult, and only partly because of the proximity of her loss and my inexperience in such modes of writing. More important, perhaps, is the fact that, in speaking of her as I have, I've of necessity spoken of us, of me, and by implication of my own shortcomings, of my inability to comprehend what was happening as it happened and, consequently, of the things I did wrong. Still more discomfiting, I fear, is the effect such candor might portend for those whose roles were more explicit, more instrumental than mine, John's in particular.[247]

We arrive here at a crux point. This concerns the veil of silence behind which victims so often shroud the facts of their victimization and its consequences. Clarity is absolutely vital in such connections: silence implies shame; shame, in turn, implies guilt. To this must be counterpoised a smattering of simple questions: Of what was Leah guilty? Or John? What was it either had done as a child to warrant what was done to them? Without guilt, there can be no basis for shame; without shame, no reason not to speak openly. By our silence, we internalize the onus of a guilt belonging not to victims but to perpetrators, effectively absolving the criminals of their crimes, letting them slide from the moral and legal hooks of their culpability.[248]

Such behavior is truly pathological, integral to the much wider pathology, or complex of pathologies, with which Native North America has become increasingly afflicted over the past half-century. The pathologies are there, unquestionably and increasingly so, yet we must refuse in acknowledging them to be "pathologized."[249] Leah was not "sick." Neither was John. Both were wounded,[250] mortally so, she by him, he

by the residential schools, each by their unwilling encapsulation within
the society of which the schools were and remain emblematic. To be sick
is one thing, wounded another; the latter requires healing, the former
a cure. To describe and assert the distinction is an act of empowerment
for native people, displacing the burden of guilt from our own shoulders
to those upon which it rightly belongs.[251]

In this way, and most likely only in this way, can those who are truly
sick be exposed for who and what they really are. They cannot be counted
among the victims. That is a certainty. Those evidencing the characteristics of psychological illness and imbalance will be found all but exclusively among the victimizers, those inflicting the wounds, presuming
that they are somehow vested with a right to do so, turning a blind eye
to the resultant suffering, inventing pretexts to revile the maimed for
the misfortune of their maiming. At issue is the virtual entirety of the
settler population. Theirs is a genuinely diseased—delusional, narcissistic, sadistic, plainly sociopathic—mental condition.[252]

There has been much banter lately, mostly from settlers, about the
need for "reconciliation" between natives and nonnatives.[253] While
this makes for glowing rhetoric, under present conditions it is about as
likely—and appropriate—as a rapist advancing a similar proposition to
his victim while the rape is still in progress. For rape victims, the most
elementary prerequisite to reconciliation with their rapist is that the rape
stop. Usually, there will also need to be unambiguous indications that
the rapist has been cured of whatever psychic disorder compelled him
to rape in the first place, and that he sincerely wishes to atone for the
injuries he's dispensed. As well, the victim will typically have had time
to heal from the trauma of her violation. Then, sometimes, a certain form
of rapprochement is possible.[254] For native people, it is no different. We
continue to suffer violation every bit as intimate, and often rape as well.

Fortunately, however, in our case a process by which victims can be
healed while perpetrators are cured of their psychoses immediately presents itself as a dialectical unity (a "reconciliation" of sorts). By speaking clearly, consistently and, above all, publicly, to the facts of what has
been/is being done to us, and by whom, native people can force admissions from the perpetrators that they have done what we contend. On
this foundation, we position ourselves to confront the question of why
such things have occurred, asserting with ever-increasing force our right
to the repossession of that which has always been ours, eroding their
fictive claims to our sovereignty and our property, incrementally compelling a relinquishment of both. While this sketch is quite simplistic, it

represents an essentially Fanonesque conception of decolonization, the material[255] and the psychological interacting in ways engendering the emancipation of colonized and colonizer alike.[256]

Is it possible to effect such a dismantlement of the internal colonial structures of North America's "super states" (or any such state, for that matter)? Of this, one cannot be certain, although the place to begin any assessment of the prospects might be with asking the leaders of the former Soviet Union. In any event, it was exactly this sort of transcendent vision that Leah was refining in her last years, conceiving for herself a transformation of quantity into quality manifested through a social order entirely different from that we now inhabit, one in which not just she but all of us might fit, a place where we might at last be both well and whole.

Were she here, I believe she would've said or written something similar to what I've produced, validating its imperative as she always did, through fragile contours of her life. Nevertheless, I've not attempted to speak for her, knowing that if I did I'd fail, as I failed her so often while she was alive. Instead, I've sought to blend her voice with my own, to achieve a synthesis, a harmony, an eternal we in the place of me. In this, too, I know I've been wanting, though perhaps not egregiously so. I will pick myself up and try again, and then again, until our tongues intertwine in explanation as once they did in passion. That is, until I get it right.

Notes

1 Roland J. Lamarine, "Alcohol Abuse among Native Americans," *Journal of Community Health*, Vol. 13, No. 3 (Fall 1988) pp. 143–55.

2 Anastasia M. Shkilnyk, *A Poison Stronger than Love: The Destruction of an Ojibwa Community* (New Haven, CT: Yale University Press, 1985); Geoffrey York, *The Dispossessed: Life and Death in Native Canada* (Boston: Little, Brown, 1992) pp. 175–200.

3 York, *Dispossessed*, p. 10; Gary Remington and Brian Hoffman, "Gas Sniffing as a Form of Substance Abuse," *Canadian Journal of Psychiatry*, Vol. 29, No. 1 (February 1984) pp. 31–35. The same pattern prevails on at least some reservations in the U.S. See, e.g., Arthur Kaufman, "Gasoline Sniffing among Children in a Pueblo Village," *Pediatrics*, Vol. 51, No. 6 (June 1973) pp. 1060–64.

4 See generally Steven Unger, ed., *The Destruction of American Indian Families* (New York: Association on American Indian Affairs, 1977); Patrick Johnson, *Native Children and the Child Welfare System* (Ottawa: Canadian Council on Social Development, 1983).

5 Deborah Jones-Saumty, Larry Hochhaus, Ralph Dru, and Arthur Zeiner, "Psychological Factors of Familial Alcoholism in American Indians and Caucasians," *Journal of Clinical Psychology*, Vol. 39, No. 5 (September 1983) pp. 783–90; Lawrence R. Burger and Judith Kitzes, "Injuries to Children in a Native American Community,"

Pediatrics, Vol. 84, No. 1 (July 1989) pp. 152–56; Carol Lujan, Lemyra M. DeBruyn, Philip A. May, and Michael E. Bird, "Profile of Abused and Neglected American Indian Children in the Southwest," *Child Abuse and Neglect*, Vol. 13, No. 4 (1989) pp. 449–61.

6   R.A. Goodman, G.R. Istre, F.B. Jordan, J.L. Herndon, and J. Kaleghan, "Alcohol and Fatal Injuries in Oklahoma," *Journal of Studies on Alcohol*, Vol. 52, No. 2 (March 1991) pp. 156–61; M.M. Gallaher, D.W. Fleming, L.R. Berger, and C.N. Sewell, "Pedestrian and Hypothermia Deaths Among Native Americans in New Mexico: Between Bar and Home," *JAMA*, Vol. 267, No. 10 (March 11, 1992) pp. 1345–48; George K. Jarvis and Menno Boldt, "Death Styles Among Canada's Indians," *Social Science Medicine*, Vol. 16, No. 14 (1982) pp. 1345–52.

7   See, e.g., Steven J. Kunitz, Jerrold E. Levy, and Michael Everett, "Alcohol Cirrhosis among the Navajo," *Quarterly Journal of Substance Abuse*, Vol. 30, No. 3 (September 1969) pp. 672–85.

8   Michael Dorris, *The Broken Cord: A Family's Struggle wit Fetal Alcohol Syndrome* (New York: Harper & Row, 1989).

9   Dwight B. Heath, "American Indians and Alcohol: Epidemiological and Sociocultural Relevance," in Danielle Spiegler, ed., *Alcohol Use among U.S. Ethnic Minorities* (Darby, PA: Diane, 1993) pp. 207–22.

10   T. Kue Young, "The Canadian North and the Third World: Is the Analogy Appropriate?" *Canadian Journal of Public Health*, Vol. 74, No. 4 (July–August 1983) pp. 239–41; Rennard Strickland, *Tonto's Revenge: Reflections on American Indian Culture and Policy* (Albuquerque: University of New Mexico Press, 1997) p. 53.

11   Strickland, *Tonto's Revenge*, p. 53.

12   T. Kue Young, "Epidemiology of Tuberculosis in Remote Native Communities," *Canadian Family Physician*, No. 28 (January 1982) pp. 67–74; Donald A. Enarson, et al., "Incidence of Active Tuberculosis in the Native Population of Canada," *Canadian Medical Association Journal*, Vol. 134, No. 10 (May 1986) pp. 1149–52; Strickland, *Tonto's Revenge*, p. 53.

13   Strickland, *Tonto's Revenge*, p. 53; U.S. Congress, Office of Technology Assessment, *Indian Health Care* (Washington, DC: 99th Cong., 2nd Sess., 1986); Brian Postl, et al., *Report of the Subcommittee on Indian Health Care* (Winnipeg: Manitoba Health Services Review Committee, 1985); Bernice L. Muir, *Health Status of Canadian Indians and Inuit: 1987 Update* (Ottawa: Health and Welfare Canada, 1987).

14   Strickland, *Tonto's Revenge*, p. 53. Also see J.A. Ward and Joseph Fox, "A Suicide Epidemic on an Indian Reserve," *Canadian Psychiatric Association Journal*, Vol. 22, No. 8 (December 1977) pp. 423–26; Thomas R. Thompson, "Childhood and Adolescent Suicide in Manitoba: A Demographic Study," *Canadian Journal of Psychiatry*, Vol. 32, No. 4 (May 1987) pp. 264–69; Task Force on Suicide, *Report on Suicide in Canada* (Ottawa: Dept. of Health and Welfare, 1987); Paul Kettl and Edward O. Bixler, "Alcohol and Suicide in Alaska Natives," *American Indian and Alaska Native Mental Health Research*, Vol. 5, No. 2 (1993) pp. 34–45.

15   Ministry of Indian and Northern Affairs, *Indian Conditions: A Survey* (Ottawa: Dept. of Indian Affairs, 1980); Yang Mao, H. Morrison, R. Semenciw, and D. Wigle, "Mortality on Canadian Indian Reserves, 1977–1982," *Canadian Journal of Public Health*, Vol. 77, No. 4 (July–August 1986) pp. 263–68; U.S. Bureau of the Census, *U.S. Census of the Population: General Population Characteristics, United States* (Washington, DC: U.S. Dept. of Commerce, Economics and Statistics Div., 1991).

16 See generally *Indian Housing and Living Conditions* (Ottawa: Assembly of First Nations, 1987); Public Health Service, *Chart Series Book* (Washington, DC: U.S. Dept. of Health and Human Services, 1988).

17 Joseph Westermeyer, "The Drunken Indian: Myths and Realities," in Mac Marshall, ed., *Beliefs, Behaviors, and Alcoholic Beverages: A Cross-Cultural Survey* (Ann Arbor: University of Michigan Press, 1979) pp. 110–16; Joy Leland, *Firewater Myths: North American Indian Drinking and Alcohol Addiction* (New Brunswick: Rutgers University Center for Alcohol Studies No. 11, 1976); Frederick A. May, "The Epidemiology of Alcohol Abuse among American Indians: Mythical and Real Properties," *American Indian Culture and Research Journal*, Vol. 18, No. 2 (1994) pp. 121–43.

18 For surveys of findings, see the booklet entitled *Alcoholism: An Inherited Disease* (Rockville, MD: National Institute on Substance Abuse and Alcoholism, 1985) and the special 1987 issue of *Progress in Clinical and Biological Research*, edited by H. Warner Goedde and Dharam P. Agrawal under the title "Genetics and Alcoholism." On AA, see Charles Bufe, *Alcoholics Anonymous: Cult or Cure?* (San Francisco: See Sharp Press, 1991).

19 The extent to which this may be true is to some extent revealed in the interviews included by Brian Maracle in his *Crazywater: Native Voices on Addiction and Recovery* (New York: Penguin, 1993).

20 See, e.g., Kirby A. Miller, *Emigrants and Exiles: Ireland and the Irish Exodus to North America* (New York: Oxford University Press, 1985) pp. 112, 319–20, 506.

21 Joan Weibel-Orlando, "Indians, Ethnicity, and Alcohol: Contrasting Perceptions of the Ethnic Self and Alcohol Use," in Linda A. Bennett and Genevieve M. Ames, eds., *The American Experience with Alcohol: Contrasting Cultural Perspectives* (New York: Plenum, 1985) pp. 201–26.

22 Dennis Calahan, *Understanding America's Drinking Problem* (San Francisco: Jossey-Bass, 1987) p. 31.

23 One can turn to rather conservative sources to find firm rebuttals of the genetic argument; see, e.g., Edward O. Wilson, *Consilience: The Unity of Knowledge* (New York: Vintage, 1998) p. 154. Also see Lillian Dyke, "Are North American Indians Biochemically More Susceptible to the Effects of Alcohol?" *Native Studies Review*, Vol. 2, No. 2 (1986) pp. 85–95; Herbert Fingarette, *Heavy Drinking: The Myth of Alcoholism as a Disease* (Berkeley: University of California Press, 1988).

24 The word "normal" is used here not in the sense of meaning "okay" but to mean "usual and predictable."

25 Frantz Fanon, *Wretched of the Earth* (New York: Grove Press, 1966) esp. pp. 206–51; Albert Memmi, *The Colonizer and the Colonized* (Boston: Beacon Press, 1967) esp. pp. 90–118.

26 Janet McDonnell, *The Dispossession of the American Indian, 1887–1934* (Bloomington: Indiana University Press, 1991); Brian Slattery, *The Land Rights of Indigenous Canadian Peoples* (Saskatoon: University of Saskatchewan Native Law Centre, 1979); Donald Purich, *Our Land: Native Rights in Canada* (Toronto: James Lorimer, 1986).

27 The extension of "trust authority" by one nation over another on a sustained basis is the clinical definition of colonialism in international law; John Howard Clinebell and Jim Thompson, "Sovereignty and Self-Determination: The Rights of Native Americans Under International Law," *Buffalo Law Review*, Vol. 27, No. 3 (Fall 1978) pp. 669–714; Thomas R. Berger, "Native Rights and Self-Government," *Canadian Journal of Native Studies*, Vol. 3, No. 2 (1983) pp. 363–75; Alvin Kienetz, "Decolonization

in the North: Canada and the United States," *Canadian Review of Studies in Nationalism*, Vol. 8, No. 1 (1986) pp. 57–77.

28   Michael Garrity, "The U.S. Colonial Empire is as Close as the Nearest Reservation," in Holly Sklar, ed., *Trilateralism: The Trilateral Commission and Elite Planning for World Government* (Boston: South End Press, 1980) pp. 238–60.

29   Teresa L. Amott and Julie A. Matthaei, *Race, Gender, and Work: A Multicultural Economic History of Women in the United States* (Boston: South End Press, 1991) pp. 56–61.

30   Ibid. Also see Fred Wien, *Rebuilding the Economic Base of Native Communities* (Montréal: Institute for Research on Public Policy, 1986); U.S. Dept. of Interior, Bureau of Indian Affairs, *Indian Service Population and Labor Force Estimates* (Washington, DC: 101st Cong., 1st Sess., 1989).

31   On the Pine Ridge Sioux Reservation in South Dakota, for example, 88 percent of all housing units were found to be "substandard" in 1990. Strickland, *Tonto's Revenge*, p. 53.

32   Rennard Strickland, "Indian Law and the Miner's Canary: The Signs of Poison Gas," *Cleveland State Law Review*, Vol. 39, No. 4 (1991) pp. 483–504.

33   Fred Beauvais, "The Consequences of Drug and Alcohol Use for Native Youth," *American Indian and Alaska Native Mental Health Research*, Vol. 5, No. 1 (1992) pp. 32–37; Roland Chrisjohn, *Suicide and Aboriginal Peoples: Professional Sins* (Toronto: Canadian Association of Suicide Prevention, 1996).

34   Raul Hilberg, *Perpetrators, Victims, Bystanders: The Jewish Catastrophe, 1944–1945* (New York: HarperCollins, 1992) pp. 170–72.

35   Donald Kenrick and Grattan Paxton, *Gypsies under the Swastika* (Hertfordshire, UK: University of Hertfordshire Press, 1995) p. 101.

36   Richard Grunberger, *The 12-Year Reich: A Social History of Nazi Germany, 1933–1945* (New York: Holt, Rinehart and Winston, 1971) p. 89.

37   For a dated but still excellent examination of the mechanics by which this psycho-social process of transference is undertaken, see William Ryan, *Blaming the Victim* (New York: Vintage Books, 1971).

38   The classic articulation of this proposition will be found in Craig MacAndrew's and Robert B. Edgerton's *Drunken Comportment: A Social Explanation* (Chicago: Aldine, 1969). Also see Dwight B. Heath, Jack O. Waddell, and Martin Topper, eds., *Cultural Factors in Alcohol Research and Treatment of Drinking Problems* (Journal of Substance Abuse Supp. No. 9, 1981) and Mary Douglas, ed., *Constructive Drinking: Perspectives on Drink from Anthropology* (Cambridge, UK: Cambridge University Press, 1987).

39   For explication, see the essay entitled "The Relativity of Privilege" in Albert Memmi, *Racism* (Minneapolis: University of Minnesota Press, 2000) pp. 197–203.

40   This dynamic is explored rather thoroughly by Memmi in his *Dominated Man: Notes Toward a Portrait* (New York: Orion, 1968).

41   Roosevelt's 1901 State of the Union Address, quoted in Laurence French, *Legislating Indian Country: Significant Milestones in Transforming Tribalism* (New York: Peter Lang, 2007) p. 92. For additional background, see Frederick E. Hoxie, *A Final Promise: The Campaign to Assimilate the Indians, 1880–1920* (Lincoln: University of Nebraska Press, 1985); John L. Tobias, "Protection, Civilization, Assimilation: An Outline History of Canada's Indian Policy," in Ian A.L. Getty and Antoine S. Lussier, eds., *As Long as the Sun Shines and the Water Flows: A Reader in Canadian Native Studies* (Vancouver: University of British Columbia Press, 1983) pp. 30–55.

42   Quoted in E. Brian Titley, *A Narrow Vision: Duncan Campbell Scott and the Administration of Indian Affairs in Canada* (Vancouver: University of British Columbia Press, 1986) p. 50.

43 "Our Indian Schools," *Calgary Herald* (February 10, 1892).

44 Richard Henry Pratt, "The Advantages of Mingling Indians with Whites," *Proceedings and Addresses of the National Education Association, 1895* (Washington, DC: National Educational Association, 1895) pp. 761–62. On Pratt's background, see his autobiography, *Battlefield and Classroom: Four Decades with the American Indian, 1867–1904* (New Haven, CT: Yale University Press, 1967 reprint of 1906 original).

45 Anonymous teacher to Deputy Minister of Education, December 1, 1918; quoted in Fraser Symington, *The Canadian Indian: The Illustrated History of the Great Tribes of Canada* (Toronto: McClelland & Stewart, 1968) p. 228.

46 For a voluminous selection of quotations drawn from the Canadian context, see J.R. Miller, *Shingwauk's Vision: The History of Residential Schools* (Toronto: University of Toronto Press, 1996). On the U.S., see, e.g., Michael C. Coleman, *American Indian Children at School, 1850–1930* (Jackson: University Press of Mississippi, 1993); Estelle Fuchs and Robert Havighurst, *To Live on This Earth: American Indian Education* (Albuquerque: University of New Mexico Press, [2nd ed.] 1983).

47 E. Brian Titley, "Red Deer Indian Industrial School: A Case Study of the History of Indian Education," in Nick Kach and Kaz Mazurek, eds., *Exploring Our Educational Past: Schooling in the Northwest Territories and Alberta* (Calgary: Detselig, 1992) p. 55. The idea that students were "caught" is lifted from Nicholas Flood Davin, reputedly nineteenth-century Canada's foremost authority on Indian education. See Nicholas F. Davin, *Report on Industrial Schools for Indians and Halfbreeds* (Ottawa: Ministry of Indian Affairs, March 14, 1879) p. 12.

48 "The children were awakened between five and six in the morning and went to bed between eight and nine at night. In between there was little time for recreation. The daily routine was much like a military school." Margaret Connell Szasz, *Education and the American Indian: The Road to Self-Determination Since 1928* (Albuquerque: University of New Mexico Press, [3rd ed.] 1999) p. 20.

49 Tuberculosis, for example, was present at a rate 6.5 times that evident among the general population. Trachoma also ran unchecked. See Lewis Meriam, ed., *The Problem of Indian Administration* (Baltimore: Johns Hopkins University Press, 1928) p. 13; U.S. Senate, Subcommittee of the Committee on Indian Affairs, *Survey of Conditions of the Indians* (Washington, DC: 70th Cong., 1st Sess., 1928) pp. 5, 217.

50 In the U.S., thirty-five cents per day was required to support each student, eleven cents spent; Meriam, *Problems of Indian Administration*, p. 12. Also see Walter W. Woehlke, "Starving the Nation's Wards," *Sunset*, No. 61 (November 1928) p. 14. On comparable conditions in Canadian institutions, see, e.g., Roland Chrisjohn and Sherri Young with Michael Maraun, *The Circle Game: Shadows and Substance in the Indian Residential School Experience in Canada* (Penticton, BC: Theytus Books, 1997) p. 75; Carl Urion, "Introduction: The Experience of Indian Residential Schooling," *Canadian Journal of Native Education*, Vol. 18, Supp. (1991) pp. i–iv.

51 Documentation in this area is substantial. See, as examples, David Wallace Adams, "From Bullets to Boarding Schools: The Educational Assault on the American Indian Identity," in Philip Weeks, ed., *The American Indian Experience: A Profile* (Arlington Heights, IL: Forum Press, 1988) pp. 218–39; Robert A. Trennert Jr., *The Phoenix Indian School: Forced Assimilation in Arizona* (Norman: University of Oklahoma Press, 1988); Robert A. Trennert Jr., "Corporal Punishment and the Politics of Indian Reform," *History of Education Quarterly*, Vol. 29, No. 4 (Winter 1989) pp. 595–617; Elizabeth M. Furniss, *Victims of Benevolence: Discipline and Death at the Williams Lake Indian Residential School, 1891–1920* (Williams Lake, BC: Cariboo Tribal Council, 1992); Assembly of

First Nations, *Breaking the Silence: An Interpretive Study of Residential School Impact and Healing as Illustrated by the Stories of First Nations Individuals* (Ottawa: Assembly of First Nations, 1994); Chrisjohn and Young with Maraun, *Circle Game*, esp. pp. 26–39, 230.

52   Chrisjohn and Young with Maraun, *Circle Game*, pp. 31–33. Also see Isabelle Knockwood, *Out of the Depths: The Experiences of Mi'kmaw Children at the Indian Residential School at Schubenacadie, Nova Scotia* (Lockeport, NS: Roseway, 1992).

53   York, *Dispossessed*, pp. 28–32. According the *New York Times*, the Anglican Church of Canada has claimed it would be bankrupted if it were compelled to pay damages to those students already proven to have suffered sexual abuse in its residential schools. The Catholic Church is in much the same position. For case studies, see Elizabeth M. Furniss, *Conspiracy of Silence: The Case of the Native Students at St. Joseph's Residential School, 1891–1920* (Williams Lake, BC: Cariboo Tribal Council, 1991); Roland D. Chrisjohn, Sherri L. Young, and Michael Maraun, "Faith Misplaced: The Lasting Effects of Abuse on a First Nations Community," *Canadian Journal of Native Education*, Vol. 18, No. 2 (1991) pp. 161–97.

54   An especially poignant treatment will be found in Ian Adams' "The Lonely Death of Charlie Wenjack," *Maclean's* (February 1967) pp. 30–31, 38–39, 42, 44. For additional details, see John S. Milloy, *A National Crime: The Canadian Government and the Residential School System, 1879–1986* (Winnipeg: University of Manitoba Press, 1999) pp. 142–46, 152–53, 285–87.

55   David Wallace Adams, *Education for Extinction: American Indians and the Boarding School Experience, 1875–1928* (Lawrence: University Press of Kansas, 1995).

56   The best overall study of Cameron and MK-ULTRA is John Marks' *The Search for the "Manchurian Candidate": The CIA and Mind Control* (New York: Times Books, 1979).

57   See, e.g., Richard Korn, MD, "Report on the Effects of Confinement in the Lexington High Security Unit," excerpted in Ward Churchill and J.J. Vander Wall, eds., *Cages of Steel: The Politics of Imprisonment in the United States* (Washington, DC: Maisonneuve Press, 1992) pp. 123–27.

58   Francis Paul Prucha, *The Churches and the Indian Schools, 1888–1912* (Lincoln: University of Nebraska Press, 1979); Charles E. Hendry, *Beyond Traplines: Towards an Assessment of the Work of the Anglican Church of Canada and Canada's Native Peoples* (Toronto: Anglican Church of Canada, 1969); Thomas A. Lascelles, "Indian Residential Schools," *Canadian Catholic Review* (May 1992) pp. 6–13.

59   Linda R. Bull, "Indian Residential Schooling: A Native Perspective," *Canadian Journal of Native Education*, Vol. 18, Supp. (1991) p. 39; Knockwood, *Out of the Depths*, chap. 3.

60   Anglican Church of Canada, brief submitted to the Royal Commission on Aboriginal Affairs (November 8–9, 1993) p. 4, quoted in Chrisjohn and Young with Maraun, *Circle Game*, p. 46.

61   The phenomenon is by no means unique, either to American Indians or to the residential school system. Rather it seems typical of all colonial settings; see Martin Carnoy, *Education as Cultural Imperialism* (New York: David McKay, 1974); Philip G. Altbach and Gail P. Kelly, eds., *Education and the Colonial Experience* (New Brunswick, NJ: Transaction, 1984). Of particular interest may be the "educational" objectives pursued by the English against the Irish: "The chief lesson to be learned by the school children was ignorance—not to say contempt—of Ireland and everything Irish, and reverence for England and everything English"; Miller, *Immigrants and Exiles*, p. 75.

62   This sort of drooling insanity has deep roots in Christian tradition. See, e.g., Richard Drinnon, *Facing West: The Metaphysics of Indian-Hating and Empire-Building*

(Minneapolis: University of Minnesota Press, 1980). Relatedly, see Miroslav Hroch and Anna Skybová, *Ecclesia Militans: The Inquisition* (New York: Dorset Press, 1990); Carol F. Karlson, *The Devil in the Shape of a Woman: Witchcraft in Colonial New England* (New York: Vintage, 1989); Anne Barstow, *Witchcraze: A New History of the European Witch Hunts* (San Francisco: Pandora, 1994).

63 Roland Chrisjohn and Sherri Young, "Among School Children: Psychological Imperialism and the Residential School Experience in Canada," included as Appendix E in Chrisjohn and Young with Maraun, *Circle Game*, pp. 237–49. Also see T. Gladwin and A. Saidin, *Slaves of the White Myth: The Psychology of Neocolonialism* (Atlantic Highlands, NJ: Humanities Press, 1980); Ashis Nandy, *The Intimate Enemy: Loss and Recovery of Self Under Colonialism* (Delhi: Oxford University Press, 1983).

64 At issue is the version of *Ostpolitik* advanced during the of spring 1940, and formalized in the notorious *Generalplan Ost* a year later. Therein, the nazi leadership detailed their intent to "reduce" the Slavic population by some 30 million people (mainly by starvation), push another 31 million into western Siberia ("resettling" their land with "ethnic Germans"), and retain the rest for use as manual labors. See Alexander Dallin, *German Rule in Russia, 1941–1945: A Study of Occupation Policies* (New York: St. Martin's Press, 1957) esp. pp. 39–40, 276–88. Also see Taras Hunczak, "Ukrainian Losses during World War II," and Georgily A. Kumanev, "The German Occupation Regime on Occupied Territory in the USSR," both in Michael Berenbaum, ed., *A Mosaic of Victims: Non-Jews Persecuted and Murdered by the Nazis* (New York: New York University Press, 1990) pp. 116–27, 128–49. (For a more recent and comprehensive examination, see Alex J. Kay, [New York: Berghahn Books, 2006] esp. pp. 53, 100–101, 162–63.)

65 Titley, "Red Deer," p. 55.

66 Hana Samek, *The Blackfoot Confederacy, 1880–1920: A Comparative Study of Canadian and U.S. Indian Policy* (Albuquerque: University of New Mexico Press, 1991) p. 140. As SS leader Heinrich Himmler put it with respect to the Slavs, it was enough for them to be able to "count to 500, sign their names, and [believe] that the essence of God's Law [was] to be subservient to the Germans." Quoted in Kumanev, "German Occupation," p. 130.

67 Meriam, *Problem of Indian Administration*, p. 13; Milloy, *National Crime*, pp. 169–71.

68 See, as examples, E. Brian Titley, "Indian Industrial Schools in Western Canada," in Nancy M. Sheehan, J. Donald Wilson, and David C. Jones, eds., *Schools in the West: Essays on Canadian Educational History* (Calgary: Detselig, 1986) pp. 133–54; Jacqueline Gresko, "Everyday Life at Qu'Appelle Industrial School," and E. Brian Titley, "Dunbow Indian Industrial School: An Oblate Experiment in Education," both in *Western Oblate Studies*, No. 2 (1991) pp. 71–94 and 95–114, respectively.

69 For a good case study, see Kenneth Coates, "'Betwixt and Between': The Anglican Church and the Children of the Carcoss (Choutla) Residential School, 1911–1954," *B.C. Studies*, No. 64 (Winter 1984–85) pp. 27–47. Also see M. Hodgson, *Impact of Residential Schools and Other Root Causes of Poor Mental Health* (Edmonton: Nechi Institute on Alcohol and Drug Education, 1990). More broadly, see Thomas Gladwin and Ahmad Saidin, *Slaves of the White Myth: The Psychology of Neocolonialism* (Atlantic Highlands, NJ: Humanities Press, 1980).

70 Chrisjohn and Young with Maraun, *Circle Game*, p. 121; York, *Dispossessed*, p. 24. According to Szasz (*Education and the American Indian*, p. 18), the proportion in the U.S. was only about one-third. She bases this only upon enrollment in a single year, 1928, however.

71   During World War I, the traumatic effects of combat were referred to as "shell shock," during World War II as "battle fatigue." See Abram Kardiner and Herbert Spiegel, *The Traumatic Neuroses of War* (New York: Hoeber, 1947). For more recent interpretations, see Herbert Hendin and Ann P. Haas, *Wounds of War: The Psychological Aftermath of Combat in Vietnam* (New York: Basic Books, 1984).

72   Robert Jay Lifton, "The Concept of the Survivor," in Joel E. Dimsdale, ed., *Survivors, Victims, and Perpetrators: Essays on the Nazi Holocaust* (New York: Hemisphere, 1980) pp. 113–26; *Death in Life: Survivors of Hiroshima* (New York: Basic Books, [2nd ed.] 1982). Also see Emmanuel Tanay, "Psychotherapy with Survivors of Nazi Persecution," in Henry Krystal, ed., *Massive Psychic Trauma* (New York: International Universities Press, 1968) pp. 219–33.

73   Ann W. Burgess and Lynda L. Holmstrom, "Rape Trauma Syndrome," *American Journal of Psychiatry*, Vol. 131, No. 9 (September 1974) pp. 981–86; D.S. Rose, "'Worse Than Death': Psychodynamics of Rape Victims and the Need for Psychotherapy," *American Journal of Psychiatry*, No. 143 (July 1986) pp. 817–24; Richard Mollica, "The Trauma Story: Psychiatric Care for Refugee Survivors of Violence and Torture," in Frank Ochberg, ed., *Post-Traumatic Therapy and Victims of Violence* (New York: Brunner/ Mazel, 1988) pp. 295–314; L. Comas-Diaz and A. Padilla, "Countertransference in Working with Victims of Political Repression," *American Journal of Orthopsychiatry*, Vol. 61, No. 1 (January 1991) pp. 125–34; Y. Fischman, "Interacting with Trauma: Clinicians' Responses to Treating Psychological Aftereffects of Political Repression," *American Journal of Orthopsychiatry*, Vol. 61, No. 2 (April 1991) pp. 179–85; Metin Basoglu, ed., *Torture and Its Consequences: Current Treatment Approaches* (Cambridge, UK: Cambridge University Press, 1992).

74   Herbert Krystal, "Trauma and Affects," *Psychoanalytic Study of the Child*, No. 33 (1978) pp. 81–116; A.H. Green, "Dimensions of Psychological Trauma in Abused Children," *Journal of the American Association of Child Psychiatry*, Vol. 22, No. 3 (May 1983) pp. 231–37.

75   Leonard Shengold, *Soul Murder: The Effects of Childhood Abuse and Deprivation* (New Haven, CT: Yale University Press, 1989).

76   Judith Herman, *Trauma and Recovery* (New York: Basic Books, [2nd ed.] 1997) pp. 115–29. On the more "standard" form of PTSD, see Bonnie L. Green, John P. Wilson and Jacob D. Lindy, "Conceptualizing Post-Traumatic Stress Disorder: A Psychosocial Framework," in Charles R. Figley, ed., *Trauma and Its Wake*, Vol. 1 (New York: Brunner/Mazel, 1985) pp. 53–72.

77   I use the term "Residential School Syndrome" with some trepidation, mindful of the critique advanced by Chrisjohn and his colleagues in *The Circle Game* (pp. 77–83). I believe, however, both that I employ the term in a manner avoiding the pitfalls described therein, and that it describes something real (which even they acknowledge at p. 81).

78   Raymond M. Scurfield, "Post-Trauma Stress Assessment and Treatment: Overview and Formulations," in Figley, *Trauma and Its Wake*, pp. 219–56.

79   It will be noted that the now discredited "good intentions" defense used to be standard with respect to several categories of child abusers. See Alice Miller, *For Your Own Good: Hidden Cruelty in Child-Rearing and the Roots of Violence* (New York: Farrar, Straus, Giroux, 1983). For analogous polemics on behalf of rapists, see Susan Brownmiller, *Against Our Will: Men, Women and Rape* (New York: Simon and Schuster, 1975) esp. pp. 283–308.

80   Ellen Bass and Laura Davis, *The Courage to Heal: A Guide for Women Survivors of Childhood Sexual Abuse* (New York: Harper & Row, 1988); J.P. Wilson, *Trauma, Transformation and*

Healing: An Integrative Approach to Theory, Research and Post-Traumatic Therapy (New York: Brunner/Mazel, 1990).

81   D.A. Pollack, P. Rhodes, C.A. Boyle et al., "Estimating the Number of Suicides Among Vietnam Veterans," *American Journal of Psychiatry*, Vol. 147, No. 6 (June 1990) pp. 772–76; Herbert Hendin and Ann P. Haas, "Suicide and Guilt as Manifestations of PTSD in Vietnam Combat Veterans," *American Journal of Psychiatry*, Vol. 148, No. 5 (May 1991) pp. 586–91.

82   See, e.g., Safiya Bukhari-Alston, "We Too Are Veterans: Post-Traumatic Stress Disorders and the Black Panther Party," *The Black Panther* (February 1991).

83   Milloy, *National Crime*, p. 302.

84   Ibid., p. 301.

85   See, e.g., the apologist gush spewed by Szasz in *Education and the American Indian*.

86   For especially astute insights in this connection, see Jimmie Durham's essay "Cowboys and . . ." in his *A Certain Lack of Coherence: Writings on Art and Cultural Politics* (London: Kala Press, 1993) pp. 170–86.

87   This is certainly true of the public school system, through which a majority of aboriginal youth are now "mainstreamed." Unfortunately, it also seems more true than not of most reserve-situated day schools, including the "Indian-controlled" ones, through which the balance are processed. "Educational 'control' is doled out to Aboriginal Peoples as they 'prove' themselves 'worthy' by performing in a manner indistinguishable from what non-Aboriginals have been doing all along. Of course, when we are indistinguishable from our oppressors, we are our oppressors." Chrisjohn and Young with Maraun, *Circle Game*, p. 145.

88   See generally the title essay in my *Fantasies of the Master Race: Literature, Cinema and the Colonization of American Indians* (San Francisco: City Lights, [2nd ed.] 1998) pp. 177–224 Daniel Francis, *The Imaginary Indian: The Image of the Indian in Canadian Culture* (Vancouver, BC: Arsenal Pulp Press, 1992).

89   It should be noted that the term "redskin" comes from a 1755 proclamation of the Massachusetts Bay Colony wherein a bounty was offered for proof-of-death of Indians in the form of their heads, scalps or "bloody red skins." See Susan Lobos and Steve Talbot, eds., *Native American Voices: A Reader* (New York: Longman, 1998) p. 176. For further analysis of the implications of the sports team mascot issue, see the essays "Let's Spread the 'Fun' Around: The Issue of Sports Team Names and Mascots" and "In the Matter of Julius Streicher," in my *From a Native Son: Essays in Indigenism, 1985–1995* (Boston: South End Press, 1996) pp. 439–54.

90   The term "squaw" derives from the Mohawk word for female genitalia. See Barbara Alice Mann, *Iroquoian Women: The Gantowisas* (New York: Peter Lang, 2000) p. 364. Used colloquially, as it is by the settler society, it is the equivalent of the English word "cunt." On prevalence of the word's current usage in place names, see Lobo and Talbot, *Voices*, p. 176.

91   Although a mass psychology of denial is at issue here, the amplifying effect upon the pathologies of trauma victims is any many ways comparable to those witnessed in instances where the denials of individual rapists, child molesters/abusers and wife batterers are treated as credible. See, e.g., Brownmiller, *Against Our Will*, pp. 228–34.

92   Analogously, see Ann W. Burgess and Lynda L. Holmstrom, "Adaptive Strategies and Recovery from Rape," *American Journal of Psychiatry*, No. 136 (October 1979) pp. 1278–82; Joel Dimsdale, "The Coping Behavior of Nazi Concentration Camp Survivors," in his *Survivors, Victims, and Perpetrators*, pp. 163–74; E. Kahana, B. Kahana, Z. Harel, et al., "Coping with Extreme Trauma," in J. Wilson, Z. Harel, and B. Kahana, eds.,

Human Adaptation to Extreme Stress: From the Holocaust to Vietnam (New York: Plenum, 1988) pp. 55–80.

93   For an overview, see the essay entitled "The Tragedy and the Travesty: The Subversion of Indigenous Sovereignty in North America," in my *Struggle for the Land: Native North American Resistance to Genocide, Ecocide and Colonization* (San Francisco: City Lights, [2nd ed.] 1999) pp. 37–92.

94   The complete text will be found in Ian Brownlie, ed., *Basic Documents on Human Rights* (Oxford, UK: Clarendon Press, [3rd ed.] 1992) pp. 31–32.

95   Ibid., p. 31.

96   Jean-Paul Sartre, "On Genocide," in John Duffett, ed., *Against the Crime of Silence: Proceedings of the Russell International War Crimes Tribunal* (New York: O'Hare Books, 1968) pp. 612–25. For critique, see Leo Kuper, *Genocide* (New Haven, CT: Yale University Press, 1981) pp. 44–46. It should be noted that while Kuper reacts almost viscerally to Sartre's formulation, he ends up accepting its validity.

97   Brownlie, *Documents*, p. 32.

98   There is a burgeoning literature on this point. See, as examples, Pierre Vidal-Naquet, *Assassins of Memory: Essays on the Denial of the Holocaust* (New York: Columbia University Press, 1992); Deborah Lipstadt, *Denying the Holocaust: The Growing Assault on Truth and Memory* (New York: Free Press, 1993); Michael Shermer and Alex Grobman, *Denying History: Who Says the Holocaust Never Happened and Why Do They Say It?* (Berkeley: University of California Press, 2000).

99   Explication will be found in Bradley F. Smith, *Reaching Judgment at Nuremberg: The Untold Story of How the Nazi War Criminals Were Judged* (New York: Basic Books, 1977).

100 See Roger Manvell and Heinrich Fraenkel, *Incomparable Crime—Mass Extermination in the 20th Century: The Legacy of Guilt* (London: Hinemann, 1967).

101 On the "Good German" thesis, see Eugene Davidson, *The Trial of the Germans, 1945–1946* (New York: Macmillan, 1966) p. 7. On the comparable culpability of euroamericans/eurocanadians, see J. Sakai, *Settlers: The Myth of the White Proletariat* (Chicago: Seeds Beneath the Snow, 1987).

102 Quoted in Bertrand Russell, *War Crimes in Vietnam* (New York: Monthly Review Press, 1967) p. 125.

103 Text will be found in Burns H. Weston, Richard A. Falk, and Anthony D'Amato, eds., *Basic Documents in International Law and World Order* (St. Paul, MN: West, 1990) p. 140.

104 This true in exactly the same sense that the personal consent and agreement of each citizen is unnecessary to bind all citizens to comply with given statutes within their country's legal codes. Such codes, of course, are themselves required to conform, at least in their generalities, to the higher body of legal articulation embodied in international law. A country is no more entitled to self-exemption from the latter than is an individual citizen from the former. A time-honored principle of international customary law, it was invoked against the nazi defendants at Nuremberg. For further explanation, see Adam Roberts and Richard Guelff, eds., *Documents on the Laws of War* (Oxford, UK: Clarendon Press, 1982) pp. 5, 10, 16. More broadly, see Theodor Meron, *Human Rights and Humanitarian Norms as Customary Law* (Oxford, UK: Clarendon Press, 1989).

105 Bradley F. Smith, *The Road to Nuremberg* (New York: Basic Books, 1981).

106 In 1986, the U.S. formally repudiated the prerogatives of the International Court of Justice with respect to matters other than resolution of trade disputes, thereby becoming the only United Nations member-state to refuse ICJ jurisdiction; "U.S. Terminates Acceptance of ICJ Compulsory Jurisdiction," *Department of State Bulletin*,

No. 86, January 1986. In 1997, it followed up by rejecting jurisdiction of the incipient International Criminal Court. Phyllis Bennis, *Calling the Shots: How Washington Dominates Today's UN* (New York: Olive Branch Press, 2000) pp. 274–79.

107 Lawrence J. LeBlanc, *The United States and the Genocide Convention* (Durham, NC: Duke University Press, 1991); text of the so-called Sovereignty Package appears as Appendix C, pp. 253–54.

108 Among many others, the Declaration on the Granting of Independence to Colonial Countries and Peoples (1960), International Covenant on Economic, Social, and Cultural Rights (1966), International Covenant on Civil and Political Rights (1966), International Convention on the Elimination of All Forms of Racial Discrimination (1966), Convention Against Torture and Other Cruel, Inhuman or Degrading Treatment or Punishment (1984), and the International Convention on the Protection of the Rights of All Migrant Workers and Their Families (1990) are at issue; a more comprehensive itemization will be found in William Blum, *Rogue State: A Guide to the World's Only Superpower* (Monroe, ME: Common Courage Press, 2000) pp. 184–99. Most recently, the U.S. refused to sign off on the 1994 Convention on Rights of the Child on the basis that the law would impair its "sovereign right" to declare kids as young as 12 "adults" for purposes of criminal prosecution/punishment (including, theoretically, imposition of the death penalty). See Bennis, *Calling the Shots*, pp. 280–81.

109 Robert Davis and Mark Zannis, *The Genocide Machine in Canada: The Pacification of the North* (Montréal: Black Rose Books, 1973) pp. 21–24.

110 Criminal Code, R.S.C. 1985, c. C-46.

111 MacPherson's preference seems to have been for the 7th College Edition of *Webster's Dictionary*, although he quotes the *OED* and *Shorter OED* as well. See *Daishowa Inc. v. Friends of the Lubicon*, Ontario Court of Justice (Gen. Div.), File No. 95-CQ-59707, Verdict of Judge J. MacPherson (April 14, 1998) p. 71.

112 Ibid., pp. 72, 76.

113 For further analysis, see the essay entitled "Last Stand at Lubicon Lake: Genocide and Ecocide in the Canadian North," in my *Struggle for the Land*, esp. pp. 226–28. Also see "Forbidding the 'G-Word': Holocaust Denial as Judicial Doctrine in Canada," in my *Perversions of Justice: Indigenous Peoples and Angloamerican Law* (San Francisco: City Lights, 2003) pp. 247–62.

114 See, e.g., see Alan T. Davies, "The Queen versus James Keegstra: Reflections on Christian Antisemitism in Canada," *American Journal of Theology and Philosophy*, Vol. 9, Nos. 1–2 (January–May 1988) pp. 99–116; Leonidas E. Hill, "The Trial of Ernst Zundel: Revisionism and the Law in Canada," *Simon Wiesenthal Annual*, No. 6 (1989) pp. 165–219.

115 The term is Adolf Hitler's. See Norman Rich, *Hitler's War Aims: Ideology, the Nazi State, and the Course of Expansion* (New York: W.W. Norton, 1973) p. 8, citing the 2-volume 1939 edition of *Mein Kampf* at pp. 403, 591. Also see *Hitler's Secret Book* (New York: Grove Press, 1961) pp. 106–8.

116 Robert Jay Lifton and Eric Markusen, *The Genocidal Mentality: Nazi Holocaust and Nuclear Threat* (New York: Basic Books, 1990).

117 At issue here are attempts to recast offenses such as those embodied in forced assimilation policies as "ethnocide," a presumptively different and lesser crime than genocide. This is mere semantic subterfuge. According to Raphaël Lemkin, who coined both terms, they are synonyms; Raphaël Lemkin, *Axis Rule in Occupied Europe: Laws of Occupation, Analysis of Government, Proposals for Redress* (Washington,

DC: Carnegie Endowment for International Peace, 1944) p. 79. A similar contrivance can be detected in dismissive observations that, "at worst," the residential
schools inflicted "only" cultural genocide upon native people, as if cultural were
that less significant than physical or biological genocide. Be it noted that Lemkin,
who devised all three classifications in the "Secretariat's Draft" of the Genocide
Convention he prepared in 1946, stated explicitly, repeatedly and emphatically that
they were of equal significance and intended to carry the same weight in law. For
background, see Matthew Lippman, "The Drafting of the 1948 Convention on the
Prevention and Punishment of the Crime of Genocide," *Boston University Journal of
International Law*, Vol. 3, No. 1 (1985) pp. 1–45.

118 Even in optimal circumstances—a decisive termination of the active source of
trauma and a social environment facilitating potential recovery—there can be no
realistic expectation that the aftershocks of traumatic damage ever completely
dissipate; see W.W. Eaton, J.J. Sigal, and M. Weinfeld, "Impairment in Holocaust
Survivors after 33 Years: An Unbiased Community Sample," *American Journal of
Psychiatry*, Vol. 139, No. 6 (June 1982) pp. 773–77; C.C. Tennant, K.G. Goulston, and
O.F. Dent, "The Psychological Effects of Being a Prisoner of War: Forty Years After
Release," *American Journal of Psychiatry*, Vol. 143, No. 5 (May 1986) pp. 618–21.

119 C. Van Dyke, N.J. Zilberg, and J.A. McKinnon, "PTSD: A 30-Year Delay in a World
War II Combat Veteran," *American Journal of Psychiatry*, Vol. 142, No. 9 (September
1985) pp. 1070–73.

120 See generally Kai T. Erikson, *Everything in Its Path: Destruction of Community in the Buffalo
Creek Flood* (New York: Simon and Schuster, 1976). For technical aspects, see J.L.
Tichener and F.T. Kapp, "Family and Character Change at Buffalo Creek, *American
Journal of Psychiatry*, Vol. 133, No. 3 (March 1976) pp. 295–99; B.L. Green, J.D. Lindy,
M.C. Grace, et al., "Buffalo Creek Survivors in the Second Decade: Stability of
Stress Symptoms," *American Journal of Orthopsychiatry*, Vol. 60, No. 1 (January 1990)
pp. 43–54.

121 There is a copious literature on this topic. See, as examples, J. Segal, E.J. Hunter
and Z. Segal, "Universal Consequences of Captivity: Stress Reactions Among
Divergent Populations of Prisoners of War and Their Families," *International Journal
of Social Science*, Vol. 28, No.3 (Summer 1976) pp. 593–609; Axel Russel, "Late Effects:
Influence on the Children of a Concentration Camp Survivor," in Dimsdale, *Survivors,
Victims, and Perpetrators*, pp. 175–99; Sarah Haley, "The Vietnam Veteran and His
Pre-School Child: Child-Rearing as a Delayed Stress in Combat Veterans," *Journal
of Contemporary Psychotherapy*, Vol. 14, No. 1 (Spring/Summer 1984) pp. 114–21;
William Niederland, "The Clinical Aftereffects of the Holocaust in Survivors and
Their Offspring," and Janice Bistritz, "Transgenerational Pathology in Families of
Holocaust Survivors," both in Randolph Braham, ed., *The Psychological Perspectives
of the Holocaust and Its Aftermath* (New York: Csengeri Holocaust Studies Institute,
CUNY, 1988) pp. 45–52 and 129–44, respectively; Norman Solkoff, "The Holocaust:
Survivors and Their Children," in Basoglu, *Torture and Its Consequences*, pp. 136–48;
Yael Danieli, "Treating Survivors and Children of Survivors of the Nazi Holocaust,"
in Ochberg, *Post-Traumatic Therapy*, pp. 278–94.

122 See, e.g., Native Women's Association of the Northwest Territories, *Communications
Strategy: Child Sexual Abuse in Residential Schools* (Yellowknife, NWT: Native Women's
Association of the Northwest Territories, n.d.); Child Advocacy Project, *New Justice
for Indian Children* (Winnipeg: Children's Hospital, 1987).

123 First Nations Health Commission, *Indian Residential School Study Draft No. 4* (Ottawa: Assembly of First Nations, May 1992) p. 3. For further discussion of the transmissive principle articulated, see Rosalyn Ing, "The Effects of Residential Schools on Native Child Rearing Practices," *Canadian Journal of Native Education*, Vol. 18, Supp. (1991) pp. 65–118.

124 See generally Tim O'Brien, *The Things They Carried* (New York: Houghton-Mifflin, 1990). For elaboration of symptomologies, see Herman, *Trauma and Recovery*, esp. 122–29. Also see L.C. Kolb and L.R. Multipassi, "The Conditioned Emotional Response: A Subclass of Chronic and Delayed Post-Traumatic Stress Disorder," *Psychiatric Annals*, No. 12 (1982) pp. 979–87; B.A. van der Kolk, R. Blitz, and W. Burr, "Nightmares and Trauma," *American Journal of Psychiatry*, Vol. 141, No. 2 (February 1984) pp. 187–90; E.A. Brett and R. Ostroff, "Imagery in Post-Traumatic Stress Disorder: An Overview," *American Journal of Psychiatry*, Vol. 142, No. 4 (April 1985) pp. 417–24; Terrence M. Keane, Rose T. Zimmering, and Juesta M. Caddell, "A Behavioral Formulation of Posttraumatic Stress Disorder in Vietnam Veterans," *Behavior Therapist*, Vol. 8, No. 1 (1985) pp. 9–12; R.J. Ross, W.A. Ball, K.A. Sullivan, and S.N. Caroff, "Sleep Disturbance as the Hallmark of Post-Traumatic Stress Disorder," *American Journal of Psychiatry*, Vol. 146, No. 6 (June 1989) pp. 697–707; W. De Loos, "Psychosomatic Manifestations of Chronic PTSD," in M.E. Wolf and A.D. Mosnaim, *Posttraumatic Stress Disorder: Etiology, Phenomenology, and Treatment* (Washington, DC: American Psychiatric Press, 1990) pp. 94–105.

125 H.B. Lewis, *Shame and Guilt in Neurosis* (New York: International University Press, 1971).

126 This is in many respects straight out of Fanon, who concluded in *Wretched of the Earth* that violence of the sort at issue was/is an inherent and thus unavoidable by-product of colonial relations. For analysis, see Hussein Abdilahi, *Frantz Fanon and the Psychology of Oppression* (New York: Plenum, 1985).

127 G.T. Hotaling and D.G. Sugarman, "An Analysis of Risk Markers in Husband-to-Wife Violence: The Current State of Knowledge," *Violence and Victims*, Vol. 1, No. 2 (Summer 1986) pp. 101–24; L.H. Bowker, M. Arbitel, and J.R. McFerron, "On the Relationship Between Wife-Beating and Child Abuse," in Kersti Yllo and Michele Bograd, *Feminist Perspectives in Wife Abuse* (Beverly Hills, CA: Sage, 1988) pp. 158–74; Steven Krugman, "Trauma in the Family: Perspectives on Intergenerational Transmission of Violence," in Bessel A. van der Kolk, *Psychological Trauma* (Washington, DC: American Psychiatric Press, 1987) pp. 127–52; K.A. Dodge, J.E. Bates, and G.S. Pettit, "Mechanisms in the Cycle of Violence," *Science*, Vol. 250, No. 4988 (December 21, 1990) pp. 1678–83.

128 See generally Lenore C. Terr, *Too Scared to Cry: How Trauma Affects Children and Ultimately Us All* (New York: Basic Books, 1990). A.H. Green, "Dimensions of Psychological Trauma in Abused Children," *Journal of the American Academy of Child and Adolescent Psychiatry*, Vol. 22, No. 3 (May 1983) pp. 231–37; Judith L. Herman, Diana E.H. Russell, and Karen Trocki, "Long-Term Effects of Incestuous Abuse in Childhood," *American Journal of Psychiatry*, Vol. 143, No. 10 (October 1986) pp. 1293–96; J.B. Bryer, B.A. Nelson, J.B. Miller, and P.A. Krol, "Childhood Physical and Sexual Abuse as Factors in Adult Psychiatric Illness," *American Journal of Psychiatry*, Vol. 144, No. 11 (November 1987) pp. 1426–30; V.E. Pollack, J. Briere, and L. Schneider, et al., "Childhood Antecedents of Antisocial Behavior: Parental Alcoholism and Physical Abuse," *American Journal of Psychiatry*, Vol. 147, No. 10 (October 1990) pp. 1290–93; L.C.

Terr, "Childhood Traumas: An Overview and Outline," *American Journal of Psychiatry*, Vol. 148, No. 1 (January 1991) pp. 10–20.

129 R.M. Clark, *The Forgotten Children* (Toronto: Alcohol and Addiction Research Foundation, 1969); Charles Deutsch, *Broken Bottles, Broken Dreams* (New York: Teachers College Press, 1982); Judith S. Seixas and Geraldine Youcha, *Children of Alcoholism: A Survivor's Manual* (New York: Harper & Row, 1985).

130 Herman, *Trauma and Recovery*, p. 101.

131 Ibid., p. 102.

132 Ibid., p. 103.

133 Mary Rogan, "Please Take Our Children Away," *New York Times Magazine* (March 4, 2001).

134 This has always been a mainstay of "conservative" settler discourse, and has over the past generation come to infest the rhetoric of liberalism as well. See the conversational and more formal snippets included in Chrisjohn and Young with Maraun, *Circle Game*, pp. 262–64.

135 Her two sisters by birth are Rhonda and Dawn, her three brothers, Mike, Byron, and Ben. The eldest, Rhonda, was born seven years before Leah. Another girl, Krissy, was adopted by the family after Leah was grown and gone. Nonetheless, Leah was very clear that she considered Krissy to be her "little sister."

136 On the Fort Frances School, see Milloy, *National Crime*, pp. 113, 240; J.R. Miller, *Shingwauk's Vision: A History of Native Residential Schools* (Toronto: University of Toronto Press, 1996) pp. 175–76, 233, 303, 346, 353. It should be noted that since she lived less that a quarter-mile from the school, Barb—unlike the bulk of her classmates—was able to reside at home. The effects of her experience may thus have been far less severe than those suffered by John. The damage inflicted on John also seems to have occurred at other schools.

137 Although John has never been able to effect a reintegration of Ojibwe tradition into his life, he long ago reconciled with his people. His route to this end was to take a leading role in organizing a boycott during the mid-1970s which resulted in Sabaskong Bay wresting control over their schools from Canada (his MA thesis was ultimately devoted to explaining the process). Having served a stint as Grand Chief of Treaty 3 during the early 1980s, he worked until his death in mid-June 2005 as an administrator in the educational system he helped create. Some of this is covered in York, *Dispossessed*, pp. 26, 282.

138 This is only partially true. Two of the children, Ben and Dawn, were still living in their parents' basement during their mid-30s. Rhonda also resides close at hand. Mike, Byron, and Leah all left at very young ages, however. Most of what I describe herein was recounted to me by Leah, although John independently corroborated much of it, and a few details were added by others.

139 One of the things that struck me early on was that, whenever she'd call on the phone, Leah would identify herself in a tone blending hope and hesitancy in a way suggesting strong doubts that I—or anyone else—might actually *want* to hear from her.

140 This would sometimes work itself out in rages concerning the fact that I and others were doing what she imagined that John might like to have done.

141 It was never completely clear to me whether the physical violence was inflicted at home, elsewhere, or both. On several occasions, she did remark upon being "smacked around" by unnamed parties outside the family. One of the problems I've had in trying to reconstruct Leah's early years is that she herself would/could provide only fragmentary glimpses. John honestly didn't recall a lot of what he

might have done to whom, or exactly when. Beyond acknowledging that "there were things that happened in her childhood," the rest of the family adopts a frozen silence on the matter. This is characteristic of those, including victims of RSS, suffering the effects of acute trauma. See Assembly of First Nations, *Breaking the Silence*; Emily Schatzow and Judith Herman, "Breaking Secrecy: Adult Survivors Disclose to Their Families," *Psychiatric Clinics of America*, Vol. 12, No. 2 (June 1989) pp. 337–49.

142 These are, of course, all classic stereotypes implanted in the residential schools and reinforced at every turn by settler discourse. See Assembly of First Nations, *Breaking the Silence*; Bull, "Residential Schools," esp. pp. 40–41. One upshot for Leah was an abiding preoccupation with personal cleanliness. She usually changed socks and underwear twice a day and washed her hands with astonishing frequency. At times I'd find her scrubbing herself so harshly that it appeared she was trying to remove her skin. Her explanation was that she was trying to rid herself of a "dingy" or "yellowish" tinge.

143 This behavior, often misleadingly characterized as "reverse racism," is a predictable reaction of those most arbitrarily victimized by the "hierarchy of color" imposed by settler society. It exists to a greater or lesser extent in virtually every community of color in North America and will undoubtedly continue to do so until the settlers' system of white skin privilege is finally abolished. For a good background reading, see Frantz Fanon, *Black Skin, White Masks: The Experiences of a Black Man in a White World* (New York: Grove Press, 1967).

144 Leah was in almost continuous—one could say obsessive—need of reassurance about her appearance. After her death I discovered a small box of photos, including school pictures taken during her early grades. On some, the face has been scribbled out with a ballpoint. Another is disfigured with horns and a Hitler mustache. Still another bears the hand-printed caption, "Ugly, Ugly, Ugly!" Yet, she was by no means unattractive.

145 John's brothers were also victims of the residential schools, where at least two were sexually abused. All four of "the Kelly boys" became serious alcoholics. One still is. A decisive majority of their children now suffer or are recovering from alcoholism, and several exhibit other forms of psychological damage. In one uncle's family, two teenagers committed suicide in a single year and it is suspected that a third, killed in a car wreck, also died by his own hand. The youngest son of another uncle, whom I'd taken as a nephew, committed suicide less than two years after Leah's death. This simple and decidedly incomplete recitation doesn't begin to convey the magnitude or quality of the senses of pain and loss swirling through this "really fucked-up family" (Leah's words). Nor is theirs an atypical situation.

146 To me, Leah mentioned only a single such incident, and only when she'd been drinking heavily. When I'd ask who had done this to her, she'd invariably look confused, and reply that it had been her "uncle." When I'd ask which uncle, she'd either claim not to remember, or confirm any name I posed, responses causing me to question whether the incident had occurred at all. It turns out, however, that she told the *whole* story to a woman friend, also sexually abused as a child—and thus inspiring of a certain intimacy—who shared it with me after Leah's death. The predator was not an actual relative, but nonetheless trusted enough to be viewed as "an uncle" by his victim. The psychological damage inflicted by his betrayal was thus to all intents and purposes the equivalent of what she described.

147 I doubt this is all there was to the incident, since it seems to have resulted in a particularly severe scarring. Leah recounted the story as I've recapitulated it here on at
least a dozen occasions, often tearfully, during the six years we were together.

148 Leah once explained to me that the only reason she'd gone to Laval was because
her "dad said it would be a good place to learn a 'useful language,' like French." She
was a quick study, picking up French in less than a year, and reasonable degrees of
fluency in Spanish and German thereafter. With her own language, however, she
was stymied, attributing her "block" to John's marked disinterest in teaching her.
Toward the end of her life she struggled valiantly to learn it anyway, spending at least
an hour each day with tapes and flashcards she'd made, increasingly frustrated that
there were no Ojibwe speakers in the Denver area with whom she could converse
or even check pronunciations. It is noteworthy, I think, that an hour spent learning
ten new words were her last sober moments.

149 These were mostly other waiters. One of them, Wendy Lewis, would become by far
the most committed and long-lasting friend in Leah's life. They talked on the phone
regularly the entire time Leah lived in Boulder, and whenever we were in Winnipeg,
there was always time spent with Wendy. More importantly, in some respects, she
always made time for Leah when we were up there, and actually undertook the effort
of visiting her in Colorado. The importance of this last, from Leah's frame of reference, cannot be overstated.

150 This was actually her second. She'd had the first during her stint at Laval. According
to Leah, the pregnancy resulted from casual sex and the loss of the child was thus
inconsequential. On the other hand, this version of events may well have been one
of her many defensive covers, the sex casual only for her partner, and the abortion
a reason she left Québec so abruptly. Either way, the fact that she'd had it, and the
Winnipeg abortion as well, induced a lingering anxiety about how her mom might
react if she found out.

151 "Why am I always such a fool? They're all laughing at me again. How is it possible
for one person to be so stupid? Nothing ever works out for me. I wish I could just
die."

152 Again, this is not quite true. She kept certain things, among them a dinner service
for two she very carefully packed away and placed in storage. I remember being
struck by the depth of the yearning this signified when she ever-so-shyly brought
them forth after coming to Boulder. I have them still: a nicely matched set of blue
plates, saucers, and wine glasses, complete with candle holders, collected for a
couple.

153 There was nothing romantic in this gesture. Bobby, although somewhat notorious
as a womanizer, sensed a deeper need in Leah and responded to it in a truly gentle
and humane fashion. She lived with him briefly after moving to San Francisco, in a
Mission district apartment shared with George Martin. Both men, to their eternal
credit, treated her with utmost respect, introduced her around and helped her find
a job, asking nothing in return.

154 She bought a few things during this period, including a pair of shoes, completely
outdated in terms of style, which she never wore but kept nonetheless kept, confid-
ing to me once with considerable embarrassment that she'd gotten them in hopes
they'd help her "fit in" once she arrived in San Francisco.

155 For those who don't know his work, former AIM leader John Trudell, perhaps the
movement's most articulate spokesperson during the 1970s, has subsequently fashioned a career for himself as a poet and spoken word performer/recording artist.

For a sample of his material, see his *Stickman: Poems, Lyrics, Talks, a Conversation* (New York: Inanout Press, 1994). Or pick up one of his numerous CDs.

156 Earth First! activist Judi Bari was a key organizer of the 1990 Redwood Summer anti-logging campaign in northern California, and, along with Darryl Cherney, the victim of an assassination attempt apparently orchestrated by the FBI. She died of cancer in 1997. See her *Timber Wars* (Monroe, ME: Common Courage Press, 1994).

157 The Onigaming First Nation paid all tuition and fees, as well as providing approximately $450 (U.S.) per month in living expenses during the entire time Leah attended the University of Colorado. I paid for everything beyond that, and gladly so. The point, of course, was that she be able to focus exclusively on her academic work and art.

158 Leah's willingness to accept an arrangement in which she did not earn an income of her own while going to school was entirely contingent upon my agreement that she'd later "pay me back" by becoming primary breadwinner. Since it was so obviously a matter of pride for her, I simply accepted the *quid pro quo* on its face.

159 During the years 1975–85, I fashioned something of a career as a painter/printmaker, exhibiting fairly widely and earning inclusion in museum collections both here and abroad. Time constraints eventually dictated that I concentrate on either my art or my writing. I opted for writing and do not regret it. I still miss the studio, however, and Leah, who liked my work, was forever encouraging me to pick up a brush.

160 During spring semester 1995, Leah enrolled as a part-time student under the university's Continuing Education Program. She did so, both to get her foot in the institutional door by establishing a GPA, and to afford me time to present a case under the Jay Treaty that she should be classified as an in-state student for tuition purposes (lower by two-thirds, than nonresident rates). Those things accomplished, she enrolled as a regular full-time undergraduate in the fall.

161 The photo, a dramatic shot of a funnel cloud moving along the skyline close to our house, was published in a Canadian magazine, *The Nation*, in September 1997.

162 "Indigena," Dennis Small Multicultural Center, University of Colorado at Boulder, April 2000.

163 The film, entitled *Barb and Harv: The Story of Two Hot Rodders*, was constrained to half-hour length by the nature of its assigned venue. Leah's condition was also such during her last semester that it never received its final edit. Her intent, in any event, was to recut the whole as a full hour documentary to be entitled *Gearheads*. I have the material she shot, am thoroughly familiar with where she was going with the piece, and for a while discussed the possibility with some of her film school friends that they might complete the latter project essentially as she'd envisioned it. Nothing ultimately came of the idea.

164 As always, there are lapses to this "truth." Leah and I had agreed, for example, to coauthor a book on the depiction of American Indians in film after she graduated.

165 This is the approach undertaken by Cherokee conceptual artist Jimmie Durham, whose work had a significant impact on Leah's thinking. See Durham, *A Certain Lack of Coherence*. Also see Dirk Snauwaert, *Jimmie Durham* (New York: Phaidon, 1998).

166 It has been suggested, wrongly, that Leah's interest in nazism was a result of my influence. Be it noted that she'd arrived at that preoccupation, long since, at the time we met (perhaps as a result of her time in Germany). It was she, not me, who insisted we sit through *The Wonderful, Horrible Life of Leni Riefenstahl*, not once but twice, during the summer of 1994. It was she, not me, who waded through Riefenstahl's massive memoir—I've still not approached the book—as well as an entire shelf of

background material. The best I can say is that my own immersion in the history of nazism placed me in a position to discuss what she was ingesting constructively and to recommend additional readings.

167 See van der Kolk, Blitz, and Burr, "Nightmares and Trauma."

168 "Explosive or extremely uninhibited anger," is listed as an indicator of Complex PTSD; Herman, *Trauma and Recovery*, p. 121.

169 So much for the notion of "congenital predisposition."

170 Leah badly needed, it seems to me now, to be able to straightforwardly bestow forgiveness upon John. For her to do so, however, it was essential that he acknowledge whatever it was he'd done. In the alternative, it was necessary that she confront him with it directly. Neither could bring themselves to that point. As indicated in note 141, the wall of silence within the family on such matters is virtually impenetrable.

171 The first time I met John was in San Francisco. He arrived proudly carrying a very nice Martin guitar he'd bought Leah when she was twelve, during one of the sober spells in which he'd sought to make up. She removed it carefully from its case, tuned it quickly, then, to my astonishment—this was the first I knew she played— "warmed up" with five flawless minutes of "Malagueña." Later, she told me how thrilled she'd been at the attention embodied in his gift, "breaking my fingers for months learning chords, because I thought it would please him. I was doing Spanish classical before I was fourteen, but he was drinking again and never noticed. With just a little encouragement I could've been really good." Then, having drifted off somewhere far away, her words quavering with loneliness, she blurted, "Oh papa, where were you?" So far as I know, although she always kept it close at hand, she never again touched the guitar.

172 This was not entirely a misperception. Leah's emotional circumstances were complicated considerably by my ex-wife's dragging out our divorce for as long as humanly possible, refusing settlement offers generous to the point of absurdity, eventually ending up, when her supposed "case" predictably collapsed under legal scrutiny, with far less than I'd willingly have paid just to be done with it a few months earlier.

173 Leah often remarked that everything in her life, including by implication herself, had been "second-rate." This translated, and she said as much, into the fear that being a second wife meant she was second-rate even in that (or, as "used goods," I was). My object in inundating her with high-quality possessions was not simply a matter of sugar daddy posturing but one of the more tangible dimensions of an overall effort to convince her that the opposite was true. In some respects it worked, in others it obviously didn't.

174 "The survivor's intimate relationships are driven by the need for protection and care and are haunted by the fear of abandonment or exploitation. In a quest for rescue, she may seek out powerful authority figures who seem to offer the promise of a special caretaking relationship. . . . Inevitably, however, the person fails to live up to her fantastic expectations. When disappointed, she may furiously denigrate the person she so recently adored. . . . In the mind of the survivor, even minor slights evoke past experiences of callous neglect and minor hurts evoke past experiences of deliberate cruelty. These distortions are not easily corrected by experience." Herman, *Trauma and Recovery*, p. 111.

175 "Abused children [often] form symbiotic relationships as adults in order to avoid reexperiencing the anxieties and vulnerabilities of childhood. . . . Feelings of helplessness, inadequacy, and low self-esteem drive them toward this symbiotic merging. Any disruption of the symbiosis causes rage. Any thought, feeling, or action that

suggests autonomy is a reminder of separateness, which reawakens memories of trauma and renders the traumatized individual to experience intolerable feelings of abandonment and helplessness. In such relationships, violence serves to punish the other for being autonomous, while also allowing intense emotional contact and the fantasy of repairing the damage bond." Steven Krugman, "Trauma in the Family: Perspectives on the Intergenerational Transmission of Violence," in van der Kolk, *Psychological Trauma*, pp. 135–36.

176 She did to others, however, including my sister and several women who sought to befriend her. An especially noteworthy incident occurred during the winter of 1997, when I received a phone call from the manager of a local stereo store explaining that she was there, very drunk, and had told him I'd come pick her up. By the time I arrived, the police were there, and Leah was being questioned—not very success-fully, from the look of it—in the parking lot. Upon seeing me pull up, and apparently deciding I'd make an excellent means of get-away, she hauled off and kicked a cop (being much dismayed when she was promptly wrestled to the ground and cuffed). It took me about twenty minutes to convince them not to charge her with assaulting an officer, in Colorado a felony carrying a potential five-year prison sentence.

177 This was actually her second, the first coming a year earlier, toward the end of a long drive from Boulder to Winnipeg. She'd been pretty far along the first time—her fifth month—and the loss hit both of us very hard. One of my major mistakes was not sharing my grief with her, figuring she had plenty to deal with already. She interpreted this, I think, as my not caring, and that may have hurt her even worse than losing the baby. The second miscarriage came during her second month, and, aside from a comment about "things never working out," she simply closed up like a fist. By the time of her third pregnancy during the winter of 1998, she was drinking heavily and all but continuously. Wishing to neither undergo another miscarriage nor deliver an FAS baby, she opted to abort. I readily—perhaps too readily—agreed. In any event, I went with her, waited at the clinic, took her home and cared for her afterward, so the event should not have seemed a replay of what had happened to her several years earlier. In her mind, nevertheless, perhaps it was.

178 I've never been certain whether Leah genuinely believed this to be true, whether the idea merely served as a useful cover for things she was feeling, or some combina-tion. Both the woman and I—we'd had an interlude a couple of years before I met Leah, subsequently becoming friends—went to great lengths to convince her that no "affair" existed, or ever really had. Leah remained unconvinced, however, or said she did, and acted-out, presumably on that basis, for years. Although I eventually jettisoned the friendship altogether, in what proved a useless attempt to quell her fears, she was still worrying to her diary that I was attracted to the "other woman" during the last month of her life. Such "persistent distrust" is a characteristic of Complex PTSD. "In the aftermath of traumatic events, survivors doubt both others and themselves. . . . The damage to the survivor's faith and sense of community is particularly severe when the traumatic events themselves involve the betrayal of important relationships" at an early age. See Herman, *Trauma and Recovery*, pp. 121, 53, 55.

179 The book was my *A Little Matter of Genocide of Genocide: Holocaust and Denial in the Americas, 1492 to the Present* (San Francisco: City Lights, 1997). Leah finished the courses with her usual "A" grades, applying the credits at Colorado.

180 It may be that Leah, as part of the "pow-wow Indian" image she was assembling, began her purposeful binge drinking during the summer, rather than the fall (when

I was first confronted with it). If so, it is probable that at some point she publicly embarrassed her lover (as she would me, often enough). For whatever reason, their affair ended with her standing in a Bemidji phone booth at two in the morning, having been refused admittance to his house, panicked, crying, calling me collect, saying she had no money for a motel and asking what to do. I covered her, as I always did, telling her to drive over to the Holiday Inn while I phoned in a credit card number for a room.

181 She said this to herself as well as me. In her diary that July—weeks before the debacle mentioned in the preceding note—there is an entry reading: "Big decision! I'm not leaving Ward for David. I'll be staying with Ward."

182 Caroline C. Fish-Murray, Elizabeth V. Koby, and Bessell A. van der Kolk, "Evolving Ideas: The Effect of Abuse on Children's Thought," in van der Kolk, *Psychological Trauma*, pp. 89–90. More broadly, see Harold Gardiner, *Frames of Mind* (New York: Basic Books, 1983).

183 Fish-Murray, Koby, and van der Kolk, "Evolving Ideas," pp. 90–95.

184 Ibid., pp. 102–3. Overall, see Frank W. Putnam, *Diagnosis and Treatment of Multiple Personality Disorder* (New York: Guilford, 1989).

185 "There is overwhelming evidence that [Multiple Personality Disorder] results from child abuse." Bessel A. van der Kolk, "The Psychological Consequences of Overwhelming Life Experiences," in van der Kolk, *Psychological Trauma*, pp. 6–7.

186 Shengold, *Soul Murder*, p. 26.

187 This, of course, indicates that she was actively visualizing these "others," at least intermittently, during waking states. Such is symptomatic of acute trauma/Complex PTSD. See Brett and Ostroff, "Imagery in Post-Traumatic Stress Disorder"; Herman, *Trauma and Recovery*, p. 121.

188 Such scenes, repeated perhaps two dozen times, are burned indelibly into my memory. Leah always said precisely the same thing, in precisely the same tone, accompanied by precisely the same gestures.

189 A hallmark of Complex PTSD is "extreme . . . inability to modulate anxiety, a pre-occupation with themes of mutilation and death, and fear of annihilation." Judith L. Herman and Bessel A. van der Kolk, "Traumatic Antecedents of Borderline Personality Disorder," in van der Kolk, ed., *Psychological Trauma*, p. 117. So are "transient dissociative episodes" of the sort described here. Herman, *Trauma and Recovery*, p. 121.

190 Oddly—since she was by no means a Christian—Leah often asked that I sing "Jesus Loves Me" (that being the only hymn I happen to know). This suggested to me that she was reclaiming some fond memory of her mom once-upon-a-time singing her to sleep with such songs. When I asked Barb about it, however, she appeared rather mystified. Following several moments of reflection, she replied that she didn't think so: "I was just too busy in those days to do things like that for her." Perhaps it was an aunt who sang, or a grandmother, or the mother of a friend. Or maybe it was simply a fulfillment of something Leah had always wished her mom had done.

191 On "alters," see Herman, *Trauma and Recovery*, pp. 102–3; Sylvia Fraser, *My Father's House: A Memoir of Incest and Healing* (New York: Harper & Row, 1987) pp. 220–21.

192 I need for obvious reasons to believe there was a difference but cannot be certain this was so.

193 This is the standard AA line. See, e.g., Margaret Bean, "Alcoholics Anonymous Principles and Methods," *Psychiatric Annals*, Vol. 5, No. 2 (February 1975) pp. 7–21.

194 Although we drank almost no hard liquor in the early days, I did keep a selection of whiskies and cognacs in a cabinet for special occasions. To celebrate the new year in 1997, I took out a bottle of single malt scotch, presumably unopened, which had been given me by one of our guests for my birthday. When Leah saw what I was doing, she quickly retired to the bedroom. Meanwhile, I poured myself and my friend a finger or so. We toasted. He then took a sip and a strange look came over his face. The bottle was filled mostly with water. So, too, was every other bottle in the cabinet—even a pint of Pernod—along with several vintage wines I'd been saving to give away at weddings and the like. Leah had drunk it all over the preceding two months. It didn't matter what it was, if there was alcohol on the premises, she'd drink it, often later apologizing profusely. Such difficulties in impulse control are characteristic of those suffering Complex PTSD. See Herman and van der Kolk, "Traumatic Antecedents," pp. III, 115.

195 We've entered an area of behavior where it is difficult to distinguish severe alcohol dependency in an anesthetic sense from efforts to use the substance as a means of achieving outright suicide. See, e.g., Shkilnyk, *Poison Stronger Than Love*, pp. 16–18.

196 This could actually be a serious problem and in some ways self-perpetuating. An emblematic example occurred in November 1999, when I took her with me to Chicago on a speaking engagement, trying for the umpteenth time to recapture some of our more magical moments (she'd been more or less dry for a couple weeks, and this was her reward). Leah liked to dance and, although I don't especially enjoy it, I was trying to please her. So I took her to a salsa night at the Heartland Café. Although she was eager to go, within a half-hour she'd drunk herself comatose. The Heartland being in a fairly remote location, I had to carry her six blocks to catch a cab, then across the hotel lobby, onto an elevator, and down a long hallway to our room. By the time this was done, I'd seriously aggravated an old spinal injury. Barely able to lift my arms by morning, I eventually required a series of medical treatments to repair the damage. Leah of course felt guilty. And when Leah felt guilty, Leah drank.

197 We went, for example, to the premiere of *Smoke Signals* so that Leah could meet the director, Chris Eyre. At the reception afterward, however—although he was more than willing—she quickly got too drunk to talk to him. Even at the opening of her own ethnographic film, which she was supposed to introduce, she passed out before the screening began. I'd cut short an awards ceremony for my own department's students so that I could be with her for her big moment. Barb and Harv Mathews, the film's subjects—having never before set foot on a university campus, this was their big night, as well—had also come to be with her. Instead of watching themselves on the silver screen, they got to help me carry her unconscious form out to my truck.

198 During the winter of 1998, for instance, Leah announced she'd like to have a dinner party to which she'd invite Melinda Barlow—a professor she admired greatly and desired to impress—as well as a very select group of women film students she'd befriended. I readily agreed. She spent two full days preparing an intricately sauced Mexican meal, while I cleaned the house from one end to the other so the "ambiance" would be just right. All was well until the women arrived. By the time we sat down at the table, however, Leah could do little but sit and smile beatifically. While making a point of sipping only a sparkling water during predinner conversation—and serving the others wine—she'd been slipping off to chug from a bottle she'd secreted in her washroom. I had to gently lead her off to bed before anyone

had taken their first bite. I then rejoined her friends, only one of whom I'd even met before, and did my best to be a good host for her.

199 One example will suffice, although there are several others that I know of. It concerns a student with whom Leah first formed a very intense relationship, then called one night in the wee hours, drunkenly berating her as a "spoiled white cunt" (the woman worked as a waiter, just as Leah had). The scenario was repeated twice more before her friend, who plainly desired to sustain it, cashed the relationship in altogether. A large part of the problem, I think, arose from the subtle, often unconscious and therefore quite insidious, eurocentrism with which even the more progressive sectors of settler society are permeated. It wasn't that the woman said or did anything overtly derogatory about Indians. It was more her bland expectation that her and Leah's connection should exist exclusively on the basis of Leah's fluency in the nuances of European/euroamerican culture. She knew nothing of Ojibwe culture and failed to see why she should. That such consignment of things native to the realm of insignificance would necessarily be received as arrogant and insulting by any native person seems never really to have crossed her mind. All of us become mortally weary of having to convince otherwise good and sensitive people that, as Indians, we're worthy of the least consideration or respect. For someone like Leah, who suffered the "heightened affect"—that is, hypersensitivity to slights resulting from Complex Trauma—the situation was impossible. She ended her days crying herself to sleep over it, and jotting little lists in her diary of women with whom she thought she might make friends. See Herman and van der Kolk, "Traumatic Antecedents," pp. 115, 117.

200 To get the drift of what I thought I was doing, see generally Peter M. Miller, *Behavioral Treatment of Alcoholism* (New York: Pergamon, 1976).

201 The taxpayer-subsidized Boulder County Alcohol Recovery Center is a misleadingly titled scam. Aside from blood pressure and breathalyzer tests administered upon check-in—Leah registered about three times the legal definition of "drunk" each time I took her—they did nothing for her aside from assigning her a cot. Clearly, by "recovery," they mean "sleep it off." Their other "services" included not so much as ensuring that Leah remained inside while intoxicated, or bothering to call me if she left (I always made sure they had my number). I quit taking her there after receiving a call from her at a little after midnight one wintry evening. She was standing in a phone booth, crying, saying she was cold and needed me to come and get her right away. I drove into Boulder in a veritable blizzard, only to find her—in a nightmarish premonition of how she'd die—running barefooted down the centerline of Valmont, a busy thoroughfare, wearing only her pajamas. For that, they tried to bill her $300.

202 One of my many heartwrenching moments in the aftermath of her death was coming across a book Leah had hidden in her dresser. It is entitled *When AA Doesn't Work for You*. Although there were times when I believed she was using AA as a sort of con to keep me off her back—alcoholics being notorious for such ploys—I was wrong. She never, ever stopped trying to find something that worked.

203 For insight into my reasoning, see Andrew Polsky, *The Rise of the Therapeutic State* (Princeton, NJ: Princeton University Press, 1991).

204 Although there are exceptions, and I've cited many of them herein, I tend to view psychiatrists as participants in a criminal enterprise, psychiatry itself as a crime against humanity. Its longstanding position at the forefront of the eugenics movement, its habitual usage of human beings as test animals, its routine employment of techniques like psychosurgery and electroshock, and its core reliance upon

psychotropics and other such drugs leave me no alternative. See generally Thomas Szasz, *The Therapeutic State: Psychiatry in the Mirror of Current Events* (Buffalo, NY: Prometheus Books, 1984); Thomas Röder, Volker Kubillus, and Anthony Burwell, *Psychiatrists: The Men Behind Hitler* (Los Angeles: Freedom Press, 1994); and Stephan Kühl, *The Nazi Connection: Eugenics, American Racism, and German National Socialism* (New York: Oxford University Press, 1994).

205 This was hardly as noble as it sounds. For the most part, such things were covered by my insurance.

206 "Bipolar Disorder," which was once and more instructively known as "Manic Depressive Psychosis," has become the state-of-the-art catch-all term of the psychiatric vernacular.

207 I'm not quite sure what was meant by this but believe it to be the same fashionably bizarre "treatment" at issue in the 2001 murder trial of self-styled "alternative therapist" Connell Watkins and her assistant, Julie Ponder, in Colorado. Their patient, a ten-year-old girl with symptoms sounding remarkably similar to Leah's, failed to survive the "rebirthing." See Julie Cart, "2 Convicted in Girl's Death During 'Rebirthing' Therapy," *Los Angeles Times* (April 21, 2001).

208 Irvin Yalom, *Love's Executioner and Other Tales of Psychotherapy* (New York: Basic Books, 1989).

209 "70 percent of patients with an established diagnosis of multiple personality disorder also qualified for the diagnosis of borderline personality disorder." Herman and van der Kolk, "Traumatic Antecedents," p. 117. Also see Herman, *Trauma and Recovery*, p. 123.

210 Letter to the Editor, *American Journal of Psychiatry*, Vol. 147, No. 10 (October 1990) p. 1390.

211 A serious problem with this approach is that those suffering Complex PTSD accruing from childhood manifest a "disguised presentation" designed to protect the traumatic source. This renders them quite suggestible to anything that might conveniently serve as a cover. Leah's case is a perfect example. A diary entry dating from the fall of 1996, when she first began to consume large amounts of alcohol, observes that, "My drinking is making my relationship with my husband crazy." After a couple of weeks with the Centennial Peaks counselors during the spring of 2000, she noted in the diary, "The craziness of my relationship with Ward makes me drink." Nowhere in her assessment questionnaires was Leah asked a single question bearing on her childhood experiences. One can only assume that the counseling sessions followed suit. By implication, she was being led toward conclusions convenient for the therapist rather than probed as to the source of her problem. The effect—with BPD, at least—is often to reinforce aspects of the problem itself. See Herman and van der Kolk, "Traumatic Antecedents," p. 116.

212 Trauma "may produce long-lasting alteration in the regulation of endogenous opioids, which are natural substances having the same effects as opiates within the central nervous system." If such organic chemical imbalances are detected by clinicians, and a patient's background of trauma is not, the tendency is to attribute their malady to the imbalance rather than vice versa. See Roger K. Pitman, Bessel A. van der Kolk, et al., "Naxoline-Reversible Analgesic Response to Combat-Related Stimuli in Post-Traumatic Stress Disorder: A Pilot Study," *Archives of General Psychiatry*, Vol. 47, No. 6 (June 1990) pp. 541–54.

213 The longterm organic chemical imbalances generated by protracted trauma and Complex PTSD are now believed to bring about physiological alterations of

brain structure. Should the deep traumatic source of imbalance go undetected in therapy—as is all but invariably the case with BPD—and abnormalities of the brain's structure discovered during postmortem examination, the tendency is to treat the abnormality as the source of symptoms rather than the other way around. This, in turn, suggests—quite erroneously—a "genetic predisposition." See Bessel A. van der Kolk, "The Body Keeps Score: Approaches to the Psychobiology of Posttraumatic Stress Disorder," in Bessel A. van der Kolk, Alexander C. McFarlane, and Lars Weisaeth, eds., *Traumatic Stress: The Effects of Overwhelming Experience on Mind, Body, and Society* (New York: Guilford, 1996) pp. 214–41.

214 Herman and van der Kolk, "Traumatic Antecedents," p. 114; quoting John G. Gunderson. *Borderline Personality Disorder* (Washington, DC: American Psychiatric Press, 1984).

215 Herman and van der Kolk, "Traumatic Antecedents," p. 118; citing, among other sources, M.H. Stone, "Borderline Syndromes: A Consideration of Subtypes and an Overview," *Psychiatric Clinics of North America*, Vol. 4 (1981) pp. 3–24; Judith L. Herman, "Histories of Violence in an Outpatient Population: An Exploratory Study," *American Journal of Orthopsychiatry*, Vol. 56, No. 1 (January 1986) pp. 137–41. Also see M.C. Zanarini, J.G. Gunderson, M.F. Marino, et al., "Childhood Experiences of Borderline Patients," *Comprehensive Psychiatry*, Vol. 30, No. 1 (January–February 1989) pp. 18–25; Judith L. Herman, J. Perry, and Bessel A. van der Kolk, "Childhood Trauma in Borderline Personality Disorder," *American Journal of Psychiatry*, Vol. 146, No. 4 (April 1989) pp. 490–95; S.N. Ogata, K.R. Silk, S. Goodrich, et al., "Childhood Sexual and Physical Abuse in Adult Patients with Borderline Personality Disorder," *American Journal of Psychiatry*, Vol. 147, No. 8 (August 1990) pp. 1008–13.

216 Herman and van der Kolk, "Traumatic Antecedents," p. 119.

217 Ibid.; citing, among other sources, Krystal, "Trauma and Affect"; Judith L. Herman, *Father-Daughter Incest* (Cambridge, MA: Harvard University Press, 1981); Bessel A. van der Kolk, *The Trauma Response as a Biopsychosocial Entity in Long-Term Effects of Violence: Cross-Cultural Treatment and Research Issues in PTSD* (Washington, DC: National Institutes of Health Monographs, 1986); Yael Danieli, "The Treatment and Prevention of Long-Term Effects and Intergenerational Transmission of Victimization: A Lesson from Holocaust Survivors and Their Children," in Figley, *Trauma and Its Wake*, pp. 295–313,

218 Szasz, *Therapeutic State*; Polsky, *Rise of the Therapeutic State*. Also see R.D. Laing, *The Politics of Experience* (New York: Ballantine, 1968); Jeffrey Moussaieff Masson, *Against Therapy* (Monroe, ME: Common Courage Press, [2nd ed.] 1994).

219 Even with Vietnam vets, where the systemic linkages to trauma cannot be denied, it can be—and usually is—argued that victimization resulted from a "mistake," since corrected—the war is over, after all—and that the system itself is sound. This is as opposed to the general, and entirely correct, recognition that what the nazis did they did for reasons of structural imperative, and that it is thus the nazi system itself which must be condemned. See generally Hendin and Haas, *Wounds of War*.

220 Herman, *Trauma and Recovery*, pp. 122–26. Also see J.B. Bryer, B.A. Nelson, J.B. Miller, and P.A. Krol, "Childhood Sexual and Physical Abuse as Factors in Adult Psychiatric Illness," *American Journal of Psychiatry*, Vol. 144, No. 11 (November 1987) pp. 1426–30.

221 Fish-Murray, Koby, and van der Kolk, "Effects of Abuse," pp. 102–3; Herman, *Trauma and Recovery*, pp. 101–7, 125; Otto Kernberg, "Borderline Personality Organization," *Journal of the American Psychoanalytical Association*, Vol. 15, No. 3 (July 1967) pp. 641–85.

222 The painting, entitled "Rug Motif #9," served as the centerpiece of group exhibition conducted in conjunction with American Indian Awareness Week at the University of Colorado, April 19–27, 2001. The show was dedicated to Leah's memory.

223 This would have been the second time I did so. Shortly after we were married in Boulder, I'd taken tobacco to Leah's uncle, Tobasonekwat Kinew (Peter Kelly), asking and he agreeing that he would perform a traditional wedding ceremony for us "when the time was right." It never was. We'd been thinking of the next summer, on the anniversary of our civil procedure, but by then she was riding on her anger. After that, there was summer school each year, and the alcohol as well. Leah would never participate in traditional things when she'd been drinking. I didn't push it, but now really wish I had. She deserved her moment to shine in that way, to be the center of attention in some ceremony other than her funeral. Till my dying day I'll wonder whether, if I'd insisted, it might have been somehow different for her.

224 Antabuse is contraindicated to alcohol in such a way as to induce nausea, headache, hot flashes, and other unpleasant side effects when the latter substance is ingested in small amounts. When combined with large amounts of alcohol, it can be dangerous, sometimes fatal.

225 Leah's impression, as she'd told me repeatedly, was that callbacks would occur within fifteen minutes. Her sense of disappointment and betrayal when we'd still received no call after an hour was palpable.

226 The coroner's report indicated that at the time of her death Leah's blood alcohol content was three and a half times the legal definition of intoxication.

227 The "pager" turned out to be a cell phone, the number to which was shortly changed or disconnected. By then, administrators at Centennial Peaks were insisting that their outpatient facility offered no such service as "emergency intervention." This hardly explains Leah's possession of Margie's number or the hand-scribbled note suggesting precisely the opposite. It also begs the glaring question of why, if the facility offered no such service, its practitioners would prescribe a potentially life-threatening drug to a patient diagnosed as suicidally ideated. Under such circumstances, a more than two-hour callback time—which Centennial Peaks itself confirmed to the Boulder County Coroner's Office—was absolutely irresponsible. That, however, hardly prevented the corporation from billing me in the amount of $1,400 for "services rendered" during the month of May.

228 According to police reports, she'd been running down the middle of Arapahoe, moving east, away from the streetlamp at our corner. She was hit by a car moving in the same direction along Arapahoe at about "45 miles per hour" (probably nearer 55). The driver, for whatever reason—he tested clean for alcohol and drugs—had not seen her until the last moment, swerving left to avoid her. At the same time, Leah tried to run in the same direction to get out of the way. She was knocked approximately one hundred feet by the impact.

229 My own traumatic baggage, carried ever since, perhaps impaired my ability to perceive the depth of hers—she did not fit my preconceived notion of a PTSD sufferer, either—but that's a story I'll take up some other time.

230 The attending physician at St. John's later told me that, had they been able to keep her alive, she'd have almost certainly have been "brain dead."

231 I am particularly indebted to Glenn Morris, Tink Tinker, and Rob Chanate in this regard.

232 This is especially true of Barb and Harv Mathews, and Barb's father, John Fallon.

233 Another reason I wanted poplar is that it degrades rapidly. Leah had not wanted to be buried, she'd wanted to go to the lakes, and I wanted her at least to return to earth as quickly as possible. In the event, as the casket was lowered into the grave, water from nearby Rainy Lake was already rising in its bottom. I know this bothered Barb, but I was happy for Leah. She'd met her mother's needs, while her own were fulfilled as well.

234 Russ Means, who'd headed for Winnipeg from Pine Ridge upon receiving word of Leah's death, met me at the airport, along with my and Leah's adoptive sister, Sharon Venne (who'd come all the way from Yellowknife), and my blood sister, Terry Friedman (from St. Louis), after my long, lonely flight up from Denver. Russ delivered a powerful tribute to Leah at her wake, naming her a "hero" for all she'd accomplished. Sharon and Terry stayed by my side the entire time, seeing me through what might otherwise have proven an impossible ordeal.

235 I've been in countless such ceremonies, and this was the most powerful by far. It was also my sister Terry's first (Sharon tended her). The next night, we sweat again, and Peter's daughter, Shawin, entered the lodge for the first time, in an altogether respectful way, expressly to be with me. One result of the strength in that moment is that Shawin received Leah's Pipe—of which Sharon served as caretaker during the intervening year—and ceremonial jacket during a memorial to be conducted at Onigaming on June 10, 2001.

236 One is not to return to an Ojibwe grave for several days after burial.

237 The proceedings were conducted by Tink Tinker, my spiritual adviser. Russ spoke again, movingly. Sharon, who'd driven me down from Winnipeg so that I might perform ceremonies at certain spots along the way, organized and helped prepare the traditional feast, explaining to those assembled how things are done in the north.

238 Sharon participated in these sweats, on instruction from Peter, sharing certain aspects of the Ojibwe version of the ceremony with the more Lakota-oriented people of this area so that Leah's spirit might always feel welcomed in our local lodges. These things have now been incorporated into the way things are done here. Her task completed, Sharon drove home to Edmonton alone. Her sort of care, concern and acceptance of responsibility is all too rare.

239 Both Ojibwes and my own Cherokee people are traditionally matrilineal (albeit, this is now contested by some Ojibwes). Had Leah and I had children, they would thus by definition have been Ojibwe rather than Cherokee. For this reason, among others, I was honored with an Ojibwe name—Kenis (Little Golden Eagle)—in a ceremony performed by Fred Kelly. During the sweat conducted the night of Leah's wake, Peter told me I might wish to consider a change of names as part of my passage into a new phase of life. Having mulled this over the summer, I sought Fred's advice in September. He was somewhat perplexed, since Ojibwe names are not subject to change. After a while, however, he inquired if Leah had said anything during her visits that struck me as peculiar. I recounted how she'd once looked up at me as we were walking together, smiled, and said the single word, "Kizhiinaabe." He looked a bit surprised. When I asked what it meant, he replied that she'd given me a second name, to be carried along with the one I already possessed. I was finally apprised of its literal meaning in a ceremony performed the following day. There is a story attending it which I will not go into here.

240 Sartre, "On Genocide"; Churchill, A Little Matter of Genocide, pp. 416, 433, 441.

241 As examples, see Drinnon, *Facing West*; Tzvetan Todorov, *The Conquest of America: The Question of the Other* (New York: Harper & Row, 1984); David E. Stannard, *American Holocaust: Columbus and the Conquest of the New World* (New York: Oxford University Press, 1992).

242 Aspects of the problem are explored quite well by Noam Chomsky, albeit in another connection, in the essay "Objectivity and Liberal Scholarship," included in his *American Power and the New Mandarins* (New York: Pantheon, 1967) pp. 23–158.

243 For elaboration, see Noam Chomsky, *Necessary Illusions: Thought Control in Democratic Societies* (Boston: South End Press, 1989); Michael Parenti, *Inventing Reality: The Politics of the News Media* (New York: St. Martin's Press, 1993).

244 For a classic example of emphasis upon personal experience to the virtual exclusion of much-needed contextualization, see Basil H. Johnson, *Indian School Days* (Norman: University of Oklahoma Press, 1988).

245 Even the best and most beautifully composed examples of the extant biographical/personal narrative literature—e.g., Rudy Wiebe and Yvonne Johnson, *Stolen Life: The Journey of a Cree Woman* (Toronto: Alfred A. Knopf, 1998)—fall about as far short of bringing out the objective conditions and processes shaping the context of their subject's lives as objective studies do in addressing more subjective considerations.

246 The point here is important insofar as one of the primary defensive strategies deployed by apologists for the status quo has been to privilege analytical individuation to the exclusion of group and systemic analyses; Rajeev Bhargava, *Individualism in Social Science: Forms and Limits of a Methodology* (Oxford, UK: Clarendon Press, 1992).

247 It should be noted that in the years before his death, John and I discussed the things said in this essay and he indicated a willingness to make them public, even to the extent of filing a damage claim against the Canadian government on the basis that what happened to Leah accrued from the trauma he himself suffered as a child in the residential schools. Whether or not he actually did so, I can't say.

248 For treatment of a somewhat analogous context, see John Duffet, ed., *Against the Crime of Silence: Proceedings of the International War Crimes Tribunal* (New York: Clarion Books, 1970). More directly, see Assembly of First Nations, *Breaking the Silence*, and Furniss, *Conspiracy of Silence*.

249 Chrisjohn and Young with Maraun, *Circle Game*, pp. 81, 255, 277.

250 This is the exactly the distinction made in behalf of combat veterans by Hendin and Haas in *Wounds of War*.

251 Had candor rather than silence been the behavioral norm among native people, or at least her family, things might well have worked out very differently for Leah. Presumptively, the same holds true for many others. See Schatzow and Herman, "Breaking Secrecy." Also see note 217.

252 "If it is sickness you seek, don't look for it in the victims of genocide; it resides in the minds and hearts of the people who planned, designed, implemented, and operated the machinery of genocide, and who now seek to cover it up. The 'meaning' of Indian Residential Schooling is not the pathology it may have created in some Aboriginal Peoples; it is the pathology it reveals in the 'system of order' giving rise to it." Chrisjohn and Young with Maraun, *Circle Game*, pp. 80–81.

253 And not just with native people here. Settler élites all over the planet have recently taken to offering apologies to and calling for reconciliation with those they've ravaged, meanwhile making no move to relinquish either the privileges or the lion's share of the spoils they obtained in the process. For a handy global survey, see Roy L.

Brooks, *When Sorry Isn't Enough: The Controversy over Apologies and Reparations for Human Injustice* (New York: New York University Press, 1999).

254 "Folk wisdom recognizes that forgiveness is divine. And even divine forgiveness, in most religious systems, is not unconditional. True forgiveness cannot be granted until the perpetrator has sought and earned it through confession, repentance and restitution. Genuine contrition in a perpetrator is a rare miracle." Herman, *Trauma and Recovery*, p. 190.

255 There is presently a tendency among the more radical native intellectuals—for which I am myself in significant part responsible—to privilege the material at the expense or even to the exclusion of the psychological. This is just as dangerous as discounting material considerations in favor of primarily "therapeutic" remedies. Leah's example offers proof positive that alterations in material circumstance alone are not sufficient.

256 Much of the material in *Wretched of the Earth* is of course relevant to this point. In some ways still more germane is Fanon's *A Dying Colonialism* (New York: Grove Press, 1967) esp. pp. 147–62. Also see Lewis R. Gordon, *Fanon and the Crisis of Western Man: An Essay on Philosophy and the Social Sciences* (New York: Routledge, 1995) esp. pp. 37–66.

FOURTEEN

The Ghosts of 9–1–1

Reflections on History, Justice and Roosting Chickens

> As ye sow, so shall ye reap.
> —*Galatians*, 6:7

September 11, 2001, will now and forever be emblazoned in the short-hand of popular consciousness as a correlation to the emergency dialing sequence, "9–1–1." On that date, a rapid but tremendous series of assaults were carried out against the paramount symbols of America's global military/economic dominance, the Pentagon and the twin towers of New York's World Trade Center (WTC), leaving about one-fifth of the former in ruins and the latter in a state of utter obliteration. Initially, it was claimed that as many as 5,000 U.S. citizens were killed, along with 78 British nationals, come to do business in the WTC, and perhaps 300 other "aliens," the majority of them undocumented, assigned to scrub the floors and wash the windows of empire.[1]

"The Ghosts of 9–1–1" is the more fully developed version of my 2001 op-ed, "Some People Push Back," which attained such an astonishing degree of notoriety three and a half years after the fact. By then, of course, the present essay had long since been published as the lead piece in my *On the Justice of Roosting Chickens: The Costs and Consequences of U.S. Imperial Arrogance and Criminality* (Oakland, CA: AK Press, 2003). In that capacity it undoubt-edly figured rather prominently in *Chickens* receiving an honorable mention for the 2003 Gustavus Myers Award for Best Book on the Topic of Human Rights. To be sure, the latter reality went conspicuously unmentioned in the media offensive mounted during the spring of 2005 by the right's talking heads, from Bill O'Reilly and Ann Coulter to Michelle Malkin and Sean Hannity, together with liberal collaborators like Marc Cooper and self-proclaimed anarchists of the Bob Black variety. Indeed, there was no mention of "Ghosts'" very existence in such circles, despite the fact that *Chickens* enjoyed a brief stint as Amazon's best-selling nonfiction paperback.

Even before the first of the Trade Center's towers had collapsed, the "news" media, as yet possessed of no hint as to who may have carried out the attacks, much less why they might have done so, were already and repeatedly proclaiming the whole thing "unprovoked" and "senseless." Within a week, the assailants having meanwhile been presumably identified, Newsweek had recast the initial assertions of its colleagues in the form of a query bespeaking the aura of wide-eyed innocence in which the country was by then, as always, seeking to cloak itself. "Why," the magazine's cover whined from every newsstand, "do they hate us so much?"

The question was and remains mind boggling in its temerity, so much so that after a lifetime of spelling out the reasons, one is tempted to respond with a certain weary cynicism, perhaps repeating Malcolm X's penetrating observation about chickens coming home to roost and leaving it at that.[2] Still, mindful of the hideous human costs attending the propensity of Good Americans, like Good Germans, to dodge responsibility by anchoring professions of innocence in claims of near-total ignorance concerning the crimes of their corporate state, one feels obliged to try to deny them the option of such pretense. It is thus necessary that at least a few of those whose ravaged souls settled in upon the WTC and the Pentagon be named.

At the front of the queue were the wraiths of a half-million Iraqi children, all of them under twelve, all starved to death or forced to die for lack of basic sanitation and medical treatment during the past ten years.[3] These youngsters suffered and died because the United States first systematically bombed their country's water purification, sewage treatment, and pharmaceutical plants out of existence, then imposed a decade-long—and presently ongoing—embargo to ensure that Iraq would be unable to repair or replace most of what had been destroyed.[4] The point of this carefully calculated mass murder, as was explained at the outset by then-president George Herbert Walker Bush, father of the current Oval Office occupant, has been to impress upon the Iraqi government—and the rest of the world as well—that "what we say, goes."[5]

In other words, though no less bluntly: "Do as you're told or we'll kill your babies."

Much has been made, rightly enough, of how U.S. governmental agencies, corporate media, and academic élites collude to provide only such information as is convenient to the status quo.[6] It is thus true that there is much of which the public is unaware. No such excuse can be advanced with respect to the fate of Iraq's children, however. Not only was the toll publicly predicted before U.S. sanctions were imposed, but two high United Nations officials, including Assistant Secretary General Denis Halliday, have resigned in protest of what Halliday described in widely reported statements as "the policy of deliberate genocide" they reflected.[7] Asked by an interviewer on 60 *Minutes* in 1996 whether the UN's estimate of child fatalities in Iraq was accurate, U.S. ambassador to the United Nations *cum* secretary of state Madeleine Albright confirmed it before a national television audience.[8]

"We've decided," Albright went on in a remark prominently displayed in the *New York Times* and most other major newspapers, "that it's worth the cost" in lives extracted from brown-skinned toddlers to "set an example" so terrifying in its implications that it would compel planetary obedience to America's dictates in the years ahead.[9] Such were the official terms defining the "New World Order" George Bush the elder had announced in 1991.[10]

One wonders how information about what was happening in Iraq could have been made much clearer or more readily accessible to the general public. Claims that average Americans "didn't know" what was being done in their name are thus rather less than credible. In reality, Americans by and large greeted Albright's haughty revelation of genocide with yawns and blank stares, returning their attention almost immediately to what they considered far weightier matters: the Dow Jones and American League batting averages, for instance, or pursuit of the perfect cappuccino. Braying like donkeys into their eternal cellphones, they went right on arranging their stock transfers and real estate deals and dinner dates, conducting business as usual, never exhibiting so much as a collective flicker of concern.

In effect, the U.S. citizenry as a whole was endowed with exactly the degree of ignorance it embraced. To put it another way, being ignorant is in this sense—that of willful and deliberate ignoration—not synonymous with being uninformed. It is instead to be informed and then *ignore* the information. There is a vast difference between not knowing and not caring, and, if Good Americans have difficulty appreciating the distinction, it must be borne in mind that there are others in the world who are quite unburdened by such intellectual impairments. They, beginning with those most directly targeted at any given moment for subjugation or eradication at the hands of American "peacekeepers," know above all else that professions of ignorance inherently preclude claims of innocence in such circumstances.

There was a time, oddly enough, when it could be said that the United States stood at the forefront of those endorsing the same principle.

How else to explain its solemn invocation at the time of the Nuremberg Trials of a collective guilt inhering in the German populace itself?[11] One would do well to recall that the crimes attributed by Americans to Good Germans were that they'd celebrated a New Order of their own, looking away while the nazi crimes were committed, never attempting to meet the legal/moral obligation of holding their government to even the most rudimentary standards of human decency.[12] For these sins, it was said, they, the Germans, civilians as well as military personnel, richly deserved the death and devastation that had been rained upon them by America's "Mighty Eighth" Air Force and its British counterpart.[13] In sum, they'd "brought it on themselves."

Some People Push Back

To be sure, I've "oversimplified," committed "reductionism" and "compared apples and oranges" in offering the preceding analogy. That was Germany, after all, while this is the United States. The situation here is of course much more "complex." America today, unlike Germany a half-century ago, is a "democratic," "multicultural" society. Its courts offer a prospect of "due process" in dispute resolution absent under the nazis.[14] Most importantly, unlike the situation in nazi Germany, there is a discernible opposition in the U.S., an active counterforce to the status quo through which progressive social, political, and economic change can ultimately be accomplished without resort to the crudities of bullets and bombs, never mind the scale of atrocity witnessed on 9-1-1.[15]

These things duly remarked, it must also be said that the implications embodied in such counterforces must be tested by their effectuality rather than their mere existence. On this score, the practical distinction between formal and functional democracy has been remarked by numerous analysts over the years.[16] As to the merits of the U.S. judicial system, one might do well to begin any assessment by asking Leonard Peltier, Mumia Abu-Jamal, Geronimo ji Jaga (Pratt), Dhoruba Bin Wahad, or any of the hundreds of other political activists who have been entombed on false charges or are now serving dramatically inequitable sentences in American prisons.[17] One might ask as well those sent to death row on racial grounds,[18] or who number among the two million predominately dark-skinned people—a proportion of the population larger than that of any country save Russia—consigned to the sprawling archipelago of forced labor camps forming the U.S. "prison-industrial" complex.[19]

Turning to America's vaunted "opposition," we find record of not a single significant demonstration protesting the wholesale destruction of Iraqi children. On balance, U.S. "progressives" have devoted far more time and energy over the past decade to combating the imaginary health effects of "environmental tobacco smoke"[20] and demanding installation of speed bumps in suburban neighborhoods[21]—that is, to increasing their *own* comfort level—than to anything akin to a coherent response to the U.S. genocide in Iraq. The underlying mentality is symbolized quite well in the fact that, since they were released in the mid-1990s, Jean Baudrillard's allegedly "radical" screed, *The Gulf War Did Not Take Place*, has outsold Ramsey Clark's *The Impact of Sanctions on Iraq*, prominently subtitled *The Children Are Dying*, by a margin of almost three to one.[22]

The theoretical trajectory entered into by much of the American left over the past quarter-century exhibits a marked tendency to try and justify such evasion and squalid self-indulgence through the expedient of rejecting "hierarchy, in all its forms." Since "hierarchy" may be taken to include "[any]thing resembling an order of priorities," we are faced thereby with the absurd contention that all issues are of equal importance (as in the mindless slogan, "There is no hierarchy to oppression").[23] From there, it becomes axiomatic that the "privileging" of any issue over another—genocide, say, over fanny-pinching in the workplace—becomes not only evidence of "elitism," but of "sexism," and often "homophobia" to boot (as in the popular formulation holding that Third World anti-imperialism is inherently nationalistic, and nationalism is inherently damaging to the rights of women and gays).[24]

Having thus foreclosed upon all options for concrete engagement as mere "reproductions of the relations of oppression," the left has largely neutralized itself, a matter reflected most conspicuously in the applause it bestowed upon Homi K. Bhabha's preposterous 1994 contention that writing, which he likens to "warfare," should be considered the only valid revolutionary act.[25] One might easily conclude that had the "opposition" not conjured up such "postmodernist discourse" on its own initiative, it would have been necessary for the status quo to have invented it. As it is, postmodernist theorists and their postcolonialist counterparts are finding berths at élite universities at a truly astounding rate.[26]

In fairness, it must be admitted that there remain appreciable segments of the left which do not subscribe to the sophistries imbedded in postmodernism's "failure of nerve."[27] Those who continue to assert the value of direct action, however, have for the most part so thoroughly constrained themselves to the realm of symbolic/ritual protest as to be self-nullifying. One is again hard-pressed to decipher whether this has been by default or design. While such comportment is all but invariably couched in the lofty—or sanctimonious—terms of "principled pacifism," the practice of proponents often suggests something far less noble.[28]

Nowhere was this more apparent than during the 1999 mass demonstrations against a meeting of the World Trade Organization (WTO) in Seattle.[29] There, notwithstanding much vociferous rhetoric denouncing the spiraling human and environmental costs attending the American-led drive to economic globalization, droves of "responsible" protesters served literally as surrogates for the police, forming themselves into cordons to protect major corporate facilities from suffering such retaliatory "violence" as broken windows.[30] Although this posture was ostensibly adopted because of a commitment to nonviolence on the part of the volunteer cops, adherence to such ideals was peculiarly absent when it came to their manhandling of Black Bloc anarchists bent upon inflicting minor property damage or otherwise disrupting business as usual in some material sense.[31] In truth, the only parties who appear to have been immunized against the physical impositions of the self-anointed "peacekeepers" were the police, WTO delegates, and other government/corporate officials.[32]

Tellingly, although the fact goes mostly unmentioned by the "peaceful protesters" involved, no less than President Bill Clinton went on television in the aftermath to complement that "great majority of the demonstrators" who, he said, did nothing at all to "interfere with the rights" of WTO delegates to coordinate an acceleration of the planetary rape and mass murder the demonstrations were supposedly intended to forestall.[33] Over the next several months, meetings and workshops were conducted among "dissidents" nationwide, most of them dedicated in whole or in part to devising ways of better containing and controlling Black Blockers at future demonstrations.[34] For its part, the government formed a special state-local-federal "counterterrorism task force" in Oregon, targeting anarchists in the cities of Eugene and Portland—each reputedly a locus of Black Bloc activity—for "neutralization."[35]

A tidier and more convivial arrangement is hard to imagine. All that was missing was something resembling a realization by participants on either side of the equation that their waltz could be continued neither indefinitely nor with impunity. So intoxicated had they been rendered by their mutual indulgence in the narcotic of American exceptionalism,[36] that they'd lost all touch with laws as basic and natural as cause and effect. "Out there," in the neocolonial hinterlands where the body count of the New World Order must mostly be tallied, no one really cares a whit that a sector of the beneficiary population has chosen to bear a sort of perpetual "moral witness" to the crimes committed against the Third World. What they *do* care about is whether such witnesses translate their professions of "outrage" into *whatever* kinds of actions may be necessary to actually put an end to the horror.[37]

When such action is not forthcoming from within the perpetrator society itself—when in fact those comprising that society's purported opposition can be seen to have mostly *joined* in enforcing at a bedrock level the very order from whence mass murder systematically emanates—a different sort of rule must inevitably come to govern.[38] There is nothing mysterious in this. The proposition is so obvious, uncomplicated, and fundamentally just that it has been often and straightforwardly articulated, usually to the accompaniment of cheers, before mass audiences in the United States. Recall as but one example the line delivered by the actor Lawrence Fishburne, portraying Prohibition-era Harlem gangster Bumpy Johnson in a 1984 movie, *The Cotton Club*: "When you push people around, *some* people [will eventually] push back."[39]

As the makeup of the historical figure upon whom Fishburne's celluloid character was based should have made equally clear, those finally forced into doing the (counter)pushing are unlikely to be "nice guys." Indeed, whoever they might otherwise have been or become, the sheer and unrelenting brutality of the circumstances compelling their response is all but guaranteed to have twisted and deformed their outlooks in some truly hideous ways.[40] Be it noted, moreover, that there is an undeniable symmetry involved when their response is in kind.[41] "What goes around comes around," it has been said.[42] In the end, "Karma is unavoidable."[43] So it was on September 11, 2001.

Trails of Tears

True, my depiction of the situation remains reductionist. This is so in many respects, perhaps, but no doubt most importantly because the ghosts of Iraq's wasted children were by no means alone in their haunting. There were others present on 9-1-1, *many* others, beginning with the 800,000 Iraqi adults—the great majority of them either elderly or pregnant—known to have died along with their youngsters as a direct result of U.S. sanctions. This makes a total of 1.3 million dead among a population of fewer than twenty million in the decade since the Gulf War supposedly ended.[44] To these must be added another 150,000-or-so Iraqi civilians written off as "collateral damage" during the massive U.S. aerial bombardment defining the war itself.[45]

Then there were the soldiers, conscripts mostly, butchered in the scores of thousands as they fled northward along what became known as the "Highway of Death," out of combat, in full compliance with U.S. demands that they evacuate Kuwait, effectively defenseless against the waves of aircraft thereupon hurled at them by cowards wearing American uniforms.[46] Also at hand were some 10,000 Iraqi guardsmen retreating along a causeway outside Basra, killed in another "turkey shoot" conducted by U.S. forces twenty-four hours *after* the "war-ending ceasefire" had taken effect.[47] Untold thousands of others were there as well, terrified teenagers, many of them wounded, refused quarter by advancing American troops who disparaged them as "sand niggers," then buried them alive while they pleaded for mercy, using bulldozers specially prepared for the task.[48]

Neither the litany nor the count ends with the suffering of Iraq, of course. Present on 9–1–1 were the many thousands of Palestinians shredded over the years by Israeli pilots flying planes purchased with U.S. funds and dropping cluster bombs manufactured in/provided by the USA.[49] There, too, were the "Intifadists," rock-throwing—or simply fist-waving—Palestinian kids mowed down with numbing regularity by Israeli troops firing hyperlethal ammunition from American-supplied M-16 rifles.[50] Also in the throng were the hundreds massacred in refugee camps like Sabra and Shatila under authority of Israel's one-time defense minister, now prime minister, and always full-time U.S. accessory, Ariel Sharon.[51] Countries, no less than individuals, will—indeed, must—be judged not only by what they do but by the company they elect as a matter of policy to keep and support (ask the Taliban).

Compared to others with whom the United States has bonded since 1950, moreover, the appalling Mr. Sharon might well purport to saintliness. Consider the 300,000 Guatemalans exterminated after the CIA destroyed their democratically elected government in 1954, installing in its stead a brutal military junta dedicated to making the country safe for the operations of U.S. corporations.[52] Consider, too, the million or more Indonesian victims of a CIA-sponsored 1965 coup in which the Sukarno government was overthrown in favor of a military régime headed by Suharto, a maneuver that led unerringly—and with uninterrupted American support—to the recent genocide in East Timor.[53] The ghosts of these victims were surely present, along with their Iraqi and Palestinian counterparts, on 9–1–1.

No less apparent are the reasons for the presence of the multitudes subjected to numerically lesser but nonetheless comparable carnage by an array of other U.S. client governments: persons tortured and murdered by Shah Mohammad Reza Pahlavi's secret police, the SAVAK, after the CIA-engineered dissolution of Iran's parliamentary system in 1954;[54] more thousands "disappeared" and summarily executed after the CIA-instigated 1973 overthrow of Chile's Allende government and installation of a military junta headed by Augusto Pinochet;[55] thousands more murdered by agents of the ghastly "public safety" programs implemented with U.S. funding and supervision throughout South America during the 1960s;[56] still more who lost their lives to the U.S.-sponsored and -orchestrated "contra" war against Nicaragua's Sandinista government during the mid-1980s.[57]

Although the list of such malignancies is still and rapidly lengthening, it is appropriate that we return to the roster of those whose fates were sealed by the U.S. in a far more direct and exclusive fashion. Of them, there is certainly no shortage. They include, quite conspicuously, three million Indochinese, perhaps more, exterminated in the course of America's savage and sustained assaults on Vietnam, Laos, and Cambodia during the 1960s and early '70s.[58] To those claimed by the war itself must be added the ongoing toll taken by America's "stay behind" legacy of land mines, unexploded artillery rounds, and cluster bomblets, as well as an environment soaked in carcinogenic-mutogenic defoliants.[59] Added, too, must be those lost to the U.S. default on its pledge to pay reparations of $4 billion in exchange for being allowed to escape with "honor" from a war it started but could not win.[60] America has never been known for paying its bills, either literally or figuratively.

Present, too, on 9–1–1 were the uncounted thousands of noncombatants massacred by U.S. troops at places like No Gun Ri amid the "police action" conducted in Korea during the early 1950s.[61] As well, there were the hundreds of thousands of Japanese civilians deliberately and systematically burned alive by the Army Air Corps during its massive fire raids on Tokyo and other cities conducted toward the end of World War II.[62] And, to be sure, these victims were accompanied by the dead of Hiroshima and Nagasaki, indiscriminately vaporized by American nuclear bombs in 1945—or left to suffer the slow, excruciating deaths resulting from irradiation—not to any military purpose, but rather to the end that the U.S. might demonstrate the technological supremacy of its "kill-power" to anyone thinking of questioning its dominance of the postwar world.[63] For all its official chatter about the necessity of preventing weapons of mass destruction from "falling into the hands of rogue states and terrorists," the United States remains the only country ever to use nuclear devices for that reason.[64]

Then there were the Filipinos, as many as a million of them, "extirpated" by American troops at the dawn of the twentieth century, as the U.S., having wrested their island homeland from the relatively benign clutches of the Spanish Empire, set about converting the Philippines into a colony of its own.[65] Nor was there an absence of "Indians," people indigenous to America itself, whose unending agony was enunciated in the silent eloquence of several hundred Lakota babies, mothers, and old men dumped into a mass grave—a crude trench, really—after they'd been annihilated by soldiers firing Hotchkiss guns at Wounded Knee in 1890.[66] Punctuating their statement were the victims of a hundred comparable slaughters stretching back in an unbroken line through Weaverville and Yreka to the Washita and Sand Creek, through the Bad Axe to Horseshoe Bend and beyond, all the way to General John Sullivan's campaign against the Senecas in 1794, a grisly affair from which his men returned proudly attired in leggings crafted from the skins of their victims.[67]

Intermixed with those massacred wholesale were many thousands of native people slain piecemeal, hunted down as sport or for the bounties placed upon their scalps at one time or another by every state and territory in the Lower Forty-Eight.[68] Many more thousands could be counted among those who'd perished along the routes of the death marches—the Cherokee "Trail of Tears," for instance, and the "Long Walk" of the Navajos—upon which they were forced at bayonet-point, "removed" from their land so that it might be repopulated by a self-anointedly superior race busily importing itself from Europe.[69] Then there were the millions dead of disease, smallpox mostly, with which they'd been infected, often deliberately, as a means of causing them more literally to "vanish."[70]

In the end, the grim column of stolen lives reached such length that it threatened to disappear into the distance. Toward its end, however, could still be glimpsed a scattering of Wappingers, a small people now mostly forgotten, eradicated by the Dutch in their founding of New Amsterdam, now New York, the victims' severed heads used for a jolly game of kickball along a street near which the WTC would later stand.[71] As for the street upon which this gruesome event took place, it is now named in honor of a prominence by which it would long be flanked, the wall enclosing the city's once-thriving slave market.[72] The lucrative trade in African flesh—that, and extraction of discount labor from such flesh—was, after all, an ingredient nearly as vital to forming the U.S. economy as was the "clearing" and expropriation of native land.[73]

Thus, the millions lost to the Middle Passage took their places among their myriad Asian and Native American cousins.[74] They, and all who perished under slavers' whips after being sold at auction in the "New World," were worked or tortured to death on chain gangs after slavery was formally abolished,[75] or were among the thousands lynched during a century-long "festival of violence" undertaken by white Americans—there were some five-to-six million active members of the Ku Klux Klan in 1924—to ensure that ostensibly "free" blacks remained "in their place" of subjugation.[76] The atrocious record of apartheid South Africa always came in a feeble second to the malignancies of Jim Crow.[77]

Intermixed, too, were a great host of others: the thousands of Chinese coolies imported during the nineteenth century, none of them standing "a Chinaman's chance" of surviving the brutal conditions into which they were impressed while laying track for America's railroads and digging its deep shaft mines throughout the West;[78] the millions of children consigned in each generation to grinding poverty and truncated lifespans across America's vast sprawl of ghettoes, barrios, Indian reservations and migrant labor camps;[79] millions upon millions more assigned the same or worse in the neocolonies of the Third World, the depths of their misery dictated by an unremitting demand for super-profits with which to fuel America's "economic miracle."[80] Truly, there seems no end to it.

Why should "they" hate "us"? The very question is on its face absurd, delusional, revealing of an aggregate detachment from reality so virulent in its evasiveness as to be deemed clinically pathological. Setting aside the wholly contrived "confusion" professed in the aftermath as to who might be properly included under the headings "we" and "they," the sole legitimate query that might have been posed on 9–1–1 was—and remains—"How could 'they' possibly *not* hate 'us'?" From there, honest interrogators might have gone on to frame two others: "Why did it take 'them' so long to arrive?" and "Why, under the circumstances, did they conduct themselves with such obvious and admirable restraint?"

On Matters of Balance, Proportion and "Security"

There can be no defensible suggestion that those who attacked the Pentagon and WTC on 9–1–1 were seeking to "get even" with the United States. Still less is there a basis for claims that they "started" something, or that the U.S. has anything at all to get even with them for. Quite the contrary. For the attackers to have arguably "evened the score" for Iraqi's dead children alone, it would have been necessary for them to have killed *a hundred times* the number of Americans who actually died.[81] This in itself, however, would have allowed them to attain parity in terms of real numbers. The U.S. population is about fifteen times the size of Iraq's. Hence, for the attackers to have achieved a proportionally equivalent impact, it would have been necessary that they kill some 7.5 million Americans.

Even this does not apprehend the reality at issue. For a genuine parity of proportional impact to obtain, it would have been necessary for the attackers to have killed 7.5 million American *children*. To inflict an overall parity of suffering for what has been done to Iraq since 1990—taking into account the million-odd dead Iraqi adults—they would have had to kill roughly 22.5 million Americans. The instrumentality by which such carnage would have been dispensed would presumably have been not just the three "300,000 pound cruise missiles" employed on September 11,[82] but also the other 49,997 airborne explosives necessary for the attackers to break even in terms of the number of bombs and missiles the U.S. expended on Iraq's cities *after* their air defense systems had been completely "suppressed."[83]

The targets, moreover, would not have been restricted to such obvious elements of what America's general staff habitually refer to as "command and control infrastructure" as the Pentagon and the WTC. Rather, the attackers of 9–1–1 would have followed the well-established U.S. pattern of "surgically" obliterating sewage, water sanitation, and electrical generation plants, food production/storage capacity, hospitals, pharmaceutical production facilities, communications centers, and much more upon which Americans are no less dependent than Iraqis for survival.[84] The result, aside from mass death, would be a surviving population wracked by malnutrition and endemic disease (just as in Iraq today).

Framed in these terms, it is immediately obvious that, were the United States somehow forced to compensate proportionally and in lives for the damage it has so consistently wrought upon other peoples over the past two centuries, it would run out of people long before it ran out of compensatory obligation. Indeed, applying such standards of "payback" vis-à-vis American Indians alone would require a lethal reduction in the U.S. population, using biological agents and comparable means, of between 96 and 99 percent.[85] Hence, no one other than the most extravagant of America's many network propagandists has claimed that the attacks upon the Pentagon and WTC were carried out as part of an effort to extract anything remotely resembling a genuine equivalency in suffering.[86]

It follows that 9-1-1 was a mostly symbolic act, a desperate bid to command attention on the part of those so utterly dehumanized and devalued in the minds of average Americans that the very fact of their existence has never been deemed worthy of a moment's contemplation. On the basis of the September 11 "wake-up call"—and perhaps only on this basis—could they position themselves to "send a message" standing the least chance of being heard by the U.S. body politic. Whether it might be understood is an altogether different matter, given the media's predictable, craven, and across-the-board compliance with official demands that the attackers' carefully articulated explanations of their actions not be placed before the public.[87]

Still, at one level, the message delivered was uncensorably straightforward and simple, assuming the form of a blunt question: "How does it feel?" The query was and remains on its face one well worth posing. Not since its own Civil War ended in 1865, after all, has the United States been directly subject to a serious taste of what it so lavishly and routinely dishes out to others (no, Pearl Harbor doesn't count; it is located in Polynesia, not North America).[88] Small wonder that, for most Americans, including even a decided majority of the troops who've served in "combat" since Vietnam, the grisly panoramas of war, mass murder, and genocide have become sanitized to the point of sterility, imbued with no more concrete reality than any other "home entertainment" offering.[89]

How else to explain the popularity of increasingly technicalized military jargon like "kill ratios," "force degradation," and "collateral damage" among the general public?[90] How else to understand the public's willingness to accept the absurd proposition that a teenager safely ensconced at a computer console while launching missiles meant to slaughter unseen/unknown others at a thousand miles distance somehow or another qualifies as a "hero"?[91] Americans have in effect collectively lost their grip, and with it all sense of the charnel stench wafting from the policies, procedures, and priorities they've consistently endorsed. The attacks of 9-1-1, while certainly designed to inflict the maximum possible material damage, given their very limited scope,[92] were even more clearly intended to force U.S. citizens into some semblance of reacquaintance with the kind of excruciation their country—and thus they themselves—have become far too accustomed to dispensing with impunity.

This brings a second level of the attackers' message into focus. If it could be anticipated that Americans would find it exceedingly painful to undergo a heavy bombing of even the most token sort—as surely they would—it could also be expected that they would begin casting about with considerable urgency for a way of ensuring that such "terrorism" would not be repeated. This, in turn, suggested that U.S. citizens might at last be receptive to embarking upon the only route to attainment of this worthy objective, a trajectory marked by Noam Chomsky's formulation, advanced shortly after the attacks, that "if you really want to put an end terrorism, you have to begin by no longer participating in it."[93] Or, more sharply, "stop killing their babies," as the matter was framed by Georgia State law professor Natsu Taylor Saito a short while later.[94]

At base, what the attackers communicated was the proposition that, from now on, if Americans wish their children to be happy and safe, they going to have to allow the children of other peoples an equivalent safety and chance for happiness. In effect, Americans will have to accord a respect for the rights of others equal to that which they demand for themselves, valuing "Other" youngsters as much as they do their own.[95] Finally, and emphatically, the United States is going to have to abide by the rules of civilized behavior articulated in international law (its own citizens shouldering the responsibility of seeing to it that it does).[96] The nature of a society rejecting such eminently reasonable terms as being "unfair" should be to a large extent self-revealing.

Unfortunately, this is precisely what the preponderance of Americans have done. Refusing the prospect that the collectivity of their own attitudes and behavior made something like 9–1–1 inevitable, they have instead bleated their "innocence" for all to hear, meanwhile reacting like a figurative Jeffrey Dahmer, enraged because the latest of his many hapless victims has displayed the effrontery of slapping his face.[97] Witness, if you will, the frenzied demands accruing from every major media outlet that those suspected of involvement in the 9–1–1 attacks—or of supporting the attackers in some fashion—be subjected to "complete extermination."[98] Witness as well the winks and chuckles with which commentators from "right" and "left" alike greeted photographic evidence that American surrogates in Afghanistan have been gleefully castrating and otherwise mutilating captured enemy soldiers before summarily executing them.[99]

Once again—this time in the name of a "crusade" to "rid the world of evil"[100]—Americans have enthusiastically embraced a policy devolving upon the systematic and potentially massive perpetration of war crimes and crimes against humanity. Here, a sublime irony presents itself: Since by no morally coherent standard—moral assessment being necessary insofar as the term employed is exclusive to the vernacular of theology/morality[101]—can the policy at issue be construed as anything but "evil," claims that it has been implemented for the above-stated purpose amount to little other than announcements of suicidal intent.[102] Still more ironic is the fact that the situation in many ways requires a more literal than metaphorical interpretation.

"Out there," amid the seething, bleeding psychic wastelands spawned by the unspeakable arrogance of U.S. imperial pretension, someone is quietly awaiting the definitive answers to questions of whether and to what extent Americans might respond constructively to the warnings posted on the WTC and Pentagon. A grim smile upon his face, her finger upon the trigger, s/he is almost certainly mouthing words to the effect of, "Go ahead, punk. Make my day."[103] What will it be next time? A far larger and more destructive wave of suicide bombings? Dispersal of biological or chemical agents? Detonation of one or more portable nuclear devices? All of these?[104] The object, no doubt, will be to attain something much closer to bona fide payback for what the United States has done, and is doing even now.

The straw-like "option" at which the great majority of Americans are presently grasping in a transparent attempt to restore their sense of exemption from responsibility—the notion that a combination of military force, intelligence gathering, and "tightened domestic security" can ultimately immunize them from the consequences of their country's actions (or their own inactions)—is purely delusional.[105] Short of setting out to kill every man, woman and child in the Third World, little can be expected of the military in terms of preventing "terrorist" responses to its own crimes. Suggestions that the CIA can somehow alter the situation, rendering applications of military force "surgically" effective against "the terrorist infrastructure" are laughable, as should be evident from the abysmal failure of the agency's Phoenix Program, undertaken for precisely the same purpose in Vietnam.[106]

Claims that measures like those described in the recent "Homeland Security Act" will produce the desired prophylactic effect are the most vacuous of all.[107] The "internal security model" most often cited by "experts" for emulation by the United States is that of Israel, a country which, although it has converted itself into a veritable garrison state over the past thirty years, has been spectacularly unable to prevent determined attackers from striking almost at will.[108] All that can be expected of such "defense" initiatives is repression of what little actual political liberty had been left to residents of "the land of the free" by the dawn of the new millennium.[109]

The "Miracle of Immaculate Genocide"

In the final analysis, it is quite reasonable that fulfillment of America's now fervent quest for security be made contingent upon its willingness to commence a process of profound national introspection that, alone, will enable it to fundamentally rework its relationship(s) with those upon whom it has heretofore proven so cavalier in visiting the worst sorts of oppression. There is much militating against attainment of so positive a development, however, not least the fact that, in the United States, a pathology often associated with clinical disorder has mutated long since into what can best be described as a normative social condition.[110] "There are," as Susan Griffin has observed, "whole disciplines, institutions, rubrics in [American] culture which serve as categories of denial."[111]

The mentality involved is in some respects multifaceted and complex, but always self-serving and convenient, each facet serving mainly to augment or complete its ostensible antithesis, producing a whole remarkable for nothing so much as the virulence of its intractability.[112] Writing of the holocaust perpetrated by U.S. troops in the Philippines a century ago—an onslaught entailing orders that every male Filipino over the age of ten be slaughtered, and the resulting deaths of one in every six inhabitants on the island of Luzon[113]—historian Stuart Creighton Miller describes "the tendency of highly patriotic Americans . . . to [vociferously] deny such abuses and even to assert that they could never exist in their country."[114] The pattern is unmistakably similar to that exhibited by severe alcoholics who, despite all evidence of the damage their behavior has caused, chronically insist that "the opposite of everything is true."[115]

More subtle than the characteristic refusal of "conservatives" to allow mere facts to in any way alter their core presumptions was/is the complementary nature of the "alternative" interpretation(s) most often posed by their "progressive" opponents. Noting that the Philippines genocide was a matter of public knowledge by 1901,[116] Miller goes on to observe that collective "amnesia over the horrors of the war of conquest . . . set in early, during the summer of 1902."[117] He then concludes by reflecting upon how "anti-imperialists aided the process by insisting that the conflict and its attendant atrocities had been the result of a conspiracy by a handful of leaders who carried out, through deceit and subterfuge, the policy and means of expansion overseas against the will of the majority of their countrymen."[118]

By refusing to acknowledge that most Americans had been bitten by the same bug that afflicted Roosevelt, Lodge, and Beveridge, anti-imperialists were letting the people off the hook and in their own way preserving the American sense of innocence. Unfortunately, the man in the street shared the dreams of world-power status, martial glory, and future wealth that would follow expansion. When the dream soured, the American people neither reacted with very much indignation, nor did they seem to retreat to their cherished political principles. If anything, they seemed to take their cues from their leader in the White House by first putting out of mind all the sordid episodes in the conquest, and then forgetting the entire war itself.[119]

So it was then, the more so today. Contemporary conservatives, whenever they can be momentarily boxed into conceding one or another unsavory aspect of America's historical record, are forever insisting that whatever they've admitted can be "properly" understood only when viewed as an "exception to the rule," an "aberration," "atypical" to the point of "anomalousness."[120] None have shown a readiness to address the question of exactly how many such "anomalies" might be required before they can be said to compose "the rule" itself. When pressed, conservatives invariably retreat into a level of diversionary polemic excusable at best on elementary school playgrounds, arguing that anything "we" have done is somehow excused by allegations that "they" have done things just as bad.[121]

Progressives, on the other hand, while acknowledging many of America's more reprehensible features, have become far more refined in offering hook-free analyses than they were in 1902. No longer much preoccupied with such crudities as "conspiracy theory,"[122] they have become quite monolithic in attributing all things negative to handy abstractions like "capitalism," "The State," "structural oppression," and, yes, "The Hierarchy."[123] Hence, they have been able to conjure what might be termed the "miracle of immaculate genocide," a form of genocide, that is, in which—apart from a few amorphous "decision-making élites"[124]—there are no actual perpetrators and no one who might "really" be deemed culpable by reason of complicity. The parallels between this "cutting edge" conception and the defense mounted by postwar Germans—including the nazis at Nuremberg—are as eerie as they are obvious.[125]

The implications of this were set forth in stark relief during the aftermath of 9–1–1, when it was first suggested that a decided majority of those killed in the WTC attack might be more accurately viewed as "little Eichmanns"—that is, as a cadre of faceless bureaucrats and technical experts who had willingly (and profitably) harnessed themselves to the task making America's genocidal world order hum with maximal efficiency—than as "innocents."[126] The storm of outraged exception taken by self-proclaimed progressives to this simple observation has been instructive, to say the least. The objections have been mostly transparent in their diversionary intent, seeking as they have to focus attention exclusively on janitors, firemen and food service workers *rather than* the much larger number of corporate managers, stock brokers, bond traders, finance and systems analysts, etc., among those killed.[127]

A few have complained of the "cold-bloodedness" and "insensitivity" embodied, not in the vocations pursued by the latter group, but in describing their attitudes/conduct as having been in any way analogous to Eichmann's. Left unstated, however, is the more accurate term we should employ in characterizing a representative 30-year-old foreign exchange trader who, in full knowledge that every cent of his lavish commissions derived from the starving flesh of defenseless Others, literally wallowed in self-indulgent excess, playing the big shot, priding himself on being "a sharp dresser" and the fact that "money spilled from his pockets . . . flowed like crazy . . . [spent] on the black BMW and those clothes—forgetting to pack ski clothes for a Lake Tahoe trip, dropping $1,000 on new stuff," and so on.[128] A "cool guy" with a "warm heart"? A "good family man"? Just an "ordinary," "average" or "normal" fellow who "happened to strike it rich"?[129] How then are we to describe Eichmann himself?[130]

Clearly, either the devastating insights concerning "the banality of evil" offered by Hannah Arendt in her 1963 study, *Eichmann in Jerusalem*, have yet to penetrate the consciousness of many American progressives,[131] or American progressives are in the main every bit as mired in the depths of denial as the most hidebound of their conservative counterparts.[132] Irrespective of whether there is an appreciable segment of the U.S. population prepared to look the matter in the face, however, the same condition of willful blindness cannot be said to prevail throughout much of the rest of the world.[133]

Excusing oneself for one's crimes is never a legitimate prerogative, nor are attempts to hide or explain them away. This is all the more true while the crimes are being repeated. Neither justice, forgiveness, nor exegesis can be self-administered or -bestowed. Of this, there should be no doubt in a country where the principle of "victims' rights" has lately been enshrined as an article of juridical faith.[134] Those who comprised the "chickens" of 9–1–1 will have their say, and it will ultimately be definitive. In this connection, the only real question confronting the U.S. polity is how in the future it will be necessary for them to say it. And that, rightly enough, will be entirely contingent upon the extent and decisiveness with which Americans prove capable of factoring such voices into the calculus of their personal and national self-concepts.

In the Alternative

In 1945, addressing a strikingly similar context of national criminality and denial—albeit one in which the state and its collaborating corporate institutions had been pounded into physical submission by external forces—the philosopher Karl Jaspers set forth a schematic of culpability, acceptance of which he suggested might allow both Germans and Germany to redeem themselves.[135] Internalizing Jaspers' four-part formulation stands to yield comparable results in America, for Americans, and thus for everyone else as well. It is therefore well worth summarizing here (in a somewhat revised form reflecting enunciation of the Nuremberg Doctrine and other subsequent developments).[136]

- First, there is the matter of *criminal guilt*. States, corporations and other such entities, while they may be criminally conceived, and employed for criminal purposes, do not themselves commit crimes. Crimes—that is, violations of customary or black letter law—are committed by individuals, those who conceive, employ or serve state and corporate institutions. Those alleged to have committed specific offenses are subject to personal prosecution and punishment.[137] If the transgressions of which they stand accused are of a sort sanctioned either explicitly or implicitly by the state under which authority they've acted, their prosecution cannot as a rule occur before tribunals controlled by that same state.[138] Nor, if mere vengeance is to be avoided, can such tribunals as a rule be placed under control of the immediate victims. Where crimes of state or state-sanctioned crime are at issue, the only appropriate judicial forum is an impartially composed international court.[139]
- Second, there is the matter of *political guilt*. It is the collective responsibility of the citizens in a modern state to ensure by *all* means necessary that its government adheres to the rule of law, not just domestically

but internationally.[140] There are no bystanders. No one is entitled to an "apolitical" exemption from such obligation.[141] Where default occurs, either by citizen endorsement of official criminality or by the failure of citizens to *effectively* oppose it, liability is incurred by all. Although degrees of onus may be assigned along a continuum traversing the distance from those who most actively embraced the crime to those who most actively opposed it, *none* are "innocent."[142] The victims thus hold an unequivocal right to receive reparation, compensation, and, where possible, complete restitution in ways and amounts deemed equitable and fair, not in the estimation of those liable, but in the judgment of an impartial international court.[143]

■ Third, there is the matter of *moral guilt*. While it may prove impractical in settings where crimes of state are at issue to try all who have committed offenses (whether by way of perpetration, or by complicity), those who go unprosecuted are not thereby absolved.[144] To them belongs the public stigma associated with their deeds and consequent existential confrontation with themselves. In this, there can be no recourse to the supposed mitigation embodied in the apology that one has "merely done one's job" or "just followed orders."[145] Still less can exoneration be found in prevarications concerning "human nature." If it were the "nature" of humans to engage in such acts, *everyone* would do so, and, self-evidently, not everyone does.[146] Each individual is thus personally responsible for his/her acts, "including the execution of political and military orders," and thus socially/morally accountable for them.

■ Finally, there is the matter of what Jaspers termed *metaphysical guilt*. This rests most heavily upon those who, while not guilty of any specific offense, averted their eyes, sitting by while crimes against humanity were committed in their name.[147] It encompasses as well all who, while we may have registered opposition in some form or degree, did less than we might have—failing thereby to risk our lives unconditionally—in our struggle to prevent or halt such crimes. Therein, incontestably, lies the guilt shared by all who opt to remain alive while Others are systematically subjugated, dispossessed, tortured, and murdered.[148]

Those who would reject such criteria out of hand might do well to bear in mind that they join company thus with Carl Schmitt, a leading light among the nazi legal philosophers, who was among the first to pronounce them "beneath attention."[149] Others, seeking to neutralize the implications by equivocation, insisting that while a Jasperian schema "makes sense for Germans," the "good offsets the bad" where America and Americans are concerned, should be aware that this is precisely the argument offered by Germany's "New Right"—neonazis, by any other name—with regard to the Third Reich itself.[150] If it can be agreed that the *Hitlerstaat* remains impervious to rehabilitation, regardless of its well-documented instigation of expressways and Volkswagens, the same holds true for the United States, irrespective of the supposed triumphs of "American civilization."[151]

Such issues must be faced straightforwardly, without dissembling, if Americans are ever to hold rightful title to the "good conscience" they've so long laid claim to owning. How they are to respond to what stares back at them from the proverbial mirror is an altogether different question, however. Transformation from beastliness to beauty can be neither instantaneous nor, in terms of its retroactive undoing, complete.[152] There is no painless, privilege-preserving pill that can be taken to effect a quick fix of what ails the U.S., no petition, no manifesto, no song or candle-lit vigil that will suffice. The terms of change must and will be harsh, inevitably so, given the propensity of those who seek to prevent it to gauge their success by the rotting corpses of toddlers.[153] This truth, no matter its inconvenience to those snugly situated within the comfort zones of political pretense,[154] is all that defines the substance of meaningful struggle.[155]

It cannot happen all at once, but it must begin somewhere, and for this there is need of nothing so much as a focal point. That, and external assistance, given Americans' abject inexperience in undertaking projects entailing the least hint of humility. Fortunately, an "action-agenda" combining both elements readily presents itself. Americans must demonstrate, conclusively and concretely, that they have at last attained a sufficient degree of self-awareness to subordinate themselves both individually and *as a country* to the rule of law.[156] Such an initiative, *only* such, and then only if it is pressed by every available means, is likely to reassure those who came on 9-1-1 that the seeds of Jaspers' wisdom have at last taken root in the U.S. to an extent making future such attacks unnecessary.

All who fancy themselves progressive—in common with every conservative who has ever mouthed the lofty rhetoric of "law enforcement"—can start by inaugurating a concerted drive to compel their government to reverse its 1986 repudiation of the compulsory jurisdiction previously held over U.S. foreign policy by the International Court of Justice (ICJ).[157]

Concomitantly, Americans can set about such action as is necessary to ensure that their country joins the rest of the world in placing itself under the jurisdiction of the newly established International Criminal Court (ICC).[158] Massive international support and assistance is virtually guaranteed to accrue to any such U.S. citizen initiative.

Following a parallel track, although much of it falls within the domain of *jus cogens* (the peremptory norms of customary law) and is thus enforceable against the U.S. without its agreement,[159] an important gesture would be embodied in Americans taking such action as is necessary to compel their government to ratify those elements of international public and humanitarian law it has, often alone, heretofore refused to endorse. High on this lengthy list,[160] is the 1948 Convention on Prevention and Punishment of the Crime of Genocide, to which the U.S. presently claims a "sovereign right" to self-exemption from compliance.[161] Recent additions include the Convention on the Rights of the Child (1989)[162] and the Convention on the Prohibition of the Use, Production, Stockpiling and Transfer of Anti-Personnel Mines (1998).[163]

Most important of all—given the abysmal record of the U.S. when it comes to bringing even those *acknowledged* to have perpetrated war crimes and crimes against humanity before its domestic bar of justice,[164] given the fact that only the most token punishments have ever been visited upon those few who have for cosmetic reasons been domestically tried and convicted of such offenses,[165] and given the imperative of establishing that Americans are finally serious about adhering to the law—such action as is necessary must be taken to compel delivery of an initial selection of present/former U.S. officials for prosecution by the ICC.[166]

Here, although the list of imminently eligible candidates is all but overwhelming, a mere threesome might constitute an adequate preliminary sample. The first, on the basis of her earlier-noted statement concerning the fate of Iraq's children and administration of attendant policies, should be former secretary of state Albright. Second, for reasons explained quite well by Christopher Hitchens and others, should be former secretary of state Henry Kissinger.[167] The third should be current North Carolina senator Jesse Helms, the bellicosity of whose threats to visit "dire consequences" upon the world community "in the event a single American is ever indicted" for violating the laws of war or international humanitarian law exemplifies the manner in which the U.S. has for decades thwarted implementation of procedures for the peaceful resolution of international disputes (this in itself offers prima facie evidence of Helms' complicity in the more direct crimes perpetrated by his codefendants).[168]

Prosecution of these three major U.S. criminals before the ICC would pave the way for a series of such trials, targeting as in the Nuremberg proceedings representative defendants drawn from each of the interactive "classes" of American offenders—governmental, military, corporate, scientific, and so on—composing the élite decision-making stratum of America's New World Order.[169] Collaterally, the criminal trials would in themselves lay a superb evidentiary groundwork for consideration of international tort claims by the ICJ, in many cases the sole procedure through which issues concerning indemnification of America's proliferate victims are likely ever to be satisfactorily addressed.[170] It may also be anticipated that, under these conditions, the principles realized in international fora will be absorbed by the U.S. judiciary, as they were in postwar Germany, to an extent sufficient for bona fide prosecutions of America's war criminals and other such terrorists to at last commence in domestic courts.[171]

Against this backdrop, otherwise preposterous assertions that recourse to "the World Court is the way to proceed" in halting America's persistently murderous aggression take on a certain coherence. The question begged in such formulations, as they stand, and as they've stood all along, concerns enforcement. A court is not a police force. Less, is it an army. Neither its jurisdiction nor its judgments are self-executing. Its decrees are vacuous without a means of exacting compliance.[172] Should it turn out that Americans were prodded by the pain inflicted on 9-1-1 to finally begin shouldering the responsibility of forcing their government to obey the law—with *all* that this implies—it may be said that a world historic corner was turned on that date. Should this not prove to be the case, however, others, especially those Others most egregiously victimized by American lawlessness, will have no real alternative but to try and do the job themselves. And, in the collectivity of their civic default, Americans, no more than the Good Germans of 1945, can have little legitimate complaint as to how they may have to go about it.[173]

To See Things Clearly

If the prescription sketched out in the preceding section offers the prospect of improving the level of security enjoyed by all Americans—mainly by drastically reducing the need for it—it contains a range of other benefits as well. Salient among them is what, with respect to Germany, former Harvard political scientist Daniel Jonah Goldhagen has described as an "internationalization of the 'national' history."[174] By this, he meant a process through which the country's apprehension of its past has been subjected to such intensive and sustained scrutiny/contributions by others that the "collective, narcissistic self-exaltation" typically marking such narratives has been preempted. This, Goldhagen concludes, has enabled contemporary Germans to attain a far more accurate—and thus healthier—conception of themselves than they were likely ever to have achieved on their own.[175]

It is exactly this kind of aggregate self-understanding that Jaspers posited as being essential to a process through which the varieties of guilt he'd so carefully delineated could be transformed into their antithesis, creating what he hoped might constitute an insurmountable psychointellectual barrier against any wholesale resurgence of the mentality from which Germany's communality of guilt had emerged.[176] There is no reason to assume that the idea holds less utility for Americans today than it did for Germans then, or that the rewards for the world of America's figurative denazification would be any less substantial than those manifest in the more literal German process.

A wealth of information necessary to redefining the character of the "American experiment" can be expected to take center stage in the above-described judicial proceedings, whether international or domestic, criminal or civil. Much of it will prove to have been available all along, publicly displayed but usually distorted beyond recognition, its meaning neatly buried in the texts, rendered alternately in terms of triumphalism or apology, that from the first have composed America's historical canon and its popular counterpart(s).[177] Reinterpreted through the lens of law, detailed at trial by those charged with assessing the culpability of individual defendants or the degree of responsibility inhering in the polity that empowered them, even that which was "known" will stand exposed in the glare of an entirely different light.

Such developments represent a good start, but by no means an end point. Even the most honest and penetrating of prosecutorial presentations is by nature erratic and uneven, skewed by the parameters of its purpose to focus in fragmentary fashion upon certain usually topical matters, emphasizing, deemphasizing, or ignoring issues of wider historical concern without regard to historiographical requirements.[178] The record made during the course of any trial, and the conclusions formally drawn from it, must therefore be compared to and combined with those obtaining in related proceedings to create a composite. This overarching iteration of what has been "discovered" through adjudication must then be broken down again in various ways, sifted and refined, its implications adduced and contextualized (that is, reinterpreted by way of their connection with or dissimilarity from "broader"—i.e., historically deeper and more diverse—processes or sequences of events).[179]

Plainly, it will be forever premature to proclaim the consummation of such a project before the most thoroughgoing reconstruction of American history, and thus a complete resignification of the codes of meaning and value residing within it, has been achieved. With this in mind, the problem confronting those who would accept it is how best to approach so monumental a devoir. A method is needed by which to deal with the surfeit of data at hand, arranging it in ways which lend coherence to its otherwise nebulous mass, tracing not just its outer contours but the inner trajectories that gave them shape, coaxing it to divulge truths too long denied.

Notes

1   All told, citizens of 86 different countries are reported to have numbered among the dead; U.S. Attorney General John Ashcroft, press briefing carried on CNBC, November 29, 2001.

2   Malcolm X with Alex Haley, *The Autobiography of Malcolm X* (New York: Ballantine, 1973) pp. 300–301.

3   See Ramsey Clark, *The Impact of Sanctions on Iraq: The Children Are Dying* (Washington, DC: Maisonneuve Press, 1996).

4   Ramsey Clark, *War Crimes: A Report on U.S. War Crimes Against Iraq* (Washington, DC: Maisonneuve Press, 1992) pp. 22, 35, 53–54. Also see Jack Calhoun, "UN: Iraq Bombed Back to Stone Age," *Manchester Guardian* (April 3, 1991); Patrick E. Tyler, "Disease Spirals in Iraq as Embargo Takes Its Toll," *New York Times* (June 24, 1991); Barston Gellman, "Storm Damage in the Gulf: U.S. Strategy went beyond strictly military targets," *Washington Post Weekly* (July 8–14, 1991).

5   Quoted by Noam Chomsky in his essay, "'What We Say Goes': The Middle East in the New World Order," in Cynthia Peters, ed., *Collateral Damage: The New World Order at Home and Abroad* (Boston: South End Press, 1992) p. 52.

6   Among the more noteworthy of such efforts is Edward S. Herman's and Noam Chomsky's *Manufacturing Consent: The Political Economy of the Mass Media* (New York: Pantheon, 1988). Also see Chomsky's *Necessary Illusions: Thought Control in Democratic Societies* (Boston: South End Press, 1989) and Herman's *The Myth of the Liberal Media: An Edward Herman Reader* (New York: Peter Lang, 1999).

7   Halliday's actions, statements, and the data upon which they were based form the core of Ramsey Clark and Others, *Challenge to Genocide: Let Iraq Live* (Washington, DC: International Action Center, 1998); see esp. pp. 79, 127, 191.

8   The interview aired on May 12, 1996.

9   Quoted in William Blum, *Rogue State: A Guide to the World's Only Superpower* (Monroe, ME: Common Courage Press, 2000) pp. 5–6.

10 See Holly Sklar, "Brave New World Order," in Peters, *Collateral Damage*, pp. 3–46.

11   Eugene Davidson, *The Trial of the Germans, 1945–1946* (New York: Macmillan, 1966).

12   For a good overview of the arguments, see Karl Jaspers, *The Question of German Guilt* (New York: Fordham University Press, 2001).

13   See the chapter entitled "The Triumph of the Bombers" in H. Bruce Franklin's *War Stars: The Superweapon and the American Imagination* (New York: Oxford University Press, 1988) pp. 101–11.

14   For purposes of comparison, see Michael Stolleis, *Law Under the Swastika: Studies on Legal History in Nazi Germany* (Chicago: University of Chicago Press, 1998).

15   For theory, see David Dellinger, *Revolutionary Nonviolence* (Indianapolis: Bobbs-Merrill, 1971); Gene Sharp, *The Dynamics of Nonviolent Action*, 3 vols. (Boston: Porter Sargent, 1973); Barbara Epstein, *Political Protest and Cultural Revolution: Nonviolent Direct Action in the 1970s and 1980s* (Berkeley: University of California Press, 1991).

16   This is covered rather well in the chapter titled "The Home Front" in Chomsky's *Deterring Democracy* (New York: Hill and Wang, 1992) pp. 69–88. Also see the chapter titled "Power in the Domestic Arena," in his *Rogue States: The Rule of Force in World Affairs* (Cambridge, MA: South End Press, 2000) pp. 188–97.

17   Former Black Panther bin Wahad served nineteen years in a New York maximum security prison after being falsely convicted of attempted murder in 1971. See Dhoruba bin Wahad, "War Within," in Jim Fletcher, Tanaquil Jones, and Sylvère Lotringer, eds., *Still Black, Still Strong: Survivors of the U.S. War Against Black Revolutionaries* (New York: Semiotext(e), 1993) pp. 9–56. Ji Jaga, another former Panther leader, served twenty-seven years in California before his false conviction was overturned. See Jack Olsen, *Last Man Standing: The Tragedy and Triumph of Geronimo Pratt* (Garden City, NY: Doubleday, 2000). American Indian Movement member Peltier continues to serve a double life sentence in federal prison despite official admissions that the evidence used to convict him was false. See Peter Matthiessen, *In the Spirit of Crazy Horse: The Story of Leonard Peltier* (New York: Viking Press, [2nd ed.] 1991). Former Panther Abu-Jamal is on death row in Pennsylvania, although his trial was an utter travesty. See Daniel R. Williams, *Executing Justice: An Inside Account of the Case of Mumia Abu-Jamal* (New York: St. Martin's Press, 2001). Overall, see my and J.J. Vander Wall's *Cages of Steel: The Politics of Imprisonment in the United States* (Washington, DC: Maisonneuve Press, 1992). **Update:** Since this was written, Mumia Abu-Jamal's death sentence was commuted to life imprisonment.

18   See the section entitled "Race and the Death Penalty," in Amnesty International, *The United States of America: Rights for All* (New York: Amnesty International, 1998) pp. 108–12.

19   For comparative incarceration rates, see Marc Mauer, *The Race to Incarcerate* (New York: Free Press, 1999) pp. 21–22. On corporatization, see Daniel Burton-Rose, Dan Pens, and Paul Wright, eds., *The Celling of America: An Inside Look at the American Prison Industry* (Monroe, ME: Common Courage Press, 1998); Joel Dyer, *The Perpetual Prisoner Machine: How America Profits from Crime* (Boulder, CO: Westview Press, 2000).

20   At the point American yuppies launched their drive to abolish smoking in public places—a social norm mainly among poor people/communities of color—it was estimated that "passive smoking" resulted in the deaths of as many as 3,000 people per year. The number could have as easily been set at three or three million since there was at the time no scientific confirmation of *any* negative effects attending exposure to "environmental" tobacco smoke. See the chapter titled "Smoke Exposure and Health," in Roy J. Shephard, *The Risks of Passive Smoking* (New York: Oxford University Press, 1982) pp. 95–108. After twenty years of intensive and

well-funded research—attended by increasingly stringent bans on ashtrays—the situation remains essentially the same. See Peter N. Lee's "Difficulties in Determining Health Effects Related to Environmental Tobacco Smoke Exposure," in Ronald A. Watson's and Mark Witten's coedited and currently definitive *Environmental Tobacco Smoke* (Washington, DC: CRC Press, 2001) pp. 1–24.

21   Stephen Burrington and Veronika Thiebach, *Take Back the Streets: How to Protect Communities from Asphalt and Traffic* (Boston: Conservation Law Foundation, [3rd ed.] 1998).

22   Clark, *Sanctions*; Jean Baudrillard, *The Gulf War Did Not Take Place* (Bloomington: Indiana University Press, 1995).

23   Terry Eagleton, *The Illusions of Postmodernism* (Oxford, UK: Blackwell, 1996) esp. pp. 93–95.

24   The eurofeminist equation of nationalism to "masculinist dominance" commenced at least as early as Barbara Burris' "The Fourth World Manifesto," in Anne Koedt, ed., *Radical Feminism* ([Chicago: Quadrangle, 1973] pp. 322–57), and has seen continued refinement in essays such as those collected by Miranda Davis in her *Third World/Second Sex: Women's Struggles and National Liberation* (London: Zed Books, 1983); those collected by Roberta Hamilton and Michèle Barrett in their coedited *The Politics of Diversity: Feminism, Marxism and Nationalism* (London: Verso, 1987); and, most recently, attempts to discredit the work of Third World anticolonial theorists like Frantz Fanon spearheaded by mainstreamers like Diana Fuss (see, e.g., her "Interior Colonies: Frantz Fanon and the Politics of Identification," in Nigel C. Gibson, ed., *Rethinking Fanon: The Continuing Dialogue* [Amherst, NY: Humanity Books, 1999] pp. 294–328).

25   Homi K. Bhabha, "Interrogating identity: Frantz Fanon and the postcolonial prerogative" in his *The Location of Culture* (New York: Routledge, 1994) pp. 40–65. Also see Bart Moore-Gilbert, *Postcolonial Theory: Contexts, Practices, Politics* (London: Verso, 1997) pp. 138–39.

26   Bhabha himself—who has yet to produce a book-length manuscript—was, as reported in the *New York Times* on November 11, 2001, hired as a reigning "star" by the literature department at Harvard.

27   Eagleton, *Illusions of Postmodernism*, p. 19. For a different and even sharper framing, see John Zerzan's "The Catastrophe of Postmodernism," *Anarchy*, No. 30 (Fall 1991) pp. 16–35; reprinted in his *Future Primitive and Other Essays* (Brooklyn, NY: Autonomedia/Anarchy, 1994) pp. 101–34,

28   For a reasonably substantial critique, see my and Mike Ryan's *Pacifism as Pathology: Reflections on the Role of Armed Struggle in North America* (Winnipeg: Arbeiter Ring, 1998).

29   The WTO was prefigured by the Trilateral Commission during the mid-1970s. See Holly Sklar, ed., *Trilateralism: The Trilateral Commission and Elite Planning for World Government* (Boston: South End Press, 1980). On its evolution during the 1990s, see Bernard Hoekman and Michael Kostecki, *The Political Economy of the World Trading System: From GATT to WTO* (New York: Oxford University Press, 2001).

30   See generally Janet Thomas, *The Battle for Seattle: The Story Behind and Beyond the WTO Demonstration* (Golden, CO: Fulcrum, 2001); Alexander Cockburn, Jeffrey St. Clair, and Allen Sekula, *Five Days That Shook the World: The Battle for Seattle and Beyond* (London: Verso, 2001).

31   The inconsistency is not especially unusual. See my and Ryan's *Pacifism as Pathology*, p. 124n135.

32   This, too, is by no mean unusual. Churchill and Ryan, *Pacifism as Pathology*, pp. 21–22.

33 The statement was made in remarks carried by the major television networks on the evening of December 1, 1997, and quoted in *USA Today* the following morning.

34 Some of this is mentioned in concluding chapters of Thomas, *Battle for Seattle*, and Cockburn, St. Clair, and Sekula, *Five Days That Shook the World*; also see the essays collected in George Katsiaficas and Eddie Yuen in their coedited volume, *The Battle for Seattle: Debating Capitalist Globalization and the WTO* (Winnipeg: Soft Skull Press, 2001). It's worth noting that, while "dissidents" were spending their time trying to figure out ways of preventing a repeat of the Black Bloc's actions, establishmentarian news organs were acknowledging that "the protesters' message was heard . . . *because of* . . . the violence [sic, emphasis added]." See "The Siege of Seattle," *Newsweek* (December 13, 1999) p. 62.

35 Rob Thaxton, an individual associated with Eugene's Anarchist Action Collective (AAO), shortly received a seven-year prison sentence for throwing a rock during a street demonstration. By June 2001, two others, Craig Marshall ("Critter") and Jeffrey Luers ("Free"), had been sentenced to five and twenty-two years respectively, ostensibly for setting fire to several SUVs at a local car dealership; see "Free Sentenced to 22 years," *Green Anarchy*, No. 6 (Summer 2001). The draconian penalties, especially that meted out to Luers, are plainly at odds with the relatively trivial nature of the offenses of which the three were convicted. They are, however, quite consistent with the sorts of pretextual sentencing guidelines suggested in the Antiterrorism and Effective Death Penalty Act of 1996 (10 Stat. 1214). Although it has never targeted humans—as opposed to property—the Earth Liberation Front (ELF), with which the AAC is allegedly overlapped, has been officially designated a "terrorist organization." See "Ecoterrorism in the United States," *ERRI Intelligence Report*, Vol. 6, No. 262 (September 18, 2000). This renders those involved either directly or indirectly open to extraordinary—that is, extraconstitutional—measures of repression. See Kenneth J. Dudonis, David P. Schulz, and Frank Bolz Jr., *The Counterterrorism Handbook: Tactics, Procedures, and Techniques* (Washington, DC: CRC Press, [2nd ed.] 2001). On the origins of the kind of "Joint Terrorist Task Force" now operating in Oregon, see my and Jim Vander Wall's *The COINTELPRO Papers: Documents from the FBI's Secret Wars on Dissent in the United States* (Boston: South End Press, 1990) pp. 309–11.

36 This goes to the notion that America is not only unique but entitled to play by a set of rules completely different from those applying to the rest of the world. See, e.g., Deborah L. Madsen, *American Exceptionalism* (Oxford: University of Mississippi Press, 1998) pp. 1–14.

37 This is by no means a novel concept. See, as examples, Malcolm X, *By Any Means Necessary* (New York: Pathfinder Press, 1992); Peter Stansill and David Zane Mairowitz, eds., *BAMN [by any means necessary]: Outlaw Manifestos and Ephemera, 1965–1970* (Brooklyn, NY: Autonomedia, 1999).

38 It is a testament to the extent to which Third Worlders are discounted in the minds of U.S. policymakers that the latter for the most part don't bother to observe the cardinal rule of domination holding that to prevent popular revolt it is necessary to present an illusion that relief is possible by other means. See generally Michael Sawad, *Co-optive Politics and State Legitimacy* (Hanover, NH: Dartmouth, 1991).

39 Interestingly, while the literature detailing activities of white—primarily Italian, Jewish and Irish—gangsters of the 1920s and '30s is vast, as of 2003 there was virtually nothing in print regarding blacks like Johnson, who not infrequently fought their more celebrated counterparts to a standstill. [Since this was written, the situation has been to some extent addressed with publication of Ron Chepesiuk's

Gangsters of Harlem: The Gritty Underworld of New York's Most Famous Neighborhood (Fort Lee, NJ: Barricade Books, 2007)—on Johnson, see pp. 89–104—as well as Mayme Johnson's and Karen E. Quinones Miller's *Harlem Godfather: The Rap on my Husband, Ellsworth "Bumpy" Johnson* (Philadelphia: Olson, 2008) and a few other books.]

40   There has been a veritable avalanche of denunciations since 9-1-1—by leftists as much as establishmentarians—of the Islamic fundamentalists in the al-Qaida organization, which allegedly carried out the attacks on the WTO and Pentagon, as well as Afghanistan's Taliban government, which supported al-Qaida, as "isla-mofascists" and "theo-nazis." While there is undoubtedly much truth to such depictions of extreme fundamentalism—Christian and Judaic, no less than Islamic—the question is how, given the manner in which the West has and continues to impose itself upon Islam, anyone might have expected things to have turned out otherwise. For the psychology at issue, see Frantz Fanon's *The Wretched of the Earth* (New York: Grove Press, 1966) esp. pp. 249–310. On the Taliban and al-Qaida, see Ahmed Rashid, *Taliban* (New Haven, CT: Yale University Press, 2001); Yonah Alexander and Michael S. Swetnam, *Usama bin Laden's al-Qaida: Profile of a Terrorist Network* (Ardsley, NY: Transnational, 2001).

41   For theory, see Fanon, *Wretched of the Earth*, pp. 35–106. Also see B. Marie Perinbam, *Holy Violence: The Revolutionary Thought of Frantz Fanon* (Washington, DC: Three Continents Press, 1982).

42   Yes, I'm quoting Charlie Manson, who, unmistakably, exemplifies the sort of systemically induced psychointellectual deformity at issue. See generally Ed Sanders, *The Family: The Story of Charles Manson's Dune Buggy Attack Battalion* (New York: E.P. Dutton, 1971).

43   See generally Rajenda Prasad, *Karma, Causation and Retributive Morality: Conceptual Essays in Ethics and Metaethics* (Calcutta: South Asia Books, 1990).

44   Actually, since the figures used here accrue from 1998, the toll stands to have ultimately been considerably higher. In any case, see Allan Connolly, M.D., "The Effect of Sanctions: A Medical Examination," in Clark and Others, *Challenge to Genocide*, p. 106.

45   For the estimate, see Ramsey Clark, "Fire and Ice: The Devastation of Iraq by War and Sanctions," in Clark and Others, *Challenging Genocide*, p. 20. For use and contextualization of the term, see Peters, *Collateral Damage*. The manner in which Iraq's cities were attacked clearly violated the 1923 Hague Rules of Aerial Warfare (Article 22) and the 1949 Geneva Convention IV Relative to the Protection of Civilian Persons in Times of War (Article 3).

46   William A. Arkin, Damian Durant, and Marianne Cherni, *On Impact: Modern Warfare and the Environment—A Case Study of the Gulf War* (Washington, DC: Greenpeace, 1991) pp. 105–15. Also see Clark, *War Crimes*, pp. 50–51, 90–93. Killing soldiers who are clearly out of combat is a war crime under terms of the Geneva Convention Common Article III. The attacks were carried out under a "no quarter" directive issued by George Bush a few days earlier. See Edward Cody, "U.S. Briefers Concede No Quarter," *Washington Post* (February 14, 1991). This also violates Article 23 (d) of the 1907 Hague Convention.

47   Clark, *War Crimes*, p. 30; citing Patrick J. Sloyan, "Pullback a Bloody Mismatch: Route of Iraqis became Savage 'Turkey Shoot,'" *New York Newsday* (March 31, 1991); "Massive Battle After Ceasefire," *New York Newsday* (May 8, 1991). Also see Clark, "Fire and Ice," pp. 18–19. Launching an assault on opposing troops after a ceasefire has taken effect is a war crime under both the Hague and Geneva Conventions.

48   Clark, *War Crimes*, p. 35; citing Patrick J. Sloyan, "U.S. Officers Say Iraqis Were Buried Alive," *San Francisco Chronicle* (September 12, 1991). Also see Clark, "Fire and Ice," p. 19. On use of the term "sand niggers," see Sklar, "Brave New World Order," p. 8. As observed in note 46, refusal of quarter to opposing troops—especially the wounded—is a war crime.

49   The best overview, in my estimation, is provided by Noam Chomsky, in his *The Fateful Triangle: The United States, Israel and the Palestinians* (Cambridge, MA: South End Press, [classics ed.] 1999).

50   Such things are exceedingly well-documented. See, as examples, Don Peretz, *Intifada: The Palestinian Uprising* (Boulder, CO: Westview Press, 1990); Middle East Watch Staff, *The Israeli Army and the Intifada: Policies that Contribute to the Killings* (New York: Middle East Watch, 1994); Roan Carey, ed., *The New Intifada: Resisting Israel's Apartheid* (London: Verso, 2001).

51   On the 1982 massacres at Sabra and Shatila, see Naseer Aruri, *Palestinian Refugees: The Right of Return* (London: Pluto, 2001) pp. 3, 127, 159. It is worth noting that Sharon "defended himself against charges of . . . complicity in the massacres by citing a similar Israeli role in [such earlier massacres as that at] Tal al-Za'tar" refugee camp in 1976; Rashid Khalidi, *Palestinian Identity: The Construction of Modern National Consciousness* (New York: Columbia University Press, 1997) p. 264.

52   On "Operation Success," as the CIA's Guatemalan intervention was codenamed, see John Prados, *Presidents' Secret Wars: CIA and Pentagon Covert Operations Since World War II* (New York: William Morrow, 1986) pp. 98–106. For insight into the consequences for grassroots Guatemalans, see Stephen Schlesinger and Stephen Kinzer, *Bitter Fruit: The Untold Story of the American Coup in Guatemala* (Garden City, NY: Doubleday, 1982); Ricardo Falla, *Massacres in the Jungle: Ixcán, Guatemala, 1975–1982* (Boulder, CO: Westview Press, 1994).

53   On the coup, see Noam Chomsky and Edward S. Herman, *The Political Economy of Human Rights, Vol. 1: The Washington Connection and Third World Fascism* (Boston: South End Press, 1979) pp. 205–9. On East Timor, John G. Taylor, *Indonesia's Forgotten War: The Hidden History of East Timor* (London: Pluto Press, 1991).

54   Prados, *Secret Wars*, pp. 91–98.

55   Armando Uribe, *The Black Book of American Intervention in Chile* (Boston: Beacon Press, 1975). For details of what happened after the coup, see Mary Helen Spooner, *Soldiers in a Narrow Land: The Pinochet Regime in Chile* (Berkeley: University of California Press, [2nd ed.] 1999); Hugh O'Shaughnessy, *Pinochet: The Politics of Torture* (New York: New York University Press, 2000).

56   A.J. Langguth, *Hidden Terrors: The Truth About U.S. Police Operations in Latin America* (New York: Pantheon, 1978); Martha K. Huggins, *Political Policing: The United States and Latin America* (Durham, NC: Duke University Press, 1998).

57   Reed Brody, *Contra Terror in Nicaragua: Report of a Fact-Finding Mission, September 1984–January 1985* (Boston: South End Press, 1985); Holly Sklar, *Washington's War on Nicaragua* (Boston: South End Press, 1988).

58   On the number killed, see H. Bruce Franklin, *Vietnam and Other American Fantasies* (Amherst: University of Massachusetts Press, 2000) p. 111. On the manner in which they were killed, see John Duffett, ed., *Against the Crime of Silence: Proceedings of the International War Crimes Tribunal, Stockholm-Copenhagen* (New York: Simon and Schuster, 1968); Vietnam Veterans Against the War, *The Winter Soldier Investigation: An Inquiry into U.S. War Crimes in Vietnam* (Boston: Beacon Press, 1972); Citizen's Commission

of Inquiry, *The Dellums Committee Hearings on War Crimes in Vietnam* (New York: Vintage Books, 1972).

59 According to Israeli journalist Amnon Kapeliouk, about a quarter-million Vietnamese children, all born during the war or after, have died of cancers or "hideous birth defects: resulting from the effects of American chemical warfare"; quoted in Noam Chomsky, "Rogue States," in his and Edward W. Said's *Acts of Aggression: Policing "Rogue" States* (New York: Seven Stories Press, 1999) pp. 41–42. For extensive—and stunning—visual confirmation of the birth defects, see Philip Jones Griffith, *Agent Orange: "Collateral Damage" in Viet Nam* (London: Trolly Ltd., 2003). For further background, see Barry Weisberg, *Ecocide in Indochina: The Ecology of War* (San Francisco: Canfield Press, 1970); John Lewallen, *Ecology of Devastation: Indochina* (New York: Penguin, 1971); Rajev Chandrasekaran, "War's Toxic Legacy Lingers in Vietnam," *Washington Post* (April 18, 2000). On land mines, and the ongoing U.S. refusal to accept their prohibition under international law, see Blum, *Rogue State,* p. 101.

60 Franklin, *Vietnam and Other Fantasies,* p. 161.

61 On the massacre mentioned, see Charles J. Hanley, Sang-Hun Choe, and Martha Mendoza, *The Bridge at No Gun Ri: A Hidden Nightmare from the Korean War* (New York: Henry Holt, 2001). More broadly, see I.F. Stone, *The Hidden History of the Korean War, 1950–51* (Boston: Little, Brown, [2nd ed.] 1988).

62 Against Germany, with the exception of its participation in the infamous 1945 incendiary attack on Dresden, the U.S. restricted itself to daylight "precision" bombing raids using high explosives. There, the stated objective was to avoid unnecessary civilian deaths. Against Japan, on the other hand—about which U.S. officials openly announced that they favored "the extermination of the Japanese people in toto"— the preferred method was nighttime saturation bombing by masses of aircraft dropping incendiaries to create "firestorms" in which vast numbers of noncombatants were deliberately cremated. In the great Tokyo fire raid on the night of March 9–10, 1945, to give but one example, more than 267,000 buildings were destroyed, a million people rendered homeless, and upward of one hundred thousand burned alive. Under such conditions, more Japanese civilians were killed in only six months than among all branches of the Japanese military during the entirety of World War II. See H. Bruce Franklin, *Star Wars: The Superweapon and the American Imagination* (New York: Oxford University Press, 1988) pp. 107–11. The public statement by U.S. War Manpower Commissioner Paul V. McNutt is quoted by John W. Dower, *War Without Mercy: Race and Power in the Pacific* (New York: Pantheon, 1986) p. 55.

63 Ronald Takaki, *Hiroshima: Why America Dropped the Atomic Bomb* (Boston: Little, Brown, 1995); Gar Alperovitz, *The Decision to Drop the Bomb* (New York: Alfred A. Knopf, 1995).

64 The same can perhaps be said with respect to biological warfare, which the United States attempted in Korea. See International Association of Democratic Lawyers, *U.S. Crimes in Korea,* 31 March 1952; annexed to a letter from the permanent member of the USSR to the president of the UN Security Council dated 30 June 1952 (UN Doc. S/2684/ADD.1/30 June 1952) Chapter 2: Bacteriological Warfare, pp. 28.7–28.9 (available at http://www.uwpep.org/Index/Resources_files/Crime_Reports_1.pdf). Also see Stephen Endicott and Edward Hagerman, *The United States and Biological Warfare: Secrets from the Early Cold War and Korea* (Bloomington: Indiana University Press, 1998). There is also a much longer history of its being selectively conducted against American Indians (see note 70), and the threat of its being employed by U.S. diplomats in their negotiations with native peoples. See, e.g., Elizabeth A. Fenn, *Pox*

Americana: The Great Smallpox Epidemic of 1775–82 (New York: Hill and Wang, 2001) esp. pp. 257–58.

65 Stuart Creighton Miller, *"Benevolent Assimilation": The American Conquest of the Philippines, 1899–1903* (New Haven, CT: Yale University Press, 1982).

66 For a very accurate—and sickening—description of what was done at Wounded Knee, see Ralph K. Andrist, *The Long Death: The Last Days of the Plains Indians* (New York: Collier, 1964) pp. 351–52.

67 All of these are covered in the essay entitled "'Nits Make Lice': The Extermination of American Indians, 1607–1996," in my *A Little Matter of Genocide: Holocaust and Denial in the Americas, 1492 to the Present* (San Francisco: City Lights, 1997) pp. 129–288.

68 On the origin and history of scalp bounties, see my "Nits Make Lice," pp. 178–88. On the hunting of Indians as sport, see David E. Stannard, *American Holocaust: The Conquest of the New World* (New York: Oxford University Press, 1992) p. 116.

69 On the Trail of Tears and related atrocities, see Grant Foreman, *Indian Removal* (Norman: University of Oklahoma Press, [2nd ed.] 1952); Russell Thornton, "Cherokee Population Losses During the Trail of Tears: A New Perspective and a New Estimate," *Ethnohistory*, Vol. 31, No. 4 (Autumn 1984) pp. 289–300. On the Navajo experience, see Clifford E. Trafzer, *The Kit Carson Campaign: The Last Great Navajo War* (Norman: University of Oklahoma Press, 1982) pp. 169–97. Regarding the explicitly racist attitudes underlying these policies, see Reginald Horsman, *Race and Manifest Destiny: The Origins of Racial Anglo-Saxonism* (Cambridge, MA: Harvard University Press, 1981).

70 Suspected instances of smallpox epidemics being deliberately unleashed among the native peoples of North America begin with Capt. John Smith's 1614 foray into Massachusetts in behalf of the Plymouth Company. Confirmed—that is to say, documentable—cases include Lord Jeffrey Amherst's order that infested blankets and other such items be distributed among the Ottawas in 1763, the U.S. Army's duplication of Amherst's maneuver at Fort Clark in 1837, and several repetitions by "private parties" in northern California during the 1850s (other examples accrue from British Columbia and the Northwest Territories in Canada during the later nineteenth century). See my "Nits Make Lice," pp. 151–57, 169–70; Peter McNair, Alan Hoover and Kevin Neary, *The Legacy: Tradition and Innovation in Northwest Coast Indian Art* (Seattle: University of Washington Press, 1984) p. 24. It should be noted that even some rather staunch apologists for the status quo have lately begun to admit that "the history of the western hemisphere has a few examples of whites deliberately releasing the [smallpox] virus among Indians." See R.G. Robertson, *Rotting Face: Smallpox and the American Indian* (Caldwell, ID: Caxton, 2001) p. 301.

71 Alan Axelrod, *Chronicle of the Indian Wars from Colonial Times to Wounded Knee* (Englewood Cliffs, NJ: Prentice-Hall, 1993) p. 39.

72 Howard Zinn, *The Politics of History* (Boston: Beacon Press, 1970) p. 67.

73 "Largely overlooked, neglected, or brushed off as a youthful indiscretion by our people is the enormous fact of slavery for over two centuries of our history," notes one progressive euroamerican analyst, "and its role as a central determinant of our economic development until at least the mid-nineteenth century." See Douglas Dowd, *U.S. Capitalist Development Since 1776: Of, By, and For Which People?* (Armonk, NY: M.E. Sharpe, 1993) p. 77. That truism uttered, he makes passing reference to slavery on exactly four other occasions in his 542-page text (American Indians are not mentioned at all, even in a section titled "Land policy"; pp. 274–75). For useful information, see Jim Marketti, "Black Equity in the Slave Industry," *Review of Black*

Political Economy, Vol. 2, No. 2 (Spring 1972) 43–66; Boris Bittker, The Case for Black Reparations (New York: Random House, 1973); Richard America, Paying the Social Debt (New York: Praeger, 1993).

74 Estimates of the aggregate mortality rate among blacks during the Middle Passage alone run as high as 40 percent, with the number of deaths from all causes associated with the transatlantic slave trade reaching as many as sixty million. See Philip D. Curtain, Slave Trade: A Census (Madison: University of Wisconsin Press, 1964) pp. 268 (Table 77), 275–82; Walter Rodney, How Capitalism Underdeveloped Africa (Washington, DC: Howard University Press, [rev. ed.] 1981) pp. 95–98; Joseph E. Inikori, "Measuring the Atlantic Slave Trade: An Assessment of Curtain and Anstey," Journal of African History, Vol. 17, No. 2 (Summer 1976) pp. 197–223; Paul E. Lovejoy, "The Volume of the Atlantic Slave Trade: A Synthesis," Journal of African History, Vol. 23, No. 4 (Winter 1982) pp. 473–501; Joseph C. Miller, "Mortality in the Atlantic Slave Trade: Statistical Evidence on Causality," Journal of Interdisciplinary History, Vol. 11, No. 3 (Winter 1981) pp. 385–423, esp. pp. 413–14.

75 For particularly useful studies, see Matthew J. Mancini, One Dies, Get Another: Convict Leasing in the American South, 1866–1928 (Columbia: University of South Carolina Press, 1996); David M. Oshinsky, "Worse Than Slavery": Parchman Farm and the Ordeal of Jim Crow Justice (New York: Free Press, 1996); Alex Lichtenstein, Twice the Work of Free Labor: The Political Economy of Convict Labor in the New South (London: Verso, 1996).

76 See Stewart Emory Tolnay, A Festival of Violence: An Analysis of the Lynching of African Americans in the American South, 1882–1930 (Urbana: University of Illinois Press, 1995); Ralph Ginzberg, 100 Years of Lynchings (Baltimore: Black Classics Press, 1997). On Klan membership, see Samuel Elliot Morrison and Henry Steele Commager, The Growth of the American Republic, 2 vols. (New York: Oxford University Press, [4th ed.] 1950) Vol. II, p. 556; Jonathan Daniels, The Time Between the Wars (Garden City, NY: Doubleday, 1966) p. 108; William Peirce Randel, The Ku Klux Klan: A History of Infamy (Philadelphia: Chilton Books, 1964) p. 220.

77 Much of what was worst about South African apartheid was based upon preexisting U.S. models. See George M. Frederickson, White Supremacy: A Comparative Study of American and South African History (New York: Oxford University Press, 1981). On the U.S. system itself, see Jerrold M. Packer, American Nightmare: The History of Jim Crow (New York: St. Martin's Press, 2002).

78 See Ronald Takaki, Strangers from a Different Shore: A History of Asian Americans (Boston: Little, Brown, 1989) pp. 80–87, 130, 240; Suchen Chan, Asian Americans: An Interpretive History (New York: Twayne, 1991) pp. 28–32.

79 See, as examples, Andrew Hacker, Two Nations: Black and White, Separate, Hostile, and Unequal (New York: Ballantine, [rev. ed.] 1995); Rodolfo Acuña, Occupied America: A History of the Chicanos (New York: Longman, [4th ed., rev.] 2000) esp. pp. 350–55, 400–410.

80 For a range of analyses, all supporting this conclusion, see Arturo Escobar, Encountering Development: The Making and Unmaking of the Third World (Princeton, NJ: Princeton University Press, 1995); Richard Falk, Predatory Globalization: A Critique (Cambridge, UK: Polity Press, 1999); Ash Narain Roy, The Third World in the Age of Globalization: Requiem or New Agenda? (Delhi/London: Madyam Books/Zed Books, 1999); David D. Newsom, The Imperial Mantle: The United States, Decolonization and the Third World (Bloomington: Indiana University Press, 2001) esp. pp. 123–202; James Petras and Henry Veltmeyer, Globalization Unmasked: Imperialism in the 21st Century (Halifax/London: Fernwood/Zed Books, 2001); Michel Chossudovsky, The

Globalization of Poverty and the New World Order (Montréal: Global Research, [2nd ed.] 2003).

81　The actual number seems to be a matter of no small controversy. During the attacks, media sources speculated that there might be upward of 17,000 dead killed at the World Trade Center alone. In the immediate aftermath, the official estimate stood at 4,500. A week later, it was ratcheted up to 5,000—the most commonly cited figure— ultimately cresting at nearly 6,000 before starting a sharp drop. By December 11, the tally, as reported on Fox News, stood at 3,040 (this should be contrasted to Sen. Orrin Hatch's assertion the same evening on *Larry King Live* [CNN] that "7,000 innocent Americans" had been killed on 9-1-1). As of January 10, 2002, the number of dead at the WTC reported by both Fox and CNN, including nearly 400 "foreigners," had fallen to 2,883. Adding in the seldom-mentioned toll at the Pentagon, and the more than two hundred aboard the four hijacked airliners, this would leave something less than 3,000 American fatalities. [As of 2014, according to Wikipedia, the tally is 2,606 dead at the WTC, 125 at the Pentagon, and 246—including the nineteen hijackers—aboard the airliners, for a total of 2,977. Of these, 373 were foreign nationals—392, counting the hijackers—leaving a total of 2,585 American dead. Given the volume of "patriotic" rhetoric devoted to decrying the deaths of food service workers, custodial and maintenance personnel, and the like, it seems instructive that Wiki's detailed statistical profile of those killed includes nothing about their occupations.]

82　This description of the airliners hijacked for the attack was offered by Secretary of Defense Donald Rumsfeld in a televised press briefing conducted on September 13, 2001.

83　The estimate is official. See Clark, *War Crimes*, pp. 17–18, 85. Bombardment of "undefended population centers"—which is what Iraq's cities were, once their "Triple A" (antiaircraft artillery) was suppressed—has been formally defined as a war crime since the Hague Convention of 1907 (under Article 25). Also see note 45.

84　For early reports on this pattern, see Jack Calhoun, "UN: Iraq Bombed Back to Stone Age," *Manchester Guardian* (April 3, 1991); Barton Gellman, "Storm Damage in the Persian Gulf: U.S. strategy against Iraq went beyond strictly military targets," *Washington Post Weekly* (July 8–14, 1991) p. 24. More comprehensively, see Clark, *War Crimes*, 22, 35, 53–58. It's worth noting that a strategy deliberately targeting *anything* other than "strictly military targets" constitutes a major war crime. See note 45.

85　The preinvasion indigenous population north of Mesoamerica has been credibly estimated as being perhaps eighteen million, the great bulk of it in what is now the Lower 48 States portion of the continent. By the time the 1890 U.S. census was taken, there were barely more than 237,000 survivors within the latter area. See Henry F. Dobyns, *Their Number Become Thinned: Native American Population Dynamics in Eastern North America* (Knoxville: University of Tennessee Press, 1983) pp. 42, 343; U.S. Department of Commerce, Bureau of the Census, *Fifteenth Census of the United States, 1930: The Indian Population of the United States and Alaska* (Washington, DC: U.S. Government Printing Office, 1937) esp. "Table II: Indian Population by States and Divisions, 1890–1930," p. 3.

86　A hue and cry was raised in the days following 9-1-1, by Fox News commentators and others, about Usama bin Laden's alleged instruction that his followers should "kill Americans wherever they may be found." While this was cast by the pundits as a desire to "exterminate" the U.S. citizenry as a whole, bin Laden's underlying intent was subsequently explained by more careful analysts—including even U.S.

Secretary of State Colin Powell—as being to make things so decisively uncomfortable for Americans that they would eventually demand a general withdrawal of the U.S. presence from Islamic countries. Problematic as the scheme may be in itself, it is very far cry from a call for genocide.

87   Segments of a videotaped statement in which Usama bin Laden explicitly linked 9–1–1 to the ongoing genocide in Iraq and the situation of the Palestinians was aired briefly, about a week after the attacks. Such broadcasts were abruptly halted when the government announced "national security" concerns, i.e., the contention that bin Laden might be using the tapes to send "coded instructions" to his followers in North America. On this ludicrous pretext, the idea that the motives underlying 9–1–1 warrant even a pretense of objective scrutiny have been abandoned in favor of official platitudes, delivered by and large in soundbite form, concerning the nature of "evil." It is quite possible that Americans would have rejected bin Laden's explanation, had they been allowed a chance to consider it. As things stand, we'll never really know, since the U.S. polity—uniquely, among its counterparts around the world—has been denied the possibility of hearing what he has to say. So much for "democratic decision-making" by an "informed citizenry." The principle/process at issue is explored very well in Chomsky's *Necessary Illusions*.

88   As noted Hawaiian rights activist Haunani-Kay Trask has observed, "Japan did not attack U.S. 'home territory' on December 7, 1941. It attacked the military forces of a foreign power engaged in the illegal occupation of my homeland. Hawaiians are not 'Native Americans,' we are Polynesians. Our country, Hawai'i, is not American; it is Polynesian. Hawai'i is not 'part of the United States'; it is a colony of the United States. These things were true in 1941, and they are just as true today. Anyone saying otherwise is either ignorant or a liar." Lecture at the University of Colorado–Boulder, March 14, 1993.

89   This is intended more literally than not. See, e.g., "Reagan Says Video Games Provide the Right Stuff," *Wall Street Journal* (Mar. 9, 1983).

90   George Cheney, "Talking War: Symbols, Strategies and Images," *New Studies on the Left*, Vol. 14, No. 3 (1991); Douglas Kellner, *The Persian Gulf TV War* (Boulder, CO: Westview Press, 1992) pp. 8–16.

91   Lynda Boose, "Techno-Muscularity and the 'Boy Eternal': From the Quagmire to the Gulf," in Amy Kaplan and Donald E. Pease, eds., *Cultures of United States Imperialism* (Durham, NC: Duke University Press, 1993) pp. 581–616; Dana L. Cloud, "Operation Desert Comfort," in Susan Jeffords and Susan Rabinovitz, eds., *Seeing Through the Media: The Persian Gulf War* (New Brunswick, NJ: Rutgers University Press, 1994) pp. 155–70.

92   The fact is that in less than two hours, nineteen men equipped with nothing more sophisticated than box cutters leveled a key command and control hub of globalization, eliminated around 2,000 of its technical personnel, put a $100 billion hole in the global economy, and knocked down a chunk of the Pentagon in the bargain. See generally Tom Templeton and Tom Lumley, "9/11 in Numbers," *The Observer* (August 17, 2002; available at http://www.theguardian.com/world/2002/aug/18/usa.terrorism). In purely military terms—as defined by U.S. strategic doctrine since at least as early as 1942—the attacks were wildly successful. See George E. Hopkins, "Bombing and the American Conscience During World War II," *The Historian*, Vol. 28, No. 3 (May 1966) pp. 451–73. Also see Ronald Schaffer, *Wings of Judgment: American Bombing in World War II* (New York: Oxford University Press, 1965);

Michael Sherry, *The Rise of American Air Power: The Creation of Armageddon* (New Haven, CT: Yale University Press, 1987).

93   *Znet Commentaries*, September 17, 2001.

94   Interview on NPR's *Powerpoint*, broadcast on Atlanta radio station WCLK, November 4, 2001.

95   For explication of the term used, see Tzvetan Todorov, *The Conquest of America: The Question of the Other* (New York: Harper & Row, 1984). Also see Homi K. Bhabha, "The other question: Stereotype, discrimination and colonial discourse," in his *The Location of Culture* (New York: Routledge, 1990) pp. 66–84; Roger Bartra, *Wild Men in the Looking Glass: The Mythic Origins of European Otherness* (Ann Arbor: University of Michigan Press, 1994).

96   This principle was set forth by the U.S.-instigated tribunal at Nuremberg in 1945. See Quincy Wright, "The Law of the Nuremberg Trials," *American Journal of International Law*, Vol. 41, No. 1 (January 1947) pp. 38–72; Bradley F. Smith, *The Road to Nuremberg* (New York: Basic Books, 1981).

97   For those unfamiliar with the case, see Anne E. Schwartz, *The Man who Could Not Kill Enough: The Secret Murders of Milwaukee's Jeffrey Dahmer* (New York: Carol, 1992).

98   It has been widely asserted, for example, that members of al-Qaida should be gunned down on the spot, even if attempting to surrender. Those making such statements are guilty of advocating criminal acts of the sort discussed in note 46. They may thus be technically subject to prosecution for war crimes in their own right. Whether or not this is so, they are certainly guilty of advocating—and thereby supporting—terrorism.

99   The photo spread appeared on p. B-1 of the *New York Times* on November 15, 2001. The response mentioned occurred on CNN's *Crossfire* the following evening. See Wayne Veysey, "I saw the killing of a Taliban Soldier," *Scottish Daily Record* (November 16, 2001).

100 Televised statements of U.S. president George W. Bush, September 12–15, 2001. All mention of a "crusade" was quickly dropped, when it became evident that the word served more than anything to validate in the eyes of Islam as a whole a 1997 al-Qaida manifesto announcing the organization had undertaken jihad against "Crusaders." See Rashid, *Taliban*, p. 134.

101 Given that the pentagon is a preeminent symbol of evil among satanists, the attackers of 9-1-1 could make a far better—or at least more literal—case for attempting to rid the world of it than can the U.S. See Genevieve Morgan and Tom Morgan, *The Devil: A Visual Guide to the Demonic, Evil, Scurrilous, and Bad* (San Francisco: Chronicle Books, 1996) p. 148. More broadly, see Paul Ricouer, *Symbolism of Evil* (Boston: Beacon Press, 1969).

102 Edwin S. Schneidman, *Definitions of Suicide* (New York: John Wiley, 1985).

103 For younger readers, it should be noted that the lines quoted—wildly popular among right-wingers everywhere—were delivered by actor Clint Eastwood during his portrayal of a homicidal San Francisco police detective in the movie *Dirty Harry* (1972).

104 On these potentials, see Jonathan B. Tucker, ed., *Toxic Terror: Assessing Terrorist Use of Chemical and Biological Weapons* (Cambridge, MA: MIT Press, 2000).

105 According to a poll reported on CNBC on December 7, 2001, 86 percent of Americans favored this recipe. On implications, see, e.g., Pamela J. Taylor, Philippa Garety, Alec Buchanan, Alison Reed, Simon Wessely, Katarzyna Ray, Graham Dunn, and Don Grubin, "Delusions and Violence," in John Monahan and Henry J. Stedman, eds.,

Violence and Mental Disorder: Developments and Risk Assessment (Chicago: University of Chicago Press, 1994) esp. the section entitled "The Nature of Delusions," pp. 161–63.

106 Some 40,000 Vietnamese were murdered and another 30,000 imprisoned by Phoenix Program operatives between 1968 and 1971, with no discernable impact on the "Viet Cong infrastructure." This was in large part because the program, which functioned on the basis of "hearsay [and] malicious gossip . . . fueled by feuds and political maneuvers," usually eliminated the wrong people; Prados, *Secret Wars*, pp. 309–11. Also see Douglas Valentine, *The Phoenix Program* (New York: William Morrow, 1990).

107 Office of Homeland Security Act of 2001 (H.R. 3026, October 4, 2001). Also see the Antiterrorism and Effective Death Penalty Act of 1996 (110 Stat. 1214).

108 Witness, for example, the wave of suicide bombings that has swept Israel since the beginning of 2001. While there had been only 25 such attacks over the entire eleven-year period since the first was carried out in July 1989, the numbers surged to 40 in 2001 and 47 the following year, falling off to 23 in 2003. Plainly, despite the best efforts of Israel's highly developed security apparatus, the attackers held the initiative throughout the campaign. It's worth noting that my contemporaneous impressions have been subsequently borne out in what may be the most comprehensive study of the relevant phenomena publicly available. See Pia Therese Jansen, *The consequences of Israel's counter terrorism policy* (PhD thesis, University of St. Andrews; available at https://research-repository.st-andrews.ac.uk/handle/10023/439).

109 See generally James X. Dempsey and David Cole, *Terrorism and the Constitution: Sacrificing Civil Liberties in the Name of National Security* (Los Angeles: First Amendment Foundation, 1999).

110 For an analogous contextualization, see Wilhelm Reich, *The Mass Psychology of Fascism* (New York: Farrar, Straus and Giroux, 1970); Peter Fritzsche, *Germans into Nazis* (Cambridge, MA: Harvard University Press, 1998).

111 Susan Griffin, *A Chorus of Stones: The Private Life of War* (New York: Anchor, 1993) p. 160. Also see E.L. Edelstein, Donald L. Nathanson, and Andrew Stone, eds., *Denial: A Clarification of Concepts and Research* (New York: Plenum, 1989); Stanley Cohen, *States of Denial: Knowing About Atrocities and Suffering* (Cambridge, UK: Polity Press, 2001).

112 In simplest terms, the condition has much in common with Sadistic Personality Disorder, that is, a "pervasive pattern of cruel, demeaning and aggressive behavior" disguised behind a sophisticated matrix of rationalization and denial. Diagnostic criteria include "(a) the use of physical cruelty or violence in establishing dominance in a relationship (e.g., not merely for the purpose of theft); (b) a fascination with violence, weapons, martial arts, injury, or torture (c) treating or disciplining others unusually harshly; (d) taking pleasure in the psychological or physical suffering of others (including animals); and (e) getting others to do what he or she wants through terror or intimidation." Thomas A. Widiger and Timothy J. Trull, "Personality Disorders and Violence," in John Monahan and Henry J. Steadman, eds., *Violence and Mental Disorder: Developments in Risk Assessment* (Chicago: University of Chicago Press, 1994) pp. 213–15.

113 The widely reported "one-in-six" estimate of fatalities on Luzon—a total 616,000 people—was offered by Brig. Gen. J. Franklin Bell during a 1902 appearance before Congress. See U.S. Senate, Committee on the Philippine Islands, *Hearings Before the Senate Committee on the Philippine Islands* (Washington, DC: 57th Cong., 1st Sess., 1902). Bell was openly referred to, both by his troops and in the press, as "The Butcher of Batangas." See U.S. Department of War, *Letter from the Secretary of War Relative to the Reports and Charges in the Public Press of Cruelty and Oppression Exercised by*

Our Soldiers Towards Natives of the Philippines (Washington, DC: 57th Cong, 1st Sess., 1902). It should be noted that, these facts being known, Bell received a Presidential Commendation for his "service" in the islands, and was later promoted Army Chief of Staff. See Miller, *"Benevolent Assimilation,"* pp. 237, 260.

114 Miller, *"Benevolent Assimilation,"* pp. 1–2.

115 William H. Chrisman, *The Opposite of Everything Is True: Reflections on Denial in Alcoholic Families* (New York: William Morrow, 1991).

116 For a clear indication of how much was known, and in what detail, see Moorfield Storey and Julian Codman, *"Marked Severities" in Philippine Warfare* (Boston: George H. Ellis, 1902).

117 Miller, *"Benevolent Assimilation,"* p. 253.

118 Ibid.

119 Ibid. The individuals named—President Theodore Roosevelt, Massachusetts Senator Henry Cabot Lodge and Indiana Senator Albert Beveridge—were key leaders among what was referred to as "The Imperialist Clique." See Richard H. Miller, *American Imperialism in 1898: The Quest for National Fulfillment* (New York: John Wiley, 1971). On the contemporaneous "anti-imperialist movement," see Robert L. Beisner, *Twelve Against Empire: The Anti-Imperialists, 1898–1900* (Chicago: University of Chicago Press, [2nd ed.] 1985). Overall, see Thomas G. Patterson, ed., *American Imperialism and Anti-Imperialism: Problem Studies in American History* (New York: Thomas Y. Crowell, 1973).

120 A cornerstone articulation came in the contention that imperialism should be treated as a "great aberration in American history" advanced by Samuel Flagg Bemis in his purportedly magisterial *Diplomatic History of the United States* (New York: Henry Holt, 1936) at p. 463. Such patent nonsense had been thoroughly refuted by the late 1960s and early 1970s. See, as examples, William Appleman Williams, *The Roots of the Modern American Empire: A Study of the Growth and Shaping of Social Consciousness in a Marketplace Society* (New York: Random House, 1969) and Sidney Lens, *The Forging of the American Empire: From the Revolution to Vietnam, A History of American Imperialism* (New York: Thomas Y. Crowell, 1969). Nonetheless, insistence that the United States has "no imperial ambitions" remains standard fare not only in the pronouncements of U.S. officials, but those of "responsible" academics as well. See, e.g., the statement of Stanford University professor of international affairs *cum* national security advisor Condoleezza Rice during a press conference conducted on July 23, 2003 (transcript available at http://www.whitehouse.gov/2003/07/20030731-7.html).

121 Often, the compensatory allegations amount to outright falsehoods, as with the much-publicized 1990 claim that Iraqi soldiers had killed hundreds of Kuwaiti babies in order to steal their incubators. See Boose, "Techno-Muscularity," p. 593.

122 There are, of course, significant exceptions to this, notably those like Mark Lane and Dick Gregory who have lost themselves forever in the mazes surrounding the Kennedy and King assassinations. See, e.g., Mark Lane and Dick Gregory, *Code Name "Zorro": The Assassination of Martin Luther King, Jr.* (Englewood Cliffs, NJ: Prentice-Hall, 1977) and Mark Lane, *Plausible Denial: Was the CIA Involved in the Assassination of JFK?* (New York: Thunder's Mouth Press, 1991).

123 This is not to argue that such concepts have no analytical value. Obviously, they do (which is of course why I employ them myself). Their insufficiency in and of themselves should be equally obvious, however. The "nazi state" committed none of the crimes of nazism; *people* subscribing to nazi "ideals" and thus embracing their manifestation in statist form committed or were complicit in the crimes. Questions

of popular culpability, accountability and even responsibility have been all but expunged from contemporary progressivist discourse, leaving it in some respects as sanitized—or disingenuous—as the conservative disquisitions it purports to critique.

124 To my knowledge, the only person attempting to define with any degree of precision who should be identified by the term "élite" has been the sociologist G. William Domhoff, in his *Who Rules America? Power and Politics in the Year 2000* (Mountainview, CA: Mayfield, 1998). Of additional interest, see his *The Power Elite and the State: How Policy Is Made in America* (Chicago: Aldine de Gruyter, 1990).

125 This is the famous stew composed in equal parts of "I didn't know," "I was only following orders"—or "I had no choice but to follow orders"—and "if I hadn't done it, someone else would have" ladled up by everyone up to and including ranking members of the nazi government. That the argument held no legal merit was clearly established at Nuremberg. Philosophically, it was rebutted rather firmly by Karl Jaspers and others at about the same time. Subsequently, it has been refuted chapter and verse both sociologically and on the grounds of historical evidence. See, e.g., Julius H. Schoeps, "From Character Assassination to Mass Murder," in Robert R. Shandley, ed., *Unwilling Germans? The Goldhagen Debate* (Minneapolis: University of Minnesota Press, 2000) pp. 79–80. In essence, knowledge of the nazi crimes was widespread, orders *could be*—and sometimes *were*—refused without personal consequence, and, had a sufficient number of Germans simply declined to go along, the Hitler régime would have had to adjust its policies accordingly. The fact is that a lopsided majority of Germans were quite comfortable with—and to a considerable extent openly celebratory of—nazism's "triumphs and accomplishments" right up to the point when the war turned decisively against them during the winter of 1942–43. See Ian Kershaw, *Hitler, 1936–1945: Nemesis* (New York: W.W. Norton, 2000) pp. 311, 367, 375, 421, 551; Michael Burleigh, *The Third Reich: A New History* (New York: Hill and Wang, 2000) pp. 266–67, 759–60. For a reserved but nonetheless very useful explication/analysis of the philosophical/legal issues involved, see Mark J. Osiel, *Obeying Orders: Atrocity, Military Discipline and the Law of War* (New Brunswick, NJ: Transaction, 1999).

126 The piece generating such controversy is my own "*Some People Push Back*: Reflections on the Justice of Roosting Chickens," *Pockets of Resistance*, No. 27 (September 2001). The term "little Eichmanns," however, was borrowed from John Zerzan's "Whose Unabomber?," *Anarchy*, Vol. 15, No. 2 (Winter 1997–98) pp. 50–51; collected in his *Running on Emptiness: The Pathology of Civilization* (Los Angeles: Feral House, 2002) p. 154.

127 Although not one of the many who raised this issue ventured a guess as to what proportion of the fatalities actually fit their description, most spoke as if there was no one in the WTC *but* such people. Alternately, their arguments imply that it is impermissible to attack a target if there is a chance *any* cleanup or food service personnel might suffer as a result. By this standard, of course, *no* targets are permissible, a principle precluding, for example, NLF mortar attacks on U.S. military compounds in Vietnam. Since none of the objectors has suggested that the latter restriction should hold true—several have in fact angrily repudiated it—their position ultimately reduces to the first sort of double standard marking any other variety of American exceptionalism. For the record, using the government's initial estimate of about 4,500 dead—roughly 4,000 at the WTC—my own arithmetic is as follows: Subtracting 300 undocumented workers, 600 documented workers,

100 temp workers, 100 bystanders (including several children), and 350 firemen from the toll leaves approximately 2,600 little Eichmanns (a tally in which 200-odd police and FBI personnel are most emphatically included). [As is observed in note 81, most of the figures used here were far too high. The *total* number killed at the WTC was barely over 2,600 (including 150 on the two airliners involved), of whom 370 were foreign nationals. All of the latter were documented, but it's doubtful that *any* of them might be accurately described as a "worker." Be that as it may, there's no indication that a single undocumented worker was among the dead. Nor is there indication that a single "random passer-by" was killed. You do the math.]

128 Obituary, *New York Times* (December 9, 2001). I wish to emphasize that by using this young man as an illustration I do not mean to single him out as having been in any way more repugnant than his peers. As I said, he is representative. I could as easily have used the obituaries in the same NYT spread for the thirty-two-year-old bond trader who had already purchased an extravagantly expensive apartment on upscale West 72nd Street and, "although it was perfectly livable"—obviously enough—had it "gutted to the slab and girders" and reassembled in a personal fashion statement costing enough to sustain an entire Third World community for years. Then there was the older corporate vice president who, at forty-eight, already owned his country estate, vacation cottage, cars, boat and collection of race horses, and was preparing to take early retirement so that he might better enjoy the "fruits of his labor." As easily, I could have used the obit spread run by the NYT on any other day since it began publishing them in September to obtain the same results.

129 The first three characterizations accrue from the obituary cited above, the last three from polemics e-mailed to me by self-styled progressives. Note how, in the second set, the wealth enjoyed by the individual in question is imputed more or less to chance, as if he'd won the lottery, rather than to the specific activities in which he'd actually engaged. The purpose of this dodge—the writer was plainly aware that happenstance played no role in the subject's income generation—is to exonerate the deceased from the onus of choices he himself had been "proud" to make, as well as from the implications of the values revealed thereby.

130 Actually, comparing him to the group in question may be in some ways unfair to Eichmann. Whatever else may be said of his motivations, they appear to have devolved upon some hideous combination of "professionalism" and perverted idealism rather than anything so crass as material greed. The "little Eichmanns" of 9–1–1, on the other hand, seem to have been suffering in varying degrees of acuteness from Antisocial Personality Disorder, a pathology marked by extreme displays of "hedonism, irresponsibility, [and] indifference to the suffering" of anyone other than themselves or a narrow circle of family and friends. See Thomas A. Widiger and Timothy J. Trull, "Personality Disorders and Violence," in Monahan and Steadman, *Violence and Mental Disorder*, pp. 208–13, 215. While many words come to mind in describing such a condition, neither "cool" nor "warm hearted" are among them. That they might go unchallenged when used in this way is evidence of the much broader pattern of dissociation/denial afflicting American social consciousness.

131 Much of the negative correspondence I've received has seemed rather visceral, as if the writers were reacting to the name, with no real clue as to who Adolf Eichmann was or what he did, and thence his significance in the present context. Let it be observed, then, that he was a mere field grade officer in the SS, by all accounts a good husband and devoted father, apparently rather mild-mannered, and never credibly accused of having personally murdered anyone at all. His crime was to have

sat at several steps remove from the holocaustal blood and gore, behind a desk, in the sterility of an office building, organizing the logistics—train and "cargo" schedules, mainly—without which the "industrial killing" aspect of the nazi Judeocide could not have occurred. His most striking characteristic, if it may be called that, was his sheer "unexceptionality" (that is, the extent to which he had to be seen as "everyman": an "ordinary," "average" or "normal" member of his society). See generally Hannah Arendt, *Eichmann in Jerusalem: A Report on the Banality of Evil* (New York: Viking, 1963).

132 I am perhaps using the term "progressive" a bit too broadly. It should be noted that *every* hostile comment I've received—or heard—has come from relatively privileged whites, mostly men, self-described as "peace activists." Such favorable commentary as I've encountered—and it's been considerable—has come mostly, though by no means exclusively, from people of color. The pattern is entirely consistent with that discussed in conjunction with notes 20–34, and one I've explored more thoroughly in *Pacifism as Pathology*.

133 Witness the oft-remarked and truly global sentiment of "anti-Americanism" which has become ever more pronounced over the past half-century. See, e.g., Alvin G. Rubinstein and Donald E. Smith, eds., *Anti-Americanism in the Third World: Implications for U.S. Foreign Policy* (New York: Praeger, 1985). Facile attributions of such resentments to "envy" are as pathologically delusional—or diversionary—as any other facet of American denial.

134 U.S. Senate, Committee on the Judiciary, *Hearing on a Proposed Constitutional Amendment to Protect Crime Victims* (Washington, DC: 105th Cong., 2nd Sess., April 28, 1998). For further discussion of the issue, as framed in the U.S., see the various contributions to Sara Flaherty and Austin Sarat, eds., *Victims and Victims' Rights: Crime, Justice and Punishment* (New York: Chelsea House, 1998).

135 Jaspers, *German Guilt*, pp. 25–26. A further elaboration of the Jasperian schematic, reframed in terms of "responsibility" rather than "guilt," is developed by David H. Jones in his *Moral Responsibility in the Holocaust: A Study in the Ethics of Character* (Lanham, MD: Rowman & Littlefield, 1999) esp. pp. 15–32.

136 See generally Geoffrey Robertson, *Crimes Against Humanity: The Struggle for Global Justice* (New York: Free Press, 2000). More technically, see Steven R. Ratner and Jason S. Abrams, *Accountability for Human Rights Atrocities in International Law: Beyond the Nuremberg Legacy* (New York: Oxford University Press, [2nd ed.] 2001).

137 "The idea that a state, any more than a corporation, commits crimes, is a fiction. Crimes are committed only by persons. . . . It is quite intolerable to let a legalism become the basis for personal immunity." U.S. Supreme Court Justice Robert H. Jackson in his role as Nuremberg prosecutor (1945), quoted in Robertson, *Crimes Against Humanity*, p. 218. Also see Lyal S. Sunga, *Individual Responsibility in International Law for Serious Human Rights Violations* (The Hague: Martinus Nijhoff, 1992).

138 A major reason the Nuremberg Tribunal was convened was because Germany had rather spectacularly defaulted on its the authority allowed it under Articles 228 and 229 of the Treaty of Versailles to prosecute its own war criminals after World War I. Of 901 individuals against whom evidence was provided by the allied powers, 888 were acquitted in German courts. Only token sentences were imposed upon the remaining thirteen, several of whom were shortly "allowed to escape by prison officials who were publicly congratulated for assisting them." See Robertson, *Crimes Against Humanity*, pp. 210–11. As will be discussed in notes 163 and 164, the U.S. record is no better.

139   The idea is neither new nor novel. See Wright, "Law of the Nuremberg Tribunal";
      Manley O. Hudson, *The Permanent Court of International Justice* (New York: Macmillan,
      1943); Maynard B. Golt, "The Necessity of an International Court of Justice," *Washburn
      Law Journal*, Vol. 6, No. 3 (Fall 1966) pp. 13–23; Leo Gross, "The International Court
      of Justice: Enhancing Its Role in the International Legal Order," in Leo Gross, ed.,
      The Future of the International Court of Justice (New York: Oceana, 1973) pp. 22–104.

140   There were those who "foresaw the disaster, said so, and warned; that does not
      count politically . . . if no action followed or it had no effect. . . . To be content
      with paper protests [or] to play riskless politics . . . is evasion of responsibility."
      Jaspers, *German Guilt*, pp. 56, 85. For a useful extrapolation based on precisely these
      principles, see Mike Ryan's "On Ward Churchill's 'Pacifism as Pathology': Towards
      a Consistent Revolutionary Practice," in *Pacifism as Pathology*, pp. 131–68.

141   "Politically everyone acts in the modern state, [if only] by voting, or failing to vote,
      in elections. . . . One might think of cases of wholly non-political persons who
      live aloof from all politics. . . . Yet they, too, are included among the politically
      liable, because they, too, live by the order of the state. There is no such aloofness
      in modern states." Jaspers, *German Guilt*, p. 56. For further elaboration, see Frank
      Harrison, *The Modern State: An Anarchist Analysis* (Montréal: Black Rose Books, 1984).

142   "A people answers for its polity [because] political conditions are inseparable from
      a people's whole way of life. . . . We are responsible for our régime, for the acts of
      our régime . . . for the kinds of leaders we allowed to arise among us. . . . Hence
      there is a two-fold guilt—first in the unconditional surrender to a leader as such,
      and second, in the kind of leader submitted to. The atmosphere of submission is a
      kind of collective guilt." Jaspers, *German Guilt*, pp. 55, 70, 72.

143   "There is liability for political guilt, consequently reparation is necessary and . . .
      loss or restriction of political rights on the part of the guilty [emphasis original]";
      Jaspers, *German Guilt*, p. 30. Also see Elazar Barkan, *The Guilt of Nations: Restitution
      and Negotiating Historical Injustices* (New York: W.W. Norton, 2000) and the material
      collected in Roy L. Brooks, ed., *When Sorry Isn't Enough: The Controversy over Apologies
      and Reparations for Human Injustice* (New York: New York University Press, 1999).

144   In some cases, the number of actual perpetrators may run into the hundreds of
      thousands, those culpable by reason of active complicity into the millions. In
      such instances, the likelihood of everyone involved being brought to trial is nil.
      For logistical reasons, if nothing else, the best hope is that a few thousand "key
      players" be prosecuted and punished. This was essentially the pattern established
      at Nuremberg. See John Alan Appleman, *Military Tribunals and International Crimes*
      (Westport, CT: Greenwood Press, 1971 reprint of 1954 original).

145   "Blindness for the misfortune of others . . . indifference toward the witnessed evil—
      that is moral guilt. The moral guilt of outward compliance, of *running with the pack*, is
      shared to some extent by a great many of us. To maintain his existence, to keep [her]
      job, to protect his [or her] chances, a man [or woman] would . . . carry out nominal
      acts of conformism. None will find an absolute excuse for doing so—notably in view
      of [those] who, in fact, did not conform, and bore the consequences. . . . It is never
      simply true that 'orders are orders.' Rather—as crimes even though ordered . . . so
      every deed remains subject to moral [and criminal] judgment [emphasis in origi-
      nal]." Jaspers, *German Guilt*, p. 64.

146   "It would, indeed, be an evasion and a false excuse if we Germans tried to exculpate
      ourselves by pointing to the guilt of being human." Jaspers, *German Guilt*, p. 94. For
      a current rehash of the bilge at issue, see Francis Fukuyama's *The Great Disruption:*

Human Nature and the Reconstruction of Social Order (New York: Simon and Schuster, 2000).

147 "Each one of us is guilty insofar as [s/he] remained inactive. . . . The conditions out of which both crime and political guilt arise [consist of the] commission of countless little acts of negligence, of convenient adaptation, of cheap vindication, and the imperceptible promotion of wrong; the participation of the creation of a public atmosphere that spreads confusion and thus makes evil possible—all that has consequences that partly condition the political guilt involved in the situation and events." Jaspers, *German Guilt*, pp. 63, 29.

148 I've consciously switched from "they" to "we" in this passage. This is because, despite my sustained, always vociferous, and at times physical opposition, and the fact that I am a citizen only by virtue of the U.S. imposition of itself upon my people, I am nonetheless *here*, in the belly of the beast, still alive and at liberty, and have thus done less than I could have. Hence, I share in the political guilt of all Americans. It follows that had I been in aboard one of the fatal aircraft on 9-1-1—or should I be similarly extinguished in the future, as is entirely possible, under present circumstances—I will have no more basis for complaint than any other American.

149 Quoted in Jürgen Habermas, "Goldhagen and the Public Use of History: Why a Democracy Prize for Daniel Goldhagen?" in Shandley, *Unwilling Germans?*, p. 265. On Schmitt's decisive role in the formulation of nazi legal theory, see Stolleis, *Law Under the Swastika*, esp. pp. 13, 92–93, 97–98, 100.

150 This concerns "attempts of the New Right ideologues around Ranier Zitelmann as well as among some of the more naive social historians to relativize the horrors of the Third Reich by reference to the supposedly 'good aspects' of the regime, which is said to have promoted a sort of 'progressive social policy,' or even have become a kind of 'welfare state' in which 'only minorities and marginal groups' were persecuted." Wolfgang Wippermann, "The Jewish Hanging Judge? Goldhagen and the 'Self-Confident Nation,'" in Shandley, *Unwilling Germans?*, p. 243.

151 The level of argumentation here descends to that embodied in claims that the lethal thugs rostering Brooklyn's Murder, Inc., during the 1930s really "weren't so bad" because, whatever else they may have done, they were always "good to their mothers." See Robert A. Rockaway, *But He Was Good to His Mother: Lives and Crimes of Jewish Gangsters* (New York: Gefen, 2000). Like it or not, the evaluative principle by which such virtues are discounted to the point of irrelevancy in assessments of Lepke Buchalter and Allie Tannenbaum—or Adolf Eichmann—is equally applicable to many of those killed on 9-1-1, as much to Cantor Fitzgerald as to Murder, Inc., to the U.S. no less than to nazi Germany.

152 The past does not simply "go away," nor can America's myriad victims just "get over it," no matter how convenient it would be for Americans if they did. See analogously, Charles S. Maier, *The Unmasterable Past: History, Holocaust, and German National Identity* (Cambridge, MA: Harvard University Press, 1988).

153 In a sense, the same could be said of America's own troops, disproportionately drawn as they are from impoverished communities of color and poor sectors of the white populace, once their more privileged countrymen have used them as fodder. Witness the ongoing official refusal to acknowledge—and thus accept responsibility for—the well-established link between dioxin exposure and the cancers/other serious maladies suffered at extraordinarily high rates by Vietnam veterans and their offspring. See Fred A. Wilcox, *Waiting for an Army to Die: The Tragedy of Agent Orange* (Santa Ana, CA: Seven Locks Press, 1989) and Institute of Medicine, *Veterans*

and *Agent Orange: Update 1998* (Washington, DC: National Academy Press, 2000). Much the same thing is now occurring with the "Gulf War Syndrome" suffered at high rates by soldiers exposed to depleted uranium and other toxins in 1991. See Akiro Tashiro, *Discounted Casualties: The Human Costs of Depleted Uranium* (Hiroshima: Chigoku Chimbum, 2001). Needless to say, the mostly affluent "progressives" of the "antismoking movement"—for all their shrieking about the illusory "health effects" of environment tobacco smoke in open air sports stadia (see note 20)—have maintained a thundering silence vis-à-vis these substantive problems.

154   See the sections titled "The Comfort Zone" and "Let's Pretend" in *Pacifism as Pathology*, pp. 46–69.

155   It should be noted that Americans are by and large as self-contradictory on this score as anything else. Although there is endless clucking about the "moral impropriety" of armed resistance to state power in the U.S., exactly the opposite is held to be true with respect to Germany. Although it's true that, as Jaspers observes, many thousands of Germans were imprisoned for resistance by the nazis ("every month of 1944 political arrests exceeded 4,000"), it's also true that these "anonymous martyrs," offered no "dangerous opposition." They resisted almost exclusively "by word" and were therefore "ineffective." See Jaspers, *German Guilt*, pp. 77, 55. Also see Peter Hoffman's massive study, *The History of the German Resistance, 1933–1945* (Montréal: McGill-Queen's University Press, [3rd ed.] 1996). The sole group consequential enough to be recollected at all in the U.S.—and quite approvingly so—are the plotters who attempted to assassinate Hitler late in the war. See, e.g., Giles MacDonogh, *A Good German: A Biography of Adam von Trott zu Solz* (Woodstock, NY: Overlook Press, 1992).

156   The "traditional Washington stance [has been] that the U.S. is above international law." Robinson, *Crimes Against Humanity*, p. 327. Suffice it here to observe that the "unilateralist" policy pursued by the U.S. in international affairs draws much of its inspiration from the theory of "the prerogative state"—a "governmental system which exercises unlimited arbitrariness and violence unchecked by any legal guarantees" other than those it elects on the basis of expedience or transient self-interest to observe—advanced by political philosopher Ernst Fraenkel, in his *The Dual State: A Contribution to the Theory of Dictatorship* (New York: Oxford University Press, 1941) p. xiii.

157   "U.S. Terminates Acceptance of ICJ Compulsory Jurisdiction," *Department of State Bulletin*, No. 86 (January 1986).

158   The U.S. refused to join 120 other states voting to affirm the ICC Charter in 1998, and continues to insist it will never do so until the Charter is revised to grant Americans "100 percent protection" against—that is, blanket immunity from—indictment and prosecution. See Blum, *Rogue State*, p. 77; Robertson, *Crimes Against Humanity*, pp. 327–28.

159   On the binding effect of customary law on all states, see Wright, "Law of the Nuremberg Tribunal."

160   For a fairly comprehensive itemization, see Blum, *Rogue State*, pp. 187–97.

161   Lawrence J. LeBlanc, *The United States and the Genocide Convention* (Durham, NC: Duke University Press, 1991); the text of the U.S. "Sovereignty Package" appears as Appendix C, pp. 253–54.

162   Article 37 of the Convention on the Rights of the Child, which has been ratified by every UN member state but the U.S. and Somalia, makes it illegal to impose the death penalty on persons who were under eighteen years of age at the time their

crime was committed. In *Tompkins v. Oklahoma* (108 S.Ct. 2687 (1988)) and *Stanford v. Kentucky, Wilkins v. Missouri* (492 U.S. 361 (1989)), however, the U.S. Supreme Court has upheld the executions of persons who were as young as sixteen when their offenses occurred. In effect, the U.S. refusal of the Convention, is expressly intended to preserve a legally fictional "sovereign right" to kill children.

163 The "Land Mine Convention," which took effect on March 1, 1999, has been affirmed by 131 states and formally ratified by more than seventy. The U.S. has stated repeatedly that it will endorse the law only if it—and it alone—is exempted from compliance. See Blum, *Rogue State*, p. 101.

164 A classic example concerns Col. John Chivington and other perpetrators of the 1864 Sand Creek Massacre. Although three separate federal investigations—one by the House, another by the Senate, the third by the Department of War—each concluded that violations of the Army's Lieber Code, several of them capital offenses, had been committed deliberately and on a massive scale, no one was prosecuted. See the final chapter of Stan Hoig's *The Sand Creek Massacre* (Norman: University of Oklahoma Press, 1961). Another concerns the 1968 My Lai Massacre in Vietnam. Only four of an already much-circumscribed list of thirty responsible officers were ever taken to trial. See Joseph Goldstein, Burke Marshall, and Jack Schwartz, *The My Lai Massacre and Its Cover-Up: Beyond the Reach of the Law* (New York: Free Press, 1976) pp. 3–4. The litany could continue, but there should be no need. The parallel to the interwar German performance described in note 138 is obvious.

165 Lt. William Calley, the only man ultimately convicted in the massacre of "at least 102 Oriental human beings" at My Lai, served only three and a half years as a result, most of it in his own quarters. Several other officers received reprimands, demoted one rank, stripped of a medal, or directed to take early retirement; Goldstein, Marshall, and Schwartz, *My Lai*, pp. ix–x, 465–67. The same pattern prevailed in 1902–3, with respect to the handful of officers found guilty of atrocities in the Philippines. See Miller "*Benevolent Assimilation*," pp. 236–38. Again, there is a striking similarity to the performance of interwar Germany described in note 138.

166 Once again, the idea is by no means new. It was first seriously proposed in 1969, as part of a broader strategy to force a halt to the U.S. war against Indochina. See Judith Cockburn and Geoffrey Cowan, "The War Criminals Hedge Their Bets," *Village Voice* (December 4, 1969); Townsend Hoopes, "The Nuremberg Suggestion," *Washington Monthly* (January 1970) pp. 18–21.

167 Christopher Hitchens, *The Trial of Henry Kissinger* (London: Verso, 2001).

168 Robertson, *Crimes Against Humanity*, pp. 446–48.

169 See Telford Taylor, *Anatomy of the Nuremberg Trials* (New York: Alfred A. Knopf, 1992).

170 The notion of "voluntary" remedies, in which offenders themselves establish either the form or the equity involved, has long since proven more than inadequate. See Hubert Kim, "German Reparations: Industrialized Insufficiency," and Roy L. Brooks, "What Form Redress?," both in Brooks, *When Sorry Isn't Enough*, pp. 77–80, 87–100.

171 Although the dispensation of justice was far from perfect or complete, more than 6,000 criminal cases were brought against former nazis in Germany's domestic courts between 1951 and 1981. See Diane F. Orentlicher, "Settling Accounts: The Duty to Prosecute Human Rights Violations of a Prior Regime," *Yale Law Journal*, Vol. 100, No. 8 (June 1991) pp. 2537–2615. One major barrier to a still more thorough process was the protection provided by the U.S. to thousands of potential defendants its CIA and military establishment saw as being useful for their own purposes;

Christopher Simpson, *Blowback: America's Recruitment of Nazis and Its Effect on the Cold War* (London: Weidenfeld and Nicholson, 1988).

172 Shortly after 9-1-1, Noam Chomsky presumed to inform the attackers of what they "should" have done instead. Astonishingly, he then goes on to posit as a "precedent" for "how to go about [obtaining] justice" the 1985 *Nicaragua v. U.S.* case in which a people "subjected to violent assault by the U.S. . . . went to the World Court, which issued a judgment in their favor condemning the U.S. for what it called 'unlawful use of force,' which means international terrorism, ordering the U.S. to desist and pay substantial reparations." What is bizarre is that Chomsky also observes how "the U.S. dismissed the court judgment with contempt, responding with an immediate escalation of the attack [in which] tens of thousands of people died. The country was substantially destroyed, it may never recover." This is how victims "should proceed"? Plainly, there's something seriously askew here. See Noam Chomsky, interviewed by David Barsamian, "The United States is a Leading Terrorist State," *Monthly Review*, Vol. 53, No. 6 (November 2001) pp. 14–15.

173 "A state [polity] which has violated natural law and human rights on principle—at home from the start, destroying human rights and international law abroad—has no claim to recognition, in its favor, of what it refused to recognize itself." Jaspers, *German Guilt*, p. 38.

174 "By 'national history,' I do not mean just the history of a given country or nation. I refer to the dominant framework for understanding that history. This is not confined to or necessarily governed by how academic history is written, though it may include that. It encompasses how a national history is represented more generally in the public sphere—in newspapers and magazines, on television and film, in textbooks and popular works of history. These shape a people's images of its past far more than do the scholarly books of academic historians." Daniel Jonah Goldhagen, "*Modell Bundesrepublik*: National History, Democracy, and Internationalization in Germany," in Shandley, *Unwilling Germans?*, pp. 275–76.

175 Ibid., pp. 277–80.

176 Jaspers, *German Guilt*, pp. 96–117.

177 For exemplars of the canonical approach, see Samuel Eliot Morison, *The Oxford History of the American People* (New York: Oxford University Press, 1965); James McGregor Burns, *The American Experiment*, 3 vols. (New York: Alfred A. Knopf, 1983–86). On its pop counterparts, see, as examples, Peter C. Rollins, ed., *Hollywood as Historian: American Film in a Cultural Context* (Lexington: University Press of Kentucky, 1983) and Robert Brent Toplin, *History by Hollywood: The Use and Abuse of the American Past* (Urbana: University of Illinois Press, 1996).

178 Although overlapping, there are significant differences between the legal and historical arenas not only with regard to the rules of evidence, but concerning the purposes to which it is put. In simplest terms, the emphasis of the former is to demonstrate culpability, the latter is upon explaining it. See generally Graham C. Lilly, *An Introduction to the Law of Evidence* (St. Paul, MN: West Wadsworth, 1996); Walter Prevenier and Martha C. Howell, *From Reliable Sources: An Introduction to Historical Methods* (Ithaca, NY: Cornell University Press, 2001).

179 This is more or less the process that has occurred with respect to Germany. See Maier, *Unmasterable Past*.

FIFTEEN

"To Judge Them by the Standards of Their Time"

America's Indian Fighters, the Laws of War, and the Question of International Order

> I want no prisoners. I wish you to kill and burn. The more you kill and burn, the better you will please me.
> —General Jacob H. Smith, Philippines, 1901

The expansion of the United States from a strip of territory situated east of the Appalachian Mountains on North America's Atlantic coast, first to continental scale, then to a position of global ascendancy, is a history replete with the use of military force.[1] Quite apart from the armed struggle by which it freed itself from English colonization, the new country's sheer bellicosity was evidenced as early as May 31, 1779, when future president George Washington issued written orders to Major General John Sullivan, instructing him to undertake a "preemptory" campaign against the Senecas and other members of the Haudenosaunee (Six Nation Iroquois Confederation) in upstate New York.[2]

Sullivan's mission was not so much to overrun Seneca territory as to destroy it, Washington wrote, and he was forbidden to "listen to any overture of peace before the total ruin of their settlements is effected."[3] The general thereupon did as he was directed. In 1838, historian William L. Stone "described in detail Sullivan's scouring the countryside, the 'war of extermination [he] waged against the very orchards.' At the town of Genesee alone Sullivan's army destroyed over a hundred houses, 'mostly large and very elegant,' laid waste extensive fields of ripening corn and beans, and 'with axe and torch soon transformed the whole of that

Originally published in my *Perversions of Justice: Indigenous Peoples and Angloamerican Law* (San Francisco: City Lights, 2003).

beautiful region from the character of a garden to a scene of drear and sickening desolation.'"[4]

Among the trophies with which Sullivan's men returned from their victorious expedition were the scalps and tanned skins of their vanquished foes, the latter neatly fashioned into leggings.[5] Small wonder, all in all, that Washington became known as "Town Destroyer" to the Haudenosaunee, and, as the Seneca leader Cornplanter remarked to America's "Founding Father" in 1792, "our women turn pale and look behind them, and our children cling close to the necks of their mothers" whenever his name was mentioned.[6]

A year after Sullivan wrought havoc upon the Six Nations, General George Rogers Clark—whose rangers still serve as the prototype after which the Army's élite units are modeled[7]—was engaged in a similar offensive against the Shawnees and other peoples in what are now the states of Ohio, Indiana, and Illinois. Clark's men, who are known to have scalped their captives alive,[8] destroyed an estimated "five hundred acres of corn . . . as well as every species of edible vegetable" at the towns of Chillicothe and Piqua alone.[9]

Clark's effort was followed by that of General Anthony Wayne, still operating under the direction of Washington, in 1794. "Mad" Anthony's troops laid waste a huge swath through the Shawnee heartland, "remaining three days on the banks of the Maumee [River] during which time all the houses and . . . immense fields of corn . . . were consumed and destroyed" for a distance of fifty miles.[10] In the aftermath, leggings crafted from tanned human skin again made their appearance, this time along the Ohio frontier.[11]

Ultimately, the Shawnees were not defeated until the Battle of Tippecanoe on November 6, 1811. There, soldiers serving under future president William Henry Harrison indulged themselves in atrocities identical in their grotesquerie to those marking the Sullivan, Clark, and Wayne campaigns a generation earlier. Emblematic of the whole was the troops' mutilation of the fallen Shawnee leader Tecumseh.

> The souvenir hunters got to work, and when the warrior had been stripped of clothing . . . Kentuckians tore the skin from his back and thigh. . . . The rapacious soldiery so thoroughly scalped the corpse that some of them came away with fragments the size of a cent piece and endowed with a mere tuft of hair. When [one of them] was interviewed in 1868 he was still able to display a piece of Tecumseh's skin.[12]

On March 27, 1814, following his massacre of the Muscogee Red Sticks at Horseshoe Bend, in Alabama, General Andrew Jackson, "supervised the mutilation of 800 or more Indian corpses—cutting off their noses to count and preserve a record of the dead, slicing long strips of flesh from their bodies to tan and turn into bridle reins."[13] Thereafter, especially during his successful bid for the presidency in 1828, Jackson, who'd meanwhile gone on record urging that the Cherokees be similarly "scurged," would frequently boast that he'd "on all occasions preserved the scalps of my killed."[14]

In 1833, general and future president Zachary Taylor—in whose militia still another president-to-be, Abraham Lincoln, was serving at the time—unleashed the massacre of around three hundred Sacs and Foxes (Mesquakis) led by Black Hawk on the Bad Axe River, in present-day Wisconsin. Taylor's men ran wild, engaging in "an eight-hour frenzy of clubbing, stabbing, shooting [and] scalping."[15] The bones of Black Hawk himself were later disinterred and put on display in a local museum in Iowaville, Iowa, for well over a century.[16]

A recounting of this sort could be extended to great length, and expanded to include related matters—the proclamation of bounties on the scalps of Indians in every one of the "Lower Forty-Eight" states[17] for instance, or the annihilation of entire native peoples by well-armed and -organized groups of "private citizens" in California[18]—but the illustrations provided above should prove sufficient to mark a conspicuous pattern of atrocity committed by the U.S. Army against American Indians during the entire period leading up to the Civil War.

They should also serve to demonstrate quite clearly that, far from being officially repudiated or socially condemned, such actions were undertaken as a matter of policy and with support by a majority of citizens enthusiastic enough to propel one perpetrator after another into the White House. Reward, not punishment or stigma, was the rule for even the worst of America's Indian-killers, any number of whom have come to be immortalized as national heroes.[19]

"To Judge Them by the Standards of Their Time"

These realities are entirely disconsonant with the carefully cultivated air of "American Innocence" adopted by the United States, both as a self-concept and as an image projected internationally.[20] Correspondingly, such "unpleasantness" has been downplayed to the point of invisibility by generations of "responsible" historians, especially those authoring popular narratives and texts intended for absorption by schoolchildren,[21] or inverted in literature, cinema, and the mass media.[22] Hence, the "tendency of [most] Americans is to deny such abuses and even to assert that they could never exist in their country."[23]

"Patriots" of this variety can of course be pinned down from time to time, usually after an infinity of hairsplitting over whether things "really" happened in the manner described, on the fact that one or even several of these "unfortunate occurrences" actually took place. The implications are seldom acknowledged, however. All but invariably, when uncomfortable facts are conceded a second level of sophistry ensues: that which threatens the sanctity of American purity of purpose is quickly consigned to the realm of aberration or anomaly.[24]

Alternately—or concomitantly—it is argued that things are being "interpreted out of context" by a process in which critics project contemporary values backward into history, imposing them upon events, persons, and entire settings where, having yet to be conceived, they bear no possible relevance. Neither actions nor implications, it is concluded, can be properly judged other than "by the standards of their time." In effect, no genuine onus can be assigned to massacres like Bad Axe and Horseshoe Bend because "everybody else was doing the same thing," or, in any event, "there was no law against it" when they happened.[25]

Strictly speaking, such arguments to technical innocence have never held water. Since its inception, the conduct of the United States, no less than that of any other country, has always been subject to the Laws of Nations.[26] More specifically, the conduct of the U.S. military has been subject to the laws of war. No recent moral innovation is involved, since "the regulation of armed conflict has occupied the attention of scholars, statesmen, and soldiers for thousands of years [and the] idea that the conduct of armed conflicts is governed by rules appears to have been found in almost all societies, without geographical limitation."[27]

> The foundation of the current legal regime is very old. . . . The Greeks and Romans customarily observed certain humanitarian principles which have become fundamental rules of the contemporary laws of war. . . . As the body of international law began to develop in Europe, early writers (such as Legnano, Victoria, Belli, Ayala, Gentili, and Grotius) gave priority to consideration of hostility in international relations. The work of Grotius, published during the Thirty Years War (1618–48) . . . has since come to be regarded as perhaps the first systematic treatment of international law, and one in which the laws of war played a principal part. Over

this period, the practice of states led to the gradual emergence of customary principles regarding the conduct of armed hostilities.[28]

The relevant body of international customary law would certainly seem to suggest a reasonable standard of contemporaneous values and legitimacy to which the actions of men like George Washington, William Henry Harrison, Andrew Jackson, and Zachary Taylor might be assessed for purposes of historical understanding.[29] Like the Germans, however, Americans, Angloamericans in particular, have always had extraordinary difficulty grasping the concept that their behavior might ultimately be subject to some set of rules other than their own.

Thus, when the argument is advanced that there was "no law against" George Rogers Clark's scalping of living human beings, or John Sullivan's making breeches from the skins of his victims, it should be understood as meaning only that the United States itself had effected no statute prohibiting such practices. The polemic is at root identical to that offered by the nazi defendants at Nuremberg in arguing that their conduct was legitimate in that it had conformed to the requirements of Germany's domestic legal code (which they themselves had written).[30] To their eternal credit, the panel of jurists presiding over the nazis' prosecution dismissed such claims to "national sovereignty" as preposterous.[31]

Instead, the Nuremberg Tribunal asserted that "international law has imposed obligations upon states to punish certain acts committed in their territory," or under their authority.[32] These obligations encompass all international customs and conventions, including the laws of war. No country possesses a right—as distinct from the power—to exempt itself from meeting this responsibility. Still less does it hold a right to "legitimate" violations of international legality by advancing formulations within its own statutes. Abridgment of these principles renders the offending state subject to international sanction and, depending on the magnitude of the issues involved, the jurisdiction of an international court.[33]

The Lieber Code

Unlike Germany, moreover, the United States has always promoted itself as being the very avatar of enlightened legality, "a nation of laws, not men."[34] Within this self-congratulatory discourse, the laws of war have featured quite prominently and the American prototype has been not infrequently offered as a model for worldwide emulation.

The most famous early example of a national manual outlining the laws of war for the use of armed forces, and one of the first attempts to codify the laws of land warfare, was the 1863 "Instructions for the Government of Armies of the United States in the Field" prepared by Dr Francis Lieber of Columbia University. This manual, which became known as the "Lieber Code," was issued to the Union Army on 24 April 1863, and was applied to the forces of the United States during the American Civil War. It became the model for many other national manuals (for example, those of the Netherlands in 1871, France in 1877, Serbia in 1879, Spain in 1882, Portugal in 1890, and Italy in 1896).[35]

The Lieber Code is highly illuminating in that it conclusively demonstrates the extent to which America's legal community was familiar with the customary laws applicable to their country's warfare. Article 22, for example, holds that "as civilization has advanced during the last centuries, so has likewise steadily advanced, especially in war on land, the distinction between the private individual belonging to a hostile country and the hostile country, with its men at arms. The principle has been more and more acknowledged that the unarmed citizen is to be spared in person, property, and honor." In Article 23, it is stated that "Private citizens are no longer murdered . . . and the inoffensive individual is as little disturbed in his private relations as the commander of the hostile troops can afford to grant."

37. The United States acknowledge and protect, in hostile countries occupied by them . . . the persons of the inhabitants, especially women. . . . Offenses to the contrary shall be rigorously punished.

44. All wanton violence committed against persons in the invaded country . . . all rape, wounding, maiming or killing of such inhabitants, are prohibited under penalty of death, or other such severe penalty as may seem adequate for the gravity of the offense.

These passages represent little more than amplifications of Emmerich de Vattel's famous observation, made a century earlier, that by the then-prevailing laws of war "the people, the peasantry, the townspeople have nothing to fear from the sword of their enemies."[37] Lieber, however, with a smugness largely absent in Vattel, then proceeded to expend two articles explaining that the extension of such protections to noncombatants proved the superiority of European and euroderivate cultures to their "savage" or "barbarous" nonwestern counterparts.

> 24. The almost universal rule in remote times was, and continues to be with barbarous armies, that the private individual of the hostile country is destined to suffer every privation of liberty and protection, and every disruption of family ties. Protection was, and still is with uncivilized peoples, the exception.
> 25. In modern regular wars of Europeans, and their descendants in other parts of the globe, protection of the inoffensive citizen of the hostile country is the rule . . .

While many of the Code's remaining articles concern matters marginal to how wars against "savages" were to be waged, there are several that bore directly on the methods traditionally employed by the Army's Indian fighters. Article 68, borrows from Clausewitz's famous dicta, first published in 1827,[38] in stating that "modern wars are not internecine wars, in which killing the enemy is the object. The destruction of the enemy in modern war, and, indeed, modern war itself, are means to obtain that objective of the belligerent which lies beyond the war."

> 60. It is [therefore] against the usage of modern war to resolve, in hatred and revenge, to give no quarter . . . [A] commander is permitted to direct his troops to give no quarter [only] in great straits, when his own salvation makes it *impossible* to cumber himself with prisoners [emphasis in original].

Prefiguring the 1864 Geneva Convention on Wounded and Sick by nearly a year[39]—it was under discussion while the Code was being written—Lieber included two articles of obvious relevance in *any* sort of armed conflict.

> 61. [Even troops compelled by circumstance to] give no quarter have no right to kill enemies already disabled on the ground . . .
> 71. Whoever intentionally inflicts additional wounds on an enemy already wholly disabled, or kills such an enemy, or who orders or encourages soldiers to do so, shall suffer death, if duly convicted . . .

He followed Montesquieu and Rousseau in Article 56,[40] stipulating that prisoners of war, whether enemy civilians or captured combatants, were "subject to no punishment for being [enemies], nor is any revenge wreaked upon [them] by the intentional infliction of suffering, or disgrace, by cruel imprisonment, want of food, by mutilation, death, or any other barbarity." Article 75 reaffirmed this point, stating that "prisoners of war are subject to confinement or imprisonment . . . but are to be subjected to no other intentional suffering or indignity." Additionally,

67. The law of nations . . . admits of no rules or laws different from those of regular warfare regarding the treatment of prisoners of war, although they may belong to the army of a government which the captor may consider as a wanton and unjust assailant.

76. Prisoners of war shall be fed upon plain and wholesome food, whenever practicable, and treated with humanity.

79. Every captured enemy shall be medically treated, according to the ability of the medical staff.

Concerning armistices, Lieber also followed long-established legal custom, noting in Article 135 that an "armistice is the cessation of hostilities for a period agreed upon between the belligerents. It must be agreed upon in writing, and duly ratified by the highest authorities of the contending parties," and, in Article 138, that it "may be general, and valid for all points and lines of the belligerents; or special, that is, referring to certain troops or certain locales only." In Article 142, he goes on to clarify that, whether general or special, "an armistice is not a partial or a temporary peace; it is only the suspension of military operations to the extent agreed upon by the parties."

There can be no claim that the Code was meant to be situational, applicable in some instances and not in others. It was clearly designed to have a universally binding effect upon the conduct of U.S. troops in the field, irrespective of who they were fighting. Article 57, for example, stipulates that "no belligerent has the right to declare that enemies of a certain class, color, or condition . . . will not be treated by him [like other enemies]." Article 58 reinforces this point, emphasizing that the "law of nations knows of no distinction on the basis of color."

Thus did the government of the United States establish, concisely and in black letter form, the set of standards by which its wartime comportment may be evaluated. Whatever legal ambiguities may have attended earlier atrocities—and, as should be apparent, things were never so murky in this respect as apologists would now have it—they were dispelled on April 24, 1863. Thereafter, intellectual honesty and the law itself require that the conduct of America's Indian fighters be judged through the lens of the Lieber Code. Hence, standards in hand, we may resume our examination of their activities.

The View from Sand Creek

On the morning of November 29, 1864, a reinforced regiment of U.S. volunteer cavalry, about nine hundred men in all, attacked a Cheyenne encampment along the Sand Creek, in southeastern Colorado. Of the seven hundred-odd Indians residing therein, a lopsided majority were women, children, and elderly men, all of them assembled on the order of territorial governor John Evans, disarmed and mostly dismounted, their safety "guaranteed" by the Army.[41] Their leader, Black Kettle, was a prominent member of the Cheyenne "peace faction" who displayed over his tipi a U.S. flag presented him by President Lincoln.[42] In addition to the stars and stripes, a white ensign of surrender flew above the village when the soldiers came storming in.[43]

Flags aside, there can be no question that the cavalrymen mistook the village for one occupied by "hostiles." Colonel John M. Chivington, in charge of all Colorado volunteer units, had assumed personal command of the assault force. He'd been present when, as the condition of a special armistice, Evans had instructed Black Kettle to place his noncombatants under the protection of military authorities at Fort Lyon.[44] They were camped close to the post, at a spot approved by the post commander. Chivington, moreover, took extraordinary precautions to prevent the defenseless Cheyennes being warned of the fate about to befall them.[45]

Nor can there be the least confusion as to whether what happened at Sand Creek was simply a "tragedy" of the sort sometimes resulting when officers "lose control" over their troops in the heat of combat. Chivington addressed his men immediately prior to the attack, directing them to "kill and scalp all, big and little"[46] under his oft-stated premise that "nits make lice."[47] The soldiers, most of whom had overstayed their enlistments to participate in the bloodletting—promised weeks beforehand[48]—can thus be said to have conducted themselves in rather strict conformity to their orders.

The exact toll taken in the orgiastic slaughter thus unleashed remains unclear. In his after-action reports, Chivington himself put the body count at "400–500." He and other officers later pushed it even higher.[49] Most estimates today place the number of killed at around 150.[50] Be that as it may, there is nothing mysterious about the manner in which the killing was done.

> The Indians fled in all directions, but the main body of them moved up the creek bed, which alone offered some protection from the soldiers' bullets. They fled headlong until they came to

a place above the camp where the banks of the [stream] were cut back by breaks. Here, the Indians frantically began digging in the loose sand with their hands to make holes in which to hide. The larger percentage of these were women and children.[51]

As the scene was later described by Robert Bent, a mixed-blood Cheyenne who had accompanied the attackers:

There were some thirty or forty [women] collected in a hole for protection; they sent out a little girl about six years old with a white flag on a stick; she had not proceeded but a few steps when she was shot and killed. All the [women] in the hole were afterwards killed. . . . [They'd] offered no resistance. Every one I saw dead was scalped. I saw one [woman] cut open with an unborn child, as I thought, lying by her side. . . . I saw quite a number of infants in arms killed with their mothers.[52]

John Smith, a veteran scout, recounted much the same.

[The soldiers] used their knives, ripped open women, clubbed little children, knocked them in the head with their guns, beat their brains out, mutilated their bodies in every sense of the word . . . worse mutilated than any I saw before. . . . [C]hildren two or three months old; all lying there; from sucking infants up to [the elderly].[53]

Even Army officers concurred.

I did not see a body of man, woman or child but was scalped, and . . . mutilated in the most horrible manner—men, women and children's privates cut out, &c; I heard one man say that he had cut out a woman's private parts and had them for exhibition on a stick. . . . [There were] numerous instances in which men had cut out the private parts of females and stretched them over saddle bows and wore them over their hats while riding in ranks.[54]

The day after the massacre, the few prisoners taken, including several women and an infant, were summarily executed.[55] The butchers then set out for Denver, the territorial capital, where they proudly paraded down Larimer Street, a main thoroughfare, displaying bloody body parts of their victims to more than a thousand wildly cheering people who'd turned out to greet them.[56] Meanwhile, the slaughter was celebrated in the *Rocky Mountain News*—which had for more than a year been championing a "war of extermination" against the Cheyennes—as "an unparalleled feat of arms [which would] live forever in the annals of martial glory."[57]

These local sentiments notwithstanding, what had occurred was a war crime—or, rather, a cluster of war crimes—of the very grossest sort. Chivington's actions, and those of most of the other officers and men at Sand Creek,[58] violated every article of the Lieber Code cited in the preceding section. Such was the finding of not one but *three* federal investigations—one each by the Senate, the House, and the War Department— in the months following the massacre.[59] Yet, although there was thus ample predication for the filing of capital charges against those responsible, no prosecutions ensued.

The rationalization adorning this outcome contained all the ingredients of a farce. Since their crimes had been committed while the perpetrators were serving in the Army, civilian authorities purported no standing upon which to try them; because they'd since returned to civilian life, the War Department disavowed jurisdiction as well.[60] It is obvious, however, that the travesty did not result from jurisdictional loopholes. Military officers, then as now, served at the discretion of the president. Their commissions, once bestowed, were permanent. Chivington and his cohorts could thus have been recalled to active duty and court-martialed at any time.[61] The case against them was both unassailable and potentially precedential. All that was required was a genuine desire to hold them accountable for what they'd done.

Given that the merit of any legal codification resides not so much in its comprehensiveness or the elegance of its phraseology as in its enforcement,[62] the fact that no such desire was evidenced highlights the gulf separating the glowing rhetoric attending U.S. policy pronouncements from the grimy reality of how those policies were actually implemented. To all appearances, neither the Army nor civilian authorities wished to see a judicial precedent which might serve to deter the perpetration of further Sand Creeks. This, of course, says quite a lot about the true nature of America's "national character."

The more so, in view of treatment subsequently accorded Colorado's war criminals. To this day, a town near the massacre site—proclaimed a "battlefield" on a marker erected by its present owner—is named in honor of John Chivington.[63] Streets in Denver similarly memorialize his principal subordinates. Until 1988, a building on University of Colorado's Boulder campus bore the name of David M. Nichols, a captain whose company was singled out for its "exceptional" performance at Sand

Creek.[64] A monument stationed just outside the state capitol building still commemorates Chivington, his officers, and his troops as "gallant men."

An "Anomaly Theory" of History?

While the example of Sand Creek can in many respects be left to speak for itself, to do so would be to beg the question of whether the massacre might be considered in some way "historically anomalous."[65] That it was not, can be readily appreciated in the nature of the "Kit Carson Campaign" conducted against the Navajos the same year. Although not so well-documented as the actions of Chivington and his troops, the record of Carson's command is replete with atrocity (e.g., soldiers playing catch with breasts hacked off living women).[66] Nor is there a shortage of comparably grisly examples.

Take, for instance, the "Battle of the Washita" on November 28, 1868, in which Lt. Colonel George Armstrong Custer's vaunted Seventh Cavalry Regiment slammed into Black Kettle's noncombatant Cheyennes for a second time. Replicating Chivington's feat almost exactly, and a day short of four years later, Custer's men left their Oklahoma killing ground strewn with 103 corpses.[67] Of these, "93 were women, old men, and children—as well as Black Kettle himself, who had been cut down with his wife as they were riding double on a pony in a desperate attempt to forestall the attack."[68] Needless to say, Custer—one of the more "glamorous" figures in U.S. military history—was not prosecuted.[69]

Then there was the Marias Massacre, in Montana, on January 23, 1870. In this "incident," two companies of the Second Cavalry under Major Eugene M. Baker slaughtered 173 Piegans, only fifteen of whom were fighting-age males.[70] Although it turned out that Baker had hit the wrong village, and that most of his victims had been incapacitated by a recent smallpox epidemic, he went unprosecuted. On the contrary, like Custer's at the Washita, Baker's actions were vigorously applauded by General Phil Sheridan, in whose military district the massacres took place and who would later serve as Army Chief of Staff.[71]

On January 9, 1879, the much-suffering Cheyennes were made to bleed again, this time when a group of about a hundred and fifty noncombatants led by Dull Knife attempted to escape from confinement at Camp Robinson, Nebraska. Sick, malnourished, afoot and almost entirely unarmed, they were quickly chased down. At least eighty-five were killed—the last thirty-two by massed soldiers firing pointblank volleys into a buffalo wallow where the Indians had sought refuge—and another twenty-three wounded. As usual, the victims were mostly old men, women, and children. With equal predictability, no one was prosecuted for murdering them.[72]

Probably the best known of all such massacres occurred at Wounded Knee, South Dakota, on December 28, 1890. There, having disarmed and immobilized a group of roughly five hundred Minneconjou Lakotas, the Seventh Cavalry, commanded at the time by Colonel George A. Forsyth, set about annihilating their captives in a manner entirely reminiscent of Sand Creek.

> [All] witnesses agree that from the moment it opened fire, [the Seventh] became a mass of infuriated men intent upon butchery. Women and children attempted to escape by running up a dry ravine, but were pursued and slaughtered—there is no other word—by hundreds of maddened soldiers, while shells from Hotchkiss guns, which had been moved up to sweep the ravine, continued to burst among them. The line of bodies was found to extend more than two miles from the camp—and they were all women and children. A few survivors eventually found shelter in brushy gullies here and there, and their pursuers had scouts call out that women and children could come out of hiding because they had nothing to fear. . . . Some small boys crept out and were surrounded by soldiers who then butchered them. Nothing Indian that lived was safe.[73]

At about the same time, several lesser massacres were perpetrated in nearby locations.[74] Afterward, as many as three hundred and fifty corpses were unceremoniously dumped in a mass grave atop a hill overlooking the primary killing field.[75] Not only was no one prosecuted for this spectacular slaughter, twenty-three soldiers were awarded medals of honor for participating in it.[76] The most prominent public criticism, moreover, appears to have been that the Army failed to "finish the job" by completing "the total annihilation of the few remaining Indians" (this from newspaper editor L. Frank Baum, gentle author of The Wizard of Oz).[77]

After adding in the myriad smaller, mostly forgotten, and always unprosecuted massacres of American Indians—that of twenty-seven Cheyennes on the Sappa Creek on April 20, 1875, to offer but one example[78]—one cannot help wondering just how many "anomalies" it takes to make a norm. The significance of such queries is accentuated when backdropped by Army Chief of Staff William Tecumseh Sherman's view, expressed in 1866, that his troops should "act with vindictive earnestness against the [Indians], even to their extermination, men, women, and children."[79] Still more, the notorious observation made three years later by Sherman's subordinate, Phil Sheridan, that "the only good Indian is a dead Indian,"[80]

These flat contradictions of the Lieber Code's noble-sounding principles represented a consensus outlook among ranking generals, field officers and troops, not to mention apparent majorities of their civilian overseers and the public.[81] Viewed in this light, can it *really* have been a matter of mere "happenstance" or "coincidence" that the Cheyennes, Arapahos, Comanches, Kiowas, and several other native peoples upon whom the Army warred during the period had all suffered population reductions in the 90th percentile by 1891, when the fighting for the most part ended, or that each experienced a dramatic numerical "rebound" thereafter?[82]

The "Indians of the Philippines"

With the notion of anomaly thus thoroughly debunked, it will be useful to address the fallback position most often assumed by apologists for the Army's consistently criminal conduct during the "Indian Wars."[83] This concerns the claim that "special" or "unique" circumstances, usually having to do with the "savage nature" of the Indians themselves,[84] necessitated resort to tactics and behaviors outlawed not only in the Lieber Code but, increasingly, by the formalism of international convention as well.[85]

Leaving aside the fact that Al Capone might well have entered a similar argument—and with tangibly more justification—concerning the rival gangsters he ordered machine-gunned on St. Valentine's Day 1929,[86] a much larger factual problem presents itself. To put it simply, were there the least substance to such victim-blaming contentions, the illegalities at issue would have been limited to North America and ceased at some point before the beginning of the twentieth-century. And, of course, neither of these things is true.

Nowhere was this more obvious than in the Philippines during the years 1899–1902. There, having "liberated" the islands from Spanish colonization in 1898, the U.S. set about converting them into a colony of its own.[87] When the Filipinos resisted, they were described as "savages no better than our Indians" by American officials, and treated accordingly.[88] "The reasoning which justifies our making war against Sitting Bull also justifies our checking the outbreaks" of Filipinos, announced incipient president Theodore Roosevelt in 1900.[89] An Army officer framed the matter more frankly still:

> There is no use mincing words. . . . If we decide to stay, we must bury all qualms and scruples about Weylerian cruelty, the consent of the governed, etc., and stay. We exterminated the American Indians, and I guess most of us are proud of it, or at least, believe the end justified the means; and we must have no scruples about exterminating this other race standing in the way of progress and enlightenment.[90]

With that end very much in mind, the War Department dispatched Major General Adna R. Chaffee, a veteran of campaigns against the Comanches, Cheyennes, Kiowas, and Apaches, to take charge.[91] As primary field commanders, Chaffee selected brigadier generals J. Franklin Bell, who'd fought the Cheyennes and Lakotas, and Jacob H. ("Hell-Roaring Jake") Smith, whose experience accrued from the Geronimo Campaign and the massacre at Wounded Knee.[92] They, in turn, brought in numerous subordinates with similar backgrounds. Small wonder that the Philippine endeavor was soon described as "just another Injun War," albeit, one waged overseas and against a vastly larger population.[93]

Bell was assigned to the Batangas region of Luzon, where he conducted "a particularly murderous campaign that depopulated large sections of the province."[94] By his own estimate, his tactics left one-sixth of the populace—some 616,000 people—dead within three years.[95] His officers were recorded as boasting that their general "had found the secret of pacification of the archipelago. . . . They never rebel in [southern] Luzon because there isn't anybody there to rebel."[96] Although one of his subordinates, General R.P. Hughes, admitted during congressional testimony that none of this comported "with the ordinary rules of civilized warfare,"[97] Bell was never prosecuted for his crimes. Instead, the "Butcher of Batangas" received a presidential commendation for his ghastly record, and was later promoted Army Chief of Staff.[98]

In the Samar district of northern Leyte, Jake Smith went even further, ordering the deaths of "all persons . . . *capable* of bearing arms in . . . hostilities against the United States [emphasis added]."[99] In response to a query from a subordinate about age limits, these instructions were refined to encompass every male "over ten years of age, as the Samar boys of that age were equally as dangerous as their elders."[100] The results were shortly reported in the press.

Our men have been relentless; have killed to exterminate men, women, children, prisoners and captives, active insurgents and suspected people, from lads of ten and up, an idea prevailing that a Filipino, as such, was little better than a dog, a noisome reptile in some instances, whose best disposition was the rubbish heap.[101]

By 1902, such exposure had begun to tarnish the U.S. image internationally, rendering the Roosevelt administration vulnerable to criticism by its liberal opponents. A Senate investigation was duly convened.[102] Hence, the War Department went through the motions of charging a total of ten junior officers with "cruelties," including murder.[103] The outcomes obtaining from the resultant courts-martial speak for themselves.

> One was convicted of "firing into a town," and "looting" and sentenced to a "reprimand." Lieutenant Bissell Thomas was found guilty of "assaulting prisoners and cruelty"; the court remarked that his cruelty had been "very severe and amounted almost to acute torture"; his sentence was a fine of $300 and "a reprimand." More appropriate was the disposition of the case of First Lieutenant Preston Brown, who was found guilty of "killing a prisoner of war" and sentenced to dismissal from the service and confinement "at hard labor for five years." . . . Brown's sentence [was, however,] commuted [on January 27, 1902] to a loss of thirty-five places in the army list and forfeiture of half his pay for nine months.[104]

Things did go a bit awry for the War Department during the trial of Littleton L.T. Waller, a Marine Corps major charged with one of the smaller slaughters he'd perpetrated while serving as Hell-Roaring Jake's right-hand man in Samar.[105] The prospects of Waller's paying much of a price were of course all but nil, the Army having appointed General William H. Bisbee, yet another of its "bald old Indian fighters," to hear the case. Unsurprisingly, although the accused candidly acknowledged presiding over not one but numerous massacres, he was promptly exonerated.[106]

Unfortunately for Smith, however, Bisbee bumbled the verdict, acquitting Waller not on the basis of his acts themselves being somehow legitimate, but because they'd been undertaken in obedience to superior orders.[107] This lapse made it necessary that the Hell-Roarer himself be charged with precipitating Waller's criminal activities. Nonetheless, "Smith was tried not for war crimes, or even for murder, but . . . for *conduct to the prejudice of good order and military discipline* [emphasis in original]."[108]

Found guilty of that remarkably trivial offense, he was sentenced to be "admonished by the President," allowing Roosevelt to "punish" the sixty-two-year-old mass murderer with a grant of early retirement on full pension.[109]

This wrist slap, if it can be called even that, represented the total penalty paid by senior officers against the staggering welter of atrocities perpetrated under their authority. Against Chaffee, who was shown to have instructed Smith—and Bell, for that matter—to use "any means" in accomplishing their objectives, there were no charges whatever.[110] Rather, in August 1903, Roosevelt rewarded his orchestration of holocaustal initiatives consuming the lives of as many as a million Filipinos by appointing him Army Chief of Staff.[111] As was mentioned above, his successor in this exalted position, appointed in 1906, was "the real terror of the islands," J. Franklin Bell.[112]

Concerning America's pitiless war against the "Indians of the Philippines," Roosevelt—whose stern visage would soon affront the face of Mount Rushmore, enshrining him for all time as one of the four "greatest" U.S. presidents—had by then declared it "the most glorious in the country's history" and "a triumph of civilization over the black chaos of savagery and barbarism."[113] General Arthur MacArthur may have come closer to the mark when he explained to the Senate that, in his opinion, the whole affair signified nothing so much as a "fulfillment of the destiny of our Aryan ancestors."[114]

The Exception as Rule

MacArthur's comment was revealing, suggesting as it did that the "special circumstances" precipitating extermination of peoples indigenous to U.S. "home" territory had little to do with anything "unique" to the victims themselves. Rather, that American Indians, like Filipinos, were *not white* was the issue. The Army, as saturated with the "scientific" racist perspectives pervading nineteenth-century American society as any other institution, simply followed the country's intellectual élite in viewing peoples of color as "species" biologically inferior to—that is, less human than—whites.[115] Hence, nonwhites were seen as being "naturally" subordinate to their European/euroderivative "betters" (of whom MacArthur's "Aryans"—Anglo-Saxons—were deemed best of the best).[116]

It follows that the measure of inhumanity believed to be incarnated in particular groups of nonwhites was adduced not from their modes of fighting, but simply from the degree and tenacity of resistance they offered to assuming their "rightful" place under white domination; the greater the resistance, the less the humanity, to the point that—as with both Native Americans and Filipinos—they were construed as something altogether *other* than human beings (i.e., "nits," "lice," "dogs," "noisome reptiles," "squaws," "savages"). In turn, this reduction of "recalcitrant" nonwhites to a repugnant, dehumanized status licensed the Army to employ "exceptional" means in waging war against them.[117]

In effect, the situation could be—and was—considered exceptional whenever the Army took the field against anyone aside from "Europeans and their descendants in other portions of the globe."[118] Thus, as a practical matter, the prohibition against treating enemies differently on the basis of color enshrined in Articles 57 and 58 of the Lieber Code were nullified at the level of military doctrine in the very moment of its promulgation. From there, the rest of the Code's lofty principles fell like dominoes every time a conflict with nonwhites occurred.

And, since the great bulk of the fighting in which U.S. troops have engaged since 1863 has been against peoples of color[119]—that is, in settings where the military has indulged in self-exemption from its own professed standards of legality—it can be seen that "exceptions" once again constitute the rule. The illegalities inherent to Indian-fighting thereby emerge as both the model and the norm of behavior for the United States Army during armed conflicts. This remains true, whether the opponent is composed of regular or irregular forces, so long as the opponent is nonwhite.[120]

The institutionalization of this implicitly racist distinction was as apparent during operations against the Japanese in World War II as it had been forty years earlier, against the Filipinos, or forty years before that, against the Cheyennes, or forty years earlier still, against the Shawnees. Although U.S. troops more or less adhered to the laws of war in the course of fighting Germans and Italians in North Africa and Europe,[121] the Pacific War against Japan was waged by very different terms. As a veteran war correspondent recounted in the *Atlantic Monthly*:

> We shot prisoners in cold blood, wiped out hospitals, strafed lifeboats, killed or mistreated enemy civilians, finished off the enemy wounded, tossed the dying into a hole with the dead, and in the Pacific boiled the flesh off enemy skulls to make table ornaments for sweethearts, or carved their bones into letter openers.[122]

Commanded by General Douglas MacArthur, Arthur's son, American soldiers "torture[d] and mutilate[d] with impunity,"[123] making a "fetish

[of] collecting grisly battlefield trophies from the Japanese dead and near dead, in the form of gold teeth, ears, bones, scalps, and skulls."[124] None of this can be said to have happened secretly, without the knowledge of responsible officers, civilian authorities, or the general public. Rather, it was widely and often pridefully publicized, as when *Life* magazine accompanied a 1944 "human interest story" with "a full-page photograph of an attractive blonde posing with a Japanese skull she'd been sent by her fiancé [serving] in the Pacific."[125] Plainly, not much had changed since 1814, when, as a celebratory gesture, Andrew Jackson encouraged his men to distribute body parts cut from the corpses of Red Sticks slain at Horseshoe Bend among "the ladies of Tennessee."[126]

Nor was this the worst of it. Following in the tradition of George Washington's order that General Sullivan "not . . . listen to any overture of peace before the total ruin of [Seneca] settlements is effected,"[127] U.S. officials steadfastly refused Japan's attempts to surrender until after a series of massive "fire raids"—culminating in the nuclear bombings of Hiroshima and Nagasaki in August—were conducted against the country's cities during the spring and summer of 1945.[128] Although not prompted by any discernable military necessity,[129] this final air offensive cost the lives of well over a half-million Japanese civilians.[130]

In 1794, Washington had referred to the infliction of such needless suffering upon those he saw as biologically lesser beings as "chastizement."[131] In 1902, General Bell described it as a "thrashing" of "unruly" natives.[132] In 1945, America's leaders framed it in terms of a mysterious requirement that Japan's surrender be "unconditional."[133] Regardless of the phrasing, however, the meaning was always the same. As President George Herbert Walker Bush would put it in 1991, such policies of systematic atrocity were and remain necessary to "send a message" to brown-skinned people—in this case, the Iraqis—that "what we say, goes."[134]

"Indian Country" (Again)

Once Japan's capitulation had converted the entire Pacific Basin into an "American lake," the U.S. turned to defending its "new frontier" on the periphery.[135] Wars fought along the Pacific Rim during the 1950s and '60s, often through surrogates, were especially brutal affairs,[136] conducted against "yellow dwarfs"[137] without regard to—and often in outright defiance of—the rule of law.[138] Although the U.S. "police action" fought in Korea from 1950 to 1953 was in many respects a worthy contender,[139] this tendency was most pronounced during America's "ten thousand day war" in Indochina, centering on Vietnam and designed to prevent the peoples of the entire region from exercising their legal rights to self-determination.[140]

After 1965, the ferocity of the assault became almost unimaginable, involving the wholesale relocation and internment of an estimated two-thirds of the entire population of South Vietnam,[141] and the massive use of white phosphorus, napalm, and other incendiary ordinance against civilian targets.[142] One small area, the Panhandle of North Vietnam, became the most heavily bombed locale in history.[143] The Plain of Jars, in Laos, and portions of Cambodia were hit almost as hard.[144] Whole new technologies of inflicting pain—cluster bombs containing fiberglass shrapnel that would not show up on x-rays, for example—were developed to achieve the goal of "pacifying" the population.[145] Eventually, the ecosystem itself was targeted for eradication.[146]

Strategically, General William Westmoreland, overall commander of U.S. forces in Southeast Asia, articulated no concept other than to cause such "attrition" among "enemy personnel"—that is, the populace—that resistance would be unsustainable.[147] General Maxwell D. Taylor, who served as personal military advisor to President John F. Kennedy and as U.S. ambassador to Vietnam under Kennedy's successor, Lyndon Johnson, drew the obvious parallel to an "Indian War."[148] "Westy" himself was more blunt, likening his mission to that of an "exterminator" killing "termites."[149] Other ranking officers concurred, describing the Vietnamese as "ants" and "flies," Vietnam itself as a "manure pile."[150]

The sentiments bound up in these restatements of Bell's attitudes and policies in Batangas—and those of Sherman, Sheridan, and Chivington on the Great Plains of North America—were lost on neither the field commanders nor their troops. From the outset, all territory other than that directly occupied by Americans was referred to by officers and men alike as "Indian Country."[151] Officers compared the tactical difficulties they faced to the "Indian Problem [in the] Old West" and announced they would "solve the . . . problem like we solved the Indian problem."[152] The indigenous population itself was habitually disparaged as being composed of "gooks," "dinks," "slopes," even "zipperheads."[153]

Unsurprisingly, a "Mere Gook Rule," otherwise known as the "MGR,"[154] was adopted by the troops, translated by one soldier as "the Indian idea . . . the only good gook is a dead gook," by another as "the only good dink is a dead dink."[155] The killing was utterly indiscriminate because, as a Marine Corps officer explained, "the troops think [the Vietnamese] are all fucking savages" anyway.[156] The techniques routinely employed in dispatching the "savages" were described rather graphically by combat veterans Varnado Simpson Jr., Gary Garfolo, and James Bergthold in 1971 (there are hundreds of such accounts, many of them officially recorded).[157]

> *Simpson:* [We'd] mutilate the bodies and everything. [We'd] hang 'em up . . . or scalp 'em.
> *Garfolo:* Like scalps, you know, like from Indians. Some people were on an Indian trip over there.
> *Bergthold:* [We] cut ears off a guy and stuff like this here, without knowing if they were [enemy combatants] or not. If you got an ear, you got an [enemy].[158]

"Anybody we saw that was over twelve years old and that we thought was a male, was to be considered an enemy and engaged as such," recounted infantryman Robert A. Kruch.[159] Thus, "anything that's dead and isn't white" was tallied as "an enemy."[160] Perhaps the best summation of the prevailing attitude was offered by Lieutenant William L. Calley, who, accused of responsibility for the massacre of "at least 102 Oriental human beings" at a hamlet known as My Lai 4 on March 16, 1968, responded that he'd not set out "to kill human beings, really. . . . We were there to kill . . . I don't know. . . . Blobs. Pieces of flesh."[161]

In actuality, Calley and his men slaughtered three hundred and forty-seven "old men, women, children, and babies," all of them unarmed, before "systematically burn[ing] their homes and huts" and reporting that they'd killed "128 enemy soldiers during an intense firefight."[162] Although the truth was known by Calley's superiors—his battalion executive officer observed the action from a helicopter and reported it to Colonel Oran Henderson, the battalion commander, who then relayed the information to the brigade commander, Major General Samuel W. Koster[163]—his unit was shortly congratulated by Westmoreland himself for its "outstanding action."[164] From there, "efforts were made at every level of command from company to division to withhold and suppress information concerning the incident."[165]

Only the unusual conscience and initiative displayed by a young ex-soldier named Ron Ridenhour forced the story into the open, nearly a year after the fact, and mainly because a growing segment of the body politic had become disenchanted with the war's spiraling costs (the administration of Richard Nixon, who replaced Johnson in 1969, was by then under a degree pressure, both domestically and internationally, making that faced by Theodore Roosevelt in 1902 seem paltry by comparison).[166] Nonetheless, after Ridenhour sent a letter detailing what had happened at My Lai to the president and twenty members of Congress on March 29, 1969,[167] the military continued to stonewall for several months.

It was not until information began to appear in the press that the Army finally charged Calley,[168] and even then it attempted to conduct his court-martial in secret.[169] By that point the story was uncontainable, however—an article by journalist Seymour Hersh appeared in thirty newspapers on November 11[170]—and the government's propaganda specialists thereupon recommended an exercise in "damage control." The resulting public relations extravaganza, beginning with a pair of "high-level reviews" of the massacre—one by the House,[171] the other by the Army[172]—was plainly intended to impress upon the world both how seriously the United States took its obligations under the laws of war, and how "aberrant" or "anomalous" the massacre had been. As the House (Hébert Committee) report concluded:

> What happened at My Lai was wrong. It was contrary to the Geneva Conventions, the Rules of Engagement, and the MACV [Westmoreland's Military Assistance Command, Vietnam] Directives. In fact it was so wrong and so foreign to the normal character and actions of our military forces as to raise a question as to the legal sanity at the time of those men involved.[173]

Soon, thirty officers, including General Koster—but not, to be sure, William Westmoreland or any of his MACV staff[174]—were charged with offenses ranging from murder to obstruction of justice. Even without resort to the insanity defense, however, the accused fared about the same as their predecessors during the Philippines Trials of 1902.

> Calley was the only person among the 30 held to account through the system of military justice. Three others were brought to trial but acquitted. Charges brought against 12 of the 30 were dismissed before trial. Administrative action . . . demotion, or reprimand, or the like . . . was taken against seven of the twelve and one of the three acquitted after trial.[175]

Like Hell-Roaring Jake Smith before him, Koster—who, because of his "exemplary service" in Vietnam had been appointed superintendent of the U.S. Military Academy at West Point—was reprimanded and placed on early retirement.[176] Also like Smith, Colonel Henderson was tried only on only relatively petty charges (dereliction of duty, failure to obey regulations); unlike Smith, he was acquitted even of those.[177] Calley's company commander, Captain Ernest Medina—who, like

Chivington at Sand Creek, had given his subordinate specific instructions to do what he did at My Lai—was charged with complicity in the massacre.[178] He, too, was exonerated.[179] The rest walked away with little more than tepid letters of censure or reprimands, remaining for the most part on active duty.[180]

As to Calley himself, barred by the Nuremberg precedent from using the "superior orders" defense employed so successfully by Littleton Waller in 1902, he was a natural scapegoat. His penalty was by no means great, however. Convicted on March 29, 1971, he was initially sentenced with much fanfare to serve "life at hard labor." Spared the labor while he appealed to the commander of the Third Army, his sentence was reduced, five months after his conviction, to twenty years imprisonment. In April 1974, Secretary of the Army Howard H. Callaway cut it to ten years, and the conviction itself was reversed on September 24. Having served three and a half years on house arrest—about three days per victim, about eight hours if the nearly two hundred and fifty unacknowledged murders at My Lai are added in—"Rusty" Calley was a free man.[181] Preston Brown would have felt right at home.

(. . . and Again)

My Lai was extraordinary only in the sense that it was publicized and therefore resulted in the token punishment of a perpetrator. As Oran Henderson put it, "every unit of brigade size has its Mylai hidden some place" although "every unit [didn't] have a Ridenhour" to make an issue of it.[182] Proof of this came, ironically enough, during the Army's field investigation of My Lai itself, when evidence was turned up that a second massacre had occurred at more or less the same time at the hamlet of My Khe 4 (or Co Luy, as it was also known), about two miles southeast of Calley's killing ground.[183]

> In this "other massacre," members of a separate company piled up a body count of perhaps a hundred peasants—My Khe was smaller than My Lai—"just flattened the village" by dynamite and fire, then threw a few handfuls of straw on the corpses. The next morning, the company moved on down the Batangan peninsula by the South China Sea, burning every hamlet they came to, killing water buffalo, pigs, chickens, and ducks, and destroying crops. And, as one of the My Khe veterans said later, "what we were doing was being done all over." Said another: "We were having a good time. It was sort of like being in a shooting gallery."[184]

General William Peers, heading up the Army's "review" of the slaughter at My Lai, "falsely stated to newsmen that no evidence had been presented of another massacre,"[185] then set about suppressing it. Hence, although the unit commander at My Khe, Captain Thomas K. Willingham, was charged with the "unpremeditated murder [of] at least twenty Vietnamese civilians" in February 1970,[186] the case against him was dismissed in June for "lack of [the very] evidence" Peers had buried.[187] To this day, the general's findings on My Khe remain highly classified.[188] So, too, are the files on Truong Khanh 2, another place "pacified" in 1968.

> "[The] troops stormed the hamlet, which was occupied mostly by old people, women, and children," going from house to house, killing everyone they found, in the end, 62 villagers. The people of the village were broom makers. When they were dead . . . "the troops put the bodies on a pile, covered them with straw, and set them on fire."[189]

Despite the best efforts of men like Peers to keep the lid on information about Truong Khanh, the massacre was described by former infantryman Daniel Notley in testimony before congressional hearings in April 1971.

> [As] we moved into the [village] nobody said anything but all of a sudden these guys start shooting. They were shooting women and kids . . . there weren't any men there. . . . It was just like cut and dried like it was understood this was going to happen. . . . [They] did this so systematically like it was something they'd done many times before, it was easy. . . . [T]here weren't any men in [the village] at all. There were some male children, but there were women and children only.[190]

"How many other incidents of this kind took place the West will never know, and in fact does not much care,"[191] although many have been recounted by American soldiers who witnessed or participated in them.[192] Even less attention is paid to the atrocities committed by the approximately seven thousand South Korean mercenaries employed from 1965 to 1973 to augment U.S. ground forces in Vietnam.[193] The standard operating procedure of these surrogates, as was certainly known to Westmoreland and other officers at MACV, included shooting one of ten civilians in villages they occupied.[194] Their record, moreover, includes at least forty-three major massacres, a dozen claiming upward of a hundred victims.[195] Australian "contributions to the war effort," actively solicited by the U.S., took much the same form.[196]

More insidious still were the sorts of ongoing massacres that never crystallized in a largescale "event" like My Lai, My Khe, or Truong Khanh. These took the form of a steady, grinding propensity of U.S. troops to carry out "innumerable, isolated killings . . . rapes and tortures,"[197] machine-gunning random peasants from passing helicopters,[198] obliterating entire villages—and their inhabitants—with artillery barrages and airstrikes (sometimes called in for no other reason than "to have something to do").[199]

> One brigade commander ran a contest, celebrating his unit's 10,000th enemy kill by giving the GI who shot him [or her, or "it"] a week's pass. . . . Many battalions staged contests among their rifle companies for the highest score in enemy kills, with the winning unit getting additional time for passes.[200]

The earlier-quoted definition of an "enemy" being "anything dead that isn't white" tells the tale, however. As *Newsweek* reporter Kevin Buckley observed with respect to an operation conducted in the single province of Kien Hoa during a six-month period of 1968:

> All the evidence I gathered pointed to a clear conclusion: a staggering number of noncombatant civilians . . . were killed by U.S. firepower to "pacify" Kien Hoa. . . . There is overwhelming evidence that virtually all [enemy combatants] were armed. Simple civilians were, of course, not armed. And the enormous discrepancy between the body count [11,000] and the number of captured weapons [748] is hard to explain—except by the conclusion that many victims were unarmed innocent civilians. . . . The death toll there made My Lai look trifling by comparison.[201]

An experienced U.S. official concurred with Buckley's assessment, stating that the "actions of the 9th Division [which conducted the Kien Hoa offensive] in inflicting civilian casualties were far worse" than those of Calley's men.[202]

> The sum total of what the 9th did was overwhelming. In sum, the horror was worse than My Lai. But with the 9th, the civilian casualties came in dribbles and were pieced together over a long period.[203]

Colonel George S. Patton, son of the legendary World War II general, also agreed with Buckley, but from a radically different perspective.

Describing his troops as "a bloody good bunch of killers,"[204] Patton went on to reflect upon how he considered their "present ratio of 90 percent killing and 10 percent pacification just about right."[205] Celebrating Christmas 1968 with a card displaying the photo of a dismembered Vietnamese over the legend "Peace on Earth," Patton returned to the U.S. carrying a polished human skull, complete with a bullet hole over the left eye, presented at his farewell party by adoring subordinates.[206] Soon to be promoted brigadier general, he'd already been awarded the Legion of Merit and characterized by Westmoreland's successor, General Creighton Abrams, as "one of our finest young officers."[207]

Fittingly, under the circumstances, U.S. troops all over Vietnam painted slogans like "Kill 'em All . . . Let God Sort 'em Out" on their helicopters and armored vehicles, along with SS death's head insignia (which also figured prominently in the impromptu patches and "beer can insignia" adopted by élite units like the Special Forces).[208] Many wore necklaces of human ears, while others posed for photos, proudly positioned beside the severed heads of those they'd killed.[209] To paraphrase another slogan popular with GIs, "killing was their business and business was good."[210]

All told, an estimated 3.2 million or more Indochinese perished as the result of U.S. actions in Southeast Asia.[211] Against that, for all practical intents and purposes, can be balanced Lieutenant William Calley's travesty of a punishment and that of First Lieutenant James Duffy, found guilty in 1970 of the premeditated murder of a prisoner. Almost immediately afterward, however, Duffy's offense was "revised" to read "involuntary manslaughter" and his sentence reduced to six months incarceration—already served—plus a $150 fine.[212] Once again, Preston Brown might have felt right at home, a circumstance underscoring how little had changed since 1902 (or 1864, for that matter).

Standards (Again)

By the time it went to war in Indochina, the U.S. military had considerably refined its Rules of Engagement. Those set forth in the Lieber Code had been updated over the intervening century to incorporate a steadily growing body of international law. The directives in effect when the massacres at My Lai and My Khe occurred indicated that "the United States recognizes the conflict in Vietnam as an international conflict to which both customary and written or conventional law apply, and . . . has declared its intent to observe this law."[213] Several elements of written law were noted as being of cardinal importance.

1. Hague Convention No. IV Respecting the Laws and Customs of War on Land and the Annex thereto which embodies the Regulations Respecting the Laws and Customs of War on Land.[214]
2. The four 1949 Geneva Conventions for the protection of the wounded and sick of armed forces in the field; wounded, sick, and shipwrecked members of the armed forces at sea; prisoners of war; and civilian persons in times of war.[215]
3. The 1929 Geneva Conventions relative to treatment of prisoners of war and the amelioration of the conditions of the wounded and sick of armies in the field.[216]

Article 6(b) of the Charter of the International Military Tribunal at Nuremberg (1945), defining "war crimes" as "violation of the laws or customs of war [including,] but not limited to, murder, ill treatment or deportation to slave labor or for any other purpose of civilian population of or in occupied territory, murder or ill treatment of prisoners of war or persons on the high seas, killing of hostages, plunder of public or private property, wanton destruction of cities, towns or villages, or devastation not justified by military necessity" was also of obvious relevance.[217]

Acknowledging that the primary purposes of these conventions devolve upon "protecting both noncombatants and combatants from unnecessary suffering" and "safeguarding certain fundamental human rights of persons who fall into the hands of the enemy, particularly prisoners of war, the wounded and sick, and civilians," the directives pledge the United States to investigate, prosecute and punish "grave breaches" of them through its own Uniform Code of Military Justice.[218] Something of the magnitude to which the Army defaulted in this regard should have been obvious in the preceding two sections.

This was but the tip of the proverbial iceberg, however. The entire strategic context in which massacres of both abrupt and protracted varieties occurred—that of using "awesome firepower" to achieve "a demographic reconfiguration" of Indochina which would deny "population resources" to the "enemy" (however defined)[219]—was illegal on its face. This would have been true even if, to advance a patently absurd hypothesis often employed by U.S. apologists,[220] not a single civilian was killed in the process.

Article 25 of the 1907 Hague Convention, for example, states that the "attack or bombardment, by whatever means, of towns, dwellings or buildings which are undefended is prohibited."[221] Article 22 of the

1923 Hague Rules of Aerial Warfare states that "aerial bombardment for purposes of terrorizing the civilian population, or of destroying or damaging private property not of a military character, or of injuring noncombatants is prohibited."[222] Article 3 of the 1949 Geneva Convention IV Relative to the Protection of Civilian Persons in Times of War affords similar protections.[223]

During the earlier-discussed 1968 Ninth Infantry offensive, codenamed "Operation Speedy Express," there were 3,183 tactical airstrikes by fighter-bomber aircraft.[224] This is aside from continuous ground support missions flown by fifty helicopter gunships equipped with rockets and miniguns (a sort of Gatling gun capable of firing three hundred rounds per second).[225] It is also aside from round-the-clock fire missions carried out by the fifty heavy and dozens of smaller artillery pieces committed to the operation,[226] and scores of "Arclight strikes"—the radio-directed saturation bombing of often unseen targets—by B-52 strategic bombers flying eight miles above the earth.[227]

The great bulk of this ordnance—something on the order of 80 percent—was expended against rural villages possessed of neither air defenses nor military installations, the residents of which were composed, even in the estimation of military intelligence analysts, all but exclusively of noncombatant peasants. As was mentioned, more than 10,000 Vietnamese civilians appear to have been killed during Speedy Express, as opposed to less than a thousand enemy combatants. More importantly, from the perspective of U.S. strategists, some 120,000 others were driven from their homes, away from the "free fire zone," and thus "denied" as a "resource" to the enemy.[228]

Speedy Express involved a single infantry division during six months of the seven-year period 1965–72, in which substantial American ground forces were deployed. At its peak, MACV had nine Army and two Marine divisions "on the ground" in Vietnam, as well as five independent infantry brigades, an independent armored regiment, and substantial elements of another airborne division.[229] There were more than two dozen offensives on the scale of Speedy Express during the war, and even this does not begin to tell the whole story, since the bombardment continued unabated during the intervals in between. All told, the quantity of aerial ordnance expended in the area of U.S. ground operations by the end of 1972 was "over 3.9 million tons . . . about double the total bomb tonnage used by the United States in all theaters during World War II."[230] The result was well over a million dead noncombatants and upward of ten million permanently "displaced" from their homes.[231]

So it was in Laos, a country against which U.S. officials insisted "no military operations [were] being conducted."[232] Although only a small number of American ground troops were committed to the "secret war" in Laos, most of them Special Forces and CIA clandestine operations personnel, the Plain of Jars and more southerly Laotian panhandle comprised one of "the most heavily-bombed regions in the history of warfare."[233] By 1969, fighter bombers were flying "an average of 200–300 sorties a day over northern Laos, and 1,200 daily over the southeast . . . bombing both day and night, dropping 500 pound bombs, delayed-action bombs, napalm, phosphorous bombs and, most of all, CBU [cluster bomb unit] antipersonnel bombs."[234] Arclight strikes by B-52s were also frequent.[235]

Although the air offensive was ostensibly designed to support the war effort in Vietnam by targeting enemy troop sanctuaries and interdicting supply routes, "everything [in Laos] was attacked—buffaloes, cows, rice fields, schools, temples . . . both the villages and their outskirts . . . and [even] tiny shelters erected outside the villages."[236] As a survivor recounted, "During the bombing, if the planes couldn't select a place to bomb, but they saw some animals or people, they would simply drop the bombs on them."[237] An American airman concurred: "The only place people could exist up there on the Plain of Jars was in caves. And we were bombing caves. A single human path was enough for us to bomb. All human activity was considered enemy activity."[238]

The goal of the saturation bombing in Laos was identical to that enunciated for Vietnam. To quote U.S. congressman Pete McCloskey, the "uncontestable conclusion is that at least 76 percent of [the] small villages in northern Laos were destroyed by bombing in 1969" alone.[239] "Cluster bombs and white phosphorous were used against the civilian population of a country with which the United States [was] not at war."[240] This served to "cause a population flow away from" the targeted areas, into locales preferred by U.S. strategic planners.[241] By 1970, an estimated "350,000 men, women and children [had] been killed . . . and a tenth of the population of three million uprooted" in the process of "destroying the social and economic infrastructure" upon which U.S. strategists believed their "enemies" depended.[242]

Yet another "secret" bombing campaign was conducted in Cambodia. Although the U.S. was "not at war" with that country either, and, according to the Pentagon itself, the targets selected usually posed at most "a potential threat to friendly forces [emphasis added],"[243] the air offensive reached a crescendo in 1973.

In all of 1972 the B-52s dropped just under 37,000 tons of bombs into Cambodia. In March 1973 they dropped over 24,000, in April about 35,000 and in May almost 36,000 tons. So with the fighter bombers. In 1972 they had loosed 16,513 tons of bombs at their targets. In April 1973 alone, they dropped almost 15,000 tons, and the figure rose monthly to over 19,000 tons in July.[244]

As in Vietnam and Laos, "the bombs were falling upon the most heavily populated areas of Cambodia,"[245] generating heavy casualties among the peasantry and destroying the basis of their economy for no purpose remotely fitting accepted definitions of "military necessity." Before the bombing ended in April 1975, an estimated 4,500 undefended villages and hamlets had been destroyed, along with half the livestock and a quarter of the farmland (cratered beyond use).[246] A minimum of 445,000 noncombatants were killed or wounded—estimates run as high as a million—and some 4 million of Cambodia's 7.7 million people driven from their homes.[247]

A quarter-century later, none of the three largest societies impacted by the onslaught—Vietnamese, Lao, and Khmer—have come close to recovering. Once comprising the "rice bowl of Asia," they remain destitute,[248] struggling with the combination of environmental devastation and intractable social trauma resulting from the sustained savagery of U.S. "pacification."[249] For the smaller "tribal" societies of the area—the upland Hmong of Laos, for example, and the so-called Montagnards of Vietnam—conditions are by all indications even worse.[250] To paraphrase the (in)famous observation of an American major after he'd leveled the town of Ben Tre in 1968, "it was necessary to destroy an entire way of life in order to save it" from existing in a manner free of American domination.[251] No American Indian familiar with his/her own history would be surprised by the expression of such sentiments.

Do as We Say (Never as We Do)

As early as 1966, England's Lord Bertrand Russell had outlined the basis upon which the overall U.S. Indochina strategy should be considered criminal.[252] A year later, he sponsored an International War Crimes Tribunal, usually referred to as the "Russell Tribunal," to hear testimony and otherwise examine matters in greater detail. Composed of noted jurists, scholars, and intellectuals and first convened in November 1967, the panel considered evidence over a period of several months, eventually concluding that the United States was guilty, as a matter of policy, not only of major war crimes, but of other offenses, including genocide.[253]

Although there was considerable "controversy" over the Russell Tribunal's findings,[254] the situation was clear enough by 1970 that even General Telford Taylor, who had served as chief counsel for the prosecution at Nuremberg, acknowledged that what was being done in Vietnam, Laos, and Cambodia was "what we hanged and imprisoned Japanese and German generals for doing."[255] Were the same standards applied to Americans as were applied against the nazis, he observed, there was "a very strong possibility" that both the military and the civilian leadership of the United States "would come to the same end [they] did."[256]

That Taylor relied upon the standards set at Nuremberg when assessing U.S. conduct was especially appropriate not only because of his experience in prosecuting violators, but because the United States had all but singlehandedly established such standards in the first place.[257] It was, after all, Supreme Court Justice Robert H. Jackson, while serving as chief U.S. prosecutor at Nuremberg, who'd articulated the principle that the laws under which the nazis were tried were as applicable to "all men [and] any other nations, including those which now sit here in judgement" as they were to Germany and the men then in the defendants' dock.[258]

> If certain acts and violations of treaties are crimes, they are crimes whether the United States does them or Germany does them. We are not prepared to lay down a rule of criminal conduct against others which we are not willing to have invoked against us.[259]

This, to be sure, proved demonstrably false. Not one U.S. airman, much less a general or high civilian official, faced charges accruing from their roles in the systematic destruction of whole Indochinese societies. On the contrary, throughout its war(s) in Indochina, representatives of the American government openly described the idea it might be bound in *any* palpable way by the Nuremberg precedent as "absurd."[260] In the astonishingly revealing estimation of one senior diplomat, "war crimes tribunals would be the worst thing that could happen, [because] they would amount to . . . a system of legal guilt for top [U.S.] officials" who violated international law.[261] Thus did the United States categorically exempt itself from the rules imposed upon those it presumed to judge.

The glaring double standard belying Jackson's rhetoric had been there all along. Germany's Grand Admiral Karl Dönitz, for instance, was convicted of war crimes at Nuremberg for having conducted a campaign of "unrestricted U-boat warfare" against Allied shipping in the North Atlantic despite an affidavit from U.S. Admiral Chester A. Nimitz admitting he'd employed the same methods against the Japanese in the Pacific.[262] Reichsmarschall Hermann Göring was also prosecuted in part for ordering the "terror bombings" of Warsaw, Rotterdam and Coventry, although these charges were quietly abandoned after the defense pointed out that the British/American strategic bombing of Germany—most especially the incendiary attacks on Hamburg and Dresden—far surpassed anything Göring's Luftwaffe had done.[263] Plainly, a crime was a crime at Nuremberg only insofar as the U.S. and its allies had not also perpetrated it (and, in the Dönitz case, even when they had).

The same was true of the "Other Nuremberg" convened in Tokyo to try Japanese war criminals.[264] Although Japan was not a signatory, several members of the Japanese general staff were executed under provision of Article 26 of the 1929 Geneva Convention Relative to the Treatment of Prisoners of War, through which they were held responsible for murders and other atrocities committed against POWs by their subordinates.[265] The best-known example is that of General Tomoyuki Yamashita, the "Tiger of Malaya" (who was actually tried in Manila).[266] Quite apart from the fact that the record of Yamashita's men pales in comparison to that of Chaffee's only forty years earlier,[267] it was common knowledge that U.S. soldiers and Marines had routinely murdered Japanese prisoners all over the Pacific.[268]

Nor was a different attitude adopted with regard to enemies of lesser rank. While American field officers and troops were nowhere charged for torturing and murdering their captured opponents—shooting hundreds of wounded Japanese on Bougainville, to provide one illustration,[269] machine-gunning "a line of unarmed Japanese soldiers who had just surrendered" on Okinawa, to offer another[270]—scores of vanquished foes were prosecuted for comparable offenses during the numerous "Little Nurembergs" that followed the main events of 1945–46.[271] SS Obersturmbannführer (Lt. Colonel) Jochen Peiper, to take the most memorable example, was sentenced to death—later commuted to thirty-five years' imprisonment—for having ordered the 1944 massacre of eighty-four U.S. POWs at Malmédy, Belgium.[272]

Unquestionably, the atrocities perpetrated by the SS and their Japanese counterparts against prisoners in their charge merited the punishments meted out. No more so, however, than those committed by U.S. troops against Japanese and, to a much lesser degree, German soldiers.[273] Nor more so than either the "water cure" and similar tortures performed by American soldiers upon thousands of Filipino prisoners decades before World War II.[274] Nor the ubiquitous "Bell telephone hour"—torture by electric shock—and other such brutalities routinely committed against the Indochinese twenty years later,[275] all of which went not just unpunished but in many cases was actively rewarded.

The same pattern can be traced much deeper in time, as when, following "Little Crow's War" in 1863, the Army conducted drumhead courts-martial of four hundred defeated Santee Dakotas and sentenced 303 of them to death for alleged crimes against white "settlers" who'd flooded into the Indians' treaty-guaranteed Minnesota homeland.[276] Only the "humanitarian intervention" of President Lincoln reduced the number to thirty-seven, all hanged together in the largest mass execution in American history.[277] The Army itself, which had slaughtered native noncombatants with its usual abandon during the war, had by then confined the bulk of the starving survivors in a concentration camp, and proclaimed a $200 bounty on the scalps of the rest.[278]

Similarly, although the Army had engaged in avowedly exterminatory campaigns against their peoples, several thousand native men of fighting age—the majority of them Cheyennes, Kiowas, Comanches, and Apaches—were accused of crimes against whites invading their territories during the 1860s, '70s, and '80s.[279] Sometimes tried, sometimes not, the warriors were consigned for long periods and with deadening regularity to the Fort Marion Military Prison in Florida. Probably the ugliest example is that of Geronimo's Chiricahua Apaches, four hundred of whom were sent first to the Florida facility, then to Fort Sill, Oklahoma, and never allowed to return to their homes.[280]

Then there was the case of Captain Henry Wirtz, a Confederate officer prosecuted for war crimes under the terms of the Lieber Code and hanged on November 10, 1865. The allegation was that while serving as its commandant, Wirtz been responsible for the hideous conditions prevailing in the Andersonville POW camp and that some thirteen thousand Union prisoners had died as a result. While the charges against the captain were accurate enough, they plainly blinked the fact that conditions in U.S. prison camps had been just as bad, the death rates therein comparable, and that "the Union had been much more capable of feeding its POWs but had deliberately reduced the amount of rations many times."[281]

Even more to the point is the reality that at the time Wirtz was tried, the Army was holding virtually the entire Navajo Nation as POWs at a concentration camp in the Bosque Redondo, outside Fort Sumner, New Mexico, and would continue to do so for another three years.[282]

Conditions there were such that, before the survivors were finally released in 1868, more than half the prisoners had died of exposure, malnutrition, and disease.[283] The death rate at Bosque Redondo was much higher than those prevailing in such infamous nazi camps as Dachau and Buchenwald eighty years later.[284] Unlike the nazis, however—or Henry Wirtz, for that matter—no U.S. officer was prosecuted for the crimes that consumed the Navajos.

On balance, it is accurate to conclude that U.S. practice concerning war crimes and related offenses has been to insist that others "do as we say, not as we do." Not only does this make a mockery of America's hallowed pretense of dispensing "equal justice before the law," it places the country in the position of conducting its affairs as a veritable outlaw state.[285] *Whatever* standards have been in effect at any given moment, the U.S. high command and its civilian counterparts have run very far afoul of them. This accounts in no small degree for what the Hébert Committee called "the normal character and actions of [American] military forces,"[286] albeit in a manner diametrically opposed to how the committee meant it.

Under Penalty of Law

Actually, where rank-and-file U.S. troops were concerned, "doing as we say" may never have entered in. No one seems to have bothered to say anything to them about the legal issues involved in combat, one way or the other. Despite the detailed references in the showpiece 1956 edition of its Rules of Engagement,[287] America's military establishment provided not even a modicum of training in such matters to junior officers or enlisted personnel. As a former artillery sergeant explained in testimony before Congress, "I was never taught anything about the Geneva Convention as far as the use of artillery goes."[288]

Graduates of the U.S. military academies were no better off, as is reflected in the recollection of an Army captain during the same hearings that, "I received no meaningful instruction whatever on the law of land warfare while I was at West Point. I did not know what the law of land warfare was until I returned from Vietnam in 1969."[289] The captain's observation was affirmed by that of a classmate: "Never in my time in the military, [and] at one time I was going to West Point, [was] I ever given training on rules of warfare, Nuremberg trials, handling of prisoners of war, or anything like that." The same was true of Marine officers:

> Never during the course of my enlisted service in boot camp and
> in infantry training nor during my cadet days in flight school nor

as an officer did I receive any instruction regarding the Hague or Geneva Conventions, the Nuremberg Principles, or the treatment of POWs.[291]

Many veterans recalled having been issued small cards upon the arrival in Vietnam inscribed with eleven general rules of behavior they were to observe while "in-country."[292] Some, however, recounted receiving manuals, classified "Top Secret," outlining the obviously illegal operational techniques they were expected to employ during prisoner interrogations.[293] In what might be described as the "best-case scenario," a two-hour briefing on the rules of engagement—heavily intermixed with information on the behavior expected of U.S. troops were they themselves to be taken prisoner—was extended to new recruits during their sixteen weeks of basic and advanced individual training.[294]

Still, in at least some cases soldiers were sufficiently conversant with the requirements of international law, and took seriously enough their obligations under the Nuremberg Principles, to refuse obedience to what they considered unlawful orders. The official response in such instances is instructive. While doing everything in its power to avoid prosecuting—or even charging—the My Lai defendants and others accused of specific war crimes, the military frequently visited what it called "the full penalty of law" upon those who resisted participation in such atrocities.[295]

A prime example is that of Captain Charles Levy, a medical officer who in 1966 refused either to serve in Vietnam or to train Special Forces personnel because he believed that doing so would make him complicit in the crimes their units were committing throughout Indochina. Levy was quickly court-martialed for, among other things, "disobedience to orders" and "conduct unbecoming an officer," then sentenced to three years at hard labor in the military prison at Fort Leavenworth, Kansas.[296] He was not alone:

> Air Force Capt. Dale Noyd [was] sentenced to a year in prison at Clovis Air Force Base, New Mexico, for refusing to train airmen for Vietnam. A private at Fort Dix, New Jersey, applied for conscientious objector status and when it was denied refused to wear his uniform. He [was] sentenced to a year at Leavenworth. A lieutenant at Shaw Air Force Base refused to assist in training for the war and [was] also convicted and sentenced.[297]

A "dozen other cases of overt resistance" involving "about forty" defendants and all resulting in convictions had been tried by April

1968.[298] Among them were the "Fort Hood Three"—Army privates Dennis Mora, David Samas, and James Johnson—who refused orders to go to Vietnam because they viewed what was happening in Indochina to be "unjust, immoral, and illegal . . . a war of extermination."[299] Like Levy, they were sentenced to hard labor at Leavenworth.[300] In several instances, the punishments were still more severe.[301]

Even the military élite was subject to sanctions. The best, or at least best-known, example is that of Lt. Colonel Anthony B. Herbert, the most decorated combat veteran of Korea and a soldier of such overall prowess that his photo appeared on the cover of the Army's Ranger Training Manual. When Herbert, assigned to the 173rd Airborne Brigade in Vietnam, objected to his superiors' condoning of conspicuous war crimes, he was strongly advised to "cease and desist" in his complaints. When he nonetheless pushed the issue "upstairs," first to MACV and then the Pentagon, he was relieved of his command and forced into early retirement.[302]

While he was still on active duty, Herbert was forbidden by Secretary of the Army Stanley Resor from testifying before a committee conducting war crimes hearings.[303] Other veterans who attempted to draw public attention to what they'd seen or done in Indochina were taken under investigation by Army's Criminal Intelligence Division (CID), although many had already been discharged from military service.[304] The FBI also became heavily involved in such cases, most notably in an illegal counter-intelligence program designed to "neutralize" Vietnam Veterans Against the War (VVAW), a group of whistle-blowing protesters organized in 1970.[305] Army intelligence personnel were assigned to collaborate with the FBI in such constitutionally prohibited operations.[306]

Yet another measure of how "The Law" was used to prevent individuals from fulfilling their obligations under the Nuremberg Principles concerns the extent to which the FBI was harnessed to enforcing the Selective Service Act (i.e., the "Draft"). By 1971, the Bureau's own records reveal that 14 percent of its time and energy was devoted to the "investigation leading where possible to successful prosecution" of young men whose only "offense" was refusing conscription by a military establishment they believed to be conducting itself in a criminal fashion.[307] A second, closely related preoccupation of both the FBI and military authorities was apprehension of active-duty soldiers who deserted rather than accept assignment to Vietnam (or rejected their orders once they got there).[308]

The virulence of this enforcement bias served for a considerable period to convince most of those who might otherwise have resisted that there was no realistic alternative to going along, obeying orders, no matter how illegitimate. When a group of thirty-five GIs at Fort Jackson, South Carolina, attempted to raise questions of legality of the war among their peers in 1968, for instance, they were warned by their commander that if they didn't stop they'd "end up in prison like Dr. Levy."[309] The result was what might be properly described as an American correlate to the oft-remarked "Good German Syndrome," even among soldiers who, despite the best efforts of the Pentagon to keep them in the dark, had become reasonably conversant with the Nuremberg Principles.

> If you are smart you will go along with it because it's the only way out, so you go along with it. You go through the basic training and [advanced individual training] and you are then in a dream world. You don't believe this is going on, but there it is. And there's no way out. . . . You have to go along with it. . . . Any moral questions in your mind about the whole thing, you just have to put those out of your mind.[310]

Major Gordon Livingston, an Army psychologist, further illuminated the process, explaining that not only did the "system [actively] discourage the assumption of individual responsibility for preventing" atrocities, it consciously fostered a "pathological association environment" making it almost impossible for lower-ranking soldiers to meet such obligations.[311]

> The system is so large and so well-organized that even an individual who finds what is happening to be morally [or legally] repugnant in some way is led to question his own values. . . . The question always arises, am I crazy or is what is going on here crazy? When it is so large and so well organized as Vietnam, it is hard for an individual to assert himself [especially when s/he is subject to harsh punishment for doing so].[312]

There was thus "a fabric, a method, a climate, call it what you will," designed to prevent soldiers "from speaking out or acting against the incredible, incredible brutality" occurring daily in Indochina,[313] even if they were not personally afflicted with the attitudes infecting the bulk of their peers. For the United States, things had progressed little since 1865, when Silas Soule, a captain in the Colorado Volunteers who had refused to allow his men to participate in the massacre at Sand Creek, was gunned down in the streets of Denver to prevent his testifying against those who had.[314] Only the mechanisms by which conformity to the country's unstated standards of inhumanity was compelled, not the underlying values themselves, had been refined in the interim.

A Certain Unmistakable Consistency

In the aftermath of the carnage in Indochina, a battery of new conventions were put in place by the international community to prevent a recurrence of what the U.S. had done there. These included the 1977 United Nations Convention on the Prohibition of Military or Any Other Hostile Use of Environmental Modification Techniques,[315] a reference to the massive use of "Agent Orange" and other chemical defoliants by the U.S. to denude vast portions of the South Vietnamese landscape.[316] In 1977, two Additional Protocols to the 1949 Geneva Conventions were also effected, prohibiting, among other things, such standard American practices as saturation ("carpet") bombing and bombardments "expected to cause incidental loss of civilian life [or] injury to civilians [i.e., 'collateral damage']."[317] Indeed, the entire U.S. Indochina strategy was declared illegal.

> It is prohibited to attack, destroy, remove or render useless objects indispensable to the survival of the civilian population, such as foodstuffs, agricultural areas for the production of foodstuffs, crops, livestock, drinking water installations and supplies and irrigation works, for the specific purpose of denying their sustenance value to the civilian population or to the adverse Party, whatever the motive, whether in order to starve out the civilians, to cause them to move away, or for any other motive.[318]

This was followed, in 1978, by the Red Cross Fundamental Rules of Humanitarian Law Applicable to Armed Conflicts,[319] and, in 1981, by the United Nations Convention on Prohibition of Certain Conventional Weapons.[320] In the latter, the use of "any weapon the primary effect of which is to injure by fragments which in the human body escape detection by X-rays"—which, as was mentioned earlier, the U.S. developed specifically for employment in Indochina—was banned altogether.[321] The use of incendiary weapons, which were employed by the U.S. more extensively in Indochina than by any other country in any other war,[322] was very sharply circumscribed, especially, under Article 2, concerning the potential impact on noncombatants.

> 1. It is prohibited in all circumstances to make the civilian population as such, individual civilians or civilian objects the object of attack by incendiary weapons.

2. It is prohibited in all circumstances to make any military objective located within a concentration of civilians the object of an attack by air-delivered incendiary weapons.

3. It is further prohibited to make any military objective located within a concentration of civilians the object of attack by means of incendiary weapons other than air-delivered incendiary weapons [i.e., by artillery or land mines], except when such military objective is clearly separated from the concentration of civilians and all feasible precautions are taken to limit the incendiary effects to the military objective.[323]

Although the United States expressed "reservations" on each of these additions to legal convention, it duly signed off and added the appropriate references when its Rules of Engagement were updated in 1984.[324] None of this mattered, however, when in August 1990 U.S. troops were deployed in the Persian Gulf against Iraq. Although President George Bush invoked the Augustinian principle of "Just War" as a basis for using overwhelming force to "roll back" what he called the "naked aggression" entailed in Iraq's recovery of Kuwait[325]—an Iraqi province until the British partition of 1916[326]—he ordered a campaign as fundamentally criminal as any in history.

This began with the opening round of "Operation Desert Storm," as the war was called, an intensive air offensive designed in part to eliminate the capacity of Iraq's military to offer meaningful resistance before U.S. ground forces began their invasion of what was once again referred to as "Indian Country."[327] This objective was easily achieved, with Iraq's air defense system "utterly obliterated" in the first days.[328] Well over a hundred thousand essentially defenseless Iraqi soldiers—"sand niggers," in the parlance of American troops—were then butchered in place, their corpses eventually bulldozed into mass graves.[329] Once the ground assault began, those who'd survived the bombing were often pinned down by machine gun fire and, thus denied the option of surrender, buried alive by tanks mounted with specially modified bulldozer blades.[330]

Given that the U.S. suffered a total of 148 killed—at least twenty of them by "friendly fire"—in the course of the "fighting," the entire campaign has been rightly described as a "massacre . . . reminiscent of the Gatling gun vs. the bow and arrow."[331] Such characterizations seem all the more apt in that, as with the Senecas in 1794, and Japan in 1945, the U.S. refused as a matter of policy to entertain any overture for peace until a certain exemplary quota of killing was completed.[332] In fact, the slaughter not only continued but escalated after Iraq had submitted, beginning the complete withdrawal of its troops from Kuwait in compliance with stated U.S. demands.[333]

The Iraqi capitulation, previously communicated to U.S. officials by Soviet intermediaries on February 21, was publicly announced by Iraqi President Saddam Hussein on February 26, 1991.[334] By then, his troops had begun a rather chaotic retreat—a "panicked flight," according to some observers—flying white flags over many of their vehicles.[335] They were plainly "out of combat" and therefore legally exempt from attack under provision of the 1949 Geneva Conventions, Common Article III.[336] Nonetheless, Bush announced that the U.S. would "continue to prosecute the war" and ordered them targeted for annihilation.[337] His specific instruction was that "no quarter be given,"[338] a gross violation of the 1907 Hague Convention, the 1864 Geneva Convention on Wounded and Sick, and even the Lieber Code.[339]

Provided such license to "find anything moving and take it out,"[340] American fliers responded with an enthusiasm that might have made Hermann Göring blush.

> The fleeing Iraqis took two roads that meet near the Kuwaiti town of al-Mutlaa and their exodus quickly became a traffic jam of immense proportions. U.S. Marines allowed the convoy of cars, trucks, and every sort of vehicle to get out of Kuwait City before bombing the front and [rear] of the convoy. Kill zones were then assigned along the seventy miles of highway so that planes would not crash into each other [as they destroyed their defenseless and immobilized prey].[341]

Thus began an "orgy of slaughter" along what is known as the "Highway of Death."[342] The pilots, in a frenzy to make second and third attacks on what they laughingly described as "fish in a barrel," didn't even bother to take time reloading with the proper ordnance; "from cluster bombs to 500 pound bombs, [they] took whatever happened to be close" at hand.[343] Anything lethal would do. Ultimately, they "continued to drop bombs on the convoy until all humans were killed."[344] Their tally was estimated at more than twenty-five thousand dead, including not only Iraqi soldiers, but thousands of Palestinians, Jordanians, and East Indian contract workers and their families attempting to escape the war zone.[345]

On March 2, a second "outright massacre"—albeit much smaller, and not involving civilians—occurred near Basra. As Ramsey Clark has observed:

On May 8, 1991, an article appeared in *New York Newsday* [describing what it called] "the largest battle of the war." The catch was that the "battle" occurred two days after Bush had ordered the final cease-fire, and eight days after Iraq had announced its full withdrawal, and fighting had ceased. It was a violation even of the cease-fire guidelines. A division of the Republican Guard withdrawing on a long, unprotected causeway, high above a swamp . . . was attacked. [U.S. Commanding] General ["Stormin' Norman"] Schwarzkopf . . . ordered the attack, claiming that a single Iraqi infantryman had fired a round at a U.S. patrol. . . . The U.S. [24th Infantry Division then deployed] attack helicopters, tanks, [and] artillery, and opened fire with laser-guided weapons.[346]

As the division's commander later and gleefully recounted, "We went right up the column like a turkey shoot. We *really* waxed 'em!"[347] In fact, while some two thousand Iraqi guardsmen were slaughtered, the U.S. suffered no casualties at all.[348] The Wounded Knee–like quality of the "Battle of Basra," especially when considered in combination with the scale of other military fatalities inflicted upon Iraq for no discernable military purpose, lends considerable credence to contentions that the overall U.S. objective was not simply to win the war, but "to so decimate the military-age male population that Iraq could not raise a substantial force for half a generation."[349]

Both the goal and the methods used in attaining it were obviously a far cry from then–defense secretary Dick Cheney's 1991 claim that the American campaign would be "remembered for its effort, within the bounds of war, to be humane," and very much within the bounds of legality.[350] There was instead, as historian Howard Zinn observed at about the same time, "a certain unmistakable consistency" uniting Desert Storm with the illegitimate modes of exterminatory warfare the U.S. had waged against American Indians and other peoples of color since its inception.[351]

"Collateral Damage"

The validity of Zinn's view, and the sheer depravity of Cheney's, is most readily confirmed by the fate imposed upon Iraqi noncombatants from the air. More than 109,000 sorties were flown by U.S. attack planes, during which 136,755 "conventional" bombs (including thousands of incendiaries), 44,922 cluster bombs and rockets, and 4,077 precision-guided ("smart") bombs—over 88,000 tons in all—were "delivered." This is aside from the launching of 217 Walleye and 2,095 HARM missiles.[352]

Much of this ordnance was expended against Baghdad, Iraq's capital and largest city, as well as the cities of Basra, Urbil, Sulamaneiya and other such obvious "concentrations of civilians."[353]

Despite the Geneva Conventions and the 1981 prohibitions on employing incendiaries in such fashion, the U.S. "used napalm against civilians. It used napalm and other heat-intensive explosives to start fires in anything that was highly [flammable]. . . . It used fuel-air explosives which can incinerate hundreds, even thousands of people at once."[354] Since fuel-air bombs are aerosol devices consuming all the oxygen in a two-square-kilometer area upon detonation, they cause death by asphyxiation as well as burning.[355] They are therefore arguably illegal under the 1925 Geneva Protocol for the Prohibition of the Use in War of Asphyxiating, Poisonous or Other Gases.[356]

In any event, much was made during the war about the precision displayed by so-called "smart bombs," which apparently hit their targets about 80 percent of the time.[357] These accounted for less than 3 percent of the bombs dropped, however. The remaining 97 percent consisted of "dumb" bombs, with a "miss rate" of approximately 75 percent.[358] This was especially true of those dropped by B-52s engaged in the legally prohibited practice of carpet bombing from their customary altitude of forty thousand feet, as was done to Basra, Iraq's second-largest city.[359] All told, U.S. "planes came in with bombs and destroyed residential neighborhoods in every city, every major town, and most villages," killing about 113,000 civilians, two-thirds of them children.[360] Some 300,000 others were wounded.[361]

Actually, the worst civilian suffering did not result from the rain of dumb bombs. It accrued instead, according to senior U.S. officials, "from precision-guided weapons that hit exactly where they were aimed—at electrical plants, oil refineries, and transportation networks."[362] To this might be added hospitals, schools, mosques, transportation centers, sanitation and water purification facilities, and pharmaceutical production facilities, as well as food production and storage capacities.[363] To again quote Ramsey Clark:

> When hostilities . . . finally ceased, the city of Urbil had only five of its forty-two community health centers functioning; Basra had five of nineteen; Sulamaneiya had six out of twenty. Likewise, in Baghdad four hospitals were destroyed. Iraq lost its only laboratory for producing vaccines as well as its available stores in the bombardment.[364]

The effects of obliterating the Iraqi power grid were, as Clark concludes, even more egregious.

> Without electricity, water cannot be purified, sewage cannot be treated, water borne diseases flourish, and hospitals cannot treat curable illnesses. This absence of electricity, coupled with direct damage to the sewage treatment facilities, has rendered the sewage treatment system as a whole inoperable. . . . The pollution of the water supply has led to epidemics of typhoid, cholera, and gastroenteritis which threaten the entire population, and children in particular.[365]

None of these "infrastructural targets" were selected to "influence the course of the conflict itself," thus meeting the minimum standard of military necessity necessary to legitimate them.[366] Nor was such damage in any way "collateral to the bombing of legitimate military targets," as U.S. officials claimed; Air Force Chief of Staff Michael J. Duggan was on record as early as September 1990 outlining plans to do exactly what was done.[367] The idea was simply to bomb the entire country "back to the Stone Age" so that the United States could "gain a post-war leverage over Iraq," especially when such calculated damage was combined with a longterm economic embargo and other such sanctions.[368] Quite predictably—indeed it *was* predicted[369]—the consequences of this "systematic destruction of the civilian infrastructure" have proven catastrophic for Iraqi noncombatants.[370]

In addition to spiraling rates of disease and thousands of deaths from otherwise treatable wounds accruing from the pinpoint bombing of Iraq's medical, electrical, and sanitation facilities, "famine [had] already begun to aggravate an already dire situation" even before the war ended.[371] According to a March 1991 United Nations report, Iraq's food supplies were by that point "critically low," in part because its food storage/production capacity had been systematically destroyed, but also because its ability to acquire foodstuffs abroad had been eliminated by the U.S.-orchestrated embargo.[372] Certain items—infant formula, for example, after a baby food factory was hit by a smart bomb[373]—had all but disappeared from Iraqi inventories, and the daily calorie intake for the population had "been cut by half and the entire [population] was beginning to suffer acute malnutrition."[374]

> Iraq now [evidences] a couple of manifestations of hunger never seen before in [the] region, [including] marasmus, the condition

that makes kids under two suddenly look like wizened old men, the bony face, the skull; and kwashiorkor, the malnutrition that turns a child's hair a rusty red and gives him a pot belly. . . . [Y]ou see it all over the place now, even in Baghdad.[375]

By May, a study conducted by the Harvard School of Public Health concluded that approximately three thousand Iraqi infants had died of malnutrition during the six months of hostilities, and that the mortality rate among children under five had subsequently doubled. The researchers projected the "deaths of an additional 170,000 children beyond normal rates of mortality among the younger age group" over the next year, unless the embargo was lifted and "humanitarian intervention" to repair the Iraqi agricultural and sanitation systems undertaken on "an emergency basis."[376] In response, the U.S. not only maintained but tightened the sanctions, with the result that by 1996 an estimated *half-million* children had perished in a country with a total population of barely twenty million.[377]

As lately as 1999, there were over ten thousand sorties by U.S. fighter-bombers over Iraq delivering more than a thousand bombs and missiles against four hundred of the usual targets, "killing and wounding many hundreds of people," while keeping the quality of life suffered by the population at the U.S.-prescribed level of misery.[378] The United States, moreover, insists that it holds "the right" to do this with what amounts to impunity. As the matter was put by Air Force Brigadier William Looney, the aptly named chief of air operations in the Gulf Region:

> If they turn on their radars we're going to blow up their goddamn [air defenses]. They know we own their country. We own their airspace. . . . We dictate the way they live and talk. And that's what's great about America right now.[379]

In 1998, UN Assistant Secretary General Denis J. Halliday resigned his position in protest of this ongoing U.S. inversion of Clausewitz (i.e., making "policy an extension of war"), describing it as not only criminal but genocidal.[380] That this is so has been openly confirmed by U.S. officials at the highest levels. In 1996, U.S. ambassador to the United Nations Madeleine Albright opined on the television program 60 *Minutes* that it is "worth the cost" of starving an entire generation of Iraqi children to death, so long as U.S. policy objectives are met.[381] Undoubtedly because of the enlightened humanitarianism and close attention to legality embodied in her views, Albright was shortly promoted by President Bill Clinton to serve as his secretary of state.

She is but one example. Her successor as at the helm of the State Department, effective January 20, 2001, was General Colin Powell, whose major job qualification appears to have been that, as chairman of the Joint Chiefs of Staff, he supervised the military's entire Gulf War strategy.[382] Asked in 1991 about Iraqi casualties, most especially among children and other civilians, he replied that it was "not a number I'm terribly interested in."[383] This response was undoubtedly honest enough, coming as it did from a man whose earlier military credentials included an active role in covering up the massacres at My Lai, My Khe, and elsewhere in Vietnam.[384]

The Penalties of Law (Again)

Even as it was running roughshod over the laws of war and every conceivable standard of international humanitarian legality in Iraq, the U.S. was once again wielding "The Rule of Law" to punish anyone attempting to obey it. Seven members of a Marine reserve unit at Camp LeJeune, North Carolina, who refused orders to participate in what they publicly denounced as a "racist war" were quickly court-martialed and "sentenced to 'bad [conduct]' discharges and prison terms ranging from one to 30 months."[385] An Air Force reservist in California was sentenced to a year's imprisonment under similar circumstances, while three noncommissioned officers in an Army reserve unit at Fort Hood received sentences of up to six years for "attempting to lead 100 fellow troopers in a work stoppage."[386]

Active-duty personnel typically fared worse than reservists, as is witnessed by two GIs at Fort Bliss, Texas, and a sergeant at Fort Riley, Kansas, sentenced to six years each.[387] This was true even of Captain Yolanda Huet-Vaughn, a medical officer who was able to muster witnesses as credible as former U.S. Attorney General Ramsey Clark to testify that since "America's military and civilian leaders are guilty of war crimes under both Nuremberg and Geneva conventions," she had no legal alternative but to refuse to accept her orders.[388]

> At a pre-trial hearing at Fort Leonard Wood, Missouri . . . Huet-Vaughn became the first resister to base her defense on international law. Her attorney, Louis Font of Boston, called [not only Clark, but] Francis Boyle, a renowned international law expert, to buttress Clark's testimony. The University of Illinois professor outlined the international laws and treaties that are binding on the U.S. government and that the U.S. forces violated during Operation

Desert Storm—including Hague and Geneva Conventions. Boyle testified that to convict Huet-Vaughn of desertion, the army had to prove that she absented herself "without authority." In his opinion, she had the necessary authority under international law.[389]

Having listened politely to this learned recitation of the Army's own Rules of Engagement and Code of Conduct, the military court promptly ruled such issues "irrelevant to the charges before us," then convicted Huet-Vaughn of "desertion with intent to avoid hazardous duty" and sentenced her to thirty months imprisonment and a dishonorable discharge.[390] By then, more than forty other soldiers, airmen, and marines had shared her fate, while an undetermined number of others were summarily handcuffed and shipped off to the war zone despite their announced intent to refuse service therein.[391]

As all this was going on, George H.W. Bush was busily pontificating on the importance of bringing Saddam Hussein, falsely accused by U.S. propagandists of ordering the removal of three hundred Kuwaiti babies from incubators, "before an international tribunal to account for this atrocity and many other crimes against humanity."[392] This was, of course, the very same George Bush who bore ultimate responsibility for the murders of so many thousands of Iraqi youngsters, openly rejecting the idea that the International Court of Justice (ICJ or "World Court") might hold any authority at all with regard to U.S. conduct abroad.[393] Indeed, he was already on record responding to queries about his own country's crimes with the bald assertion that he would "never apologize for the United States of America. I don't care what the facts are."[394]

In 1993, a year after Bush left office, a tribunal on war crimes and genocide was indeed brought into being in The Hague, organized and for the most part funded by the U.S.[395] Although Saddam Hussein was never hauled before it—it had been decided that leaving him in power would best serve U.S. interests in the Mideast, so long as his military capacity could be maintained at a properly "degraded" level through perpetual bombing and embargo[396]—it functioned mainly as an accoutrement to U.S. policy pronouncements for several years.[397] The extent to which the U.S. intended things to remain so came out when the United Nations set about converting the American-owned travesty into an actual court of international criminal law (à la Nuremberg).[398] As William Blum has noted:

> Finally, in 1998 in Rome, the nations of the world drafted the charter of The International Criminal Court [ICC]. American

negotiators, however, insisted on provisions in the charter that would, in essence, give the United States veto power over any prosecution through its seat on the [UN] Security Council. The American request was rejected, and primarily for this reason the U.S. refused to join 120 other nations who supported the charter.[399]

Senior officials have stated repeatedly and quite categorically that they will continue to reject any jurisdictional arrangement allowing international prosecution of its own civilian authorities or military personnel for war crimes as an "infringement upon U.S. national sovereignty" (thereby recapitulating the previously noted premise of the Third Reich).[400] Objections have also been raised with regard to any curtailment of self-assigned U.S. prerogatives to shield its clients—usually referred to as "friends"—from prosecution for crimes committed under its sponsorship (e.g., Suharto and other Indonesian officials responsible for the slaughter of approximately one-third of the East Timorese population from 1975 through 1995, and Turkish officials presiding over the ongoing "pacification" of Kurdistan).[401]

Concomitantly, the U.S. has become increasingly open in thumbing its nose at elements of international law it finds inconvenient, often refusing even to go through the motions of signing off. One of the more noteworthy recent examples has been the International Treaty Banning the Use, Production, Stockpiling and Transfer of Anti-Personnel Mines, which entered into force on March 1, 1999, without the United States as a signatory.[402] Here, it was argued that while every other country should be strictly bound by the treaty, the U.S. has "unique needs" entitling it—and it alone—to be formally exempted from compliance. When the signatory nations rejected this absurd proposition on its face, U.S. representatives effectively withdrew from further discussions.[403]

The same has been true with regard to a number of other important treaties, declarations and conventions over the past two decades. On December 31, 1979, for example, the U.S. was one of only three member-states voting against a UN General Assembly Resolution to implement the 1960 Declaration on the Granting of Independence to Colonial Countries and Peoples.[404] In 1981, 1982, and 1983, it was the only member-state voting against a declaration that "education, work, health care, proper nourishment and self-determination" are basic human rights.[405] In 1984, it alone voted against implementing the 1966 Convention on the Elimination of All Forms of Racial Discrimination.[406] Since 1994, it has been one of only two countries—the other is Somalia—refusing to ratify the Convention on the Rights of the Child.[407]

There are scores of comparable examples.[408] Even the 1948 Convention on Prevention and Punishment of the Crime of Genocide went unsigned by the United States for forty years, and was ratified in 1988 only after the Senate attached a "Sovereignty Package" by which the U.S. claimed a "right" to exempt itself from compliance at its own discretion.[409] Meanwhile, American diplomats have become ever more sanctimonious in advancing "international human rights enforcement" as a pretext for U.S. military interventions, both overt and covert, on a continuous and quite literally planetary basis.[410]

By far the most blatant illustration occurred in 1999, when the U.S., with an eye toward dictating the structure of Europe's internal relations, departed from its usual practice of reserving such treatment for the world's darker peoples long enough to launch "Operation Allied Force," a full-scale air offensive against Serbia.[411] Ostensibly undertaken to halt atrocities against resident Albanians in Kosovo,[412] the attack was accompanied by the filing of formal charges with the emergent ICC—at that point called the International Criminal Tribunal (ICT)—against Serbia's president, Slobodan Milošević, and other members of his régime.[413]

The worm turned a bit, however, when independent groups of international legal experts from several countries began filing criminal complaints against Bill Clinton, Madeleine Albright, Defense Secretary William Cohen, and numerous other high-ranking officials for targeting Serbia's civilian infrastructure in much the same way Bush and his cohorts had targeted Iraq's.[414] Blum writes:

> Amongst the charges filed were: "grave violations of international humanitarian law," including "willful killing . . . employment of poisonous weapons and other weapons to cause unnecessary suffering, wanton destruction of cities, towns and villages, unlawful attacks on civilian objects, [and] attacks on undefended buildings and dwellings," [all] in "open violation" of the United Nations Charter . . . the Geneva Conventions and the Principles of International Law Recognized by the International Military Tribunal at Nuremberg.[415]

The official U.S. response was "disbelief, shock, anger, and denial" at these "unjustified and appalling allegations."[416] All civilian casualties and damage to nonmilitary targets were purely "accidental and unintended," U.S. spokespersons maintained, until Canadian researchers produced a Pentagon document showing that there was actually a formal classification called "unintended civ casualties" used in strategic planning.[417] "It's a little difficult to see how civilian casualties can be both planned for *and* 'unintended,'" as one attorney put it.[418]

With that, Secretary Albright brought a bit of not-so-subtle pressure to bear on Swiss jurist Carla Del Ponte, retained by the ICT to review all charges related to the "Balkan Crisis." Still denying that the tribunal held the least jurisdiction over the United States, Albright explained to Del Ponte that unless her investigation of U.S. war crimes was immediately terminated, the U.S. would withdraw its financial support of the ICT, thereby making it impossible for the prosecutor to proceed against anyone at all. Thus confronted with the American version of how "impartial justice" is best administered, Del Ponte caved in and did as her potential defendant instructed.[419]

Much the same set of power relations have become evident in the conduct of a second tribunal, established in 1995 to try the perpetrators of the genocide carried out under French authority against the Tutsis in Rwanda a year earlier.[420] Here, as with the ICT devoted to the "Balkan Crisis," the U.S. and allied "Western governments made their support for the tribunal incumbent on the assurance that their own military and civilian representatives would escape the magistrates' scrutiny. In order to avoid any embarrassment, they even [prevented] their agents from collaborating with the court . . . refusing to cooperate with an institution they were allegedly supporting."[421] To date, although hundreds of well-publicized indictments were returned as early as 1996, there has yet to be a single prosecution.

"Indian Country" Forever?

In 1999, French Prime Minister Lionel Jospin stated publicly that the increasingly overbearing nature of U.S. behavior in its foreign relations represented "a new problem on the international scene."[422] Jospin's foreign minister, Hubert Védrine, concurred, noting with palpable irritation that "the predominant weight of the United States and the absence for the moment of a counterweight . . . leads it to hegemony,"[423] and thus an ever more imperious belief in its prerogative to dictate the terms by which the rest of the world will live or die. "Never before in modern history has a country dominated the earth so totally as the United States does today," observed the editors of the German news magazine *Der Spiegel*.[424]

The commentators were referring in part to the position of near-total economic primacy enjoyed by the U.S. at the dawn of the twentieth-first century.[425] Their main point, however, concerned the dramatic imbalance of military technology/power which followed the collapse during the late 1980s of America's greatest rival in this sphere, the Soviet Union.[426] The contest of "Gatling guns vs. bows and arrows" once defining the U.S. relationship to America's native peoples, and mentioned above with reference to Iraq—even more with respect to Afghanistan—has been extrapolated to truly global proportions. At this juncture, the entire planet can be viewed as "Indian Country" by U.S. élites, its inhabitants as "Indians" subject to extermination whenever, wherever and to whatever end their overweening sense of self-interest and entitlement may prescribe.[427]

The U.S. of course continues to seek—and to find—collaborators in pursuing even its most blatantly domineering aspirations. As Madeleine Albright bluntly informed the international community fifteen years ago, however, "we will behave multilaterally when we can, unilaterally when we must."[428] Working in concert with other nations is thus seen as a matter of mere expedience or efficiency by U.S. policymakers, and often as a purely cosmetic gesture, never as a posture devolving upon any sense of genuine reciprocity, moral commitment or the meeting of legal obligations. Should its "allies" decline to play their assigned roles at any given moment, the U.S. has made it clear that it will override any and all objections to its course of action, "going it alone," and "making it stick."[429] In other words, to repeat the earlier-quoted phrase of George Bush, "What we say, goes."[430] This, as Bush announced in 1991, parroting Adolf Hitler's pronouncement of a half-century before, is the "New World Order."[431]

That things have reached such a pass is due not only to the consistency with which the U.S. has since its first moments refused the most rudimentary adherence to law, but the manner in which it has substituted legalistic pretension for actual legality, brandishing the resultant deformity as a club with which to bludgeon those struggling to curb its criminal propensities.[432] Unchecked in such endeavors, it has by now positioned itself to consummate a final subversion of international jurisprudence, transforming it into just another weapon with which to work its will upon the world. To paraphrase Antonio de Nebrija, law, or at least the illusion of legality, has for the United States become "a perfect companion to empire."[433]

A much more fundamental layer of consideration underlies this elaborate subterfuge. It pertains to the near-universal degree of consent, only partially "manufactured" through the mechanisms of propaganda,[434] grassroots Americans have habitually extended to the unending torrent of crimes against peace and humanity perpetrated by their country. Such resonance derives from the smug "air of innocence" so eagerly personalized by average citizens—quite irrespective of factual circumstance—a ubiquitous, comfortable, and entirely self-serving affectation which readily lends itself to acceptance of even the most transparently inane official mythologies concerning the "altruism" supposedly guiding U.S. actions, ambitions and attendant policy formation.[435]

To describe the mindset at issue as "delusional" is to be clinically precise in terms of mass psychology.[436] The more so, given the virulently pathological racialism—deep-set, intractable, and for the most part vociferously denied—which now, more than ever, constitutes the institutional reality of mainstream U.S. society.[437] Add in the compulsive braggadocio and violent aggressiveness with which euroamericans in particular have sought historically to compensate for their abiding sense of cultural inferiority,[438] and the outcome is an aggregate condition which has been aptly described as a "genocidal mentality."[439] This, of course, goes a very long way toward explaining how and why the "ordinary men" of the U.S. military have so regularly and enthusiastically acquitted themselves as they have.[440]

That an objectively psychopathic collectivity such as the United States should have come to hold the physical capacity to indulge its lethal fantasies worldwide, and to do so with the knowledge that it can act without fear of retribution or accountability, bespeaks a reality far more awful in its portents than anything discussed thus far. Pretending things are otherwise will not help. Quite the opposite. Denial is the crux of the pathology itself.[441] The urgency of the need for a radical change in the existing relations of power, both globally and domestically, is not a matter subject to debate or equivocation by anyone imbued with the least sanity.[442] The only question is how best—that is, most expeditiously and completely—to achieve it.

The options on this score are limited: those in opposition may endeavor to kill the beast, to cage it, to cure it, or to undertake some combination thereof. Actually, since attempting any of the first three inevitably involves aspects of the others, it would perhaps be best to view them as forming an interactive continuum rather than as discrete and mutually exclusive components.[443] Put another way, the last option is the only viable alternative; opposition to the status quo must proceed at all times, at every possible level, and by all conceivable means, toward the common destination of abolishing it. To frame the matter in still another fashion, the goal must be to at last force judgement upon the

United States in accordance with articulated standards, and to hold it accountable to the verdict.

Although it will undoubtedly be disparaged in some quarters as a "liberal" position, there is considerable merit to the proposition that recourse to law represents the best available avenue along which to pursue a transformative agenda. While it can be conceded that explicitly revolutionary theoretical constructions hold a greater emotional appeal, it must also be acknowledged that the point of departure in any liberatory process must be where things stand, not where they "should be" or where oppositionists wish they were.[444] It is also true that the body of extant law, especially the Nuremberg Principles, can—and arguably should—be interpreted in a manner accommodating a very broad range of oppositionist objectives (including even those typically ascribed to anarchism).[445]

The point to be taken in this connection is that there is no entity "out there" to which an appeal can be made for the enforcement of international law. Tribunals of the sort convened at Nuremberg function on the basis of the military defeat of those on trial, or, as is envisioned with the ICC, their submitting more or less voluntarily to prosecution.[446] Absent such submission, and given that the aversion of armed conflict is the paramount objective of international legality,[447] the principle extended at Nuremberg is that enforcement responsibility inheres first and foremost in the citizenry of each country.[448] Oppositionists are thereby vested with not only the right, but a legal obligation to employ any means necessary to compel compliance with international law (particularly in the realm of humanitarian law).[449]

Most problematic in this respect is the question of how to motivate a sufficient number of U.S. citizens to act that the government will be forced to move in the desired direction. Even at the height of the popular mobilization against the U.S. assault on Indochina—over a million people participated in demonstrations attending the November 1969 Moratorium to End the War in Vietnam[450]—the "critical mass" was not achieved. At this point, the prospects of generating a popular response of the requisite scale seem dimmer than ever; not only is the mental imbalance of the middle-American mainstream more pronounced than ever, but increasingly larger segments of traditionally oppressed populations—African Americans, for example, and American Indians—have become locked into the military apparatus itself.[451]

Fortunately, the unprecedented degree of dominance America's élites have attained has rendered them arrogant to the point of sowing the seeds of their own potential destruction in a number of important ways. Overall, the short-run success of their economic globalization schemes has emboldened them to discount the importance of maintaining the standard of living enjoyed by three of every four Americans—dismantling social services, "rationalizing" health care, and so on—as a means of "freeing up capital" (i.e., increasing corporate profitability and the affluence of the stockholding quarter of the population).[452]

To the same end, firms operating within the U.S. have steadily "downsized," relocating their production facilities to draw upon cheap labor pools situated in neocolonial settings abroad, marginalizing the American workforce itself.[453] The specter of "runaway shops" and attendant disemployment has served as a vehicle upon which to roll back the wage gains achieved by the American labor movement over the past seventy years, as well as to cut such overhead costs as worker safety measures, pension packages, and environmental protection measures, thereby amplifying corporate profitability/élite affluence at still another level.[454]

Not even the troops upon which the élites depend have been safe from such ravages. The negative health effects of U.S. weapons technologies on successive generations of American soldiers—nuclear testing during the 1950s, for example, as well as the use of chemical defoliants like Agent Orange in Vietnam, and depleted uranium ammunition during Desert Storm—have been consistently denied and left untreated as a Pentagon "cost-cutting measure."[455] Meanwhile, despite the fact that the United States is confronted by no credible opponents, "investment" of tax dollars in the development/deployment of the technologies themselves has skyrocketed.[456] Most recently, in the face of overwhelming opposition by the international community, the U.S. announced it would "go forward" with developing a sophisticated and lavishly expensive laser "defense" system in outer space.[457]

Manifestations of social discontent accruing from these trends have been met not by the traditional methods of concession and co-optation, but by ever-harsher modes of state repression. This has been most visible in a vast proliferation of paramilitary police units since 1970,[458] and an expansion of the U.S. penal system by more than 100 percent during the same period.[459] By the late 1990s, the United States had incarcerated a greater proportion of its population than any country in the world,[460] and prison construction/administration had become the most rapidly expanding sectors of America's domestic economy.[461] Concomitantly, with one-in-four young men of color imprisoned, a literal—and very profitable—system of slave labor has reemerged in North America.[462]

"The chickens," in the words of Malcolm X, are truly "coming home to roost."[463] The U.S. domestic populace is being not-so-gradually reduced to a dehumanized status of expendability resembling that typically assigned the Third World populations to which they have so long accustomed themselves to feeling superior.[464] The potentially positive implications of this dynamic should be neither ignored nor underestimated. It was, after all, the revelation of rather analogous attitudes within the régime that finally precipitated what may otherwise have remained impossible: a generalized disenchantment of the German public with the "ideals" and policies of nazism.[465] And, notwithstanding the dissident upsurge of the 1960s, the last time a genuinely revolutionary potential was evident in the U.S. was amid the deteriorated socioeconomic environment of the Great Depression.[466]

The Ingredients of Radical Change

To the extent that the American body politic may now be more open to hearing that what has been happening is wrong than at any point in the past several generations, the question becomes how best to interpret this perceived truth so as to give it form, substance, and strike the most responsive chord among the greatest number of people. An array of moral, economic, and libertarian arguments have been employed in the past, and, while each has merit, none have worked to any appreciable degree.[467] What has not been evident, at least not in any unified and coherent form, has been an attempt to couch things in the terms the general public has been most thoroughly conditioned to believe it accepts: the Rule of Law.

As the work of Noam Chomsky in particular has long since demonstrated, depictions of circumstances as being not simply wrong, but criminally so, especially when accompanied by straightforward representations of the black letter law(s) at issue, carry with them a credibility and psychological weight with average citizens which, rightly or wrongly, is missing from other modes of articulation.[468] Bringing such analyses to bear allows oppositionists not only to connect with a wide range of people "where they are"—or where they think they are—but to preempt the rhetoric of "law enforcement" which forms a cornerstone of élite discourse, turning it against itself in an immediate sense.

More broadly, the deployment of codified law as an essential standard by which the propriety of each phase in the U.S. historical trajectory is assessed stands to challenge the "master narrative" by which America's élites purport to explain and justify themselves, introducing a serious dimension of cognitive dissonance into popular understandings of the status quo.[469] Reformulated, this goes to the notion that most approaches to remedying psychological maladies are predicated in recognition on the part of sufferers that they are not "well," much less representative of an acceptable norm, and thus in need of modifying the manner in which they perceive, understand, and act within the world.[470]

At its most basic level, the therapeutic dynamic at play embodies a conscious withdrawal of consent from the functioning of power—that is, a decay in the hegemonic structure of thought control by which élites hold sway—which leads all but inevitably to a widespread desire for some tangible rearrangement of power relations.[471] For what should be obvious reasons, these can be capitalized upon most effectively when linked over the short term to concrete goals which can at once be seen as eminently "reasonable" from the standpoint so recently occupied by those in psychointellectual transition *and* readily conceded by élite defenders in their efforts to contain and ultimately co-opt expressions of discontent.[472]

Within the analytical framework of this essay, an excellent place to begin would be with resuscitating recommendations advanced at the time of the My Lai/My Khe travesty to remove jurisdiction over war crimes from the "military justice system" and lodge it under civilian courts.[473] Mostly ignored at the time as an "insufficiently radical" idea, and now all but forgotten, the proposal was/remains important in that it would for the first time make the U.S. military even symbolically accountable to *some* entity other than itself. This, in turn, stands to significantly undermine the confidence with which real or potential war crimes perpetrators receive assurances of near-blanket immunity from punishment heretofore provided by the Pentagon (in military terms, this presents a "command, control, and morale problem" of considerable magnitude).[474]

The logic guiding this simple alteration of its domestic judicial structure, of course, points unerringly toward the far more significant adjustment embodied in U.S. acceptance of ICC jurisdiction. And that, in turn, expands the realm of legal consideration from the laws of war, per se, to that of international humanitarian law in toto, making U.S. officials subject to scrutiny and potential adjudication for noncompliance with accepted standards pertaining to child welfare,[475] penal conditions,[476] methods of policing,[477] and the like. The "trickle-down effects" from this development are obvious, bound up as they must be in the imposition of external control over the federal Bureau of Prisons and its state-level counterparts,[478] civilian rather than internal review boards to oversee the police,[479] and so on.

Each step along these lines, no matter how partial, entails a diminishment in the centralized authority/autonomy of the state and a corresponding curtailment of its capacity to exert physical force. Conversely, each represents a relative empowerment of oppositionists, as well as an incremental reorientation of the popular consciousness to embrace the constructive potentialities of legalism rather than rhetorical and repressive (mis)appropriations of it. As the latter evolves, the door is opened to a general (re)appraisal of various other matters—the lawfulness of U.S. pretensions to jurisdictional rights over indigenous national territories with its claimed boundaries, for example[480]—each of which stands to impair the ideological structure of U.S. self-legitimation and, ultimately, its geographical integrity.[481]

Tracing this devolution to its logical terminus, the United States, at least in the sense that it has been previously constructed, could no longer exist. In its stead, one would encounter a proliferation of interactive "autonomous zones," of the permanent rather than transient variety, functioning on the basis of group affinity and human scale.[482] Self-evidently the sort of military practice which has defined the flow of U.S. history and which now threatens the world with endless replications—indeed, the military itself—would be impossible in such an environment. Less still, the configuration of corporate domination which has sprouted and matured on the back of American militarism over the past century and a half.[483]

In effect, inculcating a *genuine* desire for law enforcement among the American public—that is, a demand for adherence by the state and its appendages to the baseline of international legality—could represent "the end of world order" in the sense that George Bush, Madeleine Albright, and Adolf Hitler have each used the term.[484] Ultimately, the antidote or antithesis to such cancerous behavioral/attitudinal phenomena as have been described herein may be discerned within the planetary rearrangement of relations between peoples such a prescription entails. On this basis, and probably on this basis alone, we, all of us, collectively, will be able to achieve a new set of standards, standards with which all might willingly abide. In effect, the result will at last be standards of *our* times, not "theirs," which is to say that they will be standards worthy of our children, our children's children, and theirs as well.

Postscript (2003)

This essay was completed during the fall of 2000. Approximately one year later, on September 11, 2001—a date now and forever enshrined in the American memory as corresponding to the emergency telephone sequence "9–1–1"—someone finally tired of waiting for U.S. "progressives" to stop pretending that the abolition of ashtrays in airports was a "gain" transcending the importance of doing anything tangible to halt their country's ongoing genocide in Iraq.[485] Since the five years following Madeleine Albright's open admission that the United States was consciously exterminating the youngsters of that much-battered populace had been marked by no detectable outcry from the purportedly more enlightened sectors of the perpetrator society—nothing on the scale of, say, the campaign for designer speed bumps and better bike paths in Boulder, Colorado[486]—it was deemed necessary that an emphatic sort of "wake-up call" be delivered.

Commandeering four civilian airliners, the messengers conducted a carefully coordinated and surgically precise operation in which one of the "300,000 pound cruise missiles" was flown directly into the U.S. military's central command and control complex at the Pentagon, while another pair eliminated the twin towers of New York's World Trade Center (WTC), both symbolically and in some ways more tangibly the hub of America's global economic dominance.[487] The fourth plane, reputedly targeting either the U.S. Capitol building or the White House and quite possibly shot down by Air Force interceptors, crashed in Pennsylvania.[488] Overall, some 2,977 people were killed,[489] while the technical infrastructure of U.S. finance suffered immense damage—a "hit" from which it has yet to fully recover[490]—and the economy was "degraded" by perhaps $100 billion.[491]

Even before the WTC had come crashing to the ground, all three major cable "news" networks had launched a concerted propaganda offensive, pronouncing the attacks to be "senseless," the dead both "innocent" and "Americans" (several hundred turned out to be foreign nationals).[492] By nightfall, completely ignoring the fact the U.S. had been flying daily "peacetime" combat missions over Iraq for a full decade—and that it had routinely dispensed less sustained but nonetheless comparable aggression to several other countries during the same period—officials announced that a "new and unprovoked" war had been declared against the United States.[493] A day later, President George W. Bush, unelected son of George "What We Say Goes" Bush, came out of hiding long enough to explain the motives of the "cowards" who'd willingly sacrificed their lives to give Americans a small taste of what they'd for so long—and so blithely—dished out to others. The attackers were "evil," he confided, people who "hate freedom" and whose sole objective was to destroy it.[494]

Bush the Younger's characterization seemed a bit peculiar, even for him, given that the 9–1–1 attackers had at that point been identified as members of a radical Islamist entity known as al-Qaida. The organization figured prominently among the CIA-trained and -equipped "freedom fighters"—to borrow a description from George the Elder, during his days as Ronald Reagan's vice president—who'd waged a protracted U.S. proxy war against the Soviets in Afghanistan, after the USSR invaded the country in 1979.[495] "Freedom," as employed in the vernacular of U.S. diplomacy, is a very slippery concept, however. When, in the aftermath of the 1989 Soviet defeat in Afghanistan, it turned out that al-Qaida was *genuinely* committed to Islamic self-determination—that is, as ready to fight capitalists as communists in its dedication to preventing or repealing western dominion over Islam—the group was quietly excommunicated from America's roster of "freedom-loving friends" abroad and assigned to the State Department's list of international terrorist organizations.[496]

Al-Qaida's nominal head, a wealthy Saudi named Usama bin-Laden, was quite prepared to accept responsibility for the 9–1–1 operation, as he was for earlier attacks on U.S. embassies in Nairobi and Dar es Salaam, and upon the USS *Cole* in Yemen.[497] His explanation of why the assaults been carried out, released by videotape to the Arab al-Jazeera television network in early October 2001, nonetheless stood in stark contrast to Bush's.[498] In his electronic missive, bin-Laden made it clear that the assault had been undertaken not only as a concrete response to the ongoing holocaust of Iraqi children,[499] but to the collective fate suffered by Palestinians as a result of the U.S. supporting patently illegal "settlement" policies pursued by Israel for a full generation,[500] and other such "aggression against Islam." Among the latter, he specified the continuing presence of substantial U.S. forces in Saudi Arabia, location of Mecca and others of Islam's most sacred sites.[501]

Bin-Laden might as easily have mentioned, but didn't, the shootdown of an unoffending Iranian airliner by the USS *Vincennes* on July 3, 1988, killing 290 civilians (an "accident" for which no indemnity was paid nor even a formal apology issued, and despite which both the ship's captain and the air defense officer who fired the lethal missile were awarded the Legion of Merit in 1990).[502] Or he might have remarked upon a series of U.S. provocations in the Gulf of Sidra in 1981, including the sinking of several boats and a toll of fifty dead, which provided the pretext for the subsequent downing of two Libyan fighter planes.[503] As well, there were the U.S. bombing raids on Tripoli and Benghazi on April

14, 1986, undertaken for the most spurious of reasons and resulting in massive damage and another hundred deaths (including the adopted infant daughter of Libyan president Muamar al-Qadaffi).[504] Still again, he might have noted the thousands dead in the Sudan as a result of the August 1998 U.S. bombing of that country's only pharmaceutical plant, al-Shifa, near Khartoum, "justifying" its action with the falsehood that the factory was manufacturing chemical weapons (the vacuousness of this allegation stood revealed in the subsequent U.S. refusal to allow a UN inspection of the ruins, intended to ascertain whether such activity had in fact occurred).[505] A number of other obvious possibilities offered themselves, but on these, too, bin-Laden remained mute.[506]

Despite such deficiencies in bin-Laden's formulation, the official response to the prospect that Americans might be in any way apprised of the 9-1-1 attackers' actual motives—and thus perhaps confront the possibility that they were quite "rational" in their way, their crimes against "innocent Americans" entirely consistent with those routinely perpetrated by the U.S. and its surrogates in their homelands—was to block any but the most carefully edited excerpts of bin-Laden's statements from being broadcast in the United States (this, under the preposterous pretext that airing unedited material might enable him to pass "coded instructions to his followers").[507] Considerable pressure was also brought to bear on the Emir of Qatar, where al-Jazeera is based, to "rein in" that network's coverage of al-Qaida communiqués.[508]

Meanwhile, having disgraced the dead by holding a veritable pep rally atop their corpses in the smoldering ruins of the WTC,[509] Bush declared what he called a "war on terrorism" and demanded that that the Taliban government of Afghanistan, where bin-Laden then resided, hand him over.[510] The régime, which had come into being in the first place partly as a result of the CIA's manipulation of the Afghani polity during the 1980s,[511] replied that it might comply with the "request for extradition"—albeit, the U.S. had never deigned to enter into an extradition treaty with Afghanistan—but only at such time as the United States submitted a standard offer of proof (i.e., tangible evidence of bin-Laden's guilt).[512] The U.S. reply was that in its newest global war there was/is no room for observance of such "legal niceties" and that there were/are only two real options open to any government: immediately and unconditionally "cooperate" with U.S. demands or face destruction ("What we say, goes," in clear refrain).[513]

When the U.S. assault on the Taliban was launched, early in October 2001, the first gambit was to employ air strikes to seal off Afghanistan's border with Pakistan, over which virtually all medical and food supplies to the destitute country were transported and across which an estimated 1.5 million refugees were frantically attempting to flee.[514] In short order, some 7.5 million Afghanis were placed in imminent danger of starvation, according to the UN World Food Program.[515] Under intense international criticism for its near-instantaneous creation of a "humanitarian crisis of epic proportions," the U.S. inaugurated a program of air drops so inadequate as to be dismissed even in establishmentarian publications like the *Financial Times* as "a propaganda ploy rather than a way to get aid to Afghans who really need help."[516] No solid estimate is available concerning the number of people who ultimately died as a result of this cynical maneuver, but by even the most conservative guess it would have to have been several times the number who perished on 9–1–1.

Aside from "contributing" massive airpower to its own campaign, the U.S. followed up mostly by deploying a range of special operations units[517]—Army Special Forces, Delta Force, Navy SEALs, and so on—to coordinate operations undertaken by an odd assortment of anti-Taliban Afghani groups somewhat cryptically referred to as the "Northern Alliance." In truth, the Alliance was the same amalgam of warlords and opium-smugglers who'd held power before the Taliban deposed them in 1995, largely because their three-year tenure had been "the worst in Afghanistan's history," marked as it was by "mass rapes . . . the killing of tens of thousands of civilians . . . and other atrocities."[518] Afterward, they'd mounted an unrelenting effort to undermine the new government, butchering some three thousand prisoners in a single 1997 massacre, and more generally carrying out "massive ethnic cleansing in areas suspected of Taliban sympathies."[519]

True to form, the Alliance troops, now armed, equipped, and otherwise supported by the United States—and with U.S. "advisers" overseeing their activities—proceeded to commit every conceivable variety of war crime, including the castration and summary execution of a captured Taliban fighter chronicled in full color by photojournalist Tyler Hicks.[520] Altogether, an estimated 4,770 people were killed in the direct fighting, perhaps 10 percent of them during massacres of Taliban captives at the Shiberghan prison and a school, both in or near the town of Mazar-i-Sharif.[521] The Boston-based Physicians for Human Rights has also estimated that another three thousand or so were suffocated while being transported in sealed shipping containers to the prison.[522] The Pentagon has of course denied that U.S. personnel were involved in—or even aware of—such crimes, but witnesses interviewed in the British documentary film *Massacre at Mazar* have uniformly indicated their willingness to testify to the contrary before a bona fide war crimes tribunal.[523]

As the fighting wound down toward the end of the year, it became obvious that Usama bin-Laden had quietly slipped away. Indeed, there was little indication that appreciable damage had been done to al-Qaida in any way at all. U.S. officials put a certain gloss on this potentially embarrassing situation by conflating captured Taliban fighters with al-Qaida members, declaring both to be "illegal combatants" and flying about 350 of them—allegedly the "most knowledgeable and dangerous"—halfway around the world, to the U.S. naval installation at Guantánamo Bay, Cuba.[524] There, they've been held under conditions openly defiant of the Geneva Convention's minimum standards for the treatment, not just of POWs but "of *all* persons captured during armed conflict,"[525] while they are subjected to a sustained interrogation under the guise that they possess "crucial intelligence information" about the workings of "international terrorism."

A hint as to the methods used on at least some of these unfortunates can be discerned in the fact that Brigadier General Rick Baccus, in charge of the "Camp X-Ray" facility where the prisoners are held, was recently relieved of command because of "philosophical differences" with interrogators operating therein.[526] In October 2002, moreover, the first real glimpse of the quality of the "threat" posed by those caged at Guantánamo Bay became possible when the first four were finally released. One them, Faiz Muhammad, turned out to be a seventy-eight-year-old—he believes himself to be a hundred and five—suffering from Alzheimer's, while a second, Muhammad Siddiq, is at least ninety years of age.[527]

According to Pakistani intelligence officers collaborating with their U.S. counterparts in the camp, *all* of their fifty-three countrymen presently held there are mere "Taliban foot soldiers," *none* of them privy to anything resembling an al-Qaida secret.[528] The same can likely be said of the remaining prisoners as well, but their very existence has served the dual purpose of convincing a significant segment of the U.S. populace that something "meaningful" in terms of "combating terrorism" was accomplished in Afghanistan and, by holding the threat of trial by military tribunal over the heads of the captives, consolidating a rather confused base of public support for the presidential exercise of plainly extralegal powers.[529]

Even before the first prisoner arrived at Camp X-Ray, the latter impulse had spilled over into the domestic arena, with the Senate's

passage, on October 25, 2001, of the USA PATRIOT Act. The huge tract
had obviously been in preparation long before 9–1–1—and therefore
cannot be accurately described as a "response to the attack"—but,
"under the circumstances," it was overwhelmingly endorsed without
substantive review by both U.S. legislative bodies.[530] Signed into law
on October 26, the PATRIOT Act embodied a "wish list" on the part of
America's apparatus of internal repression, the capstone to a list of earlier
statutes—the 1984 Bail Reform Act, for example, and the Antiterrorism
and Effective Death Penalty Act of 1996—which already criminalized
dissident politics and empowered the agencies involved to employ ever
more draconian techniques in eradicating them.[531]

Among other things, PATRIOT eliminates previously existing
barriers between police and intelligence agencies, vastly expands the
latitude of politically motivated surveillance—including unwarranted
bugs, phone taps, e-mail monitors, and physical searches—enjoyed by
police/intelligence agencies, formalizes guilt by association as a "legal"
concept, sanctions ethnic, gender, and ideological profiling as investigative techniques, greatly expands the ability of authorities to indulge in
the arbitrary detention of "suspects" and to impound their assets, and,
by implication, authorizes the "neutralization" rather than prosecution
of those who, for whatever reason, are secretly designated as "domestic
terrorists."[532]

This last appears especially ominous, given the marked erosion
over the past twenty years of the 1877 Posse Comitatus Act's prohibition
against the use of military personnel for domestic policing purposes[533]—
a constraint already considerably offset by the rampant militarization of
police departments around the country[534]—all the more so given the
recent revelation of a so-called Praetor Guideline (or "Praetor Protocol")
by which the past several presidents have secretly assigned themselves
an extraconstitutional "discretionary authority" to employ élite military
units like Delta Force in "quelling civil disturbances."[535] Such developments are certainly in keeping with the joint military/police/intelligence
"domestic counterinsurgency exercises" conducted under authority of
the then–newly established Federal Emergency Management Agency
(FEMA) during the mid-1980s.[536]

In any event, by the time the PATRIOT Act was effected, several of
its key ingredients were undergoing a full-fledged field test, using immigrants from Islamic countries as subjects. In short order, some five thousand students and other legal Muslim aliens were grilled by the FBI, and
six thousand others were marked for expedited deportation (all because

of minor status infractions). A further two thousand or more were simply "disappeared"—that is, indefinitely detained without charge and denied contact with either their attorneys or, in many cases, their families—in a manner so secretive that it is still impossible to ascertain with any degree of certainty who was scooped up or where they're being held.[537] Attorney General John Ashcroft has recently made it clear that, in principle, his office considers such techniques as applicable to "domestic extremists" as to foreign nationals, a matter clearly raising the specter of a proliferation of Camp X-Rays housing American citizens "guilty" of expressing— or perhaps simply holding—"objectionable" political views.[538]

Such "internal security" mechanisms well in hand, the Bush administration rapidly blurred its initial pretense that the invasion of Afghanistan had anything to do with "fighting terrorism." In this connection, bin-Laden and al-Qaida were mentioned less and less—at this point almost never—as the U.S. installed a handpicked "democratic" régime headed by Hamid Karzai, a maneuver guaranteed to result in approval of rights of way for American oil companies to build a cost-efficient pipeline from the lush but landlocked oil fields of Turkmenistan, Uzbekistan, and Kazakhstan to the Pakistani port of Gwaddar (the Taliban had been adamantly blocking the plan).[539]

The new client government is equally sure to make no objection to Afghani territory being used as a U.S. forward staging area, should military "stabilization operations" in any of the three Central Asian republics—or an invasion of neighboring Iran—become "necessary."[540] The quid pro quo, at least in part, is that those who served as U.S. proxies in 2001 have been allowed to resume opium production, which the Taliban had all but eradicated, with the result that Afghanistan has already (re) emerged as the world's leading exporter of the drug (most of it destined for North America's inner cities).[541]

Even as it disappeared as a topic in official discourse on Afghanistan, al-Qaida has continued to serve a useful propaganda purpose in other respects. Well before the end of 2001, much was being made of the "more than sixty countries" in which the "bin-Laden network" was supposedly active.[542] While these included Canada, Germany, France, England, Pakistan, Morocco, Egypt, and Saudi Arabia—as well as the U.S. itself— the "need for a military option" was expressed only with regard to countries on the official U.S. enemies list, primarily Somalia, the Sudan and, with a transparent flourish, Libya (a decisively anti-Islamist state).[543] By January 2002, Special Forces units had in fact been dispatched to the southern Philippines to combat the "al-Qaida-connected" Abu Sayyef guerrillas—generally believed by other oppositionists in those islands to be a CIA front—as well as the former Soviet republic of Georgia, to disperse "al-Qaida-linked" Chechen rebels based therein, and Yemen, where "important al-Qaida cells" were said to thrive.[544]

On January 31, 2002, Bush finally laid bare the cynicism with which U.S. policymakers were using the "war on terror" as a cover for other designs. In his State of the Union Address, the president defined an "Axis of Evil" against which he was imminently prepared to order the use of significant military force.[545] Tellingly, although Bush larded his rhetoric with references to "the continuing terrorist threat," alleged al-Qaida "hosts" were not among his three-country "Axis." Instead, the first two, Iraq and Iran, are not only mutually hostile, but emphatically so with respect to al-Qaida's brand of Islamism (and vice versa).[546] The third, North Korea, is neither Islamic nor known to support international terrorism.[547] To all appearances, the only real commonality uniting the "Axis" countries resides in the consistency with which each has rejected U.S. dictates. Ultimately, the picture painted by the president was so implausible that even Madeleine Albright publicly reproached him for it.[548]

Seemingly surprised by the such criticism, and anxious to retain his base of domestic support, Bush quickly refocused his pitch (the "Axis of Evil" line hasn't been used in months). His demotion of al-Qaida from its position of preeminence nevertheless continued, with ever-increasing emphasis placed upon "Saddam Hussein's violation of sixteen United Nations resolutions" and the "certainty" that Iraq has thereby (re) acquired "weapons of mass destruction."[549] These supposedly consist at present of both chemical and biological agents—the basis for which were secretly provided by the U.S. during the 1980s, when Saddam's brutal Ba'athist régime was considered a useful club for purposes of bludgeoning Iran[550]—although Scott Ritter, a Gulf War veteran and one of the chief UN weapons inspectors working in Iraq until 1998, has vociferously contested such contentions.

> Contrary to popular mythology, there's no evidence Iraq [ever] worked on smallpox, Ebola, or any other horrific nightmare weapons the media likes to talk about today. . . . They actually made . . . anthrax in liquid bulk agent form [and] produced a significant quantity of liquid botulinum toxin. . . . Liquid anthrax, even under ideal storage conditions, germinates in three years, becoming useless. . . . Iraq has no biological weapons today, because both the anthrax and botulinum toxin [they produced

have expired, and] they'd have to reconstitute a biological manu-facturing base.[551]

As to chemical weapons:

Iraq manufactured three kinds of nerve agents: Sarin, Tabun, and VX. Some people who want war with Iraq describe 20,000 muni-tions filled with Sarin and Tabun nerve agents that could be used against Americans. The facts, however, don't support this. Sarin and Tabun have a shelf-life of five years. Even if Iraq had somehow managed to hide this vast number of weapons from inspectors, what they're now storing is nothing more than useless, harmless goo. . . . VX is different, for a couple of reasons [but the] real ques-tion is: Is there a VX nerve agent factory in Iraq today? Not on your life. . . . Real questions exist as to whether Iraq perfected the stabilization process [and even] if Iraq had held on to stabilized VX agent, it's likely it would have degraded by today.[552]

Saddam is also alleged to be on the verge of developing nuclear weapons, although, as Ritter again points out, absolutely no evidence has been presented to substantiate the claim.[553] At any rate, conspicu-ously missing from the framing of charges against Iraq is the fact that neighboring Israel, with full and ongoing U.S. support, has over the past forty years thumbed its nose at a far greater number of UN resolutions than the Iraqis have lately disregarded,[554] and that the Israelis actu-ally—not to mention quite unlawfully—possess a substantial stockpile of nuclear weapons.[555] So does Pakistan, another country recently added to the U.S. "friends" list, and India.[556] Israel, moreover—again, compli-ments of the United States—possesses a delivery capacity vis-à-vis such weapons vastly superior to Iraq's.[557] All these illegalities notwithstand-ing, nobody in U.S. policy circles is attempting to build a case for war against Israel.

Bush has sought to finesse this blatant contradiction by claiming that in April 2001 Mohammed Atta, the man ostensibly in charge of the 9–1–1 attack teams, had met with an Iraqi intelligence officer in Prague. This "clear link" between Iraq and al-Qaida—used both to discount the sharp ideological differences separating the two, and to imply Iraqi sponsorship of the 9–1–1 attack itself—dissolved when Czech intelli-gence publicly announced that the meeting was a fiction (Atta was in Florida when the fabled liaison supposedly occurred).[558] The same sort of fate has befallen several other U.S. efforts to come up with something which might be plausibly advanced as the "smoking gun" tying Iraq into 9–1–1.[559] Still, by October 2002, a Pew Research poll revealed that fully two-thirds of all Americans were finding it convenient to "believe Saddam Hussein helped terrorists carry out the Sept. 11 attacks."[560]

A decisive majority of his constituents thus prepped, the president set about finalizing the U.S. subversion of international law, delivering an ultimatum to the UN closely resembling his "you're either with us or against us and therefore subject to immediate destruction" speeches of late 2001. On September 12, 2002, Bush appeared before the General Assembly to demand that the Security Council pass a resolution authorizing the U.S. to use whatever force it deems necessary not only to "disarm" Iraq, but to precipitate a "regime change" in the country.[561] In the alternative, he made it clear, the U.S. would no longer view the UN as a "credible" legislative and enforcement body, and he would be "compelled" to appoint his own administration its replacement. In substance, the message once again was "do as you're told, what *we* say, goes."[562]

Actually, this "UN initiative" would probably have been launched earlier, had the U.S. not had to contend with fallout resulting from Israel's having seized upon the rhetoric of "global antiterrorism" as a pretext upon which to launch yet another of its endless offensives against the Palestinian West Bank (this one lasted three months, April through June 2002, despite Bush's having openly demanded early on that Israeli premier Ariel Sharon "immediately" withdraw his forces).[563] During the invasion, which was as always carried out in defiance of urgent UN resolutions, many Israeli troops indulged in their usual behavior, committing hundreds of "unlawful killings, torture and ill-treatment of prisoners, [as well as the] wanton destruction of homes [while others regularly] blocked access to ambulances and denied humanitarian assistance, leaving the wounded and dead lying in the streets for days, and used Palestinians as 'human shields' while searching for suspected militants."[564] The pattern of atrocity appears to have been especially pronounced in the West Bank towns of Nablus and Jenin.[565]

His own ineffectuality in bringing America's primary Mideastern ally quickly to heel—a matter which, rather accurately, was widely interpreted as indicating a continuing U.S. support of Israel's systematically criminal comportment—to some extent slowed the Bushian rush to wax bellicose in condemning Iraq's illegalities.[566] It also served to seriously undermine the degree of cooperation and support the U.S. could expect from members of the Arab League during a war with Iraq. The Saudis, for example, withdrew their permission for airstrikes to be launched from bases in their territory, and several months were required to negotiate an adequate alternative with Oman.[567] By late October 2002, however, these difficulties had been for the most part resolved and Bush "turned up the heat" on the UN.[568]

The result, coming in the wake of American voters' endorsement of Bush's "don't confuse me with the facts" approach to world policy during the midterm election held on November 5, 2002, was a "compromise" resolution unanimously approved by the Security Council on November 8.[569] Predicated upon Iraq's granting "unconditional and immediate" access to any and all sites by UN weapons inspectors, the resolution contains only a pro forma requirement that the U.S. obtain Security Council approval before launching a full-scale military invasion in response to Iraqi "obstruction" (as defined, to all appearances, by the United States). The very same afternoon, an all but sexually exultant Bush displayed himself on TV, crowing that Saddam now had "no choice but to submit."[570] As he spoke, additional major U.S. forces were deploying in the Persian Gulf.

Plainly, the wake-up call delivered so forcefully on 9-1-1 has not been heeded. Rather, Americans for the most part continue to wallow in the self-serving and misbegotten notion of their own radical innocence, the same mindless outlook that has all along deformed their collective self-concept into a pathological condition.[571] Quite predictably, under these circumstances, the "Prussians" among the country's élites have moved quickly in an effort to realize the ancient and infantile fantasy of outright world domination.[572] The grim scenario described in the section of this essay titled "'Indian Country' Forever?" is coming together at breakneck speed, while the positive alternatives hinted at in the conclusion recede with equal rapidity.

True, a certain alternative potential purports to present itself in an incipient (re)emergence of a mass antiwar movement for the first time since Vietnam.[573] In the main, however, its participants have, as they did during the Vietnam era, seemed far more concerned with establishing an appearance of personal purity than with attempting anything materially disruptive to the U.S. war-making capacity.[574] Acting upon of their own vibrant sense of American exceptionalism, most have forsworn on "philosophical" grounds the range of oppositional tactics that have proven necessary—and most effective—elsewhere, arguing with all due sanctimony that circumstances unique to the United States render such methods "inappropriate" to the task of compelling transformative change on the "home front."[575] Their stance thus mirroring that of their ostensible opponents, they place themselves *a priori* in a self-neutralizing posture, leaving themselves utterly incapable of retarding—much less averting—the horrors they insist it is their purpose to halt.[576]

On the face of it, then, the normative ambit of dissent in the U.S. is being drawn, as it always has, to displace the burden of blood onto Others, "out there" somewhere (*anywhere* but here). It is to be for "Them," as ever, to do the fighting and the dying, to bear the maiming and the burns, the starvation and endemic disease, suffering all the vast and ghastly toll of American military aggression while a self-styled "resistance" within the perpetrator country performs sanitary genuflections of symbolic protest, bearing "moral witness" to Their agony. To all appearances, it is presumed that this should remain the lot of these faceless, nameless multitudes of Others to endure *whatever* may be imposed upon them for *however* long it might take for America's enlightened oppositionists, through some alchemy never quite explained, to abolish the structural basis of U.S. aggression and genocide "nonviolently" (i.e., in a manner painless to themselves).[577]

From the perspective of those on the receiving end of what the U.S. so habitually dispenses to Others, there can thus be little by which to distinguish the glaring sense of self-entitlement exhibited by America's "peace movement" from that manifested by the state/corporate edifice whose policies and comportment it ostensibly opposes.[578] The extent to which there is truth to this perception is precisely the extent to which all but the most committed and self-sacrificing sectors of the U.S. opposition have historically defaulted—and are defaulting even now—upon the most fundamental responsibilities enshrined both in the customary standards of elemental human decency and in law. Here, the premise enunciated in Nuremberg Doctrine is as irreducibly simple as it is disquieting to those who would claim virtue in their pursuit of a comfort zone politics: When *any* government defies the basic tenets of international legality—as the nazis did, and as the U.S. government always has—the citizenry is bound by the legal obligation to utilize any and all means necessary to enforce compliance.[579]

There are no lines, legal or moral, constraining citizen action in such endeavors.[580] The only illegality is entailed in shirking one's obligation to cross whatever lines have been established to ensure the stability of criminal governments.[581] Those guilty of this offense are—as more than a few Good Germans were informed in the aftermath of World War II—in certain respects no less accountable to those who've suffered their country's aggression than are the officials they wildly applauded, or quietly embraced, or in any event failed to unseat. There are no bystanders to war crimes, genocide, and other crimes against humanity. There are only victims, perpetrators, and those complicit in the perpetration by way of either their endorsement or their acquiescence. Among the last three groups, children and mental incompetents aside, *no one* is "innocent." All are to one or another extent responsible.[582]

Such was the message—a warning, really—sent on 9-1-1. The days of smugness in which Americans might anoint themselves with a "god-given right" to exemption from the pain they as a country impose on Others are over. Insofar as U.S. citizens are accepting of the proposition that the economy of another people represents a legitimate military target—as they have since John Sullivan's troops laid waste the Seneca orchards and cornfields in 1779[583]—then "infrastructural" entities like the WTC are unquestionably fair game. To the degree that Americans are comfortable with the idea that the employment of tactics and technologies resulting inevitably in the slaughter of "enemy" civilians is acceptable under the rubric of "collateral damage"—as they've been since at least as early as Anthony Wayne's 1794 campaign against the Shawnees[584]—they've no logically or morally defensible basis to complain when the same devaluation is applied to them. In the sense that Americans have been perfectly willing to condone policies targeting entire populations of Others for eradication—as they have since Indian scalp bounties were promulgated during the first moments of their republic[585]—they can have no complaint when they themselves are explicitly taken as a target and subjected to the same treatment. What goes around does in fact ultimately come around, and only the most shortsighted—and arrogant—of peoples might ever have believed they could permanently forestall actualization of that simple truth.

The lapse in comparable operations inside the United States with which "the terrorists" have followed up their carefully focused attacks of 9-1-1 seems to have been intended more than anything to afford the American public a breathing space, time to draw appropriate lessons from the bitterness of its rather minor loss. Put another way, U.S. citizens were offered one last chance to finally grasp the fact—*really* grasp it rather than paying occasional and perfunctory lip service to it—that Americans are *not* a "special" or "chosen" people, either individually or collectively, that the lowliest "sand nigger" is worth just as much as the most self-absorbed yuppie braying business transactions into his cellphone while golfing at Myrtle Beach, that every wide-eyed little waif starving to death in Iraq and the reservations of Native North America is of a value identical to that with which a Jonbenét Ramsey or Danielle van Dam is currently imbued.[586] From this realization, had it occurred, one could hope that certain conclusions might accrue, conclusions resulting not just in an American "regime change," but in an alteration of public sensibility that left the likes of Henry Kissinger and Madeleine Albright sitting where by rights they belong: in a defendants' dock overshadowed by the gallows.[587]

At the very least, it was reasonable to expect that it might at last dawn on average folk that, to quote Georgia State University law professor Natsu Taylor Saito, "if Americans want their own kids to be safe again, the way to make it happen is really not very complicated—stop killing other people's babies."[588] Even this cognitive threshold has been beyond reach, however. The public, refusing the obviousness of such formulations, has gathered itself in its usual collectivity of denial, queuing up to place its faith in the "security" offered by such absurdities as the impoundment of tweezers contained in the carry-on luggage of airline passengers, and demanded a restoration of its accustomed "right" to kill with impunity.[589] The message of 9-1-1, to all appearances, has thus been lost (another disgrace to the memory of those who died). It will therefore have to be repeated (in pedagogical theory, the technique involved is referred to as being "recursive," highly effective with slow learners).

For this reason, on November 12, 2002, Usama bin-Laden, whose long silence had lulled many into the hope that he might be dead, made a taped appearance on al-Jazeera to explain the situation in no uncertain terms. "As you kill, you will be killed," he informed those applauding the prospect of another major war in the Persian Gulf, "As you bomb, you will bombed."[590] To make it clear that al-Qaida retains the capability to deliver on its words, bin-Laden took implicit credit for a whole series of actions over the year of his invisibility, including the recent bombing of a nightclub in Bali claiming a heavy toll of Australians[591] and the even more recent Chechen takeover of a theater in Moscow which resulted in well over a hundred fatalities.[592] As a subtext, he observed that every U.S. action since September 2001 had served to solidify al-Qaida's worldwide base of grassroots support, and that any major military action against Iraq would expand its recruitment base immensely.

It is no doubt true, as U.S. officials keep reminding us, that neither al-Qaida nor any other such organization holds—or is likely ever to hold—the capacity to defeat the United States in purely military terms. Nor do they possess the means to truly destroy America's economic system. What they do have, nonetheless, is the means and the will—both of them in increasing rather than diminishing proportions—to make U.S. citizens pay in the dearest possible terms, and in numbers making 9–1–1 look like the sneak preview it actually was, for the lethal effrontery embodied in their effort to resume business as usual. As the Israelis can all too readily attest, there really is no effective defense against people driven to the depths of such despair that they will gladly sacrifice themselves, if only it means taking a few of their tormentors with them.[593] In this regard, justice sometimes assumes the most awful sort of symmetry, but it will always, and irrespective of the power relations involved, prevail.

There is no Eighth Air Force available to hammer America into the kind of humility and self-recognition that lends itself to legal compliance. Nevertheless, Americans, like the Germans before them, are now confronted with a plain and unavoidable choice concerning the measure of suffering they are willing to endure in order to maintain the delusional pretensions marking their objectively criminal way of life. One can hope they will choose correctly, and soon. The scourges of smallpox, VX, and dirty bombs would be a hideous price to pay for recalcitrance,[594] but American recalcitrance equates, as it's always equated, to mounds of rotting corpses in whatever chunk of territory the U.S. chooses to view as "Indian Country" at any given moment. Come what may, there is solace to be had in the knowledge that Americans no longer enjoy the option of pretending they can avoid the choice itself.

Notes

1   See, e.g., Edwin P. Hoyt, *America's Wars and Military Excursions* (New York: McGraw-Hill, 1987).

2   The complete text of the order will be found in John C. Fitzpatrick, ed., *Writings of George Washington* (Washington, DC: U.S. Government Printing Office, 1936), 189–93.

3   Ibid., p. 93.

4   Quoted in Richard Drinnon, *Facing West: The Metaphysics of Indian-Hating and Empire-Building* (Minneapolis: University of Minnesota Press, 1980) p. 332.

5   Anthony Wallace, *The Death and Rebirth of the Seneca* (New York: Alfred A. Knopf, 1970) pp. 141–44.

6   Quoted in Drinnon, *Facing West*, p. 332.

7   Shelby L. Stanton, *Rangers at War: Combat Recon in Vietnam* (New York: Orion Books, 1992) pp. 1–6.

8   Col. Henry Hamilton, "The Hamilton Papers," *Michigan Pioneer and Historical Collections*, No. 9 (1886) pp. 501–2.

9   Henry Howe, quoted in Richard Drinnon, *Keeper of Concentration Camps: Dillon S. Myer and American Racism* (Berkeley: University of California Press, 1987) p. 23.

10 Ibid. Also see Gerard Fowke, *Archaeological History of Ohio: The Mound Builders and Later Indians* (Columbus: Ohio State Archaeological and Historical Society, 1902) pp. 478–80.

11 For one of the better accounts of combat in the Ohio River Valley during this period, see Allan W. Eckert, *That Dark and Bloody River: Chronicles of the Ohio River Valley* (New York: Bantam, 1995).

12 John Sugden, *Tecumseh's Last Stand* (Norman: University of Oklahoma Press, 1985) p. 180.

13 David E. Stannard, *American Holocaust: Columbus and the Conquest of the New World* (New York: Oxford University Press, 1992) p. 121. Also see H.S. Halbert and T.H. Hall, *The Creek War of 1813 and 1814* (Tuscaloosa: University of Alabama Press, 1969) pp. 276–77.

14 Quoted in Stannard, *American Holocaust*, p. 121.

15 See generally Edward J. Nichols, *Zach Taylor's Little Army* (Garden City, NY: Doubleday, 1963).

16 Alan Axelrod, *Chronicle of the Indian Wars from Colonial Times to Wounded Knee* (New York: Prentice Hall, 1993) p. 151.

17 On scalp bounties, see my *A Little Matter of Genocide: Holocaust and Denial in the Americas, 1492 to the Present* (San Francisco: City Lights, 1997) pp. 178–88.

18 Robert F. Heizer, ed., *The Destruction of California Indians* (Lincoln: University of Nebraska Press, [2nd ed.] 1993).

19 I am referring here not to the men whose faces appear on U.S. currency—although several would plainly qualify—but to less overtly political figures like Daniel Boone, Davy Crockett, Kit Carson, and George Armstrong Custer. Perhaps the best analysis of how this came about will be found in Richard Slotkin's *Fatal Environment: The Myth of the Frontier in the Age of Industrialization, 1800–1890* (Norman: University of Oklahoma Press, [2nd ed.] 1998): on Boone, see pp. 65–68; on Crockett, see pp. 162–72, 269–70; on Carson, see pp. 200–207; on Custer, see pp. 369–74, 500–501, 528–30.

20 Stuart Creighton Miller, *"Benevolent Assimilation": The American Conquest of the Philippines, 1899–1903* (New Haven, CT: Yale University Press, 1982) pp. 1–2, 253–67.

21 Patricia Nelson Limerick, to name a prominent example, offers a "revised" interpretation of "how the West was won" that manages to omit all mention of such "unpleasantness"—the term is hers—as massacres. See her much-touted *The Legacy of Conquest: The Unbroken Past of the West* (New York: W.W. Norton, 1987).

22 See Richard Slotkin, *Gunfighter Nation: The Myth of the Frontier in Twentieth-Century America* (Norman: University of Oklahoma Press, [2nd ed.] 1998).

23 Miller, *"Benevolent Assimilation,"* pp. 1–2.

24 Notably, Samuel Flagg Bemis, in his supposedly magisterial study, *A Diplomatic History of the United States* (New York: Henry Holt, 1936), opined that imperialism was "a great aberration in American history." For rather more accurate views, see Richard W. Van Alstyne's *The Rising American Empire* (New York: Oxford University Press, 1960) and the first nine chapters of Sidney Lens, *The Forging of the American Empire: From the Revolution to Vietnam, A History of U.S. Imperialism* (New York: Thomas Y. Crowell, 1971) pp. 1–168.

25 Such formulations are legion. A classic illustration is J.H. Elliot's review of Stannard's *American Holocaust* published in the *New York Review of Books* on June 24, 1993. So, too, the polemics offered by James Axtell in his *The European and the Indian: Essays in the Ethnohistory of Colonial North America* (New York: Oxford University Press, 1981), *After Columbus: Essays in the Ethnohistory of Colonial North America* (New York:

Oxford University Press, 1988), and *Beyond 1492: Encounters in Colonial North America* (New York: Oxford University Press, 1992).

26 "The concept of offenses against the law of nations (*delicti juris gentium*) was recognized by classical text-writers on international law and . . . was regarded as sufficiently tangible in the eighteenth century that United States courts sustained indictments charging acts as an offense against the law of nations, even if there were no statutes defining the offense." Quincy Wright, "The Law of the Nuremberg Trial, Part II," in Jay Baird, ed., *From Nuremberg to My Lai* (Lexington, MA: DC Heath, 1972) p. 37.

27 Adam Roberts and Richard Guelff, eds., *Documents on the Laws of War* (Oxford, UK: Clarendon Press, 1982) p. 2.

28 Ibid., pp. 2–3.

29 See, e.g., Hedley Bull, Benedict Kingsbury, and Adam Roberts, eds., *Hugo Grotius and International Relations* (Oxford, UK: Clarendon Press, 1992).

30 See the opening statement of Hermann Jahrreiss, lead counsel for the defense, in *Trial of the Major Nazi War Criminals before the International Military Tribunal*, 42 vols. (Nuremberg: International Military Tribunal, 1949) Vol. 17, pp. 458–94.

31 See, e.g., Henry L. Stimson, "The Nuremberg Trial: Landmark in Law," *Foreign Affairs*, Vol. 25, No. 2 (January 1947) pp. 179–89.

32 Wright, "The Law of the Nuremberg Trial," p. 38.

33 Affirmation of the Principles of International Law Recognized by the Charter of the Nuremberg Tribunal, U.N.G.A. Res. 95(I), U.N. Doc. A/236 (1946) at 1144.

34 For an especially nauseating articulation of this thesis, see Wilcomb E. Washburn, *Red Man's Land, White Man's Law* (New York: Scribner's, 1971).

35 Roberts and Guelff, *Documents on the Laws of War*, p. 7; United States Army, *General Orders No. 100: Instructions for the Government of United States Armies in the Field* (Washington, DC: U.S. Dept. of War, April 24, 1863; hereinafter referred to as "Lieber Code").

37 Quoted in Joseph B. Kelly, "A Legal Analysis of the Changes in War," *Military Law Review*, Vol. 13, No. 5 (July 1961) pp. 89–120.

38 "War is merely the continuation of policy by other means. . . . War is thus an act of force to compel our enemy to do our will. . . . The political object is the goal, war is the means of reaching it, and means can never be considered in isolation from their purpose." Carl von Clausewitz, *On War* (Princeton, NJ: Princeton University Press, 1976) pp. 75, 87.

39 Roberts and Guelff, *Laws of War*, p. 3.

40 "Murders in cold blood after the heat of battle were condemned by all nations of the world. . . . [O]ne had the right to kill the defenders of the state as long as they bore arms, but when they surrendered they ceased to be enemies or instruments of the enemy and became men. Their killing was unnecessary to achieve the purpose of the war, namely the destruction of the enemy state. . . . The philosophical premises of the law were formulated by such philosophers of the Enlightenment as Montesquieu and Rousseau." Allan Rosas, *The Legal Status of Prisoners of War: A Study in International Humanitarian Law Applicable in Armed Conflicts* (Helsinki: Suomalainen Tiedeakatemia, 1976) p. 57.

41 On the numbers involved, and the meeting during which the protected status of the village was guaranteed, see Stan Hoig, *The Sand Creek Massacre* (Norman: University of Oklahoma Press, 1961) pp. 12, 116–17, 120.

42   Simon J. Ortiz, *From Sand Creek* (Oak Park, NY: Thunder's Mouth Press, 1981) p. 8. Also see Stan Hoig, *Peace Chiefs of the Cheyenne* (Norman: University of Oklahoma Press, 1980).

43   Hoig, *Sand Creek Massacre*, p. 150.

44   The armistice was negotiated in mid-September during a meeting conducted at Camp Weld, outside Denver, at Black Kettle's behest. Hoig, *Sand Creek Massacre*, pp. 110–28.

45   Ibid., p. 140.

46   Quoted in ibid., p. 147.

47   Chivington was paraphrasing the observation of H.L. Hall, an Indian-killer prominent in California at about the same time, that American Indian infants should be butchered whenever possible because "a knit [sic] would make a louse." See Lynwood Carranco and Estle Beard, *Genocide and Vendetta: The Round Valley Wars of Northern California* (Norman: University of Oklahoma Press, 1981) p. 63. Hall himself may well have been borrowing from a Puritan rhyme likening Indians to "rats and mice or swarms of lice," written in the aftermath of their 1637 extermination of the Pequots; Drinnon, *Facing West*, p. 55. In any event, eighty years after Sand Creek, SS Reichsführer Heinrich Himmler would extend this distinctly American rhetorical cant by comparing the extermination of Jews, Gypsies, and Slavic "untermenschen" to "delousing." Stannard, *American Holocaust*, p. 131.

48   The Third Colorado Volunteer Cavalry Regiment, comprising the bulk of Chivington's assault force, was formed during the first weeks of August 1864 for the express purpose of "exterminating" hostile Cheyennes and allied Arapahos. The term of enlistment was one hundred days. Hence, the soldiers' obligations were met by mid-November, although they'd by then come upon only a handful of Indians to exterminate, and were therefore embarrassed to be known as the "Bloodless Third." At the last moment, they were inspired to stay on—for purposes of attacking Black Kettle's noncombatants—during a visit by Gen. Patrick E. Connor, who had, on January 27, 1863, led a force of California volunteers in slaughtering several hundred Shoshones at Bear River, in southern Idaho. Reported in the *Rocky Mountain News* (November 14 and 16, 1864). On Connor's "accomplishment," see Brigham M. Madsen, *The Shoshoni Frontier and the Bear River Massacre* (Salt Lake City: University of Utah Press, 1985) esp. pp. 189–92.

49   Hoig, *Sand Creek Massacre*, pp. 172–99.

50   In *From Sand Creek*, Ortiz places the number at "105 women and children and 28 men" (p. 8).

51   Hoig, *Sand Creek Massacre*, p. 151.

52   U.S. Senate, *Reports of the Committees: The Chivington Massacre* (Washington, DC: 39th Cong., 2nd Sess., 1867) pp. 95–96.

53   Ibid., p. 42.

54   Ibid. p. 53. Corroborating testimony is too voluminous to cite adequately herein. For additional extracts, see Hoig, *Sand Creek Massacre*, pp. 177–92.

55   The infant was considered a "nuisance." Her throat was therefore slit. Jack Smith, a mixed-blood Cheyenne, was also shot. U.S. Senate, *Chivington Massacre*, p. 155.

56   *Rocky Mountain News*, December 22, 1864.

57   Gov. Evans also advocated extermination; U.S. Dept. of War, Commissioner of Indian Affairs, *Annual Report* (Washington, DC: 38th Cong., 1st Sess., 1864) pp. 239–46. Overall, see David Svaldi, *Sand Creek and the Rhetoric of Extermination: A Case-Study in Indian-White Relations* (Lanham, MD: University Press of America, 1989).

58 It should be noted that Capt. Silas S. Soule refused to allow his company to participate in the massacre; Hoig, *Sand Creek Massacre*, p. 151.

59 U.S. Senate, *Chivington Massacre*; U.S. House of Representatives, *Report on the Conduct of the War: Massacre of Cheyenne Indians* (Washington, DC: 38th Cong., 2nd Sess., 1865); U.S. Department of War, *Report of the Secretary of War: The Sand Creek Massacre* (Washington, DC: Sen. Exec. Doc. 26, 39th Cong., 2nd Sess., 1867).

60 Hoig, *Sand Creek Massacre*, p. 169.

61 Serious consideration was in fact given to recalling several officers to stand trial. They were, however, to be charged only with misappropriating horses and other booty taken at Sand Creek, a violation of Article 31 of the Lieber Code. The proposal foundered when it was realized that there was no way of bringing them under military jurisdiction for this purpose without opening them up to prosecution on the far more serious charges pending against them. Hoig, *Sand Creek Massacre*, p. 169.

62 "The state of the law cannot be properly judged by referencing the written law alone." Roberts and Guelff, *Laws of War*, p. 16.

63 There are also several thoroughly squalid books eulogizing the colonel's supposed virtues. See, as examples, Reginald S. Craig, *The Fighting Parson: A Biography of Col. John M. Chivington* (Tucson, AZ: Westernlore, 1959) and Lt. Colonel William R. Dunn, "*I Stand by Sand Creek": A Defense of Colonel John M. Chivington and the Third Colorado Cavalry* (Ft. Collins, CO: Old Army Press, 1985).

64 Patricia Nelson Limerick, "What's in a Name? Nichols Hall: A Report" (Boulder: unpublished study commissioned by the Regents of the University of Colorado, 1987).

65 Michael A. Sievers, "The Shifting Sands of Sand Creek Historiography," *Colorado Magazine*, Vol. 49 (Spring 1972) pp. 116–42.

66 See generally Clifford E. Trafzer, *The Kit Carson Campaign: The Last Great Navajo War* (Norman: University of Oklahoma Press, 1982).

67 Stan Hoig, *The Battle of the Washita* (Garden City, NY: Doubleday, 1976) p. 74. Also see Don Turner, *Custer's First Massacre: The Battle of the Washita* (Amarillo, TX: Gulch Press, 1968).

68 Axelrod, *Chronicle of the Indian Wars*, p. 209.

69 W.A. Graham, *The Custer Myth: A Sourcebook on Custerania* (Lincoln: University of Nebraska Press, [2nd ed.] 1981).

70 Robert G. Athearn, *William Tecumseh Sherman and the Settlement of the West* (Norman: University of Oklahoma Press, 1956) pp. 278–79. The best overall handling of the Marias Massacre and its backdrop will be found in James Welch, *Killing Custer: The Battle of the Little Big Horn and the Fate of the Plains Indians* (New York: W.W. Norton, 1994).

71 Paul Andrew Hutton, *Phil Sheridan and His Army* (Lincoln: University of Nebraska Press, 1985) pp. 192–94.

72 Dee Brown, *Bury My Heart at Wounded Knee: An Indian History of the American West* (New York: Holt, Rinehart and Winston, 1970) pp. 346–47.

73 Ralph K. Andrist, *The Long Death: The Last Days of the Plains Indian* (New York: Macmillan, 1964) pp. 351–52.

74 Mario Gonzalez and Elizabeth Cook-Lynn, *The Politics of Hallowed Ground: Wounded Knee and the Struggle for Indian Sovereignty* (Urbana: University of Illinois Press, 1999) pp. 177, 253.

75 As at Sand Creek, the exact number of dead is "controversial," since no accurate count was made at the time; Andrist, *Long Death*, p. 352.

76 Gonzalez and Cook-Lynn, *The Politics of Hallowed Ground*, p. 107.

77 Quoted in Elliot J. Gorn, Randy Roberts, and Terry D. Bilhartz, *Constructing the American Past: A Sourcebook of a People's History* (New York: HarperCollins, 1972) p. 74.

78 William D. Street, "Cheyenne Indian Massacre on the Middle Fork of the Sappa," *Transactions of the Kansas State Historical Society*, Vol. X (1907–1908) pp. 368–72.

79 Quoted in Axelrod, *Chronicle of the Indian Wars*, p. 203.

80 Sheridan's actual phrase was, "The only good Indians I ever saw were dead"; Hutton, *Phil Sheridan*, p. 180.

81 Svaldi, *Sand Creek and the Rhetoric of Extermination*.

82 For demographic data, see Donald J. Berthrong, *The Cheyenne and Arapaho Ordeal: Reservation and Agency Life, 1875–1907* (Norman: University of Oklahoma Press, 1976); William T. Hagan, *United States-Comanche Relations: The Reservation Years* (Norman: University of Oklahoma Press, [2nd ed.] 1990); Mildred P. Mayhall, *The Kiowas* (Norman: University of Oklahoma Press, 1962).

83 The term "Indian Wars" is itself a misnomer. In all cases, the conflicts resulted from the invasion of native nations by the United States. A more accurate characterization would therefore be "Wars of U.S. Aggression."

84 As an example: "[B]efore there were whites to rob and plunder and steal from, the [Indians] robbed and stole from each other. Before there were white men in the country to kill, they killed each other. Before there were white women and children to scalp and mutilate and torture, the Indians scalped and mutilated and tortured the women and children of enemies of their own race." Duane Schultz, *Month of the Freezing Moon: The Sand Creek Massacre, November 1864* (New York: St. Martin's Press, 1990) p. 16.

85 Although the 1868 Additional Articles to the 1864 Geneva Convention on the Wounded and Sick is certainly germane, the 1874 Brussels Declaration incorporating the "fundamental customary principle . . . that the right of belligerents to adopt means of injuring the enemy is not unlimited" goes more to the point. As formulated in the 1899 Hague Convention, this meant that "the principle of humanity prohibits any kind or degree of force not actually necessary for military purposes." Roberts and Guelff, *Laws of War*, pp. 3, 5.

86 For background on the St. Valentine's Day Massacre, see Robert J. Schoenberg, *Mr. Capone* (New York: William Morrow, 1992) pp. 207–29.

87 See generally Miller, *"Benevolent Assimilation"*; Robert E. Welch Jr., *Response to Imperialism: The United States and the Philippine-American War, 1899–1902* (Chapel Hill: University of North Carolina Press, 1979).

88 Unidentified General Officer (probably Wesley Merritt), quoted by Senator George Frisbee Hoar, *Congressional Record*, Vol. 33 (January 9, 1901) p. 714.

89 Theodore Roosevelt, *The Winning of the West*, 7 vols. (New York: Putnam's, 1907) Vol. 3, p. 145.

90 Anonymous Army officer, quoted in Moorfield Storey and Julian Codman, *"Marked Severities" in Philippine Warfare* (Boston: George H. Ellis, 1902) p. 99. The "Weylerian" reference is to the Spanish general, Valeriano Weyler, known as the "Butcher of Cuba." Miller, *"Benevolent Assimilation,"* p. 9.

91 Drinnon, *Facing West*, p. 315.

92 Ibid., pp. 324–25. Miller, *"Benevolent Assimilation,"* p. 219.

93 Ibid., pp. 196–218.

94 Slotkin, *Gunfighter Nation*, p. 119.

95   In a manner which would later become fashionable in Vietnam, Bell may have exaggerated his body count. Closer study reveals that his policies may have accounted for "only" 220,000 people (estimated as being composed of 20,000 combatants and 200,000 civilians). Glenn May, "Filipino Resistance to American Occupation: Batangas, 1899–1902," *Pacific Historical Review*, No. 48 (1979) pp. 555–56.

96   Storey and Codman, "Marked Severities," pp. 26–27.

97   Miller, "Benevolent Assimilation," p. 218.

98   Ibid., pp. 237, 260.

99   Slotkin, *Gunfighter Nation*, p. 119.

100   Drinnon, *Facing West*, p. 328.

101   *Philadelphia Ledger*, November 19, 1901.

102   U.S. Senate, Committee on the Philippine Islands, *Hearings Before the Senate Committee on the Philippine Islands* (Washington, DC: S. Doc. 331, 57th Cong., 1st Sess., 1902).

103   U.S. Department of War, *Letter from the Secretary of War Relative to the Reports and Charges in the Public Press of Cruelty and Oppression Exercised by Our Soldiers Towards Natives of the Philippines* (Washington, DC: S. Doc. 205., 57th Cong., 1st Sess., 1902).

104   Drinnon, *Facing West*, p. 522; Storey and Codman, "Marked Severities," pp. 136–37.

105   At issue were the deaths of only eleven people. Drinnon, *Facing West*, p. 327.

106   Ibid.

107   Miller, "Benevolent Assimilation," p. 232.

108   Drinnon, *Facing West*, p. 328.

109   Slotkin, *Gunfighter Nation*, p. 121.

110   Senate, *Hearings on the Philippines*, p. 1591.

111   For the best concise summary of the evidence on Filipino fatalities during Chaffee's tenure, see Luzviminda Francisco, "The Philippine-American War," in Daniel B. Schirmer and Stephen Rosskamm Shalom, eds., *The Philippines Reader: A History of Colonialism, Neocolonialism, Dictatorship, and Resistance* (Boston: South End Press, 1987) p. 19.

112   On the appointments of both Chaffee and Bell, see Miller, "Benevolent Assimilation," p. 260.

113   Quoted in ibid., pp. 250–51.

114   Senate, *Hearings on the Philippines*, pp. 867–68.

115   See William Stanton, *The Leopard's Spots: Scientific Attitudes Towards Race in America, 1815–1859* (Chicago: University of Chicago Press, 1960); Stephen Jay Gould, *The Mismeasure of Man* (New York: W.W. Norton, 1981).

116   An excellent overview of such thinking, and its effects on U.S. policy formation, will be found in Reginald Horsman, *Race and Manifest Destiny: The Origins of American Racial Anglo-Saxonism* (Cambridge, MA: Harvard University Press, 1981).

117   This is not to argue that such dynamics and sensibilities are in any way unique to the United States. For examination of analogous contexts, see, e.g., Sven Lindquist, *"Exterminate All the Brutes": One Man's Odyssey into the Heart of Darkness and the Origins of European Genocide* (New York: New Press, 1996).

118   Lieber Code, Article 25.

119   Hoyt, *America's Wars*; "That Most Peaceful of Nations."

120   For an excellent handling of the mythic aspects attending this continuity, see Slotkin, *Gunfighter Nation*, pp. 313–43, 441–86.

121   There were, of course, exceptions to this, mainly associated with the strategic bombing campaign against Germany. Probably the most notorious illustration was the incendiary attack on Dresden on the night of February 13, 1945, inflicting

an estimated 150,000 civilian casualties. See G.E. Hopkins, "Bombing and the American Conscience in World War II," *Historian*, No. 28 (1966) pp. 451–73.

122 Quoted in John W. Dower, *War Without Mercy: Race and Power in the Pacific War* (New York: Pantheon, 1986) p. 64.

123 Stannard, *American Holocaust*, p. 252.

124 Dower, *War Without Mercy*, pp. 64–65.

125 Ronald Takaki, *Iron Cages: Race and Culture in 19th-Century America* (New York: Alfred A. Knopf, 1979) p. 96. Other examples are offered in Dower, *War Without Mercy*.

126 Stannard, *American Holocaust*, p. 252.

127 See note 3.

128 "It was known that the Japanese had instructed their ambassador in Moscow to work on peace negotiations with the Allies. Japanese leaders had begun talking of surrender a year before this." Howard Zinn, *A People's History of the United States* (New York: Harper & Row, 1980) pp. 413–15.

129 "The [official] justification for these atrocities was that this would end the war quickly, making unnecessary an invasion of Japan. Such an invasion would cost a huge number of lives, the government said—a million, according to Secretary of State [James F.] Byrnes; a half-million, Truman claimed was the figure given him by General George Marshall. . . . These estimates of losses . . . seemed to be pulled out of the air to justify bombings." Zinn, *People's History*, p. 413. Also see Ronald Takaki, *Hiroshima: Why America Dropped the Atomic Bomb* (Boston: Little, Brown, 1995); Gar Alperovitz, *The Decision to Drop the Bomb* (New York: Alfred A. Knopf, 1995), esp. pp. 627–41.

130 As many as 130,000 people died in the Tokyo incendiary bombing alone. The longterm tolls of the Hiroshima and Nagasaki bombings are estimated as being 200,000 and 240,000, respectively. Lifton and Markusen, *Genocidal Mentality*, pp. 21, 24.

131 Quoted in Drinnon, *Facing West*, p. 331.

132 Ibid.

133 "On July 13, [1945,] Foreign Minister Shigenori Togo had wired his ambassador in Moscow: 'Unconditional surrender is the only obstacle to peace . . . .' If only the Americans had not insisted on unconditional surrender—that is, if they were willing to accept one condition to surrender, that the Emperor, a holy figure to the Japanese, remain in place [a stipulation the U.S. later decided was in its own interests in any event]—the Japanese would have agreed to stop the war." Zinn, *People's History*, p. 415.

134 Quoted in Noam Chomsky, "'What We Say Goes': The Middle East in the New World Order," in Cynthia Peters, ed., *Collateral Damage: The "New World Order" at Home and Abroad* (Boston: South End Press, 1992) p. 52.

135 "Modernizing Turner: The Ideology of the New Frontier," in Slotkin, *Gunfighter Nation*, pp. 491–97.

136 Consider, for example, the performance of the U.S.-backed military junta headed by General Mohamed Suharto in Indonesia, which, after overthrowing the populist President Achmed Sukarno in 1965, exterminated at least 500,000 peasant "communists" while establishing a "business-friendly climate" in the region. Noam Chomsky and Edward S. Herman, *The Political Economy of Human Rights, Vol. 1: The Washington Connection and Third World Fascism* (Boston: South End Press, 1979) pp. 205–17.

137　The characterization is of the Vietnamese, by President Lyndon B. Johnson, also known to refer to their homeland as a "damn little pissant country." Quoted in Stanley Karnow, *Vietnam: A History* (New York: Viking Press, 1983) p. 395.

138　This is true in respects well beyond the use of tactics violating the laws of war. A classic example is that of the U.S. sabotage of the 1954 Geneva Peace Accords calling for the reunification of Vietnam two years later. In the process, it violated not only the accords, but the United Nations Charter and several other elements of international legality. See Ralph Stavins, Richard J. Barnet, and Marcus G. Raskin, *Washington Plans an Aggressive War* (New York: Random House, 1971) pp. 3–18. Also see Quincy Wright, "Legal Aspects of the Vietnam Situation," in Richard Falk, ed., *The Vietnam War and International Law* (Princeton, NJ: Princeton University Press, 1968) pp. 271–91.

139　I.F. Stone, *The Hidden History of the Korean War, 1950–1951* (Boston: Little, Brown, [2nd ed.] 1988).

140　Michael MacClear, *The Ten Thousand Day War: Vietnam, 1945–1975* (New York: St Martin's Press, 1981); Noam Chomsky, *At War with Asia* (New York: Pantheon, 1970).

141　The point of this "Civic Action Program" was to "deprive the enemy of his strategic base" by forcibly driving the entire rural population into "protected hamlets," most often by employing "air and artillery to terrorize the peasantry and raze the countryside." Neil Sheehan, "Should We Have War Crimes Trials?" *New York Times* (March 28, 1971).

142　Stockholm International Peace Research Institute (Malvern Lumsden), *Incendiary Weapons* (Stockholm/Cambridge, MA: Almquist & Wiksell International/MIT Press, 1975) pp. 49–63.

143　In the area around the Marine base at Khe Sanh alone, "we delivered more than 110,000 tons of bombs [in] eleven weeks . . . the greatest volume of explosives in the history of warfare." Michael Herr, *Dispatches* (New York: Alfred A. Knopf, 1978) p. 153.

144　Noam Chomsky, *For Reasons of State* (New York: Vintage, 1973) pp. 172–76, 180–84, 187–90, 227–28.

145　Like the M-16 rifle, this type of ordnance was designed to effect technical compliance with, while achieving practical circumvention of, an unbroken line of black letter international law dating from the 1899 Hague Declaration 3 Concerning Expanding Bullets, all of it intended to prohibit the use of weapons inflicting wounds of "exceptional cruelty." Roberts and Guelff, *Laws of War*, pp. 39–42.

146　Barry Weisberg, *Ecocide in Indochina: The Ecology of War* (San Francisco: Canfield Press, 1970).

147　Karnow, *Vietnam*, pp. 17, 18, 480, 512.

148　Quoted in Drinnon, *Facing West*, p. 369.

149　Quoted in Francis Fitzgerald, *Fire in the Lake: The Vietnamese and the Americans in Vietnam* (New York: Vintage Books, 1973) p. 460.

150　Quotes in Drinnon, *Facing West*, p. 451; Karnow, *Vietnam*, p. 325.

151　Karnow, *Vietnam*, p. 325; Chomsky, *For Reasons of State*, p. 120. Also see Citizen's Commission of Inquiry, *The Dellums Committee Hearings on War Crimes in Vietnam* (New York: Vintage Books, 1972) p. 52.

152　Testimony of International Voluntary Service Director Hugh Manke before Congress, 1971. Quoted in Drinnon, *Facing West*, p. 449.

153　The term "gook" has been wrongly classified as an American corruption of a Korean word originating during the early 1950s. In actuality, it is a racial epithet invented much earlier to describe Haitians. According to the July 10, 1920, issue of *The Nation*, "officers wearing the United States uniform in the interior of Haiti talk of 'bumping off' (i.e., killing) 'Gooks' as if it were a variety of sport like duck hunting." See the chapter titled "Of Gooks and Men" in Robert Jay Lifton's *Home from the War* (New York: Simon and Schuster, 1973) pp. 189–216.

154 Unidentified junior officer from the Americal Division, quoted in the *New York Times* (March 10, 1970). Also see Sheehan, "War Crimes"; Lifton, *Home from the War*, pp. 189–216; Drinnon, *Facing West*, p. 455; Chomsky, *For Reasons of State*, p. 224; R.W. Apple, "The Real Guilt," *New Statesman* (April 2, 1971) p. 34.

155 Both quotes are taken from Joseph Strick's 1971 documentary, *Interviews with My Lai Veterans*. Also see Lifton, *Home from the War*, p. 47; Charles Levy, *Spoils of War* (Boston: Houghton-Mifflin, 1974) p. 26.

156 Quoted in Drinnon, *Facing West*, p. 457.

157 One hundred similar testimonies were read into the *Congressional Record* by Senator Mark O. Hatfield on April 6 and 7, 1971 (Vol. CXVII, pp. 2825–900, 2903–36). The same material was subsequently published as a book. See Vietnam Veterans Against the War, *The Winter Soldier Investigation: An Inquiry into American War Crimes* (Boston: Beacon Press, 1972).

158 Strick, *Interviews with My Lai Veterans*.

159 Hatfield, *Congressional Record*, p. 2928.

160 Drinnon, *Facing West*, p. 451.

161 Quoted in the *New York Times* on March 31, 1971. Also see John Sack, *Lieutenant Calley: His Own Story* (New York: Viking Press, 1971) pp. 31, 104–5. The term "Oriental human beings" was used by the Army in Calley's charge sheet. See Seymour M. Hersh, *My Lai 4: A Report on the Massacre and Its Aftermath* (New York: Random House, 1970) p. 125.

162 Drinnon, *Facing West*, p. 451. Also see Chomsky, *At War with Asia*, pp. 81–82.

163 Joseph Goldstein, Burke Marshall, and Jack Schwartz, *The My Lai Massacre and Its Cover-Up: Beyond the Reach of the Law?* (New York: Free Press, 1976) p. 47. This book contains the text of the Army's official report on My Lai, otherwise known as the "Peers Report" (see note 172, below). Citations of/quotations from that report will therefore be made from the volume cited here.

164 Quoted in Drinnon, *Facing West*, p. 451.

165 Goldstein, Marshall, and Schwartz, *My Lai Massacre*, p. 56.

166 One concern was with the mounting toll of American casualties (though never much with the millions of slaughtered Asians). Another was with the sheer fiscal cost of waging a protracted, high-tech war; see Paul Joseph, *Cracks in the Empire: State Politics in the Vietnam War* (Boston: South End Press, 1981).

167 Reproduced in Goldstein, Marshall, and Schwartz, *My Lai Massacre*, pp. 34–37.

168 Ridenhour began to put out feelers through an agent in June 1969. *Life, Look, Harper's*, and *Newsweek* magazines all expressed no interest in the story. Only the left-leaning *Ramparts* responded favorably. Hersh, *My Lai 4*, p. 115.

169 Ibid., p. 133.

170 Ibid., pp. 134–35. *Life* and *Look* were still not interested.

171 U.S. House of Representatives, Committee on the Armed Services, *Report on the My Lai Incident* (Washington, DC: 91st Cong., 2nd Sess., July 15, 1970); usually referred to as the "Hébert Committee Report," after Representative F. Edward Hébert, who chaired the subcommittee that prepared it. For analysis, see Seymour M. Hersh, *Cover-Up* (New York: Random House, 1972).

172 Lt. General William Peers, et al., *Report of the Department of the Army Review of Preliminary Investigations into the My Lai Incident*, 3 vols. (Washington, DC: U.S. Dept. of the Army, No. 13, 1974).

173 House of Representatives, *Report on My Lai*, quoted in Drinnon, *Facing West*, p. 452.

174 Years later, "Westy" would still claim, all evidence to the contrary notwithstanding, that everything that had happened "on his watch" in Vietnam would measure up "before the bar of justice and the court of history." William Westmoreland, *A Soldier Reports* (Garden City, NY: Doubleday, 1976) p. 379.

175 Goldstein, Marshall, and Schwartz, *My Lai Massacre*, pp. 3–4.

176 Koster was also demoted to brigadier general (for purposes of computing his retirement pay) and stripped of his Distinguished Service Medal (he kept the rest, including, presumably, his Good Conduct Medal). Goldstein, Marshall, and Schwartz, *My Lai Massacre*, pp. ix–x.

177 Ibid.

178 Hersh, *My Lai 4*, pp. 40–43.

179 Goldstein, Marshall, and Schwartz, *My Lai Massacre*, pp. x, 465–67.

180 Three members of Koster's staff—Brig. Gen. Young, Col. Johnson, and Maj. Johnson—were each stripped of a medal and reprimanded, but all remained on active duty. Goldstein, Marshall, and Schwartz, *My Lai Massacre*, pp. ix–x.

181 See generally Sack, *Lieutenant Calley*.

182 Quoted in Chomsky, *For Reasons of State*, p. 222.

183 Hersh, *My Lai 4*, p. 177.

184 Drinnon, *Facing West*, pp. 452–53. Also see Seymour M. Hersh, "The Army's Secret Inquiry Describes a 2nd Massacre, Involving 90 Civilians," *New York Times* (June 5, 1972).

185 Chomsky, *For Reasons of State*, p. xx.

186 Willingham had been a lieutenant when the massacre occurred. Hersh, *My Lai 4*, pp. 177–78.

187 Goldstein, Marshall, and Schwartz, *My Lai Massacre*, p. ix.

188 For background, see Hersh, *Cover-Up*.

189 Chomsky and Herman, *Washington Connection*, p. 318; quoting from Earl S. Martin, *Reaching the Other Side* (New York: Crown, 1978) p. 133.

190 Commission of Inquiry, *Dellums Hearings*, pp. 188–89.

191 Chomsky and Herman, *Washington Connection*, p. 318.

192 See note 157.

193 Chomsky, *For Reasons of State*, p. 122. The troops were paid for with supplements to the annual aid package the U.S. awarded its South Korean client régime ($134 million in 1973, for example). Chomsky and Herman, *Washington Connection*, p. 322.

194 Robert M. Smith, "Vietnam Killings Laid to Koreans," *New York Times* (January 10, 1970).

195 Chomsky and Herman, *Washington Connection*, pp. 321–22.

196 See, e.g., Alex Carey, *Australian Atrocities in Vietnam* (Sydney: self-published, 1968).

197 Chomsky and Herman, *Washington Connection*, p. 321. To illustrate, consider that Varnado Simpson, one of the soldiers quoted earlier (see note 158), admitted he'd personally "killed eight or ten Vietnamese civilians on March 16, 1968." Hersh, *My Lai 4*, pp. 179–80.

198 "Many officers stalked Vietnamese in the free fire zones from the air, shooting at anyone who moved below." Hersh, *My Lai 4*, p. 9. Also see the testimony of former

helicopter gunship pilot David Bessum in Commission of Inquiry, *Dellums Hearings*, pp. 282–94.

199   Commission of Inquiry, *Dellums Hearings*, pp. 60–61, 96–97, 190, 205, 213, 266–69.

200   Hersh, *My Lai 4*, p. 9.

201   Kevin Buckley, "Pacification's Deadly Price," *Newsweek* (June 19, 1972), quoted in Chomsky and Herman, *Washington Connection*, pp. 314–15.

202   Chomsky and Herman, *Washington Connection*, p. 316.

203   Ibid., p. 317.

204   "The Colonel Speaking of His Men," excerpts from an interview on WABC-TV (New York), in Mitchell Goodman, ed., *Movement Towards a New America* (Philadelphia/New York: Pilgrim Press/Alfred A. Knopf, 1970) p. 625.

205   Quoted in Hersh, *My Lai 4*, p. 9. On the operations of Patton's 11th Armored Cavalry Regiment, see Commission of Inquiry, *Dellums Hearings*, pp. 143–56.

206   Hersh, *My Lai 4*, pp. 9–10.

207   Chomsky and Herman, *Washington Connection*, p. 319.

208   Leroy Thompson, *Elite Unit Insignia of the Vietnam War* (London: Arms and Armour Press, 1986).

209   Herr, *Dispatches*, pp. 34–35, 198–99. Also see the photo in Goodman, *Movement*, p. 315.

210   Buckley, quoted in Chomsky and Herman, *Washington Connection*, p. 314.

211   As one of the war's principal architects, former U.S. defense secretary Robert S. McNamara, admitted in a 1995 interview, "We killed—there were killed—3,200,000 Vietnamese, excluding the South Vietnamese military." Robert Scheer, "Born of Blind Faith: Robert McNamara believed he could ascend in a meritocracy, and with good reason. So what went so 'terribly wrong'?" *Los Angeles Times* (May 16, 1995). Add in roughly a quarter-million South Vietnamese military personnel killed during "McNamara's War," and the toll reaches nearly 3.5 million. For estimated military losses, see Thomas C. Thayer, *War Without Fronts: The American Experience in Vietnam* (Boulder, CO: Westview Press, 1985) p. 106.

212   Drinnon, *Facing West*, pp. 454–55. On April 7, 1971, the *New York Times* reported that the Army claimed there had been a total of 81 soldiers prosecuted for murder as a result of their actions in Vietnam. Of these, 38 were said to have been convicted of the main charge(s), 20 of lesser charges, and 23 acquitted. Of those convicted of murder, however, it turned out that 27 had been charged with killing other Americans. Of the eleven convicted of murdering Vietnamese, none was charged with participation in a My Lai-type incident, and, as with Duffy, all were bestowed with a postconviction "revision" of the offense/reduced sentence.

213   Peers Report, in Goldstein, Marshall, and Schwartz, *My Lai Massacre*, p. 207. The formulation referenced is *Field Manual 27–10: The Law of Land Warfare* (Washington, DC: U.S. Dept. of the Army, 1956).

214   Peers Report, in Goldstein, Marshall, and Schwartz, *My Lai Massacre*, p. 207. For the full text of the 1907 Hague Convention IV, see Roberts and Guelff, *Laws of War*, pp. 43–59.

215   Peers Report, in Goldstein, Marshall, and Schwartz, *My Lai Massacre*, p. 207. For the texts of all four 1949 Geneva Conventions, see Roberts and Guelff, *Laws of War*, pp. 169–337. Of particular relevance are the 1949 Geneva Convention III Relative to Treatment of Prisoners of War (pp. 215–70) and the 1949 Geneva Convention IV Relative to the Protection of Civilian Persons in Times of War (pp. 271–73).

216   Peers Report, in Goldstein, Marshall, and Schwartz, *My Lai Massacre*, pp. 207–8.

217 Agreement for the Prosecution and Punishment of the Major War Criminals of the European Axis Powers and Charter of the International Military Tribunal (August 8, 1945). For text, see Burns H. Weston, Richard A. Falk and Anthony D'Amato, eds., *Basic Documents in International Law and World Order* (St. Paul, MN: West, 1990) pp. 138–39, quote at 138.

218 Peers Report, in Goldstein, Marshall, and Schwartz, *My Lai Massacre*, pp. 208–9.

219 See note 141. For further background, see Robert L. Gallucci, *Neither Peace nor Honor: The Politics of American Military Policy in Vietnam* (Baltimore: Johns Hopkins University Press, 1975); Neil Sheehan, *A Bright Shining Lie: John Paul Vann and America in Vietnam* (New York: Random House, 1988).

220 This goes to the oft-stated contention that where infliction of civilian casualties is not a specifically articulated policy objective—or the express goal of particular applications of tactics—they must be considered "inadvertent" and therefore not a matter of criminal culpability. Such reasoning has no basis in law (or common sense). The policies and tactical expedients at issue are prohibited because it is understood *a priori* that, if they are pursued, civilian casualties will *inevitably* result. There can thus be nothing inadvertent in their infliction. Hence, the laws of war offer no legitimate exception(s) to compliance. See generally Sydney Bailey, *Prohibitions and Restraints in War* (New York: Oxford University Press, 1972).

221 Roberts and Guelff, *Laws of War*, p. 53.

222 Text, ibid., pp. 123–35; article cited at p. 126.

223 Ibid., p. 273.

224 Buckley, quoted in Chomsky and Herman, *Washington Connection*, p. 314.

225 Ibid. On miniguns, see Herr, *Dispatches*, pp. 132–33.

226 Buckley, quoted in Chomsky and Herman, *Washington Connection*, p. 314.

227 Arclight missions "usually involved a three-ship 'cell,' bombing in close trail to saturate a target 'box' roughly one kilometer wide and three kilometers long [with overlapping craters made by 500- or 1,000-pound bombs]. Bombing from above 30,000 feet, the B-52s could be neither seen nor heard by" anyone below. See Drew Middleton, *Air War—Vietnam* (New York: Arno Press, 1978) p. 201. Also see the photos of B-52s dropping their "payload" and of bombs detonating in an Arclight box pattern at pp. 180–81.

228 Buckley, quoted in Chomsky and Herman, *Washington Connection*, p. 314.

229 Along with support units, this added up to over 525,000 men in 1968. See generally Karnow, *Vietnam*; Shelby L. Stanton, *Vietnam Order of Battle* (Washington, DC: U.S. News Books, 1981).

230 Chomsky and Herman, *Washington Connection*, pp. 311–12.

231 Noam Chomsky and Edward S. Herman, *The Political Economy of Human Rights, Vol. II: After the Cataclysm* (Boston: South End Press, 1979) pp. 66–67.

232 Hugh Toye, *Laos: Buffer State or Battleground?* (London: Oxford University Press, 1968).

233 "It is a region that has had, by conservative estimate, more than two million tons of bombs dropped on it." Commission of Inquiry, *Dellums Hearings*, p. 311.

234 Fred Branfman, "Presidential War in Laos, 1964–1970," in Nina S. Adams and Alfred W. McCoy, eds., *Laos: War and Revolution* (New York: Harper & Row, 1970) pp. 233–34.

235 Most of the B-52 strikes were conducted along the Truong Son supply route—known by Americans as the "Ho Chi Minh Trail"—in the Laotian panhandle. See the photographs in John L. Plaster, *SOG: A Photo History of the Secret Wars* (Boulder, CO: Paladin Press, 2000) pp. 53, 58, 67.

236 Branfman, "Presidential War," p. 233.

237 Quoted in Chomsky, For Reasons of State, p. 176.

238 Quoted in ibid., p. 175.

239 Quoted in Commission of Inquiry, Dellums Hearings, p. 314.

240 Ibid. Also see U.S. Senate, Committee on Foreign Relations, United States Security Agreements and Commitments Abroad: The Kingdom of Laos (Washington, DC: 91st Cong., 2nd Sess., October 20–22, 1969).

241 Commission of Inquiry, Dellums Hearings, p. 313.

242 On civilian casualties, see the New York Times, August 24, 1975. On destruction of "infrastructure," see Commission of Inquiry, Dellums Hearings, p. 313 (quoting Robert Shaplen, Foreign Affairs, April 1970).

243 U.S. Joint Chiefs of Staff, quoted in William Shawcross, Sideshow: Kissinger, Nixon and the Bombing of Cambodia (New York: Simon and Schuster, 1979) pp. 272–73.

244 Ibid., 272.

245 This is according to maps prepared for a classified Air Force history of the B-52 campaign. Shawcross, Sideshow, p. 272.

246 As reported in the New York Times on June 14, 1976, the rural populace, thus deprived of their livestock, had been reduced to working as "human buffaloes" in a desperate effort to plow what fields they had left.

247 Chomsky and Herman, After the Cataclysm, p. 165. The higher estimate was confirmed as "close" by U.S. State Department official Timothy Carney in 1976. Ibid., p. 173.

248 Chomsky and Herman, After the Cataclysm, pp. 73–77, 128–34, 160–63; David Dellinger, Vietnam Revisited: Covert Action to Invasion to Reconstruction (Boston: South End Press, 1986) pp. 166–90.

249 On March 14, 1991, Westmoreland went on record in the Boston Globe saying that the United States "won the war" because the whole of Indochina remains a "basketcase." Overall, see Chomsky and Herman, After the Cataclysm.

250 Robert L. Mole, The Montagnards of South Vietnam: A Study of Nine Tribes (Rutland, VT: Charles E. Tuttle, 1970). On the fate of the Hmong, see Chomsky and Herman, After the Cataclysm, pp. 119–26.

251 The original quote was "we had to destroy the town in order to save it." Herr, Dispatches, p. 71. Also see Clark Dougan and David Fulghum, eds., The Vietnam Experience: Nineteen Sixty-Eight (Boston: Boston Publishing Co., 1983) p. 21.

252 Bertrand Russell, War Crimes in Vietnam (New York: Monthly Review Press, 1967).

253 John Duffett, ed., Against the Crime of Silence: Proceedings of the International War Crimes Tribunal (New York: Clarion, 1970).

254 See, e.g., Judith Coburn and Geoffrey Cowan, "The War Criminals Hedge Their Bets," Village Voice (December 4, 1969).

255 Telford Taylor, Nuremberg and Vietnam: An American Tragedy (Chicago: Quadrangle, 1970) p. 169.

256 Statement made on television talk show, quoted in Drinnon, Facing West, p. 550.

257 The other participating powers—Great Britain, France, and the USSR—actually opposed the Nuremberg procedure. Winston Churchill and John A. Simon, respectively the English prime minister and lord chancellor, argued strongly for summary execution of the nazi leaders rather than risking the establishment of legal precedents at trial. See Bradley F. Smith, The Road to Nuremberg (New York: Basic Books, 1981) pp. 45–47.

258 Robert H. Jackson, "Opening Statement for the United States before the International Military Tribunal, November 21, 1945," in Jay W. Baird, ed., From Nuremberg to My Lai (Lexington, MA: DC Heath, 1972) p. 28.

259 Justice Jackson, quoted in Russell, *War Crimes*, p. 125.

260 See, e.g., Townsend Hoopes, "The Nuremberg Suggestion," *Washington Monthly* (January 1970) pp. 18–21.

261 Hoopes, quoted in Coburn and Cowan, "War Criminals."

262 Nimitz's order in fact "went far beyond the German one." Davidson, *Trial of the Germans*, p. 421. Nonetheless, it was the U.S. alternate on the tribunal, John J. Parker, who proved most insistent that Doenitz be convicted. See Bradley F. Smith, *Reaching Judgement at Nuremberg* (New York: Basic Books, 1977) pp. 260–61.

263 Robert E. Conot, *Justice at Nuremberg* (New York: Harper & Row, 1983) pp. 493–94. On Dresden, see note 121. On Hamburg, see Robert Sherry, *The Rise of American Air Power: The Creation of Armageddon* (New Haven, CT: Yale University Press, 1986) pp. 152–55.

264 Arnold C. Brackman, *The Other Nuremberg: The Untold Story of the Tokyo War Crimes Trials* (New York: Quill, 1987).

265 Ibid., pp. 409–12.

266 Ibid., p 51. Also see A. Frank Reel, *The Case of General Yamashita* (Chicago: University of Chicago Press, 1949).

267 Yamashita was accused of responsibility in the murders of 131,028 POWs and non-combatant Filipinos. Brackman, *Other Nuremberg*, p. 244. Without diminishing the significance of these deaths in any way, they should be compared to the 616,000 tallied by J. Franklin Bell in 1902 (see note 95).

268 See, e.g., George S. Andrew. Jr., "The 41st Didn't Take Prisoners," *Saturday Evening Post* (July 27, 1946). Also see Dower, *War Without Mercy*, pp. 60–71.

269 Denis Warner and Peggy Warner, *The Sacred Warriors: Japan's Suicide Legions* (New York: Avon, 1982) pp. xi, 36.

270 William Manchester, *Goodbye, Darkness: A Memoir of the Pacific War* (New York, Dell, 1980) p. 439.

271 John Alan Appleman, *Military Tribunals and International Crimes* (Westport, CT: Greenwood Press, 1954) pp. 267–89.

272 Michael Reynolds, *The Devil's Adjutant: Jochen Peiper, Panzer Leader* (New York: Sarpedon, 1995) pp. 92, 252–59.

273 Slicing open the cheeks of wounded Japanese and prying out their gold teeth with Ka-Bar knives, for example. See E.B. Sledge, *With the Old Breed at Peleliu and Okinawa* (San Francisco: Presidio Press, 1981) p. 120.

274 Drinnon, *Facing West*, pp. 316, 320; Miller, "Benevolent Assimilation," pp. 225–26, 250–51.

275 Commission of Inquiry, *Dellums Hearings*, pp. 83–156.

276 On the war and its causes, see Dee Brown, *Bury My Heart at Wounded Knee: An Indian History of the American West* (New York: Macmillan, 1970) pp. 37–65.

277 The Indians whose death sentences were overturned were not freed. Lincoln merely commuted their punishments to varying terms of imprisonment. Sidney L. Harring, *Crow Dog's Case: American Indian Sovereignty, Tribal Law, and United States Law in the Nineteenth Century* (Cambridge, UK: Cambridge University Press, 1994) p. 262.

278 Brown, *Wounded Knee*, pp. 60, 63–64.

279 Harring, *Crow Dog's Case*, p. 262.

280 Michael Lieder and Jake Page, *Wild Justice: The People of Geronimo vs. the United States* (New York: Random House, 1997).

281 Lonnie R. Speer, *Portals to Hell: Military Prisons in the Civil War* (Mechanicsburg, PA: Stackpole Books, 1997) pp. 291–92.

282 See generally Trafzer, *Kit Carson Campaign*, pp. 230–34; Lynn R. Baily, *The Long Walk: A History of the Navajo Wars, 1846–68* (Los Angeles: Westernlore Press, 1964) pp. 177–99;

Gerald Thompson, *The Army and the Navajo: The Bosque Redondo Reservation Experiment, 1863–1868* (Tucson: University of Arizona Press, 1982) pp. 98–99; Lynn R. Bailey, *Bosque Redondo: The Navajo Internment and Fort Sumner, New Mexico, 1863–68* (Tucson: Westernlore Press, 1998).

283 Roberto Mario Salmon, "The Disease Complaint at Bosque Redondo (1864–1868)," *Indian Historian*, Vol. 9, No. 3 (Summer 1976) pp. 2–7. Also see Thompson, *The Army and the Navajo*, pp. 98–99; Bailey, *Bosque Redondo*, pp. 142–51.

284 The death rate at Dachau was 36 percent, at Buchenwald, 19 percent. See Michael Burleigh, *Ethics and Extermination: Reflections on the Nazi Genocide* (Cambridge, UK: Cambridge University Press, 1997) pp. 210–11.

285 See Noam Chomsky, *Rogue States: The Rule of Force in World Affairs* (Cambridge, MA: South End Press, 2000).

286 See note 173.

287 U.S. Army, *Laws of Land Warfare* (see note 213).

288 Commission of Inquiry, *Dellums Hearings*, p. 267.

289 Ibid., p. 41.

290 Ibid., p. 329.

291 Ibid., p. 295.

292 Ibid., pp. 60, 62.

293 Ibid., p. 107.

294 Ibid., pp. 295, 304 .

295 See generally Robert Sherrill, *Military Justice Is to Justice as Military Music Is to Music* (New York: Harper & Row, 1970).

296 Andrew Kopkind, "Doctor's Plot" and "The Trial of Captain Levy II," both in his *The Thirty Years' Wars: Dispatches and Diversions of a Radical Journalist, 1965–1994* (London: Verso, 1995) pp. 72–82, 104–11.

297 Kopkind, "Levy Trial II," p. 110.

298 Ibid., pp. 109–10.

299 Dennis Mora, David Samas, and James Johnson, "The Fort Hood Three: The Case of Three GIs Who Said 'No' to the War in Vietnam," in Judith Clavir Albert and Stewart Edward Albert, eds., *The Sixties Papers: Documents of a Rebellious Decade* (New York: Praeger, 1984) p. 303.

300 Kopkind, "Levy Trial II," p. 109.

301 See Sherrill, *Military Justice*.

302 Anthony B. Herbert with James T. Wooten, *Soldier* (New York: Holt, Rinehart and Winston, 1973).

303 Commission of Inquiry, *Dellums Hearings*, pp. 83–84.

304 Ibid., pp. 154–55.

305 Fred J. Cook, "Justice in Gainesville: The Real Conspiracy Exposed," *The Nation* (October 1, 1973) pp. 295–301; Sanford J. Ungar, *FBI* (Boston: Little, Brown, 1976) pp. 483–84, 504.

306 Athan Theoharis, *Spying on Americans: Political Surveillance from Hoover to the Huston Plan* (Philadelphia: Temple University Press, 1978) pp. 120–21, 124–25, 178–79.

307 Editors, "From the Citizens Commission to Investigate the FBI," *Win*, Vol. 8, Nos. 4–5 (March 1–15, 1972) p. 9. Also see my and Jim Vander Wall's *Agents of Repression: The FBI's Secret Wars Against the Black Panther Party and the American Indian Movement* (Boston: South End Press, 1988) pp. 395–96.

308 Officially, there were 65,643 desertions from the Army alone in 1970, a half-million from all services during the years 1967–72. Army intelligence estimated that some

sixty per week were actually "crossing over to the other side" in Vietnam by early 1971. See George Katsiaficas, *The Imagination of the New Left: A Global Analysis of 1968* (Boston: South End Press, 1987) p. 141; H. Bruce Franklin, M.I.A., *or, Mythmaking in America* (Chicago: Lawrence Hill, 1992) pp. 23–24.

309 Kopkind, "Levy Trial II," p. 109.

310 Commission of Inquiry, *Dellums Hearings*, pp. 245–46.

311 Ibid., p. 37.

312 Ibid.

313 Representative Parren J. Mitchell in Commission of Inquiry, *Dellums Hearings*, pp. 118–19.

314 On Soule's performance at Sand Creek, see note 58. On his murder, see Hoig, *Sand Creek Massacre*, p. 172.

315 For the full text, see Roberts and Guelff, *Laws of War*, pp. 377–85.

316 The issues also included cloud seeding, the saturation or "carpet" bombing of rural areas, and other such techniques employed by the U.S. See Weisberg, *Ecocide in Indochina*, esp. pp. 17–32, 49–63. Also see Thomas Whiteside, *The Withering Rain: America's Herbicidal Folly* (New York: Dutton, 1971); John Dux and P.J. Young, *Agent Orange: The Bitter Harvest* (Sydney: Hodder and Stoughton, 1980).

317 Full text of Additional Protocol I will be found in Roberts and Guelff, *Laws of War*, pp. 387–446; Additional Protocol II at pp. 447–64. The language quoted accrues from Additional Protocol I, Article 51, Section 5, Clauses a and b. It will be found at p. 416 of Roberts and Guelff.

318 Additional Protocol I, Article 54, Section 2. Roberts and Guelff, *Laws of War*, p. 417.

319 For the full text, see Roberts and Guelff, *Laws of War*, pp. 465–66.

320 Full text will be found in ibid., pp. 467–82.

321 Ibid., p. 475. On the weaponry, see note 145.

322 "This was particularly so during the periods of active engagement of US ground, sea and air forces from 1961–1973," with an emphasis on napalm and white phosphorous munitions. SIPRI, *Incendiary Weapons*, pp. 49–50.

323 Roberts and Guelff, *Laws of War*, p. 481.

324 *Field Manual 31–12: The Law of Land Warfare* (Washington, DC: U.S. Dept. of the Army, 1984).

325 Quoted in George Cheney, "'Talking War': Symbols, Strategies and Images," *New Studies on the Left*, Vol. 14, No. 3 (Winter 1990–91) pp. 8–16. On the concept involved, see Michael Walzer, *Just and Unjust Wars: A Moral Argument with Illustrations* (London: Allen Lane, 1978).

326 Kuwait was first demarcated for administrative separation from Iraq, then called Mesopotamia and under Ottoman rule, by the British, in their 1916 Sykes-Picot Treaty with France. Following the defeat of the Ottomans in World War I, the partition was "finalized" by the League of Nations, with boundaries being "set" in 1922. Iraq, however, never agreed to the arrangement and began pressing claims for a formal restoration of its territory, beginning with its independence from British "protectorate" status in 1932. See Joe Stork and Ann M. Lesch, "Why War?," in Peters, *Collateral Damage*, pp. 161–62.

327 Holly Sklar, "Brave New World Order," in Peters, *Collateral Damage*, p. 8.

328 Erika Munck, "The New Face of Techno-War," *The Nation* (May 6, 1991) pp. 583–85.

329 There were forty-nine such graves filled with what may in fact have been the "hundreds of thousands" of Iraqi casualties. The Pentagon has refused to meet its legal obligation to inform the Red Cross as to their location. Ramsey Clark, et al., *War*

Crimes: A Report on United States War Crimes Against Iraq (Washington, DC: Maisonneuve Press, 1992) pp. 3, 17, 89. On use of the term "Sand Niggers," see Sklar, "New World Order," p. 8.

330   "U.S. soldiers practiced for months techniques for burying alive Iraqi soldiers." Clark, *War Crimes*, p. 35. Patrick J. Sloyan, "U.S. Officers Say Iraqis Were Buried Alive," *San Francisco Chronicle* (September 12, 1991).

331   Sklar, "New World Order," p. 15.

332   The first Iraqi attempt was made on August 12, 1990, and continued into mid-February 1991. Clark, *War Crimes*, p. 13. Also see Michael Emry, "How the U.S. Avoided the Peace," *Village Voice* (March 5, 1991) pp. 22–27.

333   These were articulated in United Nations Resolution 660, which Iraq formally accepted on February 21, 1991. Clark, *War Crimes*, p. 91.

334   Ibid.

335   Rowan Scarborough, "Pool Report Aboard the USS Blue Ridge," *Washington Times* (February 27, 1991); William M. Arkin, Damian Durrant, and Marianne Cherni, *On Impact: Modern Warfare and the Environment—A Case Study of the Gulf War* (Washington, DC: Greenpeace, May 1991) pp. 105–15.

336   "Persons taking no active part in the hostilities, including soldiers who have laid down their arms, and those placed *hors de combat* [by] any cause, shall in all circumstances be treated humanely." Roberts and Guelff, *Laws of War*, pp. 195, 217, 273.

337   Quoted in Clark, *War Crimes*, p. 91.

338   Actually, the posture had been assumed rather earlier. Edward Cody, "U.S. Briefers Concede No Quarter," *Washington Post* (February 14, 1991).

339   Article 23(d) of the 1907 Hague Convention states that "it is especially forbidden . . . to declare that no quarter will be given." Roberts and Guelff, *Laws of War*, p. 52. On the 1864 Geneva Convention, see note 39.

340   Quoted in Arkin, Durrant, and Cherni, *On Impact*, p. 109.

341   Clark, *War Crimes*, pp. 50–51.

342   Ibid., pp. 51, 90–93.

343   Randall Richard of the *Providence Journal*, quoted in Clark, *War Crimes*, p. 91.

344   Clark, *War Crimes*, p. 92. Also see "Trapped in the Killing Ground at Mutlaa," *Manchester Guardian Weekly* (March 17, 1991); Michael Kelly, "Highway to Hell," *New Republic* (April 1991) pp. 11–14.

345   Clark, *War Crimes*, p. 17.

346   Ibid., p. 30; citing Patrick J. Sloyan, "Massive Battle After Cease Fire," *New York Newsday* (May 8, 1991). Also see Sloyan's "War's Fiercest Ground Battle Was After Cease Fire," *Oakland Tribune* (May 8, 1991).

347   Quoted in Patrick J. Sloyan, "Pullback a Bloody Mismatch: Route of Iraqis Became Savage 'Turkey Shoot,'" *New York Newsday* (March 31, 1991).

348   Arkin, Durrant, and Cherni, *On Impact*, p. 112.

349   Clark, *War Crimes*, p. 17.

350   Quoted in Sklar, "New World Order," pp. 11–12.

351   Interview, radio station WBAI, New York, May 1991.

352   Clark, *War Crimes*, pp. 14, 17–18, 20, 85; Arkin, Durrant, and Cherni, *On Impact*, p. 160, n. 377.

353   Upward of three thousand bombs, including several GBU-28 devices weighing 2.5 tons each, were dropped on Baghdad alone. See Clark, *War Crimes*, p. 17–18, 85; John D. Morrocco and David Fulghum, "USAF Developed a 4,700-lb. Bomb in

Crash Program to Attack Iraqi Leaders in Hardened Bunkers," *Aviation Week & Space Technology* (May 6, 1991) p. 85.

354 Clark, *War Crimes*, p. 18.

355 Ibid., pp. 45, 86. Also see Barbara Starr, "FAEs Used to Clear Mines," *Jane's Defense Weekly* (February 23, 1991) p. 247.

356 For the full text, see Roberts and Guelff, *Laws of War*, pp. 137–45.

357 Clark, *War Crimes*, pp. 47–48.

358 Ibid., p. 48.

359 Mark Fineman, "Smoke Blots Out Sun in Bomb-Blasted Basra," *Los Angeles Times* (February 5, 1991); Clark, *War Crimes*, pp. 16, 35, 87–88.

360 Clark, *War Crimes*, pp. 35, 15.

361 Eric Hooglund, "The Other Face of War," in Peters, *Collateral Damage*, p. 183. For an early but highly detailed itemization of the impact of the air war upon Iraqi non-combatants, see Middle East Watch, *Needless Deaths in the Gulf War: Civilian Casualties During the Air Campaign and Violations of the Laws of War* (New York: Human Rights Watch, 1991).

362 Barton Gellman, "Storm Damage in the Persian Gulf: U.S. strategy against Iraq went beyond strictly military targets," *Washington Post Weekly* (July 8–14, 1991) pp. 6–7.

363 Clark, *War Crimes*, pp. 22, 35.

364 Ibid., 53–54.

365 Ibid., p. 54; citing Bill Moyers, *PBS Special Report: After the War*, Spring 1991.

366 Brig. Gen. Jack Neil, quoted in the *Washington Post* (February 2, 1991).

367 Quoted in Mark Fineman, "Eyewitnesses Describe Allied Raids' Devastation," *San Francisco Chronicle* (February 5, 1991). Also see Barbara Nimri Aziz, "Targets—Not Victims," in Anthony Arnove, ed., *Iraq Under Siege: The Deadly Impact of Sanctions and War* (Cambridge, MA: South End Press, 2000) pp. 127–36.

368 Gellman, "Storm Damage"; Jack Calhoun, "UN: Iraq Bombed Back to Stone Age," *Manchester Guardian* (April 3, 1991); Patrick E. Tyler, "Disease Spirals in Iraq as Embargo Takes Its Toll," *New York Times* (June 24, 1991).

369 E.g., a secret 1990 Air Force study, predicting that damage to Iraq's sanitation and freshwater processing facilities would generate epidemics among the civilian population, was revealed in a CNN special report titled *The Unfinished War* on January 21, 2001.

370 Clark, *War Crimes*, p. 88.

371 Ibid., p. 56.

372 U.N. Resolutions 661, 666, cited in "Hunger, Disease Stalk a Ravaged Iraq," *Manchester Guardian*, March 13, 1991. Also see George Capaccio, "Sanctions: Killing a Country and a People," in Arnove, *Iraq Under Siege*, pp. 137–48.

373 As reported in the *Washington Post* on February 1, 1991, Gen. Colin Powell, Chairman of the Joint Chiefs of Staff, claimed the factory was a "biological weapons production facility," an idea refuted even by such U.S. allies as New Zealand.

374 Joyce Price, "Embargo and Air War Diminish Iraq's Food Supply to a Record Low," *Washington Times* (February 28, 1991); Clark, *War Crimes*, p. 56, 164–69; Phyllis Bennis and Denis J. Halliday (interviewed by David Barsamian), "Iraq: The Impact of Sanctions and U.S. Policy," in Arnove, *Iraq Under Siege*, pp. 35–46.

375 Quoted in Moyers, *After the War*; Clark, *War Crimes*, pp. 56–57.

376 *Harvard Study Team Report: Public Health in Iraq After the Gulf War*; cited in Sklar, "New World Order," p. 14; Clark, *War Crimes*, p. 56, 99–101. For the most current

information, see Dr. Peter L. Pellett, "Sanctions, Food, Nutrition, and Health in Iraq," in Arnove, *Iraq Under Siege*, pp. 151–68.

377 William Blum, *Rogue State: A Guide to the World's Only Superpower* (Monroe, ME: Common Courage Press, 2000) p. 5. Also see Steven Lee Myers, "In Intense but Little-Noticed Fight, Allies Have Bombed Iraq All Year," *New York Times* (August 13, 1999).

378 Brig. Gen. George Looney III, quoted in the *Washington Post* (August 30, 1999).

379 Ibid.

380 Denis J. Halliday, "Introduction," in Phyllis Bennis, *Calling the Shots: How the U.S. Dominates Today's UN* (New York: Olive Branch Press, 2000) p. xiv. Halliday also appeared in CNN's *Unfinished War*. On the Clausewitz dictum, see note 38.

381 May 12, 1996. Quoted in Blum, *Rogue State*, pp. 5–6.

382 An excellent overview of Powell's pedigree as a war criminal will be found in ibid., p. 69.

383 Quoted in the *New York Times* on March 23, 1991.

384 "In the headquarters staff of the American Division in Chu Lai . . . a reassuring memorandum was prepared for the Adjutant General [investigating the massacres] by Major Colin Luther Powell, the assistant chief of staff (operations). . . . Showing all the signs of a soldier who had triumphed in the battle of military paperwork, Powell wrote what his superiors clearly wanted to hear. He described the Vietnamese people as being truly appreciative [of] the direct interest the division's soldiers took in their welfare and improvement of . . . standard of living. Maj. Powell . . . concluded even more complacently: 'Although there may be isolated cases of mistreatment of civilians and POWs this by no means reflects the general attitude throughout the division. In direct refutation of [allegations of the division's war crimes at My Lai and elsewhere] is the fact that relations between Americal soldiers and the Vietnamese people are excellent.'" Michael Bilton and Kevin Sim, *Four Hours at My Lai* (New York: Viking Press, 1992) p. 213.

385 The shorter sentences resulted from negotiated settlements in which defendants pled guilty to the charge of "missing a troop movement." Tod Ensign, "Military Resisters during Operation Desert Shield/Storm," in Peters, *Collateral Damage*, p. 290. Also see William Kunstler, "Harsh Government Prosecution of War Resisters," in Clark, *War Crimes*, pp. 201–3.

386 Ensign, "Military Resisters," pp. 294, 291.

387 Ibid., pp. 293–94.

388 Quoted in ibid., p. 292.

389 Ibid.

390 Ibid., p. 293.

391 Ibid., pp. 291–94.

392 Quoted in Cheney, "'Talking War,'" p. 19. On the incubator fable, see Dana Priest, "Kuwait Baby-Killing Report Disputed," *Washington Post* (February 7, 1992).

393 Bush of course served as vice president in the Reagan administration, which, when the ICJ ruled in 1985 that the U.S. had no legal right to mine Nicaraguan harbors as a "peacetime" policy expedient, replied that the ICJ held no authority to decide the matter. See Abraham Sofaer, "The United States and the World Court," *Current Policy*, No. 769 (December 4, 1985) and "U.S. Terminates Acceptance of ICJ Compulsory Jurisdiction," *Department of State Bulletin*, No. 86 (January 1986).

394 Quoted in *Newsweek* on August 15, 1988.

395 In May 1999, Secretary of State Madeleine Albright announced that the U.S. was "the major provider of funds for the Tribunal and [had] pledged even more money to it." The balance, according to NATO spokesperson Jamie Shae, was contributed by U.S. partners in the North Atlantic Treaty Alliance. See Blum, *Rogue State*, pp. 74–75.

396 Noam Chomsky, "U.S. Iraq Policy: Motives and Consequences," in Arnove, *Iraq Under Siege*, pp. 47–56. Also see Chomsky, *Rogue States*, pp. 37–38.

397 See, e.g., Francis A. Boyle, *The Bosnian People Charge Genocide: Proceedings of the International Court of Justice Concerning Bosnia vs. Serbia on the Prevention and Punishment of the Crime of Genocide* (Amherst, MA: Aletheia Press, 1996).

398 In effect, creation of the judicial venue was implied in the Affirmation of Nuremberg Principles signed by the U.S. in 1946. See note 33.

399 Blum, *Rogue State*, p. 77. Six other countries—Libya, Iraq, Sudan, China, Qatar, and Israel—also refused to sign on. Bennis, *Calling the Shots*, p. 277.

400 Blum, *Rogue State*, p. 77; Bennis, *Calling the Shots*, p. 276. Statements of Albright and others in the *New York Times* (December 2, 1998; January 3, 2000). On the dismissal of such arguments at Nuremberg, see note 31.

401 Chomsky, "East Timor Retrospective," in *Rogue States*, pp. 51–61. On Kurdistan, see, e.g., A.R. Ghassemlou, et al., *People Without a Country: The Kurds and Kurdistan* (London: Zed Press, 1980); Chomsky, *Rogue States*, pp. 41–42, 63–64.

402 Blum, *Rogue State*, p. 101; Bennis, *Calling the Shots*, p. 280.

403 Bennis, *Calling the Shots*, pp. 279–80.

404 Blum, *Rogue State*, p. 187. For the text of the Declaration, see Ian Brownlie, ed., *Basic Documents on Human Rights* (Oxford, UK: Clarendon Press, [3rd ed.] 1992) pp. 28–30.

405 Blum, *Rogue State*, pp. 189, 192–93.

406 Ibid., p. 194. For text, see Brownlie, *Basic Documents*, pp. 148–61.

407 Bennis, *Calling the Shots*, pp. 280–81.

408 A detailed itemization for the years 1978–86 will be found in Blum, *Rogue State*, pp. 185–97.

409 See Lawrence J. LeBlanc, *The United States and the Genocide Convention* (Durham, NC: Duke University Press, 1991). The text of the U.S. "Sovereignty Package" appears as Appendix C, pp. 253–54.

410 A subplot has been to use Western notions of individual rights as a lever to pry apart the group cohesion evident in nonwestern, collectivist cultural settings, especially those of indigenous peoples. See, e.g., Gustavo Esteva and Madhu Suri Prakash, *Grassroots Postmodernism: Remaking the Soil of Cultures* (London: Zed Books, 1998) pp. 110–46.

411 James Hooper, "Kosovo: America's Balkan Problem," *Current History*, Vol. 98, No. 627 (April 1999) pp. 159–64; Chomsky, "Crisis in the Balkans," in *Rogue States*, pp. 34–50.

412 For analysis of this packaging and its implications, see Noam Chomsky, *The New Military Humanism: Lessons from Kosovo* (Monroe, ME: Common Courage Press, 1999).

413 Serbia's conduct in Kosovo was indeed criminal, but by no means as extreme as the "ethnic cleansing" operations it carried out in Bosnia during the early '90s. The U.S. stood aside while the latter occurred. See Marshall Harris, "Introduction," in Boyle, *Bosnian Genocide*, pp. xi–xix; David Rieff, *Slaughterhouse: Bosnia and the Failure of the West* (New York: Simon and Schuster, 1995); Michel Feher, *Powerless by Design: The Age of the International Community* (Durham, NC: Duke University Press, 2000) esp. pp. 2–4, 70–72, 78–82, 84–92.

414 Separate actions were filed by groups of Canadian, British, and Greek international legal experts, as well as the American Association of Jurists. Blum, *Rogue State*, p. 73.

415 Ibid.

416 Quoted in ibid., pp. 75–76.

417 Quoted/paraphrased in the *Washington Post* (September 20, 1999).

418 Prof. Michael Mandel, University of Toronto Law School, September 21, 1999.

419 *The Observer* (December 26, 1999); *New York Times* (December 30, 1999); *Washington Times* (December 31, 1999).

420 Feher, *Powerless by Design*, pp. 66–67, 71–74. Also see Alaine Destexhe, *Rwanda and Genocide in the Twentieth Century* (New York: New York University Press, 1995); Gérard Prunier, *The Rwanda Crisis: History of a Genocide* (New York: Columbia University Press, 1995).

421 Feher, *Powerless by Design*, p. 86.

422 John Vincour, "Going It Alone: U.S. Upsets France So Paris Begins a Campaign to Strengthen Multilateral Institutions," *International Herald Tribune* (February 3, 1999).

423 Ibid.

424 September 1, 1997. Also see William Drozdiak, "Even Allies Resent U.S. Dominance: America Accused of Bullying World," *Washington Post* (November 4, 1997).

425 Joyce Kolko, *Restructuring the World Economy* (New York: Pantheon, 1988); Richard Barnet and John Cavanaugh, *Global Dreams: Imperial Corporations and the New World Order* (New York: Simon and Schuster, 1994); Noam Chomsky, *World Orders, Old and New* (New York: Columbia University Press, 1996).

426 Richard M. Nixon, *Seize the Moment: America's Challenge in a One-Superpower World* (New York: Simon and Schuster, 1992); Jack Nelson-Pallmeyer, *Brave New World Order* (Maryknoll, NY: Orbis Books, 1992); Michael Parenti, *Blackshirts and Reds: Rational Fascism and the Overthrow of Communism* (San Francisco: City Lights, 1997).

427 Valdas Anelauskas, *Discovering America as It Is* (Atlanta: Clarity Press, 1999) pp. 409–66.

428 Quoted in Chomsky, "U.S. Iraq Policy," p. 54. Albright repeated precisely the same formulation as recently as January 2, 2000, on NBC's *Meet the Press*.

429 George Bush, quoted in Cheney, "'Talking War,'" p. 19.

430 See note 134.

431 Bush first employed the term on January 29, 1991. Quoted in Chomsky, *World Orders*, p. 7.

432 This has been true domestically, as well as internationally. For analyses extending far beyond anything that might be offered herein, see Jerry Fresia, *Toward an American Revolution: Exposing the Constitution and Other Illusions* (Boston: South End Press, 1988), A. Leon Higgenbotham Jr., *Shades of Freedom: Racial Politics and the Presumptions of the American Legal Process* (New York: Oxford University Press, 1996), and my own "'The Law Stood Squarely on Its Head': U.S. Doctrine, Indigenous Self-Determination, and the Question of World Order," in *Acts of Rebellion: The Ward Churchill Reader* (New York: Routledge, 2003) pp. 3–22, 309–24.

433 Nebrija's 1492 observation concerned the utility of language in consolidating colonial enterprises. Quoted in Patricia Seed, *Ceremonies of Possession in Europe's Conquest of the New World, 1492–1640* (Cambridge, UK: Cambridge University Press, 1995) p. 8.

434 This is not to deny the importance of propaganda in shaping either the form or extent of apparent consensus. For analysis, see Jacques Ellul, *Propaganda: The Formation of Men's Attitudes* (New York: Vintage, 1973); Edward S. Herman and Noam Chomsky, *Manufacturing Consent: The Political Economy of the News Media* (New York: Pantheon, 1988); Noam Chomsky, *Necessary Illusions: Thought Control in Democratic Societies* (Boston: South End Press, 1989); Michael Parenti, *Inventing Reality: The Politics of the News Media* (New York: St. Martin's Press, 1993).

435 "The idea of 'altruism' has been a recurrent feature of America's love affair with itself." Blum, *Rogue State*, p. 12.

436 See R.D. Laing, *The Politics of Experience* (New York: Ballantine, 1967) esp. pp. 28–30. For broader analysis, see Wilhelm Reich, *The Mass Psychology of Fascism* (New York: Farrar, Straus & Giroux, 1970)

437 Joel Kovel, *White Racism: A Psychohistory* (New York: Columbia University Press, [2nd ed.] 1984); Michael Omi and Howard Winant, *Racial Formation in the United States from the 1960s to the 1990s* (New York: Routledge, 1994).

438 Slotkin, *Gunfighter Nation*. Also see his *Regeneration Through Violence: The Mythology of the American Frontier, 1600–1860* (Norman: University of Oklahoma Press, [2nd ed.] 2000).

439 Martin Jay Lifton and Eric Markusen, *The Genocidal Mentality: Nazi Holocaust and Nuclear Threat* (New York: Basic Books, 1988).

440 For analogs, see Christopher R. Browning, *Ordinary Men: Police Battalion 101 and the Final Solution in Poland* (New York: HarperCollins, 1992) and Daniel Jonah Goldhagen, *Hitler's Willing Executioners: Ordinary Germans and the Final Solution* (New York: Alfred A. Knopf, 1996). Among the more penetrating insights are those offered by Hannah Arendt in her oft-reviled *Eichmann in Jerusalem: A Report on the Banality of Evil* (New York: Penguin, 1964).

441 An excellent overview is presented in Stanley Cohen's *States of Denial: Knowing About Atrocities and Suffering* (Cambridge, UK: Polity Press, 2001). For more clinical appreciations of the phenomenon, see Donald A. Nathanson, "Denial, Projection, and the Empathic Wall," and Léon Wurmser, "Cultural Paradigms of Denial," both in E.L. Edelstein, Donald L. Nathanson, and Andrew M. Stone, eds., *Denial: A Clarification of Concepts and Research* (New York: Plenum, 1989) pp. 37–60, 277–86.

442 The word "radical" is used here, not in the colloquial sense of meaning "extreme"— although extreme measures may well under the circumstances be both warranted and necessary—but in accordance with its actual definition: "at the root or most elemental level."

443 For the theoretically inclined, this is a specifically dialectical reading of the possibilities. For explication, see, e.g., Michael Albert and Robin Hahnel, *Unorthodox Marxism: An Essay on Capitalism, Socialism and Revolution* (Boston: South End Press, 1978) pp. 14–16, 90–94.

444 A good forum on this point will be found in Michael Albert et al., *Liberating Theory* (Boston: South End Press, 1986) esp. pp. 127–45.

445 See generally David S. Caudill and Steven Jay Gold, eds., *Radical Philosophy of Law: Contemporary Challenges to Mainstream Legal Theory and Practice* (Atlantic Highlands, NJ: Humanities Press, 1995).

446 Bennis, *Calling the Shots*, pp. 274–79.

447 Francis Anthony Boyle, *Foundations of World Order: The Legalist Approach to International Relations, 1898–1922* (Durham, NC: Duke University Press, 1999) pp. 22–23.

448 Karl Jaspers, "The Significance of the Nuremberg Trials for Germany and the World," *Notre Dame Law Review* 22, no. 2 (January 1947): 150–60.

449 Jean-Paul Sartre, "Inaugural Statement," in Duffett, *Crimes of Silence*, esp. pp. 41–44; Richard Falk, *Human Rights and State Sovereignty* (New York: Holmes & Meier, 1981) esp. the chapter titled "Keeping Nuremberg Alive," pp. 195–201.

450 See generally Francis M. Wilhoit, *The Politics of Massive Resistance* (New York: Braziller, 1973).

451 Rachel L. Jones, "Minorities in the Military," in Peters, *Collateral Damage*, pp. 237–53.

452   Frances Fox Piven and Richard Cloward, *The New Class War: Reagan's Attack on the Welfare State and Its Consequences* (New York: Pantheon, 1988); Martin Carnoy, *Faded Dreams: The Politics and Economics of Race in America* (Cambridge, UK: Cambridge University Press, 1994); Ruth Sidel, *Keeping Women and Children Last: America's War on the Poor* (New York: Penguin, 1996); Irene Guggenmoos-Holzmann, *Quality of Life and Health* (Boston: Wiley-Blackwell, 1995); Noam Chomsky, *Profit Over People: Neoliberalism and Global Order* (New York: Seven Stories Press, 1999).

453   Barry Bluestone and Bennett Harrison, *The Deindustrialization of America: Plant Closings, Community Abandonment, and the Dismantling of Basic Industry* (New York: Basic Books, 1982); Bennett Harrison and Barry Bluestone, *The Great U-Turn: Corporate Restructuring and the Polarization of America* (New York: Basic Books, 1988); Sakia Sassen, *Mobility of Labor and Capital* (Cambridge, UK: Cambridge University Press, 1997).

454   Lawrence Mishel, Jared Bernstein, and John Schmitt, *The State of Working America, 1998–1999* (Ithaca, NY: Cornell University Press, 1999); Richard W. Judy and Carol D'Amico, *Workforce 2020: Work and Workers in the Twenty-First Century* (Indianapolis: Hudson Institute, 1997); William Julius Wilson, *When Work Disappears: The World of the New Urban Poor* (New York: Vintage, 1997).

455   As examples, see Howard I. Rosenberg, *Atomic Soldiers: American Victims of Nuclear Experiments* (Boston: Beacon, 1980); Fred Wilcox, *Waiting for an Army to Die: The Tragedy of Agent Orange* (New York: Vintage, 1983); Depleted Uranium Citizens' Network, *Radioactive Battlefields of the 1990s: The United States Army's Use of Depleted Uranium and Its Consequences for Human Health and the Environment* (Lewiston, ME: Military Toxics Project, 1996).

456   Chris Hellman, "Pentagon May Seek Substantial Increase in Fiscal Year 2000 Top-line," *Weekly Defense Monitor* (December 10, 1998); "Last of the Big Spenders: U.S. Military Budget Still the World's Largest, and Growing," *Center for Defense Information Fact Sheet* (February 1, 1999); "Administration Seeks More Money for the Pentagon," *Weekly Defense Monitor* (February 4, 1999).

457   Reported by Pacifica Network News (February 3, 2001). For background, see Anelauskas, *America as It Is*, pp. 418–20.

458   Peter B. Kraska and Victor E. Kappler, "Militarizing American Police: The Rise and Normalization of Paramilitary Units," *Social Problems*, Vol. 44, No. 1 (February 1997) pp. 1–18; Christian Parenti, *Lockdown America: Police and Prisons in the Age of Crisis* (London: Verso, 1999) pp. 139–60.

459   See, e.g., Sabina Virgo, "The Criminalization of Poverty," in Elihu Rosenblatt, *Criminal Injustice: Confronting the Prison Crisis* (Boston: South End Press, 1996) pp. 47–60.

460   Marc Mauer, "Americans Behind Bars: A Comparison of International Rates of Incarceration," in Ward Churchill and J.J. Vander Wall, eds., *Cages of Steel: The Politics of Imprisonment in the United States* (Washington, DC: Maisonneuve Press, 1992) pp. 22–37.

461   Katherine Beckett, *Making Crime Pay: Law and Order in Contemporary American Politics* (New York: Oxford University Press, 1997); Parenti, *Lockdown America*, pp. 211–42.

462   See, e.g., the section titled "Workin' for the Man: Prison Labor in the U.S.A.," in Daniel Burton-Rose, Dan Pens, and Paul Wright, eds., *The Celling of America: An Inside Look at the U.S. Prison Industry* (Monroe, ME: Common Courage Press, 1998) pp. 102–31.

463   Malcolm X as told to Alex Haley, *The Autobiography of Malcolm X* (New York: Ballantine Books, [2nd ed.] 1973) p. 329.

464   Donald L. Barlett and James B. Steele, *America: What Went Wrong?* (New York: Simon and Schuster, 1992); Michael Perelman, *The Pathology of the U.S. Economy: The Costs of a Low-Wage System* (New York: Macmillan, 1993).

465   Erosion of public support for nazism did not set in until German troop losses in the USSR rose to catastrophic levels during the winter of 1941–42. This decline in the régime's popularity became more and more pronounced over the next year, as defeats piled up, the Allied air war commenced in earnest, and the German people began to suffer the fate they'd celebrated when their military had visited it upon others. See Michael Burleigh, *The Third Reich: A New History* (New York: Hill and Wang, 2000) pp. 758–60.

466   Zinn, *People's History*, 368–97.

467   See, e.g., Ken Hurwitz, *Marching Nowhere* (New York: W.W. Norton, 1971); David Zane Mairowitz, *The Radical Soap Opera: Roots of Failure in the American Left* (New York: Discus Books, 1974).

468   For explication, see Robert F. Barsky, *Noam Chomsky: A Life of Dissent* (Cambridge, MA: MIT Press, 1998). Also see Chomsky's own *Radical Priorities*, edited by C.P. Otero (Montréal: Black Rose Books, 1981) esp. pp. 137–66; and his *Powers and Prospects: Reflections on Human Nature and the Social Order* (Boston: South End Press, 1996), as well as titles already cited.

469   On the concept of a "master" or "grand" narrative, see Jean-François Lyotard, *The Postmodern Condition: A Report on Knowledge* (Minneapolis: University of Minnesota Press, 1984) pp. xxi–xix, 31–40. As nearly as I can tell, although Leon Festinger used/developed the term somewhat earlier, the idea of "cognitive dissonance" was introduced to critical theory by C. Wright Mills, in his *The Sociological Imagination* (London: Oxford University Press, 1959). See Stephan Schmidt, "C. Wright Mills Revisited—A Rejoinder," *Scandinavian Political Studies*, Bind 12 (New Series) 3 (1989), side 270.

470   This is as true of radical alternatives to traditional psychotherapy as it is for orthodoxy itself. The one exception may be found in B.F. Skinner's behavior modification techniques. See generally Jerome Angel and the Radical Therapist Collective, *The Radical Therapist: Therapy Means Change, Not Adjustment* (New York: Ballantine, 1971). For a devastating critique of Skinner, see Noam Chomsky's "Psychology and Ideology," in *For Reasons of State*, pp. 318–65.

471   See Walter L. Adamson, *Hegemony and Revolution: A Study of Antonio Gramsci's Political and Cultural Theory* (Berkeley: University of California Press, 1980) pp. 170–79, 241–45.

472   On statist strategies of co-optation, see Katsiaficas, *New Left*, pp. 156–57, 161–64, 186–88, 195–97, 209–11.

473   Goldstein, Marshall, and Schwartz, *My Lai Massacre*, pp. 11–14.

474   Although different in configuration, the dimension of the problem is potentially analogous to that unsuccessfully confronted by the military hierarchy toward the end of the war in Indochina, when enlisted personnel began to ignore orders en masse. See, e.g., Cincinnatus, *Self-Destruction: The Disintegration and Decay of the United States Army during the Vietnam Era* (New York: W.W. Norton, 1981).

475   As of January 2001, the United States was one of only two countries—the other was Somalia—which had refused to ratify the 1994 Convention on the Rights of the Child. One of the main sticking points was an optional protocol prohibiting military service by youngsters under the age of 18. See Bennis, *Calling the Shots*, pp. 280–81.

476   A decade ago, the respected United Nations nongovernmental consultative organization Human Rights Watch conducted a survey of twenty-seven representative

U.S. prisons and documented "numerous human rights abuses and frequent violations of the [1977] U.N. Standard Minimum Rules for the Treatment of Prisoners." Human Rights Watch, *Prison Conditions in the United States* (New York: Human Rights Watch, 1991) p. 4. The Rules are an offshoot of the International Convention Against Torture and Other Forms of Cruel, Inhuman or Degrading Treatment or Punishment (1984). For text, see Weston, Falk, and D'Amato, *Basic Documents*, pp. 463–71.

477 The United Nations nongovernmental consultative organization Amnesty International recently released a report documenting chronic violation of international human rights protections by U.S. police departments; Kwame Dixon and Patricia E. Allard, *Police Brutality and International Human Rights in the United States: The Report on Hearings Held in Los Angeles, California, Chicago, Illinois, and Pittsburgh, Pennsylvania, Fall 1999* (New York: Amnesty International USA, February 2000) pp. 39–42. For further background, see Parenti, *Lockdown America*, pp. 69–139; Paul Chevigny, *The Edge of the Knife: Police Violence in the Americas* (New York: W.W. Norton, 1995) pp. 31–144; Jill Nelson, ed., *Police Brutality: An Anthology* (New York: W.W. Norton, 2000).

478 Like the military's, BoP regulations and violations thereof are not typically subject to normal judicial oversight. See, e.g., Mary K. O'Melveny, "Lexington Prison High Security Unit: U.S. Political Prison," in Rosenblatt, *Criminal Injustice*, pp. 322–33.

479 Efforts to create oversight boards to extend direct community control over the police have a long standing in the U.S., and were included as a recommendation by Amnesty International in its 2000 report. Dixon and Allard, *Police Brutality*, p. 44. For background, see Tony Platt, et al., *The Iron Fist and the Velvet Glove: An Analysis of the U.S. Police* (San Francisco: Crime and Social Justice Associates, [3rd ed.] 1982) pp. 189–90, 220–21.

480 Serious challenges have been mounted in this connection, most notably during the so-called "Sioux Sovereignty Hearing" of 1974. See John William Sayer, *Ghost Dancing the Law: The Wounded Knee Trials* (Cambridge, MA: Harvard University Press, 1997) pp. 204–5. For excerpted testimonies, see Roxanne Dunbar-Ortiz, ed., *The Great Sioux Nation: Sitting in Judgement on America* (New York/San Francisco: International Indian Treaty Council/Moon Books, 1977).

481 See the essay titled "I Am Indigenist: Notes on the Ideology of the Fourth World" in my *Struggle for the Land: Native North American Resistance to Genocide, Ecocide and Colonization* (San Francisco: City Lights, [2nd ed.] 2002) pp. 367–402.

482 Reference is made here to the concepts articulated by Hakim Bey in his *T.A.Z.: The Temporary Autonomous Zone* (Brooklyn: Autonomedia, 1991) and in Kirkpatrick Sale's *Human Scale* (New York: Coward, McCann & Geoghegan, 1980).

483 Those who would receive this formulation as evidence of a "knee-jerk radical" outlook would do well to recall that by 1961 no less conservative a figure than outgoing President—and former General of the Army—Dwight David Eisenhower was warning of the implications embodied in the "military-industrial complex" that had long since become a central feature of U.S. political and economic life. See Eisenhower's "Farewell Address," in *Annals of America, Vol. 18: 1961–1968, The Burdens of the World* (Chicago: Encyclopedia Britannica, 1968) pp. 1–5. For contemporaneous background, see C. Wright Mills, *The Causes of World War III* (New York: Simon and Schuster, 1958). For a more recent analysis, see Leah Renae Kelly, "The More Things Change, the More They Stay the Same: NSC 68, Reaganomics, and the End of the Cold War," in her *In My Own Voice: Essays on the Sociopolitical Context of Art and Cinema* (Winnipeg: Arbeiter Ring, 2001) pp. 104–7.

484 For elaboration, see Richard Falk's "Anarchism and World Order," in his *The End of World Order: Essays on Normative International Relations* (New York: Holmes & Meier, 1983) pp. 277–98. Also see the section titled "The 'Rule of Law' Versus 'Rule by Law'" in Terrance Edward Paupp, *Achieving Inclusionary Governance: Advancing Peace and Development in First and Third World Nations* (Ardsley, NY: Transnational, 2000) pp. 232–40.

485 There is absolutely no scientific basis upon which to conclude that "second-hand tobacco smoke" is a "public health hazard." For data and policy analysis, see Jacob Sullum, *For Your Own Good: The Anti-Smoking Crusade and the Tyranny of Public Health* (New York: Free Press, 1998). The most current technical summaries concerning the "problem" will be found in Ronald R. Watson and Mark Witten, eds., *Environmental Tobacco Smoke* (Boca Raton, FL: CRC Press, 2001). This is a classic instance of the personal preferences of a self-indulgently privileged sector segment being imposed under glaringly false premises upon the public as a whole, the poor and otherwise marginalized in particular.

486 Much as the drive to create "smoke-free environments" was pursued under the prevarication of "public health," the campaign to proliferate speed bumps in places like Boulder has been waged under the spurious premise that "public safety" would be increased thereby. In actuality, all that has been accomplished—aside from enhancing the already extravagant "quality of life" enjoyed by those demanding that the public wealth be expended in this fashion—is that the transit of ambulances and fire trucks has been noticeably slowed, a result which demonstrably *diminishes* public safety.

487 The "cruise missile" description was used by Defense Secretary Donald Rumsfeld during a press conference carried by CNN on September 13, 2001.

488 The story of the fourth airliner's demise is quite murky. It began with word that one passenger had managed to secretly make telephone contact with her husband from a lavatory, and that this communication was abruptly terminated by a "loud noise." Shortly thereafter, there were reports the plane had crashed. A while after that, it emerged that numerous others had supposedly contacted their loved ones by cell-phone while seated in the cabin, in full view of the hijackers. With that, all mention of the loud noise which marked the end of the first caller's conversation disappeared from the airwaves, as did reference to the caller herself. She was replaced by a young man who was said to have given his family the details of how he and several others were planning to assault their captors, recovering control of the aircraft. From there, it was an easy step to the final version, in which it is claimed that the passengers themselves dived the plane into an open field, preventing its use as a weapon and instantly converting themselves from victims into "heroes." Rousing as the latter portrayal of events may be, it cannot be accepted until the loud noise—an auditory signature consistent with the impact of an air-to-air missile—reported in the first version is explained rather than simply expunged from the narrative.

489 Apart from the 19 hijackers, there were 2,606 fatalities at the WTC, 125 at the Pentagon, and 246 on the four airliners. All told, this comes to well under half the tally of "7,000 innocent Americans" announced by Sen. Orrin Hatch on December 11, 2001, during an appearance of CNN's *Larry King Live*.

490 Those killed on the upper floors of the WTC included hundreds of the most highly skilled technicians of international finance available in the U.S. (Cantor Fitzgerald alone lost roughly 700 of 1,000 employees); Eric Roston, "A CEO's Story: All His Office Mates Gone," *Time* (September 24, 2001) p. 82. The reacquisition of such

expertise takes a considerable period of time. A clandestine intelligence-gathering facility in the WTC was also obliterated. See James Risen, "Secret C.I.A. Site in New York Was Destroyed on September 11: Attack Seriously Disrupted Spying Operations," *New York Times* (November 4, 2001).

491 The estimate is conservative. In addition to the billions in material damage resulting from the attacks, and the further billions required to clear the rubble, the already ailing air transport and related industries took a serious nosedive in the aftermath, and the stock market has yet to rebound from a period of decline first strongly manifested in the wake of September 11. For a ridiculously optimistic—or, more accurately, propagandistic—"forecast" of a rapid recovery, see Bernard Baumohl, Maggie Sieger and Adam Zagorin, "The Economy: Up from the Ashes," in the special issue of *Time* dubbed "America digs out—and digs in" (September 24, 2001) pp. 80–81.

492 People from 86 different countries, including 78 British nationals, are reported to have been killed according to Attorney General John Ashcroft during a press briefing carried by CNBC on November 29, 2001.

493 "American warplanes have methodically and with virtually no public discussion been attacking Iraq. . . . In the last eight months, American and British pilots have fired more than 1,100 missiles against 359 targets in Iraq. . . . This is triple the number of targets attacked in four furious days of strikes in December [1998]"; Myers, "In Intense but Little-Noticed Fight." "After eight years of enforcing a 'no-fly zone' in northern [and southern] Iraq, few targets remain . . . 'We're down to the last outhouse,'" one Pentagon spokesperson announced; Ronald G. Shafer, "Washington Wire," *Wall Street Journal* (October 22, 1999). A list of operations is provided in Gore Vidal's *Perpetual War for Perpetual Peace: How We Got to Be So Hated* (New York: Thunder's Mouth Press/Nation Books, 2002) 24–25. Overall, see Naseer Aruri, "America's War Against Iraq: 1990–1999," in Arnove, *Iraq Under Siege*, 23–33.

494 Such Bushian rhetoric was quickly adopted and refined by pundits like Ronald Steel, who opined in the *New York Times* on September 14, 2001, that, "They hate us because we champion a 'new world order' of capitalism, secularism and democracy that should be the norm everywhere." Meanwhile, those, like aesthetician Susan Sontag and ABC talk show host Bill Maher, who took even mild exception to the prevailing presidential idiocies were publicly savaged on "moral" grounds in the *Washington Post* and elsewhere. White House press secretary Ari Fleischer thereupon explained that those raising their voices in the "land of the free" would henceforth do well to "watch what they say." Celestine Bohlen, "In New War on Terrorism, Words Are Weapons, Too," *New York Times* (September 29, 2001).

495 For background, see John K. Cooley, *Unholy Wars: Afghanistan, America and International Terrorism* (London: Pluto Press, [2nd ed.] 2000).

496 A broad sample of the State Department material appears in Yonah Alexander and Michael S. Swetnam, *Usama bin-Laden's al-Qaida: Profile of a Terrorist Network* (Ardsley, NY: Transnational, 2001).

497 The "real assault on America would begin in earnest only in the summer of 1998, in East Africa. On the morning of August 7, 1998, truck bombs devastated the areas around the American embassies in Nairobi, Kenya, and Dar es Salaam, Tanzania. The Nairobi bomb killed 247 people, including 12 Americans in a portion of the embassy which collapsed, and wounded thousands." Cooley, *Unholy Wars*, p. 220. "Al-Qaida is also suspected of mounting the October 12, 2000, suicide bombing of

the USS *Cole*, killing 17 and wounding 39 American sailors in Aden harbor, Yemen." Alexander and Swetnam, *al-Qaida*, p. viii.

498 Reported in the *Wall Street Journal* on October 5, 2001.

499 By August 1999, UNICEF had completed an exhaustive study in which the child death toll attributable to sanctions was once again confirmed. Milan Rai, *War Plan Iraq: Ten Reasons Against War on Iraq* (London: Verso, 2002) p. 176. Also see George Capaccio, "Sanctions: Killing a Country and a People," in Arnove, *Iraq Under Siege*, pp. 137–48.

500 The "U.S. is a prime supporter of the Israeli occupation of Palestinian territory, now in its thirty-fifth year. It's been harsh and brutal from the beginning, extremely repressive. Most of this hasn't been discussed here, and the U.S. role has been virtually suppressed. . . . Even simple facts are not reported. For example, as soon as the current fighting began last September 30, Israel immediately, the next day, began using U.S. helicopters (they can't produce helicopters) to attack civilian targets. In the next couple of days they killed several dozen people in apartment complexes and elsewhere. The fighting was all in Palestinian territories and there was no Palestinian fire. . . . Meanwhile the settlement policies, which have taken over substantial parts of the territories and are designed to make it virtually impossible for an independent [Palestinian] state to develop, are supported by the U.S. The U.S. provides the funding, the diplomatic support. It's the only country that's blocked the overwhelming international consensus on condemning all this under the Geneva Convention." Noam Chomsky, interviewed by David Barsamian, "The United States is a Leading Terrorist State," *Monthly Review*, Vol. 53, No. 6 (November 2001) p. 13. For in-depth background, see Noam Chomsky, *The Fateful Triangle: The United States, Israel and the Palestinians* (Boston: South End Press, 1983); Avi Shlaim, *The Iron Wall: Israel and the Arab World* (New York: W.W. Norton, 2000); Nur Masalha, *Imperial Israel and the Palestinians* (London: Pluto Press, 2000); Naseer Aruri, ed., *Palestinian Refugees: The Right of Return* (London: Pluto Press, 2001).

501 For a full rendering of bin-Laden's/al-Qaida's position in this regard, see Alexander and Swetnam, *al-Qaida*, Appendices 1A and 1B—"Declaration of War against the Americans Occupying the Land of the Two Holy Places: A Message from Usama bin Muhammad bin Laden unto his Muslim Brethren all over the world generally, and in the Arab Peninsula specifically" (September 4, 1996) and "Jihad Against Jews and Crusaders: World Islamic Front Statement" (February 23, 1998).

502 The Iranian airliner had only just taken off and was well within a commercial air lane. According to U.S. Navy Commander David Carlson, it was shot down out of "a need to prove the viability of Aigis," the ship's state-of-the-art air defense system; quoted in Noam Chomsky, *Deterring Democracy* (New York: Hill and Wang, 1992) p. 379. In 1989, and again in 1990, the Iranians attempted to bring an action before the International Court of Justice; "Iran submits complaint over U.S. downing of airliner in '88," *Chicago Tribune* (July 25, 1990). Such recourse to legality was useless, however, since the U.S. had repudiated ICJ jurisdiction over its actions four years earlier (see note 393). Even among "progressives," there has been almost no serious expression of outrage over this blatant U.S. atrocity, a circumstance usefully compared to the outpouring of horror concerning the 1983 Soviet shoot-down of Korean Airlines Flight 007—on which there were relatively few Americans aboard, and only after the plane had deeply penetrated Soviet air space—or the Libyans' alleged 1988 bombing of Pan Am Flight 103 over Lockerbie, Scotland. On KAL Flight 007, see Edward S. Herman and Gerry O'Sullivan, *The Terrorism Industry: The Experts and the Institutions that Shape Our View of Terror* (New York: Pantheon Books, 1989) pp. 197–98.

On the destruction of Pan Am Flight 103, for which Abdel Basset Ali al-Megrahi, a Libyan intelligence officer, was sentenced to life imprisonment in January 2001—and because of which Libya recently effected a settlement with the families of the victims—see "Lockerbie lawyers said to reach 2.7-billion-dollar deal with Libya," *Agence France-Presse* (October 30, 2002).

503 The U.S. claims an "inherent right" to shoot down any "hostile" aircraft approaching within 200 miles of its coastline. By its own account, the Pentagon sent fighter-bombers within 40 miles of the Libyan coast during the 1981 Gulf of Sidra "exercise." In actuality, according to a British engineer who was monitoring a radar screen during the entire confrontation, U.S. aircraft penetrated 8 miles into the airspace over the Libyan landmass itself. "I don't think the Libyans had any choice but to hit back," he said. "In my opinion they were reluctant to do so." This reluctance prevailed despite the fact that the U.S. had already implemented a policy of firing on "any Libyan boat that enters international waters in the Gulf of Sidra for as long as the U.S. naval exercise in that region continues—no matter how far away the boat might be from U.S. ships." All quotes are in Noam Chomsky, *Pirates and Emperors: International Terrorism and the Real World* (New York: Claremont, 1986) pp. 144–45.

504 The U.S. claimed the strikes were in retaliation for Libya's sponsorship of bombings at the Rome and Vienna airports on December 27, 1985, in which a single American child, eleven-year-old Natasha Simpson, was killed. Instructively, both the Italian and Austrian intelligence agencies stated unequivocally that Libya had nothing to do with the attacks. A second pretext was that Libya was behind the April 5, 1986 bombing of the La Belle discothèque in Berlin, in which a U.S. serviceman was killed, although German intelligence was equally adamant that there was no "Libyan connection" at issue (instructively, U.S. military intelligence shared this view). See Chomsky, *Pirates and Emperors*, pp. 135, 148. In the aftermath of the U.S. raids, which clearly targeted Qadaffi himself—his home was bombed—in violation of both U.S. domestic and international law, and in which a number of children besides Qadaffi's were killed, "65 claims were filed with the White House and the Department of Defense under the Federal Tort Claims Act and the Foreign Claims Act on behalf of those killed or injured. The claimants, who were asking for up to $5 million for each wrongful death, included Libyans, Greeks, Egyptians, Yugoslavs and Lebanese. . . . [N]one of the claims got anywhere in the American judicial system, with the Supreme Court declining to hear the case"; Blum, *Rogue State*, p. 230. Arguably, it was this "due process" outcome that prompted the bombing of Pan Am Flight 103, and it should be compared to Libya's recent award of $10 million per victim who perished in that incident (see note 502).

505 All told, Al-Shifa manufactured "90 percent of Sudan's pharmaceutical products." Among other things, it "provided 50 percent of the Sudan's medicines, and its destruction has left the country with no supplies of chloroquine, the standard treatment for malaria." As well, it was the only factory "producing TB drugs—for more than 100,000 patients [as well as] veterinary drugs . . . to kill the parasites which pass from herds to herders, one of Sudan's principal causes of infant mortality." As a result of the plant's destruction, "Sudan's death toll . . . has continued, quietly, to rise . . . tens of thousands of people—many of them children—have suffered and died from malaria, tuberculosis, and other treatable diseases." According to Germany's ambassador to the Sudan, "It is difficult to assess how many people in this poor African country died as a consequence of the Al-Shifa factory, but several tens of thousands seems a reasonable guess." Noam Chomsky, *9–11* (New

York: Seven Stories Press, 2001) pp. 48–49; quoting Patrick Wintour, *The Observer* (December 20, 1998); James Astill, *The Guardian* (October 2, 2001); Jonathan Belke, *Boston Globe* (August 22, 1999); Werner Daum, "Universalism and the West," *Harvard International Review*, Vol. 23, No. 2 (Summer 2001) pp. 19–23.

506 A salient example is the staunchness with which the U.S. supported Israel after the Israeli Air Force knowingly shot down a Libyan airliner in February 1973, killing all 109 aboard. In that instance, the *New York Times*, reflecting the official U.S. stance, editorialized that, "No useful purpose is served by an acrimonious debate over the assignment of blame for the downing of a Libyan airliner over the Sinai Peninsula." The *Times*' position in the 1973 case is usefully compared to that taken on September 2, 1983, by America's "newspaper of record" concerning the Soviets' shoot-down of KAL Flight 007: "There can be no conceivable excuse for any nation shooting down a harmless airliner." This neatly-reversed "standard" was, of course, reversed again with respect to the U.S. Navy's obliteration of an Iranian airliner in 1988 (see note 501). Actually, U.S. forgiveness of its "friends'" terrorist attacks on civilian airliners is standard, having applied not only to the 1973 Israeli atrocity against Libya, but to the 1976 bombing of a Cuban airliner, killing 73, by the Cuban expatriate Orlando Bosch (a longtime CIA client), the highly lethal shoot-down of an Angola Airlines plane by Joseph Savimbi's UNITA forces on November 3, 1983 (Savimbi was from the outset CIA-supported), and the planting of a bomb aboard an Air India jumbo jet in 1985, killing 329, by Sikh extremists (one of whom had received explosives instruction at a "private" military training camp in Alabama). See Herman and O'Sullivan, *Terrorism Industry*, pp. 197–98; Chomsky, *Pirates and Emperors*, p. 136; Edward S. Herman, *The Real Terror Network: Terrorism in Fact and Propaganda* (Boston: South End Press, 1982) p. 63.

507 See, e.g., Dean E. Murphy, "With Anger and Disgust, Region Views Tape of bin Laden's Boasts," *New York Times* (December 14, 2001).

508 Chomsky, *9–11*, p. 114.

509 See, e.g., the cover of *Time*'s September 24, 2001 special issue (note 491), as well as the photo spread at pp. 24–25 therein. It should be noted that these stills do not convey the impact of the massed firemen and other emergency workers responding to the president's squalid rhetoric with chants worthy of a football locker room—a truly disgusting spectacle.

510 It should be noted that by "the summer of 1998, the leader of the Taliban, Mullah Omar [had] struck a secret deal with the Saudis to expel [bin-Laden]. But just before Mullah Omar's order . . . was carried out, President Clinton ordered an illegal missile strike on Afghanistan . . . in retaliation for the bombing of U.S. embassies in Africa. Prince Turki al-Faisal, the head of Saudi intelligence who had brokered the deal, said 'The Taliban attitude changed 180 degrees.'" Rai, *War Plan Iraq*, p. 202. For further analysis, see As'ad AbuKhalil, *Bin Laden, Islam and America's New "War on Terrorism"* (New York: Seven Stories Press, 2002).

511 The best overview is probably that provided in Ahmed Rashid's *Taliban: Militant Islam, Oil and Fundamentalism in Central Asia* (New Haven, CT: Yale University Press, 2001).

512 As Arundhati Roy put it, "The Taliban's response to U.S. demands for the extradition of bin Laden has been uncharacteristically reasonable: produce the evidence, then we'll hand him over. President Bush's response is that the demand is non-negotiable." Quoted in Chomsky, *9–11*, p. 103. Roy also points out that the U.S. has been steadfast in its refusal to honor India's extradition request, complete with a solid evidentiary offer concerning his criminal culpability, for Union Carbide CEO

Warren Anderson, an untended gas leak at whose Bhopal plant killed more than 16,000 people in 1984. Similarly, the U.S. has consistently refused Haiti's request for the extradition of Emmanuel Constant, a paramilitary leader believed to be responsible for the murders of at least five thousand people in that tiny country (i.e., close to twice the number of U.S. citizens killed on September 11, and proportionately the equivalent of several hundred thousand Americans). The pattern is not new, as is witnessed in the U.S. refusal to turn over its deposed ally, Mohammed Reza Shah Pahlavi, for trial in Iran, a matter figuring prominently in the 1980 "hostage crisis" at the U.S. embassy in Teheran. Nikki R. Keddie, *Roots of Revolution: An Interpretive History of Modern Iran* (New Haven, CT: Yale University Press, 1981) p. 270.

513   The formulation of this "stark choice" derives from that articulated by Bush himself, as quoted by R.W. Apple in the *New York Times* on September 14, 2001.

514   "UN concern as air strikes to a halt," *Financial Times* (October 9, 2001).

515   "Relief workers hit at linking of food drops with air raids," *Financial Times* (October 9, 2001).

516   Among the complainants were Oxfam International, Doctors Without Borders, Christian Aid, Save the Children, and an array of UN officials. See "Scepticism grows over US food drops," *Financial Times* (October 10, 2001).

517   Altogether, a carrier fleet, plus some "fifty thousand American military personnel and four hundred aircraft were moved from the Red Sea to the Indian Ocean, about mid-November" to participate in the Afghanistan operation. These substantial ground forces were used mainly for "mop-up" and occupation purposes, however. See Gabriel Kolko, *Another Century of War?* (New York: New Press, 2002) p. 3.

518   Joost Hilterman, a Middle East specialist for Human Rights Watch, quoted in Chomsky, 9–11, p. 96. Also see Ross Benson, "Chilling truth about the butchers who routed the Taliban," *Daily Mail* (November 14, 2001).

519   Benson, "Chilling truth." Also see the chapter titled "Mazar-E-Sharif 1997: Massacre in the North," in Rashid, *Taliban*, pp. 53–66.

520   Wayne Veysey, "I saw the killing of a Taliban Soldier," *Scottish Daily Record* (November 16, 2001).

521   Yvonne Abraham, "UN Backs Reports of Mass Execution: Says Opposition Killed Recruits Hiding at School," *Boston Globe* (November 14, 2001); Chris Brummet, "U.N. Probes Alleged Afghan Killings," *New York Times* (October 18, 2002).

522   "Afghan massacre puts Pentagon on the spot," *The Guardian* (September 14, 2001).

523   Kate Connolly and Rory McCarthy, "New film accuses US of war crimes," *The Guardian* (June 13, 2002).

524   As of October 29, 2002, there were reportedly 625 prisoners at "Gitmo." For background, see Michael Ratner, "The War on Terrorism: The Guantánano Prisoners, Military Commissions, and Torture," in Cynthia Brown, ed., *Lost Liberties: Ashcroft and the Assault on Personal Freedom* (New York: New Press, 2003) pp. 132–50.

525   Barbara Olshansky, *Secret Trials and Executions: Military Tribunals and the Threat to Democracy* (New York: Seven Stories Press, 2002) p. 47. In general, Taliban soldiers are entitled to status as POWs, and are thus subject to the protections of the Third Geneva Convention, while al-Qaida personnel fall under the heading of "unprivileged combatants," and are thus subject to the protections of Geneva IV. "Illegal combatant" is not a valid classification. In any case, the conditions prevailing at Guantánamo Bay—holding prisoners in open air cages, for example—are legally impermissible. In no instance, moreover, is the U.S. empowered under either international or its own domestic law to try prisoners before military tribunals, as, on

November 13, 2001, George Bush announced it would do (the groundwork was laid in Defense Secretary Rumsfeld's Military Commission Order No. 1, March 21, 2002). For the texts of Geneva III and IV, see Roberts and Guelff, *Laws of War*, pp. 215–70, 271–338. For relevant domestic law, see *Ex Parte Milligan* (71 U.S. (4 Wall) 2 (1866)) and *Zadvydas v. Davis* (121 S. Ct. 2491, 2500 (2001)). Overall, see Nancy Chang, "How Democracy Dies: The War on Our Civil Liberties," in Brown, *Lost Liberties*, pp. 33–51; Natsu Taylor Saito, "Will Force Trump Legality After September 11? American Jurisprudence Confronts the Rule of Law," *Georgetown Immigration Law Journal*, Vol. 17, No. 1 (Fall 2002) pp. 1–62.

526 "Detention Camp Commander Is Removed," *New York Times* (October 15, 2002).

527 "Babbling at times like a child, the partially deaf, shriveled old man was unable to answer simple questions. He struggled to complete sentences and strained to hear words that were shouted at him. His faded mind kept failing him." David Rohde, "Afghans Freed from Guantánamo Speak of Heat and Isolation," *New York Times* (October 29, 2002).

528 Ibid.

529 On the authorization of tribunals, see note 524.

530 "The bill was never the subject of Committee debate or mark-up in the Senate. There was a truncated process in the House, which heard no official testimony from opponents of the bill but at least held a full Committee mark-up. But the result of that process was put aside by the Administration and the House leadership and never brought to a vote in the full House. . . . It is virtually certain that not a single member of the House read the bill for which he or she voted." David Cole and James X. Dempsey, *Terrorism and the Constitution* (New York: New Press, 2002) p. 151.

531 Uniting and Strengthening America by Providing Appropriate Tools Required to Intercept and Obstruct Terrorism (USA PATRIOT) Act of 2001 (115 Stat. 272). The Bail Reform Act of 1984 (18 U.S.C. § 3142) empowers authorities to nullify the right of accused individuals to bail upon argument by a prosecutor that s/he represents a "danger to the community." Since the Act's passage, such arguments have been made in more than 40 percent of all cases brought before federal courts (and every single "political" case). See my introductory essay, "The Third World at Home: Political Prisons and Prisoners in the United States," in my and J.J. Vander Wall's coedited *Cages of Steel: The Politics of Imprisonment in the United States* (Washington, DC: Maisonneuve Press, 1992) pp. 9–10. The Antiterrorism and Effective Death Penalty Act of 1996 (110 Stat. 214) allows the secretary of state to define terrorism in entirely arbitrary ways, criminalizes even the most indirect support to organizations or individuals thus defined, and authorizes police and intelligence agencies to engage in previously illegal "counterintelligence" operations against those thereby criminalized. See Cole and Dempsey, *Terrorism and the Constitution*, pp. 117–46. For background on historical usage of illegal methods against domestic political targets, see "COINTELPRO: The FBI's Covert Action Programs Against American Citizens," in U.S. Senate, Select Committee to Study Government Operations with Respect to Intelligence Activities, *Final Report, Book III: Supplementary Detailed Staff Reports on Intelligence Activities and the Rights of Americans* (Washington, DC: 94th Cong., 2nd Sess., 1976) pp. 1–77. Also see my and Jim Vander Wall's *The COINTELPRO Papers: Documents from the FBI's Secret Wars Against Dissent in the United States* (Cambridge, MA: South End Press, [Classics Ed.] 2002).

532 Cole and Dempsey, *Terrorism and the Constitution*, pp. 147–75. Also see Nancy Chang, *Silencing Political Dissent: How Post-September 11 Anti-Terrorism Measures Threaten Our Civil*

Liberties (New York: Seven Stories Press, 2002). On "neutralization" of targets being the goal of counterintelligence operations, see the statements of former FBI assistant director William C. Sullivan and his subordinate, COINTELPRO supervisor George C. Moore, quoted in Senate Select Committee, *Final Report, Book III* at pp. 7 and 63, as well as the Senate staff's conclusion drawn on p. 68. Also see the statement of an unnamed counterintelligence operative quoted in Ungar, *FBI*, p. 120.

533 Posse Comitatus Act (18 U.S.C.S. § 1385). The Act is amended at 10 U.S.C. § 332, to allow the president to use the military to restore order, should enforcement of the law by civil authorities become literally "impracticable" (a very high threshold). Also at issue is an amendment accruing under Ronald Reagan's Economy Act (105 Stat. 1494), allowing the *noncombat* employment of military personnel in waging the so-called war on drugs. See generally Jim McGee, "Military Seeks Balance in Delicate Mission: The Drug War," *Washington Post* (November 29, 1996); Paul Richter, "Pentagon Plans Bigger Noncombat Role," *Los Angeles Times* (April 3, 1997).

534 On police militarization, see the chapter titled "Carrying the Big Stick: SWAT Teams and Paramilitary Policing," in Christian Parenti, *Lockdown America: Police and Prisons in the Age of Crisis* (London: Verso, 1999) pp. 111–38; Pat Cascio and John McSweeney, *SWAT Battle Tactics* (Boulder, CO: Paladin Press, 1996). On the HRT, which has never rescued a hostage, but which has repeatedly brought military tactics to bear in the U.S. domestic context, see David T. Hardy and Rex Kimball, *This Is Not an Assault: Penetrating the Web of Official Lies Regarding the Waco Incident* (San Antonio, TX: Xlibris, 2001) pp. 240–41.

535 On the Praetor Protocol, see my preface to the Classics Edition of *COINTELPRO Papers*, at pp. xlvi–xlviii. For the record here, Delta Force personnel, wearing FBI field jackets, were deployed by Ronald Reagan during the 1987 Atlanta prison riot, by George Bush (the 41st) during the 1992 insurrection in Los Angeles, and Bill Clinton during both the 1993 siege of Branch Davidians near Waco, Texas, and during the 1998 WTO demonstrations in Seattle. The quasi-official version of how all this came about is that, in 1987, Reagan secretly signed a "waiver" of the Posse Comitatus Act. According to then White House cybersecurity czar Richard Clark, "The president can waive this law at a moment's notice." Quoted in Robert Dreyfuss, "Spying on Ourselves," *Rolling Stone* (March 28, 2002) p. 34. The chief executive, of course, holds no lawful authority to "waive" *any* statute.

536 The exercises were conducted under such headings as "Rex-84." They conformed quite closely to "integrated force counterinsurgency scenarios" developed a decade earlier under the code names "Garden Plot" and "Cable Splicer" by founding FEMA director Louis O. Giufrida at the behest of then-California governor Ronald Reagan. See my and Vander Wall's *Agents of Repression*, pp. 194–95, 447.

537 David Cole, "Enemy Aliens," *Stanford Law Review*, Vol. 54, No. 5 (May 2002) p. 985.

538 The idea of using "internment centers"—concentration camps, by any other name—to neutralize the activities of politically dissident Americans is not new. Indeed, it was authorized under the Internal Security Act of 1950 (66 Stat. 163), a law that was not repealed until the early 1970s. See Thomas I. Emerson, *The System of Free Expression* (New York: Vintage, 1970) esp. p. 145; Kirkpatrick Sale, *SDS* (New York: Random House, 1973) p. 443. That preparations for such a move have been underway for some time are to some extent evidenced by the recent revelation that the Denver Police Department's intelligence unit has been compiling files on local activists under the caption "Criminal Extremist-G" for such nefarious activities as signing petitions and attending rallies. See *American Friends Service Committee, et al.*,

v. City and County of Denver (Civ. No. 02-N-0740 (D. Colo.) (2002)). Also see Sarah Huntley, "Cops have 'spy files,' groups say," *Rocky Mountain News* (March 12, 2002); "Denver Police Files Raise Rights Concerns," *New York Times* (March 14, 2002); John C. Ensslin, "Spy files have storied past," *Rocky Mountain News* (March 14, 2002); Judy Cart, "Denver Police Spied on Activists, ACLU Says," *Los Angeles Times* (March 22, 2002). Relatedly, see Katharine Q. Seelye, "Appeals Court Again Hears Case of American Held Without Charges or Counsel," *New York Times* (October 29, 2002).

539   See the chapter titled "Dictators and Oil Barons: The Taliban and Central Asia, Russia, Turkey and Israel," in Rashid, *Taliban*, pp. 143–56. Also see the map on p. xii.

540   For strategic context, see Ahmed Rashid, *The Resurgence of Central Asia: Islam or Nationalism?* (London: Zed Books, 1994).

541   David Rohde, "Afghans Lead World Again in Poppy Crop," *New York Times* (October 28, 2002); Chris Brummet, "Concerns Over Afghan Drug War," AP On-Line (October 30, 2002). For background on the historical role of Afghanistan in the international drug trade, see the chapter titled "Poppy Fields, Killing Fields and Druglords," in Cooley, *Unholy War*, pp. 127–61. For a more comprehensive view of how heroin trafficking has figured in U.S. foreign policy, see Alfred W. McCoy, *The Politics of Heroin: CIA Complicity in the Global Drug Trade* (Brooklyn: Lawrence Hill, 1991).

542   Defense Secretary Rumsfeld, quoted in Kolko, *Another Century of War?*, p. 2. "Fifty-five" is the more usual number, cited in Alexander and Swetnam, *al-Qaida*, p. viii. Either way, the implication is that the "war," as vice president Dick Cheney put it on October 18, 2001, "may never end. At least, not in our lifetime." Quoted in Kolko, *Another Century*, p. 2.

543   "Colonel Muamar al-Qadaffi had combated the Islamists in his country from the time he seized power in Libya in a coup in 1969. . . . Whenever disorders or violent opposition to his rule erupted in Libya, as it did in the eastern parts of his country during the later 1990s, travelers reaching Egypt would insist that Islamist groups had identified themselves as the authors." Cooley, *Unholy War*, p. 214. More broadly, see Jonathan Bearman, *Qadhafi's Libya* (London: Zed Books, 1986). The idea of a "Qadaffi/al-Qaida connection" can thus be viewed as a pretext for settling longstanding and completely unrelated scores. For background, see the essay titled "Libya in U.S. Demonology," in Chomsky, *Pirates and Emperors*, pp. 129–74.

544   On Abu Sayyaf, see the chapter titled "More Contagion: The Philippines," in Cooley, *Unholy Wars*, pp. 248–58. On Islamist activities in Chechnya and elsewhere in the Caucasus region, see the chapter titled "Russia: Bitter Aftertaste and Reluctant Return," esp. pp. 174–84. On the Yemen "cells," see "Bin Laden Groomed Yemen Ties for Two Years," *Gulf News* (October 21, 2000).

545   William Safire, "U.S. prepares to battle 'axis of evil,'" *San Francisco Chronicle* (February 1, 2002).

546   "Misrepresentations of bin Laden abound. For example, he is sometimes portrayed as an ally of Saddam Hussein, although he clearly despises [Saddam's] secular leadership and brutal persecution of fundamentalists in Iraq." By the same token, Iran is an all but exclusively Shi'ite country. Al-Qaida "considers Shi'ites to be infidels, and [its] unofficial spokesman, Abu Qatada, calls them *rawafid*—literally, rejectionists . . . a pejorative term applied by some Sunnis to Shi'ites." Abu Khalil, "War on Terrorism," p. 76. On the mutual hostility of Iran and Iraq, see generally Dilip Hiro, *Neighbors, Not Friends: Iraq and Iran after the Gulf Wars* (New York: Routledge, 2001).

547   Far from being a sponsor of international terrorism, the communist state of North Korea is usually described as "reclusive" or "isolationist." Like its Caribbean

counterpart, Cuba—also routinely listed as a terrorist sponsor by the State Department—North Korea's involvement in such things seems mainly to have consisted of being on the receiving end of the terrorism practiced by CIA client organizations. See Herman, *The Real Terror Network*.

548 Matthew Lee, "Former secretary of state Albright blasts Bush for 'axis of evil' tag," *Agence France-Presse* (February 1, 2002).

549 For a survey of official pronouncements, see Jonathan Wright, "Rhetoric on Iraq Tests U.S. Credibility," *New York Times* (August 20, 2002).

550 One of the conduits through which the materials necessary to Iraq's illegal armaments programs passed during the 1980s was the Halliburton Corp., a board member of which was Vice President Dick Cheney. See William Rivers Pitt, "An Interview with Scott Ritter," in William Rivers Pitts with Scott Ritter, *War on Iraq: What Team Bush Doesn't Want You to Know* (New York: Context Books, 2002) pp. 38–39. Also see Patrick E. Tyler, "Reagan Aided Iraq Despite Use of Gas," *New York Times* (August 18, 2002).

551 Pitt, "Interview with Scott Ritter," pp. 41, 42.

552 Ibid., pp. 33, 34, 36–37.

553 "The Vice President has been saying that Iraq might be two years away from building a nuclear bomb. Unless he knows something we don't, that's nonsense. And it doesn't appear he does, because whenever you press the Vice President or other Bush administration officials on these claims, they fall back on testimony by Richard Butler, my former boss, an Australian diplomat, and Khidre Hamza, an Iraqi defector who claims to be Saddam's bomb-maker. Neither of these people provide anything more than speculation to back up their assertions. The Vice President's continued claims about Iraq's nuclear weapons capability are unsubstantiated speculation. And of course that's not good enough, especially when we have the United Nations record of Iraqi disarmament from 1991 to 1998. That record is without dispute. . . . We eliminated the nuclear program, and for Iraq to have reconstituted it would require undertaking activities eminently detectable by intelligence services." Pitt, "Interview with Scott Ritter," p. 32.

554 These include the Security Council's 1967 Resolution 242, calling upon Israel to withdraw from territory beyond its borders; Security Council Resolution 338 (1973), essentially reiterating Resolution 242; Security Council Resolution 425 (1978), calling upon Israel to withdraw its forces from Lebanon; Security Council Resolution 465 (1980), calling upon Israel halt its pattern of violation of the Geneva IV Convention; and Security Council Resolution 1322 (2000), reiterating Resolution 465 in even more emphatic terms. Also at issue are General Assembly Resolution 181 (1947), establishing Israel's original borders; a 1967 General Assembly Resolution affirming the right of Palestinians to national self-determination; and a 1997 General Assembly Resolution calling for an end to all settlement activities in the Occupied Territories. During the 1988 General Assembly session alone, nearly a score of resolutions were passed—and mostly vetoed by the U.S.—condemning Israel for violations of the Geneva IV Convention during its bloody repression of the Palestinian Intifada. Israel has also been repeatedly condemned by the Security Council for specific acts of aggression beginning with the October 1953 massacre at Qibya perpetrated by Ariel Sharon's notorious Unit 101. See Shlaim, *Iron Wall*, pp. 261, 291, 303, 310, 321, 322, 338, 356, 456, 322, 338, 356, 495, 592, 25, 333, 454–55, 92; Noam Chomsky, "Terror and Just Response," in Rai, *War Plan Iraq*, p. 30.

555 Precisely when and how Israel acquired nuclear arms capability remains unclear, but it had ten operational devices by 1968; David Burnham, "U.S. Agencies Suspected Missing Uranium Went to Israel for Arms," *New York Times* (November 6, 1977). Irrespective of the details, the Israeli acquisition was—and remains—contrary to the International Treaty on Non-Proliferation of Nuclear Weapons (1970). Overall, see Seymour M. Hersh, *The Samson Option: Israel, America and the Bomb* (London: Faber and Faber, 1991).

556 India tested its first device in 1974, Pakistan a decade later. See Anna Gyorgy and Friends, *No Nukes: Everyone's Guide to Nuclear Power* (Boston: South End Press, 1979) p. 304.

557 "Prior to the Gulf War, Iraq acquired a lot of technology, as well as parts, from Germany, which has a record of precision machinery. After the war, the Iraqis tried to replicate that, but with very little success. . . . I hear people talking about Iraq having multi-staging rockets, but Iraq doesn't have multi-staging capability. They tried that once, back in 1989 when the country had full access to technology, and the rocket blew up in midair. I hear people talk about clustering, but Iraq tried that, too, and it didn't work. The bottom line is that Iraq doesn't have the capability to do long-range ballistic missiles. They don't even have the capability to do short-range ballistic missiles." Pitt, "Interview with Scott Ritter," p. 47.

558 David Rennie, "Czechs deny meeting of 9/11 leader and Iraqi official: False report was 'smoking gun' linking Saddam to terrorist attack," *National Post* (October 22, 2002).

559 David S. Cloud, "Missing Links: Bush Efforts to Tie Hussein to al Qaeda Lack Clear Evidence," *Wall Street Journal* (October 23, 2002).

560 Rennie, "Czechs deny meeting."

561 Bill Kemper with Jill Zuckman, "Bush to UN: Act on Iraq," *Chicago Tribune* (September 13, 2002).

562 Chris McCann, "U.S. Is at a 'Defining Moment' in Its History: Rule of Law or Renegade?" *Seattle Post-Intelligencer* (October 5, 2002).

563 In fairness, Sharon had probably been led to believe that his actions would receive the usual unqualified U.S. support. On December 14, 2001, for example, the U.S. vetoed a Security Council resolution calling for the introduction of UN peacekeepers to the West Bank in hopes of averting an escalation of hostilities there. Ten days earlier, it had boycotted—and thus effectively scuttled—an international conference called in Geneva to reaffirm Israel's obligation to comply with the Geneva IV Convention's requirements for protecting "enemy" civilians in times of armed conflict. See Chomsky, "Terror and Just Response," pp. 29–30.

564 "Group accuses Israel of War Crimes," *Chicago Tribune* (November 5, 2002).

565 John Ward Anderson, "Report ties Israel with war crimes: Human rights group says West Bank raids used excessive force against Palestinians," *Washington Post* (November 4, 2002).

566 Israel's pretense that it was merely "responding" to a "wave of terrorism" embodied in Palestinian suicide bombings may have played well in Peoria—and on Fox News—but virtually nowhere outside the U.S. and Israel itself. Most of the rest of the world remains rational enough to realize that suicide bombing is a tactic employed only by disempowered and utterly desperate people in a forlorn hope of gaining some sort of military parity with their oppressors. In other words, it is generally understood that it is the *Palestinians* who are "responding" to perpetual Israeli terrorism, a matter readily borne out in the lopsided fatality rates they've suffered all along. For

background, see Zachary Lockman and Joel Beinin, *Intifada: The Palestinian Uprising Against Israeli Occupation* (Boston: South End Press, 1989); Roane Carey, ed., *The New Intifada: Resisting Israel's Apartheid* (London: Verso, 2001).

567   MSNBC and CNN broadcasts, November 8, 2002.

568   Robert Holloway, "Bush turns up heat on UN Security Council to act against Iraq," *Agence France-Presse* (October 29, 2002).

569   Patrick E. Tyler, "Bush Signal: Time Is Now," *New York Times* (November 8, 2002).

570   George W. Bush, press statement broadcast of CNN, November 8, 2002. Also see David E. Sanger and Julia Preston, "President Warns Hussein to Heed a Call to Disarm: U.N. Vote Set for Today," *New York Times* (November 8, 2002).

571   See note 435.

572   McCann, "Defining Moment."

573   Monte Reel and Manny Fernandez, "100,000 Rally, March Against War in Iraq," *Washington Post* (October 27, 2002).

574   Narrower forms of crass self-interest underlay the rhetorical purity of principle marking the Vietnam era antiwar movement. Witness, for example, the rapidity with which the mass movement withered after the draft was reformed (1969) and U.S. ground forces withdrawn (1972). The war itself was continued on the basis of U.S. support for another three years—and Vietnamese died at rates as great as ever—but without substantial protest from American "antiwar" activists. In effect, once they themselves were no longer faced with the prospect of having to fight it, average protesters' "concerns of conscience" about the war abated both quickly and dramatically. See Terry H. Anderson, *The Movement and the Sixties: Protest in America from Greensboro to Wounded Knee* (New York: Oxford University Press, 1995) pp. 379–80.

575   Deborah L. Madsen, *American Exceptionalism* (Jackson: University of Mississippi Press, 1998). For framing in the dimension at issue here, see my and Mike Ryan's *Pacifism as Pathology: Reflections on the Role of Armed Struggle in North America* (Winnipeg: Arbeiter Ring, 1998).

576   For an especially biting analysis, see David Zane Mairowitz, *The Radical Soap Opera: The Roots and Failure of the American Left* (New York: Avon Books, 1974).

577   The "master work" in this connection is Gene Sharp's *The Politics of Nonviolent Action*, 3 vols. (Boston: Porter Sargent, 1973). Also see Staughton Lynd and Alice Lynd, eds., *Nonviolence in America: A Documentary History* (Maryknoll, NY: Orbis Books, 1995).

578   This critique is not new, having been advanced by the Revolutionary Youth Movement faction of Students for a Democratic Society (SDS) from 1967 onward. See, e.g., Ron Jacobs, *The Way the Wind Blew: A History of the Weather Underground* (London: Verso, 1997) pp. 1–23. Also see Karin Ashley et al., "You Don't Need a Weatherman to Know Which Way the Wind Blows," in Harold Jacobs, ed., *Weatherman* (San Francisco: Ramparts Press, 1970) pp. 51–90.

579   "In post-Nuremberg settings, a government that flagrantly violates international law is engaged in criminal behavior even on the domestic plane, and as far as internal law is concerned, its policies are not entitled to respect. To disobey is no longer, as with Thoreau, to engage in 'civil disobedience,' an initiative designed to point up the discrepancy between 'law' and 'morality,' and the priority of the latter for the person of conscience. Such a tension no longer exists. To resist reasonably a violation of international law is a matter of legal right, possibly even of legal duty if knowledge and a capacity for action exists . . . . [R]esisters who properly invoke the authority of Nuremberg stand on firm legal ground, and should not be sent off to jail, but should be exonerated. Or better, the courts should lend the weight of their authority

to the claim that a given direction of foreign policy or national security doctrine [is] incompatible with international law, and its principal executors are subject to prosecution." Richard Falk, "Introduction" to Francis Anthony Boyle, *Defending Civil Resistance Under International Law* (Dobbs Ferry, NY: Transnational, 1988) p. xxi.

580 The principle is closely related to that expressed in UN General Assembly Resolution 42/159 (1987), asserting that what would otherwise be classified as "terrorism"—that is, "the calculated and illegal use of violence or threat of violence to attain goals that are political, religious, or ideological in nature"—is permissible when its purpose is to obtain "the right to self-determination, freedom, and independence, as derived from the Charter of the United Nations, of people forcibly deprived of that right . . . particularly peoples under colonial and racist regimes and foreign occupation." Quoted in Chomsky, "Terror and Just Response," p. 23.

581 This principle is generally accepted, even in the U.S., so long as the "right" government is at issue. Witness all the recent chatter emanating from the departments of state and defense about the desirability of the Iraqis themselves "removing" Saddam Hussein (through means always left to the imagination). More classic is America's postwar valorization of the group of army officers who attempted to assassinate Adolf Hitler and seize control of Germany in 1944; see Peter Hoffmann, *The History of the German Resistance, 1933–1945* (Montréal: McGill-Queens University Press, [3rd ed.] 1996) esp. "Part VI: Assassination Attempts, 1933–1942" (pp. 251–62) and "Part VIII: Stauffenberg and the Replacement Army" (pp. 315–503). U.S. adherence to legal norms in advocating/orchestrating citizen violence against selected governments is, however, entirely situational. Consider, for instance, the immediate and massive support accruing to the openly fascist Pinochet régime in Chile, following the CIA-backed 1973 coup in which, among other things, Pinochet's insurgents assassinated Chile's duly-elected president, Salvador Allende, and committed the mass murder of some 4,000 Chilean progressives; see Mary Helen Spooner, *Soldiers in a Narrow Land: The Pinochet Regime in Chile* (Berkeley: University of California Press, [2nd ed.] 1999) pp. 17–82; Hugh O'Shaughnessy, *Pinochet: The Politics of Torture* (New York: New York University Press, 2000) pp. 49–63. Given their own record and posture, for U.S. officials to contend that it would be "wrong"—much less "illegal"—for American citizens to use force as a means of compelling governmental adherence to international human rights law and/or the laws of war is utterly ludicrous.

582 For further explication of this principle, see Karl Jaspers, *The Question of German Guilt* (New York: Fordham University Press, 2002).

583 See notes 4, 5, and accompanying text.

584 See note 11 and accompanying text.

585 See note 17 and accompanying text.

586 There are currently no fewer than two dozen books in print concerning the Jonbenet Ramsey case. See, as examples, Carlton Smith, *Death of a Little Princess: The Tragic Story of the Murder of Jonbenet Ramsey* (New York: St. Martin's, 1997); Cyril H. Wecht and Charles Bosworth Jr., *Who Killed Jonbenet Ramsey? A Leading Forensic Expert Uncovers the Shocking Facts* (New York: Signet, 1998); Lawrence Schiller, *Perfect Murder, Perfect Town: The Uncensored Story of the Jonbenet Murder and the Grand Jury's Search for the Final Truth* (New York: Harper, 1999). On the far more recent but equally sensationalized case of Danielle van Dam, see Tony Perry, "Van Dams Agree with Jury Decision," *Los Angeles Times* (September 18, 2002). It should be noted that the now seven-year-old Ramsey case was still being treated as an appropriate subject of "in-depth" media analysis as recently as November 14, 2002, when MSNBC aired a lengthy segment

featuring clips taken from the Boulder (Colorado) Police Department's interrogations of her parents.

587 Christopher Hitchens presents one case rather well in his *The Trial of Henry Kissinger* (London: Verso, 2001). The specification of charges against Albright would be similar. These two are merely representative. A long list of still-living U.S. officials are of course guilty of comparable criminality.

588 Prof. Natsu Taylor Saito, interview on the National Public Radio *Powerpoint* program, broadcast on Atlanta radio station WCLK, November 4, 2001.

589 For an itemization of the "stupid rule list," see Keith L. Alexander, "Some Rules Deserve to Go, TSA Agrees," *Washington Post* (October 16, 2002).

590 James Risen with Neil MacFarquhar, "New Recording May Be Threat from bin Laden," *New York Times* (November 13, 2002).

591 One hundred and eighty people were killed in the Bali blasts, most of them Australian tourists, targeted because of their government's endorsement of the U.S. "war on terrorism." See Ellen Nakashima and Alan Sipress, "Bombing Kills at Least 180 in Indonesian Club; Site Popular with Foreigners; 2nd Blast Hits Near U.S. Office," *Washington Post* (October 13, 2002); Mike Corder, "Al-Qaida involved in Bali bombings and more attacks to come, says Australia's spy chief," Associated Press (October 31, 2002). Bin-Laden also mentioned that a French oil tanker near the Yemen coast was heavily damaged in another recent al-Qaida operation. Sebastian Rotella and Esther Schrader, "Tanker Blast Likely a Terror Attack; Debris indicates small boat was apparently used to attack the ship off Yemen; U.S. sees incident as part of new campaign," *Los Angeles Times* (October 11, 2002); Ahmed al-Haj, "Attack on French tanker similar to USS *Cole* bombing," Associated Press (October 24, 2002).

592 The Chechens had managed to move large quantities of explosives into Moscow, despite Russia's supposedly "airtight" security, then seized a theater in which some eight hundred members of the Russian élite were viewing a performance, threatening to blow it up unless the government altered its policy of denying self-determination to Chechnya. Ultimately, the Spetznatz (Russian Special Forces) "rescued" the hostages by using a gas that killed 118 of them. Sarah Karush, "Russian lawmaker: Putin pledges to appoint official to answer lingering questions about hostage crisis," Associated Press (November 15, 2002). For insight into the "terrorists'" motives, see "Human rights groups say Russian troops have killed 20,000 Chechens in 3 years," Associated Press (November 15, 2002).

593 "Palestinian militants have carried out about 80 suicide bombings, killing almost 300 people, since the [second intifada] began just over two years ago." Laurence Copans, "Palestinian suicide bomber strikes at Jewish settlement, four killed," Associated Press (October 27, 2002). Also see "Chronology of major anti-Israeli attacks in Palestinian uprising," *Agence France-Presse* (September 18, 2002). It should be noted that several of the more significant Arab terrorist organizations were spawned in response to specific Israeli acts of aggression. The Palestine Liberation Organization (PLO) was established in 1964 with the support of Egyptian president Abdul Gamal Nasser, mainly in reaction to Israel's ongoing refusal to resolve territorial issues arising from its drive to the Suez a decade earlier. The Iranian/Syrian-backed Hizbullah (Party of God) was created in the wake of Israel's 1982 invasion of Lebanon. Hamas (Zeal) was born in 1988, as a reaction to Israel's draconian repression of the decidedly nonviolent intifada. Both Hamas and the Islamic Jihad were in decline until prime minister Benjamin Netanyahu's 1997 escalation of Israeli "settlement" efforts in the West Bank—a direct violation of the 1995 Oslo II Peace

Accords—prompted an upsurge in suicide bombings by both groups. See Shlaim, *Iron Wall*, pp. 187, 427, 459, 584. For further background, see Kameel B. Nasr, *Arab and Israeli Terrorism* (Jefferson, NC: McFarland, 1997).

594 This is not to say that it would be Iraq providing such weapons. There are several U.S. "allies"—Pakistan, for instance—possessed of them. Indeed, Scott Ritter has laid out a scenario in which he believes U.S. or Israeli actions against Iraq could lead Pakistan and Iran to "turn over nuclear capability to terrorists [and] within ten years the United States would be struck by a terrorist nuclear bomb." Pitt, *War on Iraq*, p. 65.

"*Some* People Push Back"

On the Justice of Roosting Chickens

When queried by reporters concerning his views on the assassination of John F. Kennedy in November 1963, Malcolm X famously—and quite charitably, all things considered—replied that it was merely a case of "chickens coming home to roost."

On the morning of September 11, 2001, a few more chickens—along with some half-million dead Iraqi children—came home to roost in a very big way at the twin towers of New York's World Trade Center. Well, actually, a few of them seem to have nestled in at the Pentagon as well. The Iraqi youngsters, all of them under twelve, died as a predicable—in fact, widely predicted—result of the 1991 U.S. "surgical" bombing of their country's water purification and sewage facilities, as well as other "infrastructural" targets upon which Iraq's civilian population depends for its very survival.

If the nature of the bombing wasn't already bad enough—and it should be noted that this sort of "aerial warfare" constitutes a Class I Crime Against Humanity, entailing myriad violations of international law, as well as every conceivable standard of "civilized" behavior—the

"Some People Push Back" was written on September 11, 2001, at the urgent request of the editor of *Dark Night field notes*, and was posted the following day on the journal's blog, *Pockets of Resistance* No. 27 (September 2001). Essentially an opinion piece produced from the gut, in stream of consciousness fashion against what—given my one-finger typing ability—was an all but impossible deadline, it was unannotated and made no pretense of being comprehensive. Other than minor stylistic adjustments the text appears here as originally composed. Using asterisks, I've added notes to address errors and with regard to points that were for various reasons omitted. In view of the "firestorm of controversy" belatedly ignited by my initial formulation in late January 2005—nearly three and a half years after it was posted by PR—I've also added a brief postscript discussing certain aspects of that rather peculiar circumstance.

death toll has been steadily ratcheted up by U.S.-imposed sanctions for a full decade now. Enforced all the while by a massive military presence and periodic bombing raids, the embargo has greatly impaired the victims' ability to import the nutrients, medicines, and other materials necessary to saving the lives of even their toddlers.

All told, Iraq has a population of about eighteen million. The 500,000 kids lost to date thus represent something like twenty-five percent of their age-group. Indisputably, the rest have suffered—are still suffering—a combination of physical debilitation and psychological trauma severe enough to prevent their ever fully recovering. In effect, an entire generation has been obliterated.

The reason for this holocaust was/is simple, and was stated quite straightforwardly by President George H.W. Bush, the forty-first "freedom-loving" father of the freedom-lover currently occupying the Oval Office, George the Forty-Third: The world must learn that "what we say, goes," intoned George the Elder to the enthusiastic applause freedom-loving of freedom-loving Americans everywhere.[1] How ol' George conveyed his message was certainly no mystery to the U.S. public. One need only recall the round-the-clock dissemination of bombardment videos on every available TV channel, and the exceedingly high ratings of these telecasts, to gain a sense of how much they knew.

In trying to affix a meaning to such things, we would do well to remember the wave of elation that swept America at reports of what was happening along the so-called Highway of Death: perhaps 100,000[*] "towel-heads" and "camel jockeys"—or was it "sand niggers" that week?—in full retreat, routed and effectively defenseless, many of them conscripted civilian laborers, slaughtered in a single day by jets firing the most hyperlethal types of ordnance.[2] It was a performance worthy of the nazis during the early months of their drive into the Soviet Union. And it should be borne in mind that Good Germans gleefully cheered that butchery, too. Indeed, support for Hitler suffered no serious erosion among Germany's "innocent civilians" until the defeat at Stalingrad.

There may be a real utility to reflecting further, this time upon the fact that it was pious Americans who led the way in assigning collective guilt to the German people as a whole, not for things they as individuals

---

[*]   This figure was erroneous, reflecting as it does the total number of fatalities estimated as having been suffered by the Iraqi military during the Gulf War. The number estimated as having been killed along the Highway of Death in a single day was "only" 25,000. The remainder of the sentence stands as written.

had done, but for what they had allowed—nay, empowered—their leaders and soldiers to do in their name.

If the principle was valid then, it remains so now, as applicable to Good Americans as to Good Germans. And the price exacted from the Germans for the faultiness of their moral fiber was truly ghastly. Returning now to the children, and to the effects of the post–Gulf War embargo—continued full-force by Bush the Elder's successors in the Clinton administration as a gesture of "resolve" to finalize what George himself had dubbed the "New World Order" of American military/ economic domination[3]—it should be noted that not one but two high United Nations officials attempting to coordinate delivery of humanitarian aid to Iraq resigned in succession as protests against U.S. policy.

One of them, former UN secretary general Denis Halliday, repeatedly denounced what was happening as "a systematic program . . . of deliberate genocide." His statements appeared in the *New York Times* and other papers during the fall of 1998, so it can hardly be contended that the American public was "unaware" of them. Shortly thereafter, secretary of state Madeleine Albright openly confirmed Halliday's assessment. Asked during the widely viewed TV program *Meet the Press* to respond to his allegations, she calmly announced that she'd decided it was "worth the price" to see that U.S. objectives were achieved.*

The Politics of a Perpetrator Population

As a whole, the American public greeted these revelations with yawns. There were, after all, matters far more pressing than the unrelenting misery/death of a few hundred thousand Iraqi tikes to be concerned with. Getting Jeremy and his pal Ellington to their weekly soccer game, for instance, and making sure that little Tiffany and Ashley had just the right roll-neck sweaters to go with their new cords. And, of course, there was the yuppie holy war against ashtrays—"for our kids," no less—as an all-absorbing focus.

---

* I had several facts wrong in this paragraph. Albright's televised comment was not made in response to Halliday's 1998 statements, but two years earlier, in response to UN reports, with which Halliday was only generally associated, estimating that by early 1996 some 565,000 Iraqi children under twelve years of age had died easily avoidable deaths as a result of U.S.-enforced sanctions. Her comment was made on May 12, 1996, on *60 Minutes* (CBS), not NBC's *Meet the Press*, and Clinton had not yet appointed Albright secretary of state. At the time, she was still his national security advisor. All that said, my point stands.

In fairness, it must be admitted that there was an infinitesimally small segment of the body politic who expressed opposition to what was/ is being done to the children of Iraq. It must also be conceded, however, that those involved by and large contented themselves with signing petitions and conducting candle-lit prayer vigils, bearing "moral witness" as vast legions of brown-skinned five-year-olds sat shivering in the dark, wide-eyed in horror, whimpering as they expired in the most agonizing ways imaginable.

Be it said as well, and this is really the crux of it, that the "resistance" expended the bulk of its time and energy harnessed to the systemically useful task of trying to ensure, as "a principle of moral virtue," that nobody went further than waving signs as a means of "challenging" the patently exterminatory pursuit of Pax Americana. So pure of principle were these "dissidents," in fact, that they began literally to supplant the police in protecting corporations profiting by the carnage against suffering such retaliatory "violence" as having their windows broken by persons less "enlightened"—or perhaps more outraged—than the self-appointed "peacekeepers."[4]

Property before people, or at least the equation of property to people, is, or so it seems, by no means restricted to America's boardrooms. And the sanctimony with which such putrid sentiments are enunciated turns out to be nauseatingly similar, whether mouthed by the CEO of Standard Oil or any of a swarm of comfort zone "pacifists" queuing up to condemn the black bloc after it ever so slightly disturbed the functioning of business-as-usual in Seattle.[5] Small wonder, all in all, that people elsewhere in the world—the Mideast, for instance—began to wonder where, exactly, aside from the streets of the U.S. itself, one was to find the peace America's purportedly oppositional peacekeepers claimed to be keeping.

The answer, surely, was plain enough to anyone unblinded by the kind of delusions engendered by sheer vanity and self-absorption. So, too, were the implications in terms of anything changing, out there, in America's free-fire zones. Tellingly, it was at precisely this point— with the genocide in Iraq officially admitted and a public response demonstrating beyond any shadow of doubt that there were virtually no Americans, including most of those professing otherwise, doing anything tangible to stop it—that the combat teams which eventually commandeered the aircraft used on September 11 began to infiltrate the United States.

Meeting the "Terrorists"

Of the men who came, there are a few things demanding to be said in the face of the unending torrent of disinformational drivel unleashed by George Junior and the corporate "news" media immediately following their successful operation on September 11.

They did not, for starters, "initiate" a war with the U.S., much less commit "the first acts of war of the new millennium." A good case can be made that the war in which they were combatants has been waged more or less continuously by the "Christian West"—now proudly emblematized by the United States—against the "Islamic East" since the time of the First Crusade, about 1,000 years ago.[6] More recently, one could argue that the war began when Lyndon Johnson first lent significant support to Israel's dispossession/displacement of Palestinians during the 1960s,[7] or when George the Elder ordered "Desert Shield" in 1990, or any of several points in between. Any way you slice it, however, if what the combat teams did to the WTC and the Pentagon can be understood as acts of war—and they can—then the same is true of every U.S. "overflight" of Iraqi territory since day one.

The first acts of war during the current millennium were thus carried out by U.S. aviators acting under orders from their then-commander-in-chief, Bill Clinton. The most that can honestly be said of those involved on September 11 is that they finally responded in kind to some of what this country has dispensed to their people as a matter of course. That they waited so long to do so is, notwithstanding the 1993 action at the WTC,[8] more than anything a testament to their patience and restraint. And they did not license themselves to kill "innocent civilians." There is simply no argument to be made that the Pentagon personnel killed on September 11 fill that bill. The building and those inside constituted military targets, pure and simple. As to those in the World Trade Center . . .

Well, really. Let's get a grip here, shall we? True enough, they were civilians of a sort. But innocent? Gimme a break. They formed a technocratic corps at the very heart of America's global financial empire—the "mighty engine of profit" to which the military dimension of U.S. policy has always been slaved—and they did so both knowingly and willingly. Recourse to "ignorance"—a derivative, after all, of the word "ignore"—counts as less than an excuse among this relatively well-educated élite. To the extent that any of them were unaware of the costs and consequences to others of what they were involved in—and in many cases excelling at—it was because of their absolute refusal to see. More likely, it was because they were too busy braying into their cell phones, incessantly and self-importantly, arranging power lunches and stock transactions, each of which translated, conveniently out of sight, mind, and smelling distance, into the starved and rotting flesh of infants.

If there was a better, more effective, or in fact any other way of visiting some penalty befitting their participation upon the little Eichmanns inhabiting the sterile sanctuary of the twin towers, I'd be really interested in hearing about it.

The men who flew the missions against the WTC and Pentagon were not "cowards," as George Junior described them on September 11.[9] That distinction belongs to the "firm-jawed lads" who delighted in flying stealth aircraft through the undefended airspace of Baghdad, dropping payload after payload of bombs upon anyone unfortunate enough to be below—including tens of thousands of genuinely innocent civilians—while incurring all the risk one might expect during a visit to the local video arcade. Still more, the word describes all those "fighting men and women" who sat at computer consoles aboard ships in the Persian Gulf, enjoying air-conditioned comfort while launching cruise missiles into distant neighborhoods filled with random human beings. Whatever else can be said of them, the men who struck on September 11 manifested the courage of their convictions, willingly expending their own lives in attaining their objectives.[10]

Nor were they "fanatics" devoted to "Islamic fundamentalism."* One might rightly describe their actions as "desperate." Feelings of desperation, however, are a perfectly reasonable—one is tempted to say "normal"—emotional response among persons confronted by the mass murder of their children, particularly when it appears that nobody else really gives a damn (ask a Jewish holocaust survivor about this one, or, even more poignantly, for all the attention paid their extermination in the same genocide, a Gypsy[11]).

That desperate circumstances generate desperate responses is no mysterious or irrational principle, of the sort motivating fanatics. Less

---

* The organizational affiliation of the attackers was not yet publicly confirmed when I wrote this. That they were members of al-Qaida indicates that I may have erred in my assessment of their beliefs. It should be said, however, that the joining of such an organization does not in itself "prove" that one is personally a fundamentalist, Islamic or otherwise. To the contrary, it may simply provide the most efficient infrastructural/logistical medium through which to undertake armed struggle for essentially secular reasons, and there is ample reason to suspect that this may have been the case with those composing the September 11 combat teams. For explication, see notes 12 and 13.

is it peculiar to Islam. Indeed, even the FBI's investigative reports on the combat teams' activities during the months leading up to September 11 make it clear that the members were not fundamentalist Muslims.[12] Rather, it's pretty obvious that they were secular activists—soldiers, really—who, while undoubtedly enjoying cordial relations with the clerics of their countries, were motivated far more by the grisly realities of the U.S. war against them than by any set of religious beliefs.[13]

And less still were they/their acts "insane." Insanity is a condition readily associable with the very American idea that one—or one's country—holds a "divine right" to commit genocide, and thus forever to do so with impunity.[14] The term might also be reasonably applied to anyone suffering genocide without attempting in some material way to bring the process to a halt. Sanity itself, in this frame of reference, might be defined by a willingness to try and destroy the perpetrators or their ability to commit their crimes. (Shall we now discuss the U.S. strategic bombing campaign against Germany during World War II, and the mental health of those involved in it?)

Which takes us to official characterizations of the combat teams as an embodiment of "evil."[15] Evil—for those inclined to embrace the embodiment of such a concept—was perfectly incarnated in that malignant toad known as Madeleine Albright, squatting in her studio chair like Jabba the Hutt, blandly spewing the news that she'd imposed a collective death sentence upon the unoffending children of Iraq. Evil was to be heard in that great American hero "Stormin' Norman" Schwarzkopf's utterly dehumanizing dismissal of their systematic torture and annihilation as mere "collateral damage." Evil, moreover, is a term appropriate to describing the mentality of a public that finds such perspectives and the policies attending them acceptable, or even momentarily tolerable.

Had it not been for these evils, the counterattacks of September 11 would never have occurred. And, unless "the world is rid of such evil," to lift another line from George Junior,[16] September 11 may well end up looking like a lark. There is no reason, after all, to believe that the teams deployed in the assaults on the WTC and the Pentagon were the only such, that the others are composed of "Arabic-looking individuals"—America's indiscriminately lethal arrogance and psychotic sense of self-entitlement have long since given the great majority of the world's peoples ample cause to be at war with it—or that they are in any way dependent upon the seizure of civilian airliners to complete their missions.

To the contrary, there is every reason to expect that there are many other teams in place, tasked to employ altogether different tactics in executing operational plans at least as well-crafted as those evident on September 11, and very well equipped to do their jobs. This is to say that, since the assaults on the WTC and the Pentagon were acts of war—not simply "terrorist incidents"—they must be understood as components in a much broader strategy designed to achieve specific results. From this, it can only be adduced that there are plenty of other components ready to go, and that they will be used, should this become necessary in the eyes of the strategists. It also seems a safe bet that each component is calibrated to inflict damage at a level incrementally higher than the one before (during the 1960s, the Johnson administration employed a similar policy in Vietnam, referred to as "escalation").

Since implementation of the overall plan began with the WTC/Pentagon assaults,[17] it takes no rocket scientist to decipher what is likely to happen next, should the U.S. attempt a response of the inexcusable variety to which it has long entitled itself.

About Those Boys (and Girls) in the Bureau

There's another matter begging for comment at this point. The idea that the FBI's "counterterrorism task forces" can do a thing to prevent what will happen is yet another delusion of America's infinitely delusional pathology. The fact is that, for all its publicly financed "image-building" exercises,[18] the bureau has never shown the least aptitude for anything of the sort.

Oh yeah, FBI counterintelligence personnel have proven quite adept at framing anarchists, communists, Black Panthers, sometimes murdering them in their beds or the electric chair.[19] The bureau's SWAT units have displayed their ability to combat child abuse in Waco by burning babies alive,[20] and its vaunted crime lab has been shown to pad its "crime-fighting" statistics by fabricating evidence against many an alleged car thief.[21] But actual "heavy-duty bad guys" like the sort at issue now? Heh. This isn't a Bruce Willis/Chuck Norris/Sly Stallone movie, after all, and J. Edgar Hoover doesn't get to approve either the script or the casting.

The number of spies, saboteurs, and bona fide terrorists apprehended, or even detected by the FBI in the course of its long and slimy history could be counted on one's fingers and toes. On occasion, its agents have turned out to be the spies,[22] and not infrequently terrorists as well.[23] To be fair once again, if the bureau functions at best as a carnival of clowns where its "domestic security responsibilities" are concerned, this is because—regardless of official hype—it has none. It is now, as it always has been, the national political police force,[24] an instrument created and perfected to ensure that all Americans, not just the consent-ing mass, are "free" to do exactly what they're told.[25]

They FBI and "cooperating agencies" can be thus relied upon to set about "protecting freedom" by destroying whatever rights and liberties were left to U.S. citizens before September 11 (in fact, they've already received authorization to begin).[26] Sheep-like, the great majority of Americans can also be counted upon to bleat their approval, at least in the short run, believing as they always do that the effects of what they're embracing will be felt only by others.[27]

Oh Yeah, and "The Company," Too

A possibly sicker joke is the notion, suddenly in vogue, that the CIA will be able to pinpoint "terrorist threats," "rooting out their infrastructure" where it exists or "terminating" it before it can materialize, if only it's allowed to beef up its "human intelligence-gathering capacity" in an unrestrained manner (including full-bore operations inside the U.S., of course).[28] Well, good luck with that one, boys and girls.

Since America has a collective attention-span of about fifteen minutes, a little refresher seems in order. "The Company," as the CIA is referred to by insiders, had something on the order of a quarter-million Vietnamese serving as intelligence "assets" by 1968 and it couldn't even predict the Tet Offensive.[29] God knows how many spies it was field-ing against the USSR at the height of Ronald Reagan's version of the Cold War, and it was still caught flat-footed by the collapse of the Soviet Union.[30] As to destroying "terrorist infrastructures," one would do well to recall the Phoenix Program, another product of its open season in Vietnam. In that one, the CIA enlisted élite U.S. units like the Navy Seals and Army Special Forces, as well as those of its allies—South Vietnam's rangers, for example, and the Australian SAS—to run around "neutral-izing" folks targeted by its legion of snitches as "guerrillas" (as those now known as "terrorists" were then called).[31]

Sound familiar? Upward of 40,000 people—mostly bystanders, as it turns out—were murdered by Phoenix hit teams before the guerrillas, stronger than ever, ran the U.S. and its collaborators out of their country altogether. And these are the guys who're gonna save the day, if unleashed to do their thing in North America? The net impact of all this "counter-terrorism" activity upon the combat teams' ability to do what they came to do will, of course, be nil. Instead, it's likely to make it easier for them to operate (it's worked that way in places like Northern Ireland[32]). And, since denying Americans the luxury of reaping the benefits of genocide in comfort was self-evidently a key objective of the WTC/Pentagon attacks, it can be stated unequivocally that the police state mentality already pervading this country simply confirms the magnitude of their victory.

On Matters of Proportionality and Intent

As things stand, including the 1993 detonation at the WTC, "Arab terrorists" have responded to the massive and sustained American terror bombing of Iraq with a total of four assaults by explosives within the U.S. That's less than .01 percent of the 50,000 bombs the Pentagon announced were rained on Baghdad alone during the Gulf War (add in Oklahoma City and you'll get something nearer to an actual .01 percent[33]). They've managed in the process to kill about 5,000 Americans, or roughly one percent of the earlier-mentioned number of dead Iraqi children. (The percentage is far smaller if you factor in the killing of adult Iraqi civilians, not to mention troops butchered as/after they'd surrendered *subsequent to* the "war-ending" ceasefire having been announced.)*

In terms undoubtedly more meaningful to the property/profit-minded American mainstream, they've knocked down a half-dozen buildings—albeit some very well-chosen ones—and punched a $100 billion hole in the earnings outlook of major corporate shareholders. This is as opposed, however, to the "strategic devastation" visited upon the whole of Iraq and obliteration of its entire economy.

To this extent, they've given Americans a tiny dose of their own medicine, a matter which has often been depicted as a matter of "vengeance" or "retribution." While America has unquestionably earned something of the sort, there is a serious problem such interpretations. Vengeance, after all, is usually framed in terms of "getting even," a concept that is plainly inapplicable in this instance. As the above data indicate, it would require a further 49,996 detonations killing 495,000 more Americans

---

*   Merely comparing the numbers of explosives involved would have yielded a percentage much closer to .001. I made an arbitrary upward adjustment to compensate for the 300,000 pound weight of each of the three airliners hitting the twin towers and Pentagon on September 11 vis-à-vis the average weight of the bombs dropped on Baghdad. My crude calculation thus favored the U.S. rather heavily. Similarly, based as it was upon wildly inaccurate estimates of the number of U.S. fatalities announced in the media immediately following the September 11 attacks, my 5,000 figure was grossly inflated. In actuality, the total number of American dead accruing from all five strikes, including Oklahoma City, was 2,780: 2,606 on September 11, 168 in the 1995 Oklahoma City bombing—for which, in any case, "Arabs" were in no sense responsible (see note 37)—and six in the 1993 WTC bombing. Despite these imprecisions, the pursuant thrust of my computations stands.

just to even the score for the bombing of Baghdad/extermination of Iraqi children alone. And that's merely to achieve "real number" parity. To attain *actual* parity—the U.S. being about fifteen times the size of Iraq in terms of population, even more in terms of territory—the "terrorists" would need to blow up about 300,000 more buildings and kill something on the order of 7.5 million people.

Were this the intent of those who entered the U.S. to wage war against it, it would remain no less true that America and Americans were only paying the tab on what they've already done. Payback, as they say, can be a real motherfucker (ask the Germans). There is, however, no reason to believe that retributive parity is necessarily an item on the agenda of those who planned the WTC/Pentagon operation. If it were, given the virtual certainty that they possessed the capacity to have inflicted far more damage than they did, there would be a lot more American bodies lying about right now.

Hence, it can be determined that the ravings of the "news" media since September 11 have contained at least one grain of truth: The peoples of the Mideast "aren't like Americans," not least because they "don't value life" in the same way. By this, it should be understood that Middle-Easterners, unlike Americans, have no history of exterminating others purely for profit, or on the basis of racial animus. Thus, we can appreciate the fact that they value life—all lives, not just their own—far more highly than do their American counterparts.

The Makings of a Humanitarian Strategy

In sum, one can discern a certain optimism—it might even be called humanitarianism—imbedded in the thinking of those who presided over the very limited actions conducted on September 11. Their logic seems to have devolved upon the notion that the American people have condoned what has been/is being done in their name—indeed, are to a significant extent actively complicit in it—mainly because they have no idea what it feels like to be on the receiving end. Now they do. That was the "medicinal" aspect of the attacks.

To all appearances, the idea is now to give the tonic a little time to take effect, jolting Americans into the realization that the sort of pain they're now experiencing firsthand is no different from, or the least bit more excruciating than, that which they've been so cavalier in causing others, and thus to respond appropriately. Bluntly put, that hope was, and maybe still is, that Americans, stripped of their presumed immunity from incurring any real consequences to their behavior, would comprehend and act upon a message as uncomplicated as, "Stop killing our kids, if you want your own to be safe." It's a kind of "reality therapy" approach, designed to afford the American people a chance to finally "do the right thing" on their own, without further coaxing.

Were the opportunity acted upon in good faith—a sufficiently large number of Americans rising up and doing whatever is necessary to force an immediate lifting of the sanctions on Iraq, for example, and maybe hanging a few of America's abundant supply of major war criminals (Henry Kissinger comes immediately to mind, as do Madeleine Albright, Colin Powell, Bill Clinton, and George the Elder)—there is every reason to expect that military operations against the U.S. on its domestic front would be immediately suspended.

Whether they would remain so would of course be contingent on follow-up. By that, it may be assumed that American acceptance of on-site inspections by international observers to verify destruction of its weapons of mass destruction (as well as dismantlement of all facilities in which more might be manufactured), Nuremberg-style trials in which a few thousand U.S. military/corporate personnel could be properly adjudicated and punished for their crimes against humanity, and payment of appropriate reparations to the array of nations/peoples whose assets the U.S. has plundered over the year would likely suffice.

Since they've shown no sign of being either unreasonable or vindictive, it may even be anticipated that, after a suitable period of adjustment and reeducation (mainly to allow them to acquire the skills necessary to living within their means), those restored to control over their own destinies by the gallant sacrifices of the combat teams who attacked the WTC and Pentagon will eventually (re)admit Americans to the global circle of civilized societies. Stranger things have happened.

In the Alternative
Unfortunately, noble as they may have been, such humanitarian aspirations were always doomed to remain unfulfilled. For it to have been otherwise, a far higher quality of character and intellect would have to prevail among average Americans than is actually the case. Perhaps the strategists underestimated the impact of a couple of generations' worth of full-bore media indoctrination in terms of demolishing the capacity of human beings to form coherent thoughts. Maybe they neglected to factor in the mind-numbing effects of what passes for education in the U.S. Then again, it's entirely possible they were aware that a decisive majority of American adults have been reduced by this point to a level

much closer to Pavlovian stimulus/response patterns than appeals to higher logic, and still felt morally obliged to offer the dolts an option to quit while they were ahead.

What the hell? It was worth a try. But it's becoming increasingly apparent that the dosage of medicine administered was woefully insufficient to obtain the desired result. While there are undoubtedly exceptions, Americans for the most part still don't get it. Already, they've desecrated the tomb of those who died in the WTC, staging a veritable pep rally atop the mangled remains, treating the whole affair as if it were some bizarre breed of contact sport. And, of course, there are the inevitable pom-poms shaped like American flags, school colors in the form of little red-white-and-blue ribbons affixed to lapels, sportscasters in the guise of "counterterrorism experts" drooling mindless color commentary during the pregame warm-up.

Refusing the realization that the world has suddenly shifted its axis, and that they are no longer "in charge," they have by and large reverted instantly to type, working themselves into their usual bloodlust on the now obsolete premise that the bloodletting will "naturally" occur somewhere else. "Patriotism," a wise man once observed, "is this last refuge of scoundrels."[34] And the brain-dead, he might have added.

Brain-dead scoundrel-in-chief, George Junior, lacking even the sense to be careful what he wished for, has teamed up with a gaggle of fundamentalist Christian clerics like Billy Graham to proclaim a "New Crusade" called "Infinite Justice" aimed at "ridding the world of evil." One might have easily made light of such rhetoric, remarking upon how unseemly it is for a son to thus threaten his father, or a sitting president to so publicly contemplate the murder/suicide of himself and his cabinet, but the matter is deadly serious. They're preparing once again to sally forth for the purpose of slaying brown-skinned children by the scores of thousands. Already, the B-1 bombers and missile frigates are gearing up to go.

But, to where? Afghanistan? The Sudan? Iraq again (or still)? How about Grenada (that was fun)? Any of them or all. It doesn't matter. The desire to pummel the helpless is as rabid as ever. Only, this time it's different. This time the helpless aren't, or at least not so helpless as they were before September 11. This time, somewhere, perhaps in an Afghan mountain cave, possibly in a Brooklyn basement, maybe in another locale altogether—but *somewhere*, all the same—there's a grim-visaged (wo)man wearing a Clint Eastwood smile. "Go ahead, punks," s/he's saying, "Make my day."[35]

And when they do, when they launch these airstrikes abroad—or maybe a little later; it will be at a time conforming to the "terrorists" own schedule, and at a place of their choosing—the next, more intensive dose of "medicine" will be administered here "at home."* Of what will it consist? Anthrax? Mustard gas? Sarin? A tactical nuclear weapon? That, too, is their choice to make.

Looking back, it will seem to future generations inexplicable why Americans were unable on their own, and in time to save themselves, to accept a rule of nature so basic that it could be mouthed by an actor, Lawrence Fishburne, in a movie, *The Cotton Club*. "You've got to learn," the line went, "that when you push people around, *some* people push back."

---

* In retrospect, it's clear that I greatly misjudged the nature of the strategy al-Qaida and its allies were pursuing. Based upon what appears to have been a remarkably accurate assessment of how the U.S. would respond to September 11, given the pre-existing neoconservative ambitions of key players in the Bush II régime, they seem to have counted from the outset upon the U.S. putting large numbers of "boots on the ground" in places like Afghanistan and Iraq, and that such blatant aggression would galvanize sentiment in their favor across appreciable sectors of the worldwide Islamic population. Hence, while they've made sufficient gestures toward the U.S. homeland to retain credibility as a threat in that regard, thereby perpetuating a significant drain on American resources on the domestic front, they've placed a far greater emphasis upon bleeding the U.S. militarily, financially, and politically through engagement in protracted guerrilla campaigns abroad. As of mid-2014, it must be said that by any rational assessment they've been remarkably successful. Having squandered the lives of nearly 7,000 troops and a further 7,000 military contractors in Afghanistan and Iraq since 2001, with another 52,000 troops having been severely wounded (many of them permanently disabled), untold thousands of others suffering severe combat-related psychological disorders, and $3.4 trillion expended on these efforts—$4.4 trillion when the expense of veterans' care through 2056 is added in—the U.S. has not only lost the post–September 11 wars it began in both countries, but has been unable to avert either the collapse of longtime "friendly" governments in Egypt, Tunisia, and Yemen, or to control the outcomes of revolutionary upheavals in the more hostile Libya and Syria. To say that the "other side" is winning, is merely to state the obvious. See "Human Costs of War: Direct War Death in Afghanistan, Iraq, and Pakistan October 2001–April 2015" (available at http://watson.brown.edu/costsofwar/files/cow/imce/figures/2015/SUMMARY%20CHART%20-%20Direct%20War%20Death%20Toll%20to%20April%202015.pdf) and "Summary of the Costs of War Iraq, Afghanistan, and Pakistan FY 2001–2014, Billions of Current Dollars" (available at http://watson.brown.edu/costsofwar/files/cow/imce/figures/2014/Summary%20Costs%20of%20War%20NC%20JUNE%2026%202014.pdf); Bassam Haddad, Rosie Besheer, Ziad Abu-Rish, eds., *The Dawn of the Arab Uprisings: End of an Old Order?* (London: Pluto Press, 2012); Jason Brownlie and Tarel Massoud, *The Arab Spring: The Politics of Transformation in North Africa and the Middle East* (New York: Oxford University Press, 2013).

As they should. As they must. As they undoubtedly will. There is justice in such symmetry.

Addendum (September 25, 2001)

The preceding was a first take, more of a stream-of-consciousness interpretive reaction to the September 11 counterattack than a finished piece on the topic. Hence, I'll readily admit that I've been far less than thorough, and quite likely wrong about a number of things.

For instance, it may not have been (only) the ghosts of the Iraqi children who made their appearance that day. It could as easily have been some or all of their butchered Palestinian cousins. Or maybe it was some or all of the at least 3.2 million Indochinese who perished as a result of America's sustained and genocidal assault on Southeast Asia (1959–1975),[36] not to mention the millions more who've died because of the sanctions imposed thereafter. Perhaps there were a few of the Korean civilians massacred by U.S. troops during the early '50s, and the hundreds of thousands of Japanese civilians ruthlessly incinerated in the ghastly fire raids of World War II (only at Dresden did America bomb Germany in a similar manner).[37] And of course it could've been those vaporized in the militarily pointless nuclear bombings of Hiroshima and Nagasaki.[38]

There are others as well, a vast silent queue of faceless victims, stretching from the million-odd Filipinos slaughtered during America's "Indian War" in their islands at the beginning of the twentieth century,[39] through the real Indians, America's own, massacred wholesale at places like Horseshoe Bend and the Bad Axe, Sand Creek and Wounded Knee, the Washita, Bear River, and the Marias. Was it those who expired along the Cherokee Trail of Tears or the Long Walk of the Navajo? Those murdered by smallpox at Fort Clark in 1837? Starved to death in the concentration camps at Fort Snelling and the Bosque Redondo during the 1860s? Maybe the native people killed for scalp bounties in all forty-eight of the continental U.S. states? Or the Raritans whose severed heads were kicked for sport along the streets of what was then called New Amsterdam, at the very site where the WTC once stood?[40]

One hears, too, the whispers of those lost on the Middle Passage, and of those whose very flesh was sold in the slave market outside the human kennel from whence Wall Street takes its name. And of the coolie laborers, imported by the gross-dozen to lay the tracks of empire across the scorching desert sands, none of them allotted more than "a Chinaman's chance" of surviving the ordeal. The list is simply too long, too awful to go on.

No matter what its eventual fate, the U.S. will have gotten off very, very cheap. The full measure of its guilt can never be fully balanced or atoned for.

Postscript (2015)

As is well known, this piece belatedly and rather unexpectedly triggered a media-driven "firestorm of controversy" during the spring of 2005, nearly three and a half years after it was posted. For the most part, the furor centered upon my observation that, far from being "innocent," many of those killed in the World Trade Center on September 11, 2001, were the moral equivalent of nazi technocrat Adolf Eichmann—"little Eichmanns," as I described them—individually, collectively, and in both respects willingly, pursuing personal privilege and prestige by harnessing their proficiencies to the systematic mass immiseration and death of mostly darker-skinned Others for purposes of corporate profit maximization. My argument being in this respect firmly rooted in Hannah Arendt's thesis concerning "the banality of evil," set forth in her much-celebrated—and reviled—1963 book, *Eichmann in Jerusalem*, I assumed that, irrespective of readers' reactions to my "little Eichmanns" characterization, they would at the very least be based on a general understanding of who Eichmann was (i.e., the nature of his role in the nazi judeocide). From the moment the Great Controversy commenced, however, the magnitude of my error in this regard became glaringly obvious.

Bluntly put, despite my longstanding and marked disdain for what passes as knowledge on the right, I'd profoundly underestimated the degree of sheer ignorance with which it is infused, even in élite circles. While there are literally hundreds of examples upon which I might draw by way of illustration, suffice it here to offer just one: When he was deposed by my attorney, David Lane, prior to the 2009 trial of my lawsuit against the University of Colorado for violating my First Amendment rights by firing me from a tenured professorship in retaliation for the views expressed in the present essay, former university president Hank Brown, hired specifically to oversee the process, admitted that his initial perception of my "Little Eichmanns remark" was that it was "anti-Semitic."

Why? He felt a name like Eichmann must have been that of "someone Jewish."[41]

A degree of ignorance that profound defies any possibility of rational engagement, and would be striking enough were it to have come from a stereotypical red-neck. Hank Brown, however, is neither a denizen of the proverbial Tulsa trailer park, nor, ostensibly, is he a professional motor-mouthed reactionary know-nothing, the likes of Rush Limbaugh, Sean Hannity, and Bill O'Reilly. No, he's a former Republican senator from Colorado, a founder and still a key player in the Lynne Cheney–organized American Council of Trustees and Alumni (ACTA)—an organization claiming devotion to the cause of "preserving the integrity" of academia—a tenured professor of political science, and, at the time he confused Eichmann with a Jewish victim, an ACTA-selected university president roundly applauded by the right for his staunch defense of "academic excellence."

For once, words fail. The situation speaks for itself.

Notes

1   George H.W. Bush, NBC *Nightly News*, February 2, 1991.

2   On the routine use of terms like "sand nigger" to describe Iraqis during the Gulf War, see Holly Sklar, "Brave New World Order," in Cynthia Peters, ed., *Collateral Damage: The "New World Order" at Home and Abroad* (Boston: South End Press, 1992) p. 8.

3   Although I didn't realize it at the time, the September 11 attacks marked the anniversary of Bush's "New World Order" speech. See George H.W. Bush, "Address Before a Joint Session of Congress on the Persian Gulf Crisis and the Federal Budget Deficit," September 11, 1990 (available at http://www.presidency.ucsb.edu/ws/?pid=18820).

4   Such nonsense is of course discussed in my essay "Pacifism as Pathology: Notes on an American Pseudopraxis," written and first published during the mid-1980s and available in my *Pacifism as Pathology: Reflections on the Role of Armed Struggle in North America* (Oakland, CA: AK Press, [2nd ed.] 2007) pp. 45–123. Also see Peter Gelderloos, *How Nonviolence Protects the State* (Cambridge, MA: South End Press, 2007) esp. pp. 117–34.

5   I was of course referring to the 1999 anti-WTO demonstrations in Seattle and, if anything, understated the case. "Nonviolent protest organizers" like Medea Benjamin actually did far worse than I indicated, not only denouncing those who refused to accept the tactical constraints they sought to impose, but actively collaborating in the rationalization of largescale and coordinated police violence while it was happening, facilitating the arrests of "key agitators," and in the aftermath peddling a narrative in which the victims were blamed for what had occurred. For a succinct and insightful analysis, see Alexander Cockburn and Jeffrey St. Clair, "So Who Did Win in Seattle? Liberals Rewrite History," in Eddie Yuen, George Katsiaficas, and Daniel Burton-Rose, eds., *The Battle of Seattle: The New Challenge to Capitalist Globalization* (New York: Soft Skull Press, 2001) pp. 93–98. It's worth mentioning that such behavior has persisted unabated and was very much in evidence during the 2011–12 Occupy demonstrations, a circumstance exemplified in such squalid fare as Chris Hedges' "The Cancer in Occupy," *truthdig*, Feb, 6, 2012 (available at http://www.truthdig.com/report/the_cancer_of_occupy_20120206).

6   I was off by roughly a century. The First Crusade commenced in 1095 and was followed by six others, the last beginning in 1291. In any event, the extent to which the crusader mentality was from the outset marked by sheer ferocity is revealed in a

number of ways, not least by their wholesale slaughter of the inhabitants of Maarat al-Numan 1098, whereafter, by their own accounts, they "boiled pagan adults in a cooking pots [and] impaled children on spits and ate them grilled." Anna Komnena, princess of Byzantium, quoted in Michael Foss, *People of the First Crusade* (New York: Arcade, 1998) pp. 98–99; at p. 156, the Fulk (or Fulcher) of Chartres' *Gesta Francorum* (Deeds of the Franks) is quoted to identical effect. Also see Amin Maalouf, *The Crusades Through Arab Eyes* (London: Al Saqi, 1984) p. 39.

7   While the U.S. began for its own strategic reasons to provide concrete assistance to Israel during the late 1950s, all of which might of course be considered "significant," the real point of departure in my view came in June 1964, when Johnson not only promised a substantial increase in military aid but issued a statement acknowledging the "right" of the Israeli state to "preserve [its] territorial integrity," including substantial areas contiguous to its original boundaries that had subsequently been seized from the Palestinians by force. This was followed, in May 1967, by the administration's green-lighting of Israel's surprise attack on Egypt—initiating the so-called Six-Day War—which, among other things, led to a further seizure of Palestinian territory and, in combination with Israel's follow-up victory in the 1973 war, foreclosed upon Palestinian hopes of relief from the Arab states. See Avi Shlaim, *The Iron Wall: Israel and the Arab World* (New York: W.W. Norton, 1999) pp. 222, 240–41. To appreciate the difference between Israel's national boundaries as established by the UN in 1948 and those recognized by Johnson nineteen years later—in other words, the extent of the areas from which Palestinians were massively displaced—compare the maps on pp. 102 and 315 of Shlaim's *The Politics of Partition: King Abdullah, the Zionists, and Palestine, 1921–1951* (New York: Oxford University Press, 1998). The areas seized by Israel in 1967 are shown on the map at the beginning of Michael Polumbo's *Imperial Israel: The History of the Occupation of the West Bank and Gaza* (London: Bloomsbury, 1990).

8   My reference here was to the unsuccessful attempt on February 26, 1993, to topple the twin towers by detonating a massive truck bomb parked next to a structural component in the parking garage of Tower One (North Tower). The 1,300-pound bomb was constructed by CIA-trained Kuwaiti demolitions expert Ramzi Yousef and one assistant. The operation itself was carried out by a New Jersey–based al-Qaida unit designated as the Liberation Army, Fifth Battalion. Immediately prior to the bombing, Yousef mailed a list of three demands to several New York newspapers—1) an end to all U.S. aid to Israel, 2) the severing of U.S. diplomatic relations with Israel, and 3) a formal pledge of noninterference by the U.S. in the affairs of Islamic countries—warning that failure to comply would precipitate further attacks. See generally Simon Reeve, *The New Jackals: Ramzi Yousef, Osama Bin Laden and the Future of Terrorism* (Boston: Northeastern University Press, 1999); Steve Coll, *Ghost Wars: The Secret History of the CIA, Afghanistan, and Bin Laden, from the Soviet Invasion to September 10, 2001* (New York: Penguin, 2004).

9   "Freedom itself was attacked this morning by a faceless coward. . . . Make no mistake: The United States will hunt down and punish those responsible for these cowardly acts." George W. Bush, press statement, September 11, 2001 (available at http://www.washingtonpost.com/wp-srv/onpolitics/transcripts/bushtext2_091101. htm). For the record, Bush—a Vietnam-era draft-dodger who effectively deserted from the Texas Air National Guard in May 1972—issued this statement while en route to Offutt Air Force Base, a highly secure military compound near Omaha, where he spent the next several days hiding from those he'd so bravely described as

"cowards." On Bush's evasion of the draft, see George Lardner Jr. and Lois Romero, "At Height of Vietnam, Bush Picks Guard," *Washington Post* (July 28, 1999). On his desertion, see Walter V. Robinson, "Bush fell short on duty at Guard: Records show pledges unmet," *Boston Globe* (September 8, 2004). On his stint at Offutt, see Mike Allen, "Bush Reacts to Attacks, Moves to Nebraska," *Washington Post* (September 11, 2001).

10   About the time my piece was posted, liberal comedian Bill Maher, then-host of the ABC late-night talk show *Politically Incorrect*, made observations virtually identical to those in this paragraph during an on-air discussion with conservative writer/activist Dinesh D'Sousa. While he studiously avoided comment on the U.S. military, D'Sousa also rejected the Bushian depiction of the September 11 attackers as cowards, describing them instead as "warriors." Interestingly, Maher—but not D'Sousa—was immediately taken under heavy attack from the right. Unfortunately, he immediately retreated, devoting his next week's program to apologizing for his entirely accurate remarks and otherwise seeking to demonstrate that he wasn't "anti-military" (ABC fired him anyway, and he's been attempting to atone for his momentary lapse into truth-speaking ever since). The late Susan Sontag also made the same points in a brief commentary written "within forty-eight hours" of the attack, but not published in the *New Yorker* until September 24. She, too, was quickly savaged by the right, but, unlike Maher, refused to back down. See Andrew Kirell, "If Bill Maher Made the Same Controversial 9/11 Comments Today, Would He Have Lost His Show?," *Mediaite* (October 9, 2012; available at http://www.mediaite.com/tv/if-bill-maher-made-the-same-controversial-911-comments-today-would-he-have-lost-his-show/); Vivian Gornick, "The Novelist as Metaphor: How did Susan Sontag's self-identification affect her essays?" *Book Forum* (February–March 2007; available at http://www.bookforum.com/inprint/013_05/329).

11   On the nazi extermination of the Gypsies (Sinti, Roma, Romani), see Ian Hancock, "Responses to the Porrajmos: The Romani Holocaust," in Alan S. Rosenbaum, ed., *Is the Holocaust Unique? Perspectives on Comparative Genocide* (Boulder, CO: Westview Press, 1996) pp. 39–64.

12   Activities in which at least some of the attackers were reported by the FBI to have indulged during the period leading up to September 11—consumption of alcohol and pork, visiting strip clubs, and the like—plainly suggest that they were by no means devout Muslims. See, e.g., "Manager: Men spewed anti-American sentiments," *USA Today* (September 14, 2001; available at http://usatoday30.usatoday.com/news/nation/2001/09/14/Miami-club.htm).

13   In by far the most thorough study yet undertaken—the sample included 384 of 462 or 83 percent of all suicide bombers, worldwide, between 1980 and 2003—it was determined that the motives of 57 percent were secular, only 43 percent were religiously motivated. Those acting for secular reasons would still constitute the majority—52 percent—even if it is assumed that all 78 bombers not included in the sample were religiously motivated. The extent of interaction/overlap between those motivated by religion and those propelled by secular motives was not examined. See Robert A. Pape, *Dying to Win: The Strategic Logic of Suicide Terrorism* (New York: Random House, 2005) esp. pp. 209–10.

14   A clear example is the U.S. Senate's refusal to ratify the 1948 Convention on Prevention and Punishment of the Crime of Genocide for fully forty years, on grounds that compliance with its provisions would constrain U.S. exercise of its sovereign prerogatives. Ratification finally occurred in 1988, but only on the basis of an

attached "Sovereignty Package" through which the U.S. asserted an entitlement to exempt itself from compliance with any or all of Convention's terms at its own discretion. See Lawrence J. LeBlanc, *The United States and the Genocide Convention* (Durham, NC: Duke University Press, 1991), text of the so-called Sovereignty Package (S.Exec. Rep.2, 99th Cong., 1st Sess.26–67 (1985), Adopted February 19, 1986) is annexed as Appendix C.

15 From the outset, Bush in particular seems to have fixated on the term. Witness the following passages, all of them accruing from his very brief address to the nation on the evening of September 11: "Thousands of lives were suddenly ended by evil. . . . Today our nation saw evil. . . . The search is underway for those who are behind these evil acts. . . . I will fear no evil." Such rhetoric culminated in his 2002 State of the Union Address to Congress, famously referred to as his "Axis of Evil" speech. See George W. Bush, "Address to the Nation on the Terrorist Attacks, September 11, 2001," online via Gerhard Peters and John T. Woolly, *The American Presidency Project* (http://www.presidency.ucsb.edu/ws/?pid=58057); "State of the Union Address, January 29, 2002" (available at http://millercenter.org/president/speeches/detail/4540).

16 Bush's actual line was, "We will rid the world of the evil-doers." Remarks of the President Upon Arrival [at the White House], September 16, 2001 (available at http://georgewbush-whitehouse.archives.gov/news/releases/2001/09/20010916-2.html).

17 Had I been aware that the attackers were members of al-Qaida at the time I wrote this passage, I'd have realized that implementation of the plan had commenced with the 1993 World Trade Center bombing (see note 11), and included the 1998 bombings in Nairobi (Kenya) and Dar es Salaam (Tanzania), as well as the October 2000 attack on the USS *Cole* in the Yemeni port of Aden. My point stands, although I'd have formulated the sentence accordingly. In any case, see generally Peter Bergen, *The Longest War: The Enduring Conflict Between the United States and al-Qaeda* (New York: Free Press, 2011).

18 The bureau's image-building operation began in earnest no later than the early 1930s, and thereafter mushroomed into a full-blown ministry of propaganda. See, e.g., Richard Gid Powers, *G-Men: Hoover's FBI in American Popular Culture* (Carbondale: Southern Illinois University Press, 1983) and the chapter titled "Building a Public Image" in Sanford J. Ungar, *FBI: An Uncensored Look Behind the Walls* (Boston: Little, Brown, 1975) pp. 368–90.

19 My reference to murdering people in their beds specifically concerned the FBI-orchestrated summary execution of Chicago Panther leader Fred Hampton by a special police unit during the predawn hours of December 4, 1969. With regard to murder by electric chair, I specifically had in mind the execution of Ethel Rosenberg on June 19, 1950, despite the certain knowledge of ranking bureau officials that she was innocent of any capital crime. See Jeffrey Haas, *The Assassination of Fred Hampton: How the FBI and the Chicago Police Murdered a Black Panther* (Chicago: Lawrence Hill Books, 2010) and Curt Gentry, *J. Edgar Hoover: The Man and His Secrets* (New York: W.W. Norton, 1991) pp. 419–28. For a broad overview of the bureau's engagement in political repression, see my and Jim Vander Wall's *The COINTELPRO Papers: Documents from the FBI's Secret Wars Against Dissent in the United States* (Cambridge, MA: South End Press, [classics ed.] 2002).

20 See David T. Hardy with Rex Kimball, *This Is Not an Assault: Penetrating the Web of Lies Regarding the Waco Incident* (San Antonio, TX: Xlibris, 2001).

21 See John F. Kelly and Phillip K. Wearne, *Tainting Evidence: Inside the Scandals at the FBI Crime Lab* (New York: Free Press, 1998).

22 A rather spectacular example was still recent news at the time of the September 11 attacks. See Adrian Havill, *The Spy Who Stayed Out in the Cold: The Secret Life of FBI Double Agent Robert Hanssen* (New York: St. Martin's Press, 2001). A different, little considered, but related phenomenon is that of FBI agents like John Connolly in Boston and R. Lindley DeVecchio in Boston who at the very least provided highly sensitive intelligence to the mob—often with lethal results—thus facilitating perpetuation of organized criminal enterprises. See Dick Lehr and Gerald O'Neill, *Black Mass: The Irish Mob, the FBI, and a Devil's Deal* (New York: PublicAffairs, 2000) and Peter Lance, *Deal with the Devil: The FBI's Thirty-Year Relationship with a Mafia Killer* (New York: William Morrow, 2013).

23 Actually, those who've functioned as "domestic terrorists" in behalf of the FBI have tended to be contract employees and other such surrogates, rather than "agents" per se. There are many known examples, and undoubtedly more still who remain unidentified. A classic case is that of Gary Thomas Rowe, a longterm paid bureau "informant" who, as a member of an élite "action squad" in the Alabama Klan repeatedly participated in the brutal beatings of Freedom Riders in 1961, by his own admission murdered an unidentified black man in 1963, was involved in a number of bombings in Birmingham—including, it is widely believed, the infamous Sixteenth Street Baptist Church blast on September 15, 1963, that killed four black youngsters and injured sixteen other people—and was one of the four klansmen in the car from which the fatal shot was fired at civil rights activist Viola Liuzzo on March 25, 1965 (he was later prosecuted as the shooter by the State of Alabama, but FBI noncooperation undercut the effort and it failed). See Gary May, *The Informant: The FBI, the Ku Klux Klan, and the Murder of Viola Liuzzo* (New Haven, CT: Yale University Press, 2005).

24 Or, as the inimitable Harry Truman put it in his diary on May 12, 1945, "a Gestapo or Secret Police." Quoted in Robert H. Farrell, *Harry Truman: A Life* (Columbia: University of Missouri Press, 2013) p. 302. This was not the only occasion on which Truman compared the FBI to the Gestapo. For quotes, see Gentry, *J. Edgar Hoover*, p. 326; Richard Gid Powers. *Secrecy and Power: The Life of J. Edgar Hoover* (New York: Free Press, 1987) p. 290.

25 That most Americans continue to contend, despite overwhelming evidence to the contrary, that "we are a free people," is essentially meaningless. Such mass delusions are, after all, hardly unprecedented. See Milton Mayer, *They Thought They Were Free: The Germans, 1933–45* (Chicago: University of Chicago Press, 1955).

26 The scenario has unfolded very much along the lines I anticipated. See Ivan Greenberg, *Surveillance in America: Critical Analysis of the FBI, 1920 to the Present* (Lanham, MD: Lexington Books, 2012) pp. 269–326. The erosion of civil rights, already well underway, immediately accelerated. See James X. Dempsey and David Cole, *Terrorism and the Constitution: Sacrificing Civil Liberties in the Name of National Security* (Los Angeles: First Amendment Foundation, 1999) and the essays collected in Cynthia Brown, ed., *Lost Liberties: Ashcroft and the Assault of Personal Freedom* (New York: Free Press, 2003), esp. Nancy Chang's "How Democracy Dies: The War on Civil Liberties" and Kate Martin's "Secret Arrests and Preventive Detention," at pp. 33–51 and 75–90, respectively.

27 Rather predictably, this has played out with particular virulence where those of phenotypically "Arabic" appearance are concerned. See the essays collected in Elaine C. Hagopian, ed., *Civil Rights in Peril: The Targeting of Arabs and Muslims* (Chicago/

London: Haymarket Books/Pluto Press, 2004), especially Nancy Murray's "Profiled: Arabs, Muslims, and the Post-9/11 Hunt for the 'Enemy Within,'" pp. 27–68. Also see Stephen Sheehi, *Islamophobia: The Ideological Campaign Against Muslims* (Atlanta: Clarity Press, 2011) esp. pp. 132–71.

28 When I wrote this, I had in mind as historical precedent the CIA's various domestic operations targeting antiwar activists, the Black Panther Party, and other political dissidents—Projects Merrimac and Resistance, as examples—ordered in violation of legal constraints by Lyndon Johnson in 1967 and consolidated as Operation CHAOS from 1969 until it was ostensibly terminated in 1974. Although it has repeatedly requested—but, oddly, never received—statutory authorization from Congress to resume, or more likely ramp up, operations targeting U.S. citizens on the domestic front after September 11, The Company has done so anyway. On its post–September 11 expansion of domestic operations, see, e.g., Eric Lichtblau and Mark Mazzetti, "Pentagon and CIA Expand Intelligence Role in U.S.," *New York Times* (January 14, 2007). On Operation CHAOS and its context, see Seymour Hersh, "Huge C.I.A. Operation Reported in U.S. against Antiwar Forces, Other Dissidents in Nixon Years," *New York Times* (December 22, 1974); Frank J. Donner, *The Age of Surveillance: The Aims and Methods of America's Political Intelligence System* (New York: Alfred A. Knopf, 1980) pp. 259–79.

29 See *Central Intelligence Agency: The Pike Report* (Nottingham, UK: Spokesman Books, 1977) pp. 130–38; John Ranelagh, *The Agency: The Rise and Decline of the CIA* (New York: Simon and Schuster, 1986) pp. 462–63. It should be noted that the failure to foresee Tet was by no means the CIA's alone. The Pentagon's own elaborate Military Intelligence apparatus was, if anything, even more culpable. See James J. Wirtz. *The Tet Offensive: Intelligence Failure in War* (Ithaca, NY: Cornell University Press, 1994).

30 See generally David Arbel and Ran Edelist, *Western Intelligence and the Collapse of the Soviet Union, 1980–1990: Ten Years That Did Not Shake the World* (New York: Routledge, 2003).

31 Actually, the Phoenix assassins weren't after guerrillas, as I knew perfectly well when I wrote this line (I simply couldn't resist pointing out the propagandists' change in descriptors). Rather, they were tasked with eliminating the National Liberation Front's *political* cadres, who were ensconced in virtually every village and hamlet in the country. See generally Douglas Valentine, *The Phoenix Program* (New York: William Morrow, 1990).

32 By the mid-1980s, the British had deployed a highly sophisticated counterinsurgency force in the six counties of Northern Ireland, consisting of 30,000 armed personnel drawn from the army (including substantial numbers of élite airborne troops), the Ulster Defense Regiment, and the Royal Ulster Constabulary (RUC), as well as a secret unit, Echo 4 Alpha (E4A), employing SAS, MI5, and high-level RUC operatives to conduct "surgical" assassinations. Intelligence was provided through the integrated efforts of the RUC, Army Intelligence, MI5, and the British secret service, utilizing "a vast array of electronic surveillance [and] a significant number of undercover intelligence operatives." All this was pitted against the Provisional IRA, which never numbered more than 300 core fighters with perhaps a further 450 volunteers serving in support capacities. The upshot was that in 1992, despite years of concerted and often draconian efforts by the British, the IRA carried out "282 bomb[ings], far more than in any of the preceding six years." Plainly, "the IRA [still] held the initiative," until the 1994 ceasefire declared upon Britain's acceptance of the preconditions necessary to begin peace negotiations. See Brendan O'Brien,

The Long War: The IRA and Sinn Féin (Syracuse, NY: Syracuse University Press, [2nd ed.] 1999) pp. 161–65, 301–23. On the E4A assassination program in particular, see Sean McPhilemy, *The Committee: Political Assassination in Northern Ireland* (Niwot, CO: Roberts Rinehart, 1998).

33   My reference here is of course to the April 19, 1995, bombing of the Murrah Federal Building in Oklahoma City. While major media venues like the *New York Times* and CNN immediately began peddling the idea that "Arab terrorists" were responsible— right-wing lunacy's then-preeminent motor-mouth, Rush Limbaugh, promptly used his nationally syndicated radio program to demand renewed U.S. bombing of Baghdad in "retaliation" since, he blathered, even if Saddam Hussein wasn't directly responsible for the attack, he'd "done so much to create the climate" in which it was carried out—it turned out that the conspirators were a lily-white group of Christian extremists, the bombing a response to the FBI's assault on the Branch Davidian compound near Waco, Texas, resulting in the deaths of 76 people (includ- ing nineteen infants and children) exactly two years earlier. The Arab community in the U.S. bore the early brunt of public reaction to the Oklahoma City bombing (including numerous physical assaults); however irrationally, many Americans still associate it with "Arab terrorism"; and the Limbaugh cult is still trying to pin the whole thing on Saddam or, in the alternative, "islamists." See Mark S. Hamm, *Apocalypse in Oklahoma: Waco and Ruby Ridge Revenged* (Boston: Northeastern University Press, 1997); on media coverage, pp. 54–57. For more on initial media coverage, see Penny Bender Fuchs, "Jumping to Conclusions in Oklahoma City?," *American Journalism Review* (June 1995; available at http://ajrarchive.org/article.asp?id=1980); Jim Naureckas, "Talk Radio on Oklahoma City: Don't Look at Us," FAIR (July 1, 1995; available at http://fair.org/media_criticism/talk-radio-on-oklahoma-city/). For an example of the right's ongoing effort to implicate Saddam, see Jayna Davis, *The Third Terrorist: The Middle East Connection to the Oklahoma City Bombing* (Nashville, TN: WND Books, 2004).

34   The "wise man" was Samuel Johnson, and his actual phrasing was, "Patriotism is the last refuge of a scoundrel." The comment was made on the evening of April 7, 1775, in reference to the posturing of self-proclaimed "patriot minister" John Stuart and his followers. See James Boswell, *The Life of Samuel Johnson* (London: Penguin Classics, 1979 edited reprint of 1791 original) p. 182.

35   On the outside chance there there's a reader unfamiliar with the line I've para- phrased here, among the more memorable in the history of American cinema, it was uttered on-screen by San Francisco police detective Harry Callahan, played by Clint Eastwood, in *Dirty Harry* (1971).

36   When I wrote this in 2001, 3.2 million was the standard estimate of Indochinese fatalities, accepted even by former U.S. defense secretary Robert S. McNamara, a principal architect of the war. The figure was far too low. More recent studies indi- cate that the toll among Vietnamese alone was about 3.8 million, "with the U.S.-led campaign in Cambodia resulting in 600,000 to 800,000 deaths, and Laotian war mortality estimated at about 1 million," for a grand total perhaps in the neighbor- hood of 5.5 million. See John Tirman, "Why do we ignore the civilians killed in American wars?" *Washington Post* (January 26, 2012).

37   For a brief overview, see H. Bruce Franklin, *War Stars: The Superweapon in the American Imagination* (New York: Oxford University Press, 1988) pp. 107–11. More comprehen- sively, see Kenneth P. Werrell, *Blankets of Fire: U.S. Bombers over Japan during World War II* (Washington, DC: Smithsonian Institution Press, 1996) pp. 150–223.

38 See Gar Alperovitz, *The Decision to Use the Atomic Bomb* (New York: HarperCollins, 1995) esp. pp. 627–41.

39 The estimate of a million dead is cited in neocon Max Boot's *The Savage Wars of Peace: Small Wars and the Rise of American Power* (New York: Basic Books, 2003) p. 125. Others have argued that the actual toll was closer 1.5 million. See E. San Juan Jr., "U.S. Genocide in the Philippines: A Case of Guilt, Shame, or Amnesia?" *WaybackMachine* (March 22, 2005; available at http://web.archive.org/web/20090622095234/http://www.selvesandothers.org/article9315.html). For a solid study of the manner in which the U.S. pursued the campaign, see Stuart Creighton Miller in his *"Benevolent Assimilation": The American Conquest of the Philippines, 1899–1903* (New Haven, CT: Yale University Press, 1982).

40 All of these examples and many others are covered in "'Nits Make Lice': The Extermination of American Indian, 1607–1996," in my *A Little Matter of Genocide: Holocaust and Denial in the Americas, 1492 to the Present* (San Francisco: City Lights, 1997) pp. 129–288.

41 The case is *Ward Churchill v. University of Colorado* (66 CV 1143, Denver Dist. Ct. (2009)). In his trial testimony on March 12, 2009, Brown further conceded that his view was obtained entirely from the right-wing media, and at that he'd still never bothered to read the "offending" material (transcript at pp. 899–900). For detailed background on my case—and Brown's instrumental role in it—see my "The Myth of Academic Freedom: Experiencing the Application of Liberal Principle in a Neoconservative Era," *Works and Days*, Vol. 51/52, 53/54 (2008–09) pp. 139–230; expansion published without annotation in Edward J. Carvalho and David B. Downing, eds., *Academic Freedom in the Post-9/11 Era* (New York: Palgrave Macmillan, 2010) pp. 65–113.

About the Authors

Ward Churchill (Keetoowah Cherokee) was, until moving to Atlanta in 2012, a member of the leadership council of Colorado AIM. A past national spokesperson for the Leonard Peltier Defense Committee and UN delegate for the International Indian Treaty Council, he is a life member of Vietnam Veterans Against the War and currently a member of the Council of Elders of the original Rainbow Coalition, founded by Chicago Black Panther leader Fred Hampton in 1969. Now retired, Churchill was professor of American Indian Studies and chair of the Department of Ethnic Studies until 2005, when he became the focus of a major academic freedom case. Among his two dozen books are the award-winning *Agents of Repression* (1988, 2002), *Fantasies of the Master Race* (1992, 1998), *Struggle for the Land* (1993, 2002), and *On the Justice of Roosting Chickens* (2003), as well as *The COINTELPRO Papers* (1990, 2002), *A Little Matter of Genocide* (1997), *Acts of Rebellion* (2003), and *Kill the Indian, Save the Man* (2004).

Barbara Alice Mann (Ohio Bear Clan Seneca) is a PhD scholar and associate professor in the Honors College of the University of Toledo, in Ohio. She has authored thirteen books, including the internationally acclaimed *Iroquoian Women: The Gantowisas* (2001), *George Washington's War on Native America* (2005), *Daughters of Mother Earth* (2006, released in paperback as *Make a Beautiful Way*, 2008), and *The Tainted Gift* (2009), on the deliberate spread of disease to Native peoples by settlers as a land-clearing tactic. She lives in her homeland and is the Northern Director of the Native American Alliance of Ohio.

Index

"Passim" (literally "scattered") indicates intermittent discussion of a topic over a cluster of pages.

Abbey, Edward, 283–86 passim
abortion, 59, 308, 350n150, 353n177
Abrams, Creighton, 434
Abu-Jamal, Mumia, 3, 366, 388n17
Adair, James, 170n100
Adams, Hank, 113
Adams, Richard, 186
Adamson, Joni: *American Indian Literature, Environmental Justice, and Ecocriticism,* 282–88
Adorno, Theodor, 146, 149, 165n45
Afghanistan, 376, 458, 466–69 passim, 533n
Africa, 26n55, 372–73, 509n506; U.S. embassy bombings (1998), 506n497. *See also* Burundi; Egypt; Libya; Rwanda; Somalia; South Africa; Sudan
African Americans, 12–13, 66, 252, 276n262, 372–73; imprisonment, 142; lynching, 62–65 passim, 76n38; native nations and, 128n20, 139, 140. *See also* civil rights movement
Agent Orange, 446, 461
AIM. *See* American Indian Movement (AIM)
Alaska natives, 51n66, 143
Albert, Judy, 264n134

Albright, Madeleine, xxviii, 365, 452, 456–58 passim, 465, 472, 522; as war criminal, 384–85, 478, 531
Alcatraz occupation (1969–71), 9, 147
Alcoholics Anonymous (AA), 292, 321
alcoholism, 83, 291–94 passim, 298, 299, 303–8 passim, 315–27 passim, 332, 349n145, 355–56nn194–202 passim
Aldrich, Robert: *Ulzana's Raid,* 234
al-Jazeera, 466, 467, 478
Allotment Act of 1887, xxxiv, 74n21, 115–17 passim, 121, 122, 128–29nn22–24, 130n29
Almanac of the Dead (Silko), 286
al-Qaida, 391n40, 398n100, 466–73 passim, 478, 507n497, 510n525, 513n546, 518n591; public opinion, 398n98
American Anthropological Association, 178
American Association of University Professors (AAUP), xxxiii–xxxiv, 124–25
American Council of Trustees and Alumni (ACTA), 135n65, 536
American Declaration of the Rights and Duties of Man, 61
American exceptionalism, 286, 368, 401n127, 475, 477

American Indian Chicago Conference (1961), 98

American Indian Holocaust and Survival (Thornton), 113

American Indian Literature, Environmental Justice, and Ecocriticism (Adamson), 282–88

American Indian Movement (AIM), 13, 114, 118–19, 147, 148, 248, 283; Peltier, 388n17; Wounded Knee uprising, 127n11. *See also* Colorado AIM

American Indian Quarterly, 111n, 121

American Indians, American Justice (Deloria and Lytle), 149

American Revolution, xv, 33–34, 49n30

Amherst, Jeffrey, 394n70

Amnesty International, 504n477, 504n479

Anasazi, 181, 184, 188–90 passim

Andersonville POW camp, 441

Anglican Church of Canada, 296–97, 340n53

Angola Airlines shoot-down (1983), 509n506

Anishinaabe language. *See* Ojibwe language

anthrax, 472–73, 533

anthropology, 151, 156, 166n61, 174–216 passim, 214n188, 269n190

antisemitism, xvi, xvii, 75–76n35, 192

antismoking movement, 367, 388–89n20, 465, 505n485–86, 522

Antiterrorism and Effective Death Penalty Act of 1996, 390n35, 470, 511n531

antiwar movement, 475; Vietnam, 460, 516n574

Apaches, 423, 441; in films, 232, 234, 241–42, 244. *See also* Geronimo

"apolitical" persons, 149, 301, 382, 404n141

Apted, Michael, 223, 257n43

Arapahos, 43, 482n48

archaeology, 171n111, 177–90 passim

Arendt, Hannah, xxxi, 380, 535

Arens, William, 182, 183, 185, 191–92, 206n102; *The Man-Eating Myth*, 177–79

Arizona: archaeology, 180–83 passim

Ashcroft, John, 471

assassination, 3; attempts and plots, xx, xxiv–xxvi, 351n156, 406n155, 517n581; Allende, 517n581; by FBI, 351n156, 539n19; JFK, xxviii, 520; Northern Ireland, 541n32

assimilation policy, 73, 89, 295

atrocities: Afghanistan, 468; anti-Indian, 410–11, 413, 418, 427; Crusades, 537n6; Palestinian West Bank, 474; Vietnam, 429, 434; World War II, 426–27. *See also* massacres

Atta, Mohammed, 473

Australia, 249, 478; European invasion and colonization, xviii, 15; indigenous peoples, 27n65; in UN, 14n, 70; Vietnam War, 433, 528

"Axis of Evil," 472

Axtell, James, 235–36

Aztecs, 175–77 passim, 183–87 passim, 199n23

Baccus, Rick, 469

Bad Axe Massacre, 411, 412

Bageant, Joe, 145

Baghdad, 450, 452, 496n353, 525, 529, 530, 542n33

Bahn, Paul, 177, 182, 185, 205n95

Bail Reform Act of 1984, 470

Baker, Eugene M., 420

Baldwin, George C., 180

Baldwin, Henry, 37

Baldwin, James, xxxi; *The Fire Next Time*, xviii

Balkan Crisis, 456–57

"banality of evil" (Arendt), 380, 535

Bangladesh, 71, 79n73

Bari, Judi, 285, 310, 351n156

Basques, 12, 14, 21–22n22

Basra, Iraq, 370, 448–50 passim

Bataille, Gretchen: *Native American Representations*, 280–81

battlefield trophies, 410, 426–27, 434

Battle of Bad Axe. *See* Bad Axe Massacre

The Battle of Elderbush Gulch (Griffith), 217, 227, 233–34, 253n1

Battle of Horseshoe Bend. *See* Horseshoe Bend Massacre

Battle of Little Bighorn, 228, 260n78

Battle of the Washita. *See* Washita Massacre
Battle of Tippecanoe, 410
Baudrillard, Jean, 150–51, 250; *The Gulf War Did Not Take Place*, 367
Baum, L. Frank, 421
Beals, Ralph, 186
Beck, E.M., 63, 76n38
Bell, J. Franklin, 399–400n113, 423, 425, 427, 428, 484n95
Bellecourt, Clyde, 119
Bellecourt, Vernon, 118–19
Bennis, Phyllis, 29
Bent, Robert, 418
Beresford, Bruce: *Black Robe*, 223, 225, 230, 231, 261n91
Bergthold, James, 429
Bering Strait land bridge theory, 154, 155, 156, 159, 168–69n85
Best, Steven, 277n267
Bhabha, Homi, 222, 250, 367
Bhopal disaster (1984), 509–10n512
Biddle, Francis, 89, 92, 108n122
Billman, Brian, 183
bin Laden, Usama, 396n86, 397n87, 466, 469, 478, 513n546, 518n591
Bin Wahad, Dhoruba, 366, 388n17
biological weapons, 393n64, 472–73, 497n373, 533
Biolsi, Thomas, 150
"Bipolar Disorder," 321
Bird, S. Elizabeth, 240
Birth of a Nation (Griffith), 258n54
Bisbee, William H., 424
Black Bloc, 368, 390n34, 523
Blackfeet Indians, 139, 420
Black Hawk, 411
Black Hills, 44, 109–10n133, 482n48
Black Kettle, 417, 420
Black Panther Party, 276n262, 388n17
Black Robe (Beresford), 223, 225, 230, 231, 261n91
Blood Libel, 192, 213n176, 238, 270n199
"blood quantum," xxxiv, 111–16 passim, 128n20, 129n25. *See also* half-blood quantum
"bloodthirsty savages" (trope). *See* "savages" (trope)
Blum, William, 456

boarding schools, 39, 66, 73n21, 236, 237, 295–306 passim, 334, 349n145; Chrisjohn and Young on, 361n252; John Kelly experience, 306, 361n247
bombings, suicide. *See* suicide bombings
book reviews, 139–43, 279–88
borderline personality disorder (BPD), 322–23, 357n209, 358n213
Bosnia, 71, 80n76, 499n413
Bosque Redondo, 441–42
Boulder, Colorado, 465, 505n486; Leah Kelly in, 312–28 passim, 350n149, 350n152, 356n201, 359n223. *See also* University of Colorado
Boulder County, Colorado, 321, 356n201
bounties. *See* scalp bounties
Boyle, Francis, 453–54
Brady, Ivan, 182
Branch Davidian siege (1993). *See* Waco siege (1993)
Britain. *See* Great Britain
Broken Arrow (Daves), 241–42, 245
Brown, Hank, 123, 135n65, 535–36, 543n41
Brown, Preston, 424, 434
Brownmiller, Susan, 236, 263n128
Brown v. Board of Education, 66
Brumble, H. David, 157, 158
Brussels Declaration, 1874, 484n85
Brydon, Diana, 249
Buckley, Kevin, 433
Bullock, Peter, 182–83
Bureau of Indian Affairs (BIA), 88–89, 114–17 passim, 121, 127n16, 129n25, 130n28; on education, 73n21; on sun dance, 50n56. *See also* "Indian agents"; Indian Health Service
Burma. *See* Myanmar
Burnette, Robert, 115
Burton, Michael, 145, 161n10
Burundi, 71, 79nn72–73
Bush, George Herbert Walker, 44, 45n3, 364, 365, 427, 447, 454, 521–24 passim; Afghanistan, 466; LA rebellion of 1992, 512n535; parroting of Hitler, 458; as war criminal, 80n75, 447, 454, 531

Bush, George W.: "Axis of Evil," 472; 9/11, 465–66, 524, 525, 526, 532, 537–38n9, 539n15; military tribunals, 511n525; "war on terrorism," 467
Butler, Richard, 514n553

Cabral, Amílcar, 252
California: land claims, 43, 54n96; monetary compensation, 107n106; termination, 94, 107n106, 107n108; treaties, 54n96
Callaway, Howard H., 431
Calley, William, 407n165, 429–31 passim
Cambodia, 71, 437–38, 439
Cameron, Ewen, 296
Camp McCoy bombing, Wisconsin, July 26, 1970, xxiii
Canada, 18, 27n65, 268n171, 296–309 passim, 394n70; alcoholism, 291; boarding schools, 236, 296–97; "expression of regret," 299. See also Anglican Church of Canada; Ojibwes of Onigaming First Nation; Winnipeg
cancer and Vietnam War, 393n59, 405n153
cannibalism, 174–216, 270n199; in popular culture, 194
Canyon de Chelly, Arizona, 180
capital punishment. See death penalty
captives and captivity, 235–36
carbon dating. See radiocarbon dating
Carib Indians, 174–75, 185
Carlson, David, 507n502
Carmichael, Stokely, 12, 22n23–25, 276n262
carpet bombing. See saturation bombing (carpet bombing)
Carrasco, David, 186
Carter, George, 169n85
Cartographies of Desire: Captivity, Race, and Sex in the Shaping of the American Nation (Faery), 264n135
Casas, Bartolomé de las, 31, 174, 197n7
Castaneda, Carlos, 178
Castillo, Bobby, 309, 310, 350n153
catastrophism, 152, 159
Catholic Church, 30, 31, 261n91, 296, 306, 307, 340n53
Catlin, George, 81

Center for the SPIRIT, 118
Central America. See Guatemala; Nicaragua
Central Intelligence Agency. See CIA
Césaire, Aimé, 21n15
Chacoans, 180, 189–90
Chaffee, Adna R., 423, 425
Chato's Land, 234
Chechnya, 478, 518n592
chemical weapons and warfare, 61, 393n59, 428, 446, 461, 472, 473
Cheney, Dick, 449, 514n550
Cherokees, xxxiv, 36–38 passim, 116, 129n26, 130n30, 141; naturalization of whites, 128n20; Trail of Tears, 372; Cherokee Nation v. Georgia, 36–37, 40
Cheyenne Autumn (Ford), 245
Cheyennes, 43, 128n20, 420–21, 423, 441, 482n48; in films and television, 241, 244, 245. See also Sand Creek Massacre; Washita Massacre
Cheyfitz, Eric, 125, 135n63, 136n71, 137–38n80
Chicago Conference of 1961. See American Indian Chicago Conference (1961)
child abuse, 296, 305–6, 323, 352–53n175, 354n185
child mortality, 452. See also infant mortality
children, boarding school education of. See boarding schools
children's rights convention. See Convention on the Rights of the Child
Chile, 371, 517n581
China, 15, 57, 233, 280
Chingachgook (fictional character), 239, 240
Chinese immigrants, xiv, 63, 373, 534
Chittenden, Hiram, xviii
Chivington, John M., 231, 260n83, 261n95, 407n164, 417–20 passim, 428, 482nn47–48
Chomsky, Noam, 376, 408n172, 462, 507n500
Chrisjohn, Roland, 343n87, 361n252

Christianity, 30–31, 151–52, 153, 156, 193, 532. *See also* Anglican Church of Canada; Catholic Church; Crusades

Church, Frank, 65–66

Churchill, Ward: antisemitism alleged, xvi, xvii; character assassination, xiii; death threats and hate mail, xxxv–xxxvii, 7n8; FBI surveillance and files, xxi–xxvi; *Indians Are Us?*, 111, 118; lawsuits, xxxv, 2, 123, 135–36n67, 535; Leah Kelly relationship, 289–90, 309–30, 335, 348–60 passim; *A Little Matter of Genocide*, xvii, xix, xxviii; Ojibwe name, 330, 360n239; *On the Justice of Roosting Chickens*, 363n; "Some People Push Back," xxviii–xxxiii passim, 520–43; tribal enrollment, xxxiv; University of Colorado, xxvii–xxxvii passim, 121–25 passim; in U.S. Army, xxii, xxiii, 148

Churchill, Winston, 492n257

Church of Canada. *See* Anglican Church of Canada

CIA, xxviii–xxxi passim, 296, 370–71, 377, 407n171, 528; Afghanistan, 466; airliner bombings and, 509n506; Chile, 371, 517n581; domestic operations, 541n28; Guatemala, 80n78, 370; Indonesia, 370; Iran, 371; North Korea, 514n547; Philippines, 472; Vietnam (Phoenix Program), 377, 399n106, 528, 541n31; World War II, 393n62

civilians, military targeting of: Iraq, xxix, 364, 450–53 passim, 525, 529; laws of war, 413–15 passim, 436, 446, 447, 477, 491n220; Serbia, 456–57; Sherman view, 421–22; Vietnam, 428–38 passim. *See also* "collateral damage"; My Lai Massacre; Sand Creek Massacre; Washita Massacre; Wounded Knee Massacre

Civil Rights Congress (CRC), 65

civil rights movement, 12–13, 540n23

Civil War, 414, 441

Clark, George Rogers, 410, 413

Clark, Ramsey, 449–53 passim; *The Impact of Sanctions on Iraq*, 367

Clark, Richard, 512n535

Clausewitz, Carl von, 415, 452, 481n38

Cleaver, Eldridge, 236, 264nn134–35

Clinton, Bill, 80n75, 368, 452, 456, 509n510, 512n535, 524, 531

Clinton, Robert N., 122–25, 135n61, 135n63, 136nn70–71

cluster bombs, 370, 371, 428, 437, 448, 449

Cochise, 241–42

Cochrane, John J., 90

Cody Historical Motion Picture Company, 217, 227, 228, 231

Cohen, William, 456

COINTELPRO, xxi–xxv

Cold War, 61, 114, 528

"collateral damage," xxix–xxx, xxxi, 369, 375, 526

Colmer, William M., 90

colonialism, 10–20 passim, 84, 119, 140, 165n47, 247–53 passim, 271n211, 279–80; alcoholism and, 293; "blue water" requirement, 10, 11, 19n9, 48, 148; Philippines, 422; Sartre views, 84, 246–51 passim, 260n84, 261n87, 278n272, 301, 331; white women's complicity, 265n141. *See also* decolonization; "internal colonialism"; settler states

Colorado: archaeology, 180–83 passim. *See also* Boulder, Colorado; Denver; Sand Creek Massacre; University of Colorado

Colorado AIM, xxiv–xxvii passim, 148

Columbus, Christopher, 31, 174

Columbus Day, xxvii, 299

Columbus Quincentennial, xxvii, 213–14n186

Co Luy Massacre. *See* My Khe Massacre

Coma, Guillermo, 174

Comanches, 128n20, 235, 441

Communist Party USA, 276n262

compensation, monetary, 42, 43, 86–97 passim, 103n49, 106n96, 107n97, 108n122; California bands, 107n106; Lakotas, 109–10n133. *See also* "gratuitous offsets"

compulsory schooling, 73n21

concentration camps, 288n15, 441, 494n284, 512n538

Congo, 26n55

Congress. *See* U.S. Congress

Conley, Robert, 141

Connor, Patrick E., 482n48

Connors, Chuck, 244

conquest, rights of. *See* rights of conquest

Constant, Emmanuel, 510n512

"contact" (word), xviii, xx

Convention on Prevention and Punishment of the Crime of Genocide, 50n58, 56–80 passim, 101n22, 300–302 passim, 384, 456, 538–39n14

Convention on Prohibition of Certain Conventional Weapons, 446

Convention on the Elimination of All Forms of Racial Discrimination, 20n11, 61, 455

Convention on the Prohibition of Military or Any Other Hostile Use of Environmental Modification Techniques, 446

Convention on the Rights of the Child, 345n108, 384, 406–7n122, 455–56, 503n475

Cooper, James Fenimore, 239, 245, 267n152; film adaptations, 230, 231, 232

Cornplanter, 410

corporal punishment of children, 296

Cortés, Hernan, 178, 197nn4–5

Cosmatos, George: *Tombstone*, 246

cosmology, 150, 153

Costner, Kevin: *Dances with Wolves*, 230, 231, 245

courts-martial, 419; Calley, 430, 431; Custer, 228; Lakotas, 441; Philippine-American War, 424; war resisters, 443–44, 453–54

cover-ups, 429, 432, 453

"Cowboy and Indian" movies, 217–46 passim

Crazy Horse, 120, 242, 268n170

Creek Indians. *See* Muscogees (Creeks)

Crow Indians, 128n20

Crusades, 30, 524, 532, 536–37n6

Cruse, Harold, 22n23

Cuba, 509n506, 514n547

culpability, 301, 333, 379–81 passim, 386

cultural genocide, xvii, 39, 59, 295–97, 346n117

cultural imperialism, 160

Custer, George Armstrong, 228–30, 260n78, 420

Custer Died for Your Sins (Deloria), 12, 145, 150, 151

Custer of the West (Siodmak), 229

Dances with Wolves (Costner), 230, 231, 245

Daves, Delmer: *Broken Arrow*, 241–42, 245

Davis, Robert: *The Genocide Machine in Canada*, 59

Davy Crockett (television series), 269–70n192

Davy Crockett films, 245, 269n192

Dawes Act. *See* Allotment Act of 1887

death from exposure, xvi, 83, 291, 442

death penalty, 406–7n162. *See also* Antiterrorism and Effective Death Penalty Act of 1996; execution, summary

death threats, xxxv, 7n8

Debs, Eugene, 2–3

Declaration of the Rights and Duties of Man. *See* American Declaration of the Rights and Duties of Man

decolonization, xxxvii–xxxviii, 10–18 passim, 20n12, 140, 147, 277n268, 280, 334–35; Jimmie Durham view, 247–48; Ngugi wa Thiong'o view, 252; Vine Deloria view, 160; white women and, 265n141

Deerslayer (Cooper): film and television adaptations, 239

defectors and defection, 494nn308, 514n553

dehumanization, 279, 300, 331, 375, 426, 462; in films and literature, 4, 231–33, 243, 246; Iraq, xxx, 526; Vietnam, 428, 429

De las Casas, Bartolomé. *See* Casas, Bartolomé de las

Delaware Indians. *See* Lenapes

Deloria, Vine, Jr., 3, 22n24–25, 54n94, 96, 127n16, 144–73, 271n203; *American Indians, American Justice*, 149; on apathy, 84–85; *Behind the Trail of Broken Treaties*, 147; childhood and education, 165n50; *Custer Died for Your Sins*, 12, 145, 150, 151; *God Is Red*, 151, 160; ignored by Adamson, 285; *The Metaphysics of Modern Experience*, 152–53, 160; *Red Earth, White Lies*, 153, 160, 172n124; on sovereignty, 50n53; view of Marshall opinions, 38; *We Talk, You Listen*, 12, 147

Del Ponte, Carla, 457

Delta Force, 468, 470, 512n535

DeMallie, Raymond, 146

demonization of "savages" (film trope). *See* "savages" (film trope)

demonstrations and protests. *See* protests and demonstrations

denial, xv–xvii, 219, 378, 380, 412, 459. *See also* Jewish Holocaust: denial of

Denmark, 18, 70, 309

Denver, xxv–xxvii passim; Leah Kelly memorial, 329; Sand Creek Massacre and, 418, 419–20, 445

Department of Justice. *See* U.S. Department of Justice

Department of State. *See* U.S. Department of State

depleted uranium, 406n153, 461

deportation of Muslims. *See* Muslims, detention and deportation of

Derrida, Jacques, 150

Dershowitz, Alan, 125, 137n76

desertion by soldiers, 228, 444, 454, 494n308, 537n9

Desert Storm. *See* Operation Desert Storm

detention, arbitrary, 470–71, 510n525. *See also* Guantánamo Bay, Cuba

Deutsch, Eberhard, 66

Diamond, Jared, xviii–xix

Díaz del Castillo, Bernal, 175, 186, 187

Diné people (Navajos), 12, 286, 287–88n14, 372, 441–42

"discovery," doctrine of. *See* doctrine of discovery

disease, xviii–xix, 83, 292, 295, 372, 374, 451. *See also* cancer and Vietnam War; smallpox

Disney productions, 225, 245, 269–70n195

dissidents: repression of, 368, 390n35, 512–13n538; rights and duties, 516–17n579

DiStefano, Philip, xxxiii, 121, 122

Dr. Quinn, Medicine Woman, 230, 240, 241, 245

doctrine of discovery, xxxvii, 30–35 passim, 39, 47n12, 49n34, 270n200

Dodd, Christopher, 70

domestic abuse, 304, 305–6

domestic violence, 316, 348n141

Dönitz, Karl, 439–40

Douglas, Mary, 178

Dowd, Douglas, 394n73

draft refusal, 444

Drinnon, Richard, 236; *Facing West*, 258n61

drugs, prescription. *See* prescription drugs

drug trade, 471

drug war. *See* "war on drugs"

D'Sousa, Dinesh, 538n10

Duffy, James, 434

Duggan, Michael, 451

Dull Knife, 420

Durán, Diego, 175, 186

Durham, Jimmie, 130n30, 147, 218–19, 245–48 passim, 284

Dutch colonists, 372

duty, personal. *See* responsibility, personal

Eagleton, Terry, 251, 273nn232–33, 274n240, 277n268

Earth First!, 284, 285

Earth in Upheaval (Velikovsky), 152

Earth Liberation Front (ELF), 390n35

East Timor, 370, 455

Eastwood, Clint, 532; *The Unforgiven*, 246

Echo-Hawk, Roger, 157, 171n111

Eckert, Allan W., 48n28, 99n1

Economic and Social Council (ECOSOC). *See* United Nations: Economic and Social Council (ECOSOC)

economic sanctions on Iraq, U.S., 364, 367, 369, 451–52, 521, 531 education, 73, 531. *See also* boarding schools; pedagogy

Egypt, 309, 471, 513n43, 518n593, 533n, 537n7

Eichmann, Adolf, xxix–xxxiii passim, 380, 402–3nn127–31, 525, 535

embargoes, trade, 364, 451–52, 454, 521

Environmental Modification Convention (ENMOD). *See* Convention on the Prohibition of Military or Any Other Hostile Use of Environmental Modification Techniques

environmental movement, 282–88 passim

essentialism, 273n233

"ethnocide" (word), 5, 345n117

eugenics, xxxiv, 3, 124, 125, 129n24, 151, 195, 356n204

eurofeminism, 236–37, 249, 265n138, 265n141

Europe: doctrine of discovery, 30–34, 47n12; Genocide Convention and, 70; small nations, 14; small states, 100n3. *See also* Denmark; France; Germany; Great Britain; Netherlands; Spanish explorers and conquistadors

eurosupremacism, 166n61, 167n62, 195, 196, 237, 238, 251, 296–97

"evil" (word), 526, 532, 539n15. *See also* "banality of evil" (Arendt)

execution, summary, 376, 418, 468, 492n257; by FBI, 539n19

exposure, death from. *See* death from exposure

"extermination" (word), 423, 424, 428, 482n48

extinctions, Pleistocene era. *See* Pleistocene extinctions

Faery, Rebecca Blevins: *Cartographies of Desire*, 264n135

Falk, Avner: *Anti-semitism*, xvii

Falk, Richard, 516–17n579

family abuse. *See* domestic abuse

Fanon, Frantz, 14, 120, 252, 265n138, 280, 293, 335

Farben. *See* I.G. Farben

fatal accidents, 290, 291, 327, 359n228

FBI, xxi–xxvi, 444, 470, 512n535, 526, 527–28, 538n12, 539–40nn19–23 passim; Waco siege, 527, 542n33

Federal Emergency Management Agency (FEMA), 470

federal recognition of Indians, xxxiv, 107n108, 111–17 passim, 122–24 passim, 126n4, 128n22; resistance to, 130n30. *See also* termination policy

feminism, Western. *See* eurofeminism

fetal alcohol syndrome (FAS), 292, 353n177

fiction, 141, 233, 235, 239

Filipino genocide, 372, 378–79, 399–400n113, 422–26 passim, 534

films, 4, 194, 217–46, 253–70, 300; Leah Kelly and, 313, 325, 355n197

"final solution, American-style." *See* termination policy

Finkelstein, Norman, 125, 137n76

firebombing: Dresden and Hamburg, 440, 485–86n121; Tokyo, 371, 393n62, 486n130, 534

Fleischer, Ari, 506n494

Fletcher v. Peck, 35

The Flying Torpedo (Griffith), 233

food and crop destruction (war tactic), 409, 410, 431, 438, 446, 451–52, 468, 492n246

Forbes, Jack, 14, 19n8, 113, 140, 195

forced relocation, 294, 372, 428

Ford, John, 223, 228, 243–45 passim; *Cheyenne Autumn*, 245; *The Searchers*, 234–35; *She Wore a Yellow Ribbon*, 228; *Stagecoach*, 232, 234

Fore people, 183

forgiveness, 362n254

Forsyth, George A., 421

Fort Frances, Ontario, 307

Fort Hood Three, 444

Fort Laramie Treaties. *See* Treaties of Fort Laramie (1851 and 1868)

Fort Marion Military Prison, 441

Fort Massacre (Newman), 234

Fort Wise Treaty. *See* Treaty of Fort Wise

Foster, Morris, 111n, 121

Foucault, Michel, 150, 250

Founding Fathers, xiv–xv. *See also*
Franklin, Benjamin; Jefferson,
Thomas; Washington, George
Four Corners area: archaeology, 180–84
passim
"Fourth World," 16, 149, 252
Fraenkel, Ernst, 406n156
France, 33, 457; in Rwanda, 457; in UN,
57; World War II, 114–15, 241, 492n257
Francis, Daniel, 239
Franklin, Benjamin, 235
fraud, 43, 114, 125; allegations against
Churchill, 121; anthropological,
151, 166–67n62, 183, 195; Bering
Strait theory as, 159; photographic,
205n100; *Walam Olum*, 154, 169n87
Frazier, Linn, 87
Freire, Paulo, 160, 285
Freisler, Roland, 2, 6n1
Freud, Sigmund, 194
Friedenberg, Edgar Zodiag, xxi–xxxii
Friedman, Terry, 360nn234–35
"friendly Indians." *See* "Good Indian"
(trope)
fundamentalist Islam. *See* Islamic
fundamentalism

Gaddis, John Lewis, 125, 137n78
Gajdusek, D. Carleton, 205n100
gangs and gangsters, 369, 390–91n39,
422, 540n22; Colorado AIM classed
under, xxvi
Garfolo, Gary, 429
Garment, Leonard, 29
gasoline sniffing, 242, 292, 306, 332
The Gatling Gun, 234
General Allotment Act of 1887. *See*
Allotment Act of 1887
Geneva Conventions, 61, 391n45,
392n47, 435, 446–56 passim, 507n500;
ignored in military training, 442,
443; Israeli violations, 514n554,
515n563; Prisoners of War, 435, 440,
469, 510n525; Protection of Civilian
Persons, 436, 515n563; Wounded and
Sick, 415, 435, 448, 484n85
Geneva Peace Accords (1954), 487n138
genocide, xx, 59, 140, 192–93, 278n272,
301, 331, 361n252; Bosnia, 71, 80n76;

"divine right" to commit, 526; East
Timor, 370, 455; in films, 233; Iraq,
364–65, 367, 452, 521–23 passim;
as mentality, 459; Rwanda, 71, 457.
See also Convention on Prevention
and Punishment of the Crime of
Genocide; cultural genocide; Filipino
genocide; Jewish Holocaust
"genocide" (word), xvi, xvii, 130n28
The Genocide Machine in Canada (Davis), 59
geography, 37, 243–44, 269n182
geology, 150–55 passim, 159, 168n85,
172n124
George III, King of England, 33
Georgia (country), 472
German Guilt (Jaspers), 404–5nn140–47
passim, 408n173
Germany: Berlin disco bombing of
1986, 508n504; internal criminal
cases against ex-nazis, 407n171; Iraq
relations, 515n557; Leah Kelly in, 309
Germany, nazi era: xxix–xxxiv passim,
105–6n85, 238, 380–86 passim,
400–401n123, 401n125; akin to others
in Europe, 21n15; Blood Libel, 192,
238; "delousing," 482n47; French
occupation, 114–15, 241; internal
public opinion, 462, 503n465, 521;
propaganda, 256n35; relativizing,
405n150; resistance, 406n155; Slavs
and, 297, 341n64; *Son of Paleface*
compared, 259n69; suicide, 294; U.S.
bombing of, 393n62, 440, 485–86n121,
526; U.S. influence/mirroring, 48n28,
53n80, 91–92, 97, 99n1; World War II
victory (hypothetical), 303; Wounded
Knee Massacre compared, 259n67.
See also Eichmann, Adolf; "Good
German" (trope); Hitler, Adolf;
Jewish Holocaust; Nuremberg Trials
Geronimo, 242, 295, 423, 441
Geronimo (1993 film), 245
Getches, David, 121
Gilroy, Paul, 275n255
Glasse, Robert: *Essays on Kuru*, 205n100
God Is Red (Deloria), 151, 160
Goebbels, Joseph, 256n35
Goldhagen, Daniel Jonah, 385, 408n174
Goldman, Lawrence, 196

Gómara, Francisco López de, 197n5
"Good American" (trope), 364, 365, 379, 385, 445, 522
"Good German" (trope), 260n84, 364, 366, 379, 385, 401n125, 445, 476, 521, 522
"Good Indian" (trope), 120–21, 238–43, 267n152; Sheridan opinion, 238–39, 267n150, 422, 484n80
Goodman, Jeffrey, 168n83
"Good Settler" (trope), 229–30, 245, 301
Goodwin, Francis A., 103n50
"gook" (word), 428, 487–88n153
Göring, Hermann, 440
Gramsci, Antonio, 12, 120, 140, 148, 258n55, 271n212, 276n262
"gratuitous offsets," 86–94 passim, 106n87
Great Britain: Commonwealth, 249; Kuwait partition, 447; Northern Ireland, 19n9, 541n32; in UN, 70; World War II, 492n257. See also American Revolution; Jay Treaty
Green, Rayna, 239
Green, Theodore Francis, 75–76n35
Grey, Zane: The Lone Ranger, 239
Griffin, Susan, 378
Griffith, D.W.: The Battle of Elderbush Gulch, 217, 227, 233–34, 253n1; Birth of a Nation, 258n54; The Flying Torpedo, 233
Grotius, 412
Guantánamo Bay, Cuba, 469, 510n525, 511n527
guardian and ward. See ward and guardian
Guatemala, 80n78, 370
guilt, 294, 301, 305, 379; collective, 366; Jaspers views, 381–83, 386, 404–5nn142–47 passim; Leah Kelly and, 307, 333, 334, 355n196
The Gulf War Did Not Take Place (Baudrillard), 367
Gunga Din (Kipling character), 121, 240
Gunga Din (1939 film), 240
Gunn Allen, Paula: The Sacred Hoop, 266n147
Guns, Germs, and Steel (Diamond), xviii–xix
Gypsies. See Romanis (Gypsies)

Hague Convention I (1899), 484n85, 487n145
Hague Convention IV (1907), 391n46, 396n83, 435, 448
Hague Rules of Aerial Warfare (1923), 391n45, 435–36
Haiti, 510n512
half-blood quantum, 121, 124, 129n25, 136n71
Hall, H.L., 261n95, 482n47
Halliburton, 514n550
Halliday, Denis, 365, 452, 522
Hamas, 518–19n593
Hamilton, Charles V., 22n23, 22n25
Hamza, Khidre, 514n553
Handbook of North American Indians, xviii
Harjo, Joy, 286
Harner, Michael, 176, 199n23
Harris, Marshall, 499n413
Harris, Marvin, 176, 178
Harrison, William Henry, 410
Hassler, Peter, 185
Hatch, Orrin, 68–69, 396n81, 505n489
hate mail, xxxv–xxxvii
Haudenosaunee. See Iroquois
Hawaii, 40, 397n88
health, 83, 292, 451. See also disease
Hébert Committee. See U.S. House of Representatives: Hébert Committee (My Lai investigation)
Hebrews, Indians as, 156, 170n100
Hector, Michael: Internal Colonialism, 14
Helms, Jesse, 68–69, 78n55
Henderson, Oran, 429, 430
Herbert, Anthony B., 444
Herman, Judith, 298, 352n174, 362n254
Herodotus, 177
Herr, Michael, 487n143
Hersh, Seymour, 430, 489n198
Hezbollah. See Hizbullah
Hickenlooper, Bourke B., 74n29
Hickok, Wild Bill, 242
Hicks, Tyler, 468
"hierarchy" (word), 273n232
"Highway of Death" (Iraq), 370, 448, 521
Hill, Charlie, 117, 269n188
Himmler, Heinrich, 231, 482n47
Hiroshima and Nagasaki, bombing of (1945), 298, 371, 427, 486n130, 534

historicism, 411–13

Hitchens, Christopher, 384

Hitler, Adolf, xvi, 53n80, 91, 458; assassination plot, 406n155, 517n581; on lies, 222, 256n35; *Mein Kampf*, 91, 256n35; Washington compared, 48n28, 99n1

Hizbullah, 518n593

Hodge, Frederick Webb, 180

Hogg, Gary, 176

Hohokams, 186, 190

Hollywood, 4, 194

"holocaust" (word), xvi, xvii

Holocaust, Jewish. *See* Jewish Holocaust

Homeland Security Act, 377

homosexuality, 238, 266n147

Hoover, J. Edgar, xxi, xxiii

Hope, Bob, 259n69

Hopi Indians, 97, 114, 188–89; cosmology, 153, 168n83

Horkheimer, Max, 220

horror films, 232

Horseshoe Bend Massacre, 411, 412, 427

"hostiles" (word), xxiii, 234, 241, 417

Hough, Walter, 180, 181

housing, 293

Hrdlička, Aleš, 168n85

Huet-Vaughn, Yolanda, 453–54

Hughs, R.P., 423

Human Rights Watch, 504n476

Hussein, Saddam, 448, 454, 472, 473, 474, 513n546, 517n581, 542n33

Huston, John: *The Unforgiven*, 233

ICC. *See* Indian Claims Commission (ICC); International Criminal Court (ICC)

ICJ. *See* International Court of Justice (World Court)

I.G. Farben, 286, 288n15

Images of Indians (television series), 223, 226, 253n3

immigrants, Chinese. *See* Chinese immigrants

The Impact of Sanctions on Iraq (Clark), 367

imperialism, 11, 39, 157; U.S. 377, 400n120. *See also* cultural imperialism

imprisonment. *See* prisons and imprisonment

incendiary weapons, 446–47, 450. *See also* firebombing; napalm

Incident at Oglala (Apted), 223, 257n43

income, 293

India, 26n54, 473, 509n506, 509–10n512

Indian Affairs Office. *See* Bureau of Indian Affairs (BIA)

"Indian agents," 87, 114, 116

Indian Arts and Crafts Act of 1990, 123, 130n30

Indian Citizenship Act, 74n21

Indian Claims Commission (ICC), 42–43, 81–110 passim

"Indian Country," 479; Earth as, 458; Iraq as, 449; Philippines as, 422–26; Vietnam as, 427–34

Indian Health Service, 77n48

Indian identity, xxxiv, 111–17 passim, 122–23, 126n4, 128n20

Indian languages. *See* languages, native

Indian Relocation Act of 1956, 74n21

"Indian removals." *See* forced relocation of Indians

Indian Reorganization Act (IRA), 74n21, 114, 115, 117

Indian reservations, 12, 22–23n26, 82–83, 114

Indians Are Us? Culture and Genocide in Native North America (Churchill), 111, 118

"Indian schools," residential. *See* boarding schools

Indian Self-Determination and Education Assistance Act, 131n33

The Indian Wars Refought, 217, 227–28, 229, 231

indigenous peoples worldwide, 16, 26n54, 26n56. *See also* Universal Declaration on the Rights of Indigenous Peoples

Indonesia, 71, 370, 455

infant mortality, 83, 292

inferiority (psychology), 195, 297

informers, FBI, 540n23

Innocent IV, Pope, 30, 31

"internal colonialism," 12, 14, 22n23, 84, 128, 149, 271n212, 276n262

Internal Security Act of 1950, 512n538

International Committee of the Red
Cross xxix, 446, 495n329
International Court of Justice (World
Court), 65, 67, 70, 344n106, 383, 385;
Iraq war tribunal, 454; KAL 007
shoot-down and, 507n502; Nicaragua,
78n57, 408n172, 498n393
International Covenant on Civil and
Political Rights, 20n11, 61
International Covenant on Economic,
Social and Cultural Rights, 20n11, 61
International Criminal Court (ICC), 384,
385, 406n158, 454–55, 456
International Indian Treaty Council
(IITC), 13, 16, 147, 148
international law, 29–80 passim, 376,
381–85 passim, 462; civilian courts,
463; colonialism/colonization
and, 10, 13; early history, 412–13,
481n26; enforcement, 460; Falk on,
516–17n579; Huet-Vaughn case, 454;
restitution and, 43, 110n142, 99; on
treaties, 23n31; soldiers' knowledge
or ignorance, 442–43; U.S. resistance
to, 56–80 passim, 384–85, 406n156,
454–56 passim. See also Convention
on Prevention and Punishment of
the Crime of Genocide; Geneva
Conventions; International Criminal
Court (ICC); laws of war; mental
harm (international law); Universal
Declaration on the Rights of
Indigenous Peoples
International Law Commission (ILC),
54n94
International Treaty Banning the Use,
Production, Stockpiling and Transfer
of Anti-Personnel Mines, 384, 455
international war crimes tribunals. See
war crimes tribunals
Inuits, 15, 18
Inventing the Savage (Ross), 142–43
Iola's Promise (1912 film), 244
Iowaville, Iowa, 411
Iran, 67, 371, 466, 471, 472, 507n502,
510n512, 519n594
Iraq, xxviii–xxxiii passim, 364–70
passim, 384, 472–75 passim, 506n493,
533n; bin Laden view, 397n87; Bush

I and, 44, 364, 427, 447, 454; Desert
Storm, 447–54, 461; Halliburton and,
514n550; Iran war, 67; Kuwait and, 44,
370, 400n121, 447, 448, 454, 495n326;
9/11 and, 474, 520–23 passim, 529–31
passim; weapons technology, 515n557
Irish Republican Army (IRA), 541n32
Iroquois, xv, xvi–xvii, 33, 176, 261n91,
409. See also Senecas
Islamic fundamentalism, 277n268,
391n40, 525
Israel, 399n108, 466, 473, 474, 479,
515–16n566, 518–19nn593–94, 537n7;
Chomsky on, 507n500; internal
security model, 377; LBJ and, 524,
537n7; Libyan airliner shoot-down,
509n506; massacres, 370, 392n51;
9/11 and, 370; nuclear weapons, 473,
515n555; UN and, 514n554, 515n563

Jackson, Andrew, 299, 411, 413, 427
Jackson, Helen Hunt, xvii
Jackson, Henry M. "Scoop," 93
Jackson, Robert H., 90, 92, 301–2, 439
Jacobs, Murv, 130n30, 141
Jahrreiss, Hermann, 105n85
Japan: Pearl Harbor bombing, 397n88;
U.S. war against, 371, 393n62, 426–27,
439, 440, 447–48, 486nn128–33
passim, 534. See also Hiroshima and
Nagasaki, bombing of (1945)
Jaspers, Karl, 381–83, 386, 401n125,
404–5nn140–47 passim, 406n155,
408n173
Jay Treaty, 351n160
Jefferson, Thomas, 32, 35, 156
Jenkins, Leigh, 188–89
Jeremiah Johnson (1972 film), 245
Jewish Holocaust, xv–xvi, 63, 231,
259n69, 286, 288n15; concentration
camp death rates, 494n284; denial of,
303; survivors, 298, 304, 525
Jews: Blood Libel, 192, 213n176, 238;
Indians as, 156, 170n100
Ji Jaga, Geronimo, 366, 388n17
Johnson, Bumpy, 369
Johnson, James, 444
Johnson, Lyndon Baines, 428, 524,
541n28

Johnson, William, 37
Johnson v. McIntosh, 35, 36, 40, 49n35
Jospin, Lionel, 457
Judaism, 156
Judd, Neil, 189
just war, 39–40, 447

Kagama case. See U.S. v. Kagama
Kalinagos. See Carib Indians
Karzai, Hamid, 471
Kasdan, Lawrence: Wyatt Earp, 246
Kellogg-Briand Pact, 41, 75n30
Kelly, Barbara, 307, 329
Kelly, Ellen A., 210n146
Kelly, Fred, 329, 349n145, 360n239
Kelly, John Peter, 306–7, 315, 317, 320,
    348n137, 352nn170–71, 361n247
Kelly, Leah Renae, 4, 289–91, 306–35
    passim, 348–62 passim
Kelly, Peter (Tobasonekwat Kinew), 325,
    359n223, 360n239
Kelly, Rhonda, 329, 348n135, 348n138
Kennedy, John F., xxviii, 428, 520
Khmer Rouge, 71
Kien Hoa offensive, Vietnam War, 433
"kill the Indian, spare the man," 73n21,
    295
King George III. See George III, King of
    England
King Philip's War, xxxix(n)34
Kiowas, 170n10, 244, 422, 423, 441
Kipling, Rudyard, 121, 240, 265n141
Kissinger, Henry, 384–85, 478
Klamath Indians, 87, 94, 153
Klein, Nicholas, xxxvii
Korean War, 371, 393n64, 427, 534
Korman, Sharon: Right of Conquest,
    46n10, 52n70
Kosovo, 456, 499n413
Koster, Samuel W., 429, 430
Kroeber, Alfred, 168n85
Kruch, Robert A., 429
Krugman, Steven, 353n175
Ku Klux Klan, 63–64, 258n54, 373,
    540n23
Kurdistan, 455
kuru, 205n100
Kuwait, 44, 370, 400n121, 447, 448, 454,
    495n326

Kuykendall, Jerome, 95

labor, 293, 373, 461. See also
    unemployment
LaDuke, Winona, 164n37, 284
Lakotas (Sioux), 44, 54n98, 83, 97,
    109–10n133, 114–18 passim, 147;
    cosmology, 150; in films, 228–29, 242,
    244, 245; mass execution, 441. See also
    Oglalas; Wounded Knee Massacre;
    Wounded Knee uprising (1973)
landholdings, 22–23n26, 30–34 passim,
    39–44 passim, 116, 117, 130n29;
    ceded, purchased, etc., 40, 43, 93;
    Indian Claims Commission and,
    42–43, 81–110 passim; Revolutionary
    War veterans, xvi, 49n30. See also
    Allotment Act of 1887; "gratuitous
    offsets"
land mines, 371, 384, 447, 455
languages, native, 170n101, 316, 326,
    350n148; prohibition and suppression,
    39, 59, 73n21, 99, 296
Laos, 428, 437, 439
Las Casas, Bartolomé de. See Casas,
    Bartolomé de las
Last of the Dogmen (1995 film), 245
The Last of the Mohicans (Cooper), 239;
    film adaptations, 230, 231, 239
Latinos, 252
Latter-Day Saints, 156
Laughlin, William, 155
Laval University, 308, 313, 350n148
LaVelle, John, 111–38 passim
law, international. See international law
laws of war, 413–16, 426, 435, 463,
    481n40, 484n85, 496n336; My Lai and,
    430; "no quarter," 496n339; targeting
    of civilians and, xxix, 413–15 passim,
    435–36, 446–47, 477, 491n220; U.S.
    resistance to, 384–85. See also Lieber
    Code; war crimes tribunals
lawsuits, xxxv, 2, 123, 135–36n67; land
    claims, 86, 90, 106n96
League of Nations, 40, 41, 74n26
Lebanon, 47, 59, 67, 514n554, 518n583
lebensraum, xvi, 53n80, 91
LeBlanc, Lawrence, 70

Le May, Alan: *The Searchers*, 235; *The Unforgiven*, 233
Lemkin, Raphaël, 56–57, 60, 75n35, 130n28, 346n117
Lenapes, xvi, xxx, 154
Lenihan, John H., 255n30
Leupp, Francis, 88, 89, 91
Levy, Charles, 443, 445
Lewis, Wendy, 350n149
Libya, 466–67, 471, 508nn502–4, 509n506, 513n543, 533n
Lieber Code (Francis Lieber), 413–16, 419, 422, 426, 434, 448, 483n61
Life, 427
life expectancy, 83, 292
Limerick, Patricia Nelson, 113, 126n4, 480n21
Lincoln, Abraham, 411, 417, 441
Lindenbaum, Shirley, 178, 205n100
Lipsitz, George, 237–28
Little Bighorn, Battle of. *See* Battle of Little Bighorn
Little Big Man (Penn), 229–30, 245
Little Crow's War, 441
A Little Matter of Genocide (Churchill), xvii, xix, xxviii
Livingston, Gordon, 445
Lombardo, Paul, 124
London, Jack: "The Unparalleled Invasion," 233
Lone Ranger (fictional character), 239–40, 269n189
Lone Wolf v. Hitchcock, 50n60, 84, 131n32
Looney, William, 452
Lowes, Warren, 132n36
Loyal Creeks v. U.S., 107n97
Luers, Jeffrey ("Free"), 390n35
Lugar, Richard, 68–69
lynching, 62, 65, 76n38
Lyotard, Jean-François, 150
Lytle, Clifford M., 149

MacArthur, Arthur, 425, 426
MacArthur, Douglas, 426
MacPherson, James, 302–3
Maher, Bill, 538n10
Maikov, Valerian, 144
Major Crimes Act, 117
Makah whaling, 284

Maktos, John, 58
Malcolm X, 364, 462, 520
Maltby, Richard, 244
Malmédy Massacre, 440
malnutrition: Indian Country, 23n26, 83, 295, 442; Iraq, xxviii, 374, 451–52
A Man Called Horse (Silverstein), 225, 244, 245, 270n193
Man Corn (Turner and Turner), 183–91 passim, 195–96
The Man-Eating Myth (Arens), 177–79
Manifest Destiny, xix, 53n80, 219
Manitoba, 291. *See also* Winnipeg
Mankiller, Wilma, 130n30
Mann, Anthony: *Winchester '73*, 234
Mann, Michael: *Last of the Mohicans*, 230, 231
Manuel, George, 27n65
Marcuse, Herbert, 16–17, 171n113
Margold, Nathan, 89
Marias Massacre, 420
Marshall, Craig ("Critter"), 390n35
Marshall, George, 486n129
Marshall, John, 30, 35–40 passim
Martin, George, 350n153
Marx, Karl, 194, 248
marxism and marxists, 11, 15, 16, 148, 149, 248–49, 251
mascots. *See* sports team mascots
Mashunkashey v. Mashunkashey, 50n60
Massachusetts Bay Colony, 33, 262n96, 394n70
massacres, 420–24 passim, 534; Afghanistan, 468–69; Crusades, 527n6; filmic views, 226–31 passim; Iraq, 370, 447, 448, 521; Israeli, 370, 392n51; Korean War, 371; Palestinian West Bank, 514n554; "unpleasantness," 480n21; Vietnam, 407nn164–65, 429–34, 443, 453, 498n384; World War II, 371, 440. *See also* Bad Axe Massacre; Horseshoe Bend Massacre; Marias Massacre; My Khe Massacre; My Lai Massacre; Sand Creek Massacre; Washita Massacre; Wounded Knee Massacre
master narrative, 150, 159, 218, 237, 252, 258n55, 277n265, 462

Mather, Cotton, 170n100, 236, 263–64n128

Mathias, Charles, 70

Matthews, Barb, 355n197

Matthews, Harv, 355n197

Mayans, 27n58, 80n78

McClintock, Anne, 249

McCloskey, Pete, 437

McCoy, Isabella, 236

McLaren, Peter, 277n265, 285

McMahon, Brian, 62, 63, 64, 75n35

McNamara, Robert, 72n1, 80n75, 490n211, 542n36

Means, Russell, xx, xxiv, 15, 97, 99, 111, 147, 360n234; on anthropologists, 214n188; "For the World to Live, Europe Must Die," 283

media, xxvii, 85, 521, 531; 9/11 coverage, 364, 375, 465, 524, 538n10, 542n33; World War II coverage, 427. See also al-Jazeera; films; radio; television

Medina, Ernest, 430–31

Mein Kampf (Hitler), 91, 256n35

Memmi, Albert, 120, 252, 293

Menasseh ben Israel, 156

Menominees, 94, 107n108

mental harm (international law), 50n58, 60, 66, 69, 70, 78n61, 301, 302

Meriam Commission, 89

Merritt, Edgar B., 88–89

Mesquakis. See Sacs and Foxes (Mesquakis)

The Metaphysics of Modern Experience (Deloria), 152–53, 160

Mexican-American War, xiv

Mexicans and Mexican Americans, lynching of, 76n38

Mexico: archaeology, 187–90 passim; Zapatistas, 286. See also Aztecs; Toltecs

The Middle Ground (White), xix

Mihesuah, Devon, xiv

Miles, Nelson A., 228

military academies, 442

military conscription, refusal of. See draft refusal

Miller, Stuart Creighton, 378–79

minerals and mining, 22–23n26, 84, 89, 104n59, 287–88n14

minimization (tactic), xvii–xx

Minnesota, 317, 354n180, 441

"minority" (label), 102n30

Mohawk, John, 14, 25n42

Mohawks, 128n20, 231, 268n177

Mohicans, 267n153. See also The Last of the Mohicans (Cooper)

Momaday, N. Scott, 157, 170–71n110

monetary compensation. See compensation, monetary

monster films, 232

Montana, 139, 143, 420. See also Battle of Little Bighorn

Montesquieu, 415

Monument Valley, 181, 223, 244

Mora, Dennis, 444

Mormons. See Latter-Day Saints

Morris, Earl, 180

Morris, Glenn, xxiv

Morton, Thomas J., 130

movies. See films

Muhammad Omar, Mullah, 509

Mulligan, Robert: The Stalking Moon, 232

Mundt, Karl, 93

Murrah Federal Building bombing, Oklahoma City, 1995, 529n, 542n33

Muscogees (Creeks), 107n97, 411, 427

Muslims, detention and deportation of, 470–71

mutilation of war dead. See atrocities

Myanmar, 18, 26n54

My Khe Massacre, 431–33 passim, 453

My Lai Massacre, 407nn164–65, 429–34 passim, 443, 453, 498n384

Nagasaki, bombing of (1945). See Hiroshima and Nagasaki, bombing of (1945)

napalm, 428, 437, 450

Narragansetts, 262n96

"nation" (word), 119

National American Indian Movement, Inc., 119, 132n39

"national history" (Goldhagen), 386, 408n174

The Nations Within (Deloria and Lytle), 149

Native American Representations: First Encounters, Distorted Images, and Literary Appropriations (Bataille), 280–81
native peoples worldwide. *See* indigenous peoples worldwide
naturalization of whites, 128n20
Navajos. *See* Diné people (Navajos)
Naves, Larry, 123, 136n68
nazi Germany. *See* Germany, nazi era
nazi Holocaust. *See* Jewish Holocaust
Nebrija, Antonio de, 458
Nelson, Ralph: *Soldier Blue*, 229–30, 234, 260n83
Netherlands, 33, 70, 372
New Mexico: archaeology, 180–83 passim; Navajos, 441–42. *See also* Chacoans
Newsweek, 364
Newton, Huey P., 217
New York City: atrocious history, 372
New Zealand, 18
Nez Perce Indians, 103n50
Ngugi wa Thiong'o, 252
Nicaragua, 15, 78n57, 148, 371, 408n172, 498n393
Nicaragua v. United States, 78n57, 408n172
Nickens, Paul R., 181
Nielson, Richard A., 98
Nietschmann, Bernard, 15
Nimitz, Chester A., 440
"nits make lice," 231, 262n96, 417, 482n47
Nixon, Richard M., 106n96, 115, 429
Nkrumah, Kwame, 252
"no quarter," 391n46, 415, 427, 447–48, 496n339
North Dakota, 143
Northern Ireland, 19n9, 541n32
North Korea, 472, 514n547
Northwestern Bands of Shoshone v. United States, 90, 92
Northwest Ordinance, 34, 39, 81
Northwest Passage (Vidor), 223
Notley, Daniel, 432
novels and short stories. *See* fiction
Noyd, Dale, 443
nuclear weapons, 371, 377, 473, 519n594; Iraq, 514n553; Israel, 515n555; U.S. testing of, 461. *See also* Hiroshima and Nagasaki, bombing of, 1945

Nuremberg Trials, xxxi, 41–44 passim, 56–62 passim, 75n30, 91–93 passim, 105n81, 385, 413, 439–40; Allied opposition to, 492n257; Charter/Principles, 302, 435, 443, 444, 445, 456, 460, 476; "Good Germans" and, 366; ignored in military training, 442–43; major reason convened, 403n138; precedent in Vietnam War, 431, 439; Robert Jackson, 301–2, 403n137, 439; "victor's justice" claims, 105–6n85

obscurantism, 146, 162n19
Office of Indian Affairs. *See* Bureau of Indian Affairs (BIA)
Oglalas, xx, 127n11, 242
oil industry, 471
Ojibwe language, 316, 326, 330, 350n148
Ojibwes of Onigaming First Nation, 306, 313, 329, 351n157, 360n235. *See also* Sabaskong Bay, Ontario
Oklahoma, 87, 89, 107n108, 116; Cherokee National Museum, 130n30. *See also* Murrah Federal Building bombing, Oklahoma City, 1995; Washita Massacre
O'Malley, Thomas, 90
Oneidas, 97
Onigaming First Nation. See Ojibwes of Onigaming First Nation
On the Justice of Roosting Chickens (Churchill), 363n
Operation Desert Storm, 447–54, 461
opium, 471
organized crime. *See* gangs and gangsters
origin stories, 153, 156
Ortiz, Simon J., 283
Other, 177, 222, 231–33, 279, 476
Otoes, 96

Pact of Paris. *See* Kellogg-Briand Pact
Pakistan, 468, 473, 519n594
Palestine Liberation Organization (PLO), 518n593
Palestinians, 370, 397n87, 448, 466, 474, 507n500, 514n554, 515n563; LBJ and,

524, 537n7; 9/11 and, 534; suicide bombings, 515–16n566, 518–19n593

Papua New Guinea, 183

parenting, 304

Parker, Arthur C., xvii

Parker, Cynthia Ann, 235

Parker, Quannah, 235

Parkman, Francis, xiv

The Pathfinder (Cooper): film adaptations, 239

Patriot Act. *See* USA PATRIOT Act

patriotism, 241, 532, 542n34

Patterson, William L., 65

Patton, George S., 433–34

Pawnees in films, 231

payback. *See* retribution

payouts, compensatory. *See* compensation, monetary

Peabody Coal Company, 286, 287–88n14

pedagogy, 160, 252, 478

Peers, William, 432

Peiper, Jochen, 440

Peltier, Leonard, 366, 388n17

Penn, Arthur: *Little Big Man*, 229–30, 245

Penn, William, 170n100

Pentagon (building): 9/11 attack, 465

"peoples" (word), 119, 133n43

Peoples of the Sea (Velikovsky), 168n80

Pepper, George H., 180

"permanent solution" (United States). *See* termination policy

personal responsibility. *See* responsibility, personal

Philippines, 40, 372, 378–79, 399–400n113, 422–26 passim, 441, 471–72, 534

Pickering, Michael, 205n95

Piegans, 139, 420

Pijoan Aguadé, Carmen María, 187

Piltdown hoax, 151, 166–67n62, 195

Pine Ridge Sioux Reservation, 83, 127n11, 132. *See also* Wounded Knee uprising (1973)

plagiarism, 118, 125, 132n36

Plain of Jars, Laos, 428, 437

Pleistocene extinctions, 159, 172n122

plenary power, 39, 50n60, 84, 131n32, 293

Plymouth Colony, 33, 394n70

Pocahontas, 238, 240

Poland, 11, 57, 79n68, 294, 309

police: AI report, 504n477, 504n479; Denver, 512–13n538; militarization, 470; PATRIOT Act and, 470; protester complicity, 368, 523, 536n5

political prisoners, 366, 388n17, 390n35

Poncas, 107n108

Pope Innocent IV. *See* Innocent IV, Pope

"populations" (word), 119, 133n43

population statistics, 143, 261n93, 270n201, 396n85, 422

Porter, Robert B., 138n81

Posse Comitatus Act, 470, 512n533, 512n535

"postcolonial" (word), 27n63, 140, 249, 280

postmodernism, 150, 160, 178, 249–50, 273n229, 367

posttraumatic stress disorder (PTSD), 298, 323, 353n178, 357n211, 357–58n213

poverty, 23n26, 82–83, 293

Powell, Colin, xxix, 397n86, 453, 498n384, 531

pow-wows, 317

Pratt, Geronimo. *See* Ji Jaga, Geronimo

Pratt, Richard Henry, 295, 296

Prehistoric Cannibalism at Mancos (White), 182–83, 186, 205n95

prescription drugs, 321

Price, Morton E., 110n137

prisoners of war, 415–16, 424, 435, 440–43 passim, 469, 510n525

prisons and imprisonment, 4, 142–43, 366, 461; Afghanistan, 468–69; Guantánamo Bay, 469, 510n525, 511n527; Human Rights Watch survey, 504n476; Japan, 493n267; Vietnam vets, 299. *See also* concentration camps; political prisoners

protests and demonstrations, 368, 390n35, 460, 523, 536n5

The Protocols of the Elders of Zion, 192, 238

Proxmire, William, 56

pseudoscience, xxxiv, 151, 154–55, 174–216 passim. *See also* eugenics; "scientific racism"

psychiatry, 296, 321–24 passim, 356–57n204

PTSD. *See* posttraumatic stress disorder (PTSD)

Pueblo de Taos v. United States, 106n96

Puerto Ricans, involuntary sterilization of, 65, 77n48

Puerto Rico, 40

Pufendorf, Samuel, 40

Puritans, 33, 170n100, 236, 482n47

Pushing Tin (1999 film), 244

Puyallup Indians, 97

Qadaffi, Muamar al-, 467, 508n504, 513n543

Qatar, 467

Quahadi Comanches, 235

racial segregation. *See* segregation, racial

racism, denial of, 459

racism, "scientific." *See* "scientific racism"

racism in criminal justice, 142–43

racism in warfare, proscription of, 416

radiocarbon dating, 155

radio programs, 239–40, 542n33

Rancheria Act of 1958, 107n106

rape, 233–38, 263–64n128, 299, 334; Afghanistan, 468; Vietnam War, 433

Reagan, Ronald, 72, 78nn55–58 passim, 512n535

Rebellion and Revolution (Cruse), 22n23

"reconciliation," white-native, 334, 361n253

Red Cross, International. *See* International Committee of the Red Cross

Red Cross Fundamental Rules of Humanitarian Law Applicable to Armed Conflicts, 446

Red Earth, White Lies (Deloria), 153, 160, 172n124

"red power," 22n24

Red Sticks, 411, 427

Reed, Erik, 180

Rehnquist, William, 65–66

religion, 59, 156. *See also* Christianity; Islamic fundamentalism; scientism; spiritual practices, outlawing of

relocation, forced. *See* forced relocation

Relocation Act of 1956. *See* Indian Relocation Act of 1956

reparations, 110n142, 371, 382, 404n143, 408n172, 531. *See also* compensation, monetary

reservations. *See* Indian reservations

residential schools. *See* boarding schools

Resor, Stanley, 444

responsibility, personal, 376, 382, 386, 387, 400–401n123, 403n137, 404n142, 516n579

restitution xx, 43, 98, 99, 110n142, 362n254, 382

retribution, 373–77, 508n504, 509n510, 529–30, 542n33; rules of war, 415

Revolutionary War. *See* American Revolution

Rich, Norman, 92

Ridenhour, Ron, 429–30

rights of conquest, 39–42

Ritter, Scott, 472–73, 514n553, 519n594

Roanoke and Wampum (Welburn), 139–41

Roberts, David, 210–11n157

Roberts, Frank H.H., 180

Robinson, Peter, 179, 180, 191

Rockstroh, Phil, xxxiii

Rocky Mountain News, 418–19

Rogers case. *See* U.S. v. Rogers

Romanis (Gypsies), 192, 294, 298, 525

Roosevelt, Franklin D., 90

Roosevelt, Theodore, xv, 73n21, 116, 299, 422–23, 425, 429

Rosas, Allan, 481n40

Rosenberg, Ethel, 539n19

Rosenthal, Harvey D., 82–87 passim, 96–99 passim, 103n45, 103n49, 106n87, 108–9n122

Ross, Luana: *Inventing the Savage*, 142–43

Rosse, Joseph, 134n59

Rouse, Irving, 197n3

Rousseau, Jean-Jacques, 415

Rowe, Gary Thomas, 540n23

Rowlandson, Mary, 236

Roy, Arundhati, 509–10n512

rules of engagement (war), xxix, 430, 434, 442, 443, 447, 454. *See also* laws of war

Rumsfeld, Donald, 511n525

Rusk, Dean, 64

Russell Tribunal (Bertrand Russell), 438–39
Russia, 478, 518n592
Rwanda, 71, 457

Sabaskong Bay, Ontario, 306, 348n137
The Sacred Hoop (Gunn Allen), 266n147
Sacs and Foxes (Mesquakis), 411
Sadistic Personality Disorder, 399n112
Sagan, Eli, 176
Sahagún, Bernardo de, 175, 186
Sahlins, Marshall, 176, 178, 179, 183, 206n102
Said, Edward, 258n55
Saito, Natsu Taylor, 376, 478
Sale, Kirkpatrick, 177–78, 285
Samas, David, 444
Sampson, Will, 262n105
sanctions on Iraq. *See* economic sanctions on Iraq, U.S.
Sand Creek Massacre, 231, 260n83, 417–21, 482n48, 483n61; resistance to, 445, 483n58
Sandinistas, 15, 148, 371
Santa María, Vicente de, 187
Sartre, Jean-Paul, 246–51 passim, 260n84, 261n87, 271n211, 278n272, 301, 331
saturation bombing (carpet bombing), 393n62, 436, 437, 446, 450
Saudi Arabia, 58, 474–75, 509n510
Sauks. *See* Sacs and Foxes (Mesquakis)
"savages" (film trope), 226–31, 234, 242
"savages" (word), 415, 422, 426, 428
Scalia, Antonin, 5
scalp bounties, 232, 372, 411, 441, 477
scalps and scalping, 232, 372, 411, 417, 418; Vietnam, 429
Schickel, Richard, xxxii
Schmitt, Carl, 382
schooling, compulsory. *See* compulsory schooling
schools, residential. *See* boarding schools
Schwarzkopf, Norman, 526
Schweppe, Alfred, 62–63, 64–65, 77n47
"science." *See* pseudoscience
"scientific racism," 157, 425

scientism, 151–59 passim, 171n114, 179, 196, 285
Scott, Duncan Campbell, 295
The Searchers (Ford), 234–35
Seattle WTO demonstrations (1999). *See* World Trade Organization demonstrations, Seattle (1999)
segregation, racial, 66
Selective Service Act, 444
Seminoles, 128n20, 244
Senecas, 409, 410, 427, 447–48
September 11, 2001, terrorist attacks, xxviii–xxxiii passim, 363–408 passim, 464–68 passim, 474–79 passim, 505–6nn489–94, 520–43 passim; fatality count, 505n489, 529n; "fourth airliner," 465, 505n488; World Trade Center casualties, 380, 396n81, 401–2nn127–28, 505n490, 524
Serbia, 456–57, 499n413
settler states, 15, 140, 230, 246–47, 280
sexual abuse of children, 296
sexual harassment, 367
shame, 191, 195, 333
Shane (1953 film), 246, 247
Sharon, Ariel, 370, 392n51, 474, 514n554
Shawnees, 410
Sheridan, Phil, 238–29, 267n150, 420, 422, 428, 484n80
Sherman, William Tecumseh, 421–22, 428
She Wore a Yellow Ribbon (Ford), 228
Shiva, Vandana, 285, 313
Shoshones, 87, 90, 97, 482n48
Siletz Indians, 107n108
Silko, Leslie Marmon: *Almanac of the Dead*, 286
Silverheels, Jay, 269n189
Silverstein, Elliot: *A Man Called Horse*, 225, 244, 245, 270n193
Simon, John A., 492n257
Simpson, Varnado, Jr., 429
Siodmak, Robert: *Custer of the West*, 229
Sioux. *See* Lakotas (Sioux)
Six-Day War, 537n7
Skinner, Alanson, 269n185
slaughters. *See* massacres
slavery: African American, 372–73; Indian, xviii; Mansfield Decision, xv;

Middle Passage mortality, 395n74; prisoner labor as, 461; in U.S. historiography, 394n73

Slavic genocide (nazi plan), 297, 341n64

Slotkin, Richard, 220, 236,

smallpox, xiv, 372, 394n70

"smart bombs," 449, 450, 451

Smith, H. Alexander, 75

Smith, Jacob H., 409, 423–25 passim, 430

Smith, John (1580–1631), 233, 394n70

Smith, John (scout), 418

Smith, Watson, 180

Smithsonian Institution, 81, 225, 244, 270n201; *Handbook of North American Indians*, xviii, 145

smoking, 367, 388–89n20, 465, 505nn485–86, 522

social Darwinism, 61n61

Soldier Blue (Nelson), 229–30, 234, 260n83

Somalia, 456, 471, 503n475

"*Some* People Push Back" (Churchill), xxviii–xxxiii passim, 520–43

Son of Paleface (1952 film), 259n69

Sontag, Susan, 538n10

Soule, Silas, 445, 483n58

Soul on Ice (Cleaver), 264nn134–35

South Africa, xxxii, 20n12, 142, 373

South Dakota, 143. *See also* Pine Ridge Sioux Reservation

South Koreans in Vietnam War, 432

sovereignty, 32–38 passim, 82–85 passim, 100n3, 102n30, 111–20 passim, 131n32, 147; "Christianesque" nature, 153; treaties and, 23n31, 32; of United States, 49n34, 58–70 passim, 74n29, 455; Vine Deloria on, 50n53

Soviet Union, 18, 67, 335, 458, 492n257, 528; Afghanistan, 466; KAL 007 shoot-down, 507n502; in UN, 57, 58

Spanish explorers and conquistadors, 174–75, 197nn4–7 passim

speed bumps, 367, 465, 505n486

spiritual practices, outlawing of, 38, 50n56, 73n21

Spivak, Gayatri, 237

sports team mascots, 243, 300

Squanto (1994 film), 242

"squaw" (word), 243, 268n177, 300, 308, 343n90, 426

Staden, Hans, 198n17

Stagecoach (Ford), 232, 234

The Stalking Moon (Mulligan), 232

Standing Bear case, 86

Standing Elk, Carole, 119, 132n38

starvation, xvi, 235, 247, 446, 476; Afghanistan, 468; Iraq, 364, 452, 477; Slavs, 341n64

Steel, Ronald, 506n494

stereotypes, 222–25 passim, 240

sterilization, involuntary, 65, 77n48

Stillaguamish Indians, 97

Stimson, Henry, 41

Stockbridge-Munsee Indians, 267

Stone, Willard, 130n30

Stone, William L., 409

Story, Joseph, 37–38

Strack, Herman L., 213n176

Streicher, Julius, 59, 92, 192

Strickland, Rennard, 83, 243

Sudan, 467, 471, 508n505

suicide, 83, 242, 281n9, 292, 294, 303–6 passim; Kelly family, 349n145; nazi Germany, 294; Vietnam vets, 299

suicide bombings, 377, 399n108, 515–16n566, 518–19n593; secular vs. religious motivation, 538n13; USS *Cole*, 466, 507n497. *See also* September 11, 2001, terrorist attacks

Sullivan, John, 372, 409–10, 413, 427, 477

summary execution. *See* execution, summary

Supreme Court, U.S. *See* U.S. Supreme Court

Suquamish Indians, 97

surveillance, xxiii–xxvi passim, 470, 541n32

Sutter, Keith, 20n12

sweat lodge, 329, 360n235, 360n238, 360n239

Szasz, Margaret Connell, 339n48

Taft, Robert A., 105–6n85

Tainos. *See* Carib Indians

Taliban, 467–69 passim, 509n510, 509–10n512, 510n525

taphonomy, 181, 185–87 passim, 203n73

Tarahumara Indians, 186, 188
Tarnoff, Peter, 80n76
Taylor, Maxwell, 260n82, 428
Taylor, Telford, 439
Taylor, Zachary, 411, 413
Tecumseh, 410
Tee-Hit-Ton v. U.S., 40, 41, 51n66
teen suicide, 83, 242, 292, 349n145
television, 230, 232, 240–45 passim, 300.
    See also *Images of Indians* (television
    series)
termination policy, 74n21, 93–95,
    107n106, 111
terra nullius, 31, 243–46
territorium res nullius, 31, 270n200
Thaxton, Rob, 390n35
They Died with Their Boots On (Walsh),
    228–29
Theytus Books, 132n36
Thomas, Bissell, 424
Thomas, David Hurst, 157, 158,
    171nn110–11
Thomas, Elmer, 94
Thomas, Robert K., 9–28, 148
Thompson, Smith, 37–38
Thornton, Russell, xvii, 113
Thunderheart (Apted), 223, 257n43
Tilton, Robert S., 239
Tinker, George ("Tink"), xvii, 360n237
Tippecanoe, Battle of. See Battle of
    Tippecanoe
tobacco smoking. See smoking
Togo, Shigenori, 486n133
Tolnay, Stewart E., 63, 76n38
Toltecs, 189–90
Tonto (fictional character), 239–40, 245,
    269
Torgovnick, Marianna, 177
torture, 261n91, 296, 371, 433, 440–41
trade: Indian-European, xviii. See also
    embargoes, trade
Trail of Broken Treaties, 115; Twenty-
    Point Program, 112–13, 115,
    127nn16–17
Trask, Haunani-Kay, 397n88
trauma, 298–99, 303–6 passim, 319–24
    passim, 334, 346n118, 352n174,
    357–58nn211–13

treaties, 13, 23n30–31, 29–36 passim,
    43, 44, 271n206; British, xv, 34;
    California, 54n96; fraud, 54n94;
    human rights, 61; Lakota, 44, 54n98,
    109n133; U.S. Constitution and, 75;
    Washington and, 48n28. See also Jay
    Treaty; Kellogg-Briand Pact; Vienna
    Convention on the Law of Treaties
Treaties of Fort Laramie (1851 and 1868),
    44, 109n133
Treaty of Fort Wise, 43
Treaty of Guadalupe Hidalgo, 34
Treaty of Paris, 34
"tribe" (word), 119
*Tribes, Treaties, and Constitutional
    Tribulations* (Deloria and Wilkins), 149
tribunals, war crimes. See war crimes
    tribunals
triumphalism, xv, 196, 219, 299, 300, 386
Trudell, John, 284, 310, 350–51n155
Truman, Harry, 42, 81, 93, 486n129
Truong Khanh Massacre, 432
trust (trustee) status, 39, 82–84 passim,
    89, 93, 98, 106n93, 271n204, 293;
    international law, 337n27
Turkey, 455
Turner, Christy G., II, 180–81; *Man Corn*,
    183–91 passim, 195–96, 210n146
Turner, Jacqueline, 181, 189; *Man Corn*,
    183–91 passim, 195–96, 210n146
Tuska, John, 255–56n30
Two Hawk, Webster, 115, 127n17

Ulzana's Raid (Aldrich), 234
unemployment, 82–83, 293
The Unforgiven (Le May), 233
The Unforgiven (1960 film), 233, 262n105,
    263n119
Unforgiven (1992 film), 246
United Keetoowah Band of Cherokee
    Indians, xxxiv
United Kingdom. See Great Britain
United Nations, 13–14, 41, 45, 82, 119,
    147–48, 474, 475; Charter, 52n79,
    53–54n92, 109n123, 247, 487n138;
    Commission on Human Rights,
    65; Economic and Social Council
    (ECOSOC), 56–57, 147; General
    Assembly Resolution 1514, 170n104,

247; General Assembly Resolution 1541, 10, 11, 19n9, 20n12; General Assembly Resolution 42/159, 517n580; ICC and, 454–55; Iraq war, 365, 522; Israel and, 514n554, 515n563; U.S. vetoes, 455, 514n554, 515n563; Working Group on Indigenous Populations, 14. *See also* Convention on Prevention and Punishment of the Crime of Genocide; Convention on Prohibition of Certain Conventional Weapons; Convention on the Prohibition of Military or Any Other Hostile Use of Environmental Modification Techniques; International Covenant on Civil and Political Rights; International Covenant on Economic, Social and Cultural Rights

United Nations Declaration on the Granting of Independence to Colonial Countries and Peoples, 101n21, 455

Universal Declaration on the Rights of Indigenous Peoples, 14, 55n104, 80n77, 82, 148, 163n30

University of Colorado, xxvii, xxxiii–xxxvi passim, 121–24 passim, 134n57, 134n59, 312; Leah Kelly as student, 312–14 passim, 351n160; memorial to Indian killer, 419. See also *Ward Churchill v. University of Colorado*

University of Manitoba, 316

University of South Dakota, 115, 138n81

uranium, 22n26. *See also* depleted uranium

USA PATRIOT Act, 470, 511n531

U.S. Civil Rights Commission, 12

U.S. Congress, 91–96 passim, 541n28. *See also* U.S. House of Representatives; U.S. Senate

U.S. Constitution, 36, 68, 75n29, 80n77

U.S. Department of Justice, 65–66, 87, 89, 92, 94, 96, 106n87, 108n122

U.S. Department of State, 61, 64, 80n77–78

U.S. Department of the Interior, 84, 89, 96. *See also* Bureau of Indian Affairs (BIA)

U.S. House of Representatives, 91, 93; Hébert Committee (My Lai investigation), 430, 442

USS *Cole*, 466, 507n497

U.S. Senate, 62, 65–66, 538n14

USSR. *See* Soviet Union

U.S. Supreme Court, 75n29, 80n77, 92, 131n32, 136n70; death penalty, 407n163; desegregation, 66; land claims, 35–41 passim, 51n66, 84, 90, 109–10n133; "plenary power," 39, 50n60, 84, 131n32

USS *Vincennes*, 466, 507n502

U.S. v. Kagama, 50n60, 131n32

U.S. v. Rogers, 124, 136n70

vacuum domicilium, 31, 33, 35, 46n9

Vander Wall, Jim, xxiv

Vattel, Emmerich de, 414

Védrine, Hubert, 457

Velikovsky, Immanuel, 152, 153, 159; *Peoples of the Sea*, 168n80

Venne, Sharon, 360n234, 360nn237–48

"victor's justice," 92, 105–6n85

Vidor, King, 223

Vienna Convention on the Law of Treaties, 43, 47n15, 75n29

Vietnam, 15, 26n54

Vietnam Veterans Against the War, 444

Vietnam War, 44, 260n82, 371, 427–38, 487n143, 489n198; antiwar movement, 460; B-52 strikes, 436, 437, 438, 450, 491n227, 491n235; chemical warfare, 393n59; escalation, 527; murder prosecutions, 490n212; Operation Speedy Express, 426–37; Phoenix Program, 377, 399n106, 528, 541n31; resisters, 443–45; Tet offensive, 528, 541n29; veterans, 299, 405n153, 444; Vietnamese casualty stats, 490n211, 542n36; Westmoreland view, 489n174. *See also* cancer and Vietnam War; My Lai Massacre

violence, domestic. *See* domestic violence

Vitoria, Franciscus, 31, 39

Waco siege (1993), 512n535, 527, 542n33

Walam Olum, 154, 169n87

Walker, Jerry Jeff, 145, 161n10
Waller, Littleton L.T., 424, 431
Walsh, Raoul: *They Died with Their Boots On*, 228–29
Walt Disney productions. *See* Disney productions
Wappingers, 372
war crimes (international law). *See* international law
war crimes tribunals, 71, 80n75, 91, 384–85, 460; Iraq war, 454; Japan, 41, 440; Jaspers view, 381; Rwanda, 71457; Serbia, 456–57. *See also* Nuremberg Trials; Russell Tribunal (Bertrand Russell)
ward and guardian, 36. *See also* trust (trustee) status
Ward Churchill v. University of Colorado, xxxv, 2, 123, 135–36n67, 535
Warner, Marina, 177, 178
"war on drugs," 512n533
"war on terror," 467, 472
war resisters, 443–45, 453–54
war souvenirs, body parts as, 410, 418, 426–27, 429
Washburn, Wilcomb E., 81–82, 85; *Red Man's Land, White Man's Law*, 95
Washington, George, xvi, 33, 34, 48n28, 99n1, 409–13 passim, 427
Washita Massacre, 228, 229, 230, 259n72, 420
water pollution as effect of bombings, 451, 497n369
Watkins, Arthur V., 94–95
Watson, Paul, 284, 285
Wayne, Anthony, 410, 477
Wayne, John, 234–35
"weapons of mass destruction," 371, 472, 531. *See also* nuclear weapons
Weatherford, Jack, 118, 132n36
Weinstein, Allen, 125, 137n77
Welburn, Ron: *Roanoke and Wampum*, 139–41
Westmoreland, William, 428, 429, 430, 432, 489n174
We Talk, You Listen (Deloria), 12, 147
"wétiko disease" (Forbes), 195
White, Richard: *The Middle Ground*, xix

White, Tim D., 181, 188, 196, 206n102; *Prehistoric Cannibalism at Mancos*, 182–83, 186, 205n95
white actors playing Indians, 244, 269nn187–88
The White Buffalo (1977 film), 242
white captives. *See* captives and captivity
white feminism. *See* eurofeminism
white phosphorous munitions, 428, 437
whites, naturalization of. *See* naturalization of whites
white supremacism. *See* eurosupremacism
Whyte, David, 289
Wichitas, 87
Wilkins, David E., 38, 50n53, 149
Willingham, Thomas K., 432
Wilson, Woodrow, 40
Winchester '73 (Mann), 234
Winnipeg, 308–17 passim, 330
Wippermann, Wolfgang, 405n150
Wirt, William, 32
Wirth, Tim, 80n76
Wirtz, Henry, 441
Witt, Edgar E., 94
women, involuntary sterilization of. *See* sterilization, involuntary
Worcester v. Georgia, 36, 37, 38
work. *See* labor
Work, Hubert, 89
World Council of Indigenous Peoples (WCIP), 16, 27n65
World Court. *See* International Court of Justice (World Court)
Worlds in Collision (Velikovsky), 152
World Trade Center bombing (1993), 524, 529, 537n8
World Trade Center bombing (2001). *See* September 11, 2001, terrorist attacks
World Trade Organization demonstrations, Seattle (1999), 368, 523, 536n5
World War II, 97, 114–15, 241, 393n62, 439–40; Germany, 440, 485–86n121, 503n465, 521; Japan, 371, 393n62, 426–27, 439, 440, 447–48, 486nn128–33 passim. *See also* Nuremberg Trials
Wormington, Marie, 180

Wounded Knee Massacre, 105n85,
227–28, 259n67, 372, 421, 423, 449
Wounded Knee uprising (1973), 127n11,
147, 223, 257n43
Wright, Quincy, 481n26
WTO demonstrations, Seattle (1999).
See World Trade Organization
demonstrations, Seattle, 1999
Wyatt Earp (Kasdan), 246

X, Malcolm. *See* Malcolm X

Yamashita, Tomoyuki, 440, 493n267
"Yellow Peril" literature, 233
Yemen, 466, 472, 518n591, 533n
Young, Sherri, 343n87, 361n252
Yousef, Ramzi, 537

Zannis, Mark: *The Genocide Machine in
Canada*, 59
Zapatistas, 286
Zigas, Vincent: *Laughing Death*, 205n100
Zimmerman, Larry, 150
Zinn, Howard, 449, 486n128

ABOUT PM PRESS

PM Press was founded at the end of 2007 by a small collection of folks with decades of publishing, media, and organizing experience. PM Press co-conspirators have published and distributed hundreds of books, pamphlets, CDs, and DVDs. Members of PM have founded enduring book fairs, spearheaded victorious tenant organizing campaigns, and worked closely with bookstores, academic conferences, and even rock bands to deliver political and challenging ideas to all walks of life. We're old enough to know what we're doing and young enough to know what's at stake.

We seek to create radical and stimulating fiction and non-fiction books, pamphlets, T-shirts, visual and audio materials to entertain, educate, and inspire you. We aim to distribute these through every available channel with every available technology—whether that means you are seeing anarchist classics at our bookfair stalls, reading our latest vegan cookbook at the café, downloading geeky fiction e-books, or digging new music and timely videos from our website.

PM Press is always on the lookout for talented and skilled volunteers, artists, activists, and writers to work with. If you have a great idea for a project or can contribute in some way, please get in touch.

PM Press
PO Box 23912
Oakland, CA 94623
www.pmpress.org

FRIENDS OF PM PRESS

These are indisputably momentous times—the financial system is melting down globally and the Empire is stumbling. Now more than ever there is a vital need for radical ideas.

In the years since its founding—and on a mere shoestring—PM Press has risen to the formidable challenge of publishing and distributing knowledge and entertainment for the struggles ahead. With over 300 releases to date, we have published an impressive and stimulating array of literature, art, music, politics, and culture. Using every available medium, we've succeeded in connecting those hungry for ideas and information to those putting them into practice.

Friends of PM allows you to directly help impact, amplify, and revitalize the discourse and actions of radical writers, filmmakers, and artists. It provides us with a stable foundation from which we can build upon our early successes and provides a much-needed subsidy for the materials that can't necessarily pay their own way. You can help make that happen—and receive every new title automatically delivered to your door once a month—by joining as a Friend of PM Press. And, we'll throw in a free T-shirt when you sign up.

Here are your options:

- **$30 a month** Get all books and pamphlets plus 50% discount on all webstore purchases

- **$40 a month** Get all PM Press releases (including CDs and DVDs) plus 50% discount on all webstore purchases

- **$100 a month** Superstar—Everything plus PM merchandise, free downloads, and 50% discount on all webstore purchases

For those who can't afford $30 or more a month, we have **Sustainer Rates** at $15, $10 and $5. Sustainers get a free PM Press T-shirt and a 50% discount on all purchases from our website.

Your Visa or Mastercard will be billed once a month, until you tell us to stop. Or until our efforts succeed in bringing the revolution around. Or the financial meltdown of Capital makes plastic redundant. Whichever comes first.

Pacifism as Pathology: Reflections on the Role of Armed Struggle in North America, Third Edition

Ward Churchill and Michael Ryan with a Preface by Ed Mead and Foreword by Dylan Rodríguez

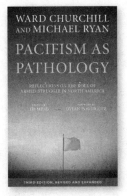

ISBN: 978-1-62963-224-7
$15.95   192 pages

Pacifism as Pathology has long since emerged as a dissident classic. Originally written during the mid-1980s, the seminal essay "Pacifism as Pathology" was prompted by veteran activist Ward Churchill's frustration with what he diagnosed as a growing—and deliberately self-neutralizing—"hegemony of nonviolence" on the North American left. The essay's publication unleashed a raging debate among activists in both the U.S. and Canada, a significant result of which was Michael Ryan's penning of a follow-up essay reinforcing Churchill's premise that nonviolence, at least as the term is popularly employed by white "progressives," is inherently counterrevolutionary, adding up to little more than a manifestation of its proponents' desire to maintain their relatively high degrees of socioeconomic privilege and thereby serving to stabilize rather than transform the prevailing relations of power.

This short book challenges the pacifist movement's heralded victories—Gandhi in India, 1960s antiwar activists, even Martin Luther King Jr.'s civil rights movement—suggesting that their success was in spite of, rather than because of, their nonviolent tactics. Churchill also examines the Jewish Holocaust, pointing out that the overwhelming response of Jews was nonviolent, but that when they did use violence they succeeded in inflicting significant damage to the nazi war machine and saving countless lives.

As relevant today as when they first appeared, Churchill's and Ryan's trailblazing efforts were first published together in book form in 1998. Now, along with the preface to that volume by former participant in armed struggle/political prisoner Ed Mead, new essays by both Churchill and Ryan, and a powerful new foreword by leading oppositionist intellectual Dylan Rodríguez, these vitally important essays are being released in a fresh edition.

"This extraordinarily important book cuts to the heart of the central reasons movements to bring about social and environmental justice always fail. The fundamental question here is: is violence ever an acceptable tool to bring about social change? This is probably the most important question of our time, yet so often discussions around it fall into clichés and magical thinking: that somehow if we are merely good and nice enough people, the state will stop using its violence to exploit us all. Would that this were true."
—Derrick Jensen, author of *Endgame*

From a Native Son: Selected Essays in Indigenism, 1985–1995, Second Edition

Ward Churchill
with an Introduction by Howard Zinn

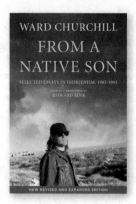

ISBN: 978-1-62963-108-0
$24.95   608 pages

From a Native Son was the first volume of acclaimed American Indian Movement activist-intellectual Ward Churchill's essays in indigenism, selected from material written during the decade 1985–1995. Presented here in a newly revised edition that includes four additional pieces, three of them previously unpublished, the book illuminates Churchill's early development of the themes with which he has, in the words of Noam Chomsky, "carved out a special place for himself in defending the rights of oppressed people, and exposing the dark side of past and current history, often forgotten, marginalized, or suppressed."

Topics addressed include the European conquest and colonization of the Americas, including the genocidal record of Christopher Columbus, the systematic "clearing" and resettlement of American Indian territories by the United States and its antecedents, academic subterfuges designed to deny or disguise the extent of Indian land rights, radioactive contamination of Indian reservations by energy corporations, government-sponsored death squads used to "neutralize" the native struggle on the Pine Ridge Reservation during the mid-1970s, the ongoing dehumanization of American Indians in literature, cinema, and by their portrayal as sports team mascots, issues of Indian identity and the expropriation of indigenous spiritual traditions, the negative effects of "postmodernism" upon understandings of contemporary circumstances of native people, the false promise of marxism in terms of indigenous liberation, and what, from an indigenist standpoint, the genuine decolonization of North America might look like. Of particular interest is Churchill's inclusion in the new version of his 1986 "On Support of the Indian Resistance in Nicaragua" concerning the Indian/Sandinista conflict along the Atlantic Coast of Nicaragua, an item which should go far in dispelling recent confusion about his thinking and actions in that regard.

"Ward Churchill points out the traditional Indian views more than anyone else."
—John Ross Jr., former principal chief United Keetoowah Band of Cherokee Indians

"Wielding his intellect like a stiletto. Churchill lays bare the evil that is Western culture."
—Haunani-Kay Trask, author of *From a Native Daughter*